Theatre
Brief Version

To Whitney Cohen

Also by Robert Cohen

Theatre, Seventh Edition
(0-0729-7-504-0)

<u>For the Acting Sequence:</u>

Acting One, Fourth Edition
(0-7674-1859-X)

Acting Power
(0-87484-408-8)

Acting Professionally: Raw Facts About Careers in Acting, Sixth Edition
(1-55934-941-7)

Advanced Acting: Style, Character, and Performance
(0-7674-2542-1)

<u>Anthologies:</u>

Eight Plays for Theatre
(0-87484-850-4)

Twelve Plays for Theatre
(1-55934-144-0)

<u>Other:</u>

Giraudoux: Three Faces of Destiny

More Power to You

Creative Play Direction (with John Harrop)

Acting in Shakespeare

The Prince (play)

Theatre
Brief Version
SEVENTH EDITION

ROBERT COHEN

Claire Trevor Professor of Drama
University of California, Irvine

Boston   Burr Ridge, IL   Dubuque, IA   Madison, WI   New York
San Francisco   St. Louis   Bangkok   Bogotá   Caracas   Kuala Lumpur
Lisbon   London   Madrid   Mexico City   Milan   Montreal   New Delhi
Santiago   Seoul   Singapore   Sydney   Taipei   Toronto

Higher Education

Copyright © 2006, 2003, 2000, 1997, 1994, 1988, 1981 by Robert Cohen. All rights reserved. Printed in the United States of America. Except as permitted under the United States Copyright Act of 1976, no part of this publication may be reproduced or distributed in any form or by any means, or stored in a database or retrieval system, without the prior written permission of the publisher.

1 2 3 4 5 6 7 8 9 0 VNH/VNH 0 9 8 7 6 5

Library of Congress Cataloging-in-Publication Data
Cohen, Robert, 1938–
    Theatre : brief version / Robert Cohen.—7th ed.
      p. cm.
    Includes bibliographical references and index.
    ISBN 0-07-297505-9 (softcover)
    1. Theater. I. Title.

PN2101.C632 2005
792—dc22
                                                 2005043791

Sponsoring editor, Caroline Ryan; *production editor,* Anne Fuzellier; *manuscript editor,* Andrea L. McCarrick; *design manager,* Preston Thomas; *cover designer,* Lisa Buckley; *interior designer,* Amy Evans-McClure; *art editor,* Emma Ghiselli; *photo editor,* Nora Agbayani; *photo researcher,* Inge King; *production supervisor,* Richard De-Vitto. This text was set in 9.5/12 Stone Serif Regular by Thompson Type and printed on acid-free, 45# Pub Matte by VonHoffmann Press.

Cover images: Clockwise from top: Ashley Judd as Margaret in *Cat on a Hot Tin Roof* by Tennessee Williams; Broadway. Photo: © Joan Marcus.

Snow in June, written by Charles Mee and adapted and directed by Chen Shi-Zheng for the American Repertory Theatre, 2003; Scene Design: Yi Li Ming. Photo © Richard Feldman.

Jude Law in *Doctor Faustus* by Christopher Marlowe, Young Vic Theatre, London, 2002. Photo: © Geraint Lewis.

Alex Jennings and Imogen Stubbs in *The Relapse* by John Vanbrugh, 1596, National Theatre, London, 2001. Photo: © Manuel Harlan.

Liz Smith and Geoffrey Hutchings in *Endgame* by Samuel Beckett, Albery Theatre, London, 2004. Photo: © Geraint Lewis.

Noh actor Otoshige Sakai (right) helps fit his son Otoharu with a mask, prior to a performance in Tokyo May 17, 2004. Photo: © Toshiyuki Aizawa/Reuters/Corbis.

The cast, six Canadian actresses, performing *Mum's the Word,* which they also wrote, in London, 2003. Photo: © Geraint Lewis.

Credits appear on a continuation of the copyright page, pages C-1–C-3.

www.mhhe.com/cohen

Preface

I am sitting in a darkened theatre correcting the galley sheets for the book you are about to read. A technical rehearsal for a play I am directing is in progress; I am seated at a make-shift desk in the back of the house, my reading illuminated by a tiny covered gooseneck lamp. Onstage stand several actors, silent and motionless, as light plays over their faces and bodies. Above me, unseen and unheard, technicians operate, adjust, and record the settings for another of the play's hundred and fifty light cues. To the outside observer, it is the dullest situation imaginable; nothing observable happens for twenty or thirty minutes at a stretch. A pool of light intensifies and then recedes, muffled conversation crackles over headsets, footsteps clang on steel catwalks lacing the ceiling, and a spotlight is carefully repositioned. This has been going on now since eight in the morning, and it is already past dinnertime.

And yet my eye is continually pulled from these pages to the dance of light upon the stage. The violet and amber hues are rich with color, and the sharp shafts of incandescence dazzle with brilliance. I am fascinated by the patient weariness of the actors, alternately glowing in and then shadowed by the lights, endlessly holding the positions that, in performance, they will occupy for only a few transitory seconds. I gaze with admiration at the followspot operator, his hands gloved, as he handles his instrument with the precision and sensitivity of a surgeon.

The silence, the stasis, is hypnotic. All is quiet but profound with held-back beats, incipient torrents of passion and exhilaration. The potential is riveting—I am alive with excitement—and I look back to these cold galley sheets with alarm.

How can I have thought to express the thrill of the theatre in these pages? How can I have hoped to make recognizable the joy and awe I feel in theatrical involvement?

The theatre is not merely a collection of crafts, a branch of literature, a collaboration of technique, or even an all-encompassing art form. It is a life. It is people. It is people making art out of themselves. Its full reality transcends by light-years anything that could be said or written about it.

What I have tried to do in these pages is not so much to introduce the theatre or to survey it as to *present* the theatre with its liveliness and humanness intact, with its incipient passion and exhilaration always present, with its potential for joy, awe, wisdom, and excitement as clear to the reader as they have been made clear to me.

Features

This is a brief version of a larger book that is published simultaneously. The larger volume includes five chapters on theatrical history that do not appear here and three chapters (instead of two) on the modern theatre. The goal of this brief version is to provide students surveying the theatrical arts and collaborative theatrical crafts—but not dramatic history—with a comprehensive text in the dramatic arts as they exist today.

I have included more than 280 theatre photographs—mostly in color—collected from all five continents. The vast majority of these are of significant recent stage productions from around the world. Other photos illustrate the processes of theatrical creation or the historical and current contexts of theatre presentation. Completing the book's art are drawings by scholar/architects that illustrate theatres both past and present as accurately as current research and skilled reconstruction can make possible. Extended captions should help readers better appreciate these images of theatre worldwide and make stronger connections to the text examples.

The text offers a number of pedagogical aids. Terms commonly used in theatre and theatre history are defined in the glossary at the back of the book, and further sources of information for the curious can be found in the selected bibliography. To help students enjoy performances, the appendix "Writing on Theatre" is available on the Online Learning Center. The appendix offers advice on observing and writing critically about plays and can be accessed at www.mhhe.com.cohen.

To help students enhance their playgoing experience further, we have revised our brief guide—*Enjoy the Play!* Co-authored with Lorna Cohen, the guide includes suggestions as to how and where students may attend live theatre—at low cost—either in their own hometowns or in major theatre centers here and abroad. It also includes pointers on how to write a play report.

To help busy instructors, there is a Test Bank, written by Marilyn Moriarty, which includes 50 multiple-choice questions and several short-answer or essay questions per chapter. A computerized version of the Test Bank is available to qualified adopters.

No study of the theatre can be truly comprehensive without seeing and reading plays. It is my belief that regular playgoing and play reading, supported by the discussions in these pages and in the classroom, will provide a good foundation for the student to develop an informed and critical enthusiasm for the art of drama.

What's New?

New to this edition is a first-ever section on the beginnings of theatre in African shamanism and ritual dance-drama, a reconsideration of ancient Greek and Roman theatre buildings and staging as discovered in recent research, a reorganized chapter on music theatre incorporating the startling directions of the past three years, new coverage on the "theatre of community" as pioneered by Bill Rauch and others, multi-language "macaronic" theatre increasingly popular in Europe and America, non-Aristotelian dramatic forms, the "verbatim theatre" of political immediacy widespread in England and the United States, a look at the major works of rising American playwrights Richard Greenberg and Neil LaBute (and emerging ones David Auburn, Doug Wright, Lynn Nottage and Tracy Butts), an examination of non-Aristotelian theatre formats in the "What is a Play?" chapter, expanded and better illustrated sections on theatre design and, especially, theatre technology, and a more sustained look at the parallels and differences between acting in theatre and cinema. Expanded space is also given to individual topics such as Greek Old Comedy, medieval morality plays, Spanish drama of the Golden Age, and Japanese *bunraku,* among others. Of course, the entire "Theatre Today" chapter is wholly revised, as are the considerations given to the careers of living American playwrights from Arthur Miller to Tony Kushner. Several new "boxes" of text, mostly illustrated, propose new "sideline" topics of discussion not previously considered.

In addition to the written text, over 140 new photographs and illustrations have been personally selected from photographers around the world, to help the reader better visualize—and experience sensually—the theatrical activity referred to in each chapter.

Acknowledgments

In all of these revisions, I have profited from literally hundreds of valuable suggestions from readers and from a dozen reviews solicited by the publisher from around the country. These include:

Joe Aldridge, University of Nevada, Las Vegas

Leo J. Van Dyke, Ph.D., University of South Alabama

Robert Gerald Levy, Clarion University of Pennsylvania

Dr. Albert F. C. Wehlburg, University of Florida

I am also very grateful for the generous counsel of my past, current, and future colleagues who have contributed to this edition. Suk-Man Kim, at the Korean National University of the Arts, has given me great insight into Korean theatre while also providing readers the image of his most fascinating dramatic work in that country. William Sun, at the Shanghai Theatre Academy, has helped me better understand the complexities of Chinese drama, as has his wife Faye (the translator of the Chinese edition of this book). Mohammed Ben Abdallah, at the University of Ghana, has opened my eyes to the splendors of both current and historic African theatre. Dan Yang was extremely helpful in clarifying and correcting passages throughout the chapter "The Theatre of Asia," as was Dennis Castellano in "The Musical Theatre" chapter, while Tom Ruzika and Tom Umfrid came to my aid with photographic support in the "Designers and Technicians" chapter. Bill Rauch and Neil LaBute were both kind and prompt in reviewing pertinent new material in the chapter "Theatre Today." I was also very pleased to enjoy the guidance of Cliff Faulkner and the inspiration of Marvin Carlson in preparing that chapter. Most of all, I am deeply indebted to the continuous and unstinting support of Lorna Cohen, and for her unerring editorial, aesthetic, and theatrical judgment which has found its way into decisions made on practically every page and image in this edition.

I am overjoyed to have had the opportunity, once again, to have the contributions of many of the finest theatre photographers in America and Europe in selecting and acquiring the many new images of current theatre work around the world. These artists of the lens include Laurencine Lot of the Comédie Française in Paris, and Geraint Lewis who covers most major theatre activity in London and Edinburgh; each of them invited me to spend a day in their studios wading through many hundreds of slides, photos, and digital images. Ryan Jensen not only contributed a photo from his files but also responded to my request to photograph the New York TKTS booth in the rain. Other fine photographers with whom I have worked in the past—Stephanie Berger, Joan Marcus and Paul Kolnick in New York, Richard Feldman in Boston, Michal Daniel in Minneapolis and Craig Schwartz in Los Angeles—were as brilliant as ever, and for the first time, Manuel Harlen in London and Frank Lin in Taipei made excellent contributions to this edition's art program.

I would also like to thank the many theatre directors and press officers who were so helpful in tracking down images that I requested: Steven Padla at the Yale Repertory Theatre, Antonio Rojas at the Almagro Theatre Festival of Spain, David Howells at the Royal Shakespeare Company, Barbara Higgs and Ronny Förster at the Zurich Schauspielhaus, James Morrison at the Guthrie Theatre, Paul Marte at Hartford Stage, Lee Lawlor at the Cornerstone Theatre, Kati Mitchell at the American Repertory Theatre, Donna Law at the Utah Shakespearean Festival, Dick Devin at the Colorado Shakespeare Festival, and Cris Gross at South Coast Repertory.

Finally, it is a pleasure to acknowledge the great workforce at McGraw-Hill Higher Education with whom I have been working very closely on this revision. Sponsoring Editor Caroline Ryan has shepherded this edition from the very outset with enthusiasm, sharp intellect and skill. Andrea McCarrick, copyeditor for the fifth edition, has once again made her expertly-crafted improvements on every page. Art editor Inge King has pored over every photograph with consummate taste and appreciation, and Production Editor Anne Fuzellier has assembled all this material with great care, concern, and keen efficiency. No author could have a better team to work with, and I am immensely indebted to each and all of them.

Support for Instructors

Please note: The supplements listed here and below in Support for Students *may accompany this text. Please contact your local McGraw-Hill representative for details concerning policies, prices, and availability as some restrictions may apply. If you are not sure who your representative is, you can find him or her by using the Rep Locator at www.mhhe.com.*

INSTRUCTOR'S MANUAL WITH TEST BANK   McGraw-Hill offers an *Instructor's Manual* to all instructors who adopt *Theatre, Brief Version* for their courses. Each chapter of the *Instructor's Manual* includes:

- an overview and outline of the text chapter
- a list of significant names and terms found in the chapter
- Lecture Launchers for student essays or discussions

The last section of the *Instructor's Manual* contains a *Test Bank,* organized by chapter containing multiple choice and true-false questions, for in-class quizzes and testing.

EZ TEXT COMPUTERIZED TEST BANK   McGraw-Hill's EZ Test is a flexible and easy-to-use electronic testing program. The program allows instructors to create tests from book specific items. It accommodates a wide range of question types and instructors may add their own questions. Multiple versions of the test can be created and any test can be exported for use with course management systems such as WebCT, BlackBoard or PageOut. The program is available for Windows and Macintosh environments.

ONLINE LEARNING CENTER: WWW.MHHE. COM/COHEN   The Online Learning Center is an Internet-based resource for students and faculty alike. The Instructor Resources are password protected and offer the complete text of the *Instructor's Manual* and a link to our customizable database of plays. To receive a password for the site, contact your local sales representative or email us at theatre@mcgraw-hill.com.

Additionally, the Online Learning Center offers chapter-by-chapter quizzes for student testing. These brief quizzes are separate from those offered in the *Instructor's Manual,* generate instant grades, and the results can be emailed directly to the instructor with the click of a button (see Student Resources below). This special quizzing feature is a valuable tool for the instructor who requires a quick way to check reading comprehension and basic understanding without using up valuable class time.

Student Resources

ENJOY THE PLAY!   This free theatre guide is packaged with every copy of the text. Revised and updated for the seventh edition, this booklet can be the ultimate tool for introductory theatre students, with information ranging from getting to the theatre to what to write in a theatre report, *Enjoy the Play!* is an excellent introduction to the art of attending a play.

ONLINE LEARNING CENTER: WWW.MHHE.COM/ COHEN   McGraw-Hill offers extensive Web resources for students with Internet access. Students will find the Online Learning Center of particular use with the seventh edition of *Theatre Brief Version,* as each chapter is equipped with: glossary terms, chapter objectives, discussion questions, and online testing. In addition, the site hosts links to promote getting involved in theatre and in conducting research on the Web.

Contents

Chapter 5   Designers and Technicians   123

Chapter 6   The Director   177

Chapter 7 Theatre Traditions: East and West   221

Chapter 8 The Modern Theatre: Realism   255

Chapter 11 The Critic   379

Introduction

I T IS EVENING IN MANHATTAN. On Broadway and the streets that cross it—from 42nd to 54th—marquees light up, "Performance Tonight" signs materialize in front of double doors, and beneath a few box-office windows placards announce "This Performance Completely Sold Out." At Grand Central and Penn stations, trains disgorge suburbanites from Greenwich, Larchmont, and Trenton; students from New Haven and Philadelphia; day-trippers from Boston and Washington. Up from the Times Square subways troop denizens of the island city and the neighboring boroughs. At the Duffy Square "TKTS" booth, hundreds line up to buy the discount tickets that go on sale a few hours before curtain time for those shows with seats yet to be filled. Now, converging on these few midtown blocks of America's largest city, come limousines, restaurant buses, private cars, and taxis, whose drivers search for a curbside slot to deposit their riders among the milling throng of pedestrians. Financiers and dowagers, bearded intellectuals, backpack-toting teenagers, sleek executives, hip Harlemites, arm-in-arm widows, out-of-town tourists and conventioneers, between-engagement actors, celebrities, honeymooners, and the precocious young—all commingle in this bizarre aggregation that is the New York Broadway audience. Even during (and perhaps *especially* during) troubled times in this vibrant city, it is as bright, bold, and varied a crowd as is likely to assemble at any single place in America.

It is eight o'clock. In close to forty theatres within two dozen blocks of each other, house-lights dim, curtains rise, and spotlights pick out performers whose lives center on this moment.

1

New York's Times Square is the heart – and heartbeat – of the Broadway theatre district. Thirty-nine major playhouses are within a five-minute walk, and most are within two or three blocks, making this the most concentrated and, hence, the most lively theatre district in the world.

Here a new musical, here a star-studded revival of an American classic, here a contemporary English comedy from London's West End, here a new play fresh from its electrifying Seattle or Atlanta premiere, here a one-woman show, here an off-Broadway hit moving to larger quarters, here a new avant-garde dance-drama, here a touring production from eastern Europe, and here the new play everyone expects will capture this year's coveted Pulitzer Prize. The hours pass.

Eleven o'clock. Pandemonium. All the double doors open simultaneously, as if on cue, and once again the thousands pour out into the night. At nearby restaurants, waiters stand by to receive the after-theatre onslaught. In Sardi's private upstairs room, an opening-night cast party gets under way; downstairs, the patrons rehash the evening's entertainment and sneak covert glances at the celebrities around them and the actors heading for the upstairs sanctuary, there to await the reviews that will determine whether they will be employed next week or back on the street looking for new jobs.

Now let's turn back the clock. It is dawn in Athens, the thirteenth day of the month of Elaphebolion in the year 458 B.C. From thousands of low mud-bricked homes in the city, from the central agora, from temples and agricultural outposts, streams of Athenians and visitors converge upon the south slope of the Acropolis, Athens's great hill and home of its grandest temples. Bundled against the morning's dampness, carrying with them breakfast figs and flagons of wine, they pay their tokens at the entrance to the great Theatre of Dionysus and take their places in the seating spaces allotted them. Each tribe occupies a separate area. They have gathered for the Great Dionysia festival, which celebrates the greening of the land, the rebirth of vegetation, and the long sunny days that stretch ahead. It is a time for revelry, for rejoicing at fertility and all its fruits. And it is above all a time for the ultimate form of Dionysian worship: the theatre.

The open stone seats carved into the hillside fill up quickly. The crowd of 17,000 people here today comprises not only the majority of Athenian citizens but thousands of tradesmen, foreign visitors, slaves, and resident aliens as well. Even paupers are in attendance, thanks to the two obols apiece provided by a state fund to buy tickets for the poor; they take their place with the latecomers on the extremities of the *theatron,* as this first of theatres is called. Now, as the eastern sky grows pale, a masked and costumed actor appears atop a squat building set in full view of every spectator. A hush falls over the crowd, and the actor, his voice magnified by the wooden mask he wears, booms out this text:

> I ask the gods some respite from the
>   weariness
> of this watchtime measured by years
>   I lie awake . . .

And the entranced crowd settles in, secure in the knowledge that today they are in good hands. Today they will hear and see a new version of a familiar story—the story of Agamemnon's homecoming and his murder, the revenge of that murder by his son, Orestes, and the final disposition of justice in the case of Orestes' act—as told in the three tragedies that constitute *The Oresteia.* This magnificent trilogy is by Aeschylus, Athens's leading dramatist for more than forty years. The spectators watch closely, admiring but critical. Tomorrow they or their representatives will decide by vote whether the festival's prize should go to this work, or whether the young Sophocles, whose plays were presented in this space yesterday, had better sensed the true pulse of the time.

Even forty years later, the comic playwright Aristophanes will be arguing the merits and demerits of this day's work.

It is noon in London, and Queen Elizabeth I sits on the throne. Flags fly boldly atop three of the taller buildings in Bankside, across the Thames, announcing performance day at The Globe, The Rose, and The Swan. Boatmen have already begun ferrying theatre-bound Londoners across the river. Meanwhile, north of town, other flocks of Londoners are headed by foot and by carriage up to Finsbury Fields and the theatres of Shoreditch: The Fortune and The Curtain. And though public theatres have been banned within the city for some time now by action of the town councilmen, an ensemble of trained schoolboys is rehearsing for a private candlelight performance before the queen in the royal palace.

Now, as the morning sermon concludes at St. Paul's Cathedral, traffic across the river increases. London Bridge fills with pedestrians hurrying to Bankside, where players at The Globe theater will present a new tragedy by Shakespeare (something called *Hamlet,* supposedly after an old play by Thomas Kyd). And The Rose theater promises a revival of the late Christopher Marlowe's *Dr. Faustus.* The noisy crowds swarm into the theatres, where the price of admission is a penny; another penny is needed for a pint of beer, and those who wish to go upstairs and take a seat on one of the benches in the gallery—the best place to see the action, both on the stage and off—must plunk down yet more pennies.

At The Globe, 2,000 spectators are on hand for the premiere. A trumpet sounds once, then again, and then builds into a full fanfare. The members of the audience exchange a few last winks with friends old and new—covert invitations to postperformance intimacies of various kinds—then turn their attention to the pillared platform stage. Through a giant door a guard bursts forth, lantern in hand. "Who's there?" he cries. Then through another door a voice responds, "Nay, answer me: stand and unfold yourself," and another guard enters. In 2,000 imaginations, the bright afternoon has turned to midnight, Bankside has given way to the outskirts of Elsinore. And a shiver from the actors onstage sets up an answering chill among the audience as the second guard proclaims to the first, " 'Tis bitter cold, and I am sick at heart." The audience strains forward. The new tragedy has begun.

It is 1629 in Edo (Tokyo), and the Shōgun has called together his advisors to discuss, with the utmost urgency, Japan's wildly pop-ular *kabuki* drama. First performed by women in Kyoto, this explosive music-drama now employs performers of both sexes and has become fabulously licentious: "Men and women sing and dance together! Their lewd voices are clamorous, like the buzzing of flies and the crying of cicadas!" an outraged Confucian has reported. Somberly, the Shōgun delivers his edict: henceforward, kabuki can be performed only by males. Little does the Shōgun realize that his edict will be absolute law at least through to the next millennium.

It is 5 A.M. in Moscow, 1898. At a cafe in the shadow of the Kremlin wall, Konstantin Stan-

In 1993, six Canadian actresses, each a mother, decided to write and perform monologues of their individual mothering experiences for Vancouver's Women in View Festival. The result, a poignant and hilarious theatre event titled *Mum's the Word*, has since been performed around the world. The exuberant moment seen here, as the "mums" recapture the infectious spirit of child's play themselves, is from a London production in 2003.

islavsky and Vladimir Nemirovich-Danchenko hotly discuss the wretched state of the current Russian theatre. It is too declamatory, they agree; it is also too insensitive, too shallow, too inartistic. Out of this all-night session the Moscow Art Theatre will be formed, bringing to the last days of czarist society the complex, gently ironic masterpieces of Chekhov and an acting style so natural as to astonish the world.

It is midnight in a basement in the East Village, or a campus rehearsal room, or a coffee shop in Pittsburgh, Seattle, Sioux Falls, or Berlin. Across one end of the room, a curtain has been drawn across a pole suspended by wires. It has been a long evening, but one play remains to be seen. The author is unknown, but rumor has it that this new work is brutal, shocking, poetic, strange. The members of the audience, by turns skeptics and enthusiasts, look for the tenth time at their programs. The lights dim. Performers, backed by crudely painted packing crates, begin to act.

There is a common denominator in all of these scenes: they are all theatre. There is no culture that has not had a theatre in some form, for theatre is the art of people acting out—and giving witness to—their most pressing, most illuminating, and most inspiring concerns. Theatre is at once a showcase and a forum, a medium through which a society displays its ideas, fashions, moralities, and entertainments, and debates its conflicts, dilemmas, and struggles. Theatre has provided a stage for political revolution, for social propaganda, for civil debate, for artistic expression, for religious conversion, for mass education, and even for its own self-criticism. It has been a performance ground for witch doctors, priests, intellectuals, poets, painters, technologists, militarists, philosophers, reformers, evangelists, prime ministers, jugglers, peasants, children, and kings. It has taken place in caves, in fields and forests, in circus tents, in inns and castles, on street corners, and in public buildings grand and squalid all over the world. And it goes on incessantly in the minds of its authors, its actors, its producers, its designers, and its audiences.

For theatre is, above all, a *living* art form—a process, an event that is fluid in time, feeling, and experience. Theatre is a matter not simply of "plays" but also of "playing"; and a play is composed not simply of "acts" but also of "acting." Just as *play* and *act* are both noun and verb, so theatre is both a thing and a happening. It is continually forming, continually present in time. In fact, that very quality of "presentness" (or, in the actor's terminology, "stage presence") defines great theatrical performance.

Unlike the more static arts, theatre presents us with a number of classic paradoxes:

It is spontaneous, yet it is rehearsed.

It is participatory, yet it is presented.

It is real, yet it is simulated.

It is understandable, yet it is obscure.

It is unique to the moment, yet it is repeatable.

The actors are themselves, yet they are characters.

The audience believes, yet it does not believe.

The audience is involved, yet it remains apart.

The theatre's actors, as you will see in later chapters, "live in the moment" during performance yet carefully study, plan, and rehearse the details of their roles beforehand. And the audience responds to this performance by rooting for dramatic "characters" to achieve their goals, then applauding the "actors" who play those roles during the curtain call. Yet these paradoxes do not represent a flaw or weakness in the logic of theatrical construction; rather, they show the theatre's essential strength, which lies in its kinship and concern with the

Theatre is a form of play, even when its subject is grim. *The Hanging Man*, about an architect who tries to kill himself but can't (Death, it seems, has gone on strike), is a playful, surrealistic meditation on death, perhaps a "comedy of the absurd." It was conceived and produced by England's Improbable Theatre as a group effort in 2003 and has toured widely in the United States; much of it is improvised each night. The maniacally hanging actor is Richard Katz.

ambiguity and irony of human life. For it is *we* —the people of the real world—who are at the same time spontaneous yet premeditating, candid yet contriving, unique yet self-repeating, comprehensible yet fundamentally unknown and unknowable. The theatre shows us, and *is* us, in all of our living complexity.

Theorists of dramatic literature and of dramatic practice often ignore the theatre's paradoxes in their attempts to "explain" a play or the art of the stage; in this they do a disservice to art as well as to scholarship, for to "explain" the theatre without reference to its ambiguities is to remove its vital dynamic tension—in other words, to kill it. And although much valuable information can certainly be discovered at an autopsy table, it is information pertinent only to the appearance and behavior of a corpse.

In this book we shall not be concerned with corpses. Our task will be the harder one—to discover the theatre in being, *alive* and with all its paradoxes and ambiguities intact. From time to time it will be necessary for us to make some separations—between product and process, for example—but we must bear in mind at all times that these separations are conveniences, not representations or fact. In the end we shall be looking at the theatre as part of the human environment and at the ways in which we fit into that environment—as participants and observers, artists and art critics, role models and role players, actors and persons. As such, this book about the theatre is also about ourselves.

1

What Is the Theatre?

W HAT IS THE THEATRE? The word *theatre* comes from the Greek *theatron,* or "seeing place." It is a place where something is seen. And the companion term *drama* comes from the Greek *dran,* "to do." It is something done, an action. Theatre: Something is seen, something is done. An action is witnessed.

Today we use the word *theatre* in many ways. We use it often to describe the building where plays are put on: the architecture, the structure, the space for dramatic performance—the place where "something is seen." We also use the term to indicate where films are shown, as in "movie theatre." And we use it metaphorically to refer to a place where wars and surgeries occur: the "theatre of operations" and the "operating theatre."

But that's just the "hardware" definition of *theatre.* The "software" definition—the *activity* involved in theatre—is far more important. For *theatre* also refers to the company of players (and owners, managers, and technicians) who perform in such a space and to the body of plays that such a company produces. This is the "something that is done." When we speak of "the Guthrie Theatre," we are referring not merely to a building in Minneapolis but also to the stage artists and administrators who work in that building and to the body of plays produced there. We are also referring to a body of ideas—a vision—that animates the artists and integrates them with the body of plays. *Theatre,* in this sense, is a combination of people, ideas, and the works of art that emanate from their collaboration.

And, finally, we also use the word *theatre* to summon up an *occupation* that is the professional activity—and often the passion—of thousands of men and women all over the world. It is a vocation, and sometimes a lifetime devotion. *A Life in the Theatre* is the title of one theatre artist's autobiography (Tyrone Guthrie, in fact, for whom the Guthrie Theatre is named), as well as the title of a play about actors by modern American dramatist David Mamet. But *A Life in the Theatre* is more universally known as the unwritten title for the unrecorded biographies of all theatre artists who have dedicated their professional lives to perfecting the special arts of acting, directing, designing, managing, and writing for "the theatre" in all the above senses.

Theatre as a building, a company, an occupation—let's look at all three of these usages more closely.

The Theatre Building

Sometimes a theatre is not a building at all but merely, in English director Peter Brook's term, an empty space. The most ancient Greek theatron was probably nothing but a flat circle where performers chanted and danced before a hillside of seated spectators. The minimal requirement for a theatre "building" is nothing but a place to act and a place to watch. And when there is a text for the performance, it is a place to hear as well as to watch. Hence the

The Guthrie Theatre in Minneapolis was founded in 1963 by distinguished director Tyrone Guthrie, who asked that it be designed like sixteenth-century Shakespearean playhouses, with actors thrust into the midst of the audience. Shown here is the curtain call from the Guthrie's 2003 production of *Pride and Prejudice*.

This watercolor depicts the opulent interior of Booth's Theatre in New York at its 1869 opening. This grand "temple of theatre" was built by America's finest actor of the time, Edwin Booth (the brother of Lincoln's assassin). Booth staged and performed in a classical repertory of Shakespearean plays at his theatre for four years. The side boxes, similar to those that still exist in older Broadway theatres today, had poor sight lines: spectators electing to sit there were more interested in being seen than in seeing the play. The luxurious seating in the orchestra made this a particularly comfortable and elegant way to see classic theatre. Charles Witham, Booth's original stage designer, painted this watercolor; part of Witham's scenery (a street scene) is shown onstage.

word *audience,* from the Latin *audientia,* "those who hear."

The empty space needs some definition, then. This includes some attention to seating a large number of people so that they can see the performers, hence the hillside presenting a bank of seats, each with a good view. It also includes some attention to *acoustics* (from the Greek *acoustos,* "heard") so that the sound is protected from the wind and directed (or reflected) toward the hearers.

Often these spaces—for performing and for seeing and hearing—can be casually defined: the audience up there, the actors down there. Occasionally, the spaces are even merged together, with the actors mingling with—and sometimes interacting with—the watchers and

THEATRE AND DRAMA

The words *theatre* and *drama* are often used interchangeably, yet they can also have distinct meanings. Although both are very general terms, *theatre* often denotes the elements of the whole theatrical production (architecture, scenery, acting), and *drama,* a more limited term, tends to refer mainly to the plays produced in such a "theatrical" environment. To use a modern metaphor, theatre is the "hardware" of play production, and drama is the "software." This reflects on the words' separate etymologies: theatre is that which "is seen," and drama is that which "is done."

Therefore, *theatre* can mean a building; *drama* cannot. *Theatre* refers to all the theatrical arts—architecture, design, acting, scenery construction, marketing, and so on—whereas *drama* focuses mainly on the written actions and the words of a play, whether acted onstage or simply read. Finally, *dramatic* suggests actions (in plays or in life) that are exceptionally compelling, whereas *theatrical*—when used pejoratively—suggests overly showy or sensationalistic behavior.

Professional theatre is not limited to major cities. Since 1973, the Montana Shakespeare in the Parks company has toured to towns and villages across this large northwestern state and its neighbors, playing to a cumulative audience of over half a million people. Here the company stages Molière's seventeenth-century French comedy *Tartuffe* on its 2004 summer tour, which spanned twenty-eight different towns, including Bozeman, Birney, Billings, Big Timber, Roundup, Cut Bank, Worland (Wyoming), and Salmon (Idaho).

listeners. When the practice of selling tickets and paying actors began (more than twenty-five hundred years ago), rigid physical separation of these spaces began to be employed.

Theatre buildings may also be very elaborate structures. Greek theatres of the fourth century B.C.—the period immediately following the "golden age" of Greek playwrights—were gigantic stone edifices, capable of holding upward of 17,000 spectators. Magnificent three-story Roman theatres, complete with gilded columns, canvas awnings, and intricate marble carvings, were often erected for dramatic festivals in the time of Nero and Caligula—only to be dis-mantled when the festivities ended. Grand freestanding Elizabethan theatres dominated the London skyline in the illustrated sixteenth-century pictorial maps of the town. Opulent proscenium theatres were built throughout Europe and in the major cities of the United States in the eighteenth and nineteenth centuries. Many are in full operation today, competing with splendid new stagehouses of every description and serving as the urban focus for metropolitan areas around the world. Theatres (the buildings) are central to modern urban architecture, just as theatre (the art) is central to contemporary life.

Shakespeare's Globe Theater has been meticulously reconstructed near its sixteenth-century location on the south bank of London's Thames River. The reconstruction was spearheaded by the late Sam Wanamaker, an American actor who labored many years to acquire the funding and necessary permits (the theatre has the first thatch roof laid in London since the Great Fire of 1666). This is scholarship's "best guess" as to the specific dimensions and features of the Globe in Shakespeare's time. Since its 1997 opening, with an acting company under the artistic direction of Mark Rylance, the Globe has produced a summer repertoire of the plays of Shakespeare's age, seen on a stage much like the ones they were written for.

The Company, or Troupe, of Players

Theatre is a collaborative art, usually involving dozens, even hundreds, of people working closely together on a single performance. Historically, therefore, theatre practitioners of various specialties have teamed up in long-standing companies, or troupes. Since the third century B.C., such troupes of players (actors, or, more literally, "playmakers") have toured the countrysides and settled in cities to present a repertory (or repertoire) of plays as a means of earning their livelihood. Generally such players have included actor-playwrights and actor-technicians as well so that the company becomes a self-contained production unit, capable of writing, preparing, and presenting whole theatrical works that tend to define the "theatre" named after it. Some of these troupes—and the works produced by them—have become legendary: the Lord Chamberlain's Men of

London, which counted actor-playwright William Shakespeare as a member, for example, and the Illustrious Theatre of Paris, founded and headed by the great actor-writer Molière. These theatres—these companies of players—have proven more long-lasting than the buildings that in some cases survived them; they represent the genius and creativity of theatre in a way that stone and steel alone cannot.

In a more general sense, we may also use the term *theatre* to indicate a general category of associated dramatic works, such as the American theatre, the Elizabethan theatre, dance-theatre, musical theatre, the theatre of the absurd, the theatre of Neil Simon, and black theatre. Any or all of these terms may serve to represent a specifically defined grouping of plays, players, authors, and buildings that form a broad identity in the minds of theatre students, critics, and enthusiasts.

The Occupation of Theatre

Finally, theatre is a principal occupation of its practitioners. It is a vocation for professionals and an avocation for amateurs, yet in either case, theatre is *work*. Specifically, it is that body of artistic work in which actors impersonate characters in a live performance of a play. Each aspect of theatre as occupation—work, art, impersonation, and performance—deserves individual attention.

Work

The "work" of the theatre is indeed hard work. Rehearsals alone normally take a minimum of four to six weeks, which are preceded by at least an equal amount of time—and often months or years—of writing, researching, planning, casting, designing, and creating a production ensemble. The labors of theatre artists in the final weeks before an opening are legendary: the seven-day workweek becomes commonplace, expenditures of money and spirit are intense, and even the unions relax their regulations to allow for an almost unbridled invasion of the hours the ordinary world spends sleeping, eating, and unwinding. The theatre enterprise may involve hundreds of people in scores of different efforts—many more backstage than onstage—and the mobilization and coordination of these efforts is in itself a giant task. So, when we think of the "work" embodied in the theatrical arts, we must think of work in the sense of physical toil as well as in the loftier sense of *oeuvre*, by which the French designate the sum of an artist's creative endeavor.

The work of the theatre is generally divisible into a number of crafts:

Producing, which includes securing all necessary personnel, space, and financing; supervising all production and promotional efforts; fielding all legal matters; and distributing all proceeds derived from receipts

Directing, which includes controlling and developing the artistic product and providing it with a unified vision, coordinating all its components, and supervising all rehearsals

Acting, in which actors perform the roles of characters in a play

Designing, in which designers map out the visual and audio elements of a production, including the scenery, properties, costumes

Part of the success of Andrew Lloyd Webber's *Phantom of the Opera* is its spectacular staging, including a famous falling chandelier and a boat ride on a lake existing underneath the Paris Opera house (which actually exists – the remains of an old water system). The celebrated production design (scenery and costumes) is by Maria Björnson, with admirable lighting by Andrew Bridge.

and wigs, makeup, lighting, sound, programs, advertising, and general ambience of the premises

Building, in which carpenters, costumers, wigmakers, electricians, makeup artists, recording and sound engineers, painters, and a host of other specially designated craftspeople translate the design into reality by constructing and finishing in detail the "hardware" of a show

Crewing, in which technicians execute in proper sequence and with carefully rehearsed timing the light and sound cues and the shifting of scenery, as well as oversee the placement and return of properties and the assignment, laundering, repair, and changes of costumes

Stage managing, which includes the responsibility for "running" a play production in all its complexity in performance after performance

House managing, which includes the responsibility for admitting, seating, and providing for the general comfort of the audience

And above all there is *playwriting,* which is in a class by itself. It is the one craft of the theatre that is usually executed away from the theatre building and its associated shops—indeed, it may take place continents and centuries away from the production it inspires.

Of course, the work of the theatre need not be divided exactly as the preceding list indicates. In any production, some people will perform more than one kind of work; for example, many of the builders will also crew. And it is not uncommon for playwrights to direct what they write, directors to act in their own productions, and designers to build at least some of what they design. There are indeed celebrated occasions where multitalented theatre artists have taken on multiple roles at the same time: Aeschylus, in ancient Greece, and Molière, in seventeenth-century Paris, each wrote, directed, and acted in their own plays, probably designing them as well; William Shakespeare was playwright, actor, and co-owner of the Lord Chamberlain's Men in Elizabethan times; Bertolt Brecht revolutionized both playwriting and acting when writing and directing his plays in Berlin after World War II; and Mel Brooks, in our own times, wrote the text and lyrics, composed the music, and produced his 2001 Broadway show, *The Producers.*

Theatre is also work in the sense that it is not "play." This is a more subtle distinction than we might at once imagine. First, of course, recall that we ordinarily use the children's word *play* in describing the main product of theatre work: while children "play games," adults may "play roles" or "put on a play." This is not merely a peculiarity of the English language, for we find that the French *jeu,* the German *Spiel,* and the Latin *ludi* all share the double meaning of the English *play,* referring both to children's games and to dramatic plays and playing. This association points to a relationship that is fundamental to the understanding of theatre: theatre *is* a kind of playing, and it is useful for us to see how and why this is so.

Theatre and games have a shared history. Both were developed to a high level of sophistication in Greek festivals: the Dionysian theatre festivals and the Olympian game—or sport—festivals were the two great cultural events of ancient Greece, each embodying the legendary Greek competition for excellence. Centuries later, the Romans merged sports and theatre in public circuses, where the two were performed side by side, often in competition with each other. And more than a millennium later, the Londoners of Shakespeare's time built "playhouses" that could accommodate dramatic productions on one day and bear-baiting spectacles (somewhat akin to more modern bullfights) on the next. The association—and popularity—of dramatic and sports entertainment continues today, where dramatizations (sitcoms, detective and courtroom dramas, even TV commercials) and games (spectator sports, quiz shows, "reality" contests) dominate television fare around the world. Meanwhile, professional athletes and stage entertainers are among the foremost (and most highly paid) celebrities of the modern age. Many a retired sports hero has even found a second career in the other type of play: acting.

This link between games and theatre is formed early in life, for "child's play" usually manifests both gamelike and dramalike aspects. Much child's play includes "dressing up" and "acting out," where children create improvisations they may call "playing doctor" or "playing cops and robbers." Like drama, this play is also educational, as it helps children prepare for the necessary role-playing of adult life. Structured games are similarly instructional: hide-and-seek, for example, while a playful and engrossing game, is also an opportunity to act out one of childhood's greatest fears—the terror of separation from the parent, or "separation anxiety," as psychologists term it. Hide-and-seek affords the child a way of dealing with separation anxiety by confronting it "in play" until it loses much of its frightening power. Such "child's play" is often grounded in serious concerns, and through the act of playing the child gradually develops means of coping with life's challenges and un-

Games and dramatic performances continue to be combined, as here in the opening ceremony of the 2000 Sydney Olympics, where a spectacular dramatic performance, directed and choreographed by Stephen Page, portrayed a little English girl "awakening" to the existence of 1,150 aborigines, the first inhabitants of Australia more than 60,000 years ago.

certainties. The theatre's plays and playing often serve the same role for adults.

Drama and games are likewise linked in that they are among the very few occupations that also attract large numbers of wholly *amateur* "players," individuals who seek no compensation beyond their sheer personal satisfaction. This is because both drama and games offer wonderful opportunities for intense physical involvement, friendly competition, personal self-expression, and emotional engagement—within limits set by precise and sensible rules. And both sport and drama also generate an audience to their activities, because the ener-gies and passions expressed by each—common enough on children's playgrounds but rarely seen in daily adult life—can prove immensely engaging to nonparticipating spectators.

But the theatre must finally be distinguished from child's play, and from sports as well, because theatre is by its nature a calculated act from beginning to end. Unlike adult games, which are open-ended, every theatre performance has a preordained conclusion. The Yankees may not win the World Series next year, but Hamlet definitely will die in the fifth act. The work of the theatre, indeed, consists in keeping Hamlet *alive* up to that

NEITHER A BOOK NOR A WORK BUT AN ENERGY

Theatrical representation is finite and leaves behind it, behind its actual presence, no trace, no object to carry off. It is neither a book nor a work, but an energy, and in this sense it is the only art of life.

— Jacques Derrida

point—brilliantly alive—to make of that foreordained end a profoundly moving, ennobling, even surprising climax.

We might say, finally, that *theatre is the art of making play into work*—specifically, into *a work of art*. It is exhilarating work, to be sure, and it usually inspires and invigorates the energies and imaginations of all who participate;

it transcends more prosaic forms of labor just as song transcends grunts and groans. But it is work. That is its challenge.

Art

As we have suggested, the work of the theatre goes beyond the mere perfecting of skills, which is, after all, a goal of professionals in every field. The theatre is *artistic* work. The word *art* brings to mind a host of intangibles: creativity, imagination, elegance, power, aesthetic harmony, and fineness of form. Furthermore, we expect a work of art to capture something of the human spirit and to touch upon sensed, but intellectually elusive, meanings in life. Certainly great theatre never fails to bring together many of these intangibles. In great theatre we glimpse not only the phys-

Richard Greenberg's prize-winning baseball play, *Take Me Out*, which won the 2004 Tony Award, is one of a great many modern dramas about sports, using the intense competitiveness of athletics to drive the dramatic conflicts essential to drama. Other successful sports plays include *The Great White Hope*, about boxing; *That Championship Season*, about basketball; *The Changing Room*, about rugby; *The Beautiful Game* and *Sing Yer Hearts Out for the Lads*, about English football; and *Fences, Damn Yankees, Cobb*, and *Bleacher Bums*, about baseball.

ical and emotional exuberance of play but also the deep yearnings that propel humanity's search for purpose, meaning, and the life well lived.

Art, of course, is one of the most supreme pursuits of humanity, integrating, in a unique fashion, our emotions with our intellects and our aesthetics with our revelations. Art is empowering, to both those who make it and those who appreciate it. Art sharpens thought and focuses feeling; it brings reality up against imagination and presses creativity to the ever-expanding limits of human potential. Although life may be fragmented, inconclusive, and frustrating, a beautiful painting, choral hymn, jazz rendition, or dance video can provide us with near-instant integration, synthesis, and satisfaction. One might, of course, find similar values in religion as well, but art is accessible without subscribing to any particular set of beliefs; it is—for everyone—an open-ended response to life's unending puzzles. It is surely for this reason that all great religions—Eastern and Western—have employed art and artworks (including dramatic art) in their liturgies and services from the earliest of times.

Impersonation

The theatrical art involves actors impersonating characters. This feature is unique to the theatre and separates it from other art forms such as poetry, painting, sculpture, music, performance art, cabaret acts, and like activities. Further, impersonation is the single most important aspect of the theatre; it is its very foundation.

Try to imagine what extreme conceptual difficulties the ancient creators of the theatre encountered in laying down the ground rules for dramatic impersonation. For how was the audience to distinguish the "real person" from the "character" portrayed—the actor-as-himself from the actor-as-character? And when the playwright was also an actor, how could onlookers distinguish between the thoughts of the playwright-as-himself and those of the playwright-as-character? Questions such as these are often asked by children today as they watch a play. Indeed, in face-to-face encounters, soap opera fans will address actors by their character names and ask them questions pertinent only to their stage lives. Given this confusion in what we like to think of as a sophisticated age, it is easy to see why the ancients had to resolve the problem of actor-character separation before the theatre could become a firmly established institution.

The solution the ancient world found was the mask. Western theatre had its true beginning that day in ancient Greece when an

Impersonation requires both internal (psychological) and external (physical) transformation, but sometimes the external comes easily: here real-life twins Peter and Paul Riopelle play the twin Dromio brothers of Shakespeare's *Comedy of Errors* (with Jeff Elam playing the waiter between them) at the 2003 Utah Shakespearean Festival.

actor first stepped out of the chorus, placed an unpainted mask over his face, and thereby signaled that the lines he was about to speak were "in character." The mask provides both a physical and a symbolic separation between the impersonator (the actor) and the impersonated (the character), thus aiding literal-minded onlookers to temporarily suspend their awareness of the "real" world and to accept in its place the world of the stage. In a play, it must be the *characters* who have apparent life; the actors themselves are expected to disappear into the shadows, along with their personal preoccupations, anxieties, and career ambitions. This convention of the stage gives rise to what Denis Diderot, an eighteenth-century French dramatist (and author of the world's first encyclopedia), called the "paradox of the actor": when the actor has perfected his or her art, it is the *simulated* character, the mask, which seems to live before our eyes, while the real person has no apparent life at all. The strength of such an illusion still echoes in our use of the word *person,* which derives from the Latin word (*persona*) for mask.

But of course we know that the actor does not die behind the mask, and herein lies an even greater paradox: we *believe* in the character, but at the end of the play we *applaud* the actor. Not only that—as we watch good theatre we are always, somewhere in the back of our minds, applauding the actor. Our appre-

Masks continue to be used in theatre. In this scene from Nicholas Wright's coming-of-age play, *His Dark Materials*, a young girl encounters fantastical creatures: rebellious angels, soul-eating ghosts, child-catching Gobblers, and the armored bears of the Arctic that are shown here. Masks (by Michael Curry) create the fantasy characters, but with the modern awareness of today's audiences, the actors' faces can be seen behind them without spoiling the image. This 2004 production at London's National Theatre was directed by Nicholas Hytner.

ciation of theatre rests largely on our dual awareness of actor and character and on our understanding that they live inside the same skin.

Masks were used throughout the ancient Greek theatre period, and as we shall see in the pages that follow, they were also staples of many other theatres of the past, including the masquerade dramas of Nigeria, the *nō* and *kyōgen* drama of Japan, and the *commedia dell'arte* of Italy. They are still seen onstage today, not only in contemporary stagings of these historic forms but in expressionist and avant-garde productions. But beyond the mask's physical presence, the *idea* of masking—of hiding the performer while displaying the character—remains at the heart of impersonation. As such, the mask endures—often as the back-to-back masks of comedy and tragedy that adorn a theatre company letterhead—as the most fundamental symbol of theatre itself.

Performance

Theatre is performance, but what, exactly, does *performance* mean? Performance is an action or series of actions taken for the ultimate benefit (attention, entertainment, enlightenment, or involvement) of someone else. We call that "someone else" the audience.

A strictly private conversation between two people is simply "communication." If, however, they engage in a conversation to impress or involve a third person who they know is in a position to overhear it, the "communication" becomes a "performance" and the third person becomes its "audience."

Obviously, performance is a part of everyday life; indeed, it has been analyzed as such in a number of psychological and sociological works. When two teenage boys wrestle on the schoolground, they may well be "performing" their physical prowess for the benefit of their peers. The student who asks a question in the lecture hall is frequently "performing" for the other students—and the professor "performs"

for the same audience in providing a response. Trial lawyers examining witnesses invariably "perform"—often drawing on a considerable repertoire of grunts, snorts, shrugs, raised eyebrows, and disbelieving sighs—for the benefit of that ultimate courtroom audience, the jury. Politicians kiss babies for the benefit of parents (and others) in search of a kindly candidate. Even stony silence can be a performance—if, for example, it is the treatment a woman metes out to an offensive admirer. We are all performers, and the theatre only makes an art out of something we all do every day. The theatre reflects our everyday performances and expands those performances into a formal mode of artistic expression.

The theatre makes use of two general modes of performance: presentational (or direct) and representational (or indirect). Presentational performance is the basic stand-up comedy or nightclub mode. Club performers directly and continuously acknowledge the presence of the audience by singing to them, dancing for them, joking with them, and responding overtly to their applause, laughter, requests, and heckling. Dramatic forms of all ages have employed these techniques and a variety of other presentation methods as well, including asides to the audience, soliloquies, direct address, plays-within-plays, and curtain calls.

Representational performance, however, is probably the more fundamental mode of drama. It is certainly the mode that makes drama "dramatic" as opposed to simply "theatrical"; in the representational mode of performance, the audience watches behavior that seems to be staged as if no audience were present at all. As a result, the audience is encouraged to concentrate on the *events* that are being staged, not on the nature of their presentation. In other words, the members of the audience "believe in" the play and allow themselves to forget that the characters are really actors and that the apparently spontaneous events are really a series of scripted scenes. This belief—or, to borrow Samuel Taylor Coleridge's famous double

Well, by Lisa Kron, is an autobiographical play of the actor-author's family history, including her mother's illness and the economically struggling neighborhood in Lansing, Michigan, where Kron grew up. Kron (*left*) plays herself, with Jayne Houdyshell as her mother, in this production; the realism of the author-as-character and the homey, acutely detailed setting by Allen Moyer and costumes by Miranda Hoffman are totally realistic to the environment Kron's text portrays. This Joseph Papp Public Theatre production enjoyed a strong off-Broadway reception in 2004.

negative, this "suspension of disbelief"—attracts audience participation through empathy: our feeling of kinship with certain (or all) of the characters, which encourages us to identify with their aspirations, sympathize with their plights, exult in their victories, and care deeply about what happens to them. When empathy is present, the audience experiences what is often called the "magic" of theatre. Well-written and well-staged dramas make people *feel*, not just think; they draw in the spectator's emotions, leaving him or her feeling transported and even somewhat changed. This is as much

magic as the modern world provides anywhere, and its effect is the same all over the world.

Occasionally, presentational and representational styles are taken to extremes. In the late nineteenth century, the representational movement known as *realism* sought to have actors behave onstage exactly as real people do in life, in settings made as lifelike as possible (on one occasion, a famous New York restaurant was completely disassembled and reconstructed on a stage, complete with its original moldings, wallpaper, furniture, silverware, and linens). At times the representational ideal so dominated in certain theatres that actors spoke with their backs to audiences, directors encouraged lifelike pauses and inaudible mumblings, playwrights transcribed dialogue from fragments of randomly overheard conversations, and house managers timed intermissions to the presumed time elapsing in the play's story.

Rebelling against this extreme representationalism, the twentieth-century German playwright-director Bertolt Brecht created its opposite: a presentational style, which, seeking to appeal directly to the audience on a variety of social issues, featured lettered signs, songs,

On the Importance of the Art of the People

"When the cannons have stopped firing, and the great victories of finance are reduced to surmise and are long forgotten, it is the art of the people that will confront future generations," said playwright Arthur Miller, accepting the Praemium Imperiale Award in 2002. Such art, said the distinguished author of *Death of a Salesman* and *The Crucible*, "can do more to sustain the peace than all the wars, the armaments, and the threats and warnings of the politicians."

Presentational styles make little pretense of mimicking ordinary life. Here, director Susan Stroman creates a wonderful farcical moment in *The Producers* as "theatre queen" director Roger De Bris (played in drag by Gary Beach) desperately tries to keep his wig on. Facial expressions around the room focus the action and intensify the hilarity. Matthew Broderick and Nathan Lane (*at left*) are the "*producers*" of the musical's title. De Bris's hangers-on (with Roger Bart as his "common-law assistant," Carmen Ghia) are perfectly arranged on the stairs by director Stroman to capture every possible droll expression. Scenic design is by Robin Wagner, costumes by William Ivey Long, and lighting by Peter Kaczorowski.

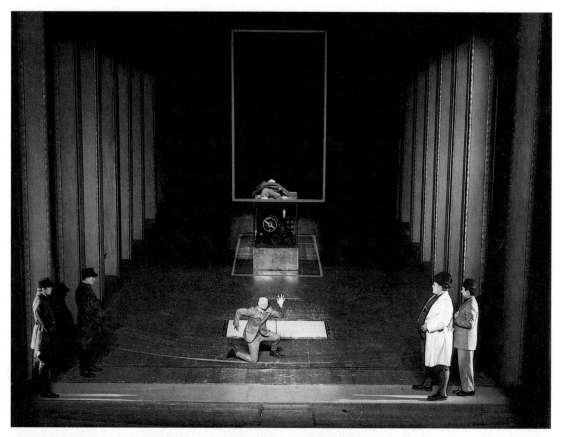

The theatre created by the great German director, theorist, and dramatist Bertolt Brecht is frankly presentational in all respects. His *Resistible Rise of Arturo Ui*, a parable of Hitler's rise to power written in 1941 (although not performed until much later), abstracts, exaggerates, and "distances" the story by setting it among some Chicago gangsters and turning it into a semifarce. This 1999 production was directed by Heiner Müller at the Berliner Ensemble, the theatre Brecht founded.

slide projections, chalk talks, political arguments directly addressed to the house, and an "alienated" style of acting that was intended to reduce empathy or theatrical "magic." These extremes, however, exist more in theory than in practice. We are always aware, during naturalistic performances, that we are watching actors perform for us, and the plays of Brecht and his followers, despite his theories, generate empathy when well performed; the fact is that theatrical performance is always *both* presentational and representational, though often in different degrees.

Two other aspects of performance distinguish theatre from certain other forms of performance: theatre is *live* performance, and it is in most cases a *scripted* and *rehearsed* event.

LIVE PERFORMANCE   Unlike video and cinema (although sometimes employing elements of both), the theatre is a living, real-time event, with performers and audience mutually

FILM STARS ON STAGE ACTING

The vast majority of film stars got their start acting onstage in high school or college, following up their training at professional drama schools or conservatories, on or off Broadway, or in regional theatres. Many of them – including the most successful – return often to live stage performing. Superstars Madonna and Gwyneth Paltrow, for example, opened in London's West End theatre district within eight days of each other in 2004 in *Up for Grabs* and *Proof*, respectively; around the same time Oscar-winning Kevin Spacey was assuming the artistic directorship of England's venerable Old Vic Theatre, where he will both act and direct. Other recent West End stars include Matt Damon (in *This Is Our Youth*) and Glenn Close (in *A Streetcar Named Desire*). On Broadway, Patrick Stewart, famed worldwide as *Star Trek*'s Captain Picard on both film and television, has at the same time been a star of the classical as well as the contemporary stage for over forty years, playing leading roles in Shakespeare, Miller, and Pinter on Broadway and the West End. Ian McKellen, renowned for his film character Gandolf in *Lord of the Rings*, also stars regularly in the theatre. McKellen was particularly celebrated for his performance as Shakespeare's

Richard III, which, after an international tour, he also filmed. Why would these actors, plus the likes of Al Pacino, Anne Heche, Ashley Judd, Christian Slater, Anthony Hopkins, Matthew Broderick, Ethan Hawke, McCauley Caulkin, Meryl Streep, Denzel Washington, and Jason Patric leave Hollywood for such vastly lower-paying stage work? Here are some of their replies:

"If my movie career was totally terminated, I would be saddened and disappointed, missing much of what goes on in movie making. But if that were to happen with the live theater, then it would be devastating. It is for me like a fountain that I have to return to."   – Patrick Stewart

"One of the glorious things about the theatre is that it cannot be preserved. You can't look at it again; it's live, it's not dead. Cinema's dead. You can laugh, you can cry, you can shout at the screen and the movie will carry on. But an audience in the theatre, whether it knows it or not, is affecting the performance. But that's the stream of life at its best, isn't it?"   – Ian McKellen

(continued)

Ian McKellen plays the Captain in this 2003 West End and Broadway production of August Strindberg's Dance of Death, with Frances de la Tour as his wife.

FILM STARS ON STAGE ACTING

(*continued*)

"There is only so long you can go from film to film to film. Theatre is a more raw experience. For an actor a live audience is creative inspiration."

— Jude Law

"My primary focus is theatre. It's the most satisfying place to be as an actor."

— Kevin Spacey

"Acting on stage was the best life experience I've had."

— Ben Affleck

"Nothing was going to stand in my way of doing that play."

— Ashley Judd, explaining why she turned down the title role of Hollywood's *Catwoman* to be onstage in the 2004 Broadway revival of Tennessee Williams's *Cat on a Hot Tin Roof.*

Ashley Judd turned down the film role of Catwoman to star as Maggie in the 2004 Broadway revival of Tennessee Williams's Cat on a Hot Tin Roof.

interacting, each fully aware of the other's immediate presence. This turns out to be an extremely important distinction. Distinguished film stars, particularly those with theatre backgrounds (as most have), routinely return to the live dramatic stage, despite the substantially greater financial rewards of film work, and invariably prefer stage acting because of the immediate audience response theatre provides, with its corresponding sensations of excitement and "presence." Beyond question, fundamental forces are at work in live theatre.

The first of these forces is the rapport existing between actor and audience. Both are breathing the same air; both are involved, at the same time and in the same space, with the stage life depicted by the play. Sometimes their mutual fascination is almost palpable: every actor's performance is affected by the way the audience yields or withholds its responses—its laughter, sighs, applause, gasps, silences. Live theatrical performance is always—even in nat-

uralistic theatre—a two-way communication between stage and house.

And second, live theatre creates a relationship among the audience members. Having arrived at the theatre as individuals or in groups of two or three, the audience members quickly find themselves fused into a common experience with total strangers: laughing at the same jokes, empathizing with the same characters, experiencing the same revelations. This broad communal response is never developed by television drama, which is played chiefly to solitary or clustered viewers who (because of frequent commercials) are only intermittently engaged, nor is it likely to happen in movie houses, where audience members essentially assume a one-on-one relationship with the screen and rarely (except in private or group-oriented screenings) break out in a powerful collective response, much less applause. In contrast, live theatrical presentations generate audience activity that is broadly social in nature:

the crowd arrives at the theatre at about the same time, they mingle and chat during intermissions, and they all depart together, often in spirited conversation about the play. Moreover, they communicate *during* the play: laughter and applause build upon themselves and gain strength from the recognition that others are laughing and applauding. The final ovation—unique to live performance—inevitably involves the audience applauding *itself,* as well as the performers, for understanding and appreciating the theatrical excellence they have all seen together. And plays with political themes can even generate collective political response. In a celebrated example, the depression-era *Waiting for Lefty* was staged as if the audience were a group of union members; by the play's end the audience was yelling "Strike! Strike!" in

A Script Is Not a Play

A play in a book is only the shadow of a play and not even a clear shadow of it. . . . The printed script of a play is hardly more than an architect's blueprint of a house not yet built or [a house] built and destroyed. The color, the grace and levitation, the structural pattern in motion, the quick interplay of live beings, suspended like fitful lightning in a cloud, these things are the play, not words on paper nor thoughts and ideas of an author.

— Tennessee Williams

response to the play's issues. Obviously, only a live performance could evoke such a response.

Finally, live performance inevitably has the quality of *immediacy.* The action of the play is taking place *right now,* as it is being watched, and anything can happen. Although in most professional productions the changes that occur in performance from one night to another are so subtle that only an expert would notice, the fact is that each night's presentation is unique and everyone present—in the audience, in the cast, and behind the scenes—knows it. This awareness lends an excitement that cannot be achieved by theatrical events that are wholly "in the can." One reason for the excitement, of course, is that in live performance, mistakes can happen; this possibility occasions a certain abiding tension, perhaps even an edge of stage fright, which some people say creates the ultimate thrill of the theatre. But just as disaster can come without warning, so too can splendor. On any given night, each actor is trying to better her or his previous

Nothing is more immediate, in the theatre, than a live animal, who (presumably at least) has virtually no self-consciousness about "acting." One of Shakespeare's classic roles is Launce in *Two Gentlemen of Verona,* who shares the stage with his dog, Crab; the actor (Michael Fitzpatrick here in the 2001 Utah Shakespearean Festival production) must seem to be as "real" and unaffected as his very real dog.

A FABULOUS INVALID?

Since the development of motion pictures, some have suggested that the theatre is an endangered species. Indeed, Broadway was called a "fabulous invalid" as early as Moss Hart and George S. Kaufman's play of that name in 1938, and the advent of television has made the theatre's predicament seem even more dire. The idea that theatre risks extinction, however, is sheer lunacy. Film and television have only *increased* the popularity of live theatre, in part by turning theatre actors—such as Marlon Brando, Meryl Streep, Dustin Hoffman, Ashley Judd, and Denzel Washington—into worldwide celebrities.

Indeed, live theatre—certainly in America—has never prospered as much as it does today. In 2003–4, for example, New York's Broadway theatre enjoyed a 20 percent–larger paid attendance than all the New York professional sports teams—Yankees, Mets, Jets, Giants, Knicks, Rangers, Islanders, and New Jersey Nets—*combined*. At the same time, dozens of glittering new theatres have opened or gone into construction around the country, including the American Airlines Theatre (on New York's Broadway), Playwrights Horizons (off Broadway), the Guthrie Theatre (Minneapolis), the Arena Stage (Washington, D.C.), the Goodman Theatre (Chicago), the Argos Stage (at South Coast Repertory in California), and the Kirk Douglas Theatre, Geffen Playhouse, and Redcat Theatre (Los Angeles). And in 2004 alone, multimillion-dollar restorations of historic but long-abandoned American theatres have reopened doors in Baltimore (the Hippodrome), San Jose (the California—after a 31-year vacancy), Chicago (the Biograph), and Boston (the Opera House, built in 1928, which reopened with *The Lion King*). Professional, not-for-profit regional theatres in America have increased from a half dozen when your author was in college to more than 425 today, in 47 states of the union, producing hundreds of new plays by dozens of new playwrights every year. The 2003–4 Broadway season opened thirteen new plays and eight new musicals and earned an all-time record ($771 million) in box-office revenue,

earning the trade paper *Variety*'s accolade as the entertainment world's "least endangered species." And while worldwide receipts for the film *Titanic* have broken all cinema records at $1.6 billion, the box-office revenue for the stage production of *Phantom of the Opera* is more than *double* that. Likewise, the worldwide revenue of the stage production of *The Lion King* now tops that of the film that preceded it.

But theatre's main importance is not its commercial appeal. Theatre truly flourishes, because even at the lowest economic end of the scale, some of the greatest and most provocative theatre has been created simply and cheaply—with neither expensive technology nor multimedia marketing. At bottom, theatre demands nothing more than brilliance, artistry, and hard work.

And such theatre is *alive*. That's why people will pay more to see a live play than a movie, just as they will pay more to see a Madonna concert than to buy a Madonna CD. Theatre is art in the flesh; it's immediate, with performers and spectators in the same space, breathing the same air, concerned (for the duration of the play, if it's a good one) with the same story, the same characters, the same ideas.

Finally, each theatre event is unique. Unlike repeated showings of a film, no stage performance is exactly like any other, which gives each performance its individual identity. When Louis Daguerre invented the daguerreotype, and hence photography, in 1839, painters feared becoming obsolete—as did some stage directors ninety years later. But Van Gogh's paintings of sunflowers—all similar but each fundamentally unique—sell for about $50 million each these days. Photographs of sunflowers may be equally pretty, but they don't spark the same price, or the same reverence. It is the unique expression of the artist, in his dabs of oils before our eyes, that makes the actual painting precious in our lives. And it is the unique life of the theatre artist, on display before a live audience, that makes the theatre eternally in demand.

performance, and no one knows when this collective effort will coalesce into something sublime. The actors' constant striving toward self-transcendence gives the theatre a vitality that is missing from performances fixed unal-

terably on videotape or celluloid. But perhaps most appropriately, the immediacy of live performance creates a "presentness," or "presence," that embodies the fundamental uncertainty of life itself. One prime function of theatre is to

Nudity, though rarely used in the theatre's history, is employed more commonly today, often to intensify the immediacy of live theatre by blurring the line between "actor" and "character," each being represented, as it were, in the same naked body. This mud-slathered Argentine production of *The Last Night of Mankind*, presented by El Periferico de Objetos (a theatre company from Buenos Aires) at the 2003 Edinburgh Festival in Scotland, created an unnerving and aesthetically powerful view of postholocaust humanity.

address the uncertainties of human existence, and the very format of live performance presents a moment-to-moment uncertainty right before our eyes. Ultimately, this "immediate theatre" helps us define the questions and confusions of our lives and lets us grapple, in the present, with their implications.

SCRIPTED AND REHEARSED PERFORMANCE

Theatre performances are largely prepared according to written and well-rehearsed texts, or playscripts. In this way they are often distinguished from several other forms of performance, such as improvisations, performance

installations, and certain other performance art projects. Although improvisation and ad-libbing may play a role in the preparation process, and even in certain actual performances, most play productions are based on a script that was established before—and modified during—the play's rehearsal period, and most of the action is permanently set during these rehearsals as well. Mainstream professional play productions, therefore, appear virtually the same night after night: for the most part, the Broadway production of *The Producers* that you see on Thursday will be almost identical to the show your friend saw on Wednesday or your mother saw last fall. And if you were to read the published text, you would see on the page the same words you heard spoken or sung on the stage.

But the text of a play is not, by any means, the play itself. The play fully exists in its performance—its "playing"—only. The script is merely the record the play leaves behind after the audience has gone home. The script, therefore, is to the play it represents only what a shadowpainting is to the face it silhouettes: it outlines the principal features but conveys only the outer margins of the complexity, the color, the smell, and the spirit of the living person.

And published scripts are an imperfect record at that. Often they carry over material left out of the actual production, or include new material the author thought of after the production was over. The published texts of Shakespeare's plays include differing versions of many of his plays, including two versions of *King Lear* now thought to have been written several years apart. When American dramatist Tennessee Williams published his *Cat on a Hot Tin Roof* after the play's premiere, he included both the third act that he originally wrote and the third act, written at director Elia Kazan's request, that was actually used, and invited his readers to select their preferred version. Moreover, even a fixed script is often as notable for what it lacks as for what it contains. Plays published before the twentieth century rarely have more than rudimentary stage directions, and even now a published play tells us almost nothing about a play's nonverbal components. For how can a printed text capture the

bead of sweat that forms on Hamlet's brow as he stabs Polonius, or Romeo's nervous laugh as he tries to part dueling adversaries, or the throbbing anxiety in Beatrice's breast when she first admits to Benedick that she loves him? The published text gives us the printed but not the spoken words: they largely fail us in providing the sounds and inflections of those words, the tones and facial expressions of the actors, the color and sweep of costumes, the play of light and shadow, the movement of forms in space —and the audience response to all this—that come together in a living production.

The chief value of playscripts, then, is that they generate theatrical production and provide an invaluable, albeit imperfect, record of performances past. Two and a half millennia of play productions have left us a repository of thousands upon thousands of scripts, some awful, many ordinary, a few magnificent. This rich store puts us in touch with theatre history in the making and allows us a glimpse back at the nature of the originals in production. It also suggests ways in which the plays of yesterday can serve as blueprints for vital theatre today.

This, then, is the theatre: buildings, companies, and plays; work, art, impersonation, and performance; living performers and written, rehearsed scripts. It is a production; an assemblage of actions, sights, sounds, ideas, feelings, words, light; and, above all, people. It consists of playing and, of course, plays.

But what is a play? That question deserves a separate chapter.

2

What Is a Play?

A PLAY IS, ESSENTIALLY, WHAT HAPPENS IN THEATRE. It is not a thing but an event.

There are other theatrical events that may be created on a theatre's stage—performance art, rock concerts, stand-up comedy, poetry readings, storytelling, and cabaret performances—and we will discuss some of these later in this chapter and later in the book as alternate theatrical presentations. But the theatre's basic unit, from the distant past to the present day, is the play. It is the theatre's *drama,* whose origin, we remember, is from the Greek *dran,* "something done." It is *action,* not just words in a book.

Action is not merely movement, however. It is argument, struggle, persuasion, threats, seduction, sound, music, dance, speech, and passion. It comprises all forms of human energy, including language, spatial dynamics, light, color, sonic shocks, aesthetic harmonies, and "remarkable things happening" from moment to moment. It is *live* action, ordinarily unmediated by videotape or cinematic celluloid.

And yet a play does not merely produce (or reproduce) live action; drama frames and focuses that action around a particular conflict, which lends the action meaning and significance. Life may be, as Shakespeare's Macbeth says, "a tale told by an idiot, full of sound and fury, signifying nothing," but drama, which is also full of sound and fury, signifies all sorts of things: if not exactly answers, then at least perspectives, vocabularies, illuminating arguments, and aesthetic illuminations. Conflict—generally between characters but also within them —shapes the action into purposeful, meaningful (and meaning-filled) human struggles, the composite of which become dramatic stories against which we can judge our own struggles. A play presents us with characters that can serve as role models, both positive and negative; it offers us themes, ideas, and revelations that we can accept, scorn, or store for future contemplation. A play is a piece of life—animated, shaped, and framed to become a work of art. It provides a structured synthesis—sometimes a critique and sometimes a celebration—of both life's glories and life's confusions.

Of course, a play is also a piece of literature. There has been a reading audience for plays at least since the time of the ancient Greeks, and play collections, such as Shakespeare's works, have been published since the Renaissance. Today, plays are often printed in literary anthologies, intermixed with poems, short stories, and even novels. But drama should not be thought of as merely a "branch" or "genre" of literature; it is a live performance, some of whose repeatable aspects (chiefly, the words) may be captured in a written and published text.*

Finally, a play is "playing," and those who create plays are "players." The theatrical play contains root notions of "child's play" in its acting-out and adventurism, of "dressing up"

in its costumes and props, and of the thrill of sportive competition in its energy and abandon. Like all play, drama is an exhibition, and its players are, in a real sense, willingly exhibitionistic. These are not fundamentally literary characteristics.

Classifying Plays

Plays may be volatile, but they are also contained. They are framed, with a beginning and an end, and no matter how original or unique, they can be seen to fall into a variety of classifications. Two of these are *duration* and *genre*. Although these classifications have been emphasized more in the past than they are today, they still play a part in our understanding of drama.

Duration

How long is a play? American playwright Arthur Miller admitted that when he first thought of writing for the theatre, "How long should it be?" was his most pressing question. The answer is far from obvious.

Historically, in Western drama, a "full-length" play has usually lasted somewhere between two and three hours. This is not an entirely arbitrary period of time; it represents roughly the hours between lunch and dinner (for a matinee) or between dinner and bedtime. The Jacobean playwright John Webster wrote that the actor "entertains us in the best leisure of our life, that is between meals, the most unfit time either for study or bodily exercise." Webster was thinking of the afternoon performances in the outdoor theatres of his day (c. 1615). A few years earlier, speaking of candlelit evening performances at court, Shakespeare's Theseus (*A Midsummer Night's Dream*) asks for a play "to wear away this long age of three hours between our after-supper and bed-time."

But plays can also be much shorter or longer. One-act plays of an hour or less, or,

---

*If the arboreal metaphor is insisted upon, drama would have to be considered the "trunk" of the literary tree, not merely a branch. Certainly no other literary form—the novel, the epic poem, the lyric poem, the short story—has the same sustained level of literary excellence over twenty-five centuries as does the written dramatic work of Aeschylus, Sophocles, Euripides, Aristophanes, Marlowe, Shakespeare, Jonson, Chikamatsu, Webster, Racine, Corneille, Lope de Vega, Calderón de la Barca, Molière, Congreve, Dryden, Farquhar, Fielding, Goethe, Schiller, Ibsen, Wilde, Yeats, Chekhov, Shaw, O'Casey, O'Neill, Pirandello, Giraudoux, Sartre, Brecht, Beckett, Williams, Churchill, Wilson, and so on.

increasingly today, "ten-minute plays," are often combined to make a full theatre program. Short plays are known from ancient times and are presented in nontraditional settings, such as lunchtime theatres, dramatic festivals, school assemblies, social gatherings, street entertainments, or cabaret performances. The shortest play on record is probably Samuel Beckett's *Breath,* which can be performed in one minute. But there are exceptionally long plays as well, particularly in Asia; for example, Chinese theatre traditionally lasts all day, and Indian dance-dramas last all night. In recent decades, six- to nine-hour productions have occasionally proven popular in the West: *Nicholas Nickleby* in London, *Brothers and Sisters* in St. Petersburg, *The Mahabharata* in Paris, *The Oresteia* in Berlin, and both Robert Schenkkan's *The Kentucky Cycle* and Tony Kushner's *Angels in America* in New York. (Indeed, it has been reported that Robert Wilson's *Ka Mountain* was once performed over 168 continuous hours.) In short, a play does not have a precisely fixed duration.

Genre

"Genre" is a more subjective means of classifying plays than is duration, and the term brings with it certain critical perspectives. *Genre* is directly derived from the Old French word for "kind" (this is also our root word for *gender*); thus, to define a play's genre is to categorize it—to say "what kind of play" it is.

Editors and publishers have often identified plays by genre as a shorthand description—even as a sort of advertising. Early publications of Shakespeare's plays, for example, bore such generic classifications on their title pages (*The Most Excellent Conceited Tragedy of Romeo and Juliet; The Most Lamentable Roman Tragedy of Titus Andronicus*), and when the first collection of Shakespeare's plays was published (the First Folio of 1623), his plays were divided into three genre classifications: comedies, tragedies, and histories.

> ## GENRE-LY SPEAKING
>
> Shakespeare has brightly parodied the division of plays into genres, a practice that in his time was already becoming almost an affectation. In *Hamlet,* Polonius describes an acting company as "the best actors in the world, either for tragedy, comedy, history, pastoral, pastoral-comical, historical-pastoral, tragical-historical, tragical-comical-historical-pastoral, scene individable, or poem unlimited."

What defines a genre is not always absolute, however, and many critics, and even more authors, including Shakespeare, have bridled at this sort of categorization (see box). But an identification of genres can generate useful distinctions—not only for the student but also for the practitioner. Russian playwright Anton Chekhov certainly guided the principal director of his works, Konstantin Stanislavsky, by pointing out that his plays were intended as comedies, thereby agreeably blunting what he thought was Stanislavsky's excessively tragic tone. And many an actor, hamstrung by considerations of psychological realism, has been freed to find a more vigorous theatricality when given to understand that the author meant the play as farce, thereby encouraging a rampaging and "over-the-top" comic style.

Two genres have dominated dramatic criticism since ancient times: tragedy and comedy. Aristotle, the ancient Greek philosopher and father of dramatic criticism, considered tragedy and comedy not as genres, however, but as wholly separate art forms, deriving from entirely unrelated sources. Tragedy, Aristotle believed, was an outgrowth of prehistoric religious rituals, whereas comedy was a secular entertainment developed out of bawdy skits and popular revels. In his monumental *Poetics* (c. 325 B.C.), Aristotle strove to define these dramatic forms and create standards for their perfection. Unfortunately, only his poetics for tragedy has survived.

Today, critics and scholars recognize a number of genre classifications by which both classic and modern plays can be roughly classified. In addition to the original tragedy and comedy (now more narrowly defined than in Aristotle's day), the interlude, mystery play, history play, tragicomedy, dark comedy, melodrama, farce, musical, and documentary have been identified as major genres into which modern plays (and, retroactively, older plays) can be classified.

A *tragedy* is a serious play (although not necessarily devoid of humorous episodes) with a topic of universal human import as its theme. Traditionally, the central character, often called the *protagonist,* is a person of high rank or stature. During the play, the protagonist undergoes a decline of fortune, leading to suffering and death. Integral to tragedy, according to Aristotle, is the protagonist's period of insightful *self-recognition* of some fundamental *hamartia*—error or sin—and a consequent reversal of his or her fortunes. The effect of a tragedy, Aristotle then claimed, is for the protagonist's self-recognition and reversal to elicit both pity and terror in the audience, which are then resolved in a *catharsis,* or purging, of those aroused emotions.

The recognition of the protagonist, his or her struggle against decline, and the conse-

Tragedy, the oldest form of recorded drama, probes archetypal problems of the human condition, always ending with death and often — as with ancient myths — dismemberment as well. Tragedy's greatest masters include ancient Greece's Aeschylus, Sophocles, and Euripides; Rome's Seneca; and England's Shakespeare. Here, Dudley Knight plays the blinded Duke of Gloucester, who has just had his eyes savagely torn from his head by the scheming son-in-law of King Lear, in Shakespeare's tragedy of that name. The bloody costume is by Dean Mogle and the stormy sky backdrop is by Chuck O'Connor in this 1999 Utah Shakespearean Festival production directed by this book's author.

quent catharsis of the audience's aroused feelings are central to the tragic experience, which is not to be confused with a merely sad or pathetic experience. Tragedy is neither pathetic nor sentimental; it describes a bold, aggressive, human attack against huge, perhaps insurmountable, odds. Tragic protagonists are often flawed in some way (indeed, classical tragic theory insists that they must be flawed or at least acting in ignorance), but they are leaders, not victims, of the play's events. Indeed, their leadership of the play's action and their discoveries during the course of that action bring the audience to deep emotional and intellectual involvement.

The notion of *protagonist* (Greek: "carrier of the action") is complemented by the notion of *antagonist* ("opposer of the action"), which gives tragedy its fundamental conflict and character struggle. The protagonists of tragedy often go forth against superhuman antagonists: gods, ghosts, fate, or the hardest of human realities. Such protagonists are heroes— or tragic heroes—because their struggle, though doomed, takes on larger-than-life proportions. Then, through the heat of conflict, the tragic heroes assume superhuman force, drawing us into the full magnitude of their thoughts and actions. Thus, tragedy offers us a link with the divine and puts us at the apex of human destiny.

A tragedy should therefore ennoble, not sadden, us. Characters that we admire may fall but not before heroically challenging the elements, divinity, and death. Tragic heroes carry us to the brink of disaster—but, finally, it is their disaster and not ours, or at least not ours yet. Seeing a tragedy is to contemplate and perhaps rehearse in our minds the great conflicts we may still have ahead of us.

There are only a few universally acknowledged tragedies. Sophocles' *Oedipus Tyrannos,* from the fifth century B.C., was Aristotle's model of a great one. Most critics also class the same dramatist's *Antigone;* Aeschylus's *Oresteia* and *Prometheus Bound;* Euripides' *The Trojan*

Tragedy lends itself to stylizations that suggest, but need not realistically portray, blood or violence. The blinded Gloucester scene shown here is from a highly elegant 1991 Japanese production at Tokyo's Globe Theatre with Kazunori Akitaya as the blinded Duke.

Women, Medea, and *The Bacchae;* Racine's *Phèdre;* and Shakespeare's *Hamlet, King Lear, Othello,* and *Macbeth* as among a handful of true tragic masterpieces. The question often arises as to whether a modern play can be termed a tragedy. Take, for example, Arthur Miller's *Death of a Salesman* (1947). Miller deliberately challenged the traditional notion of a high-ranking protagonist by naming his principal character Willy Loman (that is, *low man*). And the antagonists Willy challenges are not gods but faceless bureaucrats, insensitive children, and an impersonal capitalistic economic system. Many critics

One of the rare modern tragedies in world drama is Frederico García Lorca's 1933 *Blood Wedding,* a soaring poetic Spanish drama based on an archetypal folktale, in which Death and the Moon convey impassioned but adulterous lovers to their deaths. The doomed Spanish couple are Drew Cortese and Morena Baccarin in this Minneapolis Guthrie Theatre production of 2001.

today would deny Miller's play the classification as a tragedy on the grounds that the struggle is human, not superhuman, and that tragedy demands a larger-than-life context. If that is the case, tragedy probably belongs to an earlier world, a world in which audiences could be expected to accept without dissent the presence of divine forces mixing in with everyday human affairs.

Comedy began, according to Aristotle, in an entirely different way: as an improvised entertainment that combined satirical skits, bawdy jokes, erotic singing and dancing, and uninhibited revelry. The first known comedies were those of Aristophanes, a playwright of brilliantly funny wit and savagely penetrating political acumen. Writing in Athens a generation after Sophocles, Aristophanes set the general recipe, though not the structure, for comedies to come: interpersonal conflicts, topical issues, witty dialogue, physical buffoonery, and verbal and sexual playfulness.

Comedy is not a simple amusement, however, nor is comedy simply entertaining; comedy is always about a serious human conflict. The passionate pursuit of love, ambition, social status, and money are age-old comic themes. Indeed, the themes of many comedies are often hard to distinguish from those of tragedies; it is the plot of comedy, requiring a happy ending, and the comic style, providing human-scaled characters facing everyday—if exaggerated—problems, that allow the dramatic experience to avoid tragedy's sustained pity, terror, and cathartic shock. Gods, fate, suffering, and death rarely figure significantly in comedies, where the characters' problems are social rather than metaphysical.

The best comedies are often those in which characters foolishly overreach themselves and are hilariously shown up for their foolishness. Not only are Aristophanes' plays (*The Birds, The Frogs, Lysistrata,* for example) masterpieces of this format, but so are the great comedies of Shakespeare (*As You Like It, Twelfth Night, A Midsummer Night's Dream*) and Molière (*The Miser, The Bourgeois Gentleman, The Misanthrope*). In these plays, excesses of romantic love, intellectual pretension, physical braggadocio, or financial greed are wittily shown up, to the delight of the spectators in the audience—who can also recognize the germs of such behaviors in themselves. In this fashion, comedy seeks to advise as well as to entertain. The Roman poet Horace coined the term *utile dulce,* or "sweet instruction," to denote this deeper purpose of the comic drama.

There are many modern authors of dramatic comedy: George Bernard Shaw, Alan Ayckbourn, and Neil Simon are only a few of the twentieth-century playwrights who have succeeded brilliantly in this genre. Because they are topical, however, comedies are usually less enduring than tragedies. Because they generally probe less profoundly into the matter of human destiny, they offer less fertile ground to academic scholarship. Hence, relative to tragedies, comedies are usually less frequently

Shakespeare was also a master of comedy, and *The Taming of the Shrew* is one of his first comic dramas. Based on old Roman and medieval tales — and prejudices — the play seeks its humor by showing a man trying to "tame" the independent-minded woman he wishes to marry. Although this theme has long fallen out of public favor ("altogether disgusting to modern sensibility," said George Bernard Shaw more than a century ago), the play still draws laughs, as in this Royal Shakespeare production of 2003, directed by Gregory Doran, with Alexandra Gilbreath as the intended bride and Jasper Britton as the wooer trying to make her smile.

published in play anthologies, less frequently examined in critical literature, and even less frequently studied in most academic institutions. Nevertheless, comedy's place in the theatre is every bit as secure as is tragedy's, and its impact on audiences is as strong now as it was in Aristophanes' day.

Comedy and tragedy remained the two "official" dramatic genres through the seventeenth century, when neoclassic French critics attempted to formalize them into absolutely rigid classifications. But from the Renaissance onward, playwrights and critics began to develop new dramatic genres or to dispense with genres altogether. The medieval theatre, for example, brought to the stage *interludes* (from *inter*, "between," and *ludus*, "play"), comic entertainments presented between courses at state banquets; *mystery plays*, which dramatized Bible stories from both the Old and New Testaments; and *morality plays*, which portrayed characters representing mankind (one of whom has that very name) choosing between evil and good and in the end pronouncing the moral.

Shakespeare's editors employed a newly defined genre, the *history play*, which dramatizes the key events in the life of a king or head of state. Shakespeare himself seems to have invented this genre, and his great series of nine such plays, covering English royal history from 1377 to 1547 (inaccurate as they may be as historical documents) provides the bulk of what most people ever remember of the English kings Richard II, Henry IV, Henry V, Henry VI, and Richard III. Shakespeare's history plays combine serious scenes, brilliant poetry, battlefield pageants, and hilarious comic moments; none, however, seeks to attain the classical catharsis of tragedy or the sustained humor of comedy.

More enduring than the history play are two other mixed genres. *Tragicomedy,* as the name implies, is a form that deliberately attempts to bridge the two original genres. It maintains a serious theme throughout but varies the approach from serious to humorous and relaxes tragedy's larger-than-life scale. As such, tragicomedy has been called "tragedy that ends happily." *Amphitryon,* by the Roman playwright Plautus, is generally considered the first tragicomedy, and the play has been revised by subsequent authors—including Molière and Jean Giraudoux—into both tragic and comic versions.

Shakespeare virtually invented the history play, of which *Henry V,* based on the English king who defeated a much larger French army in the fifteenth century, is his most patriotic version of this genre. Here Adrian Lester plays the title role in Nicholas Hytner's 2004 production for England's Royal Shakespeare Company. Awareness of theatre's basic paradox allows the modern audience to accept modern rather than medieval costumes and flag and a black actor (Lester is Jamaican) as the historically white king, without diminishing the intensity of their involvement in the dramatic action. Indeed, the use of contemporary images and changes in social culture actually heightens our realization of Henry as a continuing archetype of military adventurism rather than just a long-dead man in a history book.

Dark comedy is the obverse of tragicomedy: it is an often comic but finally disturbing play that ends darkly (or ironically), leaving the impression of an unresolved universe surrounding the play's characters—and perhaps surrounding the audience as well. Dark comedies are usually funny, at least at the beginning, but they don't aim to leave us laughing. There are dark themes and ironic endings to many of Shakespeare's later plays, including *The Tempest, Measure for Measure,* and *The Winter's Tale* (these plays are also often classed as

romances), and to many of the late-nineteenth- and early-twentieth-century plays of Anton Chekhov, Bertolt Brecht, and Luigi Pirandello. In more modern times, certainly after World War II, the dark comedy has come to dominate the theatre, particularly in the work of such playwrights as Harold Pinter, Samuel Beckett, Edward Albee, and Caryl Churchill.

If histories, tragicomedies, and dark comedies are mixed genres, the next two forms are, conversely, extreme generic purifications. *Melodrama* describes plays that are outwardly serious but embellished with spectacular stagings, flamboyant dialogue ("Curse their old families—a bilious, conceited, thin lot of dried up aristocracy. I hate 'em. It makes my blood so hot I feel my heart hiss!"),* and highly suspenseful—and contrived—plotting. Melodrama presents a simple and finite confrontation between good and evil rather than a complex exposition of universal human aspirations and sufferings; such plays cannot sustain unpleasant endings or generate catharsis but can indeed provoke a deeply emotional

outpouring of audience sentiment—always a powerful theatrical response. A pure creation of the theatre, melodramas employ every possible theatrical device to generate audience emotion (the original name, "melo-drama," reveals the function music initially played in these works) and tend to reflect reality, or real human issues, only on the most superficial and sentimental level. Real melodramas are rarely performed today—when the melodramas we tend to see are usually played for laughs—but melodramatic elements frequently find their way into dramas of every sort.

Farce is similarly a pure creation of the theatre, where we expect to find a wildly hilarious

*McClosky in Dion Boncicault's *The Octoroon*, 1859.

Michael Frayn's *Noises Off* is perhaps the finest pure English-language farce of recent decades. A "backstage drama" in which we see a play being (badly) performed onstage and then again from backstage, *Noises Off* hilariously spoofs everything that can go wrong in a play production. David Ivers plays Garry and Gwyn Fawcett plays Brooke in this 2000 Utah Shakespearean Festival production.

treatment of a trivial theme—mistaken identity, illicit infatuation, physical dissolution, monetary scheming—that has been standard farce material since ancient times. Farcical plots are also drawn from stock situations and events: identical twins, lovers in closets or under tables, full-stage chases, switched potions, switched costumes (often involving transsexual dressing), misheard instructions, and various disrobings, discoveries, and disappearances. Elements of farce exist in almost all comedies, but pure farce makes no pretense toward Horace's *utile dulce*; the motto instead is "laugh 'til you cry," and in a well-written, well-staged farce the audience does just that.

There are also some new genres in the theatre. The *musical* is a dramatic style that began in the late 1800s and has become immensely and increasingly popular right up to the present time, earning an entire chapter ("The Musical Theatre") in this book. The *documentary,* a much later genre, utilizes authentic evidence as its basis for portraying recent historical events. Plays written from actual courtroom transcripts—such as the trials of Oscar Wilde, J. Robert Oppenheimer, John Scopes, and Leopold and Loeb, for example—have proven successful in twentieth-century drama, and in the twenty-first century, one play based on the transcriptions of black-box cockpit recordings taken from downed airliners (*Charlie Victor Romeo*) and another drawn from personal interviews about the Wyoming murder of young, gay Matthew Shepard (*The Laramie Project*) have taken the genre of documentary drama into newer territory yet.

Potentially, of course, there are as many theatrical genres as the diligent critic wishes to define. No system of classification should obscure the fact that each play is unique, and the grouping of any two or more plays into a common genre is only a convenience for purposes of comparison and analysis. We in the twenty-first century have learned that past formulations of tragedy and farce have had little bearing on the long-range assessment of the importance, quality, or worth—on the staying power—of any individual play. Critics who today dwell inordinately on such questions as "Is *Death of a Salesman* a true tragedy?" are doubtless spending too much time deciding what box to put the artistic work in and too little time examining and revealing the work itself.

Nevertheless, genre distinctions can be useful if we keep their limitations in mind. They can help us to comprehend the broad spectrum of purposes to which plays may be put and to perceive important similarities and differences. For the theatre artist, an awareness of the possibilities inherent in each genre—together with a knowledge of the achievements that have been made in each—stimulates the imagination and aids in setting work standards and ambitions.

Structure

Drama is action, but plays, indeed all theatre events, are *structured* actions. Unlike the actions of a street riot, say, a dramatic action (more or less) begins at a certain time, ends at a certain time, and, even when improvised or radically experimental, tends to follow certain structural patterns between its start and finish. Action provides excitement, but structure adds momentum—the feeling that the action is *consequential,* not just random, and will become even more compelling and meaningful as it goes on, heading as it must toward some sort of climax and resolution.

Plays, which constitute the vast majority of theatre events, can be analyzed structurally in two ways: by their components (that is, plot, characters, theme, and so on) and by their order of organization (exposition, development, climax, and so on). Both methods are used by most people who find it worthwhile to analyze dramatic art, and both will be used in this book.

The Components of a Play

The division of plays into components is an ancient analytical practice. Aristotle described the components of a tragedy as plot, characters, theme, diction, music, and spectacle—in that order, and, with some modification and elaboration, Aristotle's list still serves as an approximate breakdown of the major elements of all dramas, although the relative importance of each component has been a matter of continuing controversy.

PLOT   Although colloquially we may think of *plot* as synonymous with *story,* the two words are quite different: *story* is simply a narrative of what happens in the play, as might be described by someone who has seen it, whereas *plot* refers to the *mechanics* of storytelling, including the sequence of the characters' comings and goings; the timetable of the play's events; and the specific order of revelations, reversals, quarrels, discoveries, and actions that take place onstage, as in "furthering the plot." (In English theatres of the sixteenth century, a written "platte"—or "plotte"—was hung on the wall backstage, reminding the actors of the play's order of major events, entrances, and exits.) Plot is a *structure of actions:* both outer actions (such as Romeo stabbing Tybalt) and inner ones (such as Romeo falling in love with Juliet). The specific sequence and arrangement of these actions are essentially what we take away from the play; they are usually the way we describe the play to someone who has not yet seen it. This is undoubtedly why Aristotle described plot first in his list of the elements of tragedy (drama). Creating a dramatically compelling plot is one of the most difficult and demanding tests of a playwright's skill.

Traditionally, the primary demands of plot are logic and suspense. To satisfy the demand for logic, the actions portrayed must be plausible, and events must follow one upon another in an organic rather than arbitrary fashion. To sustain suspense, the actions portrayed must set up expectations for further actions, drawing the audience along in a story that seems to move inescapably toward an ending that may be sensed but is never wholly predictable. Melodramas and farces tend to rely heavily on intricate and suspenseful plots. The "well-made plays" of the late nineteenth century reflect an attempt to elevate plot construction to the highest level of theatrical art; today, murder mysteries and "whodunits" are perhaps the most plot-intensive plays.

CHARACTERS   The characters of a play are the human figures—the impersonated presences—who undertake the actions of the plot. Their potency in the theatre is measured by our interest in them *as people.* The most brilliant plotting in the world cannot redeem a play if the audience remains indifferent to its characters; therefore, the fundamental demand of a play's characters is that they make the audience care. To this end, characters cannot be mere stick figures, no matter how elaborately detailed. The great dramatic characters of the past—Hamlet, Juliet, Stanley Kowalski, Blanche DuBois, to

---

THE WELL-MADE PLAY

Pièce bien faite ("well-made play") was a term used to describe certain dramatic works, known for their complex and elegant plots, written by the popular French dramatists Eugène Scribe and Victorien Sardou (among others) during the latter part of the nineteenth century. The expression was originally complimentary but soon became a derisive reference to plays that were seen as merely mechanical, plot-heavy contrivances, holding their audience solely by a series of calculated dramatic effects. Arguing that drama should also be the vehicle for grand ideas and deep passions, playwright George Bernard Shaw coined the term "Sardoodledom" to express his contempt for Sardou's well-made but shallowly felt plays.

Anthony Sher as Iago and Sello Maake Ka Ncube as Othello radiate, through their expressions alone, the evil of the former and the innocence of the latter that are fundamental to Shakespeare's play. *Othello* is an intense character study, and Iago, though strictly a fictional character, has prompted literary scholars, psychologists, and audiences to investigate his deeper personality for four centuries. Why does Iago behave as he does? What is his *real* motivation? And why does Othello believe him? The job of the actor is not to answer these questions in an essay, but to portray the character with sufficient psychological complexity to make the audience reach their own conclusions. This 2004 Royal Shakespeare Company production was directed by Gregory Doran.

name a few—bring to an experienced theater-goer's or playreader's mind personalities as vivid and memorable as those of good friends (and hated enemies); they are whole images, indelibly human, alive with the attributes, feelings, and expectations of real people. We can identify with them. We can sympathize with them.

Character depth is what gives a play its psychological complexity, its sensuality, and its warmth. Without it, we cannot experience love, hate, fear, joy, hope, despair—any of the emotions we expect to derive from theatre—and a theatre devoid of those emotions that stem from the humanness of the characters portrayed would be a theatre without an audience in a matter of days. For this reason, many playwrights have scoffed at the notion of primacy of plot and at the often-mechanical contrivances of the well-made play. Indeed, several playwrights have fashioned plays that were arbitrarily plotted, with the story line designed simply to show various aspects of a fascinating character.

THEME The theme of a play is its abstracted intellectual content. It may be described as the play's overall statement: its topic, central idea, or message, as the case may be. Some plays have obvious themes, such as Euripides' *The Trojan Women* (the horrors of war) or Molière's *The Bourgeois Gentleman* (the foolishness of social pretense). Other plays have less clearly defined themes, and the most provocative of these have given rise to much scholarly controversy. *Hamlet, Oedipus Tyrannos,* and *Waiting for Godot* all suggest many themes, and each has spawned a great many fierce debates about which of its themes is central.

Nothing demands that a play have a single theme, of course, or even that it be at all reducible to straightforward intellectual generalization. Indeed, plays that are too obviously theme-intensive are usually considered too propagandistic or academic for theatrical success: "If you want to send a message," one Broadway saying goes, "use e-mail." Moreover, although the themes of plays address the central questions of society and humanity, a play's theatrical impact hinges always on the audience's engagement in its plot and characterization.

A play must have something to say, and that something—its theme—must seem *pertinent* to the audience. Further, the play must be sufficiently focused and limited to give the audience at least some insight into that something within its framework. Plays that try to say nothing or, conversely, plays that try to say everything rarely have even a modest impact, no

Theme dominates the intensely polemical play *Alive from Palestine,* which portrays the despair and (mostly) dashed hopes of ordinary Palestinians as they experience – and read about in the newspapers – the horrific problems of occupation, violence, poverty, and corruption in their homeland. Few were unmoved by the Arabic production (with English subtitles) mounted by the Ramallah-based Al Kasaba theatre company on its 2002 American and British tour.

The diction Aristotle considered important to drama is not limited to poetry and verse. No one mastered dramatic prose quite like Oscar Wilde, whose dialogue is filled, not only with elegant phrases, jewel-like ripostes and bon mots, and snappily comic put-downs, but cogent dramatic arguments as well. Restraint in the decor and costumes, which are formal and understated, allow the audience to concentrate on the language and inner action of Wilde's 1893 comedy *A Woman of No Importance*, as shown here in a 2003 production with Samantha Bond and Rachel Sterling.

matter how entertaining or well plotted they may be. Thus, from the beginning, playwrights working in every genre, be it tragedy, comedy, melodrama, or farce, have recognized the merit of narrowing their field of intellectual investigation when crafting a play.

DICTION Aristotle's fourth component, diction, relates to the pronunciation of spoken dialogue; to the literary character of a play's text, including its tone, imagery, cadence, and articulation; and to its use of literary forms and figures such as verse, rhyme, metaphor, apostrophe, jest, and epigram.

The value of poetry has been well established from the theatre's beginning; indeed, until fairly recent times, most serious plays were written largely in verse. Today, though the use of verse is relatively rare, all plays continue to demonstrate carefully crafted language. Many, such as those by Tom Stoppard and Richard Greenberg, feature brilliant repartee, stunning epigrams, witty arguments, and dazzling tirades. Other, quite different, sorts of plays may feature rough-textured slang, local dialects and crude vulgarities, and/or a poetry of silences and nearly inarticulate mutterings—dictions that can be no less effective than the flamboyantly crafted verbal pyrotechnics of Stoppard.

The diction of a play is by no means the creation of the playwright alone. It is very much the product of the actor as well, and for that reason throughout the history of Western theatre, an effective stage voice has been considered the prime asset of the actor. Even today, the study of voice is a primary and continuous obligation at most schools and conservatories of classical acting. The chief aim of such study is to create an acting voice capable of dealing in spectacular fashion with the broad palette of dramatic diction demanded by the works of the world's most noted playwrights.

MUSIC Any discussion of music, Aristotle's fifth component of theatre, forces us to remember that in Aristotle's time, plays were sung or chanted, not simply spoken. That mode of presentation has all but disappeared, and yet the musical component remains directly present in most plays performed today and indirectly present in the rest.

When it is directly present in a play, music can take many forms. Songs are common in the plays of Shakespeare, as well as in the works of modern writers (such as Bertolt Brecht) who employ presentational-performance techniques. Many naturalistic writers work familiar songs into their scripts, sometimes by having characters play recordings onstage. Chekhov and Tennessee Williams both make extensive use in their plays of offstage music—for example, a military marching band can be heard in Chekhov's *The Three Sisters,* and Williams provides for music from a nearby dance hall in *A Streetcar Named Desire* and from a cantina in *Night of the Iguana.* Directors also frequently add incidental music to play productions—sometimes to set a mood during intermissions or before the play begins, sometimes to underscore the play's action itself. The power of music directly present in the theatre is well known, and its effectiveness in moving an audience to ever-deeper feeling is one of its functions that few playwrights or directors wish to ignore.

Indirectly, music is present in every play. It is in the rhythm of sounds that, while not specifically tuneful, combine to create a different kind of "score"—the orchestration of sound rather than music. Vocal tones, footsteps, sighs, shouts, offstage railroad whistles, the shrilling of a telephone, muffled drumbeats, gunshots, animal cries, conversations in the next room, and amplified special effects (heartbeats, respiration, otherworldly noises, for instance) are frequently employed by authors, directors, and sound designers to create a theatrical symphony apart from, though supportive of, the plot, characters, dialogue, and theme. Moreover, the spoken word creates, in addition to its semantic impact (its meaning and connotation), an aural impact: it is an integer of pure sound, and it can be appreciated as pure musical vibration. Under the guidance of a skilled director, all of a play's sounds can be orchestrated to produce a performance of such dramatic force that it can thrill even persons wholly unacquainted with the language of the dialogue.

SPECTACLE Aristotle's last component, spectacle, encompasses the visual aspects of production: scenery, costumes, lighting, makeup, properties, and the overall *look* of the theatre and stage. It would be wrong to infer that *spectacle* is synonymous with *spectacular,* for some productions are quite restrained in their visual artistry. Rather, *spectacle* here refers to "something seen." Although this point may seem obvious, it is crucial. Theatre is as much a visual experience as it is an aural, emotional, and intellectual experience: the ancient Greeks clearly had this in mind when they chose the name *theatron* ("seeing place") to designate the site of their performances.

Much as the cinema has been called the art of moving pictures, so the theatre might be called the art of fluid sculpture. This sculpture is fashioned in part from the human body in

Robert Wilson is an American director and designer with astonishing visual creativity, and Gertrude Stein's *Four Saints in Three Acts* (1934) is an abstract avant-garde opera. The two artists were made for each other, as this spectacularly innovative 1996 staging at New York's Lincoln Center clearly demonstrates.

motion and in part from still or moving scenery and props—natural and manufactured items of both dramatic and decorative importance, all illuminated by natural or artificially modulated light. It is a sculpture that moves in time as well as in space; and although it is generally considered to be primarily a support for the plot, characters, and theme of a play, it has an artistic appeal and an artistic heritage all its own. Certainly some ardent patrons of the theatre pay more attention to settings and costumes than to any other aspect of a play, and in many a successful production, dramatic visual effects have virtually carried the play.

Memorable visual elements can be both grand and prosaic, imposing and subtle. Nineteenth-century romanticism, which survives today primarily in the form of grand opera, tends to favor mammoth stagings featuring processions, crowd scenes, palaces, animals, triumphal arches, and lavish costumes. In contrast, twentieth-century movements are more likely to go in for domestic environments and archetypal images: Jimmy and Cliff reading newspapers while Alison irons a shirt in John Osborne's *Look Back in Anger;* Laura playing with her glass animals in Tennessee Williams's *The Glass Menagerie;* Mother Courage pulling her wagon in Brecht's *Mother Courage;* and Nagg and Nell living in the ashcans of Samuel Beckett's *Endgame.* In the long run, conceptual richness and precision in a play's visual presentation are far more telling than grandeur for its own sake.

Left: Although spectacle is the last dramatic component on Aristotle's list, it is first in the minds of many theatergoers, particularly on Broadway, in London's West End, and in Tokyo's Ginza. *Bombay Dreams,* a lavish song-and-dance extravaganza about the movie industry of India's "Bollywood," has filled theatre houses in major cities mainly as a grand visual spectacle, with Mart Thomson's sets and costumes and Hugh Vanstone's lighting. Ayesha Dharker plays the movie-star diva in the play's 2002 West End opening.

Below: Spectacle can be simple but still profound. The image of the aged Nagg and Nell in their ashcans, trying to kiss, in Samuel Beckett's grimly absurdist *Endgame* is unforgettable. Shown here are Liz Smith and Geoffrey Hutchings in their 2004 performance at London's Albert Theatre.

CONVENTION To these six components of every play we should add a seventh, discrete, item that Aristotle apparently never saw reason to consider: theatrical convention. The agreement between audience and actor entails a set of tacit understandings that form the context of playwatching—conventions that make us understand, for example, that when the stage lights fade out, the play (or the act) has ended. Over the years, other common conventions of the Western stage have included the following:

A Chinese theatre convention means that a man paddling with an oar represents "boatman," "boat," and "water" alike. Here, famed Shanghai actor Liu Yilong portrays the boatman ferrying his passengers in *The Meeting by the Lake,* a classic work of the Chinese *xiqu* (traditional opera) form.

- When one actor turns directly from the others and speaks to the audience, the other characters are presumed not to hear him. This is the convention of the *aside* (to the audience).

- When the actors all leave the stage and then they or others reenter (particularly when the lights change), time has elapsed, and the locale may be changed.

- When the actors onstage freeze, we are seeing some sort of "dream state" (of one of the characters, presumably), and the words we hear are to be considered his or her thoughts, not anyone's speech.

We can see conventions more clearly in theatres unlike our own. In the *wayang kulit,* a shadow puppet theatre on the island of Bali, the play is over when the "tree of life" puppet, previously seen only in motion, finally comes to a standstill at the center of the stage. In the *nō* drama of Japan, the audience recognizes words sung by chorus members to be considered spoken by the actors who are dancing, and gestures of a fan to indicate wind, rain, or the rising moon. In the Chinese *xiqu,* or traditional opera, a character entering the bare stage while holding a boat paddle is understood to be rowing across a river. The conventions of theatre permit this sort of shorthand communication with the audience, without the encumbrance of extensive physical elaboration or acting out. If the locale can effectively be changed by the convention of a simple light shift, instead of by moving a half ton of scenery, the theatre saves money and the audience saves time. Stage violence is usually executed conventionally (that is, with little physical mayhem) rather than with lifelike (or cinematic) verisimilitude. The difficulty in realistically portraying severed torsos, rupturing intestines, and bleeding limbs onstage ordinarily outweighs any dramatic advantage in doing so; and the theatrical convention ("stab, grab, scream, collapse, and die") can be accepted fully if performed with emotional and psychological (though not physical) authenticity.

Each play sets up its own system of conventions, but in most cases they accord with the traditions of their times and therefore go largely unnoticed (doubtless that is why Aristotle, familiar with no drama other than his own, made no specific mention of them). In modern times, playwrights and directors have become increasingly aware of other traditions and possibilities; more and more play productions employ conventions of ancient times or foreign cultures and even establish new ones. Peter Shaffer's *Black Comedy,* which supposedly takes place in the dark, utilizes a convention that Shaffer attributes to the Chinese: when the lights are on they are "off," and when they are off they are "on." Eugene O'Neill's *Strange Interlude* and Steven Berkoff's *Kvetch* give us to understand that when the actors freeze and speak, we in the audience—but not the other characters in the play—hear their thoughts. Jean Anouilh's *Antigone* uses a variation on the Greek device of the chorus: a single man speaks with the author's voice as the characters onstage freeze in silence. Lanford Wilson, in *The Rimers of Eldritch,* presents a story in more than a hundred tiny scenes that jump back and forth in time; only at the play's end do we get any real sense of a story line. Arthur Miller's *After the Fall* places an imaginary psychiatrist in the midst of the audience, and the play's protagonist repeatedly interrupts the action of the drama to address his analyst in highly theatrical therapy sessions. And so it goes. There is no formal requirement for the establishment of theatrical conventions, except that the audience must "agree" to accept them (which it does, of course, unconsciously).

These seven components of every play—with the seventh framing Aristotle's six—are the raw material of drama. All are important. Indeed, the theatre could not afford to dispense with any one. Some plays are intensive in one

or more components; most great productions show artistry in all. The balancing of these components in theatrical presentation is one of the primary challenges facing the director, who on one or another occasion may be called upon mainly to clarify and elaborate a theme, to find the visual mode of presentation that best supports the action, to develop and "flesh out" the characterizations in order to give strength and meaning to the plot, to heighten a musical tone in order to enhance sensual effect, or to develop the precise convention—the relationship between play and audience—that will maximize the play's artistic impact. For as important as each of these components is to the theatrical experience, it is their combination and interaction, not their individual splendor, that is crucial to a production's success.

The Order of a Play

A play also has a temporal (time) structure. Here again, Aristotle affords some help. He tells us that drama has a beginning, a middle, and an end, and here and there in his *Poetics* he proffers a little detail about the nature of each of these elements. We can expand Aristotle's list somewhat, for by now some fairly consistent features have evolved in the orderly sequencing of a theatrical experience. These individual features can be divided into three major groupings: the preplay, the play proper, and the postplay.

The events that take place before the play proper begins are referred to as the *preplay.*

THE GATHERING OF THE AUDIENCE Dramatic theorists often either ignore the audience in considering the crucial elements of theatre or dismiss it as a "paratheatrical" (*para* meaning "only somewhat") concern. The gathering of the audience is, however, an important consideration in the presentation of a play, entailing a process that is not without its artistic and cultural significance. The chief concerns in that process have to do with publicity, admission, and seating—concerns that have preoccupied theatre producers since ancient times.

For how does the theatre attract its audience in the first place? Theatregoing, after all, is not a human necessity per se; people do not spend half their waking hours trying to supply themselves with theatre in the same way they strive to secure food, shelter, and physical security. Therefore, if it is to survive, the theatre must go out and recruit attention.

Therefore, the goal of every theatre producer is to make his or her theatre accessible, inviting, and favorably known to the widest possible public—and also, in many eras, to the *richest* possible public—and to make theatre as an art form as thrilling and spiritually *necessary* as it can possibly be.

In every era, theatre has had the responsibility of gathering its audience. The procession is one of the oldest known ways of publicizing the theatre. The circus parade, which still takes place in some of the smaller towns of Europe and the United States, is a remnant of a once-universal form of advertisement for the performing arts that probably began well in advance of recorded history. The Greeks of ancient Athens opened their great dramatic festivals with a *proagon* (literally, "pre-action"), in

Posters – on theatre walls, in subway stations and shop windows, and on special billboards – around theatre towns are universal for advertising current theatre productions. Here, in Tokyo's downtown Ginza district, theatergoers study the posters advertising the new production at the Kabuki-za theatre, the world's outstanding showcase for Japanese kabuki drama.

which both playwrights and actors were introduced at a huge public meeting and given a chance to speak about the plays they were to present on subsequent days. The Elizabethans flew flags atop their playhouses on performance days, and the flags could be seen across the Thames in "downtown" London, enticing hundreds away from their commercial and religious activities. The lighted marquees of Broadway theatres around Times Square and of London theatres in the West End are a modern-day equivalent of the flags that waved over those first great English public theatres.

Developments in the printing and broadcast media have not only spurred the growth of theatre advertising but also made it into a major theatrical craft in its own right. Splendid posters, illustrated programs, multicolor subscription brochures, full-page newspaper advertisements, staged media events, articulate press releases, and flashy thirty-second television commercials summon patrons out of the comfort of their homes and into the theatre. Far from being an inconsequential aspect of theatre, publicity today occupies a place of fundamental importance in the thinking of theatrical producers and commands a major share of the budget for commercial theatrical ventures.

Now that the patrons have been attracted to the theatre, how should they be admitted and seated? Although procedures for admitting and seating the audience are usually straightforward and conventional, they can have important—and occasionally decisive—effects on the overall theatrical presentation.

Ordinarily, theatre is supported at least in part by its admission fees, known as box-office revenue. For commercial theatres, such revenue provides the sole means of meeting production costs and providing a profit to investors. The admission charge dates from ancient Greek days, and since then only a few amateur or civic productions (such as the religious pageants of medieval England and the free Shakespeare performances in contemporary New York City) have managed to survive without it.

Seating is frequently determined by the price of admission: the best seats cost the most. What determines "best" and "poorest" seating, however, depends on many things. In modern Broadway and West End theatres, for example, the most costly seats are in the orchestra (known in the West End as the "stalls"), which is the ground-level seating area; balcony seats ordinarily cost less—the higher the balcony, the lower the price. In the public theatres of Elizabethan London, however, the ground level (which was standing room) was the cheapest space, and the "gentlemen's rooms" in the balcony—where one could be seen and visited—commanded up to twelve times as much. In the Restoration period, seats on the stage itself brought the highest prices of all, ensuring their purchasers the widest possible personal recognition (but affording a ridiculously poor view of the play's action).

Seating has not always been scaled according to price, however. In the drama festivals of ancient Athens, the front-row seats were reserved for priests, and members of the lay audience sat in sections of the theatron reserved for their particular tribe. In many noncommercial theatres today, the best seats go to the theatre company's most loyal—and long-standing—subscribers.

THE TRANSITION Gathered, admitted, and seated, the audience remains a collection of individuals preoccupied with their daily concerns. Now the theatre must transform them into a community devoted to the concerns of the play and enmeshed in the actions of imaginary characters. The theatre, in other words, must shift the audience's awareness from real life to stage life, and it must do so in a smooth and agreeable fashion.

Ushers lead the audience into the theatre, showing them where to find their seats and providing them with a written program. The program helps prepare the audience for the fiction they are about to see, giving them the locale and time of the action, the names of the play's characters and of the actors who will play them. Preshow music or perhaps an ominously pulsing sound effect may be used to set the play's mood or tone, while stage lights may "warm" a lowered stage curtain or illuminate the stage and scenery with a romantic or eerie glow, creating an anticipation of the dramatic actions about to take place.

There may be some stage activity, such as a ticking clock or flickering carnival lights or perhaps a few actors engaged in some quiet preshow activity as incoming audience members observe the scene. There is much to look at, along with the program, but above all—and this is quite different from in a movie theatre—the theatre audience is aware of *itself,* for the seating area is fully illuminated and audience members are free to greet and chat with each other. Theatre, we must always remember, is a live art, and part of its liveliness comes from the fact that the audience is part of the action and will share its responses to the actors—and to each other—with (one hopes) laughter, sighing, and applause.

Finally, a swift conclusion to the transition begins, usually these days, with an announcement for audience members to turn off their cell phones—"*now!*"—so that the outside world remains sealed out for the show's duration. Then the houselights dim, and the audience is transported into the world of new characters and a new story. To use a familiar theatrical saying, "It's magic time."

The *play proper,* particularly in contrast to other theatre events like performance art and stand-up comedy, almost always contains a structured sequence of identifiable elements, namely, exposition, conflict, climax, and denouement.

THE EXPOSITION   No important play has ever begun with a character dashing onstage and shouting, "The house is on fire!" At best, such a beginning could only confuse the audience, and at worst it could cause them to flee in panic. At that point they would have no way of knowing what house or why they should even care about it. Most plays, whatever their style or genre, begin with dialogue or action calculated to ease us, not shock us, into the concerns of the characters with whom we are to spend the next two hours or so.

Exposition is a word not much in favor now, coming as it does from an age when play structure was considered more scientific than it is today. But it is still a useful term, referring to the background information the audience must have in order to understand what's going on in the action of a play.

In the rather mechanical plotting of the "well-made plays," the exposition is handled with little fanfare, with a few characters—often servants (minor figures in the action to follow)—discussing something that is about to happen and enlightening each other (and, of course, the audience) about certain details around which the plot will turn. Consider these lines from the opening scene of Henrik Ibsen's 1884 classic, *The Wild Duck:*

PETTERSEN, *in livery, and* JENSEN, *the hired waiter, in black, are putting the study in order. From the dining room, the hum of conversation and laughter is heard.*

PETTERSEN: Listen to them, Jensen; the old man's got to his feet—he's giving a toast to Mrs. Sorby.

JENSEN: (*pushing forward an armchair*) Do you think it's true, then, what they've been saying, that there's something going on between them?

PETTERSEN: God knows.

JENSEN: He used to be quite the lady's man, I understand.

PETTERSEN: I suppose.

JENSEN: And he's giving this party in honor of his son, they say.

PETTERSEN: That's right. His son came home yesterday.

JENSEN: I never even knew old Werle had a son.

PETTERSEN: Oh, he has a son all right. But he's completely tied up at the Hoidal works. In all the years I've been here he's never come into town.

A WAITER: (*in the doorway of the other room*) Pettersen, there's an old fellow here . . .

PETTERSEN: (*mutters*) Damn. Who'd show up at this time of night?

After a few more lines, Pettersen, Jensen, and the waiter make their exits and are seen no more. Their function is purely expository—to pave the way for the principal characters. Their conversation is a contrivance intended simply to give us a framework for the action—and the information they impart is presented by means of a conversation only because a convention of realism decrees that words spoken in a play be addressed to characters, not to the audience.

In contrast, the exposition of nonrealistic plays can be handled more directly. It was the Greek custom to begin a play with a prologue preceding the entrance of the chorus and the major play episodes; the prologue was sometimes a scene and sometimes a simple speech to the audience. Shakespeare also used prologues in some of his plays. In one particularly interesting example, Shakespeare's *Henry V*, each of the five acts begins with a character called Chorus directly addressing the audience and setting the scene for the act:

CHORUS: O for a Muse of fire, that would ascend
  The brightest heaven of invention!
  A kingdom for a stage, princes to act,
  And monarchs to behold the swelling scene!
  Then should the warlike Harry, like himself,
  Assume the port of Mars, and at his heels
  (Leash'd in, like hounds) should famine, sword, and fire
  Crouch for employment. But pardon, gentles all,
  The flat unraised spirits that hath dar'd
  On this unworthy scaffold to bring forth
  So great an object. Can this cockpit hold
  The vasty fields of France? Or may we cram

Within this wooden O the very casques
That did affright the air at Agincourt?
O, pardon! since a crooked figure may
Attest in little place a million,
And let us, ciphers to this great accompt,
On your imaginary forces work.
Suppose within the girdle of these walls
Are now confin'd two mighty monarchies,
Whose high, upreared, and abutting fronts
The perilous narrow ocean parts asunder.
Piece out our imperfections with your thoughts;
Into a thousand parts divide one man,
And make imaginary puissance;
Think, when we talk of horses, that you see them
Printing their proud hoofs i' th' receiving earth;
For 'tis your thoughts that now must deck our kings,
Carry them here and there, jumping o'er times,
Turning th' accomplishment of many years
Into an hour-glass: for the which supply,
Admit me Chorus to this history;
Who, Prologue-like, your humble patience pray,
Gently to hear, kindly to judge, our play.

This famous prologue establishes setting, characters, and audience expectation of plot in a straightforward manner, and it begs the audience's indulgence for the theatrical conventions they will be called upon to entertain.

THE CONFLICT   Now is the time for the character to enter shouting, "The house is on fire!" It is a truism that drama requires conflict; in fact, the word *drama,* when used in daily life, implies a situation fraught with conflict. No one writes plays about characters who live every day in unimpaired serenity; no one would ever choose to watch such a play. Conflict and confrontation are the mechanisms by which a situation becomes dramatic.

Why is this so? Why is conflict so theatrically interesting? The reasons have to do with plot, theme, and character. Plot can hold suspense only when it involves alternatives and choices:

Conflict is what makes drama dramatic; indeed, it's what makes *life* dramatic. Conflict makes our blood boil and our anxiety gush; though painful, conflict creates many of the defining moments in our lives – and the lives of dramatic characters. In this scene from a 2004 New York production of Arthur Miller's autobiographical *After the Fall*, Quentin (Peter Krause) and Maggie (Carla Gugino) battle fiercely as their marriage dissolves in recriminations, drugs, and Maggie's eventual suicide. That Miller was married to doomed actress Marilyn Monroe gives the dramatized conflict a profound reality.

Macbeth has strong reasons to murder King Duncan and strong reasons not to; if he had only the former or only the latter, he would project no real conflict and we would not consider him such an interesting character. We are fascinated by such a character's actions largely in light of the actions he rejects and the stresses he has to endure in making his decisions. In other words, plot entails not only the actions of a play but also the inactions—the things that are narrowly rejected and do *not* happen. A character's decision must proceed from powerfully conflicting alternatives if we are to watch this behavior with empathy instead of mere curiosity. In watching a character act, the audience must also watch him *think;* a playwright gets him to think by putting him into conflict.

Conflict may be set up between characters as well as within them; it may be reducible to one central situation, or it may evolve out of many. Whatever the case, conflict throws characters into relief and permits the audience to see deeply into the human personality. To see a character at war with herself or in confrontation with another is to see how that character *works,* and this is the key to our caring.

The theme of a play is ordinarily a simple abstraction of its central conflict. In Sophocles' *Antigone,* for example, the theme is the conflict between divine law and civil law; in *Death of a Salesman,* it is the conflict between Willy's reality and his dreams. Conflicts are plentiful in farces and comedies as well; the conflicts inherent in the "eternal triangle," for example, have provided comic material for dramatists for the past two millennia. Many of the more abstract philosophical conflicts—independence versus duty, individuality versus conformity, idealism versus pragmatism, integrity versus efficiency, pleasure versus propriety, progress versus tradition, to name a few—suggest inexhaustible thematic conflicts that appear in various guises in both ancient and contemporary plays.

The playwright introduces conflict early in a play, often by means of an "inciting incident," in which one character poses a conflict or confrontation either to another character or to himself. For example:

FIRST WITCH: All hail, Macbeth, hail to thee,
    Thane of Glamis!
SECOND WITCH: All hail, Macbeth, hail to thee,
    Thane of Cawdor!
THIRD WITCH: All hail, Macbeth, that shalt be
    King hereafter!
BANQUO: (*to* MACBETH) Good sir, why do you
    start, and seem to fear
    Things that do sound so fair?

In this, the inciting incident of Shakespeare's *Macbeth* (which follows two brief expository scenes), a witch confronts Macbeth with the prediction that he will be king, thereby posing an alternative that Macbeth has apparently already considered, judging from the startled response that elicits Banquo's comment.

Once established, conflict is intensified to crisis, usually by a series of incidents, investigations, revelations, and confrontations. Sometimes even nonevents serve to intensify a conflict, as in the modern classic *Waiting for Godot,* in which two characters simply wait, through two hour-long acts, for the arrival of a third, who never comes. Indeed, with this play, Samuel Beckett virtually rewrote the book on playwriting technique by showing how time alone, when properly managed, can do the job of heightening and developing conflict in a dramatic situation.

THE CLIMAX   Conflict cannot be intensified indefinitely. In a play, as in life, when conflict becomes insupportable, something has to give. Thus every play, be it comic, tragic, farcical, or melodramatic, culminates in some sort of dramatic explosion.

As we have seen, Aristotle described that dramatic explosion, in tragedy, as a *catharsis,* a cleansing and/or purification. Aristotle's conception is susceptible to various interpretations, but it has been widely accepted and broadly influential for centuries. The catharsis releases the audience's pity and thereby permits the fullest experience of tragic pleasure, washing away the terror that has been mounting steadily during the play's tragic course. Such catharsis as accompanies Oedipus's gouging out his own eyes as he recognizes his true self illustrates the extreme theatrical explosion of which the classical Greek tragic form is capable.

For any dramatic form, the climax is the conflict of a play taken to its most extreme; it is the moment of maximum tension. At the climax, a continuation of the conflict becomes unbearable, impossible: some sort of change is mandated. Climaxes in modern plays do not, as a rule, involve death or disfiguration (although there are exceptions: Peter Shaffer's celebrated *Equus* reaches its climax with the blinding of six horses, and Edward Albee's *The Zoo Story* climaxes with one character's impaling himself on a knife held by another). However, climaxes inevitably contain elements of recognition and reversal if not of catharsis, and usually the major conflicts of a play are resolved by one or more of these elements.

THE DENOUEMENT   The climax is followed and the play is concluded by a denouement, or resolution, in which a final action or speech or even a single word or gesture indicates that the passions aroused by the play's action are now stilled and a new harmony or understanding has been reached. The tenor of the denouement tends to change with the times. In the American theatre of the 1950s and 1960s, for example, the sentimental and message-laden denouement was the rule: in Robert Anderson's *Tea and Sympathy,* a teacher's wife prepares to prove to a sensitive boy that he is not a homosexual; in Dore Schary's *Sunrise at Campobello,* a future American president makes his way on crippled legs to a convention platform. In the current theatre—in this existential age that looks with suspicion on tidy virtues and happy endings—more ironic and ambiguous denouements prevail. The current theatre also provides less in the way of purgation than do more classical modes—perhaps because the conflicts raised by the best of contemporary drama are not amenable to wholesale relief. But a denouement still must provide at least some lucidity concerning the problems raised by the play, some vision or metaphor of a deeper and more permanent understanding. Perhaps the final lines of *Waiting for Godot* best represent the denouement of the current age:

ESTRAGON: Well, shall we go?
VLADIMIR: Yes, let's go.
They do not move.

Events that take place after the play ends are referred to as *postplay.*

The curtain call is not only a chance for the cast to take their bows; it is also an opportunity for a release of emotion. This is rarely truer than in the exuberant curtain call for Jonathan Larson's 1996 Broadway musical phenomenon, *Rent.*

THE CURTAIN CALL   The last staged element of a theatrical presentation is the curtain call, in which the actors bow and the audience applauds. This convention—customary in the theatre at least since the time of the Romans—plays an important but often overlooked role in the overall scope of theatrical presentation.

The curtain call is *not* simply a time for the actors to receive congratulations from the audience, although many actors today seem to think it is. Indeed, the actor's deeply bowed head was originally an offer for his patron—the nobleman who had paid for the performance—to lop off that head with his sword if the actor had not provided satisfaction! The curtain call remains a time in which the actors show their respect for the audience that patronizes them. And aesthetically, it is a time in which the audience allows

NON-ARISTOTELIAN THEATRE EVENTS

Aristotle's influence in developing a "science" of dramatic structure has been profound, but, particularly as it focuses only on fifth-century-B.C. Greek tragedy, it is not all-inclusive. Aristotle's notion of structure does not even cover the major form of fifth-century Greek comedy (known as Old Comedy), in which the dramatic action stops around the midpoint of the play so that a character representing the author can come forward and address the audience with a speech (a *parabasis*) about current politics. The theatre of Antonin Artaud in the 1930s, "happenings" in the 1960s, and performance art in the 1980s and beyond (all discussed in the following chapters) explicitly reject Aristotelian forms in the search for something new and revolutionary. And virtually all playwrights today improvise variations on Aristotle's classic model, sometimes by presenting scenes in reverse chronological order (such as Harold Pinter in *Betrayal*) or characters in impossible situations (such as Caryl Churchill's *Top Girls*, which presents an ensemble of historical characters who lived in different centuries) or simply without expositions, climaxes, denouements, or any of the above.

Novelty – creating something fresh and, more importantly, unexpected – is a feature of all art, including drama; therefore, playwrights in all periods have tried to vary or even reverse the "conventional" notions of dramatic structure common since Greek times. Sometimes such productions directly mock classical notions: "Nothing can kill a show like too much exposition," says a character in the Broadway musical *Urinetown*. Other theatre events, often identified as plays but without making use of standard dramatic structures, may include autobiographical solo performances such as *Elaine Stritch at Liberty*, in which the veteran Broadway star recounts her life story through song and narrative; stand-up comic monologues such as Rob Becker's *Defending the Caveman* (on men and women) and Jackie Mason's *Prune Danish* and *Much Ado about Everything* (on Jews in America); satirical pieces such as Bryan Wolfson and Sam Fogel's *Jewtopia* (over-the-top sketches about Jews and gentiles); plotless music/movement/acrobatic extravaganzas such as the performances of Blue Man Group, STOMP, and De La Guarda (all discussed in the chapter titled "Theatre Today"); and eclectic works such as the multiauthored *Def Poetry Jam*, which combines slam poetry with rap, quasi haiku, and snippets of songs. All of these events have been hugely successful on today's stages – without a trace of plot, climax, or denouement. Many contemporary playwrights seek to add freshness to their own visions by borrowing techniques from these and other non-Aristotelian theatrical formulations, even when they retain other aspects of the structural model he proposed.

Nonetheless, Aristotelian-influenced drama continues to dominate the theatre, for while novelty may be crucial, it does not remain novel very long. A contemporary painting in a museum, for example, may be absolutely astonishing at first glance – possibly unlike anything you have ever seen in your life. But the average time museum visitors spend

(continued)

NON-ARISTOTELIAN THEATRE EVENTS

Director Deborah Warner's citywide installation The Angel Project *is essentially a walking tour through selected buildings in New York City, staged by Warner and designed by Tom Pye in 2003. Audience-participants are first led in groups and then sent out on their own to follow instructions in a guidebook. There is no plot whatsoever, and only a few, mainly mute, characters, but various themes, developing angel motifs, and quotations from Milton's epic poem* Paradise Lost *make the installation a stylistically coherent (if not dramatic) theatre event.*

looking at a work of art, even one they admire, is in the neighborhood of five to ten seconds. A play typically lasts for two hours. What does the audience do when the novelty passes?

Similarly, circus performers know that the practical time limit for their acts is a mere seven minutes. No matter how amazing or difficult, after seven minutes of piling acrobats on top of a bicycle, it's time to bring on the dancing elephants. Without a plot to pull us along and characters to engage us in a complexity of ideas, human relationships, and hopes dashed, attained, or deferred, the circus manager must dazzle and redazzle us with one astonishing feat after

another. It's simply too much to ask, which is why there are few truly successful circus companies left in the world today. The problem with replacing structure with novelty is that such novelty must *continue* to be novel — and be increasingly astonishing — long after the audience has grown accustomed to what they saw onstage when the show started. The invention of drama — structured action, with a story you want to follow, characters you care about, and an increasing tension in the developing events — creates a theatrical compulsion that can keep an audience on the edge of its collective seats for hours at a time.

Smaller theatres sometimes host "talk-back" sessions, during which actors and/or the playwright and director remain onstage after the show to answer questions from the audience, particularly when the play has social or political importance. When the play is new or is being "workshopped" (tested), audience feedback may lead to changes in the script or the production. Here, at New York's Culture Project, actor Richard Dreyfuss and other cast members "talk back" following *Exonerated*, a "verbatim play" composed from statements of released death-row convicts after their verdicts had been reversed.

itself to see the other side of the "paradox of the actor." The curtain call liberates the audience from the world of the play. Indeed, when there is no curtain call, audiences are often disgruntled, for this convention fulfills the last provision, so to speak, in the mutual agreement that characterizes the theatre itself—the agreement by which the audience agrees to view the actors as the characters the actors have agreed to impersonate. It is at the curtain call that actors and audience can acknowledge their mutual belonging in the human society, can look each other in the eye and say, in effect, "We all know what it is to experience these things we've just seen performed. We must all try to understand life a little better. We have enjoyed coming this far together. We are with you. We like you." In the best theatre, this communication is a powerful experience.

THE AFTERMATH: CRITICISM What follows the curtain call? The audience disperses, of course, but the individual audience members do not die. Through them the production enjoys an extended afterlife—both in talk and in print—in late-night postmortems at the theatre bar, in probing conversations and published reviews over the next few days, and sometimes in formal classroom discussions, television talk shows, letters to the editor in the local newspaper, and scholarly articles and books seen weeks, months, or years later. Indeed, in a theatre devoted to community interaction, such as Los Angeles's Cornerstone (see the chapter titled "Theatre Today"), the end of the play is the beginning of a hoped-for new life of political change. For the theatre is a place of public stimulation, both intellectual and emotional, and it should be expected that

THE STANDING OVATION

Nothing more conveys the liveliness of live theatre today than the standing ovation, when an entire audience leaps to its collective feet at the curtain call, applauding the play or, more often, its leading performer. Such an ovation is more common in America than in other countries, and probably more common on Broadway than in the rest of the country; some critics suggest that patrons paying up to $100 for their tickets want to prove (to themselves at least) that they got their money's worth. But there is no question that the standing ovation has become a sort of audience participation for theatergoers, who get to physically express their enthusiasm — particularly after a play of rousing sentiments — with both the performers who provided it and fellow audience members standing next to them.

the stimulation provided by a provocative production would generate both animated discussions and illuminating commentaries.

Both of these we may call dramatic criticism, which is the audience's contribution to the theatre. Criticism is as ancient as Aristotle and as contemporary as the essays and lectures that are presented daily in newspapers, journals, books, and academies all over the world. But criticism is not solely an expert enterprise; criticism—which combines analysis and evaluation—is everybody's job. We will look further at this key aspect of the theatre's art in the final chapter of the book.

3

The Actor

S HE STANDS ALONE IN THE DARKNESS, waiting in the wings, listening with one ear to the insistent rhythms of the dialogue played out upon the stage immediately beyond. Her heart races, and she bounces lightly on the balls of her feet, fighting the welling tension, exhilarated by the sense of something rushing toward her, about to engulf her.

The stage ahead of her is ablaze with light; dazzling colors pour on from all possible directions. The energy onstage is almost tangible: it is there in the eyes of the actors, the pace of the dialogue, the smell of the makeup, the sparkle of perspiration glittering in the lights, the bursts of audience laughter and applause, the sudden silence punctuated by a wild cry or a thundering retort.

She glances backward impatiently. Other actors wait in the backstage gloom. Some perform knee bends and roll their necks against the tension. Some gaze thoughtfully at the action of the play. Some stare at the walls. In one corner a stage manager, his head encased in electronic paraphernalia, his body hunched over a dimly lighted copy of the script, whispers commands into an intercom. The backstage shadows pulse with anticipation.

Suddenly the onstage pace quickens; the lines, all at once, take on a greater urgency and familiarity. It is the cue . . . if only there were time to go to the bathroom . . . it is the cue . . . she takes a deep breath, a deeper breath, a gasp . . . *it is the cue.* She bounds from the dimness into the dazzle: she is onstage, she is an actor!

Acting is perhaps the world's most bewildering profession. At the top, it can be extraordinarily rewarding. The thrill of delivering a great performance, the roar of validation from an enraptured audience, the glory of getting inside the skin of the likes of Hamlet, Harpagon, and Hecuba—these are excitements and satisfactions few careers can induce. Nor are the rewards purely artistic and intellectual; audience appreciation and the producer's eye for profit can catapult some actors to the highest income levels in the world, with salaries in the millions of dollars for actors achieving "star" status in films. And the celebrity that can follow is legendary. The private lives of the most universally admired actors become public property, their innermost thoughts the daily fare of television talk shows and fan magazines.

And yet, for all the splendor and glamor, the actor's life is more often than not depressingly anxious, beset by demands for sacrifice from every direction: psychological, financial, and even moral. Stage fright—the actor's nemesis—is an ever-present nightmare that often increases with experience and renown. Fear of failure, fear of competition, fear of forgetting lines, fear of losing emotional control, fear of losing one's looks, fear of losing one's audience—this list of concerns is endemic to acting as to no other profession.

Nor are the economic rewards in general particularly enticing. The six- and seven-figure salaries of the stars bear little relation to the scale pay for which most actors work: theirs is the lowest union-negotiated wage in the free-market economy, and actors often realize less income than the janitors who clean the theatres. And although the stars billed "above the title" may be treated like celebrities or royalty, the common run of actors are freely bullied by directors, bossed about by stage managers, capriciously hired and fired by producers, dangled and deceived by agents, squeezed and corseted by costumers, pinched by wig dressers, poked and powdered by makeup artists, and traduced by press agents. Certainly no profession entails more numbing uncertainties than acting, none demands more sacrifices, and none measures its rewards in such extreme and contradictory dimensions.

What Is Acting?

But what is acting? The question is not as simple as it might seem. It is, of course, the oldest of the theatrical arts. It is older than playwriting, because actors began by improvising their texts. Thespis, the first known actor (and from whose name the word *thespian,* meaning "actor," derives), was the author of the dramas in which he appeared.

Acting is also the most public art of theatre, the most visible to—and recognized by—the audience. The average theatergoer today can probably name more actors than playwrights, designers, and directors put together. The average theatergoer also thinks he or she knows more about the art of acting than the other arts of the theatre as well, because acting seems relatively simple. But it isn't.

The Two Notions of Acting

Since the first discussions of acting, which date from Greek times, theatre artists have recognized two different and seemingly contradictory notions of what acting really is. The first notion is that acting is something that the actor "presents" to the audience—through vocal skill in phrasing and projection, through an ability to imitate different characters and their individual (and social) styles, and through a variety of associated talents, which may include singing, dancing, juggling, fencing, comic improvisation, oral interpretation, and the like. Such acting is sometimes called "presentational," "external," or "technical": the actor learns to "present" a role through a program of training that customarily originates externally—not from inside the actor but from an instructional process that includes formal analy-

Training enables actors to play a variety of widely diverse characters. Kevin Kline, who studied acting at Indiana University and subsequently the Julliard School in New York, has starred in film roles as various as Shakespeare's Hamlet and Bottom the Weaver (in *A Midsummer Night's Dream*), Gilbert and Sullivan's Pirate King, and composer Cole Porter. Here he is shown in two strikingly different stage roles performed at the Vivian Beaumont Theatre in New York. *Left*, Kline is the robust, exuberant Jack Falstaff in Shakespeare's *Henry IV* in 2003; *right*, he plays the haunted ("spiritually crushed," Kline commented) title character of Anton Chekhov's *Ivanov* in 1997.

sis, technical lessons and drills, and often the imitation of teachers, well-known actors, and/or other students. Such actor training may cover technical skills in dramatic phrasing (learning rhetorical building, persuasive argumentation, and comic pointing), poetic scansion (learning to analyze and effectively accent metrical verse), vocal production (developing a multi-octave speaking range and sonorous resonance and the ability to vocally project to large audiences), stage movement (learning and practic-

ing period dances and various styles of physical combat), and both text and character analysis, from an acting standpoint, in a wide variety of dramatic styles. This list reflects the training curricula of many acting conservatories in the United States and abroad.

The second notion of acting, however, is that it emanates from somewhere *inside* the actor. By studying the role closely and entering —through her or his own imagination—the world of the play, the actor works to honestly

All Characters Are Me

I think all the characters I play are basically me.
I believe that under the right set of circumstances
we're all capable of anything, and that acting allows
the deepest part of your nature to surface – and
you're protected by the fiction as it happens.

— Willem Dafoe

and effectively "live the life of the character" within the play's situation. To do this, the actor must actually "feel" the emotions of the character portrayed and even feel that she or he "is" —during the moments of performance—the character. This is generally considered the "internal" or "representational" notion of acting; "internal" because it begins within the actor and "representational" because it asks the actor to represent all aspects—emotional as well as physical and intellectual—of the character portrayed. In the United States, this internal notion of acting is often called Method acting, or simply The Method, as it is derived from Russian actor-director Konstantin Stanislavsky's self-proclaimed System in the early years of the twentieth century. Stanislavsky's Method was made popular in America by the late Lee Strasberg at his Actors Studio in New York during the 1940s and 1950s.

The seeming opposition of these two notions of acting is still actively debated in acting circles. American actors, for example, have often felt themselves torn between the "representational" notions of Stanislavsky and the "presentational" notions put forward by traditional English actors such as Laurence Olivier and John Gielgud. But the fact is that *both* of these notions of acting—when integrated— are vital to great acting wherever it takes place. All acting is both presentational and representational, both external and internal (and, we might say, both from the head and from the heart), and all great actors must learn, or somehow acquire, the ability to present their characters in a powerful and engaging manner and

at the same time live their characters' lives fully and convincingly onstage.

The debate is by no means new. Indeed, the extent to which actors might be said to feel or not feel the emotions of their characters and believe or not believe they "are" the characters they play constitutes what Professor Joseph Roach has called "the historic, continuing, and apparently inexhaustible combat between technique and inspiration in performance theory." That actors connect emotionally with their parts was recognized in the most ancient of theatres. A Roman actor named Aesop, we are told, became so overwrought during a performance of *Orestes* that he ran his sword through a stagehand who unhappily strayed into his line of sight. Polus, another ancient actor, placed the ashes of his own dead son onstage in order to inspire himself while giving Electra's speech of lamentation. Socrates himself inquired of one Ion, a rhapsodist (poetic reciter), as to the role of real emotion in his performances:

SOCRATES: Tell me, Ion, when you produce the greatest effect upon the audience . . . are you in your right mind? Or are you not carried out of yourself [and] . . . seem to be among the persons or the places of which you are speaking?

ION: Socrates, I must frankly confess that at the tale of pity my eyes are filled with tears, and when I speak of horrors, my hair stands on end and my heart throbs.

Obviously, Ion was "living the life" of his characters, feeling the emotions of his roles, and feeling himself as in the presence of the characters in his rhapsodic tales. But, as Socrates' inquiry soon reveals, Ion was also aware of the powerful effects his acting had upon his audience:

SOCRATES: . . . and are you aware that you produce similar effects on most of the spectators?

ION: Only too well; for I look down upon them from the stage, and behold the various emotions of pity, wonder, sternness, stamped upon their countenances when I am speaking.

Thus Ion considered his acting both representational (he felt himself among the characters of his story) and presentational (he was checking out the audience all the while.) It is a paradox, not an either/or debate, Socrates realized: Ion was both in the fiction of his recitation and at the same time outside of it.

Poets and actors ever since have deliberated on this paradox. The Roman poet Horace (65–8 B.C.) turned Ion's paradox into a famous maxim of the ancient world: In order to move the audience, you must first be moved yourself. Roman orator Quintilian (c. A.D. 35–c. 100) made this into a technique, and by envisioning his wife's and children's imaginary deaths with "extreme vividness" while orating, he became "so moved" that he was brought to tears, turned pale, and exhibited "all the symptoms of genuine grief." True to acting's paradox, however, Quintilian also sought to present his characters according to appropriate stage conventions; for all his tears and passion, he urged his fellow actors to achieve the "regularity and discipline promised by calculation," cautioning, for example, that "it is never correct to employ the left hand alone in gesture" and that "the hand [may not] be raised above the level of the eyes."

Horace's notion extended right through the Renaissance; an eighteenth-century French critic even proposed that only actors who were truly in love could effectively play lovers onstage. The one great dissenter in acting theory, however, whose work remains startlingly provocative today, was also French: this was Denis Diderot, the famous encyclopedist who in 1773 directly confronted this issue in a brief but trenchant essay (in dialogue form) titled *The Paradox of Acting*. Diderot begins with the radical thesis that "a great actor . . . must [be] an unmoved and disinterested onlooker. . . . They say an actor is all the better for being excited, for being angry. I deny it. He is best when he imitates anger. Actors impress the public not when they are furious, but when they play fury well."

By contrast, Diderot explained, "actors who play from the heart . . . are alternately strong and feeble, fiery and cold. . . . Tomorrow they will miss the point they have excelled in today." Thus, Diderot maintains, "the actor who plays from thought . . . will be always at his best; he has considered, combined, learned and arranged the whole thing in his head."

Diderot's view was rooted in his confidence that all knowledge, including art, was rational and could be categorized, analyzed, alphabetized, and (given his profession) "encyclopedized." Diderot's work typifies the Enlightenment, during which he lived, with its demystification of both medieval superstition and Renaissance idealism. The coming ages of romanticism and realism, however, particularly in the theatre, brought a strong rebellion against the "objective" rationalism of Enlightenment thinking.

Stanislavsky, already considered Russia's greatest actor by the time he founded the Moscow Art Theatre in 1898, attacked Diderot's thinking with great fervor. "Put life into all the imagined circumstances and actions," Stanislavsky said, "until you have completely satisfied your sense of truth, and until you have awakened a sense of faith in the reality of your sensations." By "life" Stanislavsky meant the ambiguity of emotion, the mystery of love and death, and the confusion of experience. To create this life onstage, Stanislavsky sought to identify the separate steps of the actor's preparation. Primary to his vision was that the actor must seek, in the act of performance, to resolve his or her "character's problem" (in Russian, *zadacha*), as opposed to his or her mere "actor's problem." Thus the actor playing Juliet concentrates on winning Romeo's love (or her father's respect, or her nurse's complicity) rather than showing the audience how romantic (or poetic, or young, or pretty) she is. By this means, according to Stanislavsky, the actor represents Juliet as a real and whole person rather than simply presenting Juliet as a fictional character of the Shakespearean tragic stage. The character's *zadacha*—somewhat mistranslated into English

Most American actors are chiefly concerned with getting "inside" their characters so they can fully experience the emotions — and even the confusion — the play's situation would provoke in real life. Bryony Lavery's *Frozen* is a play that virtually requires such "internal" acting; in it, a mother visits a prison to coolly confront a serial killer with photographs of her ten-year-old daughter, whom he raped and murdered. In the play's 2004 Broadway premiere, actors Swoozie Kurtz (as the mother) and Bryan F. O'Byrne (the killer) used real family snapshots as the "props" in this scene. Their emotions were real and unpredictable. "I always find myself shocked. . . . I see those two little girls, and it breaks my heart," reported O'Byrne. Kurtz felt the same: "When I leave the apartment for the theater," she reported, "I can't breathe. I feel terrified and in pain. It's only after that scene I feel I can breathe again."

as "objective" by Elizabeth Hapgood, though her term has stuck—is Stanislavsky's key.

Stanislavsky was one of the first theatre artists to systematically investigate the notion of motivation in acting and to advance the concept that every move onstage must be seen to correspond to what the character (and not just the playwright or director) is striving to achieve. He also created the notion of "public solitude" to indicate the way in which an actor must focus her or his attention on the events of the play rather than simply on the play's impact on the audience. He established the notion that the play's text was accompanied by a "subtext" of meanings (unspoken and undescribed character goals) hidden beneath the lines. He hated all forms of empty theatricality, whereby the actor simply relies on theatrical gimmicks or conceits. He insisted that an "artistic communion" must exist among the actors into

EMOTION IN ACTING

If emotion is a state, the actor should never take cognizance of it. In fact we can never take cognizance of an emotion when we are in its grip, but only when it has passed. Otherwise the emotion disappears. The actor lives uniquely in the present; he is continually jumping from one present to the next. In the course of these successive presents he executes a series of actions which deposit upon him a sort of sweat which is nothing else but the state of emotion. This sweat is to his acting what juice is to fruit. But once he starts perceiving and taking cognizance of his state of emotion, the sweat evaporates forthwith, the emotion disappears and the acting dries up.... We cannot think "I am moved" without at once ceasing to be so. [Therefore] ... no one in a theatre should allude to the fragile phenomenon, emotion. Everyone, both players and audience alike, though under its influence, must concern themselves with actions.

— Jean-Louis Barrault

which actors must invest themselves deeply, drawing heavily, therefore, upon their own personal feelings in establishing a rapport with their characters, their fellow actors, and the fictional events of the play.

And Stanislavsky was deeply, almost obsessively, concerned with the actor's emotion. Discovering in the writings of French psychologist Théodule Armand Ribot that "all memories of past experiences are recorded by the nervous system and . . . may be evoked by an appropriate stimulus," Stanislavsky began to experiment with recalling his own past emotional states, eventually developing an acting technique known as "emotion memory" (or "emotional recall" or "affective memory"): by mentally substituting these remembered situations from his or her own life into the action of the play, the actor draws upon these memories so as to reach the emotional levels dramatically required. By this substitution of remembered emotion, Stanislavsky sought to make acting natural, truthful, and emotionally vivid for the performer and audience alike.

But emotion—and emotional memory—did not remain central to Stanislavsky's acting system for very long. True to acting's paradox, Stanislavsky was also greatly skilled and thoroughly trained in external theatre technique. Born to an affluent aristocratic family, he had performed in plays, operettas, and operas from the age of six, often in the large, fully equipped theatres his family had constructed in both their Moscow home and country estate. A promising singer, he had studied with a major Bolshoi Opera star; Tchaikovsky had proposed writing an opera for him. Like Quintilian, Stanislavsky recognized the necessity for purely rational control in performance. "Feeling . . . does not replace an immense amount of work on the part of our intellects," he said. And so he studied elocution, dance, and phrasing as passionately as emotion. By the middle of his career, Stanislavsky had even discarded emotional memory in favor of physical actions as the key to stimulating truthful acting. He began to reproach his actors for excessive wallowing in private emotions: "What's false here? You're playing feelings, your own suffering, that's what's false. I need to see the event and how you react to that event, how you fight people—how you react, not suffer. . . . To take that line . . . is to be passive and sentimental. See everything in terms of action!"

No country—not even Russia—has been as influenced by Stanislavsky's teaching as the United States. By 1919, two of Stanislavsky's disciples, Richard Boleslavski and Maria Ouspenskaya, had moved to New York and founded the American Laboratory Theatre, bringing Stanislavsky's new System to the attention of American actors. Among their converts was Lee Strasberg, an Austrian immigrant who, with others, formed the Group Theatre in 1931 and the Actors Studio shortly thereafter. Strasberg's ensuing Method, derived from the early version of Stanislavsky's System and incorporating emotional recall as a principal technique, became the standard actor-training technique

The Actors Studio

The most influential school of acting in the United States has been New York's Actors Studio, which was founded by director Elia Kazan and others in 1947 and achieved prominence following the appointment of Lee Strasberg (1901–1982) as artistic director in 1951. Strasberg, an Austrian by birth and a New Yorker by upbringing, proved a magnetic teacher and acting theorist, and his classes revolutionized American acting.

Although the Studio added commercial acting classes to its activities in 1995, it is not primarily a school but an association of selected professional actors who gather at weekly sessions to work on acting problems. The methodology of the Studio derives in part from Stanislavsky and in part from the working methods of the Group Theatre — a pre-World War II acting ensemble that included Kazan, Strasberg, and playwright Clifford Odets. But Strasberg himself proved the key inspiration of Studio teaching and of the American love affair with Method acting attributed to the Studio work.

Strasberg's work is not reducible to simple for-mulas, for the Studio is a working laboratory and the Studio work is personal rather than theoretical, direct rather than general. Much of the mythology surrounding the Studio – that actors are encouraged to mumble their lines and scratch their jaws in the service of naturalness – is fallacious. Strasberg was a fierce exponent of firm performance discipline and well-studied acting technique; insofar as the Studio developed a reputation for producing actors who mumbled and fidgeted, this seems to have been only a response to the personal idiosyncrasies of Marlon Brando, the Studio's first celebrated "graduate."

Strasberg demanded great depths of character relationships from his actors, and he went to almost any length to get them. Explanation was only one of his tools, but it is the only one that can be made available to readers. The following quote is from Strasberg himself:

> The human being who acts is the human being who lives. That is a terrifying circumstance. Essentially the actor acts a fiction, a dream; in life the stimuli to which we respond are always real. The actor must constantly respond to stimuli that are imaginary. And yet this must happen not only just as it happens in life, but actually more fully and more expressively. Although the actor can do things in life quite easily, when he has to do the same thing on the stage under fictitious conditions he has difficulty because he is not equipped as a human being merely to playact at imitating life. He must somehow believe. He must somehow be able to convince himself of the rightness of what he is doing in order to do things fully on the stage.
>
> When the actor explores fully the reality of any given object, he comes up with greater dramatic possibilities. These are so inherent in reality that we have a common phrase to describe them. We say, "Only in life could such things happen." We mean that those things are so genuinely dramatic that they could never be just made up. . . .
>
> The true meaning of "natural" or "nature" refers to a thing so fully lived and so fully experi-enced that only rarely does an actor permit him-self that kind of experience on the stage. Only great actors do it on the stage, whereas in life every human being to some extent does it. On the stage it takes the peculiar mentality of the actor to give himself to imaginary things with the same kind of fullness that we ordinarily evince only in giving ourselves to real things. The actor has to evoke that reality on the stage in order to live fully in it and with it.

in America. Perhaps because it privileged actors over the script—making their own feelings as much the "subject" of the play as their charac-ters' actions—American actors and not a few celebrities (such as Marilyn Monroe) flocked to his school. Other American acting teachers, some of whom (such as Stella Adler and Sonia Moore) studied with Stanislavsky at a later point in his career, preached the Russian mas-ter's later emphasis on physical actions rather than emotional memory.

To this day, almost all American teachers of theatre pay homage to Stanislavsky, often fram-ing the debate on acting theory as the opposition of his early teachings with his later ones. But most American stage actors agree that the technical aspects of acting are also critical to career success and that the best acting emanates from both the outside and the inside, with the two being fused in performance. Obviously a performance that failed to fulfill, in its external form, the expectations the text establishes (a performance, for example, that failed to show Prometheus as fiery, Juliet as romantic, Monsieur Jordain as comical) would prove unsatisfying. But equally unsatisfying would be a performance in which the characters' interactions, no matter how eloquently executed, seemed merely flat and mechanical, in which the passions seemed shallowly pasted on by the director or in which no sparks flew and no romance kindled between the human beings represented onstage. Mere imitation without internal conviction ("living the part") rings hollow, but conviction without definition grows tiresome. The best acting synthesizes the two notions of acting into a comprehensive art.

Beyond these two main lines of the actor's art, there are two other aspects one always finds in the greatest performers: virtuosity of technique and the ineffable "magic" that defines the greatest artists in any field.

Virtuosity

Greatness in acting, like greatness in almost any endeavor, demands a superb set of skills. The characters of drama are rarely mundane; they are exemplary, and so must be the actors who portray them. Merely to impersonate—to imitate and embody—the genius of Hamlet, for example, one must deliver that genius oneself. Similar personal resources are needed to project the depth of Lear, the lyricism of Juliet, the fervor of St. Joan, the proud passion of Prometheus, the bravura of Mercutio, or the heroics of Hecuba. Outsized characters demand outsized abilities and the capacity to project them.

Moreover, it is ultimately insufficient for an actor merely to fulfill the audience's precon-

Actors William Metzo and Jeannie Naughton play father and daughter – King Lear and Goneril – in the 1999 Utah Shakespearean Festival production of *King Lear*. While it is difficult for actors to learn to play kings and princesses, and to speak in seventeenth-century verse and wear seventeenth-century costume, the production will ultimately rise or fall mainly on the basis of how well the actors can capture the depth and intensity of something quite universal (and profound): the father-daughter relationship.

ceptions of his or her character; finally, it is necessary that the actor strive to transcend those preconceptions and to create the character afresh, transporting the audience to an understanding of—and a compassion for—the character that they never would have achieved on their own.

Both of these demands require of the actor a considerable virtuosity of dramatic technique.

Traditionally, the training of actors has concentrated on dramatic technique. Since Roman times (and probably before then), actors have spent most of their lifetime perfecting such performing skills as juggling, dancing, singing, versifying, declaiming, clowning, miming, stage fighting, acrobatics, and sleight of hand. Certainly no actor before the twentieth century had any chance of success without several of these skills, and few actors today reach the top of their profession without fully mastering at least a few of them.

Whatever the individual skills required of an actor over time, the sought-after dramatic technique that is common to history and to our own times can be summed up in just two features: a magnificently expressive voice and a splendidly supple body. These are the tools every actor strives to attain, and when brilliantly honed they are valuable beyond measure.

The actor's voice has received the greatest attention throughout history. Greek tragic actors were awarded prizes for their vocal abilities alone, and many modern actors, such as James Earl Jones, Patrick Stewart, Glenn Close, and Maggie Smith, are celebrated for their distinctive use of the voice. The potential of the acting voice as an instrument of great theatre is immense. The voice can be thrilling, resonant, mellow, sharp, musical, stinging, poetic, seductive, compelling, lulling, and dominating; and an actor capable of drawing on many such "voices" clearly can command a spectrum of acting roles and lend them a splendor the less-gifted actor or the untrained amateur could scarcely imagine. A voice that can articulate, that can explain, that can rivet attention, that can convey the subtlest nuance, that can exult, dazzle, thunder with rage, and flow with compassion—when used in the service of dramatic impersonation—can hold an audience spellbound.

The actor's use of her or his body—the capacity for movement—is the other element of fundamental technique, the second basis for dramatic virtuosity. Most of the best actors are strong and supple; all are capable of great physical self-mastery and are artists of body language. The effects that can be achieved through stage movement are as numerous as those that can be achieved through voice. Subtly expressive movement in particular is the mark of the gifted actor, who can accomplish miracles of communication with an arched eyebrow, a toss of the head, a flick of the wrist, a whirl of the hem, or a shuffle of the feet. But bold movements, too, can produce indelible moments in the theatre: Helene Weigel's powerful chest-pounding when, as Mother Courage, she loses her son, and Laurence Olivier's breathtaking fall from the tower as Coriolanus—these are sublime theatricalizations accomplished through the actors' sheer physical skill, strength, and dramatic audacity.

Virtuosity for its own sake can be appealing in the cabaret or lecture hall as well as in the theatre, but when coupled with the impersonation of character it can create dramatic performances of consummate depth, complexity, and theatrical power. We are always impressed by skill—it is fascinating, for instance, to watch a skilled cobbler finishing a leather boot—but great skill in the service of dramatic action can be absolutely transporting. Of course, virtuosity is not easy to acquire, and indeed it will always remain beyond the reach of many people. Each of us possesses natural gifts, but not all are gifted to the same degree; some measure of dramatic talent must be inborn or at least learned early on. But the training beyond one's gifts, the shaping of talent into craft, is an unending process. "You never stop learning it," said actor James Stewart after nearly fifty years of stage and film successes, and virtually all actors would agree with him.

Traditional notions of virtuosity in acting went into a temporary eclipse in the middle of the twentieth century, owing mainly to the rise of realism, which required that acting conform to the behaviors of ordinary people leading ordinary lives. The cinema vérité of the post–World War II era in particular fostered an "artless" acting style, to which virtuosity seemed intrusive rather than supportive. It is certainly true that the virtuosity of one age can seem mere affectation in the next and that modern times require modern skills, a contemporary virtuosity that accords with contemporary dramatic material. Yet even the traditional skills of the theatre have made a great comeback in recent decades: circus techniques, dance, and songs are now a part of many of the most experimental modern stagings, and multiskilled, multitalented performers are in demand as never before. The performer rich in talent and performing skills, capable not merely of depicting everyday life but of fashioning an artful and exciting theatrical expression of it as well, once again commands the central position in contemporary drama.

Magic

Beyond conviction and virtuosity (though incorporating them) remains a final acting ingredient that has been called "presence," "magnetism," "charisma," and many other terms. We shall call it "magic." It is a quality that is difficult to define but universally felt, a quality we cannot explain except to say we know it when we are under its spell.

We must always remember that the earliest actor was not a technician of the theatre but a priest—and that he embodied not ordinary men but gods. We may witness this function directly today in certain tribal dramas, in which a shaman or witch doctor is accepted by cocelebrants as the possessor of divine attributes—or as one possessed by them.

The modern secular actor also conveys at least a hint of this transcendent divinity. Elevated upon a stage and bathed in light for all to see, charged with creating an intensity of feeling, a vivid characterization, and a well-articulated eloquence of verbal and physical mastery, the actor at his or her finest becomes an almost extraterrestrial being, a "star," or, in the French expression, a *monstre sacré* ("sacred monster").

A truly great performance is occasionally said to "carry" a show, and certainly Heather Headley's sensational performance in the Broadway musical *Aida* (2000) was one of these. Appearing in almost every scene and dazzling the audience with her vivacious musicality, Headley was, for many spectators (and critics), reason enough to adore the show.

The actor's presence, the ability to project an aura of magic—does not come about as a direct result of skill at impersonation or technical virtuosity. It does, however, depend on the actor's inner confidence, which in turn can be bred from a mastery of the craft. Therefore, although "magic" cannot be directly acquired or produced, it can be approached, and its fundamental requisites can be established. For gifted individuals it might come quickly; for others, despite abundant skills and devoted training, it comes late or not at all, and they can never rise above pedestrian performances. It is perhaps frustrating to find that acting greatness depends so heavily on this elusive and inexplicable goal of magic, but it is also true that every art incorporates elements that must remain as mysteries. The best acting, like any art, ultimately transcends the reach of pure descriptive analysis; it cannot be acquired mechanically. The best acting strikes chords in the nonreasoning parts of our being; it rings with a resonance we do not fully understand, and it evokes a reality we no longer fully remember. We should extol, not lament, this fact.

Becoming an Actor

How does one become an actor? Many thousands ask this question every year; many thousands, indeed, *act* in one or more theatrical productions every year. The training of actors is now a major activity in hundreds of colleges, universities, conservatories, and private and commercial schools across the United States; and theories of actor training constitute a major branch of artistic pedagogy.

Essentially, actor training entails two distinct phases: development of the actor's instrument and development of the actor's method of approaching a role. There is no general agreement on the order in which these phases should occur, but there is a widespread understanding that both are necessary and that the two are interrelated.

The Actor's Instrument

The actor's instrument is the actor's self—mind, mettle, and metabolism are the materials of an acting performance. An actor's voice is the Stradivarius to be played; an actor's body is the sculpting clay to be molded. An actor is a portrait artist working from inside the self, creating characters with her or his own organs

and physiological systems. It is obvious that a great artist requires first-rate equipment: for the actor this means a responsive *self*, disciplined yet uninhibited, capable of rising to the challenges of great roles.

The training of the actor's instrument is both physiological and psychological; for that reason it must be accomplished under the personal supervision of qualified instructors. In the past, acting instructors were invariably master actors who took on younger apprentices; even today, students of classical French and Japanese acting styles learn their art by relentless imitation of the actors they hope to succeed. In America, however, acting instruction has expanded to include a great many educational specialists who may or may not have had extensive professional acting experience themselves; indeed, some of the most celebrated and effective acting teachers today are play directors, theatrical innovators, and academicians.

No one, however, has yet discovered the art of training an actor's instrument simply by reading books or thinking about problems of craft. This point should be borne in mind while reading the rest of this chapter.

THE PHYSIOLOGICAL INSTRUMENT Voice and speech, quite naturally, are the first elements of the actor's physiological instrument to be considered: "Voice, voice, and more voice" was the answer Tommaso Salvini, the famed nineteenth-century Italian tragedian, gave to the question "What are the three most important attributes of acting?" We already have discussed the importance of vocal skills in the acting profession. Voice- and speech-training programs are aimed at acquainting the actor with a variety of means to achieve and enhance these skills.

The basic elements of voice (breathing, phonation, resonance) and of speech (articulation, pronunciation, phrasing)—as well as their final combination (projection)—are all separate aspects of an integrated voice-training program. Such a program ordinarily takes three years or longer, and many actors continue working on their voice and speech all their lives.

As devoted as teachers and scientists have been to the problems of perfecting voice and speech, however, a certain mystery still surrounds much of their work. Even the fundamental question of how the voice actually works is still a subject of fierce dispute among specialists in anatomy and physiology. Moreover, the processes involved in breathing and speaking have acquired a certain mystique; for example, the dual meaning of *inspiration* as both "inhalation" and "spirit stimulus" has given rise to a number of exotic theoretical dictums that border on religiosity. Some of the fundamental practices of vocal and speech instruction, however, are generalized in the box on the components of voice and speech.

Movement is the second element of the actor's physiological instrument. Movement training typically involves exercises and instruction designed to create physical relaxation, muscular control, economy of action, and expressive rhythms and movement patterns. Dance, mime, fencing, and acrobatics are traditional training courses for actors; in addition, circus techniques and masked pantomime have become common courses in recent years.

Sheer physical strength is stressed by some actors. Laurence Olivier, for example, accorded it the highest importance because, he contended, it gives the actor the stamina needed to "hold stage" for several hours of performance and the basic resilience to accomplish the physical and psychological work of acting without strain or fatigue.

An actor's control of the body permits her or him to stand, sit, and move on the stage with alertness, energy, and seeming ease. Standing tall, walking boldly, turning on a dime at precisely the right moment, extending the limbs joyously, sobbing violently, springing about uproariously, and occupying a major share of stage space are among the capacities of the actor who has mastered body control through

training and confidence. In the late days of the Greek theatre, known as the Hellenistic period, actors used elevated footwear, giant headdresses, and sweeping robes to take on a larger-than-life appearance; the modern actor has discovered that the same effect can be achieved simply by tapping the residual expansiveness of the body.

Economy of movement, which is taught primarily through the selectivity of mime, permits

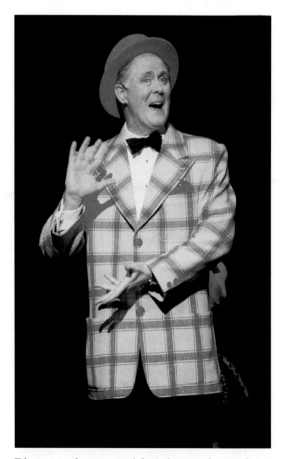

Television and screen star John Lithgow is also — and some would say primarily — a distinguished theatre actor. He is shown here as a 1940s Walter Winchell–type reporter in the serious-themed Broadway musical *Sweet Smell of Success*, for which he won the 2003 Best Actor Tony Award. Lithgow earlier won an acting Tony for *That Championship Season* and Tony nominations for the title roles in *M. Butterfly* and *Requiem for a Heavyweight*.

THE COMPONENTS OF VOICE AND SPEECH

Breathing pumps air through the vocal tract, providing a carrier for the voice. "Breath support," through the expansion of the rib cage and a lowering and controlling of the diaphragm, is a primary goal, as is natural, deep, free breathing that is sufficient to produce and sustain tone but not so forced as to create tension or artificial huffing and puffing.

Phonation is the process whereby vocal cord oscillations produce sound, a process that remains something of an anatomical and physiological mystery even today. Vocal warm-ups are essential for the actor to keep his or her vocal cords and other laryngeal (voice box) tissues supple and healthy; they also prevent strain and the growth of nodes that may cause raspiness and pain as well as phonic failure (laryngitis).

Resonance is the sympathetic vibration, or "resounding," of the voice as it is amplified in the throat, chest, and head. Resonance gives phonation its *timbre*, or tonal quality, its particular balance of bass and treble sounds. Open-throatedness – the lowering of the larynx within the neck, as by a yawn – increases the resonance in the pharynx (throat) and is a major goal in voice work. Keeping the mouth open while speaking and raising the soft palate also increase resonance and add to vocal quality.

Articulation is the shaping of vocal sound into recognizable *phonemes*, or language sounds, forty of which are easily distinguishable in the English language. Speech-training programs aim at improving the actor's capacity to articulate these sounds distinctly, naturally, and unaffectedly – that is, without slurring, ambiguous noise, or self-conscious maneuvering of the lip and tongue. A lazy tongue and slovenly speaking habits inhibit articulation and can be overcome only with persistent drilling and disciplined attention.

Pronunciation makes words both comprehensible and appropriate to the character and style of the play; clear standard pronunciation, unaffected by

regional dialect, is a crucial part of the actor's instrument, as is the ability to learn regional dialects and foreign accents when required. Occasionally actors achieve prominence with the aid of a seemingly permanent dialect – Andy Griffith and Sissy Spacek are two examples – but such actors are likely to find their casting opportunities quite limited unless they can expand their speaking range.

Phrasing makes words meaningful and gives them sound patterns that are both rhythmic and logical. The great classical actors are masters of nuance in phrasing, capable of subtly varying their pitch, intensity, and rate of speech seemingly without effort from one syllable to the next. They rarely phrase consciously; rather, they apparently develop their phrasing through years of experience with classical works and a sustained awareness of the value of spontaneity, naturalness, and a commitment to the dramatized situation. Training programs in speech phrasing aim at enabling actors to expand the pitch range of their normal speech from the normal half octave to two octaves or three, to double their clear-speaking capacity from 200 words a minute to 400, and to develop their ability to orchestrate prose and verse into effective and persuasive crescendos (where volume builds), diminuendos (where it diminishes), and sostenutos (where vowels are elongated for effect) just as if they were responding to a musical score.

Projection, which is the final element in the delivery of voice and speech to the audience, is what ultimately creates dramatic communication; it governs the force with which the character's mind is heard through the character's voice, and it determines the impact of all other components of the actor's voice on the audience. Anxiety and physical tension are the great enemies of projection because they cause shallow breathing, shrill resonance, and timid phrasing; therefore, relaxation and the development of self-confidence become crucial at this final stage of voice and speech development.

the conveyance of subtle detail by seemingly inconspicuous movement. The waggle of a finger, the flare of a nostril, the quiver of a lip can communicate volumes in a performance of controlled movement. The beginning actor is often recognized by uncontrolled behaviors—

fidgeting, shuffling, aimless pacing, and nervous hand gestures—which draw unwanted audience attention. The professional understands the value of physical self-control and the explosive potential of a simple movement that follows a carefully prepared stillness. Surprise, which is one of the actor's greatest weapons, can be achieved only through the actor's mastery of the body.

THE PSYCHOLOGICAL INSTRUMENT Imagination, and the willingness and ability to use it in the service of art, is the major psychological component of the actor's instrument. At the first level, an actress must use her imagination to make the artifice of the theatre real enough to herself to convey that sense of reality to the audience: painted canvas flats must be imag-

ined as brick walls, an offstage jangle must be imagined as a ringing onstage telephone, and a young actress must be imagined as a mother or grandmother.

At the second, far more important, level, the actor must imagine himself in an interpersonal situation created by the play: in love with Juliet, in awe of Zeus, in despair of his life. This imagination must be broad and all-encompassing: the successful actor is able to imagine himself performing and relishing the often unspeakable acts of his characters, who may be murderers, despots, or monsters; insane or incestuous lovers; racial bigots, atheists, devils, perverts, or prudes. To the actor, nothing must be unimaginable; the actor's imagination must be a playground for expressive fantasy and darkly compelling motivations.

Sean Campion and Conleth Hill play, between themselves, all sixteen male and female roles of Marie Jones's *Stones in His Pockets*.

At the third, deepest, level, the actor's imagination must go beyond the mere accommodation of an accepted role pattern to become a creative force that makes characterization a high art, for each actor creates his or her role uniquely—each Romeo and Juliet are like no others before them, and each role can be uniquely fashioned with the aid of the actor's imaginative power. The final goal of creating a character is to make it fresh by filling it with the pulse of real blood and the animation of real on-the-spot thinking and doing. The actor's imagination, liberated from stage fright and mechanical worries, is the crucial ingredient in allowing the actor to transcend the pedestrian and soar toward the genuinely original.

The liberation of imagination is a continuing process in actor training; exercises and "theatre games" designed for that purpose are part of most beginning classes in acting, and many directors use the same exercises and games at the beginning of play rehearsal periods. Because the human imagination tends to rigidify in the course of maturation—the child's imagination is usually much richer than that of the adult—veteran professional actors often profit from periodic mind-expanding or imagination-freeing exercises and games.

Discipline is the fourth and final aspect of an actor's psychological instrument, and to a certain extent it is the one that rules them all. The imagination of the actor is by no means unlimited, nor should it be. It is restricted by the requirements of the play, by the director's staging and interpretation, and by certain established working conditions of the theatre. The actor's artistic discipline keeps him or her within the established bounds and at the same time ensures artistic agility.

The actor is not an independent artist, like a writer or a painter. The actor works in an ensemble and is but one employee (paid or unpaid) in a large enterprise that can succeed only as a collaboration. Therefore, although actors are sometimes thought to be universally temperamental and professionally difficult, the truth is exactly the opposite: actors are among the most disciplined of artists, and the more professional they are, the more disciplined they are.

The actor, after all, leads a vigorous and demanding life. Makeup calls at 5:30 in the morning for film actors and nightly and back-to-back weekend live performances for stage actors make for schedules that are difficult to maintain on a regular basis. Further, the physical and emotional demands of the acting process—the need for extreme concentration in rehearsal and performance, the need for physical health and psychological composure, the need for the actor to be both the instrument and the initiator of her or his performance, and the special demands of interacting with fellow performers at a deep level of mutual involvement—do not permit casual or capricious behavior among the members of a cast or company.

Truly professional actors practice the most rigorous discipline over their work habits. They make all calls (for rehearsal, costume fitting, photographs, makeup, audition, and performance) at the stated times, properly warmed up beforehand; they learn lines at or before stipulated deadlines, memorize stage movements as directed, collaborate with the other actors and theatre artists toward a successful and growing performance, and continually study their craft. If they do not do these things, they cease to be actors. Professional theatre producers have little sympathy or forgiveness for undisciplined performers, and this professional attitude now prevails in community and university theatres as well.

Being a disciplined actor does not mean being a slave, nor does it mean foregone capitulation to the director or the management. The disciplined actor is simply one who works rigorously to develop his or her physiological and psychological instrument, who meets all technical obligations unerringly and without reminder, and who works to the utmost to ensure the success of the entire production and the fruitful association of the whole acting ensemble. The disciplined actor asks questions, offers suggestions, invents stage business, and creates characterization in harmony with the directorial pattern and the acting ensemble. When there is a serious disagreement between actor and director (a not uncommon occurrence), the disciplined actor seeks to work it out through discussion and compromise and will finally yield if the director cannot be persuaded otherwise. Persistent, willful disobedience has no place in the serious theatre and is not tolerated by it.

The Actor's Approach

As the dust clears from the last phases of the long-standing debate between external and internal acting techniques, certain elements of an integrated, or fusion, technique are nearly universal in actor training, at least in the West. The first element is Stanislavsky's primary principle: the actor creates her or his performance through the pursuit of the character's zadacha, or problem to be solved. Whether *zadacha* is further translated as "objective," "intention," "task," "victory," "want," or "goal" (this author's choice), the basic point—that the actor embodies the role by pursuing the character's goal (to marry Romeo, to displace the king of Denmark) rather than by pursuing the actor's own (to get a standing ovation, to get a better part in the next production)—is all but universally accepted. Pursuing the character's goal focuses the actor's energy, displaces stage fright, aligns the actor solidly with the character, and sets up the broadest and deepest foundation for employing all the technical skills at the actor's disposal.

It is usually best to identify the character's primary goal in relation to the other characters in the play so that acting becomes, in effect, "interacting with other people." Thus Juliet does not simply want "to marry" but "to marry Romeo," and Hamlet wants not just "to become king of Denmark" but "to replace Claudius." The acting thus becomes enlivened; it occurs in

> ### "Everybody Understands Frustration"
>
> One time I had this scene where I was to walk into this actress' dressing room and say something like "I love you; will you marry me?" We managed to make it better by having the girl go into her bathroom and close the door and I had to say those lines to a closed door. I learned to work with counterpoint. To make the material more interesting I would find ways to create obstacles for the character — frustrate him in what he wants to accomplish. That makes the character more sympathetic, because everybody understands frustration.
>
> – Jack Lemmon

real time while onstage, with moment-to-moment interplay between all the actors involved.

The second element of the actor's approach is the identification of the tactics necessary to achieve goals and avoid defeats. Romeo woos Juliet by composing love poems to her and reciting them fetchingly; he silences Mercutio's jibes by wittily humoring him. Hamlet secures Horatio's aid by speaking kindly to him; he disorients Polonius by confusing him; and he steers Ophelia out of harm's way (he believes) by frightening her. These tactics are how Romeo and Hamlet try to make their goals come to fruition, and, for the actors who play them with committed vigor, their voices and bodies should pulse with excitement, anticipation, and alarm. Actors who play tactics boldly and with enthusiasm and who allow themselves to believe that they will win their goals (even if the play dictates that they will not) convey the theatre's greatest intangible: hope. Hope achieved—as when the young deaf and blind Helen Keller finally utters the word "wawa" as her teacher splashes water on her hands in the final moments of William Gibson's *The Miracle Worker*—can be overwhelmingly thrilling. Hope dashed—as when Jim O'Connor tells Laura he won't, in fact, be

No one can say that sex appeal is not a vital part of theatre, which almost always centers on themes of erotic passion. Nicole Kidman is here the star, opposite Iain Glen, in English playwright David Hare's steamy *The Blue Room*, in the London premiere, 1998.

able to invite her on a date in Tennessee Williams's *The Glass Menagerie*—can be unbearably poignant. It is in the alternation of these sorts of climaxes that great theatrical impact is achieved.

The third and most complicated element of the actor's approach requires research into the style of the play and the mode of performance that will govern the production, in which each role is but a single integer. Some plays, and some productions, invite—indeed, require—a direct confrontation with the live audience. Some plays assume an environment in which the entire cast of characters expects and re-

wards refined speech; others assume an environment in which refined speech is ridiculed as pretentious. Some plays have several "worlds" of characters—the aristocrats, the laborers, and the fairies in Shakespeare's *A Midsummer Night's Dream,* for example—and the actor's approach must lead to an understanding of what the nature of each of the play's separate or inclusive worlds is.

The Actor's Routine

In essence, the actor's professional routine consists of three stages: the audition, the rehearsal, and the performance. The first is the way the actor gets a role, the second is the way the actor learns it, and the last is the way the actor produces it, either night after night on a stage or one time for filming or taping. Each of these stages merits independent consideration, for each imposes certain special demands on the actor's instrument and on his or her approach.

The Audition

For all but the most established professionals, auditioning is the primary process by which acting roles are awarded. A young actor may audition hundreds of times a year. In the film world, celebrated performers may be required to audition only if their careers are perceived to be declining: two of the more famous (and successful) auditions in American film history were undertaken by Frank Sinatra for *From Here to Eternity* and by Marlon Brando for *The Godfather.* Stage actors are customarily asked to audition no matter how experienced or famous they are.

In an audition the actor has an opportunity to demonstrate to the director (or producer or casting director) how well he or she can fulfill the role sought; in order to show this, the actor presents either a prepared reading or a "cold reading" from the script whose production is planned. Every actor who is seriously planning for a career in the theatre will prepare several audition pieces to have at the ready in case an audition opportunity presents itself. For the most part these pieces will be one- or two-minute monologues from plays, although sometimes short narrative cuttings from novels, short stories, and poems are used. Each audition piece must be carefully edited for timing and content (some alteration of the text, so as to make a continuous speech out of two or three shorter speeches, is generally permissible); the piece is then memorized and staged. The staging requirements should be flexible to permit adjustments to the size of the audition place (which might be a stage but could just as well be an agent's office) and should not rely on costuming or the use of particular pieces of furniture. Most actors prepare a variety of these pieces, for although auditions generally specify two contrasting selections (one verse and one prose, one serious and one comic, or one classical and one modern), an extra piece that fits a particular casting situation can often come in handy. An actor's audition pieces are as essential as calling cards in the professional theatre world and in many academies as well; they should be carefully developed, coached, and rehearsed, and they should be performed with assurance and poise.

The qualities a director looks for at an audition vary from one situation to another, but generally they include the actor's ease at handling the role; naturalness of delivery; physical, vocal, and emotional suitability for the part; and spontaneity, power, and charm. Most directors also look for an actor who is well trained and disciplined and capable of mastering the technical demands of the part, who will complement the company ensemble, and who can convey that intangible presence that makes for "theatre magic." In short, the audition can show the director that the actor not only knows her or his craft but also will lend the production a special excitement.

The Rehearsal

Plays are ordinarily rehearsed in a matter of weeks: a normal period of rehearsal ranges from ten weeks for complex or experimental productions to just one week for many summer stock operations. Much longer rehearsal periods, however, are not unheard of; indeed, the productions of Stanislavsky and Brecht were frequently rehearsed for a year or more. Three to five weeks, however, is the customary rehearsal period for American professional productions —but these entail forty-hour weeks, and they are usually followed by several days (or weeks) of previews and/or out-of-town tryouts, with additional rehearsals between performances.

During the rehearsal period the actor learns the role and investigates, among other things, the character's biography; the subtext (the unspoken communications) of the play; the character's thoughts, fears, and fantasies; the character's objectives; and the world envisioned by the play and the playwright. The director will lead discussions, offer opinions, and issue directives with respect to some or all of these matters; the director may also provide reading materials, pictures, and music to aid in the actor's research.

The actor must memorize lines, stage movements ("blocking"), and directed stage actions ("business"—precisely scripted physical behaviors) during the rehearsal period. He or she must also be prepared to rememorize these if they are changed, as they frequently are: in the rehearsal of new plays it is not unusual for entire acts to be rewritten between rehearsals and for large segments to be changed, added, or written out overnight.

Memorization usually presents no great problem for young actors, to whom it tends to come naturally (children in plays frequently memorize not only their own lines but everyone else's, without even meaning to); however, it seems to become more difficult as one gets older. But at whatever age, memorization of lines remains one of the actor's easier problems to solve, contrary to what many naive audience members think. Adequate memorization merely provides the basis from which the actor learns a part; the actor's goal is not simply to get the lines down but to do it *fast* so that most of the rehearsal time can be devoted to other things.

The rehearsal period is a time for experimentation and discovery. It is a time for the actor to get close to the character's beliefs and intentions, to steep in the internal aspects of characterization that lead to fully engaged physical, intellectual, and emotional performance. It is a time to search the play's text and the director's mind for clues as to how the character behaves and what results the character aims for in the play's situation. And it is a time to experiment, both alone and in rehearsal with other actors, with the possibilities of subtle interactions that these investigations develop.

Externally, rehearsal is a time for the actor to experiment with timing and delivery of both lines and business—to integrate the staged movements (given by the director) with the text (given by the playwright) and to meld these into a fluid series of actions that build and illuminate by the admixture of the actor's own personally initiated behavior. It is a time to suggest movement and business possibilities to the director (assuming the director is the sort who accepts suggestions, as virtually all do nowadays) and to work out details of complicated sequences with the other actors. It is also a time to "get secure" in both lines and business by constant repetition—in fact, the French word for rehearsal is *répétition.* And it affords an opportunity to explore all the possibilities of the role—to look for ways to improve the actor's original plan for its realization and to test various possibilities with the director.

Thus the rehearsal of a play is an extremely creative time for an actor; it is by no means a routine or boring work assignment—and indeed for this reason some actors enjoy the rehearsal process even more than the perfor-

mance phase of production. At its best, a rehearsal is both spontaneous and disciplined, a combination of repetition and change, of trying and "setting," of making patterns and breaking them and then making them anew. It is an exciting time, no less so because it invariably includes many moments of distress, frustration, and despair; it is a time, above all, when the actor learns a great deal about acting and, ideally, about human interaction on many levels.

The Performance

Performing, finally, is what the theatre is about, and it is before an audience in a live performance that the actor's mettle is put to the ultimate test. Sometimes the results are quite startling. The actor who has been brilliant in rehearsal can crumble before an audience and completely lose the "edge" of his performance in the face of stage fright and apprehension. Or —and this is more likely—an actor who seemed fairly unexciting in rehearsal can suddenly take fire in performance and dazzle the audience with unexpected energy, subtlety, and depth: one celebrated example of this phenomenon was achieved by Lee J. Cobb in the original production of Arthur Miller's *Death of a Salesman,* in which Cobb had the title role. Roles rehearsed in all solemnity can suddenly turn comical in performance; conversely, roles developed for comic potential in rehearsal may be received soberly by an audience and lose their comedic aspect entirely.

Sudden and dramatic change, however, is not the norm as the performance phase replaces rehearsal: most actors cross over from final dress rehearsal to opening night with only the slightest shift; indeed, this is generally thought to be the goal of a disciplined and professional rehearsal schedule. "Holding back until opening night," an acting practice occasionally employed over the past century, is universally disavowed today, and opening-night recklessness is viewed as a sure sign of the amateur, who relies primarily on guts and adrenaline to get through the evening. Deliberate revision of a role in performance, in response to the first waves of laughter or applause, is similarly frowned upon in all but the most inartistic of theatres today.

Nevertheless, a fundamental shift does occur in the actor's awareness between rehearsal and performance, and this cannot and should not be denied; indeed, it is essential to the creation of theatre art. The shift is set up by an elementary feedback: the actor is inevitably aware, with at least a portion of her mind, of the audience's reactions to her own performance and that of the other players; there is always, in any acting performance, a subtle adjustment to the audience that sees it. The outward manifestations of this adjustment are usually all but imperceptible: the split-second hold for a laugh to die down, the slight special projection of a certain line to ensure that it reaches the back row, the quick turn of a head to make a characterization or plot transition extra clear.

In addition, the best actors consistently radiate a quality known to the theatre world as "presence." It is a difficult quality to describe, but it has the effect of making both the character whom the actor portrays and the "self" of the actor who represents that character especially vibrant and "in the present" for the audience; it is the quality of an actor who takes the stage and acknowledges, in some inexplicable yet indelible manner, that he or she is there *to be seen.* Performance is not a one-way statement given from the stage to the house; it is a two-way, participatory communication between the actors and the audience members in which the former employ text and movement and the latter employ applause, laughter, silence, and attention.

Even when the audience is silent and invisible—and, owing to the brightness of stage lights, the audience is frequently invisible to the actor—the performer feels its presence. There is nothing extrasensory about this: the

England's most acclaimed actress, Judi Dench, playing the role of an acclaimed actress, here applies makeup in the 1999 Broadway production of David Hare's *Amy's View*, a story of broken relationships against a background of theatrical culture and an entertainment industry. Making up and making up are both the literal and figurative topics. Design is by Bob Crowley.

absence of sound is itself a signal, for when several hundred people sit without shuffling, coughing, or muttering, their silence betokens a level of attention for which the actor customarily strives. Laughter, gasps, sighs, and applause similarly feed back into the actor's consciousness—and unconsciousness—and spur (or sometimes, alas, distract) his efforts. The veteran actor can determine quickly how to ride the crest of audience laughter and how to hold the next line just long enough that it will pierce the lingering chuckles but not be overridden by them; he also knows how to vary his pace and/or redouble his energy when he senses restlessness or boredom on the other side of the curtain line. "Performance technique," or the art of "reading an audience," is more instinctual than learned. It is not dissimilar to the technique achieved by the effective classroom lecturer or TV talk-show host or even by the accomplished conversationalist. The timing it requires is of such complexity that no actor could master it rationally; he or she can develop it only out of experience — both on the stage and off.

Professional stage actors face a special problem unknown to their film counterparts and seldom experienced by amateurs in the theatre: the problem of maintaining a high level of spontaneity through many, many performances. Some professional play productions perform continuously for years, and actors may find themselves in the position — fortunately for their finances, awkwardly for their art — of performing the same part eight times a week, fifty-two weeks a year, with no end in sight. Of course the routine can vary with vacations and cast substitutions; and in fact very few actors ever play a role continuously for more than a year or two, but the problem becomes intense even after only a few weeks. How, as they say in the trade, does the actor "keep it fresh"?

Each actor has her or his own way of addressing this problem. Some rely on their total immersion in the role and contend that by "living the life of the character" they can keep themselves equally alert from first performance to last. Others turn to technical experiments — reworking their delivery and trying constantly to find better ways of saying their lines, expressing their characters, and achieving their objectives. Still others concentrate on the relationships within the play and try with every performance to "find something new" in each relationship as it unfolds onstage.

Some actors, it must be admitted, resort to childish measures, rewriting dialogue as they go or trying to break the concentration of the other actors; this sort of behavior is abhorrent, but it is indicative of the seriousness of the actor's problems of combating boredom in a long-running production and the lengths to which some actors will go to solve them.

The actor's performance does not end with the play, for it certainly extends into the paratheatrical moments of the curtain call — in which the actor-audience communion is direct and unmistakable — and it can even be said to extend to the dressing-room postmortem, in which the actor reflects upon what was done today and how it might be done better tomorrow. Sometimes the postmortem of a play is handled quite specifically by the director, who may give notes to the cast; more typically, in professional situations, the actor simply relies on self-criticism, often measured against comments from friends and fellow cast members, from the stage manager, and from reviews in the press. There is no performer who leaves the stage in the spirit of a factory worker leaving the plant. If there has been a shift up from the rehearsal phase to the performance phase, there is now a shift down (or a letdown) that follows the curtain call — a reentry into a world in which actions and reactions are likely to be a little calmer. There would be no stage fright if there were nothing to be frightened *about,* and the conquering of one's own anxiety — sometimes translated as conquering of the audience: "I really killed them tonight" — fills the actor at the final curtain with a sense of awe, elation . . . and emptiness. It is perhaps this feeling that draws the actor ever more deeply into the profession, for it is a feeling known to the rankest amateur in a high school pageant as well as to the most experienced professional in a Broadway or West End run. It is the theatre's "high," and because it is a high that accompanies an inexpressible void, it leads to addiction.

The Actor in Life

Acting is an art. It can also be a disease. Actors are privileged people. They get to live the lives of some of the world's greatest and best-known characters: Romeo, Juliet, Phèdre, Cyrano, St. Joan, and Willy Loman. They get to fight for honor, hunger for salvation, battle for justice, die for love, kill for passion. They get to die many times before their deaths, to duel fabulous enemies, to love magnificent lovers, and to live through an infinite variety of human experiences that, though imaginary, are publicly engaged. They get to reenter the innocence of childhood without suffering its consequences and to participate in every sort of adult villainy without reckoning its responsibility. They get to fantasize freely and be seen doing so—and they get paid for it.

Millions of people want to be actors. It looks easy, and, at least for some people, it *is* easy. It looks exciting, and there can be no question that it is exciting, very exciting; in fact, amateurs act in theatres all over the world without any hope of getting paid merely to experience that excitement. Acting addicts, as a consequence, are common. People who will not wait ten minutes at a supermarket checkout stand will wait ten years to get a role in a Hollywood film or a Broadway play. The acting unions are the only unions in the world that have ever negotiated a *lower* wage for some of their members in order to allow them to perform at substandard salaries. To the true acting addict there is nothing else; acting becomes the sole preoccupation.

The addicted actor—the actor obsessed with acting for its own sake—is probably not a very good actor, for fine acting demands an open mind, a mind capable of taking in stimuli from all sorts of directions, not merely from the theatrical environment. An actor who knows nothing but acting has no range. First and foremost, actors must represent human beings, and to do that they must know

Stage and film acting have their differences, but most American actors today hope to do both. Macaulay Culkin's first professional stage role, after starring as a child in several films, was an adolescent student seduced by his teacher – and defying his father – in Richard Nelson's *Madame Melville*, which the author also directed off-Broadway in 2001.

something about humankind. Thus the proper study of acting is life, abetted but not supplanted by the craft of the trade. Common sense, acute powers of observation and perception, tolerance and understanding for all human beings, and a sound general knowledge of one's own society and culture are prime requisites for the actor—as well as training, business acumen, and a realistic vision of one's own potential.

A lifetime professional career in acting is the goal of many but the accomplishment of very few. Statistically, one's chances of developing a long-standing acting career are quite small; only those individuals possessed of great talent, skill, persistence, and personal fortitude stand any chance of succeeding—and even then it is only a chance. But the excitement of acting is not the exclusive preserve of those who attain lifetime professional careers; on the contrary, it may be argued that the happiest and most artistically fulfilled actors are those for whom performance is only an avocation. The excitement of acting, finally, is dependent not on monetary reward, a billing above the title, or the size of one's roles but on the actor's engagement with drama and with dramatized situations—in short, on a personal synchronization with the theatre itself, of which acting is the very evanescent but still solid center.

4

The Playwright

A T HOME, AS I GAZE AT MY COMPUTER SCREEN, I am the total master of my stage. Actions cascade through my head; whole characters pop into my imagination; great words, speeches, scenes, and visions flow directly from my brain to my fingers to the words leaping onto my screen. They are *my* ideas, *my* people, *my* language, and *my* play that will soon be resounding through theatre walls around the world; it will be *me* up there receiving the critics' raves, press interviews, and speaking invitations as a result of my play's success; it will be *me* mounting the stage to accept my 'best play' award, perhaps even sitting one day in Stockholm, next to my fellow Nobel Prize winners—this year's Einstein and Marie Curie who, like me, have also rocked the modern world.

"But that's only at home. In the theatre, I am the loneliest of figures. I huddle inconspicuously in the back row, taking notes in the dark. I am unnoticed by the actors and, indeed, rarely allowed to speak directly to them. The designers look at me with condescension and suspicion. At the end of the rehearsal, when I politely offer to share my notes with the director, she at first glares at me. And when she listens, it's with a noncommittal face and a dismissive agreement that, yes, she'll 'think about all of this tomorrow.'

"I am totally convinced that the theatre is nothing more than an instrument for massacring my manuscript!"

This monologue is imaginary—and perhaps a bit extreme. Playwrights, by their creative natures, generally have vivid imaginations, which can and often do lead to both mania and paranoia.

But this inner monologue is also the great fear of every playwright, reflecting the great paradox of theatrical creation: the playwright is both the most central and the most peripheral figure in the theatrical event.

The playwright is central in the most obvious ways. She or he provides the point of origin for virtually every play production—the script, which is the rallying point around which the director or producer gathers the troops. And yet that point of origin is also a point of departure. The days when a Shakespeare or a Molière would gather actors around, read his text to them, and then coach them in its proper execution are long gone. What we have today is a more specialized theatrical hierarchy in which the director is interposed as the playwright's representative to the theatrical enterprise and its constituent members. More and more, the playwright's function is to write the play and then disappear, for once the script has been typed, duplicated, and distributed, the playwright's physical participation is relegated mainly to serving as the director's sounding board and rewrite person. Indeed, the playwright's mere physical presence in the rehearsal hall can become an embarrassment, more tolerated than welcomed—and sometimes not even tolerated.

Playwright Arthur Miller (*center*), whose 1949 *Death of a Salesman* is considered one of America's greatest plays, was one of America's busiest dramatists right up to his death in early 2005. Here Miller discusses his newly revised *Resurrection Blues* with the cast at the Old Globe Theatre in San Diego in 2004.

Fundamentally, the playwright today is considered an independent artist, whose work, like that of the novelist or poet, is executed primarily, if not exclusively, in isolation. There are exceptions, of course: some playwrights work from actors' improvisations, and others participate quite fully in rehearsals, even to the point of serving as the initial director of their plays (as Edward Albee, Sam Shepard, and George C. Wolfe often do) or, more extraordinarily, by acting in them (as Athol Fugard and August Wilson have done).

But the exceptions do not, in this case, disprove the rule; since the age of romanticism, the image of the playwright has turned increasingly from that of theatre coworker and mentor to that of isolated observer and social critic. In the long run, this change should occasion no lamentation, for if theatre production now demands collaboration and compromise, the art of the theatre still requires individuality, clarity of vision, sharpness of approach, original sensitivity, and a devotion to personal truth if it is to challenge the artists who are called upon to fulfill it and the audiences who will pay money to experience it.

It is often said that Shakespeare and Molière wrote great plays because they could tailor their parts to the talents of actors whom they knew well. It seems far more likely that they wrote great plays in spite of this, for in the hands of lesser writers, that sort of enterprise produces sheer hackwork that simply combines the limitations of the actors with those of the author. Whether writing from inside an acting company or in submission to one, the playwright strives to give life to a unique vision, to create material that transcends what has gone before, both in writing and in performance.

Therefore, the *independence* of the playwright is perhaps her or his most important characteristic. Playwrights must seek from life, from their own lives—and not from the theatrical establishment—the material that will translate into exciting and meaningful and entertaining theatre; and their views must be intensely personal, grounded in their own perceptions and philosophy, in order to ring true. We look to the theatre for a measure of leadership, for personal enlightenment derived from another's experience, for fresh perspectives, new visions. In other words, simple mastery of certain conventional techniques will not suffice to enable the playwright to expand our lives.

We Are All Playwrights

Playwriting is not just something we learn. It's something we already do. All of us. Every day —or night.

Every night, dreams come to us in our sleep. Or, rather, they *seem* to come to us: in fact, we create them, for each of us has our own "playwright-in-residence" somewhere in the back of our minds, churning out a nightly mixture of vivid, believable, and sometimes terrifying fantasies that create half-real, half-imagined characters, idealized settings, surprising plot complications, nostalgic visions, and often nightmarish climaxes and reversals. The situations and characters of our dreams are our own creations, drawn from our careful observations, colored by our unconscious phobias and fancies, stylized into associations of words, scenes, and "stagings" that ring with deep resonance of our innermost plans, fears, and secrets.

Of course there's more to playwriting than dreaming up characters and a story. As dreamers, we are only beginning playwrights. What happens next is the subject of the rest of this chapter.

Literary and Nonliterary Aspects of Playwriting

Because drama is often thought of as a form of literature (and is taught in departments of literature) and because many dramatic authors begin (or double) as poets or novelists, it may seem as if playwriting is primarily a literary activity. It is not. Etymology helps here: *playwright* is not *playwrite*. Writing for the theatre entails considerations not common to other literary forms. Although by coincidence the words *write* and *wright* are homonyms, a "playwright" is a person who *makes* plays, just as a wheelwright is a person who makes wheels. This distinction is particularly important, because some plays, or portions of plays, are never written at all. Improvisational plays, certain rituals, whole scenes of comic business, subtextual behaviors, and many documentary dramas are created largely or entirely in performance or are learned simply through oral improvisation and repetition. Some are created with a tape recorder and the collaboration of multiple imaginations and may or may not be committed to writing after the performance is concluded. And others, although dramatic in structure, are entirely nonverbal; that is, they include no dialogue, no words, and very little that is written other than an outline of mimetic effects.

So if drama is a branch of literature, it is a special and distinctive branch. It is not merely an arrangement of words on a page; it is a conceptualization of the interactions of myriad elements in the theatrical medium: movement, speech, scenery, costume, staging, music, spectacle, and silence. It is a literature whose impact depends on a collective endeavor and whose appreciation must be, in large part, spontaneous and immediate.

A play attains its finished form only in performance upon the stage: the written script is not the final play but the *blueprint* for the play,

Playwrights may draft their plays at a desk at home, but they normally revise and polish their final versions in stage rehearsals. Here Suzan-Lori Parks, who won the Pulitzer Prize for her *Topdog/Underdog* the previous year, sits on the set of her new play, *Fucking A*, as it is being rehearsed for its premiere at New York's Joseph Papp Public Theater in 2003.

the written foundation for the production that is the play's complete realization. Some of a play's most effective writing may look very clumsy as it appears in print; take, for example, the following lines from Shakespeare:

Oh! Oh! Oh!   —*Othello*

Howl, howl, howl, howl!   —*King Lear*

No, no, the drink, the drink. O my dear
   Hamlet,
The drink, the drink! I am poisoned.
                              —*Hamlet*

These apparently unsophisticated lines of dialogue in fact provide great dramatic climaxes in an impassioned performance; they are *pretexts for great acting,* the creation of which is far more crucial than literary eloquence to the art of playwriting.

Of course some formal literary values are as important to the theatre as they are to other branches of literature: allusional complexity, descriptive precision, poetic imagery, metaphoric implication, and a careful crafting of verbal rhythms, cadences, and textures all contribute powerfully to dramatic effect. But they are effective only insofar as they are fully integrated with the whole of the theatrical medium, as they stimulate action and behavior through stage space and stage time in a way that commands audience attention and involvement. Mere literary brilliance is insufficient as theatre, as a great many successful novelists and poets have learned to their chagrin when they attempted to write plays.

Playwriting as Event Writing

The core of every play is action. Unlike with other literary forms, the inner structure of a play is never a series of abstract observations or a collage of descriptions and moralizings; it is an ordering of observable, dramatizable *events*. These events are the basic building blocks of the play, regardless of its style or genre or theme.

Fundamentally, the playwright works with two tools, both representing the externals of human behavior: dialogue and physical action. The inner story and theme of a play—the psychology of the characters, the viewpoint of the author, the impact of the social environment— must be inferred, by the audience, from outward appearances, from the play's events as the audience sees them. Whatever the playwright's intended message and whatever the playwright's perspective on the function and process of playwriting itself, the play cannot be put together until the playwright has conceived of an event—and then a series of related events— designed to be enacted on a stage. It is this series of related events that constitutes the play's scenario or, more formally, its plot.

The events of drama are, by their nature, compelling. Some are bold and unusual, such as the scene in which Prometheus—in Aeschylus's tragedy—is chained to his rock. Some are subdued, as when the military regiment in Chekhov's *The Three Sisters* leaves town at the play's end. Some are quite ordinary, as in the domestic sequences depicted in most modern realist plays. But they are always aimed at creating a memorable impression. To begin playwriting, one must first conceptualize events and envision them enacted in such a way as to hold the attention of an audience.

The events of a play can be connected to each other in a strict chronological, cause-effect continuity. This has been a goal of the realistic theatre, in which dramatic events are arranged to convey a lifelike progression of experiences in time. Such plays are said to be *continuous* in structure and *linear* in chronology, and they can be analyzed like sociological events: the audience simply watches them unfold as it might watch a family quarrel in progress in an apartment across the way.

Continuous linearity, however, is by no means a requirement for play construction.

Not all plays are written by individual playwrights; increasingly common in the current era are plays written by the theatre companies that perform them. The Tectonic Theatre Company of New York, under Moisés Kaufman, created *The Laramie Project* by interviewing townspeople in Laramie, Wyoming, as they responded to the 1998 murder of gay college student Matthew Shepard; the company then transcribed, adapted, and performed the interviews in a highly successful production staged in several cities, shown here in its off-Broadway 2000 staging.

Many plays are discontinuous and/or nonlinear. The surviving plays of ancient Greece are highly discontinuous, with odes alternating with episodes in the tragedies and a whole host of nonlinear theatrical inventions popping in and out during the comedies. Shakespeare's plays are structured in a highly complex arrangement of time shifts, place shifts, style shifts, songs, and subplots ingeniously integrated around a basic theme or investigation of character. And many contemporary plays break with chronological linearity altogether, flashing instantly backward and forward through time to incorporate character memories, character fantasies, direct expressions of the play-wright's social manifesto, historical exposition, comic relief, or any other ingredient the playwright can successfully work in.

Linear, point-to-point storytelling still has not disappeared from the theatre—indeed, it remains the basic architecture of most popular and serious plays—but modern (and postmodern) audiences have proven increasingly receptive to less-conventional structures: the exuberance of the music hall, for instance, inspired the structuring of Joan Littlewood's *Oh, What a Lovely War!*; the minstrel show served as a structure for George C. Wolfe's *The Colored Museum*; and the didacticism of the lecture hall underlay much of the theatre of

Bertolt Brecht. Nonlinear, discontinuous, and even stream-of-consciousness structures can provide powerful and sustained dramatic impact in the theatre, provided they are based in the dramatization of events that the audience can put together in some sort of meaningful and satisfying fashion.

The Qualities of a Fine Play

As with any art form, the qualities that make up a good play can be discussed individually, but it is only in their combination, only in their interaction—only in ways that cannot be dissected or measured—that these qualities have meaning.

Credibility and Intrigue

To say that a play must be credible is not at all to say that it has to be lifelike, for fantasy, ritual, and absurdity have all proven to be enduringly popular theatrical modes. The demand of *credibility* is an audience-imposed demand, and it has to do with the play's internal consistency: the actions must flow logically from the characters, the situation, and the theatrical context the playwright provides. In other words, credibility is the audience's demand that what happens in act 2 makes sense in terms of what happened in act 1.

Credibility demands, for example, that the characters in a play appear to act out of their own individual interests, instincts, and intentions rather than serving as mere pawns for the development of theatrical plot or effect, as empty disseminators of propaganda. Credibility means that characters must maintain consistency within themselves: that their thoughts, feelings, hopes, fears, and plans must appear to flow from human needs rather than purely theatrical ones. Credibility also demands that human characters appear to act and think like human beings (even in humanly impossible situations) and not purely as thematic autom-

atons. Credibility, in essence, is a contract between author and audience, whereby the audience agrees to view the characters as "people" as long as the author agrees not to shatter that belief in order to accomplish other purposes.

Thus James Barrie's famous play *Peter Pan*, although undeniably fantastical, creates a cast of characters wholly appropriate to their highly imaginary situation and internally consistent in their actions within the context of their developing experience. All of their aspirations (including those of the dog!) are human ones, and their urgencies are so believable that when Tinkerbell steps out of the play's context to ask the audience to demonstrate its belief in fairies, the audience is willing to applaud its approval. At that moment, the world of the play becomes more credible, more "real," than that of the audience. So much for the power—and consequently the necessity—of dramatic credibility.

Intrigue is that quality of a play that makes us curious (sometimes fervently so) to see "what happens next." Sheer plot intrigue—which is sometimes called "suspense" in that it leaves us suspended (that is, "hanging")—is one of the most powerful of dramatic approaches. Whole plays can be based on little more than artfully contrived plotting designed to keep the audience in a continual state of anticipation and wonder. Plot, however, is only one of the elements of a play that can support intrigue. Most plays that aspire to deeper insights than whodunits or farces develop intrigue in character as well and even in theme. Most of the great plays, in fact, demand that we ask not so much "What will happen?" as "What does this mean?" Most great plays, in other words, make us care about the characters and invite us to probe the mysteries of the human condition.

Look, for example, at this dialogue from David Mamet's *Glengarry Glen Ross,* in which a disgruntled real-estate salesman proposes to a colleague that they rob their front office,

Few dramatic moments are as suspenseful as a pointed gun. In Lee Kalcheim's seriocomic *Defiled*, staged at the Geffen Playhouse in 2000, Jason Alexander plays a bibliomaniacal librarian threatening to blow up the town library – and shoot the detective (played by Peter Falk) who's trying to prevent him.

stealing some real-estate "leads" (names of potential customers) that they can then sell to a competitor.

MOSS: I want to tell you something.

AARONOW: What?

MOSS: I want to tell you what somebody should do.

AARONOW: What?

MOSS: Someone should stand up and strike back.

AARONOW: What do you mean?

MOSS: *Somebody* . . .

AARONOW: Yes . . . ?

MOSS: Should do something to *them*.

AARONOW: What?

MOSS: Something. To pay them back. (*Pause*) Someone, someone should hurt them. Murray and Mitch.

AARONOW: Somebody should hurt them.

MOSS: Yes.

AARONOW: (*Pause*) How?

MOSS: How? Do something to hurt them. Where they live.

AARONOW: What? (*Pause*)

MOSS: Someone should rob the office.

AARONOW: Huh.

MOSS: That's what I'm *saying*. We were, if we were that kind of guys, to knock it off, and *trash* the joint, it looks like a robbery, and *take* the fuckin' leads out of the files . . . [. . .] (*Pause*)

AARONOW: Are you actually *talking* about this or are we just . . .

MOSS: No, we're just . . .

AARONOW: We're just *"talking"* about it.

MOSS: We're just *speaking* about it. (*Pause*) As an *idea*.

AARONOW: As an idea.

MOSS: Yes.

AARONOW: We're not actually *talking* about it.

MOSS: No.

AARONOW: Talking about it as a . . .

MOSS: No.

AARONOW: As a *robbery.*

MOSS: As a "robbery"?! No.

AARONOW: *Well*. Well . . .

The basic action of this scene could be expressed in just two or three lines of dialogue, but since a conspiracy is being proposed each character must proceed with extreme caution —as his colleague could turn him in at any time. As each of the thirty-two short lines takes the conspiracy one tiny—but precise— step forward, the credibility is exacting while the intrigue builds to an increasingly higher level of tension.

Intrigue draws us into the world of a play; credibility keeps us there. In the best plays the two are sustained in a fine tension of opposites: intrigue demanding surprise, credibility demanding consistency. Combined, they generate a kind of "believable wonder," which is the fundamental state of drama. Credibility alone will not suffice to make a play interesting, and no level of intrigue can make a noncredible play palatable. The integration of the two must be created by the playwright in order to establish that shared ground that transcends our expectations but not our credulity.

Speakability, Stageability, and Flow

The dialogue of drama is written upon the page, but it must be spoken by actors and staged by directors. Thus the goal of the dramatist is to fabricate dialogue that is actable and stageable and that flows in a progression leading to theatrical impact.

One of the most common faults of beginning playwrights—even when the playwright may be an established novelist or poet—is that the lines lack *speakability*. This is not to say that dramatic dialogue must resemble ordinary speech. No one imagines people in life speaking like characters out of the works of Aeschylus, Shakespeare, or Shaw, or even contemporary writers like Harold Pinter or Edward Albee. A brilliantly styled language is a feature of most of the great plays in theatre history, and lifelikeness is not, by itself, a dramatic virtue—nor is its absence a dramatic fault.

Rather, speakability means that a line of dialogue should be so written that it achieves its maximum impact when spoken. In order to accomplish this, the playwright must be closely attuned to the *audial shape* of dialogue: the rhythm of sound that creates emphasis, meaning, focus, and power. Verbal lullabies and climaxes, fast punch lines, sonorous lamentations, sparkling epigrams, devastating expletives, significant pauses, and electrifying whispers—these are some of the devices of dialogue that impart audial shape to great plays written by master dramatists. Look, for example, at Andrew Undershaft's chiding of his pretentious son, Stephen, in George Bernard Shaw's *Major Barbara*, where Stephen has just said that he knows "the difference between right and wrong."

UNDERSHAFT: You don't say so! What! no capacity for business, no knowledge of law, no sympathy with art, no pretension to philosophy; only a simple knowledge of the secret that has puzzled all the philosophers, baffled all the lawyers, muddled all the men of business, and ruined most of the artists: the secret of right and wrong. Why, man, you're a genius, a master of masters, a god! At twentyfour, too!

No one would call this "everyday speech" as in the David Mamet dialogue quoted earlier, but it is immensely speakable and its cascading

TWO ENGLISH PLAYWRIGHTS

The two leading English playwrights of the past thirty years exhibit radically different styles. The plays of Harold Pinter, which are filled with abrupt, almost inexplicable transitions, intense pauses and glances, and elliptical dialogue that seems to contain innuendos we don't fully comprehend, create an almost palpable sense of foreboding and spookiness that plunges the audience deeper and deeper into Pinteresque moods and reveries. The plays of Tom Stoppard, in contrast, race glibly through brilliant rhetorical flights of language that always manage to stay one step ahead of the audience's capability to follow, keeping the audience breathless while forcing them to remain intellectually alert.

BATES: (*moves to* ELLEN) Will we meet tonight?

ELLEN: I don't know. (*Pause*)

BATES: Come with me tonight.

ELLEN: Where?

BATES: Anywhere. For a walk. (*Pause*)

ELLEN: I don't want to walk.

BATES: Why not? (*Pause*)

ELLEN: I want to go somewhere else. (*Pause*)

BATES: Where?

ELLEN: I don't know. (*Pause*)

BATES: What's wrong with a walk?

ELLEN: I don't want to walk. (*Pause*)

BATES: What do you want to do?

ELLEN: I don't know. (*Pause*)

BATES: Do you want to go somewhere else?

ELLEN: Yes.

BATES: Where?

ELLEN: I don't know. (*Pause*)

– From Pinter's *Silence* (1969)

COCKLEBURY-SMYTHE: May I be the first to welcome you to Room 3B. You will find the working conditions primitive, the hours antisocial, the amenities non-existent and the catering beneath contempt. On top of that the people are for the most part very boring, with interests either so generalized as to mimic wholesale ignorance or so particular as to be lunatic obsessions. Their level of conversation would pass without comment in the lavatory of a mixed comprehensive and the lavatories, by the way, are few and far between.

– From Stoppard's *Dirty Linen* (1976)

sarcasm develops a fiercely intimidating momentum, leaving Stephen speechless and, with a great actor playing it, the audience breathless.

Speakability also requires that the spoken line appear to realistically emanate from the character who utters it and that it contain—in its syntax, vocabulary, and mode of expression—the marks of that character's milieu and his or her personality. The spoken line is not merely an expression of the author's perspective; it is the basis from which the actor develops characterization and the acting ensemble creates a play's style. Thus the mastery of dramatic dialogue writing demands more than mere semantic skills; it requires a constant awareness of the purposes and tactics underlying human communication, as well as of the multiple psychological and aesthetic properties of language.

Stageability, of course, requires that dialogue be written so that it can be spoken effectively upon a stage, but it requires something more: dialogue must be conceived as an integral element of a particular staged situation, in which setting, physical acting, and spoken dialogue are inextricably combined. A stageable script is one in which staging and stage business—as well as design and the acting demands—are neither adornments for the dialogue nor sugarcoating for the writer's opinions but are intrinsic to the very nature of the play.

Both speakability and stageability are contingent upon human limitations—those of the actors and directors as well as those of the audience. Speakability must take into account that the actor must breathe from time to time, for example, and that the audience can take in only so many metaphors in a single spoken sentence. Stageability must reckon with the forces of gravity and inertia, which both the poet and the novelist may conveniently ignore. The playwright need not simply succumb to the common denominator—all the great playwrights strive to extend the capacities of actors and audience alike—but still must not forget that the theatre is fundamentally a human event that cannot transcend human capabilities.

A speakable and stageable script flows rather than stumbles; this is true for nonlinear plays as well as for more straightforwardly structured ones. *Flow* requires a continual stream of information, and a play that flows is one that is continually saying something, doing something, and meaning something to the audience. To serve this end, the playwright should address such technical problems as scene shifting, entrances and exits, and act breaks (intermissions) as early as possible in the scriptwriting process. Furthermore, in drafting scenes, the writer should be aware that needless waits, arid expositions (no matter how "necessary" to the plot), and incomprehensible plot developments can sink the sturdiest script in a sea of audience apathy.

Richness

Depth, subtlety, fineness, quality, wholeness, and *inevitability*—these are words often used in reference to plays that we like. They are fundamentally subjective terms, easier to apply than to define or defend, for the fact is that when a play pleases us, when it "works," the feelings of pleasure and stimulation it affords are beyond the verbal level. Certainly *richness* is one of the qualities common to plays that leave us with this sense of satisfaction—richness of *detail* and richness of *dimension*.

A play that is rich with detail is not necessarily one that is rife with detail; it is simply one whose every detail fortifies our insight into the world of the play. For going to a play

is in part a matter of paying a visit to the playwright's world, and the more vividly created that world, the greater the play's final impact. In Margaret Edson's *Wit*, for example, Vivian, a terminally ill English professor, addresses the audience from her hospital bed. Her tone is professorial, and her vocabulary is currently filled with medical terminology, little of which the average audience member will understand, but in the context of an intellectual woman struggling against a fatal disease,

Margaret Edson's *Wit* portrays English professor Vivian Bearing facing her death with courage and, yes, wit, in this powerfully affecting, Pulitzer Prize–winning play. Bearing is here played by Kathleen Chalfant, with Walter Charles as one of her doctors, in the Geffen Playhouse's 2000 production.

Edson's dialogue creates an immensely compelling and affectingly detailed portrait:

VIVIAN: I don't mean to complain, but I am becoming very sick. Very, very sick. Ultimately sick, as it were.

In everything I have done, I have been steadfast, resolute—some would say in the extreme. Now, as you can see, I am distinguishing myself in illness.

I have survived eight treatments of Hexamethophosphacil and Vinplatin at the *full* dose, ladies and gentlemen. I have broken the record. I have become something of a celebrity. Kelekian and Jason [*her doctors*] are simply delighted. I think they foresee celebrity status for themselves upon the appearance of the journal article they will no doubt write about me.

But I flatter myself. The article will not be about *me,* it will be about my ovaries. It will be about my peritoneal cavity, which, despite their best intentions, is now crawling with cancer. What we have come to think of as *me* is, in fact, just the specimen jar, just the dust jacket, just the white piece of paper that bears the little black marks.

Vivian's free use of seven-syllable words, her refining of words on the spot (from "very sick" to "very, very sick" to "ultimately sick"; from "steadfast" to "resolute"), her public style of presentation ("ladies and gentlemen"), parallel phrases ("I have . . . I have . . . I have . . . ," "just the . . . just the . . . just the . . ."), alliteration of consonants ("just . . . jar . . . just . . . jacket, just"), and use of antithesis ("white piece of paper . . . little black marks") tell us volumes about her character and how she is "distinguishing" herself in illness. Richness of linguistic detail lends a play authority, an aura of sureness. It surrounds the play's characters as a city surrounds homes and gives them a cultural context in which to exist. It lends a play specificity: specific people are engaged in specific tasks in a specific place. Going to (or even reading) a play rich with texture is like taking a trip to another world—it is an adventure no travel agent could possibly book.

Richness is not an easy quality to develop in writing. It demands of its author a gift for close observation, an uninhibited imagination, and an astute sense of what to leave out as well as what to include. A person who can recollect personal experiences in great detail; who can conjure up convincing situations, peoples, locales, and conversations; and who is closely attuned to nuance can perhaps work these talents into the writing of plays.

Depth of Characterization

Depth of characterization presents perhaps the greatest single stumbling block for novice playwrights, who tend either to write all characters "in the same voice" (normally the author's own) or to divide them into two camps: good characters and bad. But capturing the depth, complexities, and uniqueness of real human beings, even seemingly ordinary human beings, is a more difficult task.

Depth of characterization requires that every character possess an independence of intention, expression, and motivation; moreover, these characteristics must appear sensible in the light of our general knowledge of psychology and human behavior. In plays as in life, all characters must act from motives that appear reasonable to *them* (if not to those watching them or those affected by them). Moreover, the writer should bear in mind that every character is, *to himself or herself,* an important and worthwhile person, regardless of what other people think. Thus even the great villains of drama—Shakespeare's Richard III, Claudius, and Iago, for example—must be seen to believe in themselves and in the fundamental "rightness" of their cause. Even if we never completely understand their deepest motivations (as we can't fully understand the motives of real villains such as Hitler, Caligula, or John Wilkes Booth), we should be able to sense at the bottom of any character's behavior a validity of purpose, however twisted or perverse we may find it.

The realistic theatre—Chekhov, Williams, Miller, and the like—has provided many works in which the psychological dimensions of the characters dominate all other aspects of the theatrical experience. Look, for example, at this speech of Big Mama in Tennessee Williams's *Cat on a Hot Tin Roof:*

BIG MAMA [*outraged that her son-in-law, Gooper, is offering her a written trusteeship plan which would give him and his wife control over the estate of Big Daddy, Mama's ailing husband*]: Now you listen to me, all of you, you listen here! They's not goin' to be any more catty talk in my house! And Gooper, you put that away before I grab it out of your hand and tear it right up! I don't know what the hell's in it, and I don't want to know what the hell's in it. I'm talkin' in Big Daddy's language now; I'm his *wife,* not his *widow,* I'm still his *wife!* And I'm talkin' to you in his language an'—

Williams has brilliantly crafted Big Mama's rage with aggressive verbs ("grab," "tear"), local vernacular ("they's"), clause repetitions ("I'm his wife . . . I'm still his wife"), loaded adjectives ("catty"), profanities rare for a southern woman ("hell's"), dialectical contractions ("goin'", "talkin'"), and individual word emphases as marked by italics. But he has also undermined her rage by having her admit to assuming her husband's vocabulary—so that while she states that she's not Big Daddy's widow, her language indicates that she knows, even if only unconsciously, that it shall soon be otherwise.

Modern dramatists have even made psychotherapy part of their dramatic scheme in many cases: psychiatrist characters may be seen (or are addressed) in plays such as Williams's *Suddenly, Last Summer,* Miller's *After the Fall,* Peter Shaffer's *Equus,* and the 1941 American musical *Lady in the Dark,* each of which portrays a principal character undergoing psychotherapy and discussing what he or she learns. Certainly the psychological sophistication of modern theatre audiences has afforded playwrights expanded opportunities to explore and dramatize characters' psyches, and it has helped to make the "case study" drama a major genre of the current theatre.

Gravity and Pertinence

Gravity and *pertinence* are terms used to describe the importance of a play's theme and its overall relevance to the concerns of the intended audience. To say that a play has gravity is to say simply that its central theme is one of serious and lasting significance in humanity's spiritual, moral, or intellectual life. The greatest dramas —comedies as well as tragedies—are always somehow concerned with what is sometimes called the human predicament: those universal problems—aging, discord, love, insecurity, ambition, loss—for which we continually seek greater lucidity. Gravity does not mean somberness, however; it requires only a confrontation with the most elemental tasks of living. When an audience truly understands and identifies with a play's experiences, even the darkest tragedy radiates power and illumination.

Look, for example, at Bynum's speech in August Wilson's *Joe Turner's Come and Gone.* Bynum is what Wilson calls a rootworker (conjuror). A younger man, Jeremy, has just praised a woman as knowing "how to treat a fellow," and Bynum chastises him for his shallowness:

You just can't look at it like that. You got to look at the whole thing. Now, you take a fellow go out there, grab hold to a woman and think he got something 'cause she sweet and soft to the touch. It's in the world like everything else. Touching's nice. It feels good. But you can lay your hand upside a horse or a cat, and that feels good too. What's the difference? When you grab hold to a woman, you got something there. You got a whole world there. You got a way of life kicking up under your hand. That woman can take and make you feel like something. I ain't just talking about in the way of jumping off into bed together and rolling around with each other. Anybody can do that. When you grab hold to that woman and look at the whole thing and see what you got . . . why she can take and make something of you. Your mother was a woman. That's enough right there to show you what a woman is. Enough to show you what she can do. She made something out of you.

Using only simple words (see, for instance, Vivian's speech in *Wit*), Wilson's Bynum probes at the heart of a profound subject: the most meaningful relationship between a man and a woman. When well acted, these lines will stay with us long after we have left the theatre.

Pertinence refers to the play's touching on current audience concerns, both of-the-moment and timeless. Plays about current political situations or personalities are clearly pertinent; they may, however, quickly become outdated. Plays whose concerns are both ephemeral and universal, however, such as Miller's *The Crucible*—which, in treating the Salem witch trials of 1692, pertains as well to the McCarthy trials of the 1950s as well as to corrupt investigations in all eras—will have a more enduring relevance. The greatest plays are not merely pertinent to a given moment but also serve as archetypes for all time.

Compression, Economy, and Intensity

Compression, economy, and intensity are also aspects of the finest plays. *Compression* refers to the playwright's skill in condensing a story (which may span many days, even years, of chronological time) into a theatrical time frame; *economy* relates to an author's skill in eliminating or consolidating characters, events, locales, and words in the service of compression. Unlike other literary or visual art forms that can be examined in private and at the leisure of the observer, a play must be structured to unfold in a public setting and at a predetermined pace.

Many beginning playwrights attempt to convert a story to a play in the most obvious way: by writing a separate scene for every event described in the story (and sometimes including a different setting and supporting cast for each scene). Economy and compression, however, require that most stories be restructured in order to be dramatically viable. If the play is to be basically realistic, the playwright has traditionally reworked the story so as to have all the events occur in one location, or perhaps in two locations with an act break between to allow for scenery changes. Events that are integral to the story but cannot be shown within the devised settings can simply be reported (as in Shaw's *Misalliance*, for example, in which an airplane crash occurs offstage as the onstage characters gawk and exclaim). More common today is the use of theatricalist techniques that permit an integration of settings so that events occurring in various places can be presented on the same set without intermission. Similarly, economy and compression commonly dictate the deletion or combination of characters and the reduction of expository passages to a few lines of dialogue.

The effects of economy and compression are both financial and aesthetic. Obviously, when scenery changes and the number of characters are held to a minimum, the costs of production are minimized as well. But beyond that, compression and economy in playwriting serve to stimulate intrigue and focus audience expectation: a tightly written play gives us the feeling that we are on the trail of something important and that our quarry is right around the next bend. Thus, economy and compression actually lead to *intensity*, which is one of the theatre's most powerful attributes.

Dramatic intensity can take many forms. It can be harsh, abrasive, explosive, eminently physical, or overtly calm. It can be ruminative, tender, or comic. But whenever intensity occurs and in whatever mood or context, it conveys to the audience an ineradicable feeling that this moment in theatre is unique and its revelations are profound. Intensity does not come about by happy accident, obviously,

Intensity of passion – alternating with abrupt, enigmatic silences – characterizes the plays of Harold Pinter. Here, in a 2003 Broadway production of *The Caretaker*, Patrick Stewart (*right*) and Aidan Gillen are seen in one of the play's violent outbreaks.

but neither can it be simply injected at the whim of the playwright. It must evolve out of a careful development of issues, through the increasing urgency of character goals and intentions and the focused actions and interactions of the plot that draw characters and their conflicts ever closer to some sort of climactic confrontation. A play must spiral inward toward its core; that is, its compression must increase and its mood must intensify as it circles toward its climax and denouement. Too many tangential diversions can deflect a play from this course, rendering it formless and devoid of apparent purpose.

Celebration

Finally, a fine play celebrates life; it does not merely depict or analyze or criticize it. The first plays were presented at festivals that—though perhaps haunted by angry or capricious gods—were essentially joyful celebrations. Even the darkest of the ancient Greek tragedies sought to transcend the more negative aspects of existence and to exalt the human spirit, for the whole of Greek theatre was informed by the positive (and therapeutic) elements of the Dionysian festival: spring, fertility, the gaiety and solidarity of public communion.

The theatre can never successfully venture too far from this source. A purely didactic theatre has never satisfied either critics or public, and a merely grim depiction of ordinary life has little to offer this art form. Although the word *theatrical* usually suggests something like "glittery" or "showy," it better accords with the theatre's most fundamental aspirations: to extend our known experience, to illuminate life, and to raise existence to the level of art: the art of theatre.

This celebration can easily be perverted. Dramas intended to be merely "uplifting"—with a reliance on happy endings and strictly noble sentiments—or written in self-consciously "elevated" tones do not celebrate life; they merely whitewash it. The truest and most exciting theatre has always been created out of a passionate, personal vision of reality and a deep devotion to expressing life's struggles and splendors, for the theatre is fundamentally an affirmation. Writing, producing, and attending plays are also acts of affirmation: attesting to the desire to share and communicate and celebrating human existence, participation, and communion. Purely bitter plays, no matter how justly based or how well grounded in history or experience, remain incomplete and unsatisfying as theatre, which simply is not an effective medium for nihilistic conveyance. Even the bleakest of modern plays radiates a persistent hopefulness—even joyousness—as represented archetypally by Samuel Beckett's two old men singing, punning, and pantomiming so engagingly in the forlorn shadow of their leafless tree as they wait for Godot.

The Playwright's Process

How does one go about writing a play? It is important to know the elements of a play (as discussed in Chapter 2) and the characteristics of the best plays—credibility, intrigue, speakability, stageability, flow, richness, depth of characterization, gravity, pertinence, compression, economy, intensity, and celebration—as discussed in the preceding sections. But that is not enough; one must still confront the practical task of writing.

The blank sheet of paper is the writer's nemesis. It is the accuser, the goad and critic that coldly commands action even as it threatens humiliation. There is no consensus among writers as to where to begin. Some prefer to begin with a story line or a plot outline. Some begin with a real event and write the play to explain why that event occurred. Some begin with a real character or set of characters and develop a plot around them. Some begin with a setting and try to animate it with characters and actions. Some begin with a theatrical effect or an idea for a new form of theatrical expression. Some write entirely from personal experience. Some adapt a story or a legend, others a biography of a famous person, others a play by an earlier playwright; others simply expand upon a remembered dream.

A documentary might begin with a transcript of a trial or a committee hearing. Other documentary forms might begin with a tape recorder and a situation contrived by the playwright. Some plays are created out of actors' improvisations or acting-class exercises. Some are compilations of material written over the course of many years or collected from many sources.

START AT THE BEGINNING

All those awards, all that stuff, I take them and I hang them on my wall. But then I turn around and my typewriter's sitting there, and it doesn't know from awards. I always tell people I'm a struggling playwright. I'm struggling to get the next play down on paper. You start at the beginning each time you sit down. Nothing you've written before has any bearing on what you're going to write now.

— August Wilson

The fact is, writers tend to begin with whatever works for *them* and accords with their immediate aims. Because playwrights usually work alone, at least in the initial stages, they can do as they please whenever they want: there is no norm. On the other hand, certain steps can be followed as introductory exercises to playwriting, and these may in fact lead to the creation of an entire play.

Dialogue

Transcription of dialogue from previous observation and experience—that is, the writing down of *remembered dialogue* from overheard conversations or from conversations in which the author has participated—is a fundamental playwriting exercise; probably most finished plays contain such scenes. Because we remember conversations only selectively and subjectively, a certain amount of fictionalizing and shading inevitably creeps into these transcriptions; and often without even meaning to do so, authors also transform people in their memory into characters in their scenes.

Writing scenes of *imagined dialogue* is the logical next step in this exercise, for all the author need do now is to extend the situation beyond its remembered reality into the area of "what might have happened." The dialogue then constructed will be essentially original yet in keeping with the personalized "characters" developed in the earlier transcription. The characters now react and respond as dramatic figures, interacting with each other freshly and under the control of the author. Many fine plays have resulted from the author's working out, in plot and dialogue, hypothetical relations between real people who never confronted each other in life; indeed, many plays are inspired by the author's notion of what *should* have happened among people who never met. In this way, the theatre has often been used as a form of psychotherapy, with the patient-playwright simply acting out—in imagination or with words on paper—certain obligatory scenes in life that never occurred.

Conflict

Writing scenes of *forced conflict* accelerates the exercise and becomes a third step toward the creation of a play. Scenes of separation, loss, crucial decision, rejection, or emotional breakthrough are climactic scenes in a play and usually help enormously to define its structure. If a writer can create a convincing scene of high conflict that gets inside *each* of the characters involved and not merely one of them, then there is a good chance of making that scene the core of an exciting play—especially if it incorporates some subtlety and is not dependent entirely on shouting and denunciation. What is more, such a scene will be highly actable in its own right and thus can serve as a valuable tool for demonstrating the writer's potential.

Exercises that result in scripted scenes—even if the scenes are just a page or two in length—have the advantage of allowing the writer to test her or his work as it progresses, for a short scene is easily producible: all it requires is a group of agreeable actors and a modest investment of time, and the playwright can quickly assess the total impact. The costs and difficulties of testing a complete play, on the other hand, may prove insurmountable for the inexperienced playwright. Moreover, the performance of a short original scene can sometimes generate enthusiasm for the theatrical collaboration needed for a fuller theatrical experience.

Structure

Developing a complete play demands more than stringing together a number of scenes, of course, and at some point in the scene-writing process the playwright inevitably confronts the need for structure. Many playwrights develop outlines for their plays after writing a scene or two; some have an outline ready before any scenes are written or even thought of. Other playwrights never write down anything except dialogue and stage directions yet find an overall structure asserting itself almost unconsciously as the writing progresses. But the beginning playwright should bear in mind that intrigue, thematic development, compression, and even credibility depend on a carefully built structure and that it is an axiom of theatre that most playwriting is in fact *rewriting*—rewriting aimed principally at organizing and reorganizing the play's staged actions and events.

A strong dramatic structure compels interest and attention. It creates intrigue by establishing certain expectations—both in the characters and in the audience—and then by creating new and bigger expectations out of the fulfillment of the first ones. A good dramatic structure keeps us always wanting more until the final curtain call, and at the end it leaves us with a sense of the inevitability of the play's conclusion, a sense that what happened onstage was precisely as it had to be. A great structure makes us comfortable and receptive; we feel in good hands, expertly led through whatever terrain the play may take us. And we are willing, therefore, to abandon ourselves to a celebration of vital and ineffable matters.

The Playwright's Rewards

There will always be a need for playwrights, for the theatre never abandons its clamor for new and better dramatic works. Hundreds of producers today are so anxious to discover new authors and new scripts that they will read (or instruct an associate to read) everything that comes their way; thus a truly fine play need not go unnoticed for long. Moreover, playwrights are the only artists in the theatre who can bring their work to the first stage of completion without any outside professional help at all; they do not need to be

auditioned, interviewed, hired, cast, or contracted to an agent in order to come up with the world's greatest dramatic manuscript.

The rewards that await the successful playwright are absolutely staggering: they are the most fully celebrated artists of the theatre, for not only do they receive remuneration commensurate with their success, but they also acquire enormous influence and prestige on the basis of their personal vision. The public may adore an actor or admire a director or designer, but it *listens* to the playwright, who in Western culture has always assumed the role of prophet. Playwriting at its best is more than a profession, and it is more than a component of the theatrical machine. It is a creative act that enlarges human experience and enriches our awe and appreciation of life.

Contemporary American Playwrights

America was the site of some of the most exciting playwriting in the twentieth century. Eugene O'Neill was America's first internationally celebrated dramatist, both for his realistic works (most notably his autobiographical *Long Day's Journey into Night*) and his experiments in antirealism (such as the expressionist *Hairy Ape*, about workers in a boiler room). Tennessee Williams and Arthur Miller followed, energizing the American theatre beginning in the 1940s with their blend of realism, poetry (Williams's forte), and political insight (most notably in Miller). At the beginning of the current century, literally dozens of American playwrights have been defining their society to a worldwide theatre audience. Seventeen are listed here, in order of their birthdates.

Arthur Miller (born 1915)

The legendary Arthur Miller, author of the modern classics *All My Sons* (1947), *Death of a Salesman* (1949), and *The Crucible* (1953), was certainly America's most distinguished living dramatist until the time of his death in February, 2005, his reputation burnished by major New York and London restagings of virtually all of his works—including Broadway revivals of *Death of a Salesman* (with Brian Dennehy) in 1999, *The Crucible* (with Liam Neeson and Laura Linney) in 2002, and *After The Fall* (with Peter Krause) in 2004. Even Miller's first play, *The Man Who Had All the Luck,* quickly dismissed in its 1944 Broadway premiere, returned to Broadway (at the American Airlines Theatre) in 2002.

But Miller, even as he approached his nineties, remained to the end a vibrant and contemporary playwright who simply could not be ignored. In his final plays—all premiering in the current century—Miller made his final investigations of where his country has come since he began writing more than fifty years ago. *The Ride Down Mount Morgan,* which had its Broadway premiere in 2000 and was being made into a film in 2004, covers almost every topic Miller had written about before—and much more. Centered on themes of bigamy and generational dissonance, *Mount Morgan* is also concerned with American views of pleasure, guilt, marriage, money, children, race, sex, death, business, Jewishness, non-Jewishness, socialism, Christianity, suicide, political and sexual betrayal, men versus women, humans versus animals, the Reagan-Bush administration versus Arthur Miller, and, almost as an afterthought, capital-T Truth—all delivered in exquisitely Millerish agony: "Only the truth is sacred," Miller's male protagonist declares to one of his two wives at the play's end. And, working virtually right up to his death, Miller came forth with *Resurrection Blues,* produced at Minneapolis' Guthrie Theatre in 2002 and revised for its Old Globe production in Spring 2004, and *Finishing the Picture,* produced at Chicago's Goodman Theatre in the Fall of that year—the first play exploring the often unnamed South American country where 2% of the population enjoys 96% of the wealth, and

the second revisiting the ending of the author's famously disastrous marriage with the film star, Marilyn Monroe, and the artistic frauds that he felt surrounded and betrayed her. No other playwright in the current theatre has so aggressively called society to task for its failures nor so passionately told the audience to pay attention to the world around them.

Neil Simon (born 1927)

It can be argued that Neil Simon is not only America's most successful commercial playwright but also the most successful playwright in the entire history of theatre. Beginning as a TV comic writer in the early 1950s, Simon quickly spun off a staggering series of hit Broadway comedies in the '60s and '70s, including consistently revived works such as *Barefoot in the Park, The Odd Couple, Plaza Suite, The Last of the Red Hot Lovers, The Sunshine Boys,* and *California Suite,* not to mention the books for musicals such as *Little Me* and *Sweet Charity* and the screenplays for dozens of films. Virtually all of his plays "work," at least in the sense that they make the audience laugh, and they have made Simon, among other things, enormously rich.

In the late 1980s, Simon turned decidedly more serious, however, and his deeply felt trilogy of autobiographical plays, *Brighton Beach Memoirs, Biloxi Blues,* and *Broadway Bound,* have proved astute and compassionate works that have attracted a more sober appreciation of Simon's gifts. Since that time, he has continued writing semiautobiographical works, including the highly unconventional *Jake's Women,* a revisitation of various women, living and dead, in the author's life and mind; *Laughter on the 23rd Floor,* recalling the experiences of Simon and his colleagues as gag writers for the 1950s TV comic Sid Caesar; and *Lost in Yonkers,* a profoundly powerful work about a Holocaust survivor and her family, for which Simon has received the Pulitzer Prize and the widespread critical acclaim that, for the most part, had previously eluded him.

Simon's most recent works are his 2001 *Café Edison,* a loving tribute to the old-timer Broadway theatre crowd that takes its lunches and coffee breaks at a hotel coffee shop (informally known as the "Polish Tea Room" after its immigrant owners), and his 2003 *Rose's Dilemma,* a fable of two characters modeled on the famous mid-twentieth-century American writers (and lovers) Lillian Hellman and Dashiell Hammett. Both plays are set in Simon's New York City, and each displays a typically late-Simon mix of gags and reminiscences. Both, however, are also glimpsed through an unmistakable patina of gloom. Indeed, *Rose's Dilemma* (like *Jake's Women*) is a ghost story, since one of the characters has been dead five years before the play's events begin. Typically for a Simon play, the characters spend most of their time together scrapping with each other (Rose: "Sex with a dead man isn't half as good as I was led to believe"); atypically, the play enjoyed only a brief run, plus some unwanted publicity when Simon fired his intended "Rose," the beloved actress Mary Tyler Moore, during rehearsals for not learning her lines—a decision he quickly regretted.

Simon is a consummate New York playwright, whose work has captivated Broadway in the past and remains popular in dinner and community theatres. His work is rarely per-

Neil Simon's wistful and nostalgic comedy *Rose's Dilemma* is set in a Long Island beach house. In this 2003 production at the Manhattan Theatre Club, Patricia Hodges plays a writer like Lillian Hellman and John Cullen plays the ghost of a writer like Hellman's lover, Dashiell Hammett. The setting is by Thomas Lynch.

formed in regional or college theatres, however; it is almost a mark of pride for such theatres to say "we don't do Neil Simon" as a shorthand way of saying that they don't produce conventional, commercial, or well-made comedies. Simon probably has more fans and more detractors than any other living playwright, but his early comedies are unmatched in their craftsmanship and easygoing humor, and his recent work shows evidence of a deep and lasting theatrical achievement.

Edward Albee (born 1928)

The Zoo Story, a one-act, two-character play set in New York's Central Park, brought Edward Albee to prominence in 1959. The play concerns a chance meeting between a married publisher (Peter) and a young drifter (Jerry), both male; at play's end, Jerry impales himself on a knife he gave to Peter. The odd story, its electrifying dialogue, its gingerly oblique treatment of homosexuality, and, particularly, its initial pairing on a double bill with Samuel Beckett's *Krapp's Last Tape* gave Albee immediate national attention that would be almost impossible to achieve today. And with his first full-length play, *Who's Afraid of Virginia Woolf?,* premiering on Broadway in 1962, Albee quickly assumed the mantle of America's leading new playwright in the early 1960s.

Subsequent Albee plays have had both great success—*A Delicate Balance* (What happens when a married couple mysteriously gets frightened and moves in with their best friends?) and *Seascape* (What happens when a pair of lizards pop in on a married couple at the beach?) won the Pulitzer Prizes in 1967 and 1975—and failure—*Tiny Alice* (provoked outrage along with mild admiration in its Broadway debut), and *The Man with Three Arms* (scathingly attacked by New York critics and has not been performed since). But Albee's trenchant and autobiographical *Three Tall Women* in 1994 thrust the author squarely back into the limelight and virtually restarted his career, winning him his third

Pulitzer and a chance to laugh at his critics once again. This two-act disquisition on Albee's own mother, as a person and as a spirit, tempers anger with compassion as Albee had not previously done and places its author back in the front ranks of American dramatists.

The Play about the Baby, opening off-Broadway in 2000 (after a very successful premiere in London), wittily recapitulates some of Albee's earlier themes and techniques (an older couple sarcastically taunting a younger one; a baby that may or may not exist), adding doses of quite postmodern nudity and self-referential disjunction (including the title). And his extraordinarily provocative *The Goat, or Who Is Sylvia?* (treating a married man who falls in love with, yes, a beast of that description) followed in quick succession, winning the 2003 Tony Award for Best Play and going on to enjoy stunningly successful runs throughout America. *The Goat,* which Albee subtitles "Notes Toward a Definition of Tragedy," posits itself between the Greek tragic mode (the original meaning of *tragedy* is "goat song") and Shakespearean comedy ("Who is Sylvia?" is a line from *Two Gentlemen of Verona*). But the play, which ends bloodily, is funny as well, at least in its opening segments. It is a play—like most of Albee's—judged as either masterful or awful, depending on the spectator's taste.

Albee's most recent venture has been to "complete" his first play, *The Zoo Story,* by giving it a first act, titled *Homelife,* which shows Peter at home with his wife, Ann, prior to going to the park. The new play, opening on Broadway in 2004, is titled *Peter and Jerry,* and Albee has now "retired" *The Zoo Story* as an independent play. "I am the guardian of the plays that are sitting in my head that want to come out," he says, and *Peter and Jerry,* which seems to have been in Mr. Albee's head for more than forty years, has now been released to a waiting public. We can be assured that this gifted and prolific dramatist will continue to both captivate and consternate the American stage.

Edward Albee's newest work is an expansion of the author's 1959 one-act play *The Zoo Story.* Here, in the Hartford Stage Company 2004 premiere of the refashioned *Peter and Jerry*, Frank Wood (*seated*) plays Peter, a middle-aged businessman, and Frederick Weller plays Jerry, a younger vagrant who accosts Peter in New York's Central Park, with dire consequences for both.

Lanford Wilson (born 1937)

Lanford Wilson emerged as a pioneer playwright in the heady days of New York experimental theatre in the 1960s. His first plays, many produced at the Cafe La MaMa and Caffé Cino theatre bars, were evocative and sometimes profound studies of male homosexuality (*The Madness of Lady Bright*), interracial marriage (*The Gingham Dog*), and small-town small-mindedness (*The Rimers of Eldritch*). Joining with director Marshall Mason and other Caffé Cino colleagues, Wilson helped create the Circle Repertory Theatre in New York, which produced his finely crafted *The Hot l Baltimore*, about the comings and goings of a down-and-

out hotel (the missing "e" in the title indicates a burnt-out letter in the hotel's neon sign), and a series of emotionally affecting plays about the fictional midwestern Talley family: *The Fifth of July, Talley's Folly* (which won the 1980 Pulitzer Prize), and *A Tale Told.*

In 2002–3, the Signature Theatre in Manhattan devoted its entire season to a repertory of Wilson's plays, including his two newest ones: *Rain Dance* (2001), about the creation of the atomic bomb at Los Alamos, New Mexico (a play described as "a thoughtful and emotionally resonant wartime character study"), and *The Book of Days* (2003), in which the author returns to his Missouri roots and echoes many of the themes (crime, religion, and small-mindedness in a south-midwestern town) of his earlier *The Rimers of Eldritch.*

Wilson is an extraordinarily prolific playwright, having written, thus far, over forty plays. His writing for the most part (*Burn This* is an exception) is gentle, poetic, natural, and wise; increasingly, his works focus on the larger social and philosophical contexts of contemporary life. And although he is dramaturgically innovative, his plays rarely call attention to their structures or to the author's subtle stylistic departures.

Terrence McNally (born 1939)

The first produced play of Terrence McNally, the angry and nightmarish *And Things That Go Bump in the Night,* was virtually booed off its Broadway stage when it premiered in 1965—with the theatre management reduced to loudly hawking tickets for $1 apiece on New York street corners to passersby who "wanted to see a Broadway play." McNally was quickly pigeonholed as a raging young avant-gardist, having little in common with the audiences of his time. Both time and McNally changed. A series of hilarious and provocative comedies, often on sexual themes, followed in the 1970s (*Next* and *The Ritz* became widely popular), yielding to a defter and more delicate comic collection in the 1980s and 1990s. *Frankie and Johnnie at the Claire de Lune* (1987) is a landmark study of a couple—he a short-order cook and she a waitress—in a postcoital moment after their first date, trying to decide how or if they should build a deeper relationship. What is novel in this play is that both characters are totally naked during large portions of the performance. The 2002 Broadway revival with Edie Falco and Stanley Tucci was an electrifying illustration of how nudity, as novelty, can virtually "disappear" under the intensity of great acting. *The Lisbon Traviata* (1989) explores a gay male couple's relationship, in which their passion for opera masks a fundamental void in

their capacity for affection. *Lips Together, Teeth Apart* (1992) explores the relationships of and between two married couples summering in a beach house where a relative of one of them has just died of AIDS; it is a comedy with a poisonous snake under the pretty terrace.

Subsequently, *Kiss of the Spider Woman* (1993) got McNally—who wrote the book—his first Tony Award, and *Love! Valour! Compassion!* (1994) got him his second. The first is a darkly brilliant musical about sexual and political betrayal in a South American prison, and the second is a wicked and sensitive portrayal of eight gay men—bright, urban, and urbane—weekending in the country, occasionally in the buff.

Much of McNally's recent work has been, like *Lisbon Traviata* and *Kiss of the Spider Woman,* involved with music. *Master Class* (1995), portraying a music lesson by Maria Callas, won McNally a third Tony in 1996, and his book for the musical *Ragtime* (1998) won him his fourth, while his books for musicals *The Full Monty* (2000) and the opera *Dead Man Walking* (2000) have earned him even further acclaim. Yet McNally's highly controversial *Corpus Christi* (1998), about a contemporary Christ-like figure (see the chapter titled "Theatre Today"), made clear that the much-lauded author retains the capacity, and probably also the desire, to shock as well as to entertain. McNally's most recent play, a pair of one-acts collectively titled *The Stendhal Syndrome,* recapitulates some of his earlier themes and his preoccupations with sexual power and artistic force. The first play, *Full Frontal Nudity,* is set in the Florence Accademia, where Michelangelo's nude statue of David is the focus; the second, *Prelude and Liebestod,* portrays a hugely egocentric conductor, rapturously in love with himself (played by Richard Thomas in the 2004 premiere), as he furiously conducts Wagner's *Tristan und Isolde.* At the time of this writing, McNally is opening his newest play, *Dedication or the Stuff of Dreams,* at the 2004

Actor Richard Thomas conducts a fantasy orchestra in Terrence McNally's dramatic study of art and ego, *Stendhal Syndrome*, which premiered at New York's Primary Stages in 2004.

Williamstown Theatre Festival and working on a new play about musical-theatre star Chita Rivera.

McNally has the gift of blending passion with humor and tracking the universal emotions within a variety of lifestyles and belief systems. No longer just an angry young playwright, McNally has become a superb theatrical craftsman and a powerful innovator of new dramatic idioms without compromising his investigation of controversial and immensely provocative subjects.

Sam Shepard (born 1943)

Like Lanford Wilson, Sam Shepard came to prominence in the coffeehouses of Greenwich Village in the 1960s. He then received great acclaim in the 1970s and 1980s for his suc-

cessful full-length plays *The Tooth of Crime, The Curse of the Starving Class, Buried Child* (which won the Pulitzer Prize), *True West, Fool for Love,* and *A Lie of the Mind.*

Shepard's plays are basically prose poems; the language is musical, and the subject matter, which is generally contemporary and American, suggests modern myth more than everyday reality. His plays, which invariably involve sex and violence, create arresting (and often inexplicable) images and tantalize the audience with moments of extreme surface realism that ultimately open into something more abstract. His early plays are wildly surreal and dreamlike, but these qualities diminished in his more realistic plays of the late 1980s, during which period Shepard also became well known for his acting performances in films such as *The Right Stuff, Frances,* and his own *Fool for Love.* Shepard has continued to both act and write for the theatre over the past decade and has scored significant playwriting successes in recent years for his Broadway revision of *Buried Child* as well as for his new plays *Simpatico* (1995), *Eyes for Consuela* (1998), and *States of Shock* (1998). Shepard's latest work, *The God of Hell,* opened off-Broadway in New York in 2004. A sharp political satire, the very dark comedy treats a rural Wisconsin farming couple (played in the premiere by Randy Quaid and J. Smith-Cameron) who, responding to a salesman's entreaties, soon find themselves bullied and tortured by a U.S. government agent. Satirical and surrealistic like much of his earlier work, *The God of Hell* is also intended to sound a political alarm.

August Wilson (born 1945)

Absolutely no American dramatic project has been as ambitious as August Wilson's all-but-complete decalogy—a ten-play cycle, whose ninth segment, *Gem of the Ocean,* opened in Chicago in 2003. When complete, by 2005, Wilson's ten-play dramatic cycle will portray black American life within each decade of the twentieth century. Astonishingly, each of the nine already-completed plays is superb. Two (*Fences* and *The Piano Lesson*) have won Pulitzer Prizes, six have won New York Drama Critics Circle Awards, seven have won Tony nominations, and all have become fixtures in American theatrical repertoires. Wilson has virtually redefined the American theatre as it goes into the twenty-first century. There can be little question but that he, at this moment, is America's greatest active playwright.

Born to an interracial couple in Pittsburgh, Wilson began his rise as a dramatist there when, in 1968, he founded the Black Horizons on the Hill Theatre, creating, as he remembers, "an explosion of poetry and black art that made the Harlem Renaissance look like a tea party. . . . Suffice it to say, we were *bad.*" When, later on, Wilson submitted a dramatic

Ethan Hawke holds up Arliss Howard in Sam Shepard's *The Late Henry Moss,* at New York's Signature Theatre. The play, involving two brothers in New Mexico coming to terms with their father's legacy, was directed by Joseph Chaikin for the theatre's 2001–2 season, which was entirely devoted to Shepard's plays.

manuscript to the Eugene O'Neill Theatre Center in Waterford, Connecticut, in 1981, it came to the attention of the center's director, Lloyd Richards. Richards, already a major figure in the American theatre (he had directed the major African American play of the postwar era, Lorraine Hansberry's *A Raisin in the Sun,* in 1959), was quick to see Wilson's writing potential. In the ensuing years, Richards encouraged and directed a series of brilliant Wilson plays that won Wilson major standing in the American theatre.

Wilson's dramaturgy takes many forms. *Fences* (set in the 1950s) and *Jitney* (the 1970s) are in the mainstream of American realism (*Fences* is indeed in many ways a black *Death of a Salesman*), while *Ma Rainey* (set in the 1920s), the story of a black jazz singer, and *Seven Guitars* (the 1940s), concerning a black singer-guitarist, blend musical, racial, tragic, and romantic themes. In contrast, *The Piano Lesson* (set in the 1930s) and *Joe Turner's Come and Gone* (set in the 1910s, and Wilson's masterpiece) are profoundly emotive family dramas that draw deeply upon black American history and ancient African roots. The eighth play in Wilson's decalogy, *King Hedley II* (set in the 1980s), which played on Broadway in 2001, is the first of these works to incorporate characters from the earlier plays: *Hedley* tracks people first seen in *Seven Guitars* and reports the death—at age 366!—of a mythic "Aunt Ester," who appeared in the 1960s-set *Two Trains Running*.

Wilson's most recent play is *Gem of the Ocean,* which is also, chronologically, the first "chapter" of his story. Set in the 1910s and located in the Pittsburgh Hill district, where the author was raised, *Gem* is one of his most eloquent and moving works, probing ever more deeply into Wilson's primary subject: slavery's horrendous crush of the black American spirit. In *Gem,* we meet Aunt Ester for the first time, as a mythic 285-year-old seer whom we had heard of in earlier plays but never seen until now. A young man has come to Ester to have his soul "washed" by her divine ministrations; in the play's climactic scene, the overloaded slave ship that gives this play its title sinks into the ocean. Creaking and groaning, it becomes a "city of bones" and a symbol of the entombment of all slaves everywhere—and their spiritual heirs. Now we see that while the century of Wilson's decalogy has passed, its central issue—slavery's hideous aftermath—has yet to even approach closure. "It's a war and you're always on the battlefield," says one character, forty years after the end of the Civil War.

In August Wilson's *Gem of the Ocean*, Solly Two Kings (Anthony Chisholm, in voodoo mask) leads the character of Citizen Barlow (John Earl Jelks) on an imagined ritual journey to the "City of Bones" – the undersea grave of a sunken slave ship in which Citizen can "wash his soul." The play was directed on Broadway by Kenny Leon in 2004.

Wilson's decalogy will conclude with the yet-unknown *Radio Golf,* which should premiere at the Yale Repertory Theatre around the time this book will appear. It is expected to be no less than a monumental reckoning of the horrors of American slavery and their unending consequences.

Yet prior to completing the decalogy, Wilson forged a wholly new path for himself, writing and then performing as the sole actor in a new autobiographical play, *How I Learned What I Learned.* In it, Wilson explains to his audience that "We are an African people. We have our own history and we are not black by the accident of our birth." He then shares stories from his early life and his interactions within and across white and black societies. The play was a popular success at the Seattle Repertory Theatre premiere in 2003. Wilson's commitment to exploring African American culture is both broadly political and deeply aesthetic. He glories, though not always uncritically, in black life and is not at all interested in synthesizing races or glossing over cultural differences. A poet still, Wilson blends drama with profound observation and glorious, though disturbing, humanity.

David Mamet (born 1947)

David Mamet is called a Chicago playwright because Chicago is his birthplace, his home, the setting of most of his plays, and the city where his plays have most often been premiered; moreover, Mamet served for some time as an associate artistic director of Chicago's Goodman Theatre. He is, however, a truly national figure. Mamet's plays, like some of Shep-

ard's, employ at least fragments of intensely realistic writing and feature rhythmic language patterns that, though brutal, seem almost musical. Indeed, Mamet's dialogue is often strung out of mere language fragments: the tortured syntax of everyday speech rather than the turned phrases of eloquent discourse, often consisting of a series of frustrated stammerings, grunts, curses, repetitions, trail-offs, and the hemmings and hawings of nervous conversation. In all, there might not be but one or two complete sentences in an entire Mamet play. *Sexual Perversity in Chicago* brought Mamet broad attention in 1974, and *American Buffalo* (1977), *A Life in the Theatre* (1977), and the Pulitzer Prize–winning *Glengarry Glen Ross* (a scathing depiction of greed, deceit, and crime

David Mamet's *Oleanna*, a two-character drama about a student who accuses her college professor of sexual harassment, has become increasingly popular as the issue has moved from the immediate headlines to a deeper and more complex understanding in the American consciousness. Shown here is the 1998 South Coast Repertory production, with Lynsey Mcleod and Michael Canavan.

in an all-male real-estate office, premiering in 1984) solidified it. All four of these plays were written to be performed with all-male casts, however, confronting Mamet with questions as to whether he could write women's roles as well—questions to which he responded with a new play, *Speed-the-Plow,* which featured the actress Madonna in its 1988 Broadway premiere.

In the 1990s, Mamet turned some of his attention to the cinema, with screenplays such as *Hannibal, Heist,* and *The Spanish Prisoner.* But in 1992 he strongly returned to the theatre with the scorching play *Oleanna,* a masterful and intense drama about a charge of sexual (and academic) harassment brought by a college student (female) against her professor (male). Mamet's latest works include *Boston Marriage* (2001), a surprisingly elegant, epigrammatic drama about a long-term relationship between two unmarried women, *Dr. Faustus* (2004), a classically-based disquisition on morality after Christopher Marlowe, and the wonderfully hilarious *Romance* (2005), which might be considered the theatre's first example of "courtroom farce." These, together with Mamet's intriguing books on theatre theory and practice—*True and False: Heresy and Common Sense for the Actor* (1997) and *Three Uses of the Knife: On the Nature and Purpose of Drama* (1998)—reveal that Mamet has not merely returned to the theatre but is eager to play a revolutionary role in both its dramaturgy and production.

Wendy Wasserstein (born 1950)

After receiving her bachelor's and master's degrees from Mount Holyoke College and City College of New York, respectively, Wendy Wasserstein wrote her first important play, *Uncommon Women and Others,* while a graduate student at the Yale Drama School (1976). Since then she has been highly admired for her successful off-Broadway play *Isn't It Romantic?* and subsequently *The Heidi Chronicles,* which won both the Tony Award and Pulitzer Prize for 1989.

Wasserstein is concerned with the situation of American women, particularly those struggling with what they see as the dialectics of marriage and career, romance and politics, activism and traditionally passive "feminine" roles. Though her characters mostly come from the upper-middle-class Jewish intelligentsia from which the author herself springs, her writing aims at universality; there are no easy answers in Wasserstein's work, but there is a deep level of investigation and a powerful dramatic momentum.

Wasserstein's 1993 play *The Sisters Rosensweig* is in some ways her most accomplished: a neo-Chekhovian comedy about three sisters who meet in London (where one of them lives) and compare their ongoing lives and loves. Themes of Jewishness, feminism, career versus home, and the theatricalization of everyday life are melded into a brilliant comic stew. With triumphant performances by Jane Alexander and the late Madeline Kahn, *Rosensweig* was a Broadway hit and has moved into regional theatre with considerable success. In more recent years, Wasserstein has begun to move into films, television, magazine essays, and, notably, motherhood, but she has continued writing for the stage. Like Neil Simon, Wasserstein writes comfortable and accessible dramas, always wise, funny, and compassionate. Whether she will continue in this trend or expand her dramaturgical horizons (which *Old Money* seems to attempt) is one of the questions that make current theatergoing an always-fascinating adventure.

Paula Vogel (born 1951)

Paula Vogel is one of America's outstanding newer playwrights, winning the 1998 Pulitzer Prize for Drama with her powerful and unnerving *How I Learned to Drive,* which excoriates the implications of a long-standing incestuous relationship between a young Maryland girl, L'il Bit, and her adult uncle, Peck. L'il Bit, it turns out, learned to drive while sitting on her uncle's lap, her hands on the steering wheel and his

AMERICAN WOMEN PLAYWRIGHTS

Two of America's leading women playwrights talk about the start of their careers:

[The women's movement] enabled me to leave New York and give up that whole careerism business – the man's world of career stuff. I was always acting as the woman behind a man anyway, I was giving my energies to male careers. That's what the women's movement freed me from, and it also made me see really clearly that there's a necessity to write about very strong women so women can know that there have been strong women in the past.

— Megan Terry
author of *Viet Rock* with the Open Theatre,
Calm Down Mother, Keep Tightly Closed in a Cool Dry Place, and *Approaching Simone*

In one of my early conversations about writing plays, before I had ever written one, that is, Jon Jory, of Actors Theatre of Louisville, told me, "Go back at least ten years and write about some time when you were really scared."

Getting Out, my first play, was the result of that advice. The scary time was the two years I spent teaching in the children's unit of a state mental hospital. . . . The most frightening thing was the realization that once a violent child got into the system, there was no way out for her. The children were also aware of this, and consequently ran away as often as they could. . . . Later, when I sat down to write, I wondered what would happen if one of our girls ever found herself some place she couldn't get out of. Like solitary confinement in federal prison.

— Marsha Norman
author of *Getting Out, 'Night, Mother,*
and *The Secret Garden*

Paula Vogel won the 1998 Pulitzer Prize for her extraordinary dramatization of sexual abuse in childhood, *How I Learned to Drive*. Shown here are Mary Louise Parker as the seventeen-year-old L'il Bit and David Morse as her Uncle Peck, who teaches L'il Bit how to drive – and a few other things as well. This sometimes funny, sometimes searing play premiered at the off-Broadway Vineyard Theatre in 1997 and has quickly become a staple of the international repertoire.

hands on her. Prior to her Pulitzer, Vogel had earned a strong playwriting reputation with *Hot 'n' Throbbing, Desdemona, And Baby Makes Seven, The Oldest Profession,* and, her own favorite, *The Baltimore Waltz,* each of which has been produced at close to a hundred regional and international theatres. More recently, her *Mineola Twins*—a story about two identical (but emotionally and politically dissimilar) sisters set over the course of three Republican administrations—has had wide visibility.

Vogel's plays delve into profoundly disturbing social and cultural issues, including AIDS, incest, eroticism, betrayal, and mental disturbance, but her tones and techniques include broad satire and whimsy; sudden juxtapositions of popular music, signs, and slide projections; and bold theatricalizations of her characters' unconscious thoughts. *Baltimore Waltz, Hot 'n' Throbbing* (which concerns a female pornographer), and *Mineola Twins* all include dream sequences in which the characters' fantasies become, for a time, the core of the play's present action. *How I Learned to Drive* is written for two characters plus a three-person "Greek chorus" whose members play all the subsidiary roles and make announcements; one of the chorus even speaks for L'il Bit herself at the play's conclusion.

Able to sustain audience interest without step-by-step linear plot construction, Vogel's plays seem to circle their subjects gingerly at first, then spiral sharply inward to propel the audience into a shocking, deeply unsettling, and extraordinarily powerful conclusion. A master at her craft, Vogel also heads a master's-level playwriting program at Brown University and has taught in a women's prison as well. Her most recent play is *The Long Christmas Ride Home,* which premiered at Trinity Repertory in Providence in 2003. Using puppets as well as live actors, the play depicts the aftermath of a Christmas Day car crash, as family members struggle with the conflicts of their past and present lives. Vogel is certain to provide fascinating drama in the years to come.

Tony Kushner (born 1956)

Surely no play has burst upon the contemporary American theatre scene with such thrilling panache as the seven-hour, two-part *Angels in America* by Tony Kushner. Initially commissioned by the Eureka Theatre in San Francisco, *Angels* was subsequently developed at the Mark Taper Forum in Los Angeles and (part one only) at the Royal National Theatre in London. The two parts had separate openings on Broadway in 1993 (under the direction of George C. Wolfe) and received rapturous critical acclaim. Part one, *Millennium Approaches,* took the Tony Award and Pulitzer Prize in 1993, and part two,

Perestroika, took the Tony in 1994—an unprecedented achievement. By 1995 the play had fully entered the international repertoire and was featured in major productions in theatre capitals and drama festivals throughout the world.

Angels fully merits this extraordinary attention: it is a true masterpiece of modern drama; many critics consider it the finest American play of the present generation. Dealing unstintingly with the AIDS crisis, Kushner has laid bare still-unsettled issues in American culture that touch upon race, religion, gender, politics, economics, and sexual orientation. Pairing a heterosexual couple (Joe and Harper Pitt, Mor-

Tony Kushner's brilliant, two-part *Angels in America* is thought by many critics to be the finest American play in years or even decades. A complex work of comedy, sagacity, and fantasy, it casts a wicked eye on American politics, religion, economics, medicine, and racial and sexual bigotry – but it is also a moving story of human affection and alienation. In this 1993 Broadway production, an angel visits Prior Walter, who is dying of AIDS.

mons from Utah) with a homosexual couple (Louis Ironson, a New York Jew, and Prior Walter, afflicted with both AIDS and a lineage that goes back to the *Mayflower*), Kushner interweaves their stories and shakes up their lives within a vast medical-political "America," which is run in Kushner's imagination by Roy Cohn — the (real) self-hating, self-baiting, one-time gay Jewish lawyer in raging self-denial right up to his awful AIDS-ravished demise. A black nurse (male) and a white angel (female) also play sustained roles in this adventure, which is additionally peopled with another twenty-five characters, real and imagined and all played by the eight actors in the cast: a rabbi, an Eskimo, a travel agent, a real-estate saleswoman, the ghost of Ethel Rosenberg, various doctors, nurses, angels, and a man we are told is "the

world's oldest Bolshevik." What is astonishing about Kushner's work is its explosive humor; this is one of the funniest American plays of the twentieth century. But it's also one of the saddest. Though not meant for all audiences (rejected by many theatre producers in conservative cities, the play includes frontal nudity, grisly depictions of AIDS suffering, savage religious satire, the blatant miming of homosexual acts, and a good deal of in-your-face hurling of loathing invectives), *Angels* has a transporting and transforming effect on spectators who are attuned to its rhythms and subject. Most claim to come out of the seven-hour performance ennobled. Many more experienced the same feelings when a cable-television version of the play, directed by Mike Nichols, premiered on HBO in 2003.

Linda Emond plays the title role in Tony Kushner's *Homebody/Kabul*, about Afghanistan in the late 1990s.

And just who is this Tony Kushner? Born in New York City and raised in Louisiana, Kushner had been known, pre-*Angels,* almost entirely for his clever adaptation of Pierre Corneille's French classic *The Illusion.* After *Angels* he resurfaced with a brilliant short play on a Russian theme, *Slavs! Thinking about the Longstanding Problems of Virtue and Happiness,* and a new translation of S. Ansky's Yiddish classic *The Dybbuk;* neither of these works received the acclaim of *Angels in America,* but what could? Many wondered whether Kushner would remain a major theatrical force after the millennium actually arrived. The answer came quickly at the top of the century, with *Homebody/Kabul,* a three-act, sixteen-actor, 210-minute extravaganza, written in English, French, Pashto, Dari, Arabic, Esperanto, and international computerese. Set in London, Kabul, and the Afghan desert, *Homebody/Kabul* spans a global, mythic history that covers the history of central Asia, from Cain's burial to the present day. When the play debuted in 2001 it was considered astonishingly prescient ("You love the Taliban so much? . . . don't worry, they're coming to New York!" cries a Pashtun woman, in lines written before the World Trade Center attack). As events in that part of the world have proceeded in subsequent years, the play's impact has grown, as has the author's genius for combining the foreign with the familiar, the ancient with the contemporary, and dope-laden ecstasy with passionate intellectuality. (Has there ever before been a play in which the word *dichlorodiphenyltrichloroethane* came trippingly off a character's tongue? or the verbal compound *synchitic expegeses?*) Kushner followed *Kabul* with a musical about a black maid in a Jewish Louisiana family like his own. *Caroline, or Change,* set in the 1960s, digs deeply but not polemically into America's complicated race relations, finding, amid the misery, nuances of grace, humor, and hope. Already a giant among American playwrights, Kushner will surely be a major force in the world's theatre for decades to come.

David Henry Hwang (born 1957)

Growing up in San Gabriel, California, David Henry Hwang began writing—"on a lark," he says—while an undergraduate at Stanford University. His first play, *FOB* (for "Fresh Off the Boat"), is a biting, honest, angry reaction to hidden (and not-so-hidden) American racism; it was first produced at Stanford and subsequently at the Eugene O'Neill Theatre Center in Connecticut and at the New York Public Theatre, for which it won the Obie Award.

Hwang's subsequent *M. Butterfly* (1988), his most celebrated work, explores the bizarre (and apparently true) relationship between a French diplomat and his Chinese mistress: bizarre because the mistress is revealed, during the play, to be—unbeknown to the diplomat—a male in disguise. Hwang's main subject is "Orientalism," the ingrained sense of deprecation with which Western culture views the East. In *Butterfly,* Hwang, of Chinese heritage, brilliantly interweaves gritty Western romanticism (including portions of the Puccini opera that gives the play its name) with Asian theatre and Chinese Opera technique, lending it current-political and timeless-mythic proportions. *Butterfly* won Hwang the Tony Award in 1988 and international fame. His subsequent *Golden Child* (1998), a play about a traditional Chinese family assimilating to Westernizing influences after World War I, was also a Broadway critical success, earning its author another Tony nomination for Best Play. Hwang's prominence continues into the twenty-first century as the adapter of Rodgers and Hammerstein's *Flower Drum Song,* for which he transformed the glib fable of a young Chinese woman's assimilation into American life into a far more nuanced—though still optimistic—voyage through struggle and hardship; Hwang also revised an earlier (1983) play into a new opera, *The Sound of a Voice,* blending fantasies and superstitions of ancient Japan.

The Sound of a Voice, the latest work by David Henry Hwang, is an opera (with music by Philip Glass) about the dreams and fantasies of a writer (played by Susan Hansen) and an aging Japanese warrior (Herbert Perry). Its 2003 world premiere was directed by Robert Woodruff at the American Repertory Theatre, with scenery by Robert Israel, costumes by Kasia Walicka Maimone, and lighting by Beverly Emmons.

Richard Greenberg (born 1958)

In the fall of 2003, Richard Greenberg became the first American playwright in more than a decade to have two plays running on Broadway simultaneously: *Take Me Out,* for which he won the Tony Award for Best Play, and *The Violet Hour.* These were Greenberg's third and fourth Broadway plays, but the New York–based playwright is more closely associated with off-Broadway, particularly the Manhattan Theater Club, and even more with South Coast Repertory (SCR) in Costa Mesa, California, where seven of his plays (including *The Violet Hour)* have enjoyed their world premieres.

Born in Long Island, New York, and educated at Princeton, Harvard, and the Yale Drama School, Greenberg is an intellectual playwright, perhaps the only major American dramatist whose characters you are not surprised to hear talking about Reinhold Niebuhr or Boolean algebra, as they do in *Three Days of Rain.* But Greenberg is an adept comedian as well. His first Broadway show, *Eastern Standard,* was a breakthrough hit, and his first SCR play, *The Extra Man,* had him pegged as a new Neil Simon (or, as John Simon noted, "the gay heir to Neil Simon").

Simon he is not, however, as his 1994 *Night and Her Stars* (about the television quiz-show scandals) suggested and his 1997 *Three Days of*

Rain conclusively demonstrated; the latter earned Greenberg his first Pulitzer Prize nomination. Set in a Greenwich Village apartment, *Rain* covers—in reverse chronology—two distinct generations: one of two male architects and the woman they both loved in 1960, and the successor generation (though the first we see) of three children of their two resulting families in 1995, all seeking to make sense of their parents' confused affairs—and of their own. The sins of the father(s) is one of Greenberg's themes, but so are the sins of the mother and, more important, the virtues of each. Greenberg's *Rain* characters are masterfully created; each is sympathetic, droll, and intelligent. And while the playwright's acute wit is fully evident here, the bleakness of his characters' plights—as sodden as the rain that constantly falls on the grating outside their apartment—gives Greenberg's play an emotional gravity that had previously not been recognized in his work.

It is his second Pulitzer-nominated play that has garnered Greenberg his greatest acclaim, however. *Take Me Out* took virtually every best-play citation in New York, including the Tony, New York Drama Critics Circle, and Outer Critics Circle awards. That the play initially debuted in the United Kingdom (at London's Donmar Warehouse) was particularly interesting because of the play's main theme: the public outing (pun intended) of a gay baseball player. In addition to Greenberg's usual comic wit and wry philosophizing, *Take Me Out* has a vigorous locker-room earthiness, virtually dictated by the extensive (and essential) frontal nudity when the play's half-dozen players take long and very real showers fully facing the audience, snapping towels at each other's bottoms like overgrown boys. This, however, is not a peekaboo play; it is a searching and continually provocative exploration of the relationship between conflicting American interests: sports, money, celebrity, and bigotry. Baseball becomes a metaphor for all of this. "Baseball is better than democracy," says the play's accountant-philosopher (and the author's obvious alter ego); because it "acknowledges loss," it "achieves the tragic vision that democracy evades." Greenberg's intellectualizing, however, is balanced by his lively use of humor ("Any young man can go out there and become a ball player. Or an interior decorator."), along with his sensitive depiction of always-striving but usually failing characters.

Neil LaBute (born 1963)

Neil LaBute burst into the public eye in his early thirties, when his eerily violent film *In the Company of Men,* first written as a stage play, took the Filmmakers Trophy at the 1997 Sundance Film Festival. Yet although LaBute followed *Company* with other films, his greater success has come with a rapid series of highly successful plays—*Bash* (1999), *The Shape of Things* (2001), *The Distance from Here* (2002), *The Mercy Seat* (2002), and *Autobahn* (2004)—all of which explore, in ways both shocking and revelatory, the hidden violence that can lie beneath seemingly stable human relationships.

Bash consists of three self-contained but thematically linked one-acts, all set within the context of the Church of Jesus Christ of Latter-Day Saints, to which LaBute himself once belonged. Although the word *bash* occurs only in the sense of "party" during the play, it also suggests murder, and indeed each of the three separate acts reports a savage killing—monstrous, certainly, but also a bit giddy. The first two plays, each monologues for a single actor, have classic roots. In *Medea Redux,* a young Mormon woman sits at a bare steel table speaking to a presumed interrogator in the back of the house; by play's end she has confessed the details of a truly Medean infanticide: she has electrocuted her child in a motel bathtub. LaBute's unnamed young woman nonetheless lays out her horrifically ordinary story with seductive appeal, drawing upon the Greek notions—once taught to her by her predator-teacher—of fate and "atoxia," or world disorder.

Shown here is Neil LaBute's *The Distance from Here* in its 2004 American premiere at New York's Duke Theatre, with actors (*left to right*) Anna Paquin, Josh Charles, and Melissa Leo.

As played by a willowy-armed and bloody-eyed Calista Flockhart at its premiere, the woman's performance is momentous, making the banal significant, the inelegant profound. In the following act, titled *Iphigenia in Orem,* a hard-drinking corporate middle-manager, fooled into thinking he is facing job termination and depressed because of company downsizing and reciprocally escalating feminism, conspires in the fatal suffocation of his baby daughter—hoping for a sympathy response from his bosses. His odd chuckles as he relates his story—to a boozy stranger in his hotel room—make his incapacitating guilt both resonant and palpable. And in the concluding act, *A Gaggle of Saints,* a young, newly engaged Mormon couple cheerfully recount an event of the previous night's bash (in both senses) at a New York hotel, where the groom-to-be beat a gay man to death in a public restroom while his future bride slept blithely in their suite. Each of *Bash's*

three murders is appalling, but with brilliant dramaturgical finesse, LaBute has increased the charm of each narrator in parallel with our disgust level of his or her criminal behavior, so that at play's end we walk out in an absolutely perplexed tension of horror and dizziness.

LaBute's subsequent plays, coming at more than one a year, are equally grim treatments of contemporary America but lack *Bash's* Mormon underpinnings. *The Shape of Things* portrays a young female art student in a midwestern university who cunningly charms and flatters a young male museum guard until he falls hopelessly in love with her—whereupon she dumps him. "Watching *The Shape of Things,* you think you're watching an episode of 'Friends,' comfortable with your popcorn—and then the chair gets pulled away from you," said Rachel Weisz, who played the young girl in the premiere (and the subsequent film). *The Distance from Here* depicts three teenagers and their assorted parents and stepparents and the empty relationships among them all. The play is situated in various suburban haunts—the monkey cage at a zoo, a bus stop at a mall, a school parking lot and detention hall, and in front of a living-room TV; the dialogue consists mainly of conversations about food, car problems, and allowance cutbacks—spiced up with frequent "faggot" and "slut" insults. But when a girl makes the mistake of getting pregnant, her "boyfriend" smashes his fist into her stomach until she miscarries. And when a baby cries too much, he gets hurled over the fence of the zoo's penguin enclosure, to drown in the freezing pool. "Whatever!" is the principal explanation for all of this macabre behavior.

LaBute's most recent international success is his 2002 *The Mercy Seat,* in which a married man in his early thirties and a woman in her mid-forties, coworkers in a downtown Manhattan office, are engaged in a secret liaison in the woman's loft—on September 11, 2001. Since their office was in the World Trade Center, no one—certainly not the man's wife and children—knows that either of them is still alive. In the course of the play's single act, which takes place the following day, the couple confront the possibilities of running away and creating new lives, versus acknowledging and thus ending their adulterous relationship. The situation gives rise to a varied and intense spiral of guilt, sadness, lust, and recrimination—a virtual road map of middle-aged angst in the affluent urban jungle.

LaBute's great contribution to the stage is his coruscating dialogue—vivid, penetrating, desperate, and palpably *real* in the mouths of his characters. The high-velocity flow of his dialogue seems as lifelike (and as "nonliterary") as normal speech (normal, at least, within the imagined world of his characters), including startling profanity, pauses, sentence trail-offs, nongrammatical syntax, and rapidly overlapping speeches—which he sometimes denotes by a slash within the lines. All of these techniques can be seen in this sample from *Mercy Seat:*

BEN: We've been given something here. A chance to . . . I don't know what, to wash away a lot of the, just, rotten crap we've done. More than anything else, that's what this is. A chance. I know it is.

ABBY: Yeah, but it's tainted . . . / . . . it's a fluke.

BEN: What? / No, it's not that, no, it's . . .

ABBY: We got lucky. Or, more specifically . . . *you* did. But you didn't earn it.

BEN: What are you talking about?

ABBY: I'm just saying that it was a happy coincidence that you managed to be over here at my place yesterday morning, getting your proverbial cock sucked, when it happened . . . that's all. (*Beat.*) Right?

BEN: I guess. Yes.

ABBY: The one day out of the year you're supposed to be down there for us and you decide to skip out, come over, get some head . . . that's not bad.

BEN: So?

ABBY: So . . . there's probably a lot of spouses out there right now who wish their dearly departed would've stopped to pick up a nice Frappuccino or dropped off that roll of film they were carrying around in their pocket . . . hell, maybe paid for a *blow job,* even. Whatever it takes to stay alive. (*Beat.*) I'm saying you really dodged a bullet there.

BEN: Plane. I dodged a plane.

ABBY: Ooooohhh. Careful with the humor thing, remember?

BEN: Yeah . . . (*Beat.*) That's a shitty thing to say.

As we go to press, LaBute's very affecting *Fat Pig* has opened to rave reviews at the Lucille Lortel Theatre in New York, and his *This Is How It Goes* is readying for a 2005 premiere at the New York Public Theatre. Clearly, LaBute should be expected to remain a major force in the American theatre for years to come.

Suzan-Lori Parks's *Fucking A* is one of this playwright's most provocative, and also most accessible, dramas.

Suzan-Lori Parks (born 1964)

In the summer of 2001, *New York Times* drama critic Ben Brantley declared Suzan-Lori Parks "ferociously talented," while rating the first act of her *Topdog/Underdog* "as exciting as any new play from a young American since Tony Kushner's *Angels in America*." Donald Lyons in the *New York Post,* on the other hand, called the same play "clumsy" and "glib," a mix of "incredible and pretentious ideas." Such fiercely mixed reaction is highly characteristic of Parks's work, which typically meets with both angry walkouts and standing ovations.

Raised in both the United States and Germany, Parks studied with the great American writer James Baldwin at Mount Holyoke College; it was Baldwin who, hearing Parks read her stories aloud in class, first suggested she write for the stage. Parks's first play, *The Sinners' Place,* earned her cum laude honors in English—but was turned down for production by Holyoke's theatre department on the grounds that "you can't put dirt onstage! That's not a play!" Her next play, however, *Imperceptible Mutabilities in the Third Kingdom* (1989), won her a coveted Obie Award, leading to subsequent positions as resident dramatist at both the Yale Repertory Theatre and the New York Public Theatre, each of which has produced several of her plays.

Parks's plays are not easy to read, however, and it is easy to sympathize with her theatre department not immediately seeing their merit. Writing about the black experience in America —slavery, lynchings, poverty, discrimination, minstrelsy, and racism are common themes— she rejects both realism and easy polemics, preferring a savagely comic irony and freshly minted language to diatribes or bald recountings. With the speech of Mrs. Aretha Saxon from *Mutabilities,* for example,

Six seven eight nine. Thupp. Ten eleven twelve thirteen fourteen fifteen sixteen. Thupp. Seventeen. Eighteen nineteen twenty twenty-one. And uh little bit. Thuuup. Thuup. Gotta know thuh size. Thup. Gotta know thuh size exact. Thup. Got people comin. Hole house full. They gonna be kin? Could be strangers. How many kin kin I hold. Whole hold full. How many strangers. Depends on thuh size. Thup. Size of thuh space. Thuup. Depends on thuh size of thuh kin. Pendin on thuh size of thuh strangers. Get more mens than womens ssgonna be one number more womens then mens ssgonna be uhnother get animals thuup get animals we kin pack em thuup. Tight. Thuuup. Thuuuup. Mmmmm. Thuuup.

Suzan-Lori Parks's *Topdog/Underdog* (2001) returns to a common Parks' theme, the reenactment of Abraham Lincoln's assassination as a public amusement. Jeffrey Wright (*right*) is a contemporary "Lincoln," who also plays the role of Lincoln in a sideshow, and Don Cheadle is his brother "Booth," who also plays Booth. Con games and crooked gambling (the sidewalk "three-card monte" ruse) are the brothers' preoccupations and escape from wretched conditions. The sets were designed by Riccardo Hernandez and the costumes by Emilio Sosa for this New York Public Theatre production.

The Playwright's Career

How does a person become a playwright? Writing plays, naturally, is the first (and most important) step. But getting that original play produced is almost as challenging.

There are hundreds of "break-in" opportunities for playwrights to develop their scripts in open rehearsals or in developmental workshop productions or staged readings. And sometimes a playwright can realize (or can produce herself or himself) a fully staged production. Many of these developmental opportunities are available through colleges and universities. David Henry Hwang's *FOB* was first presented at his college dormitory at Stanford University, and Wendy Wasser-

stein's *Uncommon Women and Others* was first presented at the Yale Drama School.

Virtually all regional professional theatres present new plays from time to time, and many — if not most of them — actively solicit new works, usually presenting them first in script-in-hand readings or special workshops, where the works are presented and critiqued by other writers and company artists. The annual publication *Dramatists Sourcebook* (published by Theatre Communications Group in New York) lists such theatres that solicit new works and identifies any special areas of interest they might have (such as a theatre dedicated to Spanish-speaking plays).

Parks vividly—but in an indelible style—describes the process of packing human cargo into an English slave ship.

Two subsequent Parks plays, both set in nineteenth-century sideshows, have created startling themes that have continued in her work. In *The America Play* (1993), her main character, "The Foundling Father," is so obsessed with Abraham Lincoln that he leaves his family to play the role of America's sixteenth president in a sort of traveling carnival, soliciting spectators to come up onstage and, for a fee, pick up a prop gun and, as John Wilkes Booth, shoot him. And *Venus* (1996) portrays a nineteenth-century African woman, Saartjie Baartman, who, because of her enormous buttocks, was displayed throughout America as a freak. The basic situations—as well as Parks's savagely comic and ironic style—of both plays have been transmuted to current times in two of Parks's more recent works. *Fucking A,* which Parks directed in Houston in 2000, is a present-day *Venus,* though the character is now an abortionist. And *Topdog/Underdog,* staged by playwright-director George C. Wolfe at the Public Theatre in 2001, while set in present-day America, concerns a violently contentious pair of brothers named Lincoln and Booth, and once again Lincoln, now a retired master of three-card monte, New York's sidewalk con game, is playing President Lincoln in an arcade show, while Booth, a shoplifter, is his assassin in a fugue of sibling and status rivalry. Inner identities, outer roles, and status levels all continuously shift and jostle in these newest Parks plays, which are more generally accessible than her earlier work (she was working on a new Disney musical about the Harlem Globetrotters basketball team), but no less controversial in their reception than her earlier work. And the 2002 restaging of Parks's *Topdog/Underdog* on Broadway coincided with her winning of the coveted Pulitzer Prize for Drama for that same work, crowning her playwriting accomplishments with broad public and critical acceptance.

Lynn Nottage's *Intimate Apparel* depicts a young black lingerie seamstress trying to make her way – in both livelihood and love life – in 1905 Manhattan. Shané Williams (*right*) is the seamstress, and her landlady is played by Brenda Pressley, in this South Coast Repertory pre-Broadway production of 2003, directed by Kate Whoriskey.

And a Host of Others . . .

These playwrights hardly constitute all of the new playwrights making names for themselves in the current American theatre. Margaret Edson's first—and thus far only—play, *Wit* (discussed earlier in this chapter), won the Pulitzer Prize in 1999. First-time playwright David Auburn's *Proof* won the Pulitzer Prize and Tony Award in 2002 and became the longest-running Broadway play in two decades. Tracy Letts's *Bug,* a chilling study of paranoia, was an off-Broadway hit in 2004, and his *Man from Nebraska* earned him a finalist spot for the 2004 Pulitzer Prize. Nilo Cruz won the 2003 Pulitzer for *Anna in the*

Tropics, about a Cuban-American cigar factory, and Doug Wright took both the 2004 Pulitzer Prize and Tony Award with his *I Am My Own Wife,* a captivating play about a gay German survivor of both Nazism and communism. And Lynn Nottage won the 2004 New York Drama Critics Circle Award for her *Intimate Apparel,* about a black seamstress in nineteenth-century New York; Nottage followed brilliantly with *Fab-*

ulation, or the Re-education of Undine, about an upper-class black woman reduced to poverty by her scoundrel husband. (Many of these plays are discussed elsewhere in this edition.) Never before, in this author's opinion, has American drama been so richly endowed with skillful, meaningful, and provocative playwrights as in this first decade of the twenty-first century.

5

Designers and Technicians

THE ACTOR AND THE PLAYSCRIPT MAY BE AT THE CORE of the theatrical experience, but they are by no means the sum of it. Indeed, in the view of many spectators and participants, the primacy of acting and playwriting is extremely debatable, for acting and textual brilliance are not isolated components capable of full expression in and by themselves. In even the most primitive of dramas the theatrical experience always has a look and a sound and a shape—a visual and aural impact—that can be achieved only through *design*. And the execution of that design always entails a measure of *technology*. In many ways and at many times the theatre has had occasion to celebrate the artistic talent of its designers and the engineering capability of its technicians, for many of the world's great aesthetic and technological innovations have been made public primarily through theatrical exploitation.

Therefore, in examining a play it is hardly sufficient to inquire, What is it about? We must also ask, How does it look? How does it sound? How is it built? How does it run? These questions bring us face-to-face with an army of backstage personnel: the artists and technicians who create and make possible what Aristotle called the spectacle of theatre, the individuals responsible for the overall appearance, orchestration, and management of the theatrical experience.

It is customary for purposes of discussion to divide design functions into a series of components—scenery, lighting, costume, makeup, and so forth—and to a certain extent this categorization is appropriate; most productions involve separate "departments" of design, each with its own designers, assistants, and crews. Yet in fact all design functions of a production are closely interrelated: the appearance of scenery, for example, is heavily dependent on the light that falls upon it, and the look of a costume is greatly affected by the actor's makeup and hairstyle, to say nothing of his or her acting and bearing. Designers tend, therefore, to work as a design "team," in close collaboration with each other and with the director, from the outset of the production process. In the following listing of the various contributing "arts" of theatrical design, therefore, we must recognize that in examining

Thomas Umfrid's scenery for a production of Noel Coward's *Hay Fever,* set in a well-to-do acting family's English country home in the mid-1920s, is beautifully realized for the 2003 Utah Shakespearean Festival. Umfrid's set forcefully projects the action of the play forward by a skillful arrangement of staircase, doors, and landing. The showy 1920s costumes were designed by Kevin Alberts and the summery lighting by Lonnie Alcaraz.

Gloriously exotic scenery and costumes (by Bob Crowley) and spectacular lighting (by Natasha Katz) create the throbbingly colorful North African panorama that is fundamental to the 2000 Disney musical, *Aida*.

each function separately we are attempting only to clarify certain traditional practices and that no single design art can be fully realized in isolation. Similarly, the ordering of these separate arts can only be arbitrary, for no fundamental hierarchy exists among them. We will begin with the theatre's architecture, scenery, and lighting and then move on to costuming, makeup, sound design, special effects, and the new computer technologies that affect all of them. Finally, we will discuss the many and varied theatre technicians who, jointly, play a crucial role in every theatrical production.

Theatre Architecture

Theatre architecture has long been one of the glories of the Western world. The Greek theatres, which evolved out of a pagan rite celebrated on a hillside, rank high among the magnificent relics of antiquity: the surviving theatre at Epidaurus is only one of many from the fourth century B.C. that still resound from time to time with revivals of the same great plays that thrilled audiences in the Hellenistic age. The theatres of ancient Rome were so grandiose in conception and execution that only hyperbole, it appears, could convey their proper character. For example, can we believe Pliny's account of an 80,000-seat theatre built in three stories, one each of marble, glass, and gilt? or of the two theatres built back-to-back that, filled with spectators, rotated on a pivot to join in a huge amphitheater that was then flooded for sea battle scenes?

Later times have given us many more fine theatres. Of Peter Street, the architect of Shakespeare's Globe and Henslowe's Fortune theatres, historical documentation unfortunately tells us little more than that his theatres were provocative of the best in dramatic art. The Teatro Olimpico in Vicenza, Italy, was designed by the famed Andrea Palladio; built in 1584, it not only survives intact but is still occasionally used for dramatic presentations. Other theatres surviving from earlier eras, such as the elegant eighteenth-century court theatre at Drottningholm, Sweden, and the opulent nineteenth-century romantic structure built for the Paris Opera, are cultural landmarks as well as theatrically significant sites of contemporary production.

The last half of the twentieth century experienced an explosion of theatre construction that began just after the end of World War II. Since that time, theatres and performing arts centers have sprung up in virtually every major city in North America, Europe, and Asia. Indeed, the past half century may well be considered a golden age of theatrical architecture. It is an age marked by a growing public willingness to lend financial support to the theatre and by a greatly increased understanding of the need for extensive collaboration between theatre artists and architects in order to reconcile the needs for theatrical "tone" and atmosphere with those for practical flexibility and operational ease.

Staging Formats

The two principal types of modern theatre building are the "proscenium" stage design and the "thrust" stage design. These two basic types, and their various combinations, account for more than 95 percent of the professional theatres in Europe and America today and for the bulk of amateur stages as well. The *proscenium* theatre is essentially a rectangular room, with the audience on one side facing the stage on the other; separating the two areas is an arch (the "proscenium arch") through which the audience peers. This creates the well-known "picture-frame" stage, with the arch serving as the frame for the action going on within. The proscenium format was developed in Italy during the Renaissance as a mode of presenting elaborate masques and other court entertainments; because it put the audience on but one side of the action, it allowed extensive hidden areas backstage for the scene shifting and trickery involved in creating the illusions and fantasies so admired at the time. The proscenium theatre achieved its fullest realization in the Baroque era, and some of the surviving court theatres and opera houses of Europe testify eloquently to the splendor of that age. Modern proscenium theatres have proven particularly serviceable for the use of realistic scenery and for the presentation of scenic spectaculars. Virtually all Broadway theatres feature the proscenium format.

The *thrust* design, pioneered in North America by Tyrone Guthrie, was in fact the favored format in ancient Greece and Elizabethan England. Because it places much of the action in the midst of the audience, the thrust stage is a more actor-centered (rather than scenery-centered) theatre configuration. In the thrust format the members of the audience are more aware of each other than they are in a darkened proscenium "fan," and their viewing perspectives differ radically, depending on their seating locations. When the acting platform, or thrust, can be accessed from tunnels (*vomitoria*) that come up through the audience, the stage can be flooded by actors in a matter of seconds, creating a whirlwind of movement that is dazzling and immediate—the thrust stage's alternative to elaborate stage machinery

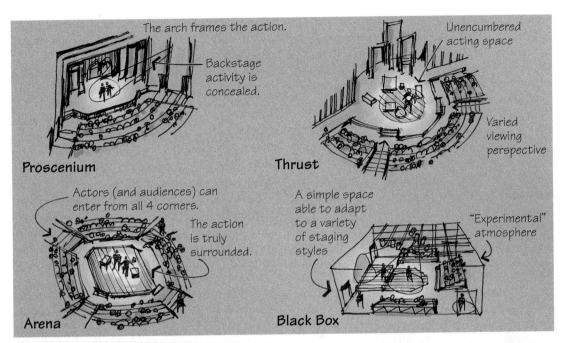

Illustrated here are the four basic staging formats: proscenium, thrust, arena, and black box. Deciding where to locate the stage in relation to the audience is the architect's first consideration in theatre design.

and painted scenes. That is not at all to say that there can be no scenery on a thrust stage but merely that scenic pieces tend to be placed behind the action rather than surrounding it to leave a relatively unencumbered acting space that projects into the center of the audience. In a thrust stage, the treatment given to the stage floor may in fact become the dominant scenic element.

Combined proscenium and thrust stage theatres, which can be converted from one format to another depending on the nature of the production, have increasingly come into fashion since the 1960s, particularly in academic-based theatre structures such as the Loeb Drama Center at Harvard and the Loretto-Hilton Center at Webster College. In these cases, mechanical lifts raise a thrust stage into the midst of the audience or lower it for an orchestra pit or additional seating in the proscenium mode.

A third theatrical configuration is the *arena* format (also known as "theatre-in-the-round"), in which the audience surrounds the action on all sides. One American regional theatre, the Arena Stage in Washington, D.C., has presented an arena season regularly since 1950. Arena staging dispenses with all scenery except floor treatments, furniture, and out-of-the-way hanging or standing pieces, and it focuses audience attention sharply and simply on the actors.

A final staging alternative is the so-called *black box* theatre, a formatless space that can be adjusted to any desired arrangement and is therefore particularly useful in experimental, environmental, or academic stagings. Usually painted black (hence the name), this type of theatre consists of a bare room fitted with omniflexible overhead lighting; in this room, the stage and seating can normally be set up in a variety of ways—proscenium, thrust, arena, or two-sided "alley" configuration—or the action can be staged *environmentally,* so as to occur at several locales interspersed variously throughout the room and perhaps above or below the audience as well. The black-box theatre allows the director/creator to develop a near-infinite variety of actor-audience interactions and to make use of highly unusual scenic designs and mechanisms. Performance art, participatory dramas and rituals, and seminar plays—all of which demand active audience involvement—are well suited to these sorts of spaces.

Other Architectural Considerations

Designing a theatre involves a great deal more than choosing a staging format. It involves creating a seating space that is suited to the requirements of the expected audience; this may mean one thing in a sophisticated urban area, another in a rural setting, and yet another on a college campus. It involves providing for effective communication systems, sightlines, and stage mechanisms for the sorts of productions the theatre will handle. This means there must be adequate wiring, soundproofing, and rigging, as well as a good use of backstage and onstage spaces, both open and enclosed—often that means calling in a consultant to ascertain the most practical design for the widest variety of uses.

Architectural design also involves principles of acoustics, which can determine whether actors' voices will be heard, given a normal volume level, in all parts of the house and whether singers' voices can be heard when the orchestra is playing. As a science, acoustics is maddeningly inexact; the best results come only after much experience and testing. Theatre architecture also involves the art of lighting, for no lighting designer can possibly overcome the limitations imposed by poorly located, permanently installed lighting fixtures. One of the sadder sights in many older theatres is the snarls of exposed pipes and lighting instru-

ments awkwardly strapped to gilded cupids in a latter-day attempt to make up for antiquated lighting systems.

And finally, designing a theatre building involves a love of theatre, an emotional and aesthetic understanding that a theatre is not merely a room, a hall, or an institutional building with certain features but a permanent home for the portrayal of human concerns and a repository of 2,500 years of glorious tradition. Such a place must be functional and flexible, to be sure, but it should also be a welcoming environment—for both artists and audiences—and a place that inspires us to focus our attention on the concerns of the dramatic production. Whether that implies the cushy velvet seats of a Broadway playhouse, the hard, backless wooden benches of Peter Brook's Bouffes du Nord in Paris, or the standing-room pit of the newly restored Globe Theater in London, the theatre's architectural structure powerfully orients us toward our ultimate perception of the play.

Scenery

Scenery is often the first thing we think of under the general category of theatrical design. It is usually what we first see of a play, either at the rise of the curtain in a traditional proscenium production or as we enter the theatre where there is no curtain. The scene designer is usually listed first among designers in a theatre poster or program. But scenery is a relatively new design area, historically speaking. Costume, makeup, and masks are far more ancient; scenery was not needed at all in the *Abydos Passion Play* or the Greek dithyramb, and it probably played little part in early Greek or Roman drama, save to afford entry, exit, and sometimes expanded acting space for actors (such as rotating prisms and rolling platforms) or to provide a decorative backdrop later in the period. In much Asian theatre, scenery remains rare or even nonexistent; this is the case in most Chinese Opera and—apart from the elaborate stagehouse itself—in nō drama as well. Nor was scenery of paramount importance in the outdoor medieval or public Elizabethan theatres, apart from a few painted set pieces made to resemble walls, trees, caves, thrones, tombs, porches, and the occasional "Hellmouth"; virtually all visual aspects of staging prior to the seventeenth century were dictated by the architecture of the theatre structure itself.

It was the development of European indoor stages, artificially illuminated, that fostered the first great phase of scene design: the period of painted, flat scenery. Working indoors, protected from rain and wind, the scenic designers of Renaissance court masques and public spectacles were free for the first time to erect painted canvases and temporary wooden structures without fear of having the colors run and the supports rot out or blow away. And with the advent of controllable indoor lighting, designers could illuminate their settings and acting areas as they wished, leaving other parts of the theatre building, such as the audience seating, in the dark. Designers could, in short, create realistic illusion and extravagant visual spectacle and have the audience focus on this work in decent comfort.

The result was a series of scene-design revelations that brought the names of a new class of theatre artists to public consciousness: designers such as the Italians Sebastiano Serlio (1475–1554), Aristotile da Sangallo (1481–1551), and Giacomo Torelli (1608–1678); the Englishman Inigo Jones (1573–1652); and the Frenchman Jean Bérain (c. 1637–1711). By the beginning of the eighteenth century, the scene designer's art had attained a prominence equal to (or perhaps greater than) the playwright's; and for almost two hundred years thereafter, flat scenery, painted in exquisite perspective, took on even greater sophistication under the brilliant artists of the theatre's baroque, rococo, and romantic epochs. The proscenium format, which was developed primarily to show off elegant settings, dominated theatre architec-

---

THE HIDDEN ENERGY

A stage setting has no independent life of its own. Its emphasis is directed toward the performance. In the absence of the actor it does not exist. Strange as it may seem, this simple and fundamental principle of stage design still seems to be widely misunderstood....
A scene on the stage is ... like a mixture of chemical elements held in solution. The actor adds the one element that releases the hidden energy of the whole. Meanwhile, wanting the actor, the various elements which go into the setting remain suspended, as it were, in an indefinable tension. To create this suspense, this tension, is the essence of ... stage designing.

—Robert Edmund Jones

---

ture for two hundred years, and it remains the most widely used theatre format in the world. But the painted flat scenery that the proscenium gave rise to has been only one of many competing scenic formats in the modern era, which began at the end of the nineteenth century.

Modern scenery is generally either realistic or metaphoric—or (most often these days) a combination of both. Realistic scenery attempts to depict, often in great detail, a specific time and place in the real world where the play's events are presumed to take place. Metaphoric scenery favors, instead, visual images that seek to evoke (or to suggest, abstract, or make a visual statement about) the production's intended theme, mood, or social/political implications. Metaphoric scenery tends to remind us —at least when we first see it—that we are in a theatre, not in a bedroom or butcher shop; generally its intention is to draw us more deeply into the play's larger issues and concerns. And although stage design today most often combines realism with metaphor—these terms are better described as end points on a continuum rather than purely exclusive categories—these complementary design goals have each contributed mightily to the important position of scenery in the theatrical experience today.

Hayden Griffin's scenery and costume design for Roy Williams's *Sing Yer Heart Out for the Lads,* which concerns race relations in present-day England, transformed the Cottesloe stage of the National Theatre into a totally realistic sports pub, with a projection TV, pool table, and working bar taps for the 2004 revival; members of the audience, in fact, were seated and served at the bar tables. Ashley Walters plays the put-upon Barry in the foreground. Lighting is by Andy Phillips.

Realistic settings carry on the tradition of illusionism established in eighteenth-century painted scenery; at that time, an ingeniously arranged assembly of "wings" (vertical, flat scenery pieces standing left and right of the stage), "borders" (horizontal, flat scenery pieces hung above the stage), and "drops" (short for *backdrops:* large, flat scenery pieces at the rear of the stage), painted in perspective, created the lifelike illusion of drawing rooms, conservatories, ballrooms, reception halls, parlors, libraries, servants' quarters, professional offices, and factory yards of many a dramatist's imagination. By the nineteenth century, this "wing-and-drop

set," as it was known, yielded to the "box set": a three-dimensional construction of interconnected hard-covered "flats" (representing the walls and ceilings of a real room), which was then filled with real furniture and real properties taken from ordinary real-world environments. The box set is very much alive today and is indeed the major scenic format for the contemporary domestic drama (particularly comedy) of New York's Broadway, London's West End, and most community and college theatres across America. Although no longer particularly voguish (the box set rarely wins design awards), it fulfills the staging requirements of a great many domestic comedies, thrillers, and serious, linearly structured dramas, particularly those requiring interior settings. Advances in scenic construction and technology have made the box set a marvel of lifelike appearance and detail.

Box sets do more than merely designate a play's locale. By adding three-dimensional features, they allow for acting and playwriting opportunities previously unachievable: staircases to descend, doors to slam, windows to climb through, bookcases to stash revolvers in, and grandfather clocks to hide characters in. The public fascination with realistic scenery reached its high-water mark in the ultrarealistic "theatre of the fourth wall removed," in which the box set was used to such advantage that it helped foster a uniquely architectural theory of theatre—that it should represent life as it is normally lived but with one wall removed so that the audience could look in upon it.

Metaphoric scenic design, however, tends to be more conceptual than literal, more kinetic than stable, more theatrical than photographic. The use of scenic metaphor is hardly new; in the *Abydos Passion Play,* two maces represent Set's testicles and a red stone, the Eye of Horus. Shakespeare, in his prologue to *Henry V,* apologizes for the "unworthy scaffold" of his stage and begs his audience to use their "imaginary forces" to complete the scenic picture; for example, with the help of two or three scaling ladders placed against the stage balcony the audience could imagine the English army storming a castle wall in France. These are scenic "abstractions" in the most elemental sense: they present reality by a sign rather than trompe-l'oeil ("eye-deceiving") realism. But the modern sense of metaphoric scenery began with the theoretical (and occasionally practical) works of designers Adolphe Appia (1862–1928) and Gordon Craig (1872–1966), both of whom urged the fluid use of space, form, and light as the fundamental principle of dramatic design. Today, aided by technological advances in motorized, computer-controlled lighting and scene shifting, the movement toward a more conceptual, abstract, and kinetic scenography has inspired impressive stylizations around the world. Shafts and walls of light, transparent "scrims," sculptural configurations, wall-sized photo reproductions, mirrored and burlapped surfaces, "floating" walls and rising staircases, and "found" or "surreal" environments have all become major scenic media over the past fifty years.

Metaphoric settings can of course establish locales (as with Quince's "wall," mentioned in the accompanying box), but they are even

---

QUINCE'S SIGNIFICANT MOON

Shakespeare understood and at times apologized for the pictorial limitations of the scenery of his time ("Piece out our imperfections with your thoughts," he advised the audience in the prologue to *Henry V*), but he also appreciated its capacity to signify – rather than merely depict realistically – the world of his plays. In Shakespeare's *A Midsummer Night's Dream*, the character of Peter Quince is seen directing a play of *Pyramus and Thisbe* with a group of amateur actors and pondering the "hard things" that this *Pyramus* requires, mainly the effect of moonshine in a bedroom chamber. One actor, finding that the moon will be shining on the night of performance, suggests they simply open the window and let the real moon shine in.

Quince, however, prefers that an actor hold up a lantern to "disfigure, or to present" the moon. The created "scenic" moon is preferred to the real one because it *signifies* moonshine; it is intentional and consequently meaningful rather than accidental and meaningless. To indicate a "wall" in the same play – the other "hard thing" – Quince abjures bringing in a real wall and instead has another actor put on "some plaster or some loam" so as "to signify wall." Life may be a tale, as Shakespeare's *Macbeth* says, "full of sound and fury, signifying nothing," but the theatre tells tales that signify a great many things. Thus scenery's function is not merely to depict but to signify – to "make a sign," to be "significant."

more effective in establishing moods and styles. Of course, a play's mood can be established by realistic scenery as well; for example, by creating a theatrical space that is tall and airy (or cramped and squat) or by using certain colors or shapes, the designer can create an environment in any mode so that the play's action delivers a strikingly defined tone. But with a determined metaphoric extension, the designer can greatly elaborate upon this tone and translate it into a highly specific sensory impact.

Bert Neumann's sterile 1950s German bungalow set for *The Insulted and Injured,* for example, both oriented and disoriented audiences, keeping them at arm's length from the story and reminding them of the often-arbitrary grimness of daily life; its modern walls, plastic furniture, frozen-over wading pool, and projection screen on the roof, surmounted by billowing smoke from the chimney, contrasted brutally with the warmly lit interior seen behind the windows, where parties were held and music played and life seemed happier. In contrast, Bob Crowley's exotic Broadway design of *Aida* (see page 451) stimulated thoughts of African heat, ritual, and ancient manual labor, while John Gunter's design for the English National Theatre's *Love's Labor's Lost* gave the audience a profound sensory appreciation of the civilly tamed pre–World War I English parkland, where this production was set. And Tim Hatley's ravishing three-story hotel for Noel Coward's *Private Lives* (see page 475) beautifully set the mood of witty elegance, extravagance, and refinement of a 1920s Riviera hotel facade as the curtain rose on Broadway for the first act.

Specifically postmodern design elements, too, have made their appearance in the theatre of the 1980s and 1990s. Because the postmodern emphasizes disharmonies and associations, it travels a somewhat different path from the departures of modernist innovators Craig and Appia; postmodern design is identifiable by its conscious disruption of "unifying" stylistic themes, replacing them with what may at first seem random assemblages of

Bert Neumann's set for the Berlin Volksbühne production of *The Insulted and Injured* (adapted from a Dostoevsky novel of the same title) is a bleak, rotating 1950s German bungalow, topped off with a projection screen (here rotated with its back to the audience) that shows events occurring within the bungalow, as well as seemingly irrelevant TV commercials.

different and unrelated styles, some "quoting" other historical periods or intellectual sources and others disrupting the linear flow of consistent imagery or effect. Postmodern design also tends to reconfigure, or refer to, the theatre facility itself with (for example) painted scenery made to look specifically scenic, particularly in contrast to seemingly arbitrary found objects strewn about the set, and with designed units meant to comment on—and to mock—their own "theatricality."

Bob Crowley's setting for Tom Stoppard's *The Invention of Love,* portraying the English poet and classical scholar A. E. Housman, is a postmodern deconstruction of Roman architectural and sculptural forms, reflected in the River Styx in Stoppard's version of the classical Hades (the mythological Greek world of the dead). And Richard Hudson's 1997 *The Lion King* filled Broadway's New Amsterdam Theater—stage and house alike—with multiple and ingenious recapitulations of African, Asian, and American avant-garde design in a joyous celebration of the theatre's truly global virtuosity.

The best scenic design today is so much more than mere "backing" for the action of a play; it is instead the visual and spatial architecture of the play's performance, an architecture that when fully realized is *intrinsic to the play's action:* it is the place *where* the play exists; it also determines exactly *how* the play exists and, along with other factors, helps reveal the play's deepest meanings.

Scenic Materials

Scene designers work, most fundamentally, with space, time, and images. The traditional materials with which these have been created over the past four centuries—wood, canvas, and paint—were in the twentieth century extended to include virtually every form of matter known to (or created by) humankind: metals, plastics, masonry, and fabrics; earth, stone, fire, and water; fog, smoke, rain, and light projections. Designing scenic components that employ any or all of these materials is the first area of training for every scene designer.

Platforms, flats, and draperies are the traditional building blocks of fixed stage scenery, and no changes in aesthetics or technology have in any way diminished their importance in the contemporary theatre. *Platforming* serves the all-important function of giving the actor an elevated space from which to perform, making her or him visible over the heads of other actors and stage furniture. A stage setting that utilizes several artfully arranged platforming levels (normally of increasing height toward the back of the stage), together with appropriate connecting staircases and ramps or "raked" platform units, can permit dozens of actors to be seen simultaneously. Platforms can be created in any size and shape; moreover, with the growing use of steel in stage-platform construction, platform support can be fairly open, allowing for huge but still "lacy" settings of great structural stability.

Flats, which today are normally sturdy wooden frames covered in various hard surfaces (such as plywood) and then painted or otherwise treated, are generally used to indicate vertical walls and to define space. In a realistic design, such flats can be pierced with windows, doors, and open archways; adorned with moldings, paintings, hangings, bookcases, or fireplaces; or turned horizontally to serve as ceilings. They can be "tracked" onto the stage in grooves, as they were in the eighteenth century, or "flown" down from the overhead "flies" (rope-and-pulley or counterweight systems for moving hanging scenery), as they often still are in repertory theatres that store many different settings. The flat is an immensely versatile workhorse that until recently had almost become a symbol of the theatre itself.

Drapery, on the other hand, is widely used as the great neutral stuff of stage scenery. Black hanging drapery is conventionally used to mask (hide) the backstage areas and the lighting instruments; in such cases it is not formally considered part of the scenic picture. Sometimes, in fact, a full set of neutral black drapery—which is standard equipment in most proscenium theatres—can be employed as the entire surround for a staged reading or chamber production. The stage curtain of the proscenium theatre is another form of conventional hanging drapery. When the curtain rises vertically or parts horizontally or is pulled diagonally upward (the "opera drape") at the beginning of a play, it

John Gunter's set for Trevor Nunn's production of Shakespeare's *Love's Labor's Lost* is a breathtaking Edwardian English green park, with a huge beech tree, surrounded by moss and foliage, that frames the seated actors but does not overpower them. Joseph Fiennes and Olivia Williams play the seated Berowne and the Princess of France in this 2003 London National Theatre production.

normally signals the drama's first engagement of the audience.

A final type of drapery found in most well-equipped theatres is the "cyclorama," a hanging fabric stretched taut between upper and lower pipes and curved to surround the rear and sides of the stage. Colored white, gray, or gray-blue, the "cyc" can be lighted with stronger colors to represent a variety of "skyscapes" with great effectiveness; it can also be used for abstract backgrounds and projections.

In addition to the three primary components of stage settings, many productions make use of the special objects, or *set pieces,* which frequently become focal points for an overall

setting design or even for the action of a whole play. The tree in *Waiting for Godot,* for example, is the primary scenic feature of that play's setting, symbolizing both life and death. The moment when Vladimir and Estragon "do the tree"—a calisthenic exercise in which each man stands on one leg and tries to assume the shape of the tree—is a profound moment of theatre in which set piece and actors coalesce in a single image echoing the triple crucifixion on Calvary, where two thieves died alongside Christ. Similarly, the massive supply wagon hauled by Mother Courage in Bertolt Brecht's epic play of the same name gives rise to a powerful visual impression of struggle and travail

Tom Stoppard's *Jumpers* was a critical success in its 2004 Broadway revival in part because of its spectacular designs: startling scenery by Vicki Mortimer, eye-popping costumes by Nicky Gillibrand, starburst lighting by Paule Constable, and high-flying aerial choreography by Aidan Treays. Pictured is Essie Davis as the philosopher's wife, swinging on the moon in a starry nighttime sky.

Ming Cho Lee's great realistic setting for Patrick Meyer's adventure drama *K-2* portrays a ledge in the Himalaya mountains. It even feels cold.

that may last long after the words of the characters are forgotten. And what would *Prometheus Bound* be without its striking set piece, which represents Prometheus's rock and chains? No matter how stylized this element may have been in its original realization, it must have radiated to the Athenian audience a visual poetry every bit as eloquent as the verbal poetry with which Aeschylus supported it. Individual set pieces indeed tax the imagination of author, director, designer, and scene technician alike,

The horticultural set, dominated by a giant beehive at its center, was designed by Tim Hatley and proved the virtual star of Charlotte Jones's *The Humble Boy*, which played at the New York City Center in 2003.

and the masterpieces of scenic invention can long outlive their makers in the memory of the audience.

A host of modern materials and technological inventions add to the primary components and set pieces from which scenery is created. *Light* as scenery (as opposed to stage lighting, discussed later) can create walls, images, even (with laser holography) three-dimensional visualizations. Banks of sharply focused light sent through dense atmospheres (enhanced by smoke or dust or fog) can create trenches of light that have the appearance of massive solidity and yet can be made to disappear at the flick of a switch. Carefully controlled slide projections can provide images either realistic or abstract, fixed or fluid, precise or indefinite.

Scrim has been a staple of theatre "magic" for years. This loosely woven, gauzy fabric looks opaque when lit from the front (the audience side) and transparent when lit from behind, allowing actors and even whole sets to suddenly appear or disappear simply by a shift in the lighting.

Stage machinery—turntables, elevators, hoists, rolling carts and wagons, and the like— can be used to create a veritable dance of scenic elements to accompany and support dramatic action. The ancient Greeks apparently understood the importance of mechanical devices quite well, as did Shakespeare, with his winched thrones and disappearing witches. Tricks and sleight of hand (called in the medieval theatre "trucs" and "feynts") have always imparted a certain sparkle of mystery to the theatre and hence will always play a part in the designer's art.

Sound also must be taken into consideration by the designer, who must plan for the actors' footfalls as well as for the visual elements behind, around, and underneath them. The floor of a Japanese nō stage, for example, has a characteristic look and produces a characteristic sound; it is meant to be stamped upon, and it must sound just so. The European scenographer Joseph Svoboda designed a stage floor for *Faust* that could be either resonant or silent depending on the arrangement of certain mechanisms concealed underneath; when Faust walked upstage his steps reverberated; when he turned and walked downstage his steps were silent—and from this we knew that Mephistopheles had taken his body.

Properties and furniture, which are often handled by separate artists working under the guidance of the scene designer, are crucial not only in establishing realism but also in enhancing mood and style. Although furniture often functions in the theatre as it does in real life—to sit upon, lie upon, and so forth—it also has a crucial stylistic importance; often stage furniture is designed and built in highly imaginative ways in coordination with the setting to convey a special visual impact. Properties such as ashtrays, telephones, letters, and tableware are often

For Patrick Marber's *Closer,* a contemporary British drama about adult couplings and decouplings, designer Vicki Mortimer created a candle-lit mausoleum backdrop that framed the disquieting drama with its incipient mortality. Liza Walker plays Alice and Clive Owen is Dan in the 1997 English National Theatre Cottesloe production, directed by the author.

Top: Neil LaBute's *The Mercy Seat,* about a couple presumed killed in the September 11 World Trade Center attack but who were actually having a secret affair in an apartment across town, lends itself to both realistic and highly stylized stagings. Robert Jones's entirely realistic setting beautifully sets off Sinead Cusack's effusive exhilaration as Abby (with John Hannah as Ben).

Left: Alex Hard's setting for the Zurich Schauspiel-haus production of *The Mercy Seat* in the same year (2003) focuses on the situation rather than the characters, making the play – as directed by Christina Paulhofer – less personal but more intensely political.

1.

British-born Tony Walton has become, over a forty-plus-year career, one of America's premier theatre designers. In addition to his extraordinary design accomplishments in stage scenery (for which he has won three Broadway Tony Awards), Walton is noted for his work in stage costumes as well as innumerable designs for films, ballets, operas, posters, books, and record albums.

Born in Surrey in 1934, he found his way to classically oriented Radley College (a prep school near Oxford), London's Slade School of Fine Art, and, at age twenty-one, the hard-knocks post of assistant designer at a provincial theatre in Wimbledon, where he was expected to design, assistant-design, and paint scenery for a new production every week. British military service took him to Canada the following year, and upon his discharge Walton settled in New York, earning his living by designing caricatures and illustrations for *Harpers* and *Vogue* magazines. He subsequently passed the exam—in all three areas of scenery, costumes, and lighting—for admission to the United Scenic Artists,

America's sole professional union for theatre designers.

By 1957 Walton had designed his first New York play, Noel Coward's *Conversation Piece,* and by 1999 he had designed sets for more than forty New York productions, plus many more in London, Los Angeles, Seattle, New Haven, Washington, and other cities. Among his most celebrated stage designs have been the Broadway or Lincoln Center premiere productions of *A Funny Thing Happened on the*

1. Tony Walton is shown here in his New York studio, with one of his design assistants. The model for his 1998 revival of *1776,* for which he is preparing to unroll a set of plans, is to the left.

2. Walton's drawing of the wedding scene for his 1992 Broadway revival of *Guy and Dolls* is complete with characters as he imagines them in the show's finale.

3. Here is the actual wedding scene from that production of *Guys and Dolls,* directed by Jerry Zaks. (Walton won the Tony Award for this design.)

2.

3.

4.

6.

5.

Way to the Forum (for which he also designed the 1996 revival), *Pippin* (for which he received his first Tony), *Chicago, Streamers, The Real Thing, Hurlyburly, I'm Not Rappaport, Lend Me a Tenor, Grand Hotel, Six Degrees of Separation, Death and the Maiden, Laughter on the 23rd Floor, Waiting for Godot, Four Baboons Adoring the Sun, Steel Pier, Conversations with My Father,* and *The Beauty Queen of Leenane,* as well as Broadway revivals of *Anything Goes, Guys and Dolls, She Loves Me, Company,* and *1776.*

On a 1998 visit to his labyrinthine upper West Side (New York) home and studio—a virtual beehive of constant activity—this author asked Walton what he was working

on at the moment. Having prepared himself for this question at a Chinese restaurant the night before, Walton pulled from his pocket a chopsticks wrapper on which he had listed his current projects. "Let's see," he began. "At the moment I'm designing a production of *Noel and Gertie* for the Bay Street Theatre on Long Island, plus an off-Broadway production of a new play by Terrence McNally and Jon Robin Baitz called *House,* plus a production of Harold Pinter's *Ashes to Ashes* for Broadway." While catching his breath, he turned over the wrapper. "Then of course I'm also redesigning this massive *Christmas Carol* for Madison Square Garden again, plus designing the interior of the Roundabout Theatre company's new 42nd Street stagehouse. Also I'm directing a production of my wife, Gen's, new play, *Missing Footage.* I think there's more, but I ran out of room here."

In the studio wing of Walton's apartment, two design assistants—both professional designers themselves—were busily at work. One was touching up the *Ashes* model; the other was carefully cutting out some simulated tile squares to use on the model for *House.* Around the room, in addition to stacks of books, drawings, photos, scripts, and material samples, were the models of just-completed projects: the Broadway sets for *Leenane* and *1776.* The workmanship for the latter production was admirable, and one of Walton's assistants said that the ceiling moldings, which had to be precisely carved to account for the forced perspective of the illusion, had been hand-shaped by a team of specialist woodsmiths from Germany. "Getting it right in the model saves countless hours in the shops," Walton explained.

One looks in vain for a "signature style" in Walton's many works, and Walton himself

7.

8.

4. Walton's set model for *Grand Hotel* shows the orchestra's position above the play's action.

5. Here is the actual set of the play as realized in this 1989 production, directed by Tommy Tune.

6. Walton's set design for Martin McDonagh's 1998 Irish-themed off-Broadway hit *The Cripple of Inishman* beautifully captured the dank chill of rural Irish mudplaster.

7. Moldings in Walton's model for the Roundabout Theatre's 1998 revival of the musical *1776* were meticulously carved in perspective, and the furniture was precisely scaled.

8. The actual setting reverses two wall hangings but otherwise retains the balance and scale of the model.

agrees: "For me it is preferable to try and start out as a blank slate—completely available to the special nature of the piece. I hope to let the piece itself—via the director's approach to it—dictate the design," he says in his entry in *Contemporary Designers*. His amazing virtuosity over a wide range of dramatic and aesthetic styles, as well as the sureness of his technique, is illustrated in the photographs of his designs shown here.

functional in realistic plays, but they can also have aesthetic importance and are therefore carefully selected—or else specially designed. Frequently, furniture pieces or properties have considerable symbolic significance, as in the case of the thrones in Shakespeare's *Richard III* or the glass figurines in Tennessee Williams's *Glass Menagerie;* indeed, on occasion they are raised to titular metaphoric importance (in which cases their design may be enhanced), as in Elmer Rice's expressionistic play *The Adding Machine.*

The Scene Designer at Work

The scene designer's work inevitably begins with a reading and rereading of the play, normally followed by research on the play and its original period (and the periods in which it may be set), a consideration of the type of theatre in which the play is to be produced, and extensive discussions with the director and other members of the design and production team. It is usually by a mutual, collaborative process—among the director, other designers, and the technical staff—that scenic design proceeds in the modern professional and academic theatre. (We'll examine this process in more detail in the next chapter.)

This discussion phase normally proceeds, almost simultaneously, with the designer's preparation of a series of visualizations, which may begin with collected illustrations (for example, clippings from magazines, notations from historical sources, color ideas, spatial concepts) and move on to sketches, color renderings, and/or three-dimensional models. Eventually, this process results in a full set of working drawings or other materials, approved by the director and producer, that will serve as a guide for construction. Throughout the process, of course, the designer must reckon with budgetary constraints and the skills of the construction staff available to execute and install the finished design. Part architect, part engi-

neer, part accountant, and part interpretive genius, the scene designer today is one of the theatre's premier artists/craftspeople.

Lighting

The very word *theatre,* meaning "seeing place," implies the crucial function of light. Light is the basic condition for theatrical appearance. Without light, nothing can be seen.

The use of light for dramatic effect, as distinct from pure illumination, can be traced back to the earliest surviving plays: *Agamemnon,* by Aeschylus, was staged so that the watchman's spotting of the signal fire heralding Agamemnon's return to Argos coincided with the actual sunrise over the Athenian skene (stagehouse); it is also probable that the burning of Troy at the conclusion of Euripides' *Trojan Women* was staged to coincide with the sunset that reddened the Attic sky. Modern plays commonly use light in metaphoric and symbolic ways: the blinking neon light that intermittently reddens Blanche's quarters in Williams's *A Streetcar Named Desire* and the searching "follow-spot" (a swivel-mounted lighting instrument that can be pointed in any direction by an operator) demanded by Samuel Beckett to train upon the hapless, trapped characters in his *Play.*

Although it is customary to think of theatre lighting as dating from the invention of electricity, nothing could be more misleading. Lighting has always been a major theatrical consideration. In addition to coordinating the timing of their plays to the sunrise and sunset, the ancient Greeks paid a great deal of attention to the proper orientation of their theatres to take best advantage of the sun's rays. The medieval outdoor theatre, although as dependent on sunlight as was the Greek theatre, made use of several devices to redirect sunlight, including halos made of reflective metal to surround Jesus and his disciples with a focused and intensified illumination; in one production a brightly polished metal basin was held over Jesus' head to concentrate the sun's rays—and surviving instructions indicate that medieval stagehands substituted torches for the bowl in the case of cloudy skies!

It was in indoor stagings as early as the Middle Ages, however, that lighting technology attained its first significant sophistication. In a 1439 production of the *Annunciation* in Florence, one thousand oil lamps were used for illumination, plus a host of candles that were lighted by a "ray of fire" that shot through the cathedral. One can imagine the spectacle. Leonardo da Vinci designed a 1490 production of *Paradise* with twinkling stars and backlit zodiac signs on colored glass. And by the sixteenth century the great festival lighting of indoor theatres, located in manor houses and public halls, would serve as a symbol of the intellectual and artistic achievements of the Renaissance itself, a mark of the luxury, technical wizardry, and ostentatious, exuberant humanism of the times. People went to the theatres in those times simply to revel in light and escape the outside gloom—in rather the same way that Americans, from early in the twentieth century, populated air-conditioned movie theatres largely to escape the heat of summer days.

By the Renaissance, the sheer opulence of illumination was astonishing—though the entire effect was created simply from tallow, wax, and fireworks. Raphael "painted" the name of his patron, Pope Leo X, with thirteen lighted chandeliers in a 1519 dramatic production; Sebastiano Serlio inserted sparkling panes of colored glass, illuminated from behind, into his flat painted scenery to create glistening and seductive scenic effects. And, as the Renaissance spirit gave way to the lavish Royal theatre of the age of the Sun King, Louis XIV, artificial illumination—calculated to match Louis's presumed incendiary brilliance—developed apace: one 1664 presentation at Versailles featured 20,000 colored lanterns, hundreds of transparent veils and bowls of colored water, and a massive display of fireworks.

It was the invention of the gaslight in the nineteenth century and the development of electricity shortly thereafter—first in carbon arc and "limelight" electrical lighting and then in incandescence—that brought stage lighting into its modern phase and made it less strictly showy and more pertinent to individual works and dramatic action. Ease and flexibility of control are the cardinal virtues of both gas and electric lighting. By adjusting a valve, a single operator at a "gas table" could raise or dim the intensity of any individual light or of a preselected "gang" of lights—just as easily as we can raise or lower the fire on a gas range with the turn of a knob today. And, of course, with electricity—which was introduced in American theatres in 1879 and in European theatres the following year—the great fire hazard of a live flame (a danger that had plagued the theatre for centuries and claimed three buildings a year on average, including Shakespeare's Globe) was at last over. The fire crews, which were round-the-clock staff members of every major theatre in the early nineteenth century, were dismissed, and the deterioration of scenery and costumes from the heat, smoke, and carbon pollution similarly came to a halt. Incandescent lighting also had the great advantage of being fully self-starting—it did not need to be relit or kept alive by pilot lights—and it could easily be switched off, dimmed up and down, and reranged or reconnected simply by fastening and unfastening flexible wires. Within a few years of its introduction, electricity became the primary medium of stage lighting in the Western world, and great dynamo generators—for electricity was used in the theatre long before it was commercially available from municipal power supplies—were installed as essential equipment in the basements of theatres from Vienna to San Francisco.

Electricity provides an enormously flexible form of lighting. The incandescent filament is a reasonably small, reasonably cool point of light that can be focused, reflected, aimed, shaped, and colored by a great variety of devices invented and adapted for those purposes, and electric light can be trained in innumerable ways upon actors, scenery, audiences, or a combination of these to create realistic and/or atmospheric effects through dimensionality, focus, animation, distortion, diffusion, and overwhelming radiance. Today, thanks to the added sophistication of computer technology and microelectronics, it is not uncommon to see theatres with nearly a thousand lighting instruments all under the complete control of a single technician seated in a comfortable booth above the audience.

Modern Lighting Design

Today, the lighting for most productions is conceived and directly supervised by a professional lighting designer, a species of theatre artist who has appeared as a principal member of the production team only since the mid-twentieth century. By skillfully working with lighting instruments, hanging positions, angles, colors, shadows, and moment-to-moment adjustments of intensity and directionality, the lighting designer can illuminate a dramatic production in a great variety of subtle and complex ways. The manner in which the lighting designer uses the medium to blend the more rigid design elements (architecture and scenery) with the evolving patterns of the movements of the actors and the meanings of the play is normally a crucial factor in a production's artistic and theatrical success.

Visibility and *focus* are the primary considerations of lighting design: visibility ensures that the audience sees what it wants to see, and focus ensures that it sees what it is supposed to see without undue distraction. Visibility, then, is the passive accomplishment of lighting design, and focus is its active accomplishment. The spotlight, a development of the twentieth century, has fostered something

In this 1991 Adrian Hall production of *King Lear* at the American Repertory Theatre, Natasha Katz's intense downlighting keeps our attention on Edmund (Jonathan Fried), his sword drawn before his duel with Edgar (*deep background*).

akin to a revolution in staging. Contemporary productions now routinely feature a darkened auditorium (a rarity prior to the 1880s) and a deliberate effort to illuminate certain characters (or props or set pieces) more than others —in other words, to direct the audience's attention toward those visual elements that are dramatically the most significant.

Realism and *atmosphere* also are common goals of the lighting designer, and both can be achieved largely through the color and direction of lighting. Realistic lighting can be created

Individual pools of light illuminate the parasols and costumes – and the isolation – of ladies waiting for the soldiers' return at the beginning of *Much Ado about Nothing*. This 1994 Indiana Repertory Theatre production was directed by Libby Appel, with lighting design by Robert Peterson.

to appear as if emanating from familiar sources: from the sun, for example, from "practical" (real) lamps on the stage, or from moonlight, fire, streetlights, neon signs, or the headlights of moving automobiles. Atmospheric lighting, which may or may not suggest a familiar source, can be used to evoke a mood appropriate to a play's action: sparkly, for example, or gloomy, oppressive, nightmarish, austere, verdant, smoky, funereal, or regal.

Sharp, bold lighting designs are frequently employed to create highly theatrical effects — from the glittery entertainments of the Broadway musical tradition to harsher experimental stagings like those often associated with the plays and theories of Bertolt Brecht. Brecht's concept of a "didactic" theatre favors lighting that is bright, cold (uncolored), and specifically

"unmagical." Brecht suggested, in fact, that the lighting instruments themselves be made part of the setting, placed in full view of the audience; this "theatricalist" use of the lighting instruments themselves is now widespread even in nondidactic plays. Moodier plays may employ dense or unnatural colors, "gobo" filters that break light beams into shadowy fragments (such as leaf patterns), or atmospheric "fog" effects that make light appear misty, gloomy, or mysterious. The Broadway-type musical, on the other hand, often makes splashy use of banks of colored footlights and border lights, high-intensity follow-spots that track actors around the stage, "chaser" lights that flash on and off in sequence, and a near fuse-busting incandescence that makes a finale seem to burn up the stage; in fact, this traditional exploitation

Lighting designer Rainer Casper's radically contrasting lighting colors – even in the same scene – create wholly different indoor and outdoor environments in Bert Neumann's set for *The Insulted and Injured*.

of light has done as much to give Broadway the name Great White Way as have the famous billboards and marquees that line the street.

Stylized lighting effects are often used to express radical changes of mood or event; indeed, the use of lighting alone to signal a complete change of scene is an increasingly common theatrical expedient. Merely by switching from full front to full overhead lighting, for example, a technician can throw a character into silhouette and make her or his figure appear suddenly ominous, grotesque, or isolated. The illumination of an actor with odd lighting colors, such as green, or from odd lighting positions, such as from below, can create mysterious, unsettling effects. The use of follow-spots can metaphorically put a character "on the spot" and convey a specific sense of unspeakable terror. Highly expressive lighting and projections, when applied

to a production utilizing only a cyclorama, a set piece, sculpture, or stage mechanism and neutrally clad actors, can create an infinite variety of convincing theatrical environments for all but the most resolutely realistic of plays; it is here, in the area of stylization and expressive theatricality, that the modern lighting designer has made the most significant mark.

The Lighting Designer at Work

The lighting designer ordinarily conceives a lighting design out of a synthesis of many discrete elements: the play, discussions with the director and other members of the design team as to the approach or concept of the production, the characteristics of the theatre building (lighting positions, control facilities, and wiring system), the scenery and costume de-

LIGHT AS MUSIC

Light and shadow in the course of the drama achieve the same significance as a musical motif which, once stated and developed, has an infinite range of variation. Tristan's agony is sufficient motivation for carrying this kind of lighting to its greatest degree of expressiveness, and the audience, overwhelmed vicariously by the spiritual tragedy of the hero and heroine, would be disturbed by any form of stage setting which did not incorporate this element of design. The audience would really suffer for lack of the kind of staging I have indicated, because it needs to get through its eyes a kind of impression which, up to a given point, can equal the unexampled emotional power of the score. Light is the only medium which can continuously create this impression and its use is motivated and justified by the score itself.

— Adolphe Appia

signs, the movements and behavior of the actors, and the available lighting instruments. Occasionally the availability of an experienced lighting crew must also be a consideration. Because not all of these variables can be known from the outset (the stage movement, for example, may change from one day to the next right up to the final dress rehearsal), the lighting designer must be skilled at making adjustments and must have the opportunity to exercise a certain amount of control, or at least to voice concerns with regard to areas affecting lighting problems.

Ordinarily, the two major preparations required of the lighting designer are the light plot and the cue sheet. A *light plot* is a plan or series of plans showing the placement of each lighting instrument; its type, wattage, and size; its

The lighting by Peter Mumford makes Tim Hatley's setting for Noel Coward's *Private Lives* an enchanting hotel facade, whose Mediterranean-facing balconies offer the promise of an elegant – but perhaps empty – life. Alan Rickman and Lindsay Duncan star in this production on Broadway in 2002.

1.

Chris Parry's interest in lighting began in his native England, where, as a talented physics student, he was tapped to run the lighting for his high school's plays and then for several amateur theatre groups. "I had no idea at the time that you could do this for a living, though," Parry recalls, and so he began his professional life as an apprentice telephone repairman. The theatre still beckoned, however, and, while still in his early twenties, he wrote to the distinguished lighting designer Richard Pilbrow, inquiring how one might start a professional lighting career. Pilbrow suggested applying for an apprenticeship at a regional British theatre, and before long Parry had landed an electrician's post "at the very bottom rung" of the Royal Shakespeare Company's lighting department. Hanging and focusing lights for the company's many resident and guest designers was "an incredible learning experience," and working the daily changeovers from

one show to another in the company's rotating repertory schedule gave him a sure command of his craft. By the late 1970s Parry was beginning to freelance as a designer outside the company and by the early 1980s as an RSC resident designer himself, creating the lighting for major productions of the classics (*Othello, King Lear, The Plantagenets, Macbeth, Hamlet, The Winter's Tale*) as well as modern plays (*The Master Builder, Les Liaisons Dangereuses, The Blue Angel, The Crucible*) at England's two greatest theatre companies: the RSC and the Royal National Theatre.

It was the RSC *Les Liaisons* that brought Parry to the United States; when the production came to the Music Box Theatre in 1987, he received a Tony Award nomination for his lighting and a few years later moved permanently to America, where he continues to reside while designing widely in both countries. Among Parry's internationally visible productions since moving to the United States have been *The Who's Tommy* (1995), which won him the Tony Award, *Not about Nightingales* (1999), winning him another Tony nomination, and *Translations* (1995), all on Broadway, plus *Jane Eyre* in Toronto, and London productions of *The Secret Garden* (RSC, 2000) and *The Way of the World*

2.

3.

(Royal National Theatre, 1995). And for America's regional market, the very busy Parry has designed more than sixty productions for companies including the Seattle Repertory, Hartford Stage, Geffen Playhouse (Los Angeles), South Coast Repertory, La Jolla Playhouse, Milwaukee Repertory, Mark Taper Forum, Pasadena Playhouse, Oregon Shakespeare Festival, Shakespeare Theatre (Washington), Guthrie Theatre, and Yale Repertory, plus operas in Los Angeles, Houston, Lucca (Italy), and Buxton (UK). He also heads the graduate lighting program at the University of California, San Diego, and teaches master classes in New York City.

Parry considers himself half artist and half craftsman, remarking that "I still struggle as to where the art actually comes from; I was always told I wasn't 'artistic' in school . . . !" Working in his Beverly Hills, California, studio, decorated with posters from his productions and, discreetly tucked into a bookshelf, his Tony Award, he drafts detailed and comprehensive light plots for shows opening in London, Seattle, and San Diego. "Sometimes it's an agonizing

process," he admits, "and then sometimes it comes almost immediately." Three elements figure prominently in Parry's design process: the script, the director, and the set. As to the latter, "I try to make it look like the scenery and lighting were designed by the same person," he explains, aiming at a seamless integration of scenic objects and their illumination. I'm always interested in any lighting ideas the scenic designer has too—after all, he's the one who designed it, and who presumably sees the set already illuminated in his mind's eye." Parry acknowledges, however, that audiences and critics are not quick to "see" the lighting. "The curtain goes up and they say 'what a beautiful set.' But what would it look like just under work lights?" Not much.

As for the script, Parry tries to be guided by the director's vision, seeking to arrange early conversations with his directors. "Of course, some directors have very little time to give you. With Trevor Nunn or Adrian Noble [artistic directors of the Royal National Theatre and Royal Shakespeare Company, respectively] you might just get fifteen minutes. But then fifteen minutes with Trevor or Adrian can get you everything you need, whereas two hours with someone else might leave you wondering if you have anything at all!" Parry relishes directors who can make concrete assessments of how they see a scene and provide him with images as opposed to abstractions. "To say that the lighting should be 'optimistic' doesn't really help very much, does it?" he inquires,

4.

1. Parry lives and works in a pleasant, contemporary apartment in Beverly Hills, California, which is decorated with, among other things, posters and award certificates from the many shows he has designed in his career – which marked its twenty-fifth anniversary at the time of this 2001 interview.

2. At his drafting table in the studio of his apartment, Parry, using a plastic template (in green), inks a new instrument into the light plot for an upcoming production of *A Little Night Music* for Seattle's Fifth Street Theatre. On the left side of the plot, Parry has taped swatches of the basic colors he intends to use in the final plot.

3. Parry searches for an additional color from one of the several manufacturer's swatch books he keeps in his studio.

4. On the wall opposite his drafting table, Parry has taped up samples of the colors used in the costume and set designs and samples of wallpaper used in the set.

5.

answering his own question with a wry grimace. "But tell me it should look like cotton candy—well, I can do something with that. I know what that looks like, feels like, and what it means."

Parry frequently speaks of lighting as painting ("I can't

5. In a separate office, Parry, like most designers today, works out many details of his lighting design on CAD (computer-aided-design) programs on his computer.

6. Chris Parry won the coveted Tony Award for his brilliantly florid and tightly focused lighting – emphasizing the electronic atmosphere and the lighting instruments themselves – in the 1993 Broadway production of *The Who's Tommy*, a rock musical set in and around a somewhat mythical pinball parlor. Stage settings by John Arnone; costumes by David C. Woolard.

7. Toplighting – focusing lights from directly overhead – isolates the prisoners and guards, leaving some in sight and some in shadow, in Parry's lighting design for the 1999 Royal Shakespeare production of Tennessee Williams's recently rediscovered *Not about Nightingales*.

actually paint or draw, and so this is how I do it . . ."), referring to lighting instruments as "light paintbrushes." And, like a painter, he enjoys having a wide array of different brushes to work with. Designers in England, he explains, have a greater variety of instruments at their disposal than do their American counterparts, and he is often hard-pressed to find some of the specialty lights he wants, such as the supersized 2000-watt or even 5000-watt fresnels (a lamp with a broad beam), which he prefers to the banks of the more tightly focused lekos or PAR lamps most American designers use. "A large single-source instrument focused on an actor on a big stage gives one single shadow. It can feel very 'lonely,' and that's beautiful," he points out, while dozens of smaller instruments "give you dozens of smaller shadows that wash each other out." Shadows figure prominently in many of Parry's designs, as in his Broadway/Royal National Theatre

6.

production of *Not about Nightingales,* a recently rediscovered Tennessee Williams play set in a prison, for which Parry relied, at times exclusively, on selective but intense "toplighting" (lighting from directly above the stage), with dark spaces between the lighted ones to convey the isolation and control of a prison environment.

7.

And while Parry's lighting is normally quite subtle, underlining but—from the audience's viewpoint—seeming to disappear underneath the action, there are times when a production calls for big, splashy, and dominant lighting, as in his Tony-winning *The Who's Tommy,* which centers on a pinball game—a garishly illuminated object in its own right. For shows like this one, Parry designs more aggressively and enjoys having "a lot of toys" with which to work. "Light curtains"—of low-voltage, high-intensity instruments—and intense light that penetrates through the wispy smoke he uses in battle scenes are among his particular favorites.

Above all, Parry considers himself an essentially intuitive designer. When your craft is secure, "lots of things play into your creativity." He prefers setting cues during technical rehearsals rather than working them all out on paper beforehand, believing that the lighting designer needs to see and hear all the elements of the scene—actors, set, costumes, sound—before deciding what must be created to complete the picture. "You have to work fast, but it's so instinctual that you don't get time to second-guess yourself. Your first response is

8. Parry's low lighting instruments are angled upward to create colorful and expressive shadows on both the walls and the ceiling of Ming Cho Lee's grotesquely skewed set in South Coast Repertory's 2000 world premiere production of Howard Korder's *The Hollow Lands.* The play, directed by David Chambers and with costumes by Shigeru Yaji, fantasizes America's western expansion in the nineteenth century; Mark Harelik, standing on the bed, plays a spellbinding pioneer who projects his distorted visions to others – as underlined by all aspects of the production's design.

8.

9. Contrasting colors from floodlights, spotlights, and direct sources provide the distinctive design elements in Parry's Olivier-nominated 1994 production of *A Midsummer Night's Dream* at the Royal Shakespeare Company, with settings and costumes by Anthony Ward.

10. In this Old Globe (San Diego) 2000 production of *Love's Labor's Lost*, directed by Roger Rees, the patterns of James Joy's setting are created by Parry's "gobos" — filters placed in the lighting instruments to scatter and variegate the light — creating a romantically dappled effect. The ominous figure in black silhouette at bottom center is Mercade, not yet discovered by the others onstage, who will shortly prove a messenger of death.

9.

10.

usually the best," he says. Of course, it helps that he is at a point in his work where he has sufficient confidence to trust those instincts. "I'm a great believer in intuition," Parry asserts. "But when that fails, your craft is still there to support you."

wiring and connection to an appropriate dimmer; its color; and sometimes its movement, as lighting instruments are increasingly being programmed to pan, tilt, or change color by remote, motorized control. A *cue sheet* is a list of the occasions, referred to by number and keyed to the script of the play (or, in final form, the more fully annotated stage manager's script), when lights change in intensity or color or move. The light plot and cue sheet are developed in consultation with the director and other members of the design team, who may take major or minor roles in the consultation, depending on their interests and expertise. Inasmuch as some productions use hundreds of lighting instruments and require thousands of individual cues, the complexity of these two documents can be extraordinary; weeks and months may go into their preparation.

The lighting designer works with a number of different sorts of lighting instruments and must know the properties of each instrument well enough to anticipate fully how it will perform when hung and focused on the stage. Few theatres have the time or space flexibility to permit much on-site experimentation in lighting design; thus the development of the light plot and cue sheet takes place primarily in the imagination and, where possible, in workshop or free experimentation apart from the working facility. This requirement places a premium on the designer's ability to predict instrument performance from various distances and angles and with various color elements installed; it also demands a sharp awareness of how various lights will reflect off different surfaces.

Once the light plot is complete, the lights are mounted (hung) in appropriate positions, attached to the theatre's wiring system (or wired separately), "patched" to proper dimmers, focused (aimed) in the desired directions, and colored by the attachment of frames containing plastic color media. Ideally, the stage setting is finished and in position when all of this occurs, but it rarely works this way,

Top: The ellipsoidal reflector spotlight (sometimes called "leko" after its two inventors, Joe Levy and Ed Kook) is the lighting designer's workhorse instrument, offering an intense and precisely focused circular light beam that is easily reconfigured by shutters (which make straight-line cuts "shuttering" the beam), irises (which diminish the beam's diameter), gobos (which create silhouette patterns of any type), and color media. The ETC (Electronic Theatre Control) company's Source Four model is an outstanding example of such an instrument, with interchangeable lens tubes and a rotating barrel.

Bottom: Lights are controlled by a board that can turn individual instruments – or hundreds at a time – on, off, or to any mid-level with a simple button or lever. ETC's Obsession II control board, with its ergonomic lines and Pentium processor, is a leader among such devices, with which a single operator can control literally tens of thousands of individual lighting changes during a production.

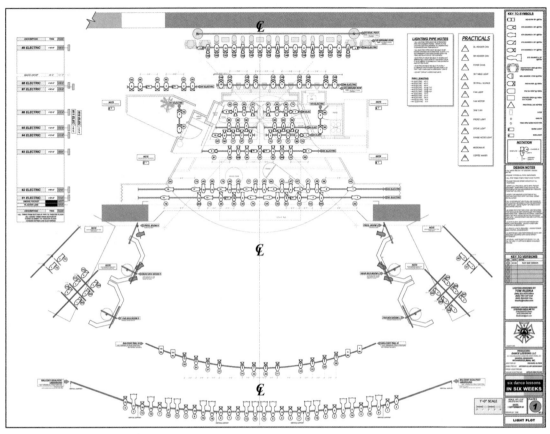

Shown here is Tom Ruzika's light plot for the 2003 Broadway production of *Six Dance Lessons in Six Weeks* (reduced in size to fit this page). You are looking down from the theatre's ceiling; the stage is at the top of the drawing, and the audience area (the "house") is at the bottom. Gray rectangles on each side indicate the vertical sides of the proscenium; the "CL" symbol is the center line of the stage and house, and each bomb-shaped symbol is an individual and specific lighting instrument. "Practicals" are lighting or other working electrical instruments that are part of the scenery but are also connected ("wired") into the lighting control system (the "board"). The light plot tells the electrical staff where instruments are to be hung, where (roughly) they are to be aimed, and how they are wired to the board.

particularly on Broadway, where theatres are often rented only a short time before the opening performance. Once the instruments are in place and functioning, the lighting designer begins setting the intensities of each instrument for each cue, a painstaking process involving the recording of thousands of precise numerical directions on a series of track sheets (or charts) for the technicians who must effect the cues.

Computer technology has vastly simplified this process for most theatres; with or without computers, however, much time and care inevitably go into this process, which is vital to the development and execution of a fully satisfying lighting design. Finally, the lighting designer presides over the working and timing of the cues, making certain that in actual operation the lights shift as subtly or as boldly, as grandly

Shown here is Tom Ruzika's lighting as seen in the actual production of *Six Dance Lessons*. The actors are Mark Hamill and Polly Bergen; the setting is by Roy Christopher.

or as imperceptibly, as is appropriate for the play's action and for the design aesthetic.

It is out of thousands of details, most of which are pulled together in a single final week, that great lighting design springs. Gradations of light, difficult to measure in isolation, can have vastly differing impacts in the moment-to-moment focus and feel of a play. Because light is a medium rather than an object, audience members are rarely if ever directly aware of it; they are aware only of its illuminated target. Therefore, the lighting designer's work is poorly understood by the theatergoing public at large. But everyone who works professionally in the theatre—from the set and costume designers to the director to the actor—knows what a crucial role lighting plays in the success of the theatre venture. As the

Old Actor says as he departs the stage in off-Broadway's longest-running hit, *The Fantasticks:* "Remember me—in light!" The light that illuminates the theatre also glorifies it; it is a symbol of revelation—of knowledge and humanity—upon which the theatrical impulse finally rests.

Costume

Costume has always been a major element in the theatrical experience; it is a vehicle for the "dressing up" that actors and audiences alike have always considered a requirement for the fullest degree of theatrical satisfaction. Costume serves both ceremonial and illustrative functions.

The costumes by Gabriel Berry for Andrei Serban's 2003 production of Shakespeare's romantic fantasy *Pericles* at the American Repertory Theatre are, like the play, colorful, exotic, and sensual. Set and video design are by Dan Nutu, and lighting is by Beverly Emmons; the actors are Will Lebow as Cleon, Karen MacDonald as his murderous wife, and Gilbert Owuor as a henchman.

The Functions of Costume

The first theatrical costumes were essentially ceremonial vestments. The himation (a gown-like costume) of the early Aeschylean actor was derived from the garment worn by the priest-chanter of the dithyramb; the comic and satyr costumes, with their use of phalluses and goat-skins, were likewise derived from more primitive god-centered rites. The priests who first enacted the *Quem Queritis* trope (liturgical text) in medieval Europe simply wore their sacred albs, hooded to indicate an outdoor scene but otherwise unaltered. And the actors of the classic Japanese nō drama even today wear costumes that relate more to spiritual sources than to secular life. Ancient and original uses of costuming have served primarily to separate the actor from the audience, to "elevate" the actor to a quasi-divine status. The thick-soled footwear (kothurnoi) worn by Greek actors in the fourth century B.C. were calculated to enhance this ceremonial effect by greatly increasing the height of the wearers, thereby "dressing them up" both figuratively and literally.

The shift of stress in costuming from a "dressing up" of the actor to a defining of the character came about gradually in the theatre's history. In the Elizabethan theatre, the costumes often had an almost regal, ceremonial quality because the acting companies frequently solicited the cast-off raiment of the nobility; English theatre of this time was known throughout Europe for the splendor of its costuming, but apparently little effort was made to suit costume to characterization. Moreover, it was not unusual in Shakespeare's time for some actors to wear contemporary garb onstage while others wore costumes expressive of the period of the play. In Renaissance Italy, costuming developed a high degree of stylization in the commedia dell'arte, in which each of the recurring characters wore a distinctive and arresting costume that instantly signified a particular age, intelligence, and disposition. The same characters and the same costumes can be seen today in contemporary commedia productions, and they are still as eloquent and entertaining as they were four hundred years ago.

Modern costuming acquired much of its present character during the eighteenth and nineteenth centuries, when certain realistic considerations took control of the Western theatre. These centuries witnessed a great deal of radical social change that led to, among other things, the widespread acceptance of science and its methods and a great fascination with detail and accuracy. These trends coalesced in the European (and eventually the American) theatre with a series of productions in which historical accuracy served as the guiding principle. For the first time, painstaking effort ensured that the design of every costume in a play (and every prop and every set piece as well) accorded with an authentic "period" source. Thus a production of *Julius Caesar* would be intensively researched to re-create the clothing worn in Rome in the first century A.D., a *Hamlet* would be designed to mirror the records of medieval Denmark, and a *Romeo and Juliet* would seek to re-create, in detail, the world of Renaissance Verona.

The movement toward historical accuracy and the devotion with which it was pursued led ultimately to a widespread change in the philosophy of costume design that persists to this day, for although historical accuracy itself is no longer the ultimate goal of costume design, stylistic consistency and overall design control have proven to be lasting principles. Costuming today stresses an imaginative aesthetic creativity as well as a coordinated dramatic suitability; thus the influence of realism, with its attendant emphasis on historical accuracy, has fostered coherent and principled design in place of the near anarchy that once prevailed.

Modern costume design might then be said to serve four separate functions. First, in concert with its ancient origins, it retains at least a hint of that ceremonial magic once conjured by ancient priests and shamans. Costume, even today, bespeaks a primordial theatricality. As Theoni Aldredge said of the costumes for *A Chorus Line,* they "had to look real and yet theatrical enough for an audience to say, 'Okay, I'm in the theatre now.'"

Second, in aggregate, the costumes of a play show us what sort of world we are asked to enter, not only by its historical place and period but by implication its social and cultural values as well. The word *costume* has the same root as *custom* and *customary;* as such it indicates the "customary" wearing apparel (or the "habitual habit") of persons living in a particular world. For example, the Mexican American characters in Luis Valdez's *Zoot Suit,* set in the 1940s, are seen as virtual extensions of their overly long pegged trousers and looping watch chains. Tennessee Williams, in *A Streetcar Named Desire,* specifically directed the poker players to wear shirts of "bright primary colors," to contrast their primary sexuality with Blanche DuBois's dead (and gay) husband, whom the dramatist had named "Allan Grey." The ensemble of costumes in a play production generally reveals the production's style, at least as it emanates from the play's characters.

Third, the individual costumes can express the specific individuality of each character's role; they reveal at a glance, for example, the character's profession, wealth, age, class status, tastes, and self-image. More subtly, costume can suggest the character's vices, virtues, and

Plays often indicate design colors for symbolic importance. In *A Streetcar Named Desire*, playwright Tennessee Williams emphasizes the ethnic pride of card-playing New Orleans workingmen by specifying that they wear "bright primary colors," while the delicate lady who visits them has the name of Blanche – French for "white" – and she dreams of her deceased gay husband, named Grey. In this 2002 London production, designer Bunny Christie underlines Williams's color symbolism by clothing Glenn Close, as Blanche, in a white dress, white hat, and sheer white gloves and accessorizing her with a sheer white handkerchief and white rosebuds in her hair.

IMPORTANCE OF SMALL DETAILS

The task of subtly distorting uniformity, without destroying the desired illusion, is a difficult one. Anton Chekhov's play *The Three Sisters* presents a case in point. The characters of the male players are clearly defined in Chekhov's writing, but because the men are all wearing military uniforms they are theoretically similar in appearance. One of the few ways in which the designer can help to differentiate between characters is by the alteration of proportion; alterations such as these, which do not show enough from the "front" to make the uniforms seem strange to the audience, can be extremely effective, as well as helpful to the actor. In a London production of *The Three Sisters*, Sir Michael Redgrave wore a coat with a collar that was too low; Sir John Gielgud one that was too high. No one in the audience was unaware of the characters' individuality, the talents of these actors being what they are, but the small details added to the scope of their performances.

— Motley

hidden hopes — or fears. By the judicious use of color, shape, fabric, and even the *sound* a fabric makes, costume designers can imbue every character with individual distinctiveness, particularly in contrast to the standard dress in which other characters of his or her class are seen. When Hamlet insists on wearing his "inky cloak" in his uncle's presence, he silently signifies his refusal to accept his uncle's authority; he refuses to "fit" into the world of the Danish court, which becomes both a mark of Hamlet's character and a significant action in the play. When Monsieur Jourdain in Molière's *The Bourgeois Gentleman* dons his fancy suit with the upside-down flowers and, later, his Turkish gown and grotesque turban, he is proclaiming (foolishly) to his peers that he is a person of elegance and refinement. And Estragon's unlaced shoes in *Waiting for Godot* represent—pathetically, to be sure—his great wish to be unfettered, not "tied to Godot" but simply free, fed, and happy.

Finally, the costume serves as wearable clothing for the actor! For a costume, of course, is indeed clothing; it must be functional as well as meaningful and aesthetic. The actor does not model his costume; he walks in it, sits in it, duels in it, dances in it, tumbles downstairs in it. Indeed, unless the character is a prisoner or a pauper, we are supposed to believe that he chose the costume himself and really *wants* to wear it! The costume designer thus cannot be content merely to draw pictures on paper but must also design workable, danceable, *actable* clothing, for which cutting, stitching, fitting, and quick changing are as important considerations as color coordination and historical context. Thus costume designers generally collaborate very closely with the actors they dress.

The Costume Designer at Work

The costume designer works primarily with fabric, which comes in a variety of materials and weaves and can be cut, shaped, stitched, colored, and draped in innumerable ways. Jewels, armor, feathers, fur, hair (real or simulated), and metallic ornamentation also commonly figure into costume design. The costume designer both selects and oversees the acquiring or building of costume elements, usually in combination. The costumes for some plays are assembled entirely out of items ready at hand. For contemporary plays with modern settings, the costumes are often selected from the actors' own wardrobes or from department store racks. Sometimes a costume designer will acquire clothing from thrift shops and used-clothing stores, particularly for plays set in the recent past; indeed, this is not unusual even for high-budget professional productions. In one celebrated instance, Louis Jouvet appealed to the citizens of Paris to donate costumes for the posthumous premiere of Jean Giraudoux's *The Madwoman of Chaillot,* and the clothing that poured into the Athénée theatre for that brilliant 1945 Parisian production signaled to the world that France had survived the scourge of the Nazi Occupation with its devotion to the theatre intact.

Even in a "fully designed, fully built" production, some costume elements are usually purchased, rented, or taken from costume storage; shoes, for example, are not ordinarily built from scratch for theatrical productions. Nonetheless, it is the productions that are designed

Costumes are not always created from ordinary fabrics. Here, Janet Swenson has designed a garment of fishnet and flesh-colored latex, augmented by seashells, flotsam and jetsam, mottle-dyed spandex stretched over pieces of plastic, and hand-crocheted pieces of "hairy yarn" to create the blistered, bee-stung, and "fishified" flesh of the monstrous Caliban, as performed (and in part codesigned) by David Ivers for the 2001 Utah Shakespearean Festival production of *The Tempest.*

and built for a given set of performances that test the full measure of the costume designer's imagination and ability. In these productions, the costume designer can create a top-to-toe originality. The comprehensive design for such a production begins with a series of sketches and material choices—these usually proceed

1.

For more than forty years, Patricia Zipprodt—working mainly in the sunny Greenwich Village penthouse apartment pictured on these pages—designed award-winning costumes for New York and regional theatres as well as opera and ballet companies, winning Tony Awards in design for the original Broadway productions of *Fiddler on the Roof, Cabaret,* and *Sweet Charity.* She also received dozens of other awards and nominations for her fifty-five

Broadway productions, including the world or American premieres of *Sunday in the Park with George, The Blacks, Plaza Suite, Shogun, Pippin, Chicago, Alice in Wonderland, Fools, Brighton Beach Memoirs, The Little Foxes, Mack and Mabel, 1776, Zorba, King of Hearts,* and *Picasso at the Lapin Agile* and revivals of *My Fair Lady* and her own *Cabaret* and *Fiddler on the Roof.* Additionally, she found time to design for films, television, ballet, opera, and ice skating spectaculars; to head the MFA costume program at Brandeis University; and to help found the National Theatre of the Deaf. Sadly, Ms. Zipprodt died in the summer of 1998, just as this photo essay was published in a previous edition of this book and within months of what turned out to be her final design, the Wilshire Theatre (Los Angeles) production of *Picasso at the Lapin Agile,* which the *Variety* critic praised as

1. Shown here is costume designer Patricia Zipprodt in her New York studio. Behind her are masks and posters from her breakthrough production of Jean Genet's *The Blacks,* which she designed off-Broadway in 1962.

2. One of Zipprodt's most masterful designs was the Broadway *Sunday in the Park with George,* the first half of which details the life and, in part, the work of French artist Georges Seurat.

3. The rich textures of Zipprodt's costumes, shown in this detail, brought to life not only the play's period but Seurat's painting — the subject of the act — *La Grande Jatte.*

2.

3.

"evoking a wonderful sense of being in another time and place."

Born in Chicago, where she studied painting as a high school student at an annex of the famous Art Institute, Zipprodt headed for Wellesley College for premedical studies. After graduation, however, she moved to New York rather than going on to medical school. There she waited on tables at Schrafft's and ushered at Carnegie Hall to pay the rent; at the same time, she resumed her painting studies at the Art Students League. But ballet and theatre soon competed for her attention, and discovering that "a play is a painting that moves," Zipprodt changed her medium from paint to fabric. After taking some classes at the Fashion Institute of Technology, she embarked on what was to become a legendary career. Beginning right at the top, she started her career by designing the highly successful Broadway production of Gore Vidal's *Visit*

4.

to a Small Planet in 1957, then two more Broadway shows the same year (*The Potting Shed* and *The Rope Dancers*), but all of these were small-cast, realistic modern plays, which Zipprodt termed "go to Macy's" jobs. Her original talent more fully emerged in the celebrated off-

Broadway production of Jean Genet's *The Blacks* in 1962, which led to increasingly important assignments, ranging from avant-garde theatre to major Broadway musicals—particularly those directed and choreographed by Bob Fosse, for whom she became an inextricable professional partner.

ZIPPRODT AT WORK: 1957–1998

Zipprodt's achievements span virtually every dramatic style, but she is best known for highly textured fabrics, aesthetically harmonious color balances, and meticulous research. Her working method begins with an assemblage of a huge "bible" of preliminary drawings and fabric swatches ("I think I must have done at least eighteen different sketches of the Tevye family [for *Fiddler on the Roof*], just to get going on them and find out who they were," she said). Zipprodt selected her fabrics—which included cottons, rayons, silks, gold-threaded brocades,

5.

4. In 1998, forty-one years after her Broadway design debut, Zipprodt designed three productions for Washington's Arena Stage, including the one pictured here: Kaufman and Hart's classic and eccentric American comedy *You Can't Take It with You*, directed by Douglas C. Wager.

5. Zipprodt's collection of fabrics included literally thousands of swatches, which she kept organized in a wall-sized color-coded "card catalogue" that formed the heart of her New York design studio.

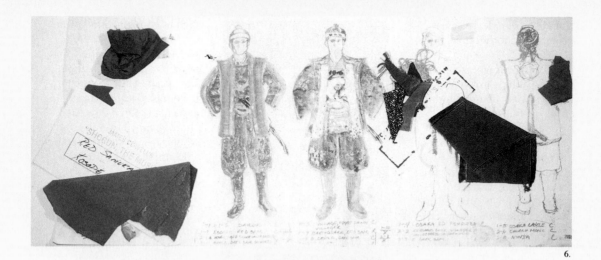

6.

tie-dyes, muslins, leather—from the thousands she kept on file in a wall cabinet in her studio. For color palettes, Zipprodt assembled onto a single sheet of black construction paper the major color swatches in each scene, to assess their harmony and avoid color clashes. Considering the number of costumes involved in a major production—her *Shogun* had over 350—helps explain the importance of these steps.

Zipprodt marveled at the evolution of costume construction shops, which handle the cutting, stitching, dyeing, and assemblage of costumes and are better now than at any time in memory: "What we're having now is a renaissance of skilled artisans." And she appreciated the ensemble work that theatre artistry provides. "I love the process. I think we are very privileged people . . . to be able to start something every time and not know what we are going to do . . . [to] put a whole new network of people together and start again on the process. It is thrilling to work constantly and collaboratively in that kind of newness and fresh discovery, because who else has that opportunity, except those of us in the theatre?"

6. Zipprodt collected swatches and paint samples on a single "color palette" for each scene in the plays she designed so that she could keep track of color complementarity and balance for each one. This example is from *Shogun*.

7. For the Broadway musical *Shogun*, Zipprodt designed over 350 costumes, many with fabrics purchased in Japan. This sketch was one of hundreds in her collection.

7.

hand in hand—based on a thorough knowledge of the play, a clear agreement with the director on interpretation and style, research into necessary historical sources, and a firm understanding of the production monies and "build time" available to the costume shop. Generally, a separate costume sketch is made for each character, although choruses and extras are sometimes represented in a single sketch. Once approved, the sketches are developed into full-color renderings with sample fabric swatches attached. Construction details are frequently included on the rendering itself so that a single document conveys both the general look and specific construction of each costume.

The purchase of fabric is of course a crucial stage in costuming, for fabric is the basic medium of the costumer's art. Texture, weight, color, suppleness, and response to draping, dyeing, folding, crushing, twirling, and twisting are all considerations. Velvet and velveteen, silks and woolens are the costumer's luxury fabrics; cottons, felt, burlap, and even painted canvas are less expensive and often appropriate for theatrical use. Coloring, "aging" (making a new fabric appear old and used), and detailing are often achieved with dyes, appliqués, and embroidery and sometimes with paint, glues, and other special treatments (for example, the costume designers Motley—three women working under a single professional name—simulate leather by rubbing thick felt with moist yellow soap and spraying it down with brown paints). Frequently, of course, fabrics with designs

Frances Kenny's wedding dress in Alfred Uhry's *Last Night of Ballyhoo* has, like wedding dresses everywhere, an archetypal meaning, projecting marriage and everything that goes (and goes away) with it. Blair Sams plays the bride-to-be, with Guilford Adams and Kandis Capell, at South Coast Repertory in 2003. Scenery is by Michael Olich and lighting by Tom Ruzika.

Bold colors suggest fantasy realms, particularly in theatre for children. The gilt mask and costume, the shining red rectangle held by elegant masked stagehands, and the deep purple hues on the floor and sky were designed by Jeremy Herbert (sets) and Kandis Cook (masks and costumes) for the 2004 Royal Shakespeare Company production of *Beauty and the Beast*. Adam Levy plays the beast and Aoife McMahon the beauty in this show, intended for "seven-year-olds and upward."

printed, embossed, or woven in are purchased for women's costumes or for male period attire.

The cutting, fitting, draping, and stitching of original costumes are equally important steps in costume design. Most designers are very involved with all these procedures, for the cutting of a fabric determines the manner in which it drapes and moves, and the fitting and draping of a costume determine its shape and silhouette. Needless to say, cutters, stitchers, and drapers are full-time professionals in the theatre, and the designer must work in close collaboration with them to achieve worthy results. Fitting and stitching (as well as refitting, restitching, and often re-refitting and re-restitching) are part of the obligatory and

time-consuming backstage process by which the costume becomes a wearable garment for the actor and the actor "grows into" the theatrically costumed characterization.

Finally, the accessories of costume can greatly affect the impact of the basic design; occasionally they may even stand out in such a way as to "make" the costume or to obliterate it. Hairstyles (including beards and mustaches) and headdresses, because they frame the actor's face, convey a visual message every time the actor speaks a line; they are obviously of paramount importance. Jewelry, sashes, purses, muffs, and other adornments and badges of various sorts have considerable dramatic impact insofar as they "read" from the audience—

that is, insofar as the audience can see them clearly and understand what they may signify about the character. The lowly shoe, if unwisely chosen, can destroy the artistry of a production, either by being unsuitable for the character or style of the play or by being so badly fitted (or so unwieldy) that the actor exhibits poor posture or even stumbles about the stage.

Whether arrived at through design and fabrication or through careful selection from the Army surplus store, good costume design creates a sense of character, period, style, and theatricality out of wearable garments. In harmony with scenery, makeup, and lighting and with the play's interpretation and performance, costuming can have its maximum impact in a subtle way—by underlining the play's meaning and the characters' personalities—or it can scream for attention and sometimes even become the "star of the show." Not a few musicals have succeeded primarily because the audience "came out whistling the costumes," as a Shubert Alley phrase reminds us. Certainly the magnificently attired principals of Chinese Opera, the gloriously patchworked Arlecchino of the commedia dell'arte, and the stunningly garbed black-and-white mannequins of Cecil Beaton's creation in *My Fair Lady* have dominated stages past and present. But even in the most naturalistic drama, well-designed and well-chosen costumes can exert a magical theatrical force, lending a special magnitude to the actor's and the playwright's art.

Makeup

Makeup, which is essentially the design of the actor's face, occupies a curiously paradoxical position in the theatre. In much modern production, certainly in the realistic theatre, makeup seems sorely neglected. It tends to be the last design technology to be considered; indeed, it is often applied for the first time at the final dress rehearsal—and sometimes not until just before the opening performance. Indeed, makeup is the only major design element whose planning and execution are often left entirely to the actor's discretion. And yet, ironically, makeup is one of the archetypal arts of the theatre, absolutely fundamental to the origins of drama. The earliest chanters of the dithyramb, like the spiritual leaders of primitive tribes today, invariably made themselves up—probably by smearing their faces with blood or the dregs of wine—in preparation for the performance of their holy rites; their resulting makeup subsequently inspired the Greek tragic and comic masks that are today the universal symbols of theatre itself. The ancient art of face painting remains crucial to the Chinese Opera, as well as to other traditional Asian, African, and Native American theatre forms.

The reason for makeup's paradoxical role resides in the changing emphasis of theatre aims. Makeup, like costuming, serves both ceremonial and illustrative functions. The illustrative function of makeup is unquestionably the more obvious one today—so much so that we often forget its ceremonial role entirely. Illustrative makeup is the means by which the actor changes her or his appearance to resemble that of the character—or at least the appearance of the character as author, director, and actor imagine it. Makeup of this sort is particularly useful in helping to make a young actor look older or an old one look younger and in making an actor of any age resemble a known historical figure or a fictitious character whose appearance is already set in the public imagination. Makeup gives Cyrano his great nose and Bardolph his red one; it reddens *Macbeth*'s "bleeding captain" and blackens Laurence Olivier's Othello; it turns the college sophomore into the aged Prospero, the Broadway dancer into one of T. S. Eliot's cats, and Miss Cathy Rigby into Master Peter Pan. Artificial scars, deformities, bruises, beards, wigs, sunburn, frostbite, and scores of other facial embellishments, textures, and shadings can contribute significantly to realistic stagecraft when needed or desired.

A subtler use of makeup, but still within the realistic mode, is aimed at the evocation of psychological traits through physiognomic clues: the modern makeup artist may try to suggest character by exaggerating or distorting the actor's natural eye placement, the size and shape of her mouth, the angularity of her nose, or the tilt of her eyebrows. There can be no question that we do form impressions of a character's inner state on the basis of observable physical characteristics—as Caesar notices and interprets Cassius's "lean and hungry look," so do we. And the skilled makeup artist can go far in enhancing the psychological texture of a play by the imaginative use of facial shapings and shadings.

Still another use of makeup, also within the realistic and practical spectrum, seeks merely to simplify and embolden the actor's features in order to make them distinct and expressive to every member of the audience. Using a theatre term mentioned earlier, this is known as creating a face that "reads" to the house—a face that conveys its fullest expression over a great distance. To achieve this effect the makeup artist exaggerates highlights and shadows and sharply defines specific features such as wrinkles, eyelashes, eyebrows, and jawlines. Such simplified, emboldened, and subtly exaggerated makeup, combined with stage lighting, creates an impression of realism far greater than any that could be achieved by makeup or lighting alone;

Makeup reflects ancient roots. These young African women have applied bold geometric face paint in a centuries-old design for their performance of a traditional dance-drama of the Ivory Coast based on an ancient hunting ritual. The design, originally intended not merely to entertain an audience but to suggest a magical transformation into the spirit realm, continues to carry at least the resonance of that meaning today.

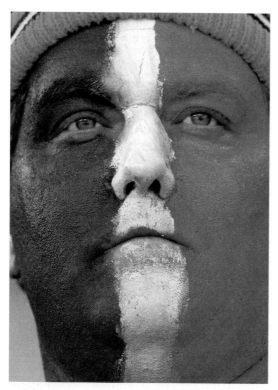

Makeup has a ritual and power-enhancing aspect in Western daily life as well. Here a Cleveland Browns fan, following tribal traditions of which he may be wholly unaware, has "war-painted" his face to provide what he might imagine as spiritual support for his team as it plays the archrival Cincinnati Bengals in 2003. Similarly, football players often paint black grease swipes beneath their eyes, and soldiers paint brown and green splotches on their faces; although these colorations are ostensibly to prevent glare and provide camouflage, they are no doubt also intended to convey fiercer, even superhuman images to their adversaries.

the chanters of the dithyramb—and the face painting of the ancient Chinese actor—that endowed them with the same aspect of spiritual transcendence that warpaint provides for the celebrant of tribal rituals: by making himself "up," the actor was preparing to ascend to a higher world; he was self-consciously assuming something of the power and divinity of the gods, and he was moreover offering to guide the audience on a divine adventure.

Today one still sees some obvious examples of such traditional makeup and "making up," particularly in European and Asian theatre. The makeup of the circus and the classic mime, two formats that developed in Europe out of the masked commedia dell'arte of centuries past, both use bold colors: white, black, and sometimes red for the mimist and an even wider spectrum for the circus clown. Avant-garde and expressionist playwrights also frequently utilize similar sorts of abstracted makeup, as does French dramatist Jean Genet in *The Blacks* (which features black actors in clownish whiteface) and German playwright Peter Handke (whose *Kaspar* features stylized facial painting similar to Genet's conception). And Asian theatre has always relied on the often dazzling facial coloring (and manelike wigs and beards) of certain characters in Japanese kabuki, Indian kathakali, and Chinese Opera—not to mention the violently expressive makeup often seen in contemporary avant-garde productions in Tokyo. The American theatre, which so far has witnessed only a small sampling of stylized makeup, is perhaps due for an awakening to this fascinating approach to theatrical design.

In most cases, makeup and hairstyle design fall to the costume designer, whose final renderings include all aspects of the character's appearance. But because the actual makeup is normally applied night after night by each actor, the costume designer, director, and actor often collaborate on the precise makeup details. In the Broadway production of *Cats*, for example, John Napier designed the makeup for each "cat" along with its costume and worked with each actor to "tweak" that design for

in fact, most directors and actors consider a minimum level of makeup to be a necessity, if only to prevent the actor from looking washed out in the glare of the stage lights.

Yet none of these realistic or practical uses of makeup truly touch upon its original theatrical use, which was aimed at announcing the actor as a performer and at establishing a milieu for acting that was neither realistic nor practical but rather supernatural, mysterious, and calculatedly theatrical. It was the ritual makeup of

Basic makeup consists of a foundation, color shadings, and various special applications. The foundation is a basic color that is applied thinly and evenly to the face and neck and sometimes to other parts of the body as well. Creme makeup, formerly (and still commonly) known as greasepaint, is a traditional foundation material; a highly opaque and relatively inexpensive skin paint, it comes in a variety of colors. Cake makeup, or "pancake" as it is also known, is another type of foundation; it is less messy than creme but also less flexible. Cake makeup comes in small plastic cases and is applied with a damp sponge. Most theatrical foundation colors are richer and deeper than the actor's normal skin color so as to counteract the white and blue tones of stage lights.

Color shading defines the facial structure and exaggerates its dimensions so as to give the face a sculptured appearance from a distance; ordinarily, the least imposing characteristics of the face are put in shadow and the prominent features are highlighted. Shading colors – universally called "liners" – come in both creme and cake form and are usually chosen to harmonize with the foundation color, as well as with the color of the actor's costume and the color of the lighting. Shadows are made with darker colors and highlights with lighter ones; both are applied with small brushes and blended into the foundation. Rouge, a special color application used to redden lips and cheeks, is usually applied along with the shading colors. When greasepaints are used, the makeup must be dusted with makeup powder to "set" it and prevent running. A makeup pencil is regularly used to darken eyebrows and also to accentuate eyes and facial wrinkles.

Special applications may include false eyelashes or heavy mascara, facial hair (beards and mustaches, ordinarily made from crepe wool), nose putty and various other prosthetic materials, and various treatments for aging, wrinkling, scarring, and otherwise disfiguring the skin. A well-equipped actor has a makeup kit stocked with glue (spirit gum and liquid latex), solvents, synthetic hair, wax (to mask eyebrows), and hair whiteners – in addition to the standard foundation and shading colors – to create a wide variety of makeup effects.

maximum individual expression. For highly complicated makeup, however, specialist designers may be employed, such as Jon Dodd, who designed the beast's prosthetics in *Beauty and the Beast* in collaboration with costume designer Ann Hould-Ward, and Jean Begin, who designed the highly stylized makeup of the Cirque du Soleil's *Saltimbanco*. Specialists in hair and wig design are also engaged for major Broadway productions, such as David H. Lawrence for *Guys and Dolls,* Angela Gari for *Carousel,* and Paul Huntley for *Once upon a Mattress* and *Laughter on the 23rd Floor.* Still, makeup, because it must be reapplied for every performance, also relies in most cases on the actor's ability to execute the design—and the makeup kit is a fundamental part of each actor's professional equipment.

The realistic and symbolic functions of makeup are probably always combined to some extent in the theatre, for even the most stylized makeup is ultimately based on the human form and even the most realistic makeup conveys an obvious theatricality. The theatre, after all, is never very far from human concerns, nor is it ever so immersed in the ordinary that it is completely mistaken for such. When the American actor sits at a makeup table opening little bottles and tubes, moistening Chinese brushes, and sharpening eyebrow pencils, more is going on than simple, practical face making: atavistic forces are at work, linking the actor not merely to the imagined physiognomy of his or her character or to the demands of facial projection in a large arena but also, and more fundamentally, to the primitive celebrants who in ages past painted their faces to assure the world that they were leaving their temporal bodies and boldly venturing into the exalted domain of gods.

Sound Design

Music and sound effects have been in use in the theatre since ancient times; Aristotle considered music one of the six essential components of tragedy, and offstage thunder, trumpet "flourishes" and "tuckets," and "a strange hollow and confused noise" are all called for in Shakespeare's original stage directions. Before the electronic age, theatres were routinely equipped with such devices as rain drums (axis-mounted barrels that, partly filled with pebbles or dried seeds, made rain sounds when revolved), thundersheets (hanging sheets of tin that rumbled ominously when rattled), and thunder runs (sloping wooden troughs down which cannonballs rolled and eventually crashed). Since 1900, most theatres have also used an electric telephone ringer (a battery-powered bell mounted on a piece of wood) and a door slammer (a miniature doorframe and door, complete with latch) to simulate the sounds of domestic life. All of these "sound effects" were ordinarily created by an assistant stage manager, among many other duties. But the development of audio recording and playback technologies in the 1970s and 1980s has led to a virtual revolution in the area of sound design and the emergence of an officially designated sound designer in theatres around the world. As with musical underscoring in cinema and sound balancing and enhancement in rock concerts, theatre sound is now almost entirely an electronic art.

Augmented sound is now routinely used in theatrical performances. Musical theatre and larger theatres increasingly employ electronic sound enhancement to reinforce the actors' voices and create a "louder than life" sonic ambiance for certain plays; in such cases the actors usually wear miniature wireless microphones (ordinarily concealed in their hair). The use of live or recorded offstage sounds may establish locale (such as foghorns), time of day (midnight chimes), time of year (birdsong), weather conditions (thunder and rain), and onstage or offstage events in the play (a ringing telephone, an arriving taxi, an angel crashing through the ceiling). Music, as well as sound, is often used to evoke a mood, support an emotion, intensify an action, or provide a transition into or between scenes. Stage

sounds can be realistic (an ambulance siren), stylized (an increasingly amplified heartbeat), stereophonically localized (an airplane crossing overhead from one side of the stage to the other), or pervasive and "in-your-head" (a buzzing mosquito). Music accompanying a play can be composed for the production and played "live" during the performance or derived from (legally acquired and paid-for) copyrighted recordings, which are then played back through a theatre's sound system (or, sometimes, through onstage "prop" boom boxes). Naturally, many combinations are possible. The sound designer designs and oversees the implementation of all of these elements, and, particularly if she or he is also the play's musical composer, this work may be of immense importance in the overall production.

Sound design has rapidly escalated in importance over the past two decades as playwrights and directors have sought to incorporate the new sound technologies that have swiftly expanded the theatrical potential, first with audio tape-recording, which permitted accurate recording and playback; then with audio cartridges, which provided exact cuing of individual sounds; and most recently with digital samplers, which permit an operator to program dozens of individually recorded sounds onto a control keyboard, where each can be instantly recalled and played, individually or in any combination, simply by pressing the appropriate keys, which are, moreover, volume responsive, as are those on a piano. Almost any sound can be programmed into a sampler, except for gunshots—which are usually performed "live," with blanks, because they are too loud for most sound systems and all but impossible to synchronize with the necessarily simultaneous fireflash.*

Contemporary sound design is not without its detractors. The electronic amplification of speaking and singing voices in most Broadway

---

Note: Any stage gunshot, even with blanks, must meet precise conditions as specified by authorized fire and safety officers.

musicals, and many nonmusical plays as well, is often derided by critics who prefer—or claim to prefer—the more natural unamplified sound. The sound mixing board, which is now commonplace in the back orchestra rows of most Broadway and larger regional theatres, is a visual reminder of the modern technology that some feel mediates the "liveness" of "live theatre." Extended musical underscoring in some plays raises objections that it turns drama into cinema and suffuses the articulation of ideas in the syrup of generalized emotion. Nonetheless, sound design—as well as original music composition—is definitely here to stay.

Special Effects

Theatre "magic" implies special effects not easily described as simply lighting or sound, such as fire, explosions, sudden apparitions, mysterious disappearances ("Witches vanish," Shakespeare writes in a stage direction in *Macbeth*), fog, smoke, wind, rain, snow, lightning, and a whole host of blood effects—all of which must be accomplished, of course, without burning down the theatre or puncturing the actors. (It was the firing-off of an offstage cannon that burned down Shakespeare's Globe theatre in 1613!) Commercial devices can

Falling snow is one of the special effects – and also underlines the major theme and title – of *Snow in June*. The play, which depicts the ghost of a young Chinese girl returning to earth, was inspired by a thirteenth-century Chinese legend. Written by Charles Mee and adapted and directed by Chen Shi-Zheng for the American Repertory Theatre in 2003, *Snow in June* blends ancient Chinese theatre techniques with contemporary technology. The play's accompanying music, composed by Paul Dresher, mixes bluegrass, Tex-Mex, Chinese, and Cajun elements. Scenic design is by Yi Li Ming, costumes by Anita Yavich, and lighting by Rick Fisher.

Theatrical smoke is commonly used with stage lighting to provide atmospheric and supernatural effects, and also to create a level of stylization that permits a suspension of realism – as in a battle scene that would be dangerous to stage with greater physical authenticity. Here, smoke and lighting combine to create the chaos and violence of battle in the Utah Shakespearean Festival production of *War of the Roses*, a compilation by Howard Jensen of Shakespeare's three plays of *Henry VI*. Lighting is by Donna Ruzika.

achieve all of these effects, but each requires its own on-the-spot ingenuity to be both credible and effective. There are also one-of-a-kind tricks, such as having Hans's armor suddenly fall off his body in Jean Giraudoux's *Ondine,* that must be individually designed and perfected. Effects designers are not universally employed in the theatre, but their day may not be far off.

Computer Technologies in Theatre Design

Designers—like other visual artists—have always used the technologies available to them. For centuries, designers have worked with such basic drawing implements as charcoal, colored paints, rulers, squares, and drafting tables. Complicated "drawing machines" came into play during the Renaissance: Leonardo da Vinci invented a "perspectograph" to help artists transform their perceived earthly realities into two-dimensional sketches and engravings in the early 1500s, and Canaletto's detailed paintings of eighteenth-century Venice were executed with the aid of a room-sized "camera obscura." The computer of today is only the most recent in a long list of technological tools used by visual artists, but it is a tool of far-reaching potential for the theatre. Becoming widespread in industry in the mid-1980s, computer-aided design (CAD) and computer-aided manufacture (CAM) were securely established by the 1990s as the fastest-growing technology of the current stage.

What do computers offer over pencil and paper? Computers don't think and can't create. Nor can they analyze a text, imagine an environment, suggest a costume, conceive a style, or even make an audience laugh. But what they can do is aid those artists who can do these things. In its capacity for combining and configuring (and then reconfiguring) ideas, angles, shapes, colors, spaces, perspectives, and measurements, which designers uncover through research or create through imagination, the computer consolidates a vast realm of experimental possibilities with the technical assurance of a mathematician or an engineer. Perhaps no "machine" of any era has so successfully counterpoised reality's hard facts with the artist's free-floating imagination.

Computers are useful—and becoming invaluable—to the contemporary designer on a variety of levels. First, they can assist with or even replace much of the drudgery of sheer drawing mechanics. With a click of the mouse, straight lines, angles, circles, shapes, colors, and typefaces can be selected from a menu of choices and placed where desired. Moreover, all of these design elements can be reconfigured in an instant: colors can be changed, lines lengthened, walls thickened, floors raised, furniture moved, sightlines adjusted, dimensions measured, and texts edited and resized. Individual design elements can be instantly replicated: an elaborately drawn banister post can become a dozen such posts in a matter of seconds. Indeed, whole drawings can be rescaled, zoomed in or out, printed and reprinted. Whole designs —or designated portions of them—can be rotated or relocated freely about the page. And working designs can be instantly sent around the world by digital electronic transmission. Instant and virtually unlimited "clean" revisions and instantaneous communications are the hallmarks of the computer revolution, in art as well as in text processing.

Second, computers enable designers to draw upon vast visual databases: virtual libraries of art that can be found in commercial clip-art palettes or on CD-ROMs. Designers themselves may create such libraries and store them for later use. These libraries give instant access to thousands of existing drawings and photos— such as "virtual catalogues" of eighteenth-century chandeliers, Victorian drapery, or Roman statuary—that have been digitized for computer retrieval and can be, subject to legal copyright considerations, incorporated into stage designs. Computerized data banks have already revolutionized costume management in theatre shops and film studios, permitting designers to access pictures of, for example, hundreds of blouses currently available in various wardrobe collections. Computerized libraries are also replacing the plastic templates used by scenic and lighting designers to configure furniture on the set or lighting instruments on the light pipes, saving many hours of painstaking pencil and plastic copywork, particularly when multiple revisions are necessary. Even far more advanced computing capabilities are now coming into the art and craft of theatre design.

Third, computerized cutting and pasting allow the designer to combine visual forms on the screen; for example, a costume designer can "virtually sew" the sleeves of one garment onto another without requiring a single stitch; a wig designer can have an actor "virtually try on" wigs by combining a photo of the actor with drawings of wigs of different colors and styles—all without having to buy a single strand of hair or calling the actor in for a fitting. Actors, indeed, can be "virtually dressed" in entire costume designs long before any fabric is purchased.

Fourth, computerized scenographic modeling supplements traditional ground-plan and elevation drawings by creating, on a computer screen, three-dimensional models of the stage set that can demonstrate perspectives from any vantage: from the left, right, and center of the house or from a bird's-eye position that may clarify lighting and offstage storage positions. With sufficient computing power and memory, designers, directors, and actors can then "walk through" the designed set, which at that point exists only as a "virtual reality," not as a hard construction of steel, wood, and fabric. Although computing equipment for such modeling is expensive, it is surely—in the long run—much cheaper than building and rebuilding stage scenery until it's just right. And integrated computer design—which might enable a design team to design a scenic model, inhabit it with actors wearing designed costumes, and throw colored light upon the scene from precisely calibrated lighting positions—is already with us in some places and is likely to become a regular part of design conferences in many new theatres over the coming decade. The opportunity to "storyboard" scenery, costumes, and lighting, together with text and music and sound, is an extraordinary advance in the art of production planning wherever time and money are involved, as they almost always are.

Finally, dedicated database programs permit lighting and sound technicians to save innumerable hours in storing, sorting, and printing the dozens of dimmer schedules, cue sheets, and loudspeaker assignments needed in multi-production repertory assignments.

Will computer-aided design reduce the creativity and imagination that go into the designer's art? Veteran designers often voice this concern, apprehensive about the encroachment of binary numbers and microelectronics on what has generally been considered a more freehand, soul-expressive art. But there is little question that in the first decade of the twenty-first century most young designers are trained in—and employ—a wide variety of CAD techniques, and many senior designers are switching over to them as well. Imagination, most designers now believe, is not a function of one's tools—pen and paper or keyboard and screen—but of the mind that guides them.

Computer adherents are resoundingly supportive of the computer revolution. To its professional devotees, computers are tools—superpencils, really—not ends in themselves; they provoke experimentation and innovation as well as (or even in lieu of) mere craft precision and mechanics. The computer age has, of course, long since arrived in all major areas of commerce and culture, and it already has a substantial history in the theatre; indeed, one of the first commercial uses of computing was in theatrical lighting, which has been largely computerized since at least the mid-1960s. And the theatre has been one of the testing places for many of the world's emerging technologies, including hydraulic elevators, gas lighting, electricity, and air-conditioning. It

seems inevitable that the computer screen will become a principal conveyor of design creativity and communication in the immediate years to come.

Technical Production

Far outnumbering all the others—actors, designers, writers, and directors—put together are the artisans or "technologists" who get the production organized, built, installed, lit, and ready to open, and who then make it run.

Because of their numbers, theatrical technicians are ordinarily marshaled into a hierarchical structure, headed by stage, house, and production managers, technical directors, and shop supervisors, all of whom are charged with guiding and supervising the work of a virtual army of craftspersons. A typical breakdown of these functions—which you might find detailed in the theatre program of any major theatre—could be something like this:

The production manager (PM) is a position that has grown mightily in importance over the past two decades. The PM coordinates the scheduling, staffing, and budgeting of every element of the production, from the acting rehearsals to the building, installation ("load-in"), and operation ("running") of all the design and technical elements. Expert in legal codes, safety procedures, and accounting policies and sensitive to the varying artistic needs of actors, directors, designers, and technicians, the PM wrestles with the complex problems of integrating the play's disparate elements, determining, for example, whether the lights should be hung and focused before or after the scenery is installed (there can be reasons for going either way on this) and anticipating how long it will take to train the stage crew or set the light cues.

The stage manager (SM) (now often called the "production stage manager") has the highly responsible position of coordinating the director's work with that of the actors and the technical and design departments. At the beginning of rehearsals, the SM is involved primarily in organizational work: scheduling calls and appointments, recording the blocking of actors, anticipating technical problems of quick costume changes, set shifts, and the like, and organizing the basic "calling" of the show—that is, the system by which lighting, sound, and scene-shift cues are initiated. During performance, the SM actually runs the show, having final authority over the entire onstage and backstage operation; moreover, it is the SM who ordinarily conducts understudy and replacement rehearsals in a professional run and who assumes the functions of the director when the director is absent or no longer employed by the production.

Working for the SM are normally one or more assistant stage managers. In rehearsals, ASMs typically will set out props, follow the script and prompt actors who are "off book" (no longer rehearsing with script in hand) if they forget their lines, take line notes when actors say lines incorrectly, and substitute for actors who may be temporarily away, as at costume fittings. During performance, with the SM normally calling the show from a booth above the audience, ASMs—on their two-way headset connections—implement the SM's calls by transmitting them as visual "go" signs for scene shifts, actor entrances, and effect cues. ASMs also serve as the backstage eyes and ears of the SM, who is out front, watching the stage.

The technical director (TD) is generally in charge of the building and operation of scenery and stage machinery and is often in charge of the lighting crews as well. The TD must oversee the moving of scenery into and out of the theatre; ensure that all technical departments have adequate "stage time" to do their jobs; establish policies and directives for scene shifting, special effects, and "strike" (the final removal of scenery from the theatre after a run); and, most important, make certain that everything is ready on time—no small order, considering the massive technical complexities of theatre today.

During actual production, the technical crews, working under the SM and trained by the TD, are often a virtual backstage army, hoisting, lowering, and pushing scenery pieces exactly on cue to precisely predetermined locations; shifting props and furniture to the right places at the right times; relaying the SM's cues to actors awaiting their entrances or offstage cries; and, in general, making the carefully preplanned scene changes, prop appearances, and actor entrances appear to flow effortlessly, to ensure that the audience will concentrate on the play's action rather than the theatre's mechanics.

One particularly special tech assignment is flying actors through the air, which is usually done by only a few professional companies with patented equipment and expertly trained personnel. The most prominent American company, Flying by Foy, was created by Peter Foy in 1950 and has achieved preeminence in aerial choreography of astonishing beauty and complexity.

Working in the scene shop—normally under the TD, a shop foreman, or a scenery supervisor—are carpenters (and master carpenters) and scenic artists (painters), with welders required when steel—commonly used today for weight-bearing constructions—is to be joined. In the costume shop, a wider array of specialists is required (though many costume designers and technologists assume more than one of these roles):

- the costume director (or costume shop manager), who coordinates the entire operation, supervising personnel, work spaces, and schedules.

- dyers, who dye fabrics to the color specified by the design and may also be skilled at fabric painting, aging, distressing, and other fabric modifications.

- drapers, who drape fabrics on an actor, or a dummy, testing and choosing the way the fabric falls—either with the grain or on the bias—to create the desired look of

The wardrobe supervisor searches through the multilevel costume storage room at the Canadian Shakespeare Festival in Stratford, Ontario.

the eventual garment both at rest and on a moving (and possibly dancing, tumbling, or fencing) actor.

- cutters, who cut the fabric according to the selected grain direction, either from a flat paper pattern or with no pattern at all, often first on a cheap muslin prototype. (Most often today, draping and cutting are performed by the same person: a draper/cutter).

- first hands, who, working directly for the cutter, correct the pattern after the muslin prototype has been fitted to the actor and then "hand off" the work to the stitchers.

- stitchers, who sew the garment.

- craft specialists, who make costumes or costume elements involving more than

fabric—such as armor, belts, masks, and so forth. Specific specialists such as milliners to make hats and cobblers to make shoes, may be added. Other specialists may also be involved in distressing costume elements (making them look older and well used) or adding decorations—badges, military ribbons, gold braid, and the like.

- hairstylists and wigmakers, who coif the actors as the designers specify.

- wardrobe supervisors, who ensure that costumes are cleaned and maintained during the run of a show and delivered to the appropriate backstage areas during dress rehearsals and performances. Wardrobe (or storage) supervisors and technicians also oversee the costume storage area and help determine which existing costumes can be taken from storage and rebuilt to serve a new design.

- dressers, who work backstage during dress rehearsals and performances, helping the actors when necessary with quick changes between the scenes.

In the area of lighting, master electricians and electricians hang, focus, and gel (put color media in) lights prior to and during technical rehearsals and maintain the lighting technology during the run of a show, while trained lighting-board and follow-spot operators execute the lighting cues called by the stage manager. For the sound department, one or more sound engineers work with the sound designer in recording the sound cues and placing the speakers, and a soundboard operator executes the cues during technical and dress rehearsals and performances. And in the makeup room, makeup artists may provide assistance to actors requiring it, or they may indeed apply full makeup to the actors as specified by the designers.

Each of these "backstage" technicians plays an absolutely crucial role in theatrical presentation—and the "stage fright" of the actor playing Hamlet is not necessarily any greater than that of the stagehand who must pull the curtain. For backstage work, though technical, is never simply mechanical, and every stage production poses a host of problems and situations in each area that are new to the people who deal with them and, sometimes, new to the theatre itself. Technological innovation takes place when a sound knowledge of craft combines with creative imagination in the face of unanticipated problems. The technical artists of the theatre have always manifested an impressive ingenuity at meeting unprecedented challenges in creative ways. Each of the theatre's shops—scene shop, costume shop, prop shop, and makeup room—is therefore a creative artistic studio and a teaching laboratory for all its members, as well as a theatrical support unit.

Indeed, in contemporary theatre, particularly under the influences of Bertolt Brecht and then postmodernism, the theatre's technology—such as lighting instruments and sound-enhancing devices—has increasingly been taken out of hiding and placed right on the stage itself. And with follow-spot operators (and sometimes stage managers) often placed in direct public view, sound operators plopped right in the midst of the audience, and puppeteers visibly manipulating their animals right on the stage, the theatre's technicians themselves have increasingly been drawn into direct public awareness—in some cases, with the "backstage" crew taking onstage curtain calls with the rest of the cast. A popular fascination with technology, together with a diminishing interest in stage "magic" or naturalistic illusion, has led to a scenography that deliberately incorporates technology as a visible aesthetic component of the theatre itself. Given this trend and the theatre's increasing use of the most recent technical innovations—lasers and holograms, air casters, large-screen video, motorized lights and projections, to name but a few—the theatre technologist is becoming widely recognized (as cinematographers are in cinema) as not merely implementors but full-fledged stage artists and creators.

Throughout history, theatrical crafts have been learned through apprenticeship; even today, although beginning theatre technologists are often trained in universities before their first employment, much of their learning is necessarily on the job, as each job is somewhat unique to the play that prompts it. And although written and unwritten "textbooks" of stage practice can illustrate the traditional means of building a flat, cutting a pattern, organizing a rehearsal, laying out a prop table, and painting a prop, it is artistic sensitivity that ultimately determines the technical quality of a production, and it is artistic imagination that brings about the technical and technological advances that further theatrical creativity.

6

The Director

THE ROOM IS ALREADY FILLED WITH PEOPLE when she enters, a bit fussily, with a bundle of books and papers under her arm. Expectation, tension, and even a hint of panic can be sensed behind the muffled greetings, loose laughter, and choked conversation that greet her arrival.

She sits, and an assistant arranges chairs. Gradually, starting at the other end of what has suddenly become "her" table, the others seat themselves. An edgy silence descends. Where are they going? What experiences lie ahead? What risks, what challenges are to be demanded? What feelings, in the coming weeks and months, are going to be stirred to poignant reality?

Only she knows—and if she doesn't, no one does. It is in this silence, tender with hope and fear, that the director breaks ground for the production. It is here that plan begins to become work and idea begins to become art. It is the peak moment of directing and of the director.

This is an idealized picture, to be sure. There are many directors who deliberately avoid invoking an impression of "mystique" and whose primary efforts are directed toward dispelling awe, dread, or any form of personal tension among their associates. Nonetheless, the picture holds a measure of truth for every theatrical production, for the art of directing is an exercise in leadership, imagination, and control; in the director's hands, finally, rest

177

the aspirations, neuroses, skills, and ideas of the entire theatrical company.

Directing is an art whose product is the most ambiguous, perhaps the most mysterious, in the theatre. The direction of a play is not visible like scenery or costumes; and unlike the actor's voice or the sound designer's score, it cannot be directly heard or sensed. And yet direction underlies everything we see and hear in the theatre. Utterly absorbed by the final theatrical experience, direction animates and defines that experience. A whole class of theatrical artists in our time have reached international eminence in this particular art. But what, exactly, is involved?

At the *technical* level, the director is the peson who organizes the production. This involves scheduling the work process and supervising the acting, designing, staging, and technical operation of the play. This is the easiest part of the directorial function.

At the more fundamental, *artistic,* level, the director inspires a creation of theatre with each production. He or she conceptualizes the play, gives it vision and purpose—both social and aesthetic—and inspires the company of artists to join together in collaboration.

It is in the conjunction of these levels, the technical and the artistic, that each director defines the directorial function anew. And it is

Directors often create their own theatre companies, as did Simon McBurney, cofounder and current director of Complicite (formerly Theatre de Complicité), one of the most exciting theatres performing regularly in Europe and America. Almost all of McBurney's work is written by the ensemble he has assembled; this production of *The Elephant Vanishes* is a coproduction between Complicite and Tokyo's Setagaya Public Theatre. The play, based on short stories of Japanese author Haruki Murakami, was performed in New York in 2004, employing high-tech, antirealistic staging innovations. The designer was Michael Levine.

At the first reading, the director normally discusses the play and its production, after which the cast reads through their parts and, if available, the playwright shares his or her desires and answers cast and director questions. Shown here in a New York rehearsal studio are director Pamela MacKinnon (*far left*), playwright Edward Albee (*standing*), and cast members Johanna Day, Frank Wood, and Frederick Weller, who have gathered for the first reading of the playwright's newest play, *Homelife*. The play is part of Albee's newly combined *Peter and Jerry*.

with one foot in each that the director creates—through an adroit synthesis of text, materials, and available talent—a unique and vivid theatrical experience.

The Arrival of the Director: A Historical Overview

Directing has been going on ever since theatre began, but there has not always been a director—that is, there has not always been a sole individual specifically charged with directorial functions and responsibilities. The evo-

lution of the director as an independent theatre artist, in just the past century has had as much to do with the development of modern theatre as has any dramatic innovation. The gradual process of this evolution can be roughly divided into three phases.

Phase One: The Teacher-Directors

In the earliest days of the theatre and for some time thereafter, directing was considered a form of teaching. The Greeks called the director the *didaskalos*, which means "teacher," and in medieval times the director's designation, in all the various European languages, was "master." The underlying assumption of teaching, of course, is that the teacher already knows and understands the subject; the teacher's task is simply to transmit that knowledge to others. The earliest directors, therefore, were simply asked to pass along the accumulated wisdom and techniques of "correct" performance within a "given" convention. Often the playwrights themselves served as directors, for who would be better qualified to "teach" a play than the person who wrote it? In one famous dramatic scene, Molière delightfully depicts himself directing one of his own plays; this is surely an effective model of the author-teacher-director for the seventeenth century and indeed for much of the theatre's history.

The teacher-director reached a pinnacle of influence, albeit anonymously, during the late Enlightenment and the Victorian era—during the eighteenth and nineteenth centuries— partly in response to the remarkable fascination of those times with science, scientific method, and humanistic research: the same dedication to rationalism that fostered a profusion of libraries, museums, and historic preservation also emphasized accuracy, consistency, and precision in the arts. The temper of the times led to major directorial changes in the theatre, for on the one hand audiences were demanding revivals of classic plays—whose authors were no longer around to direct them—and on the other hand they were demanding that these revivals be historically edifying, that they have a museumlike authenticity. All of this required research, organization, and comprehensive coordination; in other words, it demanded an independent director.

Most of the directors of this time—virtually all of them until the latter part of the nineteenth century—received no more recognition for their efforts than the museum director who created historical dioramas. Sometimes the directing was attributed to a famous acting star, such as the Englishman Charles Kean or

the American Edwin Booth, when in fact the work was done by a lesser functionary; in Booth's case, for example, one D. W. Waller was the true director, but his name was all but buried in the program and never appeared in the reviews or publicity. Nevertheless, these teacher-directors who labored largely in the shadows began the art of directing as we know it today. They organized their productions around specific concepts—independently arrived at—and they dedicated themselves to creating unified and coherent theatrical works by "directing" an ensemble of actors, designers, and technicians toward established ends.

Phase Two: The Realistic Directors

The second stage in the development of modern-day directing began toward the end of the nineteenth century and brought to the fore a group of directors who restudied the conventions of theatrical presentation and strove in various ways to make them more lifelike. George II, Duke of Saxe-Meiningen, was the first of this breed and is generally regarded as the first modern director. The duke, who headed a provincial troupe of actors in his rural duchy, presented a series of premieres and classical revivals throughout Europe during the late 1870s and 1880s that were dazzling in their harmonized acting, staging, and scenery. Although still historically "correct," the duke's productions featured an ensemble of performances rather than a hierarchy of "star, support, and supernumerary." All of his performers were vigorously rehearsed toward the development of individual, realistically conceived roles—which were then played out in highly organic, even volatile, patterns of dramatic action. The stodgy lineup of spear carriers that had traditionally looked on while the star recited center stage was conspicuously absent from the Meiningen productions; so was the "super" who was customarily hired on the afternoon of performance, squeezed into a costume, and set upon the stage like so much living scenery. The totality of the Meiningen theatre aesthetic, embracing acting, interpretation, and design, was acclaimed throughout Europe: when the Meiningen troupe ceased touring in 1890, the position of a director who would organize and rehearse an entire company toward a complexly and comprehensively fashioned theatrical presentation was firmly established.

In 1887 André Antoine began a movement of greater realism in Paris with his Théâtre Libre, and Konstantin Stanislavsky initiated his even-more-celebrated Moscow Art Theatre in 1898. Both of these directors, amateurs like Meiningen at the start of their careers, went on to develop wholly innovative techniques in acting and actor-coaching based on the staging concepts of the duke; both also theorized and worked pragmatically at the organizing of theatre companies, the development of a dramatic repertory, the reeducation of theatergoing audiences, and the re-creation of an overall aesthetic of the theatre. Although both Antoine and Stanislavsky were known primarily as naturalists—somewhat to their disadvantage, perhaps, for they had many other interests as well—they were above all idealists who sought to make the theatre a powerful social and artistic instrument for the expression of truth. Their ideals and their commitment virtually forced them to expand the directorial function into an all-encompassing and inspirational art.

The importance of these directors—and of certain other pioneers of the same spirit, including Harley Granville-Barker in England, David Belasco in America, and Otto Brahm in Germany—was not merely that they fostered the developing realist and naturalist drama but also that they opened up the theatre to the almost infinite possibilities of psychological interpretation. Once the psychology of the human individual became crucial to the analysis and acting of plays, directors became

more than teachers: they became part analyst, part therapist, and even part mystic; their *creative* function in play production increased substantially. The rise of realism in the theatre of the late nineteenth and early twentieth centuries and the rise of directors capable of bringing out realistic nuances and patterning them into highly theatrical productions brought about an irreversible theatrical renovation that in turn irrevocably established the importance of the director.

Phase Three: The Stylizing Directors

Right on the heels of the realist phase of direction came a third phase—one that brought the director to the present position of power and recognition. This phase arrived with the directors who joined forces with nonrealist playwrights to create the modern antirealistic theatre. Their forces are still growing. They are the ones who demand of directing that it aim primarily at the creation of originality, theatricality, and style. The stylizing directors are unrestrained by rigid formulas with respect to verisimilitude or realistic behavior; their goal is to create sheer theatrical brilliance, beauty, and excitement and to lead their collaborators in explorations of pure theatre and pure theatrical imagination.

Paul Fort, one of the first of these third-phase directors, launched his Théâtre d'Art in Paris in 1890 as a direct assault upon the realist principles espoused by Antoine. Similarly, Vsevolod Meyerhold, a one-time disciple of Stanislavsky, began his theatre of "bio-mechanical constructivism" (an acting method characterized by bold gestures and rapid, near-acrobatic movement) in Moscow to combat the master's realism. The movement toward stylized directing occasioned by these innovators and others like them introduced a lyricism and symbolism, an expressive and abstract use of design, an explosive theatricality, and certain intentionally contrived methods of

Anne Bogart is one of America's foremost directors, distinguished in part by her adaptation of Mary Overlie's precise choreographic-dramatic methodology known as "viewpoints." Here Bogart has staged a scene from Pierre Marivaux's *La Dispute* for the American Repertory Theatre in 2003, with costumes by James Schuette.

acting that continue to have a profound effect on today's theatre and its drama.

Perhaps the most influential proponent of this third-phase position of the director, however, was not himself a director at all but an eminent designer and theorist: Gordon Craig. In a seminal essay titled "The Art of the Theatre" (1905), Craig compared the director of a play to the captain of a ship: an absolutely indispensable leader whose rule, maintained by strict discipline, extends over every last facet of the enterprise. "Until discipline is understood in a theatre to be willing and reliant obedience to the manager [director] or captain," wrote Craig, "no supreme achievement can be accomplished." Craig's essay was aimed at a full-scale "Renaissance of the Art of the Theatre,"

in which a "systematic progression" of reform would overtake all the theatre arts—"acting, scenery, costuming, lighting, carpentering, singing, dancing, etc."—under the complete control and organizing genius of this new-comer to the ranks of theatrical artistry, the independent director.

The Contemporary Director

Craig's renaissance has surely arrived: this indeed is the "age of the director," an age in which the directorial function is fully established as the art of synthesizing script, design, and performance into a unique and splendid theatrical event that creates its own harmony and its own ineffable yet memorable distinction. If, as J. L. Styan says, "the theatre persists in communicating by a simultaneity of sensory impressions," it is above all the director who is charged with inspiring these impressions and ensuring this simultaneity.

Today, in a world of mass travel and mass communications, the exotic quickly becomes familiar and the familiar just as quickly becomes trite. Nothing is binding; the directorial function has shifted from teaching what is "proper" to creating what is stimulating and wondrous. At the beginning of a production, the director faces a blank canvas but has at hand a generous palette. At his or her disposal are not only the underlying conventions of the time but also all those of the past, which can

be revived for novel effects and stunning juxtapositions: our conglomerate theatre of today allows Shakespeare in modern dress, Greek tragedy à la kabuki spectacle, theatre of the absurd as vaudevillian buffoonery, and romantic melodrama as campy satire. Thus, at the conception of a theatrical idea today—in the first moments of imagining a specific production—no question can be answered automatically, no style is obligatory, no interpretation is definitive. Jean-Paul Sartre has said about the whole of modern life that "man is condemned to be free"; in the theatre the director's freedom in the face of almost limitless possibilities leads to a certain existential anxiety that is both chilling and thrilling in its challenge.

Legendary German director Peter Stein staged this production of Chekhov's *The Seagull* at the 2003 Edinburgh Festival, with the play's sexual and psychological betrayals enhanced with bold symbolic images. Here Madame Arkadina – the overwrought actress, mother, and lover as played by Fiona Shaw – retreats inside her luggage in a paranoid frenzy far bolder than Chekhov specified but with profoundly, even tragically, unsettling effect.

Directorial Functions

Directing is not simply a craft; it is *directing* in the dictionary as well as in the theatrical sense: it is to lead, to supervise, to instruct, to give shape. In other words, it is to do what is necessary to make things "work." The director has final responsibility for *everything* that happens in a production; therefore, the "function" of a director must be, at least in part, subject to day-to-day demands and continuous improvisation.

Producer and Director

Part of what the director does in any given production is determined by the possible existence of a *producer*. The producer is the person (or the institution) responsible for the financial support of the production: the producer may be a resident theatre, a university theatre, or, as in Broadway or off-Broadway productions, an independent individual or partnership of individuals. In the regional theatre, the artistic director normally serves as the producer of each production in the theatre's season as well as the director of one or more plays; associate and/or freelance directors may be hired to direct other individual productions.

Where there is an active producer, separate from the director, it is the producer who is generally responsible for hiring the director, for establishing the production budget, and for determining the theatre facility and the production dates. The producer also normally plays an important role (if not *the* dominant role) in selecting the play, engaging the artistic staff (designers and technicians), and possibly even casting the actors.

As a result, functions listed below as "directorial" may in fact be divided between the director and the producer. They remain directorial functions, however, inasmuch as they "direct" the artistic product that will finally appear on the stage.

Directorial Vision

Principally, the directorial function is one of *envisioning* the main lines of the production and providing the artistic *leadership* necessary to realize that vision. Envisioning, however, does not mean plotting out every detail in advance, nor does leadership mean dictatorship or tyranny. Directing means, quite literally, "giving direction," which implies choosing a point of focus and guiding everyone to face the same way. The talents of the play director are, in this regard, not unlike those of the bank director or the director of a research team: to provide goals, establish procedures, facilitate communication, drive the schedule, monitor the progress, encourage the timid, rein in the errant, heighten the stakes, refine the objectives, build the morale, and inspire absolute excellence from every participant. No two individuals will fulfill each of these functions in

---

"ALWAYS AN IMPOSTOR"

When I hear a director speaking glibly of serving the author, of letting a play speak for itself, my suspicions are aroused, because this is the hardest job of all. If you just let a play speak, it may not make a sound. If what you want is for the play to be heard, then you must conjure its sound from it. This demands many deliberate actions and the result may have great simplicity. However, setting out to "be simple" can be quite negative, an easy evasion of the exacting steps to the simple answer.

It is a strange role, that of the director: he does not ask to be God and yet his role implies it. He wants to be fallible, and yet an instinctive conspiracy of the actors is to make him the arbiter, because an arbiter is so desperately wanted all the time. In a sense the director is always an impostor, a guide at night who does not know the territory, and yet he has no choice — he must guide, learning the route as he goes. Deadliness often lies in wait when he does not recognize this situation, and hopes for the best, when it is the worst that he needs to face.

— Peter Brook

the same way nor to the same degree. Directing clearly involves a confident and natural way of working with other people, as well as learned directorial technique. Artistic sensitivity, interpersonal skills, and an eagerness to accept responsibility (and exercise authority) should always be expected of the professional play director.

For purposes of discussion, individual directorial functions can be viewed as so many separate steps in the process of play production. The process, in fact, takes place over a period of weeks and sometimes years and is at no time as orderly as a schematic listing might suggest. Nonetheless, such a listing can help us see the basic architecture of the directorial process and the progression of decisions and actions that bear upon the final production.

The steps divide easily into phases: a preparatory phase, which involves play selection, conceptualizing, designer selection, designing, and casting; and an implementation phase, which involves staging, actor-coaching, pacing, coordinating, and presenting. All of these steps are continuous rather than segmented—a director conceptualizes the production right up to the last minute and begins pacing it from the instant the play is chosen—but they

are generally centered in a time frame of relatively set order and organization.

Preparatory Phase

The preparatory phase of a production may take days or months or years; it is the director's dreamworld, wherein ideas germinate and begin to flower. Most directors are "in preparation" for several productions at once: even as one production is in rehearsal, others are taking shape in her or his mind. Eventually, however, preparation moves from dreaming to planning, from visions to details.

PLAY SELECTION   The selection of a script is unquestionably the most critical act of any director. The play is the essential theatrical product, so to speak: it is the basic element to which the audience responds—or thinks it responds—and it is universally perceived as the core of the theatrical experience. For this reason, play selection is the one directorial decision over which the producer—the provider of a production's financial support—invariably reserves the right of review.

Three basic considerations go into play selection: the director's interest, the interest of

Moisés Kaufman, founder and artistic director of the Tectonic Theatre Project, both wrote and directed *Gross Indecency: The Three Trials of Oscar Wilde,* based on the transcripts of Wilde's trials (essentially for sodomy) during the 1890s. Kaufman's directorial style for this production may be described as declaratory: actors all face the audience and hoist their "transcripts" as they speak them to the jury-audience. Despite the lack of face-to-face confrontation, the play develops extraordinary emotional power. It ran for more than 600 performances in New York in 1997, winning many awards and then touring to Los Angeles, San Francisco, Toronto, and London's West End.

the intended audience, and the capability of the director and producer to acquire, conceptualize, and produce the play. The director's interest is important because no director, save by chance, can create theatrical excitement from a script he or she finds dull and uninteresting. Nonetheless, it is also the director's job to seek the excitement latent in a script and to imagine its various theatrical possibilities. Often a director who can envision the improvements to be gained by script revision, adaptation, or reinterpretation can discover plays that other-wise would be ignored; indeed, one of the marks of a great director is the ability to make us recognize the brilliance or beauty of a script we have unwittingly passed over.

The audience's interest is of even greater importance. It is the audience, after all, that makes the theatre possible, and the ability to assess an audience's needs and wants is absolutely fundamental to directing, both for pragmatic reasons (to ensure that an audience turns out to see the play) and for artistic reasons (to ensure that the play is satisfying and

George C. Wolfe wrote, directed, and produced *Harlem Song*, staging it not on Broadway or even at his own downtown theatre (the Joseph Papp Public Theatre, which he then helmed as artistic director) but in Harlem's fabled Apollo Theatre, a longtime showplace for black entertainers. Wolfe's stated goal with this 2002 production was not so much to create dramatic innovation (for which he is well known) as "to make a populist piece that is very theatrical and entertaining." Indeed, *Harlem Song* drew thousands of New Yorkers and tourists to the city's vibrant and newly redeveloped African American neighborhood, raising public consciousness of the great literary and artistic contributions of the Harlem community over the past century.

pertinent to those who come to see it). A director directs not only the actors and designers but the audience members as well, by giving direction to their feelings and perceptions through the intellectual focus of the production. A director who discounts or ignores the interests—and the intelligence—of the audience stands little chance of creating any genuine theatrical impact.

Play selection that considers audience interest does not necessarily mean a reliance on the tried and true; quite the contrary, it means providing the audience with theatrical work that is fresh, fascinating, vigorous, and exciting. For some audiences, these ingredients can be provided by musicals, thrillers, and domestic comedies; for others, by works of the European avant-garde, by plays of social protest and reform, or by new plays hot off the laptops of yet unknown authors. There is an audience for every sort of good play, and it is the director's job to find that audience and attract it to the theatre. The audience demands to be challenged as well as confirmed—and, in the long run, directors who lead their audiences are far more likely to gain artistic recognition than are those who either follow the audience or ignore them completely.

The capability of the director to produce the play adequately with available resources is the final requisite for sound play selection. Can the production rights to the play be acquired? Can a cast be brought together? a production staff? a theatre? Is there enough money? Interest alone—the director's and the audience's—will not buy the scripts, rent the theatre, pay for the electricity, or perform the roles. Considerations of quality must also be factored in: Are the available actors experienced enough to master the play's style? Is the costume budget adequate for the size of the cast and the period of the play? And, finally, does the director understand this play well enough to bring out its ideas? A realistic consideration of one's own capabilities, together with an ability to assess the potential of one's expected collaborators, must be a significant factor in the critical decisions of play selection.

CONCEPTUALIZING More has been written in modern times about the director's role in conceptualizing a play than about any other directorial task; entire books have been devoted to the "directorial image," or the creation of the central concept that focuses and informs an entire production. Particularly through those concepts that give unexpected and fresh insights into character, story, or style, the modern director has seized the imagination of the public. Like it or not (and there are many who do not), audiences and critics today are much more likely to admire (and remember) "high-concept" productions, such as Silviu Purcărete's *Oresteia* or Andrei Serban's *Taming of the Shrew*, than they are "traditional" stagings of these plays. Although the director runs a considerable risk with this kind of undertaking—for indeed Wild West Romeos, homosexual Hamlets, and Watergate Macbeths have more often been laughable than laudable—a brilliantly appropriate concept can completely captivate an audience by focusing a play production with such pertinence and meaning that it transcends time, place, and stylistic artifice to create profound, moving, and illuminating theatricalization.

The formation of a directorial concept takes place at both the conscious and the unconscious level; it takes place, in fact, whether the director wants it to or not. There is no avoiding it: it begins when the director first hears of a certain play, and it grows and develops as she or he reads the play, considers producing it, imagines its effects on an audience, and mentally experiments with possible modes of staging. The directorial concept is a product not only of the director's personal intelligence and vision but also of the director's personal experiences that relate to the matters portrayed by the play, as well as personal likes and lusts, appreciations and philosophical leanings, and desires concerning audience reaction

to the final directorial product. The thought processes by which the concept develops are both deductive and inductive, and they are set in motion with the first impressions the director receives from a play.

Concepts can be expressed in many ways. Often they are social statements ("this is a play about tyranny") or philosophical ones ("this is a play about self-knowledge"). Often they involve specific interpretations ("this is a play about a man who cannot make up his mind"), and often they invoke a particular genre of theatricality ("this is a revenge melodrama"). Frequently a director will state the concept psychodramatically ("this is a primitive ritual of puberty"), and frequently the concept is predominantly historical ("this is a play about fratricide in the Middle Ages") or imagistic ("this is a play about swords, sables, and skulls") or metatheatrical ("this is a play about playing"). Often the conception of a play includes a basic tone ("sad," "heroic," "royal"), often a basic texture ("rich," "cerebral," "stark"). Diverse as

Left, top: Eastern European theatre produced many brilliantly original "high-concept" directors during the cold-war years, since straightforward theatre with liberal themes was discouraged by political authorities. Since the fall of the iron curtain, many of these directors have brought their stylistic innovations to the world stage, including Romanian director Silviu Purcărete, who staged this abstract and ritualized 1998 production of *The Oresteia* at the Edinburgh Festival in Scotland.

Left, bottom: Romanian American director Andrei Serban has long been a stimulating and high-concept director. In this 1998 production at the American Repertory Theatre, he tackles Shakespeare's *Taming of the Shrew*, a play that poses serious problems for modern audiences as it ends with Katherine (the now-tamed "shrew" of the title) urging present and future wives to "place your hands below your husband's foot." Many directors try to find ironies or contradictions in Katherine's apparent conversion to male chauvinism; Serban, conversely, emboldens it – making the final scene, as one critic termed it, a "noisy, politically incorrect, irresistibly funny romp." The setting is by Christine Jones.

these examples may seem, they all fall within the range of possibility in conceptualizing a single play: indeed, any one of them could be applied to Shakespeare's *Hamlet,* and probably at one time or another every one of them has been, as have hundreds of others besides.

The concept is the director's creation, and to a certain extent it remains primarily his or her own concern. It constitutes a personal organizing focus, the means of keeping the production aimed in a *specific* direction and impervious to deflection by tempting possibilities that might come to mind over the course of a production period. Therefore the concept, expressed succinctly but comprehensive in its implications, becomes the director's starting point in choosing designers and actors, in initiating design discussions, and in setting the direction for the first rehearsals. Directing, of course, means giving *direction,* and the concept is the first and most decisive step in getting a particular production under way.

A great directorial concept has many qualities. It is specific, appropriate, evocative, visual, theatrical, concrete, and original, as well as a bit mysterious and a bit amusing. It *leads* the actors and the designers; and if it is truly inspired, it leads the director as well.

DESIGNER SELECTION   The concept is the director's own creation, but its refinement and realization finally rest in the hands of collaborators whose personal artistry and inclinations will inevitably play an enormous role in the shape and impact of the final product. Hence the selection of these individuals is by no means a mechanical or arbitrary task; it is a central directorial concern of great artistic consequence.

Ordinarily directors make every effort to find designers with whom they feel not only a personal compatibility but also a mutual respect and a synchrony of artistic and intellectual vision. Like all true collaborations, the most effective director-designer relationships result in a give-and-take of ideas, plans, feelings, and

Andrei Serban's radically contemporized production of *Twelfth Night*, in which Orsino arrives with bodyguards on a military helicopter, reveals Shakespeare's romantic comedy — if we buy into Serban's vision — as a play of darker political complexity. This American Repertory Theatre production featured sets by Derek McLane and costumes by Catherine Zuber.

hypotheses—a sense of sharing and complementary support.

DESIGNING   The design phase of production marks the first step toward transforming vision into actuality: at this stage, people turn ideas into concrete visual realizations. The director's work in designing a production is generally suggestive and corrective; how well she or he succeeds in this delicate task is highly dependent on the personalities and predilections of the individuals involved. In theory, the director's and designer's goals in this phase are identical: actable space, wearable costumes, and an evocative, memorable, and meaningful appearance of the whole. In practice, each of the principals will have an inde-

pendent perspective on what is actable, what is memorable, and what is evocative; moreover, each may have a different sense of the importance of sometimes contradictory values. A costume designer, for example, may place a higher value on the appearance of a garment than will the director, who may be more concerned with the actor's ability to move in it. A lighting designer may be greatly interested in the aesthetics of murkiness, whereas the director may be more concerned that an actor's face be clearly seen at a particular moment. These are the sorts of artistic perspectives that must be reconciled in the design phase, which is essentially a collaboration whose decisions are acknowledged to be subjective rather than right or wrong; it is a

Longtime avant-garde American director Richard Foreman has a directorial "signature" — wires strung across the stage — as seen here in his harshly penetrating production of Bertolt Brecht's *The Threepenny Opera* at New York's Lincoln Center. Brecht's theatre, which is boldly presentational and direct, lends itself to Foreman's technique. Raul Julia (*left*) played Mack the Knife.

phase that demands qualities of leadership and artistic inspiration that are as sensitive as any the director may ever be called upon to exercise.

The design phase normally takes place in a series of personal conferences between director and designers, sometimes on a one-on-one basis and sometimes in group meetings. These are give-and-take affairs, for the most part, with the director doing most of the giving at the beginning and the designers taking over shortly thereafter. Often the first step is a collective meeting—the first design conference— at which the director discusses his or her concept in detail and suggests some possibilities for its visual realization: colors, images, spaces, textures, and technological implementations.

In the ensuing conferences, which are often conducted one-on-one and sometimes on an ad hoc basis, designers normally present their own conceptions and eventually provide the director with a progressive series of concrete visualizations: sketches (roughs), drawings, renderings, models, ground plans, working drawings, fabrics, technical details, and devices. During these conferences the design evolves through a collaborative sharing, in which the director's involvement may range from minimal to maximal depending on how well the initial concept and the developing design seem to be cohering. Periodically—whenever the overall design effort reaches a stage requiring coordinated planning—full design conferences are called to review and compare current plans for scenery, costume, lighting, and properties; these conferences afford opportunities for the designers to collaborate with each other instead of simply with the director.

The director's function at this stage of design is to approve or reject, as well as to suggest. As the person who sits at the top of the artistic hierarchy, the director has the last word on design matters, but that does not mean she or he can simply command the show into being; theatre design, like any creative process, cannot be summoned forth like an obedient servant. Moreover, wholesale rejection of a designer's work after the initial stages inevitably involves serious time loss and budgetary waste—not to mention the risk of provoking some important staff resignations. For these reasons, the directorial effort must be committed from the outset to sound collaborative principles. Once under way, the director-designer collaboration must take the form of shared responsibility in a developing enterprise, not confrontation between warring artists attempting to seize the reins of aesthetic control.

CASTING   The cliché "casting is 90 percent of directing" undeniably contains more than a germ of truth. The people in a play—the actors—not only attract more audience attention than any other aspect of the play but also represent what the audience *cares* about and will remember the next day. They garner about 90 percent of all the interest an audience expends on a play, and if they squander that interest they can destroy the effectiveness of any theatrical presentation.

The theatre as a medium has many individual elements that are standardized and predictable: flats are made according to formula, lighting instruments are factory-calibrated to conform to precise specifications, color media are mathematically measured and numbered, and one theatre's black "velours" are identical to those of another. But the one unique ingredient of the theatre—as the audience sees it—is the actor. Actors are people, and as people they are exquisitely individual; moreover, the audience, being human itself, is particularly attuned to the actor's human and idiosyncratic uniqueness. We would never mistake the Hamlet of Mel Gibson for the Hamlets of Kenneth Branagh, Ethan Hawke, Kevin Kline, or Val Kilmer. The actor's personality, physical and vocal characteristics, technical abilities, and sheer talent and "presence" weigh mightily in the final realization of every individual performance and in every ensemble of performances. A miscast or untalented or untrained actor can mar the effectiveness of any production, even in a minor role; in a major role a poor performance simply ruins the play. Casting may not, in the end, account for 90 percent of the director's contribution, but there can be no doubt that bad casting renders all other efforts immaterial.

Most casting takes place in auditions, where the actor can be seen and heard by the director and associates either in a "cold reading" of material from the play to be produced or in a prepared presentation of previously developed material not necessarily related to the production at hand. Although "star" performers are often cast apart from auditions, owing to their known ability to attract audiences to any production, most veteran professional actors regularly submit to auditioning. The director's ability to detect an incipiently brilliant performance in the contrived audition format is a critical factor in effective casting.

Depending on the specific demands of the play and the rehearsal situation, the director may pay special attention to any or all of the following characteristics: the actor's training and experience, physical characteristics and vocal technique, suitability for the style of the play, perceived ability to impersonate a specific character in the play, personality traits that seem fitted to the material at hand, ability to understand the play and its milieu, personal

Theatre is an art that people make out of themselves. But that art doesn't simply arise out of thin air; it must be created, afresh, in every instance. That creation requires both inspiration and organization, which together turn ideas and wishes into an actual dramatic production, comprising many separate ingredients.

THE FOUR INGREDIENTS OF THEATRE . . .

To make theatre—that is, to produce a play—two ingredients are absolutely required: *space* and *people.* Two additional ingredients are almost certainly needed: a *text* and various *materials,* such as scenery, costumes, and props. Of course, It's nice to have money as well, but money, after all, is only useful for acquiring the previously mentioned ingredients; indeed, great productions have been created by unpaid volunteers who improvised their texts in available spaces, using materials already in their possession. So money facilitates but is not an absolute requirement of theatrical art.

AND A FIFTH . . .

But there is one vital, intangible component of theatrical art that animates and drives the other four: *purpose.* Purpose asks the question, *Why* do you want to make theatre? To create a work of art? to entertain an audience? to convey a message? to ritualize a sacred belief? to build a community? to investigate drama more deeply? or, for more personal and social reasons, to meet new people? to impress your friends? to build a dramatic

career? All productions are driven by an individual mix of such purposes, some idealistic, some social, and some career-centered. Any and all of these purposes can motivate and anchor a play's production, and none of them are inimical to theatre art.

PUTTING IT TOGETHER

Putting a play production together is an art in itself. Although the end product may appear to be seamlessly assembled, the ingredients are many, and the process of bringing them all to individual excellence—and then fusing them into an integrated artistic whole—takes time, experience, and skill.

SEQUENCE OF ASSEMBLY

There is no "normal" order in which a play's text, space, people, and materials are brought together. In what we might call the twentieth-century European model, a director might simply choose a play and begin rehearsing it with a company of actors, designers, and technicians, all of whom would work simultaneously and collaboratively toward an ultimate production. Staging possibilities are suggested, explored, and tested in rehearsal, and designs are developed to support the emerging stage action. When (and if) a viable production appears, an opening performance date is announced, and eventually the production is placed in the theatre's repertory. This European model was standard for directors Konstantin Stanislavsky at the Moscow Art Theatre and Bertolt Brecht at the

Berliner Ensemble, each of whom spent up to a year rehearsing his individual productions; it is still common in many state-subsidized European theatre companies. But this model is dependent on a number of factors rarely available outside of those state-run theatres that maintain a large company of permanent artists (on year-round salaries) and enjoy a budget unconstrained by commercial (box-office) pressures. Even in Europe, such theatres are becoming increasingly rare.

In the much more common model, virtually universal in America, productions are largely assembled on paper and in meetings well before rehearsals even begin. Plays are selected with production schedules (and opening dates) already determined; they are often designed before the roles have been cast. Rehearsal and construction periods are often as short as three weeks or less. This "American model," as we'll call it here, is obviously more efficient with regard to up-front costs, as the great bulk of theatre workers (actors and most technicians) need be hired for only a few weeks of concentrated work prior to the opening performance, when box-office receipts start coming in to cover expenses. And while many theatre artists lament the decreased opportunity to make creative changes in rehearsal, the American model challenges those who lead theatrical productions—chiefly directors and designers—to become visionaries: to create in their heads, to communicate quickly and easily in writing (and sketching), to organize productively, to anticipate wisely and surely, and to inspire in a void.

Using the American model, then, we will examine the play production process by dividing it into two parts: *conception* and *execution*. Because the former is essentially done in the minds of the leadership team (the producer, director, and designers), we will discuss this process in general terms. For the latter, however, we will examine through photographs an actual play production.

Conception

The conception phase is generally headed by a producer, who ordinarily has final responsibility for choosing a script, securing the financing and the theatre facility, hiring the staff, and overseeing all aspects of the production.

Once a director and design team are in place, however, these individuals become a fundamental part of the conceptualizing process. They are the ones responsible for making—and integrating—the initial decisions about the bringing in and bringing together of the first four ingredients of play production. We'll look at these ingredients separately, keeping in mind, however, that they are meaningful only in their eventual combination.

Text Unless you are hoping to present a totally improvised play, making the words up as you go along (and such works have existed since the begin-

ning of theatre history, though not always labeled as plays), your drama will be built around a specific dramatic text: perhaps a recognized classic, a play from the modern repertoire, an adaptation or translation of either of these, or an original play to be seen for the first time. What questions should you, as a potential producer-director, consider when selecting a text?

- Who is the potential audience for this play? Are there enough people in the community who would be interested in seeing it?
- Does the play have meaning for a contemporary audience? Does it have relevance to contemporary issues? Will the play entertain the audience, not only in the comedic sense but also in the root sense of the word (in French, *entretenir*); that is, will the play hold the audience's attention?
- Can I—and the staff I can attract—pull it off? Do I understand this play, and can I imagine its theatrical possibilities well enough to make it a "success" with the resources available to me?
- Can I get *performance rights* to the play? If it's an original play, you will need the author's written permission. If it's a published play and still protected by copyright, you will need the permission of the author's legal representative. Published plays and play translations written before 1978 are protected for seventy-five years from the date of publication. Plays

published after that date are protected for seventy years following the author's death. Thus if the play you want to produce was written within the past seventy-five years, it's probably covered by copyright. Fortunately, play-leasing companies—such as Samuel French, Inc., and Dramatists' Play Service—normally make rights available for such plays, at a reasonable cost, after their initial professional runs have been completed.

Space Where might the play be staged? In a school auditorium? an outdoor amphitheater? a leased theatre in the city? a public plaza? a back room in a restaurant? or a "site-specific" venue, such as a train station or a woody grove? Whatever location you choose will have profound influence on the way the play will be staged, seen, and received. You should certainly consider the following:

- How large an audience do I anticipate? The number of seats times the number of performances will determine the theatre's maximum capacity for this play; you will certainly want a seating area large enough to accommodate those who come, but you won't want a house so large as to leave a sea of empty seats.
- What *scale* and *style* of production am I considering? A bustling farce with several sets and a huge cast would overwhelm a small theatre; conversely, an intimate play

would get lost if staged in a cavernous dining hall.

- How do I want to stage the play? If you want to use flying scenery, you'll obviously need a theatre with the appropriate equipment. If you want to stage the play throughout the audience space, you might look for a theatre without a fixed seating area.
- Is the theatre available for rehearsal time? for loading in scenery? Is the theatre heated? air-conditioned? reasonably free from traffic noise? too expensive?

People How many people does it take to put on a play? Consider the original program for Claudia Shear's semi-autobiographical drama, *Blown Sideways through Life*. This one-woman, one-set, one-act play was written and performed by Shear at the Cherry Lane Theatre in New York in the late 1990s. What might amaze you is the number of persons listed in that program: there were eight producers, two assistants to the producers, a director, an assistant director, four designers (set, costumes, lighting, and sound), two assistant designers, a composer, a choreographer, a production stage manager, an assistant stage manager, two general managers, one assistant to the general managers, three press representatives, a company manager, a production manager, a technical director, an assistant technical director, three painters, a production electrician, a production photographer, a legal counsel, an accountant, a comptroller, and two management interns. Then there was Cherry Lane Theatre's general manager, plus its house manager, box-office treasurer, assistant treasurer, and house carpenter. Finally, there were six business firms (general management, insurance, advertising, banking, payroll service, press representation) plus three production firms (scenery, lighting, and sound). And after all of this, the program gave "special thanks" to fifteen additional persons and institutions.

So this small, off-Broadway "one-woman" show required no less than seventy named individuals and nine firms—in addition to the author-performer—to make its way to the public. And that figure doesn't even include the ushers, the ticket takers, the concession personnel, or the maintenance crew. It actually took over a hundred people to put on this "one-woman" show. And if it takes a hundred people to mount *Blown Sideways through Life,* you can imagine what it takes to mount the Broadway *Phantom of the Opera.* Here are some things you'd want to consider before assembling the people who will help to put the play together:

- How many people (and in what roles: actors, stage managers, carpenters, running crew, and so on—perhaps all of those job titles listed in the program just mentioned, plus some others unique to your play) will I actually need? Where can I find them?

- What sort of a company do I want to assemble? Professionals? students? amateur enthusiasts? family members? There are pros and cons for each choice.
- Will they be able to work together? Will they be able to work with me? Putting on a play necessarily involves collaboration; all the people engaged must work in close harmony for the play to succeed. Will the people I want, individually, prove compatible with each other in their respective roles?
- Do the people I want (whom I believe I have access to) have the skills I need for the play? Will they be available for rehearsals, work calls, and performances? Can I afford their services—that is, will they work for free, or, if not, will I be able to hire them within my budget? Are there legal or union provisions governing such hirings?

Materials Most play productions include manufactured items such as scenery, costumes, props, and lighting. Many productions also include music and/or sound, which can be recorded or played "live" on instruments or other implements. Some of these materials can be purchased, rented, or built. If materials are to be built, you may also need shop space for building, painting, and assembling. Some considerations include the following:

- *Style:* What kind of look do I want for this production? Elegant? lavish? shocking?

experimental? naturalistic? political? Every look should be reflected in the mix of materials you choose.

- *Cost:* Can I afford what I'm looking for? What are my resources for creating it—from purchasing to renting to building? If I build, do I have the people, the space, the funds, and the time to do it the way I want?
- *Safety:* What safety measures do I need to take? Anything an actor or audience member walks on (or under or near) or sits on must meet all local codes for structural soundness and fireproofing. Aisles and exits must be kept clear at all times.

Execution

To illustrate the execution part of a play's production process, we will look at the 1998 production of *Measure for Measure,* directed by the author of this book at the Colorado Shakespeare Festival. The CSF, which has operated continuously on the campus of the University of Colorado in Boulder since 1957, employs about 175 persons each summer, mounting four productions in two theatres, including the outdoor Mary Rippon Theatre, where *Measure for Measure* was staged.

The production process lasts roughly a year, with initial staff hirings (directors and designers) occurring in the previous summer, consultations (generally by mail or e-mail) between directors and designers beginning in the fall, full-scale and on-site design and production meetings in January and March, casting and rehearsals beginning in mid-May, and a seven-week performance season beginning at the end of June—when the whole process begins all over again for the following year.

The CSF is considered a semi-professional" theatre company because the directors, designers, and many of the senior managers and technicians are professionals (members of professional stage unions and/or academic theatre faculties) and a number of the actors (two in 1998) are members of the Actors Equity Association; the remaining company members are selected in a national search, including exhaustive auditions, from current students and recent graduates of leading American graduate theatre programs.

1. *Planning meetings.* We get started. The director meets regularly with the designers and staff – beginning nearly six months before rehearsals begin – to create the basic production concepts, designs, staging plans, and building/rehearsal schedules that will bring the production into being.

1.

2.

for" roles in (that is, read aloud from) each play. The site shown here is the outdoor stage where the play will ultimately be presented; Tyler Layton and Andrew Shulman audition for the roles of Isabella and Angelo, which they will get.

4. *First reading.* When the play is cast, the director gathers the actors around a table, introduces them to the design staff and each other, explains the initial production concepts that have already been developed, and invites the designers to show their designs to the company. Then, still around the table, the actors read the play aloud. Layton, having highlighted her character's lines in green, reads aloud from her text as designer Forrester looks on and Courtney Peterson — who will play five different roles in this production (Francesca, Marianna, a dancer, a prisoner, a whore) — highlights lines she is assigned at this reading.

2. *Design meeting.* Continuing design "mini-meetings" are essential to make certain that design and directorial goals are integrated and consistent. Here, scene designer William Forrester and costume designer Madeline Kozlowski compare their individual renderings to ensure that the colors harmonize effectively.

3. *Auditions.* Actors in the company first present prepared monologues and then are asked to "read

3.

4.

5.

6.

5. *Scene shop.* Designer Forrester, using the three-dimensional model he has developed, explains its mechanics to master carpenter Michael Dombroski.

6. *Set construction.* On the stage, technical director Stancil Campbell oversees the welding together of structural pieces in the central scenic unit.

7. *Set detail.* In the scene shop, property artisan Janelle Baarspul sculpts and sands the statuary that is to be part of the scenic architecture.

8. *Costume shop.* Designer Kozlowski arranges the sash on the duke's costume while cutter Andrea Johnson works on a garment. Behind Kozlowski are the renderings (colored drawings) that guide the shop in creating each costume.

7.

8.

9.

9. *Fittings*. With Kozlowski looking on, Layton is fitted into a preliminary costume, made with an inexpensive fabric but on the pattern of the final garment; this will serve as a model for the actual costume.

10. *Checking the call-board*. Because four plays are rehearsing simultaneously in this company,

rehearsal schedules are extremely complicated. Actor Greg Ungar checks the call-board, where all schedules are posted at least twenty-four hours in advance.

11. *Blocking*. One of the most fundamental directorial functions is to "block" the actors' movements – to determine from which side of the stage they enter; where, when, and

MEASURE FOR MEASURE

10.

11.

how they sit, stand, walk, fall down, or leave the stage; and, in general, how they create the physical action of the play. Here, at an early rehearsal on the outdoor stage – with the yet-unbuilt scenery indicated by lines taped onto the stage floor – the director blocks a scene between Mikel McDonald, playing the duke, and Layton; both are still carrying and reading from their scripts, into which they will also write down their blocking.

12. *Rehearsing.* Once the actors are "off book" (have memorized their lines and basic moves), they can begin to fully embody their roles, filling them with passion and intensity. Wearing rehearsal costumes (that is, clothing that approximates the shape – though not necessarily the look – of their costumes), and working in an indoor rehearsal hall (with the lines of the set again taped onto the floor), Layton and Shulman rehearse one of their confrontations. Shulman is wearing prop eyeglasses in order to get used to them. This rehearsal is just for a single scene; subsequent rehearsals will run whole acts at a time, and, eventually, "run-through" rehearsals will be called for the whole play.

13. *Choreography.* Directors call in specialist directors when required. Here, in a dance studio, choreographer David Capps (*center*) stages the Viennese waltz with which the production will begin.

12.

13.

14. *Hanging lights*. On and around the stage, technicians hang and mount the hundreds of lighting instruments that will be used in the production. Here, master electrician Kevin Feig mounts an ellipsoidal reflector at the side of the stage.

15. *Cabling*. Atop the "diving board," apprentice technician Tiffany Williams wires up a string of overhead lights twenty-four feet above the ground.

16. *Prop shop*. The director has requested a stand-up desk for the play; it will hold the papers, pens, official stamping devices, sealing wax, envelopes, and several other items to be used during performance. But it also must stand straight on a raked (tilted) stage floor and have a device that will hold props steady in a high wind — the production will be staged in an outdoor theatre! Scenic designer Forrester has designed the unit; it remains for property master Jolene Obertin and master property artisan Sean McArdle to determine exactly how it will be used onstage and to make and paint it accordingly.

15.

14.

16.

17.

18.

17. *Craft shop*. The area of crafts encompasses everything that falls between props and costumes, particularly nonfabric items that are worn, such as shoes, armor, and insignia. Here, crafts artisan Abbey Rayburn glues together the leather epaulets that will be part of Angelo's costume.

18. *Sound studio*. Sound design creates all the non-actor-generated music and sound effects – prerecorded or performed live – heard by the audience. In this production, Strauss waltzes, 1930s jazz, medieval religious chants both male and female, coarse German drinking songs, gloomy "prison music," an extended royal trumpet fanfare, amplified door knockings and key-lock turnings, and the sound of a 1930s propeller airplane flying across the stage will be heard. Sound designer Kevin Dunayer must acquire, record, and establish the cuing (timing) of all these effects and determine how they will emanate from his various tape decks and amplifiers to the myriad speakers on and around the stage.

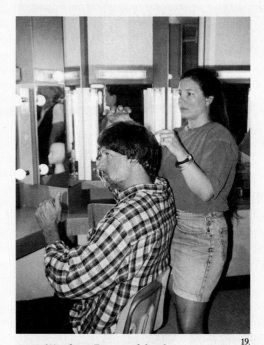

19.

19. *Wig shop*. For part of the play, the duke disguises himself as a friar, and so McDonald must be fitted for a friar's wig, complete with "baldpate" in the center, by wig shop manager Lee Barnette-Dombrowski.

20.

20. *Paper tech*. To this point the show has been created in separate spaces: acting in the rehearsal room, choreography in the dance studio, lighting on the stage, and scenery, costumes, props, wigs, crafts, and sound in their separate shops and studios. Now it is time to start putting them together and under the control of the stage manager, Richard Ballering (*second from left*), who will "call" the show moment-by-moment. At the "paper tech," every light and sound event, every scenery and prop move, and every actor entrance and exit is precisely identified and written into the stage manager's production book. These are the "cues" that the stage manager will time and call — ordinarily through headsets — during every performance.

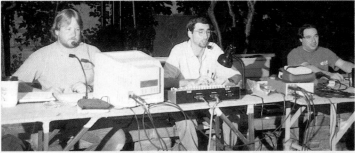

21.

21. *Tech table*. At the subsequent technical rehearsal (known as "tech" — of which there may be many more than one), acting is finally combined with the technical elements of scenery, lighting, props, and sound. For tech, a special table is set up in the back of the audience; there, stage manager Ballering and the lighting and sound designers can communicate over headsets, write notes about what must be corrected, and still watch every second of what is happening onstage.

22.

22. *Tech rehearsal is under way*. Onstage, actors rehearse the play on the basic set and under stagelights; they are still in rehearsal clothes, though some actors wear pieces of their actual costumes. The set is not yet fully completed or painted, but enough elements are in place that the lighting and sound can be roughly established — and later perfected during the two dress rehearsals and preview that are to follow.

23.

24.

23. Scene painting. Charge artist Heidi Hoffer gives the set its final coats of paint and texture.

24. "Quick-change" rehearsal. Because some actors must change costumes in a matter of seconds without having time to get back to the dressing room, offstage clothing changes are carefully choreographed and rehearsed before full dress rehearsals. A team of backstage "dressers" are essential to the process. Here, Alex Ward and his dressers rehearse one of his quick changes — from Antonio to Barnardine.

25. Stage manager's booth. In preparation for dress rehearsal, stage manager Ballering moves from the tech table to his hidden perch above the audience where he will call the show. His headset connects him with the sound and light operators and to the assistant stage manager backstage who will coordinate the cuing of actors and scenery shifters.

25.

26. Makeup room. Readying for dress rehearsal, actors Laurie G. Lapides and Layton share a makeup mirror; behind them actor Robert May, playing old Escalus, has just put on his baldpate.

27. First dress rehearsal. "First dress" is where costumes and (usually) makeup are added to the mix. Everything is coming together, in fact, except for the audience. Here, backstage, as Francesca (*far right, facing us*) leaves the stage proper, the provost (*his back to us*) prepares to make his entrance, while assistant stage manager Stephanie Dulaney cues a stagehand to rotate the "office wall" into position. Not everything will work perfectly tonight: one quick change won't get completed on time, and Isabella's veil will come off prematurely. But this is what tech and dress rehearsals are for: to find the problems and then fix them.

26.

27.

28.

28. Director's notes. From run-throughs on, the director (*standing at right*) meets with the cast after every rehearsal to suggest how the production can be improved. Do we need faster pacing? clearer diction? heightened intensity? revised blocking? Because rehearsal time is quite limited in a repertory company as opening night nears (the actors are preparing another production simultaneously with this one), almost all of these changes will have to be made in such a note session, held in the theatre's rehearsal hall, rather than in a full re-rehearsal. Actors write down their notes. Because tomorrow is opening night, there will be no further chance to get everything right before facing the audience — and the critics.

29.

29. The house manager. It's time to open. In the final act of preparation, one of the house managers instructs the ushers how to seat the patrons. The actors are in the dressing rooms, the stage manager is in his perch, the technicians are at their booths and offstage positions, and the director (typically) is nervously pacing at the back of the house. The show is just about to begin.

30.

30 and 31. *The final production.*
Top: The Duke and his officers over-
look the Viennese waltz at his farewell
party, with which the production begins. *Bottom:* A waiter and three
patrons drink, smoke, and argue in
an outdoor cafe at the beginning of
the following scene.

31.

liveliness and apparent stage "presence," past record of achievement, general deportment and attitude, apparent cooperativeness and "directability" in the context of an ensemble of actors in a collaborative enterprise, and overall attractiveness as a person with whom one must work closely over the next four to ten weeks. And the director might well be looking for a great many other things besides.

What is ultimately astonishing about the casting process is that most of the decisions based on these complex criteria are made not in agonizing conferences but in two- to four-minute auditions among perfect strangers! Indeed, this practice is often looked upon as a regrettable theatrical fact, but its very persistence indicates that a great many valid casting judgments can be made in a very short time— provided that time is used with wisdom and sensitivity.

Most of the decisions that are made in the two- to four-minute initial audition are "no" decisions; that is, those actors who are immediately perceived as wrong for the play, wrong for the part, or lacking in the desired level of proficiency are winnowed out. Others may be winnowed out on the subjective ground of apparent attitude—a dangerous ground, because the director might mistake shyness for hostility or "audition jitters" for an exaggerated reserve.

Actors who survive the first audition then "read" again, sometimes several times, and at this stage the director is involved more and more in the audition process, often coaching the actors to determine how rapidly they can acquire the qualities needed. Such "callbacks" can go on for days and even weeks in the professional theatre, limited only by the union requirement that actors receive pay after a certain point; the frequency with which such payments are made amply attests to the care that attends final casting decisions in the professional theatre.

There is good casting and bad casting, of course, and there is also inspired casting. Many of the greatest performances in theatre history have been achieved by actors who at first glance appeared unsuited to their roles: gangly Janet McTeer seemed to many an odd choice to play Nora, whose husband calls her his "little lovebird" in Ibsen's *A Doll's House,* but her dazzling performance in that role received an enthusiastic reception in London and New York and won her the 1997 Broadway Tony Award for Best Actress. Diminutive Michael Emerson was more than a foot shy of Oscar Wilde's stature but played him to sensational acclaim in Moisés Kaufman's award-winning 1997 play *Gross Indecency.* The ability to perceive an actor's unique and unexpected relationship to a specific role—and to chance that casting in place of a "safer" and more traditional choice—has always been the mark of the most daring and most successful film and play directors.

Implementation Phase

With the play selected and conceptualized, with the designers chosen and the designs under way, and with the actors auditioned and cast, the production moves from its preparatory phase to its implementation. It is here that the meeting described at the beginning of this chapter occurs; it is here in the silence between the completion of a plan and its execution that conversation and ink on paper turn into blood, sweat, and tears. The pressure is on. Now the director's ability to maintain both leadership and creative inspiration under pressure—always an important element of professional skill—becomes crucial.

From the time of that first company meeting, the director controls the focus and consciousness of the entire cast and staff. As head of an ambitious and emotionally consuming enterprise, the director will be the repository of the company's collective artistic hopes—the focal point for the company's collective frustration, its anxiety, and, on occasion, its despair. The company's shield against the intrusions of an outside world, the director is also the spokesperson for the enterprise to which the

Trevor Nunn's 2004 production of *Hamlet* at the Old Vic in London employed the revolutionary casting of a very young man, 23-year-old Ben Whishaw, in the title role. Foregoing the standard practice of using a famous older actor, Nunn's production – with a consequently younger-than-usual actress, Imogen Stubbs, as Hamlet's mother – made Hamlet's sulkiness and indecision far more affecting than is customary in this play.

company has collectively dedicated itself. Directorial power or influence cannot be substantially altered by any attempt the director may make to cultivate or repudiate it—it simply comes with the job and with the need for every theatrical company to have a head, a focus, a direction. The manner in which the director uses that power, and the sensitivity with which she or he now brings the production into being, determines the nature of each director's individual brand of artistry.

STAGING   Staging—which essentially involves positioning actors on the set and moving them about in a theatrically effective manner—is certainly the most obvious of directorial functions. It is the one thing directors are always expected to do and to do well, and it is the one they are most often *seen* doing; it is no wonder that traditional textbooks on directing tend to be largely devoted to this function.

The medium of staging is the actor in space and time—with the space defined by the acting area and the settings and the time defined by the duration of the theatrical event and the dynamics of its dramatic structure. The goals of staging are multiple and complementary: to create focus for the play's themes, to lend cred-

One of the director's major problems in staging realistic plays is letting the audience see the expressions of important characters – and hence the faces of the actors playing them – while still maintaining the credibility of those characters, who are (supposedly) talking to each other and not to the audience. Director Guy Masterson solves this by having all actors focus on a key prop in this jury-room scene in Reginald Rose's *12 Angry Men*, produced at the Edinburgh Festival in 2003.

ibility to the play's characters, to generate interest in the play's action, to impart an aesthetic wholeness to the play's appearance, to provoke suspenseful involvement in the play's events, and, in general, to stimulate a fulfilling theatricality for the entire production.

The basic architecture of staging is called "blocking," which refers to the timing and placement of a character's entrances, exits, rises, crosses, embraces, and other major movements of all sorts. The "blocking pattern" that results from the interaction of characters in motion provides the framework of an overall staging; it is also the physical foundation of the actors' performance—and many actors

have difficulty memorizing their lines until they know the blocking that will be associated with them.

The director may block a play either by preplanning the movements ("preblocking") on paper or by allowing the actors to improvise movement on a rehearsal set and then "fixing" the blocking sometime before the first performance. Often a combination of these methods is employed, with the director favoring one method or the other depending on the specific demands of the play, the rehearsal schedule, rapport with the acting company, or the director's own stage of preparation: complex or stylized plays and settings and short rehearsal periods usually dictate a great deal of preblocking; simple domestic plays and experienced acting ensembles are often accorded more room for improvisation. Each method can produce highly commendable results in the right hands and at the right time; both can present serious problems if misapplied or ineptly handled.

For the most part, the blocking of a play is hidden in the play's action; it tends to be effective insofar as it is *not* noticed and insofar as it simply brings other values into play and focuses the audience's attention on significant aspects of the drama. By physically enhancing the dramatic action and lending variety to the play's visual presentation, a good blocking pattern can play a large role in creating theatrical life and excitement. But beyond this, there are moments when inspired blocking choices can create astonishing theatrical effects—effects that are not hidden at all but are so surprising and shocking that they compel intense consideration of specific dramatic moments and their implications. Such a *coup de théâtre* was achieved, for example, by director Peter Brook in his celebrated 1962 production of *King Lear,* when Paul Scofield, as Lear, suddenly rose and, with one violent sweep of his arm, overturned the huge oak dining table at which he had been seated, sending pewter mugs crashing to the floor as he raged at his daughter Goneril's treachery. This stunning action led to a reevaluation of the character of both Lear and Goneril and of the relationship between this tempestuous and sporadically vulgar father and his socially ambitious daughter.

Some plays require specialized blocking for certain scenes—for duels, for example, or dances. Such scenes demand more than nuts-and-bolts blocking and are frequently directed by specialists, such as dueling masters or fight choreographers, working with the director. These specialized situations are not at all rare in the theatre—almost every play that was written before the nineteenth century includes a duel or a dance or both—and the ability to stage an effective fight scene or choreographic interlude (or at least to supervise the staging of one) is certainly a requisite for any director who aspires to work beyond the strictly realistic theatre.

"Business" is a theatre term that refers to the small-scale movements a character performs within the larger pattern of entrances and crosses and exits. Mixing a cocktail, answering a telephone, adjusting a tie, shaking hands, fiddling with a pencil, winking an eye, and drumming on a tabletop are all "bits of business" that can lend a character credibility, depth, and fascination. Much of the stage business in a performance is originated by the actor—usually spontaneously over the course of rehearsal—although it may be stimulated by a directorial suggestion or command. The director ultimately must select from among the rehearsal inventions and determine what business will become a part of the finished performance; when this determination is made, bits of business become part of the blocking plan.

Staging, then, in the largest sense, includes both hidden and bold blocking effects, specialized movements, and small idiosyncratic behaviors, all combined into a complex pattern that creates meaning, impact, and style. Skillful staging unites the design elements of a production with the acting, creating an omnidynamic spatial interaction between actors, costumes, scenery, and audience, infusing the stage with life. Getting a play "on its feet," as the theatrical jargon puts it, is usually the first step in making it breathe; and the best staging is that which gives the actors the chance to breathe the air of the playwright's world and to awaken to the true vitality of the playwright's characters.

ACTOR-COACHING The director is the actor's coach, and in practice the director is likely to spend the largest share of her or his time exercising this particular function. The coaching begins at the first meeting with the cast.

Aaron Beall takes a characteristic director's pose as he stages Mark Greenfield and Melora Griffis in a production of Chekhov's *Vaudevilles* at New York's 42nd Street Show World Center.

Initially, it is the director who conveys the direction the production is expected to take: the concept, the interpretation, the intended "look" and style of the theatrical product. It is also the director who determines the schedule and process of work that will lead up to that final product. The director is the rehearsal leader and decides what activities—discussions, improvisations, games, exercises, lectures, research, blocking, or polishing—will occupy each rehearsal period; the director leads such activities with an eye to their ultimate goal.

Further, like the manager of an athletic team, the director is responsible for stimulating the best efforts of the cast and for instilling in them a high regard for teamwork (which in the theatre is called "ensemble") as well as for individual craft excellence and artistry. And because the work of the theatre inevitably demands of the actor a good measure of emotional, psychological, even irrational investment, the director has an opportunity (if not an obligation) to provide an atmosphere in which actors can feel free to liberate their powers of sensitivity and creativity. Good directors lead their cast; great directors inspire them.

The ways in which directors go about coaching actors are various and probably more dependent on personality than on planning. Some directors are largely passive; they either "block and run," in the jargon of commercial theatre, or function primarily as a sounding board for actors' decisions about intention, action, or business. Conversely, there are directors closer to the popular stereotype, mercurial directors whose approaches at times verge on the despotic: they cajole, bully, plead, storm, and rage at their actors; involve themselves in every detail of motive and characterization; and turn every rehearsal into a mixture of acting class, group therapy session, and religious experience. Both methods, as experience teaches, can produce theatrical wizardry, and both can fail utterly; probably the determining factors either way are the strength of the director's ideas and the extent to which the cast is willing to accept his or her directorial authority.

Too little direction, of course, can be as stultifying to an actor as too much; the passive director runs the risk of defeating an actor's performance by failing to confirm it, that is, by withholding constructive response. Similarly, the extremely active director may, in a whirlwind of passion, overwhelm the actor's own creativity and squelch his efforts to build a sensitive performance, thereby condemning the production to oppressive dullness. For these and other reasons, most directors today strive to find a middle ground, somewhere between task mastery and suggestion, from which they can provide the actor with both a goal and a disciplined path toward it while maintaining an atmosphere of creative freedom.

Directors need not be actors themselves, but they must understand the paradoxes and ambiguities inherent in that art if they are to help the actor fashion a solid and powerful performance. The greatest acting braves the unknown and flirts continuously with danger (the danger of exposure, of failure, of transparency, of artifice); the director must give the actor a careful balance of freedom and guidance in order to foster the confidence that leads to that kind of acting. Directors who are insensitive to this requirement—no matter how colorful their stormings and coaxings or how rational their discussions of the playwright's vision—are virtually certain to forfeit

"This Is How It's Done!"

Publicity photographs taken in rehearsal frequently show a director onstage with a few actors, demonstrating a bit of business and "showing them how it's done." This kind of publicity has probably fostered a certain misunderstanding of the director's role among the general public, for demonstration is only a part of directing, and a distinctly small part at that. Indeed, some directors scrupulously avoid it altogether.

Demonstration as a way of teaching an actor a role has a long history in the theatre and was a particularly common practice in those periods when directing was carried out chiefly by retired actors. Even today, young actors rehearsing for classical plays at the Comédie Française (founded in 1680) are expected to learn their parts by mimicking the performance of their elders down to the last detail of inflection, tone, gesture, and timing. And, of course, many contemporary American directors occasionally give "line readings" to an actor or demonstrate the precise manner of gesturing, moving, sitting, or handling a prop if they perceive that a specific desired behavior might not come naturally from the actor himself.

But demonstration as an *exclusive* method of coaching an actor in a role is very much a thing of the past. Most contemporary directors make far greater use of discussion, suggestion, and improvisation. These methods seek to address the inner actor and to encourage him to distill his performance out of self-motivated passions and enthusiasms. Because they know that a purely imitative performance is all too likely to be a mechanical performance, today's directors tend to rely on more creative methods than "getting up there and showing how it's done."

the performance rewards that arise from the great actor-director collaborations.

PACING   Despite all the director's responsibilities, pace is perhaps the only aspect of a theatrical production for which general audiences and theatre critics alike are certain to hold the director accountable. Frequently, newspaper reviews of productions devote whole paragraphs of praise or blame to the actors and designers and evaluate the director's contribution solely in terms of the play's pace: "well paced" and "well directed" are almost interchangeable plaudits in the theatre critic's lexicon; and when a critic pronounces a play "slow" or "dragging," everyone understands he or she is firing a barrage at the director.

To the novice director (or critic), pace appears to be primarily a function of the rate at which lines are said; hence a great many beginning directors attempt to make their productions more lively simply by instructing everyone to speak and move at a lively clip: "Give it more energy!" "Make it happen faster!" But pace is fundamentally determined by a complex and composite time structure that must be developed to accommodate many variables, such as credibility, suspense, mood, style, and the natural rhythms of life: heartbeat, respiration, the duration of a spontaneous sob or an unexpected laugh. How much time is properly consumed, for example, by a moment of panic? a pregnant pause? a flash of remembrance? an agonized glance? a quick retort? These are the ingredients of pace, and they are not subject to the generalized "hurry-up" of the director who has not first discovered the pattern of rhythms inherent in a play.

The pace of a play should be determined largely by the quantity and quality of the information it conveys to the audience, and the director must decide how much time the audience requires to assimilate that information. In a farce, of course, the audience needs almost no time to synthesize information— therefore, farce generally is propelled rapidly, with information coming as fast as the actors can get it out. A psychological drama, on the other hand, may require a slower pace to convey a deeper understanding of its characters and issues; sympathy is engendered when audience members have an opportunity to compare the characters' lives with their own, to put themselves in the characters' situations, and to engage in introspection even as they observe the action onstage. Similarly, political drama commonly demands of us a critical inquiry into our own societies and our own lives as part of our understanding of what is happening onstage; this form, too, demands time to linger over certain perfectly poised questions—and the pace of a production must give us that time.

Just as a symphony is composed of several movements, so a well-paced theatrical production will inevitably have its adagio, andante, and allegro tempos. Faster tempos tend to excite, to bedazzle, and to sharpen audience attention; slower ones give audience members a chance to consider and to augment the play's actions and ideas with their own reflections. Often directors speak in terms of "setting up" an audience with a rapid pace and then delivering a "payoff" with a powerful, more deliberately paced dramatic catharsis. The sheer mechanics of theatrical pacing demand the greatest skill and concentration on the part of both actor and director, and for both, the perfection of dramatic timing (and most notably comic timing) is a mark of great theatrical artistry.

Directors vary in their manner of pacing plays, of course. Some wait until final rehearsals and then, martinet-like, stamp out

Directing comedy is an art in itself, and Dominique Serrand scored a brilliant success in a Shakespearean play that demands theatrical humor in its very title: *The Comedy of Errors*. Serrand, an artistic director at the Theatre de la Jeune Lune, guest-directed this play at the Guthrie Theatre in 2002 with what one reviewer called "fantastical . . . madcap panache" — as clearly shown in the mouth-stuffing scene between Laura Esping as an irate Luciana and Judson Pearce Morgan as a bewildered Antipholus.

rhythms on the stage floor with a stick or clap their hands in the back of the house. Some work out intricate timing patterns in the early rehearsals and explore them in great detail with the actors as to motivation, inner monologue, and interpersonal effect. Directorial intervention of some sort is almost always present in the achievement of an excellent dramatic pace; it rarely occurs spontaneously. Actors trained to the realist manner often tend to work through material slowly and to savor certain moments all out of proportion to the information they convey; actors trained in a more technical manner just as often are "off to the races" with dialogue, leaving the audience somewhat at sea about the meaning or importance of the matters at hand. And when a variety of actors, trained in different schools, come together in production for the first time, they can create such an arrhythmic pace that the play becomes unintelligible until the director steps in to guide and control the tempo.

COORDINATING   In the final rehearsals the director's responsibility becomes more and more one of coordination: of bringing together the concept and the designs, the acting and the staging, the pace and the performance. Now all the production elements that were developed separately must be judged, adjusted, polished, and perfected in their fuller context. Costumes must be seen under lights, staging must be seen against scenery, pacing must include the shifting of sets, acting must coalesce with sound amplification, and the original concept must be reexamined in light of its emerging realization. Is the theme coming across? Are the actions coming across? Can the voices be heard and understood? Do the costumes read? Is the play focused? Is the play interesting? Do we care about the characters? about the themes? about anything? Does the production seem to *work*?

Timing and wholeness are governing concepts in this final coordinating phase of production. In assessing the play's overall timing, the director must be prepared to judge the play's effectiveness against its duration and to modify or even eliminate those parts of the production that overextend the play's potential for communicating information, feelings, or ideas. Last-minute cutting is always a painful process—much labor and creative spirit have gone into those parts that will be cut—but many a production has been vastly improved by judicious pruning at this time. And in the interest of providing wholeness—that quality which unifies a play and gives it the stamp of taste and aesthetic assurance—the best and bravest directors are willing in these final moments to eliminate those elements that fail to cohere with the play's overall appearance and significance. Often these elements hold a special meaning for the director; they may even have figured into his or her earliest conception of the production. But now, in the cold light of disciplined analysis, they look painfully like directorial indulgence or extraneous showing off. The best directors are those who can be most rigorous with themselves at this stage, for they are the ones who are capable not only of generating ideas but also of refining and focusing artistic form.

In the final rehearsals—the "technical rehearsals," when scenery, lighting, and sound are added, and the "dress rehearsals," when the actors don costumes and makeup for the first time—the director arrives at a crossroads: although remaining fundamentally responsible for every final decision about the timing and balance of theatrical elements, she or he must now "give over" the production to the actors and technicians who will execute it. Beyond this junction the director will be consumed by the production and will disappear within it in a matter of days: it will reflect the director's personal conceptions and directorial skills without reflecting the director's own persona. After contributing to everything that appears upon the stage and initiating much of it, the director must accept the fact that he or she will not be recognized in any single moment, any single act, any single costume or lighting cue. In these final rehearsals the director's presence normally becomes more a force for organization than a source of inspiration—clipboard in hand, she or he delivers hundreds of last-minute notes to actors, technicians, and stage managers in an effort to give the production that extra finesse that distinguishes the outstanding from the mediocre.

What an extraordinary exchange of power has taken place between the first meeting of the cast and director and these final days! Whereas earlier the entire production was in the director's head and the cast waited in awe and expectation, now the actors hold the play in their heads and everyone confronts the unknowns of the play's reception. The actors have a new master now: the audience. It is in these days that even the most experienced actors confront their fundamental nakedness in performance: they must face the audience, and they must do it without benefit of directorial protection, with nothing to shield them save their costumes, characters, and lines. To the actor, the director is no longer a leader but a partner, no longer a parent but a friend. Actors may indeed experience a certain feeling of betrayal; the director, after all, has abandoned them to face the audience alone, just as in the medieval play Good Deeds accompanied Everyman only to the brink of the grave. But then acting, like death, is a trial that cannot be shared.

PRESENTING   It is an axiom of the theatre that nobody is more useless on opening night than the director. If all has progressed without major catastrophe and the production has successfully been "given over" to those who will run it and perform in it, the director's task on opening night consists chiefly in seeing and evaluating the production and gauging the audience response. This night may, of course, prove to be nothing but a calm between storms: in the professional theatre it may simply be the first of a series of opening nights, one calculated to serve as a guide to future rehearsals, rewritings, and rethinkings. Still, at this time the major work has reached a stopping point, and the director must shift perspectives accordingly.

The director in this last phase sometimes takes on certain responsibilities of a paratheatrical nature, such as writing directorial notes for use in newspaper stories and interviews and overseeing the house management, the dress of the ushers, the lobby decorations, the concession stands, or the "dressing of the house" (the spacing of audience members in a less than full house). The director may also play an active role as audience member by greeting patrons, chatting with critics, or leading the laughter and applause—although all of these activities are more common in community theatres than in professional ones.

More central to the directorial function in this final stage is the director's continuing evaluation of every production element in an effort to improve the audience impact. This may lead to changes at any time during the run of a play. In the professional theatre, new productions commonly go through a tryout period of two weeks or more—up to a year in a few cases—when the play is rehearsed and re-rehearsed daily between performances and ma-

terial is deleted, revised, restaged, and freshly created in response to audience reception. Some quite famous plays have succeeded only because of such "doctoring" during tryout periods, and it is not at all uncommon in the contemporary commercial theatre for a director to be replaced during this phase in order to accelerate revision.

Even after the final opening, however, and throughout the run of a play, most directors attend performances periodically and follow up their visits with notes to the actors—either to encourage them to maintain spontaneity or to discourage them from revising the original directorial plan. One perhaps apocryphal show-business story has it that the American director George Abbott once posted a rehearsal call late in a play's run in order to "take out the improvements."

Just as the actor might feel alone and somewhat betrayed in those empty moments prior to opening performance, so might the director feel a twinge of isolation at the ovation that follows the first performance. For it is in that curtain-call ovation that the audience takes over the director's critic-mentor function and the director is consigned to anonymity. The actors, heady with the applause, suddenly remember that it is they who provide the essential ingredient of theatre, while the director, cheering the ensemble from the back of the house, suddenly realizes he or she is now just one of the crowd, one witness among many to the realization of his or her own intangible and now remote plans and ideas. In the professional theatre, it is at this moment that the director's contract expires—a fitting reminder of the "giving over" that occurs in the direction of all plays. Only those directors who can derive genuine satisfaction from creating out of the medium of others' performance will thrive and prosper in directorial pursuits; those who aspire to public acclaim and adulation will most likely face perpetual frustration as practitioners of this all-encompassing and yet all-consuming art.

The Training of a Director

Traditionally, directors have come to their craft from a great many areas, usually after achieving distinction in another theatrical discipline: for example, Elia Kazan was first an actor, Gower Champion was a choreographer, Harold Prince was a producer, Peter Hunt was a lighting designer, Franco Zeffirelli was a scene designer, Robert Brustein was a drama critic, Harold Pinter was a playwright, Mike Nichols was an improvisational comedian, and Robert Wilson was an architectural student. Still, in addition to a specialty, most of these directors have brought to their art a comprehensive knowledge of the theatre in its various aspects. Having distinction in one field is important chiefly insofar as it gives directors a certain confidence and authority—and it gives others a confidence in their exercise of that authority. But it is comprehensive knowledge that enables directors to collaborate successfully with actors, designers, managers, playwrights, and technicians with facility and enthusiasm.

New directors entering the profession today are more likely than not to have been trained in a dramatic graduate program or conservatory—and often they have supplemented this training with an apprenticeship at a repertory theatre. One of the most remarkable recent developments in the American theatre has been the emergence of a cadre of expertly trained directors: men and women with a broad understanding of the theatre and a disciplined approach to directorial creativity.

Well-trained directors will possess—in addition to the craft mastery of staging, actor-coaching, pacing, and production coordinating—a strong literary imagination and an ability to conceptualize intellectually and visually. They will be sensitive to interpersonal relationships, which will play an important role in both the onstage and offstage activities under their control. They will have a sound working knowledge of the history of the theatre, the various styles and masterworks of dramatic literature, the potential of various theatre technologies, and the design possibilities inherent in the use of theatrical space. They will have at their command resources in music, art, literature, and history; they will be able to research plays and investigate production possibilities without starting at absolute zero; and they will be able to base ideas and conceptions on sound social, psychological, and aesthetic understandings.

All of these advanced skills can be effectively taught in a first-rate drama program, and for that reason today's top-flight theatre directors, more than any other group of stage artists, are likely to have studied in one or another of the rigorous drama programs now in place across the country. The accomplished director is perhaps the one all-around "expert" of the theatre; this is not to deride the director's function as a creative and imaginative force but to emphasize her or his responsibility over a broad and highly complex enterprise. Nothing is truly irrelevant to the training of a director, for virtually every field of knowledge can be brought to bear upon theatre production. The distinctiveness of any production of the contemporary theatre is largely a reflection of the unique but comprehensive training of its director, who is responsible not only for the overall initiative and corrective authority that infuse the production but also for the personal vision that inspires its singular direction.

7

Theatre Traditions: East and West

THEATRE, WHICH CONSISTS OF LIVE ACTORS who perform in real time before live audiences, is a unique art form because it exists "in the present." Theatre, however, is also deeply rooted in its past; plays seen today are often revivals, adaptations, or parodies of earlier ones. Even when they're wholly original, new plays will inevitably be compared to earlier works. Likewise, contemporary actors—like contemporary baseball players—will also be compared to their predecessors. Theatre is a living art but also a living tradition.

Some plays travel through time effortlessly, reappearing in new guises at dozens of points throughout history. A fourth-century-B.C. Greek comedy named *The Lot Drawers*, by Diphilis, concerning an old man foolishly in love with a young girl, was revised more than a hundred years later by the Roman comic dramatist Plautus under the title of *Sorientes;* another Roman dramatist revised it some years later into a play called *Casina;* and more than a thousand years later this play became the basis for a fifteenth-century Italian comedy by Niccolò Machiavelli titled *Clizia*. Thereafter, major elements of the plot appeared in early-sixteenth-century Italian *commedia dell'arte* farces, in the sixteenth- and seventeenth-century plays of Shakespeare and Molière, and more recently in American comedies on stage, film, and television.

Indeed, many of the world's greatest plays—in both the East and the West—are closely based on preceding ones. Dozens of eighteenth-century Japanese *kabuki* dramas are based on fourteenth-century Japanese *nō* scripts (often bearing the same titles), and most traditional Indian and Chinese plays are based on dramas from prior millennia. French neoclassic tragedies of

221

the seventeenth century, as well as French comedies of the twentieth century, were often based on Greek and Roman models more than two thousand years old. At least three of William Shakespeare's best-known plays—*King Lear, Hamlet,* and *The Taming of the Shrew*—were revisions of earlier English plays of virtually the same names by other authors. And Shakespeare's plays, in turn, have been a source for literally hundreds of modern dramas, including Tom Stoppard's *Rosencrantz and Guildenstern Are Dead,* Lee Blessing's *Fortinbras,* Paul Rudnik's *I Hate Hamlet,* Richard Nelson's *Two Shakespearean Actors,* Ann-Marie McDonald's *Goodnight Desdemona (Good Morning Juliet),* Amy Freed's *The Beard of Avon,* Stephen Sondheim's *West Side Story,* and Neil Simon's *The Goodbye Girl* and *Laughter on the 23rd Floor,* all of which parody or creatively extend portions of Shakespeare's plays. Indeed, the theatre continually resurrects its past traditions, just as it always seeks to extend and surpass them.

Therefore it is helpful, in looking at the theatre of today, to look to the traditions of the theatre in the past, from both the West (Europe and the Americas) and the East (Asia and the subcontinent). What follows is a capsule history of eleven important theatre traditions, from both East and West, that together outline the major world developments prior to the start of the modern theatre in the nineteenth century.*

The Origins of Theatre

How did drama begin?

No one knows for sure, but the theatre, along with human civilization itself, almost

_____

*Readers searching for expanded information on the theatre's past should consult the long edition of this book or, for a detailed accounting of the theatre's history, surveys and guides such as those by Martin ˙nham and Oscar Brockett (see the Selected Bibliog-
˙ y at the back of this book).

certainly began in Africa. The first known dramatic presentations occurred in northern Africa alongside the Nile River in ancient Egypt, as much as five thousand years ago, possibly as early as 3300 B.C.

But African theatre is far older than that. Indications of ritual performances can be seen in the activities of literally hundreds of African tribal groups dating as far back as 6000 B.C. And while we know very little about such performances—which, unlike the arts of painting and sculpture, left behind no permanent records—it is very likely they resembled tribal performances widely seen in rural Africa today. And from such present-day performances, we can see the two foundations of the theatre as it has been known and enjoyed throughout the course of human civilization. These two foundations of theatre are *ritual* and *storytelling.* Both have existed since ancient times, and both can be seen—though in different forms—wherever theatre is performed today.

Ritual

A ritual is a collective ceremony performed by members of a society, normally for religious or cultural reasons. The most ancient rituals were primarily intended to summon gods and influence nature, as with rain dances and healing ceremonies. But tribal rituals also arose to worship important life events, such as the changing of the seasons, and to provide public witness to life passages, such as birth, death, marriage, and the coming of age. Contemporary rituals of Christian baptism and Jewish bar mitzvah (coming of age) and funeral rites in virtually all cultures are descendants of these ancient tribal rites-of-passage ceremonies. Other rituals reenact defining moments of a culture's religious history—such as the birth, death, or resurrection of divine beings—allowing adherents to directly experience the passion of their culture's sacred heritage.

The early tribal rituals soon grew to involve elements we now consider theatrical crafts, in-

DNA studies have shown that the San bushmen, seen here in a ritual trance-dance in their native Botwsana, are direct descendants of the first evolved *Homo sapiens* from more than 100,000 years ago. The San remain hunter-gatherers; after a kill, the whole group chants and dances in a prehistoric desert ritual, summoning spiritual powers into their stomachs so as to heal both physical and psychological illnesses.

cluding staging, costuming, makeup, music, dance, formalized speech, chanting, and singing, as well as specific physical "props" (objects such as staffs, spears, skulls, and so on), often with totemic or spiritual properties that would prove crucial to the staged event. And while initially performed solely for the collective worship of the participants themselves, such theatricalized rituals played a role in impressing, educating, and evangelizing observers, including the children of the tribe and tribal visitors.

Not all rituals are based in religion. Secular rituals exist in Western culture today to give a spiritual or larger-than-life dimension to more worldly events. Such secular rituals may be seen in the black robes of courtroom judges, the precisely choreographed changing of the guard at the Tomb of the Unknown Soldier, the daily recitation of the formal Pledge of Al-

legiance in certain American classrooms, and even the lowering of the ball in New York's Times Square on New Year's Eve. Perhaps the most common collective ritual in Western culture is the wedding ceremony, with its formal costumes (tuxedo or tie-dyed), elevated language (psalms or sonnets), symbolic gift exchanges (ring or rings), and traditional music (Mendelssohn or McCartney). And the gravely cadenced march down the aisle transmits the ancient symbolism of bride handed from father to groom, even though such symbolism has lost much (if not all) of its original meaning over the years.

Whether sacred or secular, rituals dignify the events they represent, giving them enhanced meaning and authority. Most brides, for example, would feel shortchanged if their intended husband were to respond "uh-huh"

The mudmen of Papua New Guinea in the South Pacific, isolated from the rest of the world until the twentieth century, still cover their bodies in mud and wear home-made clay masks for their ancient hunting ritual, performed in their villages and also, as shown here, at a biannual September gathering of tribes in the town of Goroka.

Dogon performers of the *dana* ritual, dancing on six-foot stilts, represent larger-than-life forces in the most literal way: by being double human size.

instead of "I do," for while the literal meaning of "uh-huh" is perfectly clear, its everyday casualness implies a lack of public—and hence permanent—commitment.

Ritual is at the very origin of theatre. It is the act of performers re-creating, intensifying, nd making meaningful the myths, beliefs, ends, and traditions common to their col-e lives.

Storytelling

Coming almost immediately after ritual, however, and quickly blended into it, is the art of storytelling. Since humans developed coherent speech, they have sought to recount their (and others') daily adventures, including stories of the hunt and histories of the tribe. Indeed, such storytelling surely went hand in glove with the development of speech itself, for why invent words like *glorious* and *brave* and *beautiful* if not to augment a story being told?

Such storytelling is more personal and individual than collective ritual performance, since it generally relies on a single voice—and there-

Storytelling, an art more ancient than theatre, is still practiced as a public performance form, nowhere more successfully than at the annual Jonesborough, Tennessee, storytelling festival.

fore a single point of view. And while rituals may attract an audience, storytelling *requires* an audience: "hearer-spectators" who either don't know the story being told or are eager to hear it again with new details or fresh expression. Storytelling thus generates elements of character impersonation—the creation of voices, gestures, and facial expressions that reflect the personalities of the individuals portrayed—and seeks means to convey character emotions to the hearer-spectators. It also seeks to entertain, and thus it provides a structured *story*—rather than a random series of observations—which makes the narrative flow so as to compel audience engagement through suspense, varied graphic details, and a calculated momentum of escalating events that, in theatre, will be called a *plot*. We can see all of these

features in great storytelling today, both in surviving tribal cultures and in modern storytelling performances.

If ritual makes an event larger than life, storytelling makes it personal and affecting. While wedding rituals give wedlock a halo of dignity, marrying couples today generally humanize their own ceremony through their personal decisions about dress, language, music, setting, and staging, so that the resulting event combines collective ritual formality with the marrying partners' "telling their story" of their own uniqueness—as individuals and as a couple.

Shamanism, Trance, and Magic

Ancient dramas, or, more commonly, dance-dramas, began in the combination of ritual and storytelling, first on the African continent and afterward in tribal cultures around the world; they continue to be performed in, among other places, Siberia, South America, Southeast Asia, Australia, and Native American enclaves. Storytelling provided these performances with an audience-attracting narrative, a link to events in daily human life, the freshness of detail, and the individuality of each performer's special creativity. But ritual provided the intensity of the celebrants who could commit, body and soul, to the impersonation of divine spirits and the reenactment of what they believed to be real—if otherworldly—events. Belief in the power of such spirits to animate objects has been called *animism,* a catchall term describing the basic religious impulse of tribal culture in the world's prehistory. Humans who assume an animist role, mediating between spirit and earthly realities, are—in a similarly general way—called *shamans* (the word is originally Siberian), or go-betweens to the spirit world.

Shamans have been identified in tribal cultures since at least 13,000 B.C. In the eyes of his community, the shaman (almost always male in the ancient world) can cure the sick, aid the hunter, make the rain come and the crops grow. Shamans may also appear as mediums, taking the forms of otherworldly spirits, often animal and/or demonic. In most shamanic practices, the shaman performs his mastery—his travel between the human and spirit worlds and his incarnation of spiritual presences—in a state of trance.

Since the shaman's trance leads him to otherworldly presences, his performance takes on a magical appearance. Ecstatic dancing and rapturous chanting are often primary features of shamanism, usually climaxing in violent shaking at astounding speeds. Astonishing acrobatics are common: in the *pegele* dance of Nigeria, shamans leap high in the air, spin around horizontally, and then come down far from where they left the ground. Sleight of hand may be involved in this "magic," as when the Formosan shaman "stabs" himself but really only pierces a blood-filled animal bladder hidden beneath his clothes. But genuine transformation, both physical and psychological, apparently takes place as well, permitting normally inhuman feats. The San bushmen of Namibia and Botswana eat live snakes and scorpions during hunting rituals. The Indian fakir (Arabic for "poor man"; the word is not related to fakery) hangs suspended from a hook through his flesh, and the Muslim dervish places glowing coals in his mouth, seemingly anesthetized from pain.

Costumes, body paint, headdresses, and—above all—masks disguise the shaman-performer, sometimes completely, transforming him (often to himself as well as to observers) into a spirit presence. The mask, common in virtually all tribal cultures, was initially derived from the ecstatic contortion of the shaman's face during trance and subsequently served to represent the particular spirit that the trance-liberated shaman inhabited. But the mask has outlived the rituals that spawned it and remains today as the primary symbol of drama around the world.

The Beginnings of Traditional Drama

When spoken dialogue comes into shamanistic rites, true traditional drama begins. The Ceylon *sanniyakuma,* a traditional all-night curing ceremony of drumming and "devil dancing," portrays a suffering patient who seeks exorcism of the devil and includes this exchange:

YAKKA (*demon*): What is going on here? What does this noise mean?

DRUMMER: Somebody has fallen ill.

YAKKA: What are you going to do about it?

DRUMMER: We will give him a medicine.

YAKKA: That will not be of any use! Give me twelve presents and I will cure him."*

---

*The source for this dialogue and other information in this section is largely E. T. Kirby, *Ur-Drama: The Origins of Theatre* (New York: NYU Press, 1975).

The dialogue creates suspense, conflict, danger, and action.

African Traditional Drama

But it is in sub-Saharan Africa where we can see—even today—the vast variety of traditional drama, where ritual and storytelling continually interweave. More than eight hundred languages are spoken in sub-Saharan Africa, and each represents a culture with roots in the past and social community in the present. Many have long-standing traditions of dance-dramas. The Dogon performers of Mali are celebrated for their stilt walking and brightly colored masks. The Senufo of the Ivory Coast and Burkina Faso have animal masks—with the tusks of wild boars, the teeth of alligators, and the horns of antelopes—to frighten witches—and brightly colored masks for women characters (played by men). In the Yacouba country of the Ivory Coast, traditional performers may wear elaborate beaded headdresses and full-face makeup instead of masks or, as in the panther dance-drama, cover their entire heads in painted cloth with panther ears. Acrobatics are a feature of Burundi performers, while rain dance rituals are common in Botswana.

Egyptian Drama

While theatrical performances almost certainly began in sub-Saharan Africa, they soon drifted northward, up the Nile River to what we now know as Egypt. From there they spread to Mesopotamia, Canaan, and eventually throughout

The antiwitchcraft *kponiugo* mask of the Poro secret society of the Senufo tribe in West Africa's Ivory Coast is believed to protect the community from sorcerers and soul-stealers. Groups of Poro maskers seem to spit fire between the alligator teeth of their open jaws. Wild boar tusks and antelope horns represent ferocity and gentleness.

the Middle East. The first written records we have of this activity are in Egypt, dating at least as far back as 2500 B.C. and perhaps as much as 800 years before that. Known as the *Abydos Passion Play,* this drama was apparently staged each spring in a boat procession along the Nile, with performances taking place at several temples along the way. The play tells the story of the murder of the wheat god, Osiris, by his enemy Set (death). Scenes of lamentation by the priestesses Isis and Neptys, the tearing asunder of Osiris's body (which is then thrown into the Nile), Osiris's resurrection in the person of the god Horus, and a combat between Horus and Set are the ingredients of this drama, portrayed through dialogue, dance, animal sacrifices, mimed violence, a coronation ceremony, and the performance of sacred fertility rites. Bold effects complement the symbolic actions: beads of carnelian (a translucent red stone) represent the great Eye of Horus, which is bloodied when Set plucks it out in the combat between the two demigods. Two maces represent Set's testicles, which Horus tears off and engrafts upon his own body to become stronger. The lowering and raising of ceremonial pillars into the Nile represent the burial and resurrection of Osiris.

Modern anthropology has made clear that this Egyptian springtime resurrection drama—and other similar Middle Eastern texts of that time that employed the same plot elements, such as the Babylonian play *Baal* (in which the god Baal dies, goes to Purgatory, and rises again on the third day) and the Hittite play *Snaring of the Dragon*—derives from even more ancient ritualized reenactments of the coming of spring that celebrated the rebirth of vegetation in the fields. The death of Osiris, like the death of the wheat sheaf he represents, is not permanent; when his body is torn apart and thrown into the river, Osiris is resurrected, as is the wheat sheaf when its seeds are scattered by the wind and irrigated by the annual springtime flooding of the Nile. The tragedy of death, therefore, yields life, and the tears of

tragic lamentation become nourishment for the seeds of life's renewal. Such tragedy, therefore, however painful, brings with it rejuvenation and hope. To emphasize the connection between the drama and nature's annual process of renewal, the *Abydos Passion Play* was performed at temples oriented so that their doorways faced the sun's rising on the vernal equinox, the first day of spring.

Theatre in the West

Drama did not continue to flourish in the Middle East, however; much of the ancient theatre tradition there had disappeared by the third century B.C., and the religion of Islam, which originated early in the seventh century A.D., viewed depictions of humans—in both the visual and performing arts—as irreligious. But dramatic art was not stifled: from its Middle Eastern origins, it spread rapidly both east and west. In both India and Attica (now Greece), cultic rituals took place well before the first millennium B.C. And by the middle of that millennium, in the West, there arose a spectacular theatre in the city-state of Athens, which over the course of 150 years produced four of the greatest playwrights and the most important dramatic theorist of the theatre's long history. Greek drama ushered in the Western strain of theatre, establishing its major modes of tragedy and comedy and characters and plot lines that underlie much of Western drama as we know it today.

Greek Drama

The drama of Athens in the fifth century B.C. still stands as one of the greatest—some would say *the* greatest—bodies of theatrical creation of all time. A magnificent and vigorous blend of myth, legend, philosophy, social commentary, poetry, dance, music, public participation, and visual splendor, Athenian drama created the forms of both tragedy and comedy, peopling

Euripides' *The Trojan Women*, shown here in Matthias Langhoff's 1998 production at the French National Theatre of Rennes, Brittany, is the all-time masterpiece of war's horror and ruin. Hecuba, here played by Evelyne Didi, cries out against her country's destruction from an ancient Trojan theatre laid to waste by Greek armies. Thus, Langhoff employs a "stage theatre" to face the real one in which the audience sits. Certainly, no one in the French audience will fail to grasp the parallels to contemporary struggles elsewhere in Europe.

them with characters that have become cultural archetypes in successive eras and laying thereby the foundation not only of future Western drama but also of continuing debates as to how —and to what purposes—life should be lived.

Aristotle and later scholars tell us that Greek tragedy derived from ancient, orgiastic rites, filled with wine drinking, phallus worshipping, and the chanting of ancient poems, called *dithyrambs,* in honor of the Greek demigod Dionysus (the Greek god of fertility and wine and, eventually, the god of theatre as well). Thought to have come to Greece by way of the Middle East, Dionysus was the counterpart of Egypt's Osiris and, like the Egyptian wheat god, was believed to have been dismembered in the winter and resurrected in the spring, proving a demi-divine analogue to the rebirth of vegetation on the Attic peninsula. And when classic Greek dramas came to be staged on the Athenian acropolis by the latter part of the sixth century B.C., it was at the Great Theatre of Dionysus, during the annual springtime festival known as the City Dionysia (or Great Dionysia), that the demigod's apparent rebirth was celebrated. Dionysus has, ever since, been considered the founding deity of Western drama.

Although the transition from orgiastic celebrations to tragic drama is decidedly obscure, we do know that by the end of the fifth century three great tragedians—Aeschylus, Sophocles, and Euripides—had written and produced close to three hundred plays, of which thirty-three have come down to us, most of which are on every theatre scholar's list of the world's greatest dramatic masterpieces. Furthermore, there was a brilliant author of comic dramas—Aristophanes—from whom eleven plays survive, one of which (*The Frogs*) is a biting and vastly informative satire about the three great tragedians who shared his times. Other authors of Greek comedy, including Menander, and literary theorists, including Aristotle (with his *Poet-*

ics, a treatise on tragedy), plied their trades in the century that followed, making for one of the richest bodies of dramatic work ever created.

Greek tragedies explored the social, psychological, and religious meanings of the ancient gods and heroes of Greek history and myth, as well as current events; the comedies presented contemporary issues affecting all Athenians. Both types of drama were first staged in a simple wheat-threshing circle on the ground (the *orchestra*), with a dressing hut (*skene*) behind it; the audience was seated on an adjacent hillside (the *theatron*). As Greek culture expanded, however, huge amphitheaters—the largest of which sat upward of 15,000 people—were built in Athens and subsequently throughout the grow-

The Greek theatre of Priene, in modern-day Turkey, dates from about 300 B.C. Unlike most Greek theatres, Priene was never rebuilt by the Romans and thus remains one of the best examples of a hillside Greek *theatron*. The standing row of columns and connecting lintel once made up the front of the stone *skene*, or stagehouse.

In the dithyrambs that preceded ancient Greek tragedy, there was a chorus of fifty performers. Romanian director Silviu Purcărete, at the National Theatre of Craiova, actually
employed a chorus of double that number – with fifty men and fifty women – in his innovative production of *Les Danaïdes*, adapted from Aeschylus's war tetralogy, *The Sup-
pliants*. Purcărete's highly stylized production, performed (in French) in Manhattan's
Damrosch Park as part of the Lincoln Center Festival in 1997, had clear overtones of
current problems in eastern Europe and the Balkans and a strong emphasis on political
terrorism, sexual assault, and the ambiguity of gender and cultural identity.

ing Greek empire. Many of those later theatres remain today, in various stages of ruin and renovation, in parts of Greece, Italy, and Turkey; and of course the terms *orchestra, scene,* and *theatre* remained to define the theatre of future eras.

Ancient Greek actors were all male. They performed in masks, partly to indicate the age, gender, personality, and social standing of the characters they were playing and partly to amplify their voices. (The word *person,* which derives from the Latin *per son,* or "for sound," originally referred to the amplification provided by an actor's mask, as used in the phrase *dramatis personae,* or "cast of characters.") Each tragic actor wore elevated shoes (*kothurnoi*), an elaborate headdress (*onkos*), and a long, usually colorful gown (*himation*) with a tunic over it (*chlamys*) to enhance the larger-than-life struggles between royal heroes, gods, and demigods. Plays were performed with only two (later three) principal actors, who, by changing masks, could play several parts each during the course of a play. The actors were supported by a Greek invention, a chorus of twelve or fifteen singer-dancers (usually representing the local populace) who chanted their lines in unison or through a single chorus leader. When the skene became an elevated stage for the principal actors, the chorus members remained in the orchestra below, separating them from the main interactions of the principals.

Greek tragedy was chanted and/or sung, not spoken; unfortunately, the music has not survived. And the chorus danced, as it did in the dithyrambic ceremonies, sometimes formally, sometimes with wild abandon. Greek tragedy, therefore, is the foundation not merely of Western drama but of Western musical theatre, including opera, as well. Greek comedy, in contrast, is the foundation of burlesque, satire, and television sitcoms. The plays of Aristophanes, referred to as Old Comedy, are filled with broad physical humor, gross sexual gags and innuendos, and brilliant wordplay and repartee, often at the expense of contemporary politicians and celebrities. The later plays of Menander, known as New Comedy, gave rise to "stock characters" (such as the bumbling suitor and the timid warrior) and comic plot devices (such as mistaken identity), both of which are recurrent elements of thirty-minute network television.

The City Dionysia was a weeklong festival of celebrations and dramatic competitions. On the first day, introductory ceremonies were held; at these ceremonies, each playwright (selected in advance by civic authorities) introduced his cast and announced the theme of his work. The second day featured processions,

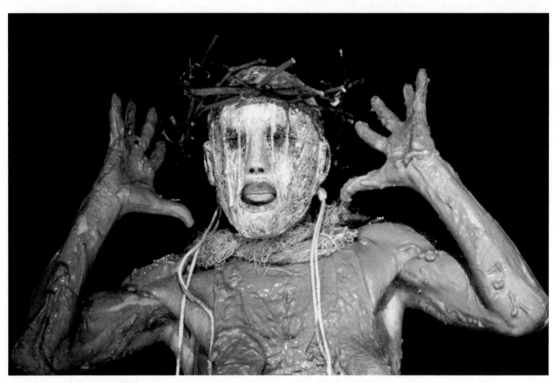

The most ancient theatre is often the most modern. This 1996 English production of Sophocles' *Oedipus Tyrannos*, with Gregg Hicks shown here as Tiresias, premiered at the ancient Greek theatre of Epidaurus before reopening at the National Theatre in London. Packed houses greeted it with rousing acclaim in both locations.

Kate Whoriskey's 2004 production of Sophocles' *Antigone* at the South Coast Repertory Theatre included imagery of the September 11, 2001, attacks and resulting war on terror.

sacrifices, and the presentation of ten dithyrambs; and on the third day, five comedies were played. On the fourth, fifth, and sixth days, the three competing playwrights presented—each on a separate day—three related tragedies (a *trilogy*), followed by a comic variation or parody (a *satyr play*) on the same theme. The authors served as the directors of their works. On the seventh, and final, day, judging took place, and prizes for the best play and best leading actor were awarded. It appears that the entire population of freeborn males, and perhaps of freeborn females (we don't know this for certain), attended these performances and rooted for their favorites; judging by later commentaries, outstanding dramatists and actors

were as famous then as are today's best-known film directors and movie stars. Clearly the City Dionysia of fifth-century Athens was a monumental and glorious undertaking, which led to some of the most thrilling dramas and theatrical spectacles in history.

Roman Drama

Greek civilization, battered by internal wars, had lost its leading edge by the end of the fifth century B.C., and the power balance in the Mediterranean shifted, in succeeding centuries, to the growing Roman Empire. Excelling in architecture and engineering, more than in dramatic creativity, the Romans created some astonishing stage buildings, of which more than two hundred (most dating from the first centuries A.D.) survive to the present day. Roman architects dispensed with the Greek hillside theatron and threshing-circle orchestra and designed a theatre that was an entirely integrated structure set on a level plain. They also cut the orchestra in half and created tunnel entrances to it (*vomitoria*) on both sides. The simple Greek skene had become a very elaborate three-story wall (the *frons scaenae*), which was decorated by dozens of statues.

Roman dramatists, however, were rarely as impressive as Roman architects and almost always drew upon Greek sources for their work; indeed, most Roman plays are about Greek characters and Greek struggles. The Roman comic playwrights Plautus and Terence were quite popular in their time, however, and many of their works survive and are performed occasionally today, as are (albeit more rarely) the chamber tragedies of Seneca, a protégé (and victim) of Emperor Nero. All three of these Roman dramatists, in fact, were very popular and much admired by writers and audiences during the European Renaissance. Roman theatre, however, degenerated into sheer spectacle and decadence by the end of the empire, as many theatres were converted into arenas for gladiatorial combat, pitched sea battles, and gruesome public massacres. Together, Greek and Roman drama form a "classical theatre" tradition that has been referenced over and over in Western drama since the Renaissance and right up to the present day.

Medieval Drama

The Fall of Rome (around the middle of the first millennium A.D.) brought to an end the classical era of theatre, and both the early Christian and new-founded Islamic religions of those times banned theatrical representation altogether, partly in reaction to the excesses of late Roman theatre. And when Western drama reappeared, as it did in Europe shortly before the year 1000, it was an altogether different product, sponsored by the same Christian Church that had once banned it. The earliest known dramatization of that period was not a play in the ordinary sense but rather a brief moment in the church's Easter service, when officiating monks reenacted the biblical story of the Virgin Mary and her two companions (also named Mary) as they visit the tomb of Jesus. "Whom seek ye?" (*Quem queritis?*) an angel asks. "Jesus of Nazareth," reply the Marys, whereupon they are told, "He is not here, He

Adam and Eve (Alessandro Mastrobuono and Erin Jellison) take their instructions from God (Tom Fitzpatrick) in Brian Kulick's 2003 *The Mysteries* in Los Angeles. The actors would probably have worn flesh-colored body stockings in medieval times, but contemporary theatre is able, on this occasion, to express their innocence before the Fall more literally.

Bill Buell and Jennifer Roszell battle the floodwaters as Noah and his Wife in Kulick's *The Mysteries*.

has risen." They then break into a chorus of hallelujahs. It is fascinating, of course, that European drama of the Christian era, like the drama of ancient Egypt and ancient Greece, began with the springtime celebration of a divine resurrection. This simple liturgical playlet, now known as the *Quem Queritis,* became the first of literally hundreds of church-sponsored dramatizations depicting and celebrating the Judeo-Christian story of humankind—from the Creation of the Universe and Adam and Eve to Doomsday and the Harrowing of Hell.

Medieval drama remained in church liturgy for nearly two centuries, but by about 1250, Bible-based drama had moved outdoors into the churchyards and then into the public streets of every country in Europe. By this time the medieval "mystery plays," as they were then called, were performed in the emerging modern languages of French, English, Spanish, German, and Italian rather than Latin and included scenes that were more secular than purely religious, often with contemporary political overtones. The actors were no longer monks but ordinary citizens, some of whom—those who had mastered the leading parts—were well paid for their efforts. The authors, though anonymous to us, were highly prized by their communities, as they converted the formal prose of the Bible to comic interplay, jesting repartee, swashbuckling bluster, and intricate versification.

Entire festivals of such plays, numbering in the dozens, were presented in hundreds of European towns every spring, dominating city life where and when they were played and attracting rural audiences from all around. On the European continent, such drama festivals lasted for many days or even weeks, with huge casts performing on a series of stages (known as *mansions*) set up next to each other in the town plaza or marketplace; audiences could stroll from one play to the next, as the plays were performed in sequence. In England, however, the plays were performed on wagon-mounted stages, one for each playlet, that wheeled from one audience site to another during a daylong springtime festival known as Corpus Christi.

At first glance, these mystery plays may appear stylistically primitive (see box), at least in contrast to the splendor of the classic Greek tragedies, but twentieth-century productions have demonstrated their tremendous dramatic impact, even to a religiously diverse contemporary audience. And the scale of medieval theatre production—with its mansions, rolling stages, and casts of hundreds—was simply astonishing. Like the great Gothic cathedrals—also created anonymously and at roughly the same time—the Bible-based medieval theatre was a monumental enterprise that affected the lives of the entire culture that created and experienced it.

MEDIEVAL VERSE — AND A SHAKESPEAREAN PARODY

Medieval English drama was written in verse employing irregular line lengths, an extensive use of alliteration (neighboring words that begin with the same consonant), and rhymes that were seemingly forced into place. This excerpt (with archaic words but modernized spellings) is from the anonymous *Fall of Lucifer* play, written and performed in York, England, in the fourteenth century. It exemplifies early English dramatic verse:

LUCIFER: (*in Heaven*) Oh, certain, how I am worthily
    wrought with worship, iwis!
  For in glorious glee, my glittering gleams!
  I am so mightily made, my mirth may not miss —
  E'er shall I bide in this bliss through brightness of
    beams!
  Me needs no annoyance to neven,
  All wealth in my world I am wielding!
  Above yet shall I make by building
  Oh high in the highest of heaven!
    (*Lucifer falls into Hell.*)
  Ow! Deuce! All goes down!
  My might and my main all is marring.
  Help, fellows! In faith, I am falling!
  Out! Out! Harrow! Helpless, such heat is there here

This is a dungeon of dole in which I can't delight!
What has my kind become, so comely and clear?
Now I am loathsome, alas who was light.
My brightness is blackest and blue now,
My bale is e'er beating and burning.
I hie me a-howling and churning.
Out! Ay, welaway! I wallow in woe now!

Shakespeare parodied this style of writing two centuries later in *A Midsummer Night's Dream*, in which a group of village craftsmen write and produce a play called "Pyramus and Thisbe," which includes such lines as:

PYRAMUS: Sween moon, I thank thee for thy sunny
    beams.
  I thank thee, moon, for shining now so bright;
  For by thy gracious, golden, glittering gleams,
  I trust to take of truest Thisbe sight.
    But stay, O spite!
    But mark, poor knight,
  What dreadful dole is here!
    Eyes, do you see?
    How can it be?
  O dainty duck! O dear!

An eighteenth-century illustration of Italian *commedia dell'arte.*

Like its predecessor, the modern Globe Theater replica in London schedules performances by daylight, come rain or shine. As in Shakespeare's day, a sizable portion of the audience (the "groundlings," as they were called in Elizabethan times) observes from a standing-room pit in front of the stage; everyone else sits on hard wooden benches in the surrounding galleries. Shown here, the concluding dance of the Globe's 1998 *As You Like It* enchants the audience on all sides of the stage, which is "thrust" into their midst.

Renaissance Drama

Medieval drama was created in ignorance of its classical predecessors, but when, in the High Middle Ages, Roman and then Greek texts began to be translated and published, their influence—on all arts and culture, not merely the theatre—proved overwhelming. We call this the Renaissance: the period when ancient culture was "reborn" and fused—sometimes uneasily—with the medieval and Gothic forms that had been dominant for centuries.

The Renaissance began, by most reckonings, in Italy, where the plays of Plautus and Seneca were first translated in the 1470s. Amateur productions of these Italian translations soon became popular, giving rise to freer adaptations, which are now known as *commedia erudita*, or "learned comedies." By the 1520s, the Florentine diplomat and essayist Niccolò Machiavelli was famous throughout Italy for his learned comedies based on—and taking off from—Roman forebears, and by the middle of the sixteenth century a semi-improvised variation of that comedy, known as *commedia dell'arte*, was performed by itinerant professional actors throughout the Italian peninsula and even beyond. Soon both commedia dell'arte and scripted plays in modern European languages—based on classic or

Above: All actors in Shakespeare's day were male, by law. The laws were overturned to permit women on the English stage in 1660, and by the nineteenth century some women – Sarah Bernhardt for example – had, on occasion, begun to play male roles. By the late twentieth century, men were often playing women's roles, both to make modern statements on the "performative" nature of gender (a belief that gender is a role, not a fixed identity) and also to return to the roots of Shakespearean acting. Here Mark Rylance (*left*), artistic director of the London Globe Theater, plays Queen Cleopatra in this gender-crossing 1999 production of Shakespeare's *Antony and Cleopatra* at that playhouse.

Right: Mark Rylance, in the title role of the history play *Richard II* at the Globe Theater, meditates upon the importance of gaining, or losing, his royal crown.

Matthew Rhys (*left*) as Romeo and Tam Mutu as Tybalt duel in this 2004 Royal
Shakespeare Company production of *Romeo and Juliet,* directed by Peter Gill.

Romeo (Tom Burke) discovers Juliet (Kananu Kirimi) on her bier between wax-dripping
candles in this production, featuring costumes of the play's period, at the reconstructed
Globe Theatre in London in 2004.

DID SHAKESPEARE WRITE SHAKESPEARE?

Students occasionally wonder about the so-called "authorship question," which challenges the commonly held belief that Shakespeare's plays were written by Shakespeare. Yet while several books have argued against Shakespeare's authorship, and some distinguished thinkers (among them Mark Twain and Sigmund Freud) have shared their doubts as well, there is simply no question to be posed: the evidence that Shakespeare wrote Shakespeare's plays is absolutely overwhelming. Nor has a shred of evidence appeared thus far to indicate that anyone else wrote them. Not a single prominent Elizabethan scholar has accepted the "anti-Stratfordian" (as proponents of other authors are called) argument, which America's most noted Shakespearean scholar, Harold Bloom, simply dismisses as "lunacy."

How can there be a question? Shakespeare is named as author on the title page of seventeen separate publications during his lifetime and is cited as the author of eleven known plays in a book published when he was thirty-four. He is credited as the author of the First Folio in its title, *Mr. William Shakespeare's Comedies, Histories, and Tragedies*, published just seven years after his death; the Folio's editors were his acting colleagues, who describe Shakespeare as fellow actor, author, and friend, and their preface also includes four poems — one by dramatist Ben Jonson — each unequivocally referring to Shakespeare as the author of plays. Surviving records show him performing in his plays at the courts of both Queen Elizabeth and King James, and he was buried, along with his wife, daughter, and son-in-law (and no one else), in the place of greatest honor in his hometown church. An inscribed funeral monument, mentioned in the Folio and showing him with pen in hand, looks down on Shakespeare's grave and was regularly visited in the coming years by persons wishing to see, as one wrote, the last resting place of "the wittiest poet in the world." Birth, marriage, death, heraldic, and other legal records, plus dozens of citations during and shortly after his life tell us more about dramatist William Shakespeare than we have collected for all but a few common-born citizens of his era.

So, what is left to argue? Anti-Stratfordians maintain that the evidence doesn't paint the picture we should expect of such a magnificent playwright: He apparently didn't go to college; his name was spelled in several different ways and sometimes hyphenated; his signatures indicate poor handwriting; his wife and daughters were probably illiterate; he didn't leave any books in his will; no ceremony marked his death; he never traveled to Italy, where many of his plays were set; and an early engraving of the Stratford monument looks different — lacking its pen — than the monument does now.

Little of this is provable, however, and none of it is remotely convincing even if true. Aeschylus,

current themes, not biblical ones—were common throughout Europe.

It was in England that the Renaissance brought forth the greatest dramatic masterpieces of that (or perhaps any) era, in the works of William Shakespeare. Coming of age during the reign of Queen Elizabeth I, Shakespeare began his career in a vibrant world of palatial court theatres, freestanding outdoor "public theatres" that dominated the London skyline, and companies of professional actors who entertained court and public at home and on tour. This "Elizabethan" theatre featured dozens of playwrights whose works remain popular today; Christopher Marlowe, Ben Jonson, and John Webster are three of Shakespeare's most prominent contemporaries, but none, however, was fully comparable to Shakespeare himself. Alone among the world's great authors, Shakespeare was equally adept at producing exemplary postclassical masterpieces of both comedy and tragedy. Four centuries after they were written (approximately 1580–1610), his plays are the most-produced dramas in literally thousands of theatres around the world; they are, indeed, the primary reper-

Euripides, and George Bernard Shaw didn't go to college, either. Shakespeare's knowledge of Italy is nothing an intelligent person couldn't have picked up in an afternoon's conversation – and it wasn't that accurate, (Shakespeare writes of one who could "lose the tide" facilitating a trip from Verona to Milan – where no water route exists). Many people have unreadable signatures, and in Shakespeare's day neither spelling nor hyphenation was standardized, nor was literacy a norm among country women. That we don't know of a memorial ceremony doesn't mean there wasn't one, and evidence clearly indicates the engraving of a pen-less monument was simply one of many errors in a too-hastily-prepared book. And if Shakespeare maintained a library, he could simply have given it to his son-in-law (a doctor) before his death or left it to be passed on to his wife along with his house and furnishings, or perhaps he kept books in a private office at The Globe theatre in London, which burned to the ground three years before his death. And who actually knows that he didn't travel to Italy or even study at a university for that matter? We know absolutely nothing about Shakespeare between the ages of twenty-one and twenty-eight; he could have been anywhere and done anything.

But we do know he was a man of the theatre. And obviously a genius. What else need we know? Why must we insist that he have good handwriting? or literate relatives? Because *we* do? But we're not Shakespeare, and Shakespeare doesn't have to be like us.

And absolutely no evidence exists that anyone *else* wrote any of the plays – which explains why there are nearly a half dozen claimants to this phantom position of the "real" Shakespeare.

It is impossible to represent the entirety of either argument in a few paragraphs (one of the books, proposing the Earl of Oxford, runs over 900 pages), but the entire anti-Stratfordian case, diverting as it may be, is painstakingly and effectively refuted in Irvin Leigh Matus's relentlessly straightforward *Shakespeare, IN FACT* (1994).

It is, of course, possible that all the evidence we now have – *all* of it – has somehow been fabricated. This would mean Shakespeare managed to fool – or buy off – virtually everyone in his town, everyone in his church, everyone in his theatre company, everyone at two royal courts, everyone in the London theatre world, most of the printers and booksellers in England, and everyone they talked to. We would be asked to believe that this gigantic lie (for which we have not a trace of evidence) *never* got out, not through the revival of his plays after his death and then later during the Restoration era. It would have been the most stupendous hoax in human history, incomparable to the insignificant hoax proffered to us by anti-Stratfordians today.

toire of over a hundred theatre companies named after him.

Shakespeare was not only an author; he was also an actor and part owner of his own theatre company, the King's Men, and of The Globe theatre in London, which his company built and operated; a new Globe, in fact, has been built near the original site and, since its 1997 opening, has been used for the presentation of Shakespearean-era (and occasionally other) plays. With its "thrust stage" and standing-room "pit" open to the sky and surrounded by thatched-roof seating galleries on three levels, the modern Globe may not—because of fire regulations—seat the three thousand people accommodated by the original building, but its restoration helps us better understand the vigor of Shakespearean-era staging and the potential of the drama to electrify a large and diverse audience with profound intelligence and passion, as well as comically expressive hijinks. Shakespeare's plays are well known to literary scholars for their poetic brilliance, relentless investigation of the human condition, and deeply penetrating character portrayals, but they are also filled with music, dancing, ribaldry, puns, satire,

Priest and playwright Pedro Calderón de la Barca (1600–1681) was Spain's great court dramatist, whose philosophical and theological plays were deemed more elegant and refined than those of his Renaissance predecessors Lope de Vega and Miguel Cervantes. Calderón's masterpiece, *Life Is a Dream* (c. 1638), treats moral responsibility in a royal (courtly) context; this scene is from the Denver Theatre Center's 1998 production, staged as part of a summer festival of Spanish golden-age drama.

pageantry, and humor, which only performance brings to life. They are both great dramatic art and magnificent theatrical entertainment.

The Royal Theatre

If the Renaissance was the rebirth of classical civilization, the age that followed was a vast consolidation and refinement of what had come before; it was an era organized intellectually by the then-emerging empirical sciences and rational philosophies and politically by the increasing importance of European royalty. The seventeenth-century theatre of this so-called Royal era featured the dramas of Pedro Calderón de la Barca at the court of King Philip IV in Spain, the tragedies of Jean Racine and

Pierre Corneille and the comedies of Molière under King Louis XIV in France, and the Restoration comedies of William Wycherley and William Congreve under English king Charles II, who was crowned when the royal family was restored to the throne after eighteen years of English civil war and Puritan rule.

Plays of the Royal era were generally aimed more at the aristocracy than at the general populace and reflected the gentility of the seemingly refined taste of courtly patrons. Rational sensibility dominated the times: theories of drama, adapted from Aristotle and hence called "neoclassic," sought to regularize plays within "reasonable" frameworks of time and place, establish strictly measured structures for dramatic verse, unify styles around set genres,

The romantic spirit encompasses more than romance; it is also swashbuckling swordplay, picaresque characters, poetic elaborations, and period costumes — all of which come together in the famous dueling-rhyming scene between the long-nosed Gascon poet-soldier Cyrano and his aristocratic rival, the Compte de Guiche, in Edmond Rostand's *Cyrano de Bergerac* (1898), produced here by South Coast Repertory in 2004.

and eliminate onstage depictions of physical violence. Indoor theatres, lit by candles instead of sunlight, replaced the outdoor public theatres of earlier times, providing more intimate and comfortable surroundings for an increasingly well-dressed audience. Furthermore, protection from wind and weather permitted elaborately painted scenery and stage machinery. Several of these theatres are architectural gems that have remained in continuous use to the present day. Style, wit, grace, and class distinction became not merely the framework of drama but its chief subject, and the fan and the snuffbox became signature props. This was also the Western world's first era of extensive theatrical commentary and thus the first from which we have detailed commentaries and evidence—both textual and visual—of the era's

dramatic repertoires, acting styles, artists' lives, and manifestos and controversies that continue to define, in sum, the art of drama.

The Romantic Theatre

Every era in theatre is, to some extent, a rebellion against the previous one, and the romantic theatre of the eighteenth and nineteenth centuries was, in the main, a bold rejection of the rational decorum of the preceding Royal era and its spirit of ordered, elegant, and enlightened debate. Romanticism, in contrast, was florid, exotic, grotesque, sprawling, and imbued with the free-flowing spirit of the individual rather than the social organization of class, court, or scientific or aesthetic academy. Compassion, rather than style and wit, was central to the romantic creed, and authors, such as Johann Wolfgang von Goethe and Friedrich von Schiller in Germany and Victor Hugo in France, intrigued audiences with their deep humanitarian concerns in plays that dealt with devils and monsters, robbers and priests, hunchbacks and heroes.

Romanticism gave rise to melodrama and grand opera and much of the anarchic passion and sprawling sentiment of modern realism as well. Moreover, the romantic quest for the foreign and exotic represented Western drama's first serious reengagement with the theatre of the East. This, then, is a good point at which to return to drama's earlier years—to the Eastern strain of theatre that sprang from Egyptian and Canaanite beginnings and soon resurfaced on the Indian subcontinent and thereafter throughout Asia.

Theatre in the East

It is misleading to refer to *an* "Asian theatre," for drama in Asia is as rich and diverse as—if not more so than—theatre in the West. Asia, after all—with three-fifths of the world's population—comprises dozens of countries, hundreds of languages, and thousands of identified theatre forms. Nevertheless, although Asian dramatic forms differ markedly from each other, they generally adhere to many fundamental principles, mostly in strong contrast to Western traditions:

- Asian drama is almost never just "spoken"; rather, it is danced, chanted, mimed, and very often sung. Mere spoken drama, when it does occur in the East, is generally recognized as Western in origin or influence.
- Asian dramatic language is invariably rhythmic and melodic; it is appreciated for its sound as much as (or more than) for its meaning. Alliteration, imagery, rhyme, and verbal juxtaposition are often as important in Asian dramatic dialogue as logic, per-

suasive rhetoric, and realism are in Western drama; and the sonic value of words is as valued by an Asian audience as their semantic value is by a Western audience.

- Asian theatre is ordinarily more visual and sensual than literary or intellectual. Although some Asian dramatists are known for their literary gifts (and several are mentioned in the following discussion), few Asian plays have been widely circulated for general reading or academic study. Most Asians would consider the act of reading a play—separate from seeing it in performance—a rather odd pastime. Rather, Asian drama is inextricable from the arts of performance that bring it to life: dance, song, mime, gesture, acrobatics, puppetry, music, sound, costume, and makeup.
- Asian theatre has a strong emphasis on storytelling and myth, yet it is not tightly plotted, as Western drama is, and rarely leads to escalating incidents, stunning reversals, crescendoing climaxes, or elaborate plot closures. Asian theatre, whose metaphysical roots lie in those timeless meditations on human existence that are at the very heart of Hindu and Buddhist cultures, instead may seem, to Western tastes, leisurely and almost wandering. Certainly, Asian theatre's dramatic appeal is more continuous and rapturous than cathartic or arresting.
- Asian theatre is broadly stylized. As one might expect of a dramatic form imbued with music and dance, slice-of-life realism is virtually unknown. Brilliantly colored costumes and makeup, long and obviously artificial beards, elegantly danced battle scenes, and live instrumental accompaniment are virtually standard in traditional Asian theatre.
- Actors train in traditional Asian dramatic forms through an intense apprentice system beginning in early childhood and lasting into early middle age. Most Asian

actors, indeed, are born or adopted into their trade.

- The Asian theatre is deeply traditional. Although there are modern and avant-garde theatre movements in most Asian countries—and some Western influence is evident in many of them—what is most remarkable about Eastern theatre is its near-universal consonance with folk history, ancient religions, and cultural myths.

Indian Sanskrit Drama

Asian drama began in India, where it sprang from the same Middle Eastern roots as its Western counterpart; some scholars even believe that the Greek Dionysus had an Indian heritage. Indeed, there are tantalizing connections between ancient India and Greece, which, one scholar argues, suggests an "Indo-Greek theatre" of the first millennium B.C.; these include fragments of Indian archeological remains that seem to be based on Greek dramatic texts and intriguing anecdotes of Greek theatre productions mounted by officers of Alexander the Great during his Indian invasion in 326 B.C.

Despite its connections to Greek theatre, Indian theatre is very much an independent Asiatic creation, which was first known to us in the form of a native Sanskrit dance theatre that achieved a solid foothold on the subcontinent somewhere around 200 B.C. and remained popular for more than a thousand years thereafter.* Sanskrit plays survive from about A.D. 100, and a comprehensive book of dramatic theory, the *Natyasastra,* or "treatise on theatre," ascribed to Bharata Muni, dates from somewhere between 200 B.C. and A.D. 200. The *Natyasastra,* the most comprehensive study of theatre surviving from the ancient world, contains detailed analyses of Sanskrit dramatic texts, theatre buildings, acting, staging, music, gesture, dance, and even theatre-company orga-

nization. The treatise describes ten major genres of Sanskrit drama, including two primary ones: the *nataka,* which was based on well-known heroic stories of kings or sages, and the *prakarana,* based on the theme of love. The greatest Sanskrit poet, Kalidasa, wrote his masterpiece, *Shakuntala and the Ring of Recognition,* in the nataka style somewhere around the fifth century A.D. *The Little Clay Cart,* attributed to Sudraka, is the best known of two surviving examples of prakarana.

Sanskrit theatre, as far as we can tell (no ruins or drawings survive), was performed indoors, within a roofed building. Rectangular in structure and fitted with a stage of about forty-eight by twenty-four feet, these buildings could seat somewhere between two hundred and five hundred spectators. Two doors, with an onstage orchestra between them, provided access to the dressing area behind the stage, and four columns held up the roof or an upper pavilion. Carved wooden elephants, tigers, and snakes adorned the pillars and perhaps the ceiling. Sanskrit drama was danced and acted with an onstage instrumental and percussion accompaniment. Performers, all from priestly castes and trained from very early childhood, were absolute virtuosos of their particularly demanding art.

Sanskrit drama died out around the tenth century, as the broad-based Hindu court culture fragmented in the wake of repeated Mongol invasions and the peoples of India fell back into preexisting regional cultures and languages. In succeeding centuries, dozens—even hundreds—of provincial theatre forms became popular throughout the subcontinent, a vast number of which remain to the present day. Despite their many differences, all Indian drama forms share many of the fundamental theatre aesthetics of their Sanskrit predecessors and the doctrines of the ancient *Natyasastra.*

Indian Kathakali

Today the most widely known of these regional dance-drama forms is the *kathakali* ("story play"), which originated in rural villages in the

---

*All dates in early Indian drama are extremely approximate, within a plus-or-minus margin of sometimes up to four or five *centuries.*

province of Kerala in the seventeenth century; it currently plays in many urban centers in the province and often abroad. Kathakali is a drama based on any of thousands of stories from the two great Indian epics, the *Ramayana* and the *Mahabharata*. Kathakali performance itself is somewhat of an epic as well, with its outdoor performances lasting from about ten at night until well beyond dawn the next day. Traditionally, audience members are free to leave, take naps, and eat during the performance; today, however, kathakali is more often performed in the three-hour evening time blocks common to Western theatre.

In kathakali, the text is sung—to a percussion accompaniment of gongs, drums, and cymbals—by two singers seated at the side. Actors dance and pantomime the dramatic action; by employing precise and elaborate hand gestures, footwork patterns, distinctive eye and eyebrow movements, and postural contortions, they reveal subtleties of meaning and characterization that are barely suggested by the text. Consequently, actors train rigorously for kathakali performance from early childhood, achieving mastery—if at all—only by about age forty. Highly stylized makeup and costuming also convey characterization and attitude: red- or black-bearded characters represent evil, and white-bearded ones the divine. No scenery is used in kathakali, as plays are presented in arbitrary sites, with four simple poles defining the acting area.

Chinese Xiqu

China, Asia's largest nation, is Asia's oldest continuous culture, as well as the home of Asia's oldest continuous theatre tradition. As with all Asian drama, Chinese theatre is more sung than spoken, but since even Chinese speech is itself semimusical—as it is based on tonal changes as well as syllabic pronunciation—all traditional Chinese theatre is known by the Chinese term *xiqu* ("tuneful theatre"), which we translate as "Chinese Opera."

In the Indian kathakali dance-drama, royal characters wear an elaborate *kiritam*, or crown, which frames the actor's eye movements – one of the most intensively studied skills of kathakali performers. Kalamandalam Gopi, a senior kathakali maestro, is shown here in the role of King Rugmangada in *Rugmangadacharitam*, performed in Trichur, Kerala (India) in 1993.

Although forms of xiqu existed in China before the first century, the first well-defined Chinese Opera form, known as *zaju* ("various plays"), appeared in China during the Song dynasty in the tenth century, reaching its golden age in the thirteenth century under the Mongol emperor Kublai Khan. Zaju was a comedic music-dance-drama, with acrobatics and clowning; it was so popular that a single amusement park in thirteenth-century Keifeng (then China's northern capital) featured at least fifty indoor zaju theatres, the largest holding several thousand people.

Circus-style acrobatics have always been a great feature of the stylized battle scenes in Chinese *xiqu*, as shown here by the brilliant leaps and flips of the *wu sheng* (acrobat warrior) performers of China's Hebei Opera Company during their 1998 international tour.

By the end of the Ming dynasty, in 1644, zaju had been succeeded by a more stately, poetic, and aristocratic opera known as *kunqu*, originating from the town of Kunshan; soon thereafter kunqu became the favored theatre entertainment of the Chinese court. Kunqu is still performed today. More popular theatre developed around the same time in the form of a more boisterous "clapper opera," characterized by the furious rhythmic beating of drumsticks on a hardwood block. And in subsequent years, many regional theatre styles, influenced by the zaju, kunqu, and clapper opera forms, arose throughout the country. Today there are as many as 360 variations of Chinese Opera in the People's Republic, most of them—such as Cantonese Opera, Sichuan Opera, Hui Opera— known by their regional origins.

The most famous Chinese Opera in modern times, however, is the Beijing (Peking) Opera, which is known in Chinese as *jingju*, or "theatre of the capital." Jingju was founded in 1790, when, in celebration of the emperor's eightieth birthday, a group of actors from the mountains of Anhui—led by one Cheng Chang-geng— came to Beijing and amazed the court with their brilliant and innovative style of singing, music, and (in particular) acrobatics and martial arts. As local actors assimilated the Anhui style with their own, a new "capital" style was developed, reaching its current form by about 1850, by which time it had become the dominant popular theatre of all China. Beijing Opera remains not just one of the great glories of the world's traditional performing arts but— after a nearly thirteen-year hiatus occasioned

The Monkey King – a ferocious scamp – is the most enduring character in xiqu; he is always dressed in yellow, as shown here in this Shanghai Jingju Theatre production of *Pansi Cave*.

by the Chinese Cultural Revolution in the 1960s and 1970s—a highly popular national entertainment in China and around the world.

Because the stories and plots of Chinese Opera are normally ancient and well known, the actual staging of such works becomes, above all, a celebration of the performers' individual skills (*gong*); in particular, actors must master the classic fourfold combination of singing (*chang*), speech (*nian*), acting and movement (*zuo*), and martial arts and acrobatics (*da*). Virtually all Chinese Opera performers are proficient in all four of these arts; the greatest performing artists—who are famous throughout China—have mastered each of them to

virtuoso standards. Indeed, it might be said that the equivalent of a great Chinese actor in the West would be someone who could perform for the American Ballet Theatre, La Scala Opera, the Royal Shakespeare Company, the Ringling Brothers Circus, and the French foreign legion—all on the same evening.

Chinese Opera is a spectacular visual feast, with dazzling costumes, huge glittery headdresses, and brilliantly colorful face painting. Actors of both sexes wear multilayered gowns in bold primary colors, many of which have "water-sleeves," which fall all the way to the floor. Chinese Opera singing, much of which is in an extreme falsetto (originally employed so that actors could be heard over the din of people talking during the performance), is accompanied by the near-constant clanging of gongs and cymbals, clapper claps, drumbeats, and the furious strumming of various two-stringed fiddles. Movement skills include a rapid heel-to-toe walk, contortionist bendings and swayings, sudden jerks and freezes, and thrilling displays of full-stage acrobatics: continuously back-springing performers bound across the stage in a literal blur, and in battle scenes combatants repel spear thrusts—sixteen at a time, all from different directions—with both hands and both feet. Chinese Opera has never been dependent on scenery—an actor who enters holding a paddle behind him is assumed to be on a boat; an actor entering with a riding crop is assumed to be on horseback—but its storytelling conventions and its spectacular musical, visual, and acrobatic displays offer

audiences one of the world's most thrilling and magnificent theatrical experiences.

Japanese Nō

The island nation of Japan has created two great theatre forms, *nō* and *kabuki*. Each is virtually a living museum of centuries-old theatre practice—nō and kabuki are performed today in very much the same fashion as in earlier times—yet each is also an immensely satisfying theatre experience for modern audiences attuned to the Japanese culture.

Nō is Japan's most revered and cerebral theatre. It is also the oldest continuously performed drama in the world. Perfected in the fourteenth and fifteenth centuries almost solely by a single father-son team (Kan'ami and Zeami), who between them wrote and produced approximately 240 of the surviving plays, nō is a highly ceremonial drama, mysterious and tragic, that almost always portrays supernatural events and characters. All nō plays center on a single character, known as the *shite* (the "doer"), who is interrogated, prompted, and challenged by a secondary character, called the *waki*. Whereas waki characters are always living male humans—usually ministers, commoners, or priests—shite characters may be gods, ghosts, women, animals, or warriors; the shite role, unlike the waki, is played in a mask. Nō actors—all of whom are male—train for only one of these role types, which they normally perform throughout their careers. Long training provides actors with the precise choreography and the musical notations required of their danced and chanted performance.

The actual nō stage is a precisely measured square of highly polished Japanese cypress flooring, about eighteen feet across, supported from below by large earthenware jars that resonate with the actors' foot-stompings. A bridge-like runway (*hashigakari*) provides stage access from stage right; it is used for the solemn entrances and exits particularly characteristic of nō. An ornate, curved roof covers the stage and

Nō actors usually come from long-standing nō families that operate nō schools. Here one of Japan's "living national treasures," the venerable Otoshige Sakai of the Kanze Nō-gakudo school, which was founded in the fourteenth century, helps mask his son, Otaharu, before a 2004 performance in Tokyo.

is reminiscent of the time when the stage was housed in a separate building, which the audience observed from a distance; the nō roof is supported by four wooden pillars, each with its own name and historic dramatic function. A wooden "mirror wall" at the rear of the stage bounces back the sounds of music and singing to the audience; on the wall, a painted pine tree, delicately gnarled and highly stylized, provides the only scenery. A four-man orchestra—whose instruments include a flute, small and large hand drums, and a stick drum—provides continuous musical accompaniment at the rear of the stage, and a chorus of six to ten singer-chanters is positioned on a platform addition at stage left. The absolute precision of

the theatre design and the stately performance choreography and musicality give nō a ceremonial quality that is unique in world drama.

Nō has never been a theatre of mass entertainment, and first-time patrons today—including many Japanese—often find it bewildering. Plotting, even in comparison to other Asian forms, is weak or virtually nonexistent. The language is medieval, elliptical, and often forbiddingly obscure. The cast is small, the action relatively static, and the pace, by modern standards, virtually glacial: the basic nō walk, said to be derived from tramping through rice paddies, is an agonizingly deliberate slip-slide shuffle, with the feet barely leaving the ground. The actors are trained to keep their faces immobile and expressionless at all times, even when unmasked. Certainly nō is produced today more for enthusiasts than for the general public, but it is notable that the number of such enthusiasts—at least in Japan—is currently growing, not falling; in fact, one scholar claims that "performances are at their most popular level in the history of the art." Like the study of martial arts, flower arranging, and the tea ceremony, nō remains a Japanese national passion. Its sublime mystery and serenity—reflective of deep Buddhist and Shinto values—resonate profoundly in contemporary Japanese life and have proven increasingly influential to Japanese as well as Western dramatists of the current era.

Japanese Kabuki

Created two hundred years after nō, kabuki has always been a more spectacular and accessible form of theatrical entertainment. Whereas nō is refined, dignified, and designed for small, studious audiences, kabuki is gaudy and exhilarating; from its earliest days, it was created to delight large crowds of merchants, traders, courtesans, and ordinary city dwellers. Whereas nō is sober and ascetic and staged on a relatively small, bare platform, kabuki is a theatrical extravaganza of dazzling colors, flamboyant dance and recitation, passionate emotion, and elaborate stage machinery and effects. Japanese audiences often respond by shouting their favorite actors' names or other words of encouragement at key moments in the play.

Kabuki was created in Kyoto around 1600 by the legendary shrine maiden Izumo Okuni, whose flamboyant and dramatic style of dancing became hugely popular in Kyoto's brothels and teahouses. The outlandish extravagance of Okuni's costumes and the fact that women performed both male and female parts invited the term *kabuku,* meaning "askew" (we might translate it today as "punk"). This fast-developing and exotic entertainment was transformed by midcentury—in a series of government edicts —from an all-female to an all-male performing art. More complex dramatic storytelling—with themes based on traditional myths, historical incidents, local sex scandals and suicides, and already-ancient nō drama—was adapted into the evolving format, which was by then renamed *kabuki,* a term made up of three ideographs: *ka* ("song"), *bu* ("dance"), and *ki* ("skill"), the three major ingredients of kabuki.

By the century's end, kabuki staging had incorporated curtains and scenery, playwrights' names were being printed in kabuki programs, and star actors had emerged, creating the two principal kabuki acting styles: *wagoto* (the elegant and naturalistic "soft style" of actor Sakata Tōjūrō I, from Kyoto) and *aragoto* (the thundering "rough style" of Ichikawa Danjūrō I, from Edo, now Tokyo). The traditions of both these actors remain central to kabuki to the present day, as all kabuki actors are members of but eleven famous families and all can trace their lineage—familial and professional—back to their kabuki-performing ancestors. The current star Ichikawa Danjūrō XII, for example, is the great-great-great-great-great-great-great-great-great-grandson of Ichikawa Danjūrō I, born in 1660; the celebrated Danjūrō style has been directly passed, father to son, down through the centuries.

There are many types of kabuki dramas, but the major works fall generally into two categories: history plays (*jidaimono,* or "period things") and domestic plays (*sewamono,* or "common things"). The history plays dramatize—usually in spectacular fashion—major political events of the remote past; often, however, the historical distance was little more than a protective cover for past playwrights and actors, who were in fact reflecting—under the guise of an apparently historical depiction—various controversial issues of nobles and political officials of their own time. Domestic plays, in contrast, deal with the affairs of the townspeople, merchants, lovers, and courtesans of the playwright's own era, often focusing on the conflicts—intense throughout Japanese

In kabuki's famous dance-drama *Kagami Jishi* (The Lion Dance), the lion (played by Nakamura Kankuro V) is teased by butterflies (played by his sons Nakamura Kantaro II and Nakamuro Schichinosuki II).

culture—between affairs of the heart and the call of duty. A great many domestic plays end in suicide (many, in fact, end in double suicides), with the lovers vowing to meet again in the world to come; such plays have been the subject of attempted bannings, as they have led to real suicides in consequence.

Kabuki is mainly an actor's theatre; many of its plays are of unknown authorship and have been augmented over the centuries by actors' additions. One notable exception, however, is the kabuki author Chikamatsu Monzaemon (1653–1725). Considered the greatest Japanese dramatist of all time, Chikamatsu was also a famous playwright of the Japanese puppet theatre *bunraku*.

The Theatrical Tradition Today: East and West

These eleven great theatre traditions of the past—Greek, Roman, medieval, Renaissance, Royal, and romantic in the Western world; Sanskrit, kathakali, xiqu, nō, and kabuki in the East—are all alive today, either in the form of regular and careful revivals or, happier yet in the case of the last four (and, to some extent,

One of kabuki's most celebrated moments is Tomomori's suicide, which ends the 1747 history play *Yoshitsune Sembon Zakura* (Yoshitsune and the Thousand Cherry Trees). Tomomori, a defeated Heike warlord, ties a ship's anchor to his waist and throws it back over his head, following it overboard to a watery death. The role is performed here by Ichikawa Danjūrō XII.

This bunraku performance of *Yoshitsune and the Thousand Cherry Trees* was performed at the National Theatre of Osaka, Japan.

the plays of the Royal and romantic eras as well), by a continuous tradition of performance. All of these traditions have influenced the modern theatre, as we will see in the next chapter. Increasingly, that influence crosses and recrosses the East-West divide that has existed in theatre history since the decline of the Egyptian resurrection dramas two thousand years ago.

8

The Modern Theatre

T HE THEATRE HAS EXPERIENCED MANY GREAT PERIODS, as we have seen, but one of its greatest is still going on. This is the period we call the modern, to which can be added the onrush of avant-garde movements we call (for the time being) the post-modern. Together, these make up the theatre of our times, a theatre that will likely be her-alded for *all* times.

Modern drama can be said to date back to about 1875, and its roots lie deep in the social and political upheavals that developed in the eighteenth and nineteenth centuries, a time charac-terized by revolution. Political revolution in the United States (1776) and France (1789) irrev-ocably changed the political structure of the Western world, and industrial-technological revolution cataclysmically overhauled the economic and social systems of most of the world. In the wake of these developments came an explosion of public communication and trans-portation, a tremendous expansion of literacy, democracy, and public and private wealth, and a universal demographic shift from country to town. These forces combined to create in Europe, the United States, and elsewhere mass urban populations hungering for social com-munion and stimulation: a fertile ground for the citified and civilized theatre of our times.

Simultaneously, an intellectual revolution—in philosophy, in science, in social understand-ing, and in religion—was altering human consciousness in ways far transcending the effects of revolutionary muskets and industrial consolidation. The intellectual certainty of Louis XIV, whose divine right to rule was unquestioned in the seventeenth and early eighteenth centuries, appeared ludicrous in an age governed by secular scientific investigation. The clear-sightedness of a playwright such as Molière seemed simplistic in an age of existentialism signaled by the soul-searching, self-doubting analyses of Søren Kierkegaard. The intellectual revolution was an exceedingly complex phenomenon that occurred in many spheres of thought and was to gain momentum with each passing decade. It continues to this day.

The Copernican theory had already made clear that human beings do not stand at the geographic center of the universe but rather that our world, indeed our universe, is swept up in a multiplicity of interstellar movements. Later scientists would press further than that, until eventually the revelations of Albert Einstein, Werner Heisenberg, and others would remove all of our "hitching posts in space" and establish the human animal as little more than a transformation of kinetic energy, wobbling shiftily in a multigravitational atomic field marked by galaxies and black holes, neutrinos and quarks, matter and antimatter, all in a vast dance of inexplicable origin and doubtful destiny.

Nor was that "human animal" so vastly privileged over other species, it would seem. Darwin would argue that we *Homo sapiens* are directly linked to other mammals—descended not from Adam and Eve or pre-Hellenic demigods but from primal apes and prehistoric orangutans. Our morals and religions, anthropologist Ruth Benedict would argue, were not handed down to all humanity from a single source but are instead a ranging complex of laws and traditions, wholly relative to the climes and cultures we inhabit. The work of Freud would disclose the existence of the unconscious, a dark and lurking inner self aswarm with infantile urges, primordial fantasies, and suppressed fears and rages. The writings of Karl Marx would contend that all social behavior has its basis in economic greed, class struggle,

and primal amorality. "Everlasting uncertainty and agitation" is the nature of human intercourse, according to Marx, and society comprises "two great hostile camps" continually engaged in civil war.

These and scores of other serious challenges to traditional thinking were accompanied everywhere by public debate and dispute. By the turn of the twentieth century, an investigative ferment had seized Western civilization: data were being collected on every conceivable topic, and scientific questioning and testing replaced intuition and dogma as the accepted avenues to truth. Experimentation, exploration, documentation, and challenge became the marching orders of the artist and intellectual alike.

The modern theatre has its roots in these political, social, and intellectual revolutions. Ever since its outset it has been a theatre of challenge, a theatre of experimentation. It has never been a theatre of rules or simple messages, nor has it been a theatre of demigods or of absolute heroes and villains. It has reflected, to a certain degree, the confusions of its times, but it has also struggled to clarify and to illuminate, to document and explore human destiny in a complex and uneasy universe.

Realism

Thus far, the movement that has had the most pervasive and long-lived effect on modern theatre is, beyond question, realism. Realism has sought to create a drama without conventions or abstractions. *Likeness to life* is realism's goal, and in pursuit of that goal it has renounced, among other things, idealized or prettified settings, versifications, contrived endings, and stylized costumes and performances.

Realism is a beguiling aesthetic philosophy. Indeed, the theatre has *always* taken "real life" as its fundamental subject, and so realism seems at first glance to be an appropriate style with which to approach the reality of existence. In-

Tennessee Williams's 1947 masterpiece, *A Streetcar Named Desire*, depicts with intense, aching realism the tragic flight of Blanche DuBois, a once-wealthy but now homeless southern belle, to the New Orleans tenement apartment of her sister Stella and Stella's rough-hewn husband, Stanley Kowalski, played here by Iaian Glen in a 2002 National Theatre production, with Glenn Close as Blanche.

stead of having actors represent characters, the realists would say, let us have the actors *be* those characters; instead of having dialogue stand for conversation, let us have dialogue that *is* conversation; instead of having scenery and costumes that convey a sense of time and place and atmosphere, let us have scenery that is genuinely inhabitable and costumes that are real clothes.

But, of course, realism has its limits: any dramatic piece must inevitably involve a certain shaping and stylization, no matter how lifelike its effect; the advocates of theatrical realism are well aware of this inevitability. Nevertheless, the ideology of realism was tested, during the last years of the nineteenth century and the first

years of the twentieth, in every aspect of theatre—acting, directing, design, and playwriting—and the results of those tests form a body of theatre that is both valid and meaningful and a style that remains enormously significant.

A Laboratory

In essence, the realistic theatre is conceived to be a laboratory in which the nature of relationships, the ills of society, the symptoms of a dysfunctional family are "objectively" set down for the final judgment of an audience of impartial observers. Every aspect of realistic theatre should strictly adhere to the "scientific method" of the laboratory; nothing must ring false. The setting is to resemble the prescribed locale of the play as closely as possible; indeed, it is not unusual for much of the scenery to be acquired from a real-life environment and transported to the theatre. Costumes worn by characters in the realistic theatre follow the dress of "real" people of similar societal status; dialogue re-creates the cadences and expressions of daily life.

Early on in the realist movement, the proscenium stage was modified to accommodate scenery constructed in box sets, with the walls given full dimension and with real bookcases, windows, fireplaces, swinging doors, and so forth built into the walls just as they are in a house interior. In the same vein, realistic acting was judged effective insofar as it was drawn from the behavior of life and insofar as the actors seemed to be genuinely speaking to each other instead of playing to the audience. A new aesthetic principle was spawned: the "theatre of the fourth wall removed," in which the life onstage was conceived to be the same as life in a real-world setting, except that, in the case of the stage, one wall—the proscenium opening—had been removed. Thus the theatre was like a laboratory telescope and the stage like a microbiologist's slide: a living environment set up for judicious inspection by neutral observers.

And so realism presents its audience with an abundance of seemingly real-life "evidence" and permits each spectator to arrive at his or her own conclusions. There is some shaping of this evidence by author and performer alike, to be sure, but much of the excitement of the realistic theatre is occasioned by the genuine interpretive freedom it allows the audience and by the accessibility of its characters, whose behaviors are familiar enough to the average spectator that they may be easily assimilated and identified.

Moreover, in presenting its evidence from the surface of life, realism encourages us to delve into the mystery that lies beneath—for the exploration of life's mystery is the true, if unspoken, purpose of every realistic play. Real-

ism's characters, like people in life, are defined by detail rather than by symbol or abstract idealization: like people we know, they are ultimately unpredictable and humanly complex rather than ideologically absolute.

The success of realism is well established; indeed, realism remains one of the dominant modes of drama to this day. At its most profound, when crafted and performed by consummately skilled artists, realistic theatre can generate extremely powerful audience empathy by virtue of the insight and clarity it brings to real-world moments. In giving us characters, the realist playwright gives us *friends*: fellow travelers on the voyage of human discovery with whom we can compare thoughts and feelings. In the uncertainties and trepidations, the wistfulness, the halting eloquence and conversational syntax of these characters we recognize ourselves, and in that recognition we gain an understanding of our own struggles and a compassion for all human endeavors.

Pioneers of Realism

The realistic theatre had its beginnings in the four-year period that saw the premieres of three shocking plays by Norwegian playwright Henrik Ibsen: *A Doll's House* (1867), *Ghosts* (1881), and *An Enemy of the People* (1882). Already famous for historical and poetic dramas, including the magnificent *Peer Gynt* (1867), Ibsen (1828–1906), soon to be known as the "father of dramatic realism," had in these works turned his attention to more contemporary and day-to-day themes: woman's role in society, hereditary disease and mercy killing, and political hypocrisy. Ordinary people populate Ibsen's realistic world, and the issues addressed in these dramas affect ordinary husband-wife, mother-son, and brother-brother relationships and are played out in the interiors of ordinary homes. Controversial beyond measure in their own time, these plays retain their edge of pertinence even today and still have the power to inform, move, and even shock. The reason for their

Patrick Stewart is the visionary architect in the title role of Ibsen's *The Master Builder*, here playing opposite Lisa Dillon in a production directed by Anthony Page at the Albery Theatre (London) in 2003.

lasting impact lies in Ibsen's choice of issues and his skill at showing both sides through brilliantly captured psychological detail.

The realistic theatre spread rapidly throughout Europe as the controversy surrounding Ibsen's plays and themes stimulated other writers to follow suit. The result was a proliferation of "problem plays," as they were sometimes called, which focused genuine social concern through realistic dramatic portrayal. In Germany, Gerhart Hauptmann (1862–1946) explored the plight of the middle and proletarian classes in several works, most notably in his masterpiece *The Weavers* (1892). In England, Irish-born George Bernard Shaw (1856–1950) created a comedic realism through which he addressed issues such as slum landlordism (in *Widowers' Houses*, 1892), prostitution (in *Mrs.*

Warren's Profession, 1902), and urban poverty (in *Major Barbara*, 1905). In France, André Antoine (1858–1943) created his Théâtre Libre in 1887 to encourage stagings of realistic dramas, including Ibsen's *Ghosts* and *Wild Duck*, Hauptmann's *Weavers*, and the French plays of Eugène Brieux (1858–1932), including *Damaged Goods* (1902), about syphilis, and *Maternity* (1903), about birth control. By the turn of the century, realism was virtually the standard dramatic form in Europe.

If the realistic theatre came to prominence with the plays of Henrik Ibsen, it attained its stylistic apogee in the major works of Anton Chekhov (1860–1904). Chekhov was a physician by training and a writer of fiction by vocation. Toward the end of his career, in association with realist director Konstantin Stanislavsky

"This mass of vulgarity, egotism, coarseness, and absurdity...This disgusting representation...An open drain; a loathsome sore unbandaged; a dirty act done publicly...Absolutely loathsome and fetid... Crapulous stuff." These were the *London Daily Telegraph*'s comments on the 1891 English premiere of what they described as "Ibsen's positively abominable play entitled *Ghosts*."

The *Telegraph* was hardly alone. "Unutterably offensive...Abominable...Scandalous," said the *Standard*. "Naked loathsomeness...Most dismal and repulsive," said the *Daily News*. "Revoltingly suggestive and blasphemous," said the *Daily Chronicle*. "Morbid, unhealthy, unwholesome, and disgusting," said *Lloyds*. "Most loathsome of Ibsen's plays...Garbage and offal," said *Truth*. "Putrid," said *Academy*. "A wicked nightmare," said *Gentlewoman*. "As foul and filthy a concoction as has ever been allowed to disgrace the boards of an English theatre," said *Era*.

Why such outrage? What offense, precisely, did *Ghosts* commit? This is a play without a single obscene word, without a single undraped bosom, without a single sexual act, and without a single double entendre.

What *Ghosts* does is to explore ruthlessly, honestly, and *realistically* the fullest implications of a hypocritical Victorian marriage, one behind whose seeming serenity exists a chaotic history of promiscuity, incest, disease, and deceit. In the play, Mrs. Alving maintains the outward shell of her marriage, thought by society to be an "ideal" one, despite the profligacy of her husband. When her son, Oswald, loses his mind at the end of the play—a mind destroyed by the syphilitic spirochetes (the literal "ghosts" of the play) inherited from his father's sins—the high spirit of European romanticism was forcibly retired in favor of a more searching, more demanding, ground-level analysis of contemporary life in a postindustrial age.

tlety: *The Seagull* (1896), *Uncle Vanya* (1899), *The Three Sisters* (1901), and *The Cherry Orchard* (1904). The intricate craftsmanship of these plays has never been surpassed; even the minor characters seem to breathe the same air we do.

Chekhov's technique was to create deeply complex relationships among his characters and to develop his plots and themes more or less between the lines. Every Chekhovian character is filled with secrets that are never fully revealed by the dialogue.

As an example of Chekhov's realist style, examine particularly the dialogue in the following scene from *The Three Sisters*. In this scene, Vershinin, an army colonel, meets Masha and her sisters, Irina and Olga, whom Vershinin dimly remembers from past years in Moscow:

VERSHININ: I have the honor to introduce myself, my name is Vershinin. I am very, very glad to be in your house at last. How you have grown up! Aie-aie!

IRINA: Please sit down. We are delighted to see you.

VERSHININ: (*with animation*) How glad I am, how glad I am! But there are three of you sisters. I remember—three little girls. I don't remember your faces, but that your father, Colonel Prozorov, had three little girls I remember perfectly. How time passes! Hey-ho, how it passes! . . .

IRINA: From Moscow? You have come from Moscow?

VERSHININ: Yes. Your father was in command of a battery there, and I was an officer in the same brigade. (*To* MASHA) Your face, now, I seem to remember.

MASHA: I don't remember you.

VERSHININ: So you are Olga, the eldest—and you are Masha—and you are Irina, the youngest—

OLGA: You come from Moscow?

VERSHININ: Yes. I studied in Moscow. . . . I used to visit you in Moscow.

Masha and Vershinin are destined to become lovers; their deepening, largely unspoken com-

(1863–1938) and the Moscow Art Theatre, he also achieved success as a playwright through a set of plays that portray the end of the czarist era in Russia with astonishing force and sub-

Realistic plays do not necessarily require realistic scenery. In Alfred Uhry's *Driving Miss Daisy*, the elderly southern Jewish woman of the title is driven around town by her African American chauffeur; over the years, they develop a profound – though mostly unstated – emotional relationship. It would be impossible, however, to stage the moving car realistically, so this vital element must simply be mimed. But the costumes, dialogue, and acting are acutely realistic. Patricia Frasier and Ernest Perry, Jr., are the actors in this 2000 Utah Shakespearean Festival production.

munion will provide one of the most haunting strains in the play. And how lifelike is the awkwardness of their first encounter! Vershinin's enthusiastic clichés ("How time passes!") and interjections ("Aie-aie!") are the stuff of everyday discourse; the news that he comes from Moscow is repeated so that it becomes amusing rather than informative, a revelation of character rather than of plot.

Masha's first exchange with Vershinin gives no direct indication of the future of their relationship; it is a crossed communication in which one character refuses to share in the other's memory. Is this a personal repudiation, or is it a teasing provocation? The acting, not simply the text, must establish their developing rapport. The love between Vershinin and Masha will tax to the maximum the capabilities of the actors who play their parts to express deep feeling through subtle nuance, through the gestures, the glances, the tones of voice, and the shared understandings and sympathetic rhythms that distinguish lovers everywhere. It is a theme that strongly affects the mood of the play but is rarely explicit in the dialogue.

The late Arthur Miller's *Death of a Salesman* is often considered America's finest tragedy. While largely realistic, it is also a memory play, and some scenes take place only inside the head of its title character, Willy. (Indeed, Miller first wanted to call the play "The Inside of His Head.") But the dreams, though dreams, are real — at least as Willy dreams them. Here Brian Dennehy as Willy (*center*) talks to the dream figures of his two sons (Kevin Anderson, *left*, and Ted Koch) as he remembers them to have been, in this 1999 Goodman Theatre production.

Naturalism

Naturalism, a movement whose development paralleled but was essentially independent of realism, represents an even more extreme attempt to dramatize human reality without the appearance of dramaturgical shaping. The naturalists, who flourished primarily in France during the late nineteenth century (Émile Zola, 1840–1902, was their chief theoretician), based their aesthetics on nature, particularly humanity's place in the natural (Darwinian) environment. To the naturalist, the human being was merely a biological phenomenon whose behavior was determined entirely by genetic and social circumstances. To portray a character as a hero, or even as a credible force for change in society, was anathema to the naturalist, who similarly eschewed dramatic conclusions or climaxes. Whereas realist plays at that time tended to deal with well-defined social issues—women's rights, inheritance laws, worker's pensions, and the like—naturalist plays offered nothing more than a "slice of life," in which the characters of the play were the play's entire subject; any topical issues that arose served merely to facilitate the interplay of personalities and highlight the characters' situations, frustrations, and hopes.

The naturalists sought to eliminate every vestige of dramatic convention: "All the great successes of the stage are triumphs over convention," declared Zola. Their efforts in this direction are exemplified by August Strindberg's (1849–1912) elimination of the time-passing intermission in *Miss Julie* (instead, a group of peasants, otherwise irrelevant to the plot, enter the kitchen setting between acts and dance to fill the time Miss Julie is spending in Jean's offstage bedroom) and by Arthur Schnitzler's (1862–1931) elimination of conventional scene beginnings, endings, and climaxes in the interlocking series of cyclical love affairs that constitute the action of *La Ronde*.

Inasmuch as sheer verisimilitude, presented as "artlessly" as humanly possible, is the primary goal of the naturalist, the term *naturalism* is often applied to those realistic plays that seem most effectively lifelike. This is not a particularly felicitous use of the term, however, because it ignores the fundamental precept of naturalism—that the human being is a mere figure in the natural environment. Naturalism is not merely a matter of style; it is a philosophical concept concerning the nature of the human animal. And naturalist theatre represents a purposeful attempt to explore that concept, using extreme realism as its basic dramaturgy.

Eugene O'Neill (1888–1953), America's first great playwright, pioneered an earthy naturalistic style in his early plays, returning to that style in his autobiographical masterpiece, *Long Day's Journey into Night*—a play so true to life that O'Neill forbade its production or publication until many years after his death. In our times, the dramas of Arthur Miller, Tennessee Williams, Robert Anderson, William Inge, David Mamet, and Lorraine Hansberry are all strongly influenced by both realism and naturalism, which continue to have a commanding presence on the American stage.

Antirealism

Realism and naturalism were not the only new movements of the late nineteenth century to make themselves strongly felt in the modern theatre. A counterforce, equally powerful, was to emerge. First manifest in the movement known as symbolism, this counterforce evolved and expanded into what we will call antirealistic theatre, which moved across Europe and quickly began contesting the advances of realism step-by-step.

The Symbolist Rebellion

The symbolist movement began in Paris during the 1880s as a joint venture of artists, playwrights, essayists, critics, sculptors, and poets. If realism was the art of depicting reality as ordinary men and women might see it, symbolism would explore—by means of images and metaphors—the *inner* realities that cannot be directly or literally perceived. "Symbolic" characters, therefore, would not represent real human beings but instead would symbolize philosophical ideals or warring internal forces in the human (or the artist's) soul.

Symbolism had another goal as well: to crush what its adherents deemed to be a spiritually bankrupt realism and to replace it with traditional aesthetic values—poetry, imagery, novelty, fantasy, extravagance, profundity, audacity, charm, and superhuman magnitude. United in their hatred for literal detail and for all that they considered mundane or ordinary, the symbolists demanded abstraction, enlargement, and innovation; the symbolist spirit soared in poetic encapsulations, outsized dramatic presences, fantastical visual effects, shocking structural departures, and grandiloquent speech. Purity of vision, rather than accuracy of

Realism as Blindness: Craig's View

Realism is a vulgar means of expression bestowed upon the blind. Thus we have the clear-sighted singing: "Beauty is Truth, Truth Beauty — that is all ye know on earth, and all ye need to know." The blind are heard croaking: "Beauty is Realism, Realism Beauty — that is all I know on earth, and all I care to know — don't ya know!" The difference is all a matter of love. He who loves the earth sees beauty everywhere: he is a god transforming by knowledge the incomplete into the complete. He can heal the lame and the sick, can blow courage into the weary, and he can even learn how to make the blind see. The power has always been possessed by the artist, who, in my opinion, rules the earth....

The limited section of playgoers who love beauty and detest Realism is a small minority of about six million souls. They are scattered here and there over the earth. They seldom, if ever, go to the modern theatre. That is why I love them, and intend to unite them.

— Gordon Craig

observation, was the symbolists' aim, and self-conscious creative innovation was to be their primary accomplishment.

The first symbolist theatre, founded in 1890 by Parisian poet Paul Fort (1872–1960), was intended as a direct attack on the naturalistic Théâtre Libre of André Antoine, founded three years earlier. Fort's theatre, the Théâtre d'Art, was proposed as "a theatre for Symbolist poets only, where every production would cause a battle." In some ways, Antoine's and Fort's theatres had much in common: both were amateur, both gained considerable notoriety, and each served as a center for a "school" of artistic ideology that attracted as much attention and controversy as any of its theatrical offerings.

But the two theatres were openly, deliberately, at war. While Antoine was presenting premieres of naturalistic and realistic dramas by August Strindberg, Émile Zola, and Henrik Ibsen, Fort presented the staged poems and poetic plays of both contemporary and earlier writers such as the French Arthur Rimbaud and Paul Verlaine, the Belgian Maurice Maeterlinck, and the American Edgar Allan Poe. Whereas Antoine would go to great lengths to create realistic scenery for his plays (for example, he displayed real sides of beef hung from meathooks for his presentation of *The Butchers*), Fort would prevail upon leading impressionist easel painters — including Pierre Bonnard, Maurice Denis, and Odilon Redon — to dress his stylized stage. Silver angels, translucent veils, and sheets of crumpled wrapping paper were among the decors that backed the symbolist works at the Théâtre d'Art.

Fort's theatre created an immediate sensation in Paris. With the stunning success in 1890 of *The Intruder,* a mysterious and poetic fantasy by Maeterlinck, the antirealist movement was fully engaged and, as Fort recalled in his memoirs, "the cries and applause of the students, poets, and artists overwhelmed the huge disapproval of the bourgeoisie."

The movement spread quickly as authors and designers alike awakened to the possibilities of a theatre wholly freed from the constraints of verisimilitude. Realism, more and more critics concluded, would never raise the commonplace to the level of art; it would only drag art down into the muck of the mundane. It ran counter to all that the theatre had stood for in the past; it throttled the potential of artistic creativity. In fact, such naturalistic and realistic authors as Henrik Ibsen, August Strindberg, Gerhart Hauptmann, and George Bernard Shaw soon came under the symbolist influence and abandoned their social preoccupations and environmental exactitude to seek new languages and more universal themes. As an added element, at about this time Sigmund Freud's research was being published and discussed, and his theories concerning dream images and the worlds of the unconscious provided new source material for the stage.

By the turn of the century, the counterforce of theatrical stylization set in motion by the

No playwright more boldly represents antirealism than Samuel Beckett, whose characters inhabit a world like nothing we have ever seen but that, at a symbolic level, we can fully understand. In *Happy Days*, Beckett's main character is buried deep in the earth – and sinking further as the play goes on – but she still pursues happiness at every waking moment. Shown here is Felicity Kendal as the entombed Winnie, in Sir Peter Hall's 2003 London production, with scenery by Lucy Hall and lighting by Paul Pyant.

symbolists was established on all fronts; indeed, the half decade on either side of 1900 represents one of the richest periods of experimentation in the history of dramatic writing. Out of that decade came Hauptmann's archetypal fairy tale *The Sunken Bell* (Germany, 1896), Alfred Jarry's outrageously cartoonish and scatological *Ubu Roi* (France, 1898), Ibsen's haunting ode to individualism *When We Dead Awaken* (Norway, 1899), Strindberg's metaphoric and imagistic *The Dream Play* (Sweden, 1902), William Butler Yeats's evocative poetic fable *Cathleen ni Houlihan* (Ireland, 1903), Shaw's philosophical allegory *Man and Superman* (England, 1903), and James Barrie's whim-

sical, buoyant fantasy *Peter Pan* (England, 1904). Almost every dramatic innovation that has followed since that time has been at least in part prefigured by one or more of these seminal works for the nonrealist theatre.

The realist-versus-symbolist confrontation affected every aspect of theatre production. Symbolist-inspired directors and designers, side by side with the playwrights, were drastically altering the arts of staging and decor to accommodate the new dramaturgies that surged into the theatre. Realist directors such as Antoine and Stanislavsky suddenly found themselves challenged by scores of adversaries and renegades: a school of symbolist and poetic directors

Robert Wilson (the director) and John Conklin (the costume designer) codesigned
the scenery for this dreamlike American Repertory Theatre production of Ibsen's
When We Dead Awaken in 1991.

rose in France, and a former disciple of Stanislavsky, the "constructivist" Vsevolod Meyerhold (1874–1940), broke with the Russian master to create a nonrealist "biomechanical" style of acting and directing in sharp contrast to that established at the Moscow Art Theatre; by 1904 Stanislavsky himself was producing the symbolist plays of Maeterlinck at the Moscow Art Theatre. With the advent of electrical stage lighting, opportunities for stylizing were vastly expanded: the new technology enabled the modern director to create vivid stage effects, starkly unrealistic in appearance, through the judicious use of spotlighting, shadowing, and shading. Technology, plus trends in postimpressionist art that were well established in Europe by 1900, led to scenery and costume designs that departed radically from realism. Exoticism, fantasy, sheer sensual delight, symbolic meaning, and aesthetic purity became the prime objectives of designers who joined the antirealist rebellion.

In some respects, the symbolist aim succeeded perhaps beyond the dreams of its originators. Fort's Théâtre d'Art, although it lasted but a year, now has spiritual descendants in every city in the Western world where theatre is performed.

The Era of "Isms"

The symbolist movement itself was short-lived, at least under that name. *Symbolism,* after all, was coined primarily as a direct contradiction of *realism,* and movements named for their oppositional qualities—called for what they are not—are quickly seen as artistically limited, as critiques of art rather than as art itself.

Within months of the symbolist advances, therefore, symbolism *as a movement* was deserted by founders and followers alike. Where did they go? Off to found newer movements: avant-gardism, futurism, Dadaism, idealism, aestheticism, impressionism, expressionism, constructivism, surrealism, formalism, theatricalism, and perhaps a hundred other "isms" now lost to time.

The first third of the twentieth century, indeed, was an era of theatrical isms, an era rich with continued experimentation by movements self-consciously seeking to redefine theatrical art. Ism theatres sprang up like mushrooms, each with its own fully articulated credo and manifesto, each promising a better art—if not, indeed, a better world. It was a vibrant era for the theatre, for out of this welter of isms the aesthetics of dramatic art took on a new social and political significance in the cultural capitals of Europe and America. A successful play was not merely a play but rather the forum for a *cause,* and behind that cause was a body of zealous supporters and adherents who shared a deep aesthetic commitment.

Nothing quite like that ism spirit exists today, for we have lost the social involvement that can turn an aesthetic movement into a profound collective belief. But the experiments and discoveries of those early days of the twentieth century and the nonrealistic spirit of symbolism itself survive and flourish under a variety of formats: ritual theatre, poetic theatre, holy theatre, theatre of cruelty, existentialist theatre, art theatre, avant-garde theatre, theatre of the absurd, and theatre of alienation. These present-day groupings, unlike the isms, are critic-defined rather than artist-defined; indeed, most theatre artists today reject any "grouping" nomenclature whatever. However, the formats these groupings pursue can be shown to reflect the general approach to structure, style, and experimentation that began with the symbolists in the late nineteenth century.

Stylized Theatre

We have chosen the rather loose term *antirealistic theatre* or, occasionally, the *stylized theatre* to embrace the entire spectrum of nonrealistic modern theatre, which, although disparate in its individual manifestations, exhibits a universal insistence on *consciously stylizing reality* into larger-than-life theatrical experience. Any theatre mode in any era, of course, has its distinctive style, but in past eras that style was always largely *imposed* by current convention and technological limitations. Modern dramatists, in contrast, have consciously *selected and created* styles to satisfy their aesthetic theories, their social principles, or simply their desire for novelty and innovation.

Antirealistic theatre attempts to create new theatrical formats, not merely to enhance the portrayal of human existence but also to disclose fundamental patterns underlying that existence: patterns of perception, patterns of association, patterns of personal and environmental interaction. The styles employed by this modern theatre come from anywhere and everywhere: from the past, from exotic cultures, and from present and futuristic technologies. The modern theatre artist has an unprecedented reservoir of sources to draw upon and is generally unconstrained in their application by political edict, religious prohibition, or mandated artistic tradition. The modern stylized theatre is undoubtedly the freest in history: the dramatist, director, actor, or designer is limited only by physical resources and individual imagination. Virtually anything can be put upon a stage, and in the twentieth century it seems that virtually everything was.

Antirealistic theatre does not altogether dispense with reality but wields it in often unexpected ways and freely enhances it with symbol and metaphor, striving to elucidate by parable and allegory, to deconstruct and reconstruct by language, scenery, and lighting. Further, it makes explicit use of the theatre's very theatricality, frequently reminding its audience members, directly or indirectly, that they are watching a performance, not an episode in somebody's daily life. Stylization inevitably reaches for universality. It tends to treat problems of psychology as problems of philosophy, and problems in human relations as problems of the human condition. Stylization reaches for patterns, not particulars; it explores abstractions and aims for sharp thematic focus and bold intellectual impact.

In the stylized theatre, characters usually represent more than individual persons or personality types. Like the medieval allegories, modern stylized plays often involve characters who represent forces of nature, moral positions, human instincts, and the like—entities such as death, fate, idealism, the life force, the earth mother, the tyrant father, and the prodigal son. And the conflicts associated with these forces, unlike the conflicts of realism, are not responsive to any human agency; they are, more often than not, represented as permanent discords inherent in the human condition. The stylized theatre resonates with tension and human frustration in the face of irreconcilable demands.

But that is not to say the antirealistic theatre is necessarily grim; on the contrary, it often uses whimsy and mordant wit as its dominant mode. Although the themes of the antirealistic theatre are anxious ones—for example, the alienation of humanity, the futility of communication, the loss of innocence, the intransigence of despair—it is not on the whole a theatre of pessimism or of nihilistic outrage. Indeed, the glory of the stylized theatre is that, at its best, it refuses to be swamped by its themes; it transcends frustration; it is the victory of poetry over alienation, comedy over noncommunication, and artistry over despair. The antirealistic theatre aims at lifting its audience, not saddling them; and even if it proffers no solutions to life's inevitable discords, it can provide considerable lucidity concerning the totality of the human adventure.

The diversity of stylized theatrical works precludes further generalization about their shared characteristics. To help us understand this diversity, however, we will examine brief examples from plays written over the past hundred years that serve to establish the main lines of the antirealistic theatre.

THE FRENCH AVANT-GARDE: *UBU ROI* The opening of Alfred Jarry's *Ubu Roi* (King Ubu) at the Théâtre Nouveau in Paris on December 11, 1896, was perhaps the most violent dramatic premiere in theatre history: the audience shouted, whistled, hooted, cheered, threw things, and shook their fists at the stage. Duels were even fought after subsequent performances. The avant-garde was born.

The term *avant-garde* comes from the military, where it refers to the advance battalion, or the "shock troops" that initiate a major assault. In France the term initially described the wave of French playwrights and directors who openly and boldly assaulted realism in the first four decades of the twentieth century. Today the term is used worldwide to describe any adventurous, experimental, and nontraditional artistic effort.

Jarry (1873–1907), a diminutive iconoclast ("eccentric to the point of mania and lucid to the point of hallucination," says critic Roger Shattuck), unleashed his radical shock troops from the moment the curtain rose. Jarry had called for an outrageously antirealistic stage—painted scenery depicting a bed, a bare tree at its foot; palm trees, a coiled boa constrictor around one of them; a gallows with a skeleton hanging from it; and falling snow. Characters entered through a painted fireplace. Costumes, in Jarry's words, were "divorced as far as possible from [realistic] color or chronology." And the title character stepped forward to begin the play with a word that quickly became immortal: *"Merdre!"* or "Shrit!"

This *mot d'Ubu* ("Ubu's word") more than anything else occasioned scandal, for although Ibsen had broken barriers of propriety in subject matter, no one had tested the language barriers of the Victorian age. Vulgar epithets, common enough in the works of Aristophanes and Shakespeare, had been pruned from the theatre in the Royal era and abolished entirely in the lofty spirit of romanticism; far from trying to sneak them back in, Jarry simply threw them up, schoolboy-like, in the face of the astonished audience. The added "r" in *merdre,* far from "cleansing" the offending obscenity, only called more attention to it and to its deliberate intrusion onto the Parisian stage.

Ubu Roi was, in fact, a schoolboy play; Jarry wrote the first version at the age of fifteen as a satire of his high school physics teacher. Jarry was only twenty-three years old when the play astounded its Parisian audiences, and the juvenile aspects of the play's origins were evident throughout the finished product, which proved to be Jarry's sole masterwork.

Ubu Roi is a savage and often ludicrous satire on the theme of power, in which Father (later King) Ubu—a fat, foul-mouthed, venal, amoral, and pompous Polish assassin—proves one of the stage's greatest creations. The play sprawls; its thirty-three scenes are often just crude skits barely linked by plot, but the interplay of farce and violence is inspired, as in the famous eating scene:

FATHER UBU, MOTHER UBU, CAPTAIN BORDURE *and his followers.*

MOTHER UBU: Good day, gentlemen; we've been anxiously awaiting you.

CAPTAIN BORDURE: Good day, madam. Where's Father Ubu?

FATHER UBU: Here I am, here I am! Good lord, by my green candle, I'm fat enough, aren't I?

CAPTAIN BORDURE: Good day, Father Ubu. Sit down boys. (*They all sit.*)

FATHER UBU: Oof, a little more, and I'd have bust my chair.

CAPTAIN BORDURE: Well, Mother Ubu! What have you got that's good today?

MOTHER UBU: Here's the menu.

FATHER UBU: Oh! That interests me.

Mother Ubu pokes her strikingly made-up face through an abstractly colored backdrop in Babette Masson's 1993 French production of Jarry's *Ubu Roi.*

MOTHER UBU: Polish soup, roast ram, veal, chicken, chopped dog's liver, turkey's ass, charlotte russe . . .

FATHER UBU: Hey, that's plenty, I should think. You mean there's more?

MOTHER UBU: (*continuing*) Frozen pudding, salad, fruits, dessert, boiled beef, Jerusalem artichokes, cauliflower à la shrit.

FATHER UBU: Hey! Do you think I'm the Emperor of China, to give all that away?

MOTHER UBU: Don't listen to him, he's feeble-minded.

FATHER UBU: Ah! I'll sharpen my teeth on your shanks.

MOTHER UBU: Try this instead, Father Ubu. Here's the Polish soup.

FATHER UBU: Crap, is that lousy!

CAPTAIN BORDURE: Hmm—it isn't very good, at that.

MOTHER UBU: What do you want, you bunch of crooks!

FATHER UBU: (*striking his forehead*) Wait, I've got an idea. I'll be right back. (*He leaves.*)

MOTHER UBU: Let's try the veal now, gentlemen.

CAPTAIN BORDURE: It's very good—I'm through.

MOTHER UBU: To the turkey's ass, next.

CAPTAIN BORDURE: Delicious, delicious! Long live Mother Ubu!

ALL: Long live Mother Ubu!

FATHER UBU: (*returning*) And you will soon be shouting, "Long live Father Ubu." (*He has a toilet brush in his hand, and he throws it on the festive board.*)

MOTHER UBU: Miserable creature, what are you up to now?

FATHER UBU: Try a little. (*Several try it, and fall, poisoned.*) Mother Ubu, pass me the roast ram chops, so that I can serve them.

MOTHER UBU: Here they are.

FATHER UBU: Everyone out! Captain Bordure, I want to talk to you.

THE OTHERS: But we haven't eaten yet.

FATHER UBU: What's that, you haven't eaten yet? Out, out, everyone out! Stay here, Bordure. (*Nobody moves.*) You haven't gone yet? By my green candle, I'll give you your ram chops. (*He begins to throw them.*)

ALL: Oh! Ouch! Help! Woe! Help! Misery! I'm dead!

FATHER UBU: Shrit, shrit, shrit! Outside! I want my way!

ALL: Everyone for himself! Miserable Father Ubu! Traitor! Meanie!

FATHER UBU: Ah! They've gone. I can breathe again—but I've had a rotten dinner. Come on, Bordure.

They go out with MOTHER UBU.

The elements of deliberate scatology, toilet humor, juvenile satire, and a full-stage food fight make clear that *Ubu Roi* is a precursor of American teen films such as *American Pie;* it is a little more difficult, however, to see the play as a precursor of a serious art and literary movement like surrealism, but such is the case. *Surrealism,* a word that means "beyond realism" or "superrealism," was officially inaugurated by André Breton in 1924 but can be said to date from this play—which, its advocates claim, reaches a superior level of reality by tracing the unconscious processes of the mind rather than the literal depictions of observable life.

EXPRESSIONISM: *THE HAIRY APE* Of all the isms, expressionism is the one that has given rise to the most significant body of modern theatre, probably because of its broad definition and its seeming alliance with expressionism in the visual arts. The theatrical expressionism that was much in vogue in Germany during the first decades of the twentieth century (particularly in the 1920s) featured shocking and gutsy dialogue, boldly exaggerated scenery, piercing sounds, bright lights, an abundance of primary colors, a not very subtle use of symbols, and a structure of short, stark, jabbing scenes that built to a powerful (and usually deafening) climax.

In America, expressionist writers addressed the growing concern that the country's rapid industrial and financial successes were crushing human freedom—and human nature itself.

Elmer Rice's *The Adding Machine* (1923) is one of America's most important expressionistic plays, showing the dehumanization of employees trapped in a corporate accounting department. Anne Bogart directed this rambunctious version for the 1995 Classics in Context festival of the Actors Theatre of Louisville.

During the 1920s, in the boldly expressionist dramas *Subway, The Adding Machine,* and *Street Scene,* Elmer Rice (1892–1967) angrily attacked what he considered the dehumanization of modern American life. And Eugene O'Neill, who had begun as a realistic playwright in the previous decades, wrote a play that became a landmark of expressionist theatre in 1921. O'Neill's *The Hairy Ape* is a one-act play featuring eight scenes. Its workingman-hero Yank meets and is rebuffed by the genteel daughter of a captain of industry. Enraged, Yank becomes violent and eventually crazed; he dies at play's end in the monkey cage of a zoo. Scene 3 illustrates the tenor of the writing:

The stokehold. In the rear, the dimly outlined bulks of the furnaces and boilers. High overhead one hanging electric bulb sheds just enough light through the murky air laden with coal dust to pile up masses of shadows everywhere. A line of men, stripped to the waist, is before the furnace doors.

They bend over, looking neither to right nor left, handling their shovels as if they were part of their bodies, with a strange, awkward, swinging rhythm. They use the shovels to throw open the furnace doors. Then from these fiery round holes in the back a flood of terrific light and heat pours full upon the men who are outlined in silhouette in the crouching, inhuman attitudes of chained gorillas. The men shovel with a rhythmic motion, swinging as on a pivot from the coal which lies in heaps on the floor behind to hurl it into the flaming mouths before them. There is a tumult of noise—the brazen clang of the furnace doors as they are flung open or slammed shut, the grating, teeth-gritting grind of steel against steel, of crunching coal. This clash of sounds stuns one's ears with its rending dissonance. But there is order in it, rhythm, a mechanical regulated recurrence, a tempo. And rising above all, making the air hum with the quiver of liberated energy, the roar of leaping flames in the furnaces, the monotonous throbbing beat of the engines.

As the curtain rises, the furnace doors are shut. The men are taking a breathing spell. One or two are

O'Neill's Expressionism

In the scene [in *The Hairy Ape*] where the bell rings for the stokers to go on duty, you remember that they all stand up, come to attention, then go out in a lockstep file. Some people think even that is an actual custom aboard ship! But it is only symbolic of the regimentation of men who are the slaves of machinery. In a larger sense, it applies to all of us, because we all are more or less the slaves of convention, or of discipline, or of a rigid formula of some sort.

The whole play is expressionistic. The coal shoveling in the furnace room, for instance. Stokers do not really shovel coal that way. But it is done in the play in order to contribute to the rhythm. For rhythm is a powerful factor in making anything expressive. You can actually produce and control emotions by that means alone.

– Eugene O'Neill

arranging the coal behind them, pulling it into more accessible heaps. The others can be dimly made out leaning on their shovels in relaxed attitudes of exhaustion.

PADDY: (*from somewhere in the line—plaintively*) Yerra, will this divil's own watch nivir end? Me back is broke. I'm destroyed entirely.

YANK: (*from the center of the line—with exuberant scorn*) Aw, yuh make me sick! Lie down and croak, why don't yuh? Always beefin', dat's you! Say, dis is a cinch! Dis was made for me! It's my meat, get me! (*A whistle is blown—a thin, shrill note from somewhere overhead in the darkness.* YANK *curses without resentment.*) Dere's de damn engineer crackin' de whip. He tinks we're loafin'.

PADDY: (*vindictively*) God stiffen him!

YANK: (*in an exultant tone of command*) Come on, youse guys! Git into de game! She's gettin' hungry! Pile some grub in her. Trow it into her belly! Come on now, all of youse! Open her up! (*At this last all the men, who have followed his movements of getting into position, throw open their furnace doors with a deafening clang. The fiery light floods over their*

shoulders as they bend round for the coal. *Rivulets of sooty sweat have traced maps on their backs. The enlarged muscles form bunches of highlight and shadow.*)

YANK: (*chanting a count as he shovels without seeming effort*) One—two—tree— (*His voice rising exultantly in the joy of battle*) Dat's de stuff! Let her have it! All togedder now! Sling it into her! Let her ride! Shoot de piece now! Call de toin on her! Drive her into it! Feel her move. Watch her smoke! Speed, dat's her middle name! Give her coal, youse guys! Coal, dat's her booze! Drink it up, baby! Let's see yuh sprint! Dig in and gain a lap! Dere she go-o-es. (*This last in the chanting formula of the galley gods at the six-day bike race. He slams his furnace door shut. The others do likewise with as much unison as their wearied bodies will permit. The effect is of one fiery eye after another being blotted out with a series of accompanying bangs.*)

PADDY: (*groaning*) Me back is broke. I'm bate out—bate— (*There is a pause. Then the inexorable whistle sounds again from the dim regions above the electric light. There is a growl of cursing rage from all sides.*)

YANK: (*shaking his fist upward—contemptuously*) Take it easy dere, you! Who d'yuh tink's runnin' dis game, me or you? When I git ready, we move. Not before! When I git ready, get me!

VOICES: (*approvingly*) That's the stuff!
Yank tal him, py golly!
Yank ain't affeerd.
Goot poy, Yank!
Give him hell!
Tell 'im 'e's a bloody swine!
Bloody slave-driver!

YANK: (*contemptuously*) He ain't got no noive. He's yellow, get me? All de engineers is yellow. Dey got streaks a mile wide. Aw, to hell wit him! Let's move, youse guys. We had a rest. Come on, she needs it! Give her pep! It ain't for him. Him and his whistle, dey don't belong. But we belong, see! We gotter feed de baby! Come on! (*He turns and flings his furnace door open. They all follow his lead.*

At this instant the SECOND *and* FOURTH ENGINEERS *enter from the darkness on the left with* MILDRED *between them. She starts, turns paler, her pose is crumbling, she shivers with fright in spite of the blazing heat, but forces herself to leave the* ENGINEERS *and take a few steps nearer the men. She is right behind* YANK. *All this happens quickly while the men have their backs turned.)*

YANK: Come on, youse guys! (*He is turning to get coal when the whistle sounds again in a peremptory, irritating note. This drives* YANK *into a sudden fury. While the other men have turned full around and stopped dumbfounded by the spectacle of* MILDRED *standing there in her white dress,* YANK *does not turn far enough to see her. Besides, his head is thrown back, he blinks upward through the murk trying to find the owner of the whistle, he brandishes his shovel murderously over his head in one hand, pounding on his chest, gorilla-like, with the other, shouting.)* Toin off dat whistle! Come down outa dere, yuh yellow, brass-buttoned, Belfast bum, yuh! Come down and I'll knock yer brains out! Yuh lousy, stinkin', yellow mut of a Catholic-moiderin' bastard! Come down and I'll moider yuh! Pullin' dat whistle on me, huh? I'll show yuh! I'll crash yer skull in! I'll drive yer teet' down yer troat! I'll slam yer nose trou de back to yer head! I'll cut yer guts out for a nickel, yuh lousy boob, yuh dirty, crummy, muck-eatin' son ofa— (*Suddenly he becomes conscious of all the other men staring at something directly behind his back. He whirls defensively with a snarling, murderous growl, crouching to spring, his lips drawn back over his teeth, his small eyes gleaming ferociously. He sees* MILDRED, *like a white apparition in the full light from the open furnace doors. He glares into her eyes, turned to stone. As for her, during his speech she has listened, paralyzed with horror, terror, her whole personality crushed, beaten in, collapsed, by the terrific impact of this unknown, abysmal brutality, naked and shameless. As she looks at his gorilla face, as his eyes bore into hers, she utters a low, choking cry and shrinks away from him, putting both hands up before her eyes to shut out the sight of his face, to protect her own. This startles* YANK *to a reaction. His mouth falls open, his eyes grow bewildered.)*

MILDRED: (*about to faint—to the* ENGINEERS, *who now have her one by each arm—whimperingly*) Take me away! Oh, the filthy beast! (*She faints. They carry her quickly back, disappearing in the darkness at the left, rear. An iron door clangs shut. Rage and bewildered fury rush back on* YANK. *He feels himself insulted in some unknown fashion in the very heart of his pride. He roars.)* God damn yuh! (*And hurls his shovel after them at the door which has just closed. It hits the steel bulkhead with a clang and falls clattering on the steel floor. From overhead the whistle sounds again in a long, angry, insistent command.)*

Curtain

O'Neill's forceful combination of visual and auditory effects lends this expressionistic play a crude, almost superhuman power. The use of silhouette in the staging and lighting, the "masses of shadows everywhere," the "tumult of noise," the "monotonous throbbing beat of the engines," the "fiery light," the "rivulets of sooty sweat," the massed chanting and the movements in unison, the "peremptory, irritating note" of the "inexorable whistle," the shouting of curses and bold ejaculations, the animal imagery, and the "horror, terror . . . of . . . unknown, abysmal brutality, naked and shameless" are all typical of the extreme stylization of early-twentieth-century expressionism. The scene also demonstrates how O'Neill and his followers in the American theatre turned away from realism and romanticism in their effort to arrive at a direct presentation of social ideology and cultural criticism.

METATHEATRE: *SIX CHARACTERS IN SEARCH OF AN AUTHOR* First produced in 1921, *Six Characters in Search of an Author* expresses from its famous title onward a "metatheatrical" motif by which the theatre itself becomes part of the content of play production, not merely the vehicle. "All the world's a stage," said Shakespeare, but in this play Luigi Pirandello (1867–1936) explores how the stage is also a world—and how the stage and the world, illusion and reality, relate to each other. In this still-stunning play, a family of dramatic "characters"—a father, his stepdaughter, a mother, and her children—appear as if by magic on the "stage" of a provincial theatre where a "new play" by Pirandello is being rehearsed. The "characters," claiming they have an unfinished play in them, beg the director to stage their lives in order that they may bring a satisfactory climax to their "drama." This fantasy treats the audience to continually shifting perceptions, for clearly a play-within-the-play is involved, but which is the real play and which the real life? There are actors playing actors, actors playing "characters," and actors playing "actors-playing-characters"; there are also scenes when the actors playing "characters" are making fun of the actors playing actors-playing-"characters." It is no wonder that most audiences give up trying to untangle the planes of reality Pirandello creates in this play; they are simply too difficult to comprehend except as a dazzle of suggestive theatricality.

Pirandello contrasts the passionate story of the "characters"—whose "drama" concerns a broken family, adultery, and a suggestion of incest—with the artifice of the stage and its simulations; in the course of this exposition Pirandello's performers discuss the theatricality of life, the life of theatricality, and the eternal confusions between appearance and reality:

THE FATHER: What I'm inviting you to do is to quit this foolish playing at art—this acting and pretending—and seriously answer my question: WHO ARE YOU?

THE DIRECTOR: (*amazed but irritated, to his actors*) What extraordinary impudence! This so-called character wants to know who I am?

THE FATHER: (*with calm dignity*) Signore, a character may always ask a "man" who he is. For a character has a true life, defined by his characteristics—he is always, at the least, a "somebody." But a man—now, don't take this personally—A man is generalized beyond identity—he's a nobody!

THE DIRECTOR: Ah, but me, me—I am the Director! The Producer! You understand?

PIRANDELLO: THE PLANE OF REALITY TRANSFORMED

A stage which accommodates the fantastical reality of these six characters is not, itself, a fixed or immutable space, nor are the events of the play preconceived in a fixed formula. On the contrary, everything in this play is created freshly as it happens; it is fluid, it is improvised. As the story and the characters take shape, so the stage itself evolves, and the plane of reality is organically transformed.

– Luigi Pirandello

THE FATHER: Signore—Think of how you used to feel about yourself, long ago, all the illusions you used to have about the world, and about your place in it: those illusions were real for you then, they were *quite* real— But now, with hindsight, they prove to be nothing, they are nothing to you now but an embarrassment. Well, signore, that is what your present reality is today—just a set of illusions that you will discard tomorrow. Can't you feel it? I'm not speaking of the planks of this stage we stand on, I'm speaking of the very earth under our feet. It's sinking under you—by tomorrow, today's entire reality will have become just one more illusion. You see?

THE DIRECTOR: (*confused but amazed*) Well? So what? What does all that prove?

THE FATHER: Ah, nothing, signore. Only to show that if, beyond our illusions (*indicating the other characters*), we have no ultimate reality, so your reality as well—your reality that touches and feels and breathes today— will be unmasked tomorrow as nothing but yesterday's illusion!

These lines illustrate Pirandello's use of paradox, irony, and the theatre as metaphor to create a whimsical drama about human identity and human destiny. By contrasting the passion of his "characters" and the frequent frivolity of his "actors," Pirandello establishes a provocative juxtaposition of human behavior and its theatricalization—and the whole fantastical style is nothing but an exploitation of the theatrical format itself.

THEATRE OF CRUELTY: *JET OF BLOOD*

Antonin Artaud (1896–1948) was one of drama's greatest revolutionaries, although his importance lies more in his ideas and influence than in his actual theatrical achievements. A stage and film actor in Paris during the 1920s, he founded the Théâtre Alfred Jarry in 1926, producing, among other works, Strindberg's surrealist *A Dream Play* and, in 1935, an adaptation of Shelley's dramatic poem *The Cenci*. His essays, profoundly influential in the theatre today, were collected and published in 1938 in a book titled *The Theatre and Its Double*.

The theatre envisaged by Artaud was a self-declared theatre of cruelty, for, in his words, "Without an element of cruelty at the root of every performance, the theatre is not possible." The "cruel" theatre would flourish, Artaud predicted, by "providing the spectator with the true sources of his dreams, in which his taste for crime, his erotic obsessions, his savagery, his illusions, his utopian ideals, even his cannibalism, would surge forth."

In Artaud's vision, ordinary plays were to be abolished; there should be, in his words, "no more masterpieces." In place of written plays there should be

cries, groans, apparitions, surprises, theatricalities of all kinds, magic beauty of costumes taken from certain ritual models; . . . light in waves, in sheets, in fusillades of fiery arrows. . . . Paroxysms will suddenly burst forth, will fire up like fires in different spots.

In a famous metaphor, Artaud compared the theatre to the great medieval plague, noting that both plague and theatre had the capacity to liberate human possibilities and illuminate the human potential:

The theatre is like the plague . . . because like the plague it is the revelation, the bringing forth, the exteriorization of a depth of latent cruelty by means of which all the perverse possibilities of the mind, whether of an individual or a people, are localized. . . .

One cannot imagine, save in an atmosphere of carnage, torture, and bloodshed, all the magnificent Fables which recount to the multitudes the first sexual division and the first carnage of essences that appeared in creation. The theatre, like the plague, is in the image of this carnage and this essential separation. It releases conflicts, disengages powers, liberates possibilities, and if these possibilities and these powers are dark, it is the fault not of the plague nor of the theatre, but of life.

Artaud's ideas were radical, and his essays were incendiary; his power to shock and inspire is undiminished today, and many contemporary theatre artists claim an Artaudian heritage. It is not at all clear, however, what final form the theatre of cruelty should actually take in performance, and it is readily apparent even to the casual reader that the theatre Artaud speaks of is much easier to realize on paper than on an actual stage. Artaud's own productions were in fact failures; he was formally "expelled" from the surrealist movement, and he spent most of his later life abroad in mental institutions. His one published play, *Jet of Blood* (1925), illustrates both the radically antirealistic nature of his dramaturgy and the difficulties that would be encountered in its production. This is the opening of the play:

THE YOUNG MAN: I love you, and everything is beautiful.

THE YOUNG GIRL: (*with a strong tremolo in her voice*) You love me, and everything is beautiful.

THE YOUNG MAN: (*in a very deep voice*) I love you, and everything is beautiful.

THE YOUNG GIRL: (*in an even deeper voice than his*) You love me, and everything is beautiful.

THE YOUNG MAN: (*leaving her abruptly*) I love you. (*Pause*) Turn around and face me.

THE YOUNG GIRL: (*she turns to face him*) There!

THE YOUNG MAN: (*in a shrill and exalted voice*) I love you, I am big, I am shining, I am full, I am solid.

THE YOUNG GIRL: (*in the same shrill tone*) We love each other.

THE YOUNG MAN: We are intense. Ah, how well ordered this world is!

A pause. Something that sounds like an immense wheel turning and blowing out air is heard. A hurricane separates the two. At this moment two stars crash into each other, and we see a number of live pieces of human bodies falling down: hands, feet, scalps, masks, colonnades, porches, temples, and alembics, which, however, fall more and more slowly, as if they were falling in a vacuum. Three scorpions fall down, one after the other, and finally a frog and a beetle, which sets itself down with a maddening, vomit-inducing slowness . . .

Enter a knight of the Middle Ages in an enormous suit of armor, followed by a nurse holding her breasts in both hands and puffing and wheezing because they are both very swollen.

Artaud's apocalyptic vision has stimulated many subsequent theatre directors, including Jean-Louis Barrault and Roger Blin in France, Peter Brook in England, Jerzy Grotowski in Poland, and André Gregory in America; his influence can also be seen in the plays of Jean Genet and the productions of Robert Wilson. His notion of a theatre of cruelty, although not fully realized onstage in his lifetime, has been more closely approached by each of these artists and may still be achieved.

PHILOSOPHICAL MELODRAMA: *NO EXIT*   *No Exit* is one of the most compelling short plays ever written. In this one-act fantasy written in 1944, Jean-Paul Sartre (1905–1980), the well-known French existentialist philosopher, establishes a unique "Hell," which is a room without windows or mirrors. Into it come three people, lately deceased, all condemned to this netherworld because of their earthly sins. The three are brilliantly ill matched: Garcin, the sole man, tends toward homosexuality, as does Inez, one of the two women; Estelle, the final occupant

Jean-Paul Sartre's *No Exit* is a philosophical study of three characters locked together in "Hell" – which is discovered to be "other people." Shown here is the 1993 Comédie Française production.

of this bizarre inferno, tends toward heterosexual nymphomania. Estelle pursues Garcin, Garcin pursues his fellow spirit, Inez, and Inez pursues the beautiful Estelle in a triangle of misdirected affection that, one presumes, will continue maddeningly through all eternity. The infinite bleakness of this play's fantastical situation and the numbing futility of each character's aspirations provoke Garcin to beg for some good old-fashioned torture—but nothing quite so simple is forthcoming. Instead, he is forced to conclude: "Hell is other people." And the play ends with a curtain line that is characteristic of the modern stylized theatre:

GARCIN: Well, well, let's get on with it.

This line suggests that although the play concludes, the situation continues, eternally, behind the drawn curtain.

No Exit is a classic dramatic statement of existentialism, of which Sartre was the twentieth century's leading exponent. Remove the fantastical elements—that this is Hell and the characters are ghosts—and we have Sartre's vision of human interaction: every individual forever seeks affirmation and self-realization in the eyes of the Other. Each character in the play carries with him or her a baggage of guilt and expectation, each seeks from another some certification of final personal worth, and each is endlessly thwarted in this quest. We are all condemned to revolve around each other in frustratingly incomplete accord, suggests Sartre; we are all forced to reckon with the impossibility of finding meaning in the unrelated events that constitute life.

One can accept or reject Sartre's view—which is perhaps more than usually pessimistic for having been written during the Nazi Occupation of Sartre's Paris—but no one can dispute the brilliance of his dramatic stylization: the fantastical Hell, an amusing "valet" who brings each character onto the stage, and the highly contrived assemblage of mismatched characters all serve to focus the intellectual argument precisely. Sartre's characters are philosophically

---

ALBEE ON THE ABSURD

As I get it, The Theatre of the Absurd is an absorption-in-art of certain existentialist and post-existentialist philosophical concepts having to do, in the main, with man's attempts to make sense for himself out of his senseless position in a world which makes no sense – which makes no sense because the moral, religious, political, and social structures man has erected to "illusion" himself have collapsed.

– Edward Albee

---

representative rather than psychologically whole; there is no intention on Sartre's part to portray individual people with interesting idiosyncrasies, and there is no feeling on our part that the characters have a personal life beyond what we see in the play. Biographical character analysis would be useless for an actor assigned to play one of these roles, and the interlock of psychological motivation, even in this sexually charged atmosphere, is deliberately ignored by the author. What Sartre presents instead is a general understanding of human affairs: a philosophy of interpersonal relations.

THEATRE OF THE ABSURD: *WAITING FOR GODOT* The name *theatre of the absurd* applies to a grouping of plays that share certain common structures and styles and are tied together by a common philosophical thread: the theory of the absurd as formulated by French essayist and playwright Albert Camus (1913–1960). Camus likened the human condition to that of the mythological Corinthian king Sisyphus, who because of his cruelty was condemned forever to roll a stone up a hill in Hades, only to have it roll down again upon reaching the top. Camus saw the modern individual as similarly engaged in an eternally futile task: the absurdity of searching for some meaning or purpose or order in human life. To Camus, the immutable irrationality of the universe is what makes this task absurd. On the one hand,

EXISTENTIALISM, ABSURDISM, AND WORLD WAR II

Both Jean-Paul Sartre's existentialism and Albert Camus's philosophy of the absurd were forged largely in the outrages of World War II, when both men were leading figures in the French Resistance movement. A hellish world that affords "no exit" and in which human activity is as meaningless as Sisyphus's torment seems perfectly credible during such desperate times, times of national occupation and genocidal slaughter. After the war, Jean-Paul Sartre, who was France's foremost exponent of existentialism and one of that country's leading dramatists during the 1940s and 1950s, spoke eloquently of his first experience as playwright and director, which occurred when he was a prisoner of war:

My first experience in the theatre was especially fortunate. When I was a prisoner in Germany in 1940, I wrote, staged and acted in a Christmas play which, while pulling the wool over the eyes of the German censor by means of simple symbols, was addressed to my fellow prisoners.... No doubt it was neither a good play nor well acted: the work of an amateur, the critics would say, a product of special circumstances. Nevertheless, on this occasion, as I addressed my comrades across the footlights, speaking to them of their state as prisoners, when I suddenly saw them so remarkably silent and attentive, I realized what theatre ought to be – a great collective, religious phenomenon.

human beings yearn for a "lost" unity and lasting truth; on the other hand, the world can only be seen as irrecoverably fragmented—chaotic, unsummable, permanently unorganized, and permanently unorganizable.

The plays that constitute the theatre of the absurd are obsessed with the futility of all action and the pointlessness of all direction. These themes are developed theatrically through a deliberate and self-conscious flaunting of the "absurd"—in the sense of the ridiculous. Going beyond the use of symbols and the fantasy and poetry of other nonrealists, the absurdists have distinguished themselves by employing in their dramas, for example, clocks that clang incessantly, characters that eat pap in ashcans, corpses that grow by the minute, and personal interactions that are belligerently noncredible.

The theatre of the absurd can be said to include mid-twentieth-century works by Jean Genet (French), Eugène Ionesco (Romanian), Friedrich Dürrenmatt (Swiss), Arthur Adamov (Russian), Slawomir Mrozek (Polish), Harold Pinter (English), Edward Albee (American), Fernando Arrabal (Spanish), and the Irish poet, playwright, and novelist Samuel Beckett. And although Paris is the center of this theatre—so much so that the works of Ionesco, Adamov,

Arrabal, and Beckett are all written in French rather than in their native tongues—its influence is felt worldwide.

Samuel Beckett (1906–1989), the unquestioned leader of the absurdist writers, eschewed all realism, romanticism, and rationalism to create works that are relentlessly unenlightening, that are indeed committed to a final obscurity. "Art has nothing to do with clarity, does not dabble in the clear, and does not make clear," argued Beckett in one of his earliest works, and his theatre was based on the thesis that man is and will remain ignorant regarding all matters of importance.

Born in Dublin, Beckett emigrated in 1928 to Paris, where he joined a literary circle centered on another Irish émigré, James Joyce. Beckett's life before World War II was an artistic vagabondage, during which he wrote several poems, short stories, and a novel; following the war and his seclusion in the south of France during the Occupation, he produced the masterworks for which he is justly famous: the novels *Molloy, The Unnamable,* and *Malone Dies,* and the plays *Waiting for Godot* and *Endgame.* By the time of his death in 1989, Beckett had received the Nobel Prize in Literature, and his works had become the subject of hundreds of critical

Samuel Beckett's *Waiting for Godot* is generally considered the great classic of theatre of the absurd. In this 1997 Paris production – directed by Patrice Kerbrat – Pierre Arditi and Marcel Maréchal (*left to right*) play the two old men, Vladimir and Estragon, while Pozzo (Robert Hirsch, *seated*) holds his bag-carrier, Lucky (Jean-Michel Dupuis), on a leash around his hapless servant's neck. The writing projected above the backdrop explains the play's famously minimal setting: "a country road, with tree." The scenery is by Édouard Laug.

books and essays. It was *Godot* that first brought Beckett to worldwide attention: the play's premiere in Paris in 1953 occasioned a great stir among French authors and critics, and its subsequent openings in London and New York had the same effect there.

Waiting for Godot is a parable without a message. On a small mound at the base of a tree, beside a country road, two elderly men in bowler hats wait for a "Mr. Godot," with whom they have presumably made an appointment. They believe that when Godot comes they will be "saved"; however, they are not at all certain

that Godot has agreed to meet with them or if this is the right place or the right day or whether they will even recognize him if he comes. During each of the two acts, which seem to be set in late afternoon on two successive days (although nobody can be sure of that), the men are visited by passersby—first by two men calling themselves Pozzo and Lucky and subsequently by a young boy who tells them that Mr. Godot "cannot come today but surely tomorrow." The two old men continue to wait as the curtain falls. Although there are substantial references in the play to Christian symbols and beliefs, it is not clear whether these imply positive or negative associations. The only development in the play is that the characters seem to undergo a certain loss of adeptness while the setting blossoms in rebirth (the tree sprouts leaves between the acts).

What Beckett has drawn here is clearly a paradigm of the human condition: an ongoing life cycle of vegetation serving as the background to human decay, hope, and ignorance. Beckett's tone is whimsical: the characters play enchanting word games with each other, they amuse each other with songs, accounts of dreams, exercises, and vaudevillian antics, and in general they make the best of a basically hopeless situation. Beckett's paradigm affords a field day for critical investigators: *Waiting for Godot* has already generated a veritable library of brilliantly evocative discussions, and few plays from any era have been so variously analyzed, interpreted, and explored for symbolic meaning and content. Owing largely to the international critical acceptance of this play and its eventual public success, absurdist drama, as well as the whole of modern stylized theatre, was able to move out of the esoteric "art theatre" of the world capitals and onto the stages of popular theatres everywhere.

THEATRE OF ALIENATION: *THE GOOD PERSON OF SZECHUAN* Contrasting vividly with the theatre of the absurd is the theatre of alienation (or of distancing). Whereas the hermetic, self-contained absurdist plays highlight the essential futility of human endeavors, the sprawling, socially engaged "epic" theatre of alienation concentrates on humanity's potential for growth and society's capacity to effect change.

The guiding genius of the theatre of alienation was Bertolt Brecht (1898–1956): theorist, dramatist, and director. No single individual has had a greater impact on post–World War II theatre than Brecht. This impact has been felt in two ways. First, Brecht introduced theatre practices that are, at least on the surface, utterly at variance with those in use since the time of Aristotle; second, his accomplishments

invigorated the theatre with an abrasive humanism that reawakened its sense of social responsibility and its awareness of the capacity of theatre to mold public issues and events.

Brecht, who was born in Germany, emerged from World War I a dedicated Marxist and pacifist. Using poems, songs, and eventually the theatre to promote his ideals following the German defeat, Brecht vividly portrayed his country during the Weimar Republic as caught in the grips of four giant vises: the military, capitalism, industrialization, and imperialism. His *Rise and Fall of the City of Mahagonny,* for example, an "epic opera" of 1930, proved an immensely popular blending of satire and propaganda, music and expressionist theatricality, social idealism and lyric poetry; it was produced all over Germany and throughout most of Europe in the early 1930s as a depiction of a rapacious international capitalism evolving toward fascism.

Brecht was forced to flee his country upon Hitler's accession to the chancellorship. Thereafter he moved about Europe for a time and then, for much of the 1940s, settled in America. Following World War II he returned in triumph to East Berlin, where the East German government established for him the Berliner Ensemble Theatre; there Brecht was allowed to consolidate his theories in a body of productions developed out of his earlier plays and the pieces he had written while in exile.

Brecht's theatre draws upon a potpourri of theatrical conventions, some derived from the ancients, some from Eastern drama, and some from the German expressionist movement in which Brecht himself played a part in his early years. Masks, songs, verse, exotic settings, satire, and direct rhetorical address are fundamental conventions that Brecht adopted from other theatre forms. In addition, he developed many conventions of his own: lantern-slide projections with printed "captions," asides and invocations directed to the audience to encourage them to develop an objective point of view, and a variety of procedures aimed at demystifying theatrical techniques (for example, lowering the lights so that the pipes and wires would be displayed) became the characteristics of Brecht's theatre.

Brecht deplored the use of sentimentality and the notion of audience empathy for characters and attempted instead to create a performance style that was openly "didactic": the actor was asked to alienate himself, or distance himself, from the character he played—to "demonstrate" his character rather than to embody that character in a realistic manner. In Brecht's view, the ideal actor was one who could establish a *critical objectivity* toward his or her character that would make clear the character's social function and political commitment. In attempting to repudiate the "magic" of the theatre, he demanded that it be made to seem nothing more than a place for workers to present a meaningful "parable" of life, and he in no way wished to disguise the fact that the stage personnel—actors and stagehands—were merely workers doing their jobs. In every way possible, Brecht attempted to prevent the audience from becoming swept up in an emotional, sentimental bath of feelings: his goal was to keep the audience "alienated" or "distanced" from the literal events depicted by the play so that they would be free to concentrate on the larger social and political issues that the play generated and reflected. Brecht considered this theatre to be an "epic" one because it attempted, around the framework of a parable or an archetypal event, to create a whole new perspective on human history and to indicate the direction that political dialogue should take to foster social betterment.

Brecht's theories were to have a staggering impact on the modern theatre. In his wholesale renunciation of Aristotelian catharsis, which depends on audience empathy with a noble character, and his denial of Stanislavsky's basic principles concerning the aims of acting, Brecht provided a new dramaturgy that encouraged playwrights, directors, and designers to tackle social issues directly rather than through the implications of contrived dramatic situations. Combining the technologies and aesthetics of other media—the lecture hall, the slide show, the public meeting, the cinema, the cabaret, the rehearsal—Brecht fashioned a vastly expanded arena for his *dialectics:* his social arguments that sought to engender truth through the confrontation of conflicting interests. These ideas were played out, in Brecht's own works and in countless other works inspired by him, with a bold theatricality, an open-handed dealing with the audience, a proletarian vigor, and a stridently entertaining, intelligently satirical, and charmingly bawdy theatre. This theatre has proven even more popular today than it was in Brecht's time, because since then the world seems to have grown even more fragmented, more individualistic, and more suspicious of collective emotions and sentimentality.

No play better illustrates Brecht's dramatic theory and method than *The Good Person of Szechuan* (1943). This play, set in western China (of which Brecht knew virtually nothing, thus adding to the "distancing" of the story), concerns a kindhearted prostitute, Shen Te, who is astounded to receive a gift of money from three itinerant gods. Elated by her good fortune, Shen Te uses the money to start a tobacco business. She is, however, quickly beset by petty officials seeking to impose local regulations, self-proclaimed creditors demanding payment, and a host of hangers-on who simply prey upon her good nature. At the point of financial ruin, Shen Te leaves her tobacco shop to enlist the aid of her male cousin Shui Ta, who strides imperiously into the tobacco shop and rousts the predators, making it safe for Shen Te to return. But the predators come back, and Shen Te again has to call on the tyrannical Shui Ta to save her. A simple story—but Brecht's stroke of genius is to make Shui Ta and Shen Te the same character: Shui Ta is simply Shen Te in disguise! The aim of the play is not to show that there are kindhearted people and successful people but that a person must choose to be one or the other. What kind of society is it, Brecht asks, that forces us to make this sort of choice?

Brecht was no mere propagandist, and his epic theatre is not one of simple messages or

Brechtian "epic" design techniques – masks for the actors, a wrinkled curtain with obvious stage lights and wires, a bare platform, and frontal address to the audience – distinguish this 2004 production of *The Good Person of Szechuan* at the Théâtre de Chaillot in Paris. The designs were by Noëlle Ginefri (sets) and Sylvie Martin-Hyszka; the play was directed by Irina Brook (Peter Brook's daughter) and featured Maryse Poulhe (*front left*) as Shen Te disguised as her male cousin Shui Ta.

easy conclusions. At the end of *The Good Person of Szechuan*, Shen Te asks the gods for help, but they simply float off into the air reciting inane platitudes as the curtain falls. The gods do not have the answer—so the audience must provide it. In the play's epilogue, a character comes forward and addresses us:

Hey, honorable folks, don't be dismayed
That we can't seem to end this play! You've
    stayed
To see our shining, all-concluding moral,
And what we've given you has been this
    bitter quarrel.
We know, we know—we're angry too,
To see the curtain down and everything
    askew.
We'd love to see you stand and cheer—
    and say
How wonderful you find our charming play!
But we won't put our heads into the sand.
We know your wish is ever our command,
We know you ask for *more:* a firm conclusion
To this alarming more-than-mass confusion.
But what is it? Who knows? Not all your
    cash
Could buy your way—or ours—from this
    mishmash.
Do we need heroes? Dreams? New Gods?
    Or None?
Well, tell us—else we're hopelessly undone.
The only thing that we can think to say
Is simply that it's *you* must end this play.
Tell us how our own good woman of
    Szechuan
Can come to a good ending—if she can!
Honorable folks: you search, and we will
    trust
That you will find the way. You must, must,
    must!

Brecht's parables epitomize the conflicts between social classes; they do not presume to solve these conflicts. Indeed, the social problems he addresses are to be solved not on the stage but in the world itself: the audience must find the appropriate balance between morality and greed, between individualism and social responsibility. Brecht's plays reenact the basic intellectual dichotomy posed by Marx's dialectical materialism; thus they are, in a sense, Marxist plays, but they certainly are not Leninist, much less Stalinist. They radiate a faith in the human potential. Yet although they are both socially engaged and theatrically eclectic —qualities not particularly noticeable in the theatre of the absurd—they still resound with the fundamental human uncertainty that pervades all of modern stylized theatre.

COMEDY OF CONTEMPORARY MANNERS: *BEDROOM FARCE* Comedy has always been one of the greatest staples of the theatre; since the days of Aristophanes in ancient Greece and Plautus in Rome, comedians have entertained the public with puns, antics, lighthearted social commentaries, and a host of other amusing reflections on the human struggle. It is an axiom of the theatre that "comedy is serious business," and the true comedian is understood to be as inspired an artist as any who labors under the lights. Yet comedy is rarely accorded its fair share of academic consideration, partly because comedy tends to be topical and therefore less than universal and partly because the very thing that makes comedy popular—its accessibility—also makes it relatively simple, and academicians adore complexity. But simple does not mean simple-minded, and the relative scarcity of fine comic plays originating in any generation attests to the enormous talent it takes to write, direct, and act comedically.

In America, Neil Simon (born 1927) has for four decades exhibited enormous talent and success as a writer of light comedy for the stage (and film), and in England, Alan Ayckbourn (born 1939) has demonstrated a comparable skill at the form. Ayckbourn's *Bedroom Farce* was first produced in 1975 by the Library Theatre in Scarborough, England, with which Ayckbourn is associated; the play was subsequently produced by the National Theatre in London in 1977 and came to Broadway and various other American cities shortly thereafter.

Like all of Ayckbourn's works, *Bedroom Farce* is an ingenious comedy of current manners, novel in its dramatic structure and reasonably true to life in its concerns. The setting for

Shown here is Alan Ayckbourn's delightful three-bedroom comedy, *Bedroom Farce*, as directed by Loveday Ingram for London's Aldwych Theatre in 2002.

Bedroom Farce is three bedrooms, all in view simultaneously; the characters consist of four couples who, for reasons cleverly worked out in the plot, find themselves in one bedroom after another by turns. Although the innuendos of this play are highly sexual, the action consists primarily of animated verbal exchanges and comic business and pratfalls; thus the play lives up to the farcical structure promised by its title.

The opening scene of *Bedroom Farce*—an exchange of dialogue between Ernest and Delia, the oldest couple in the play—typifies the witty and very British repartee mastered by Ayckbourn. The scene takes place in a bedroom described as a "large Victorian" room "in need of redecoration":

. . . DELIA *sits in her bedroom at her dressing table mirror. She is going out. She is in her slip and finishing her make-up. An elaborate operation.* ERNEST *wanders in. Birdlike, bumbling, nearly sixty. He is in evening dress. He stares at* DELIA. *They are obviously going to be late but* ERNEST *has learnt that impatience gets him nowhere.*

DELIA: It would appear that things between Susannah and Trevor are coming to a head.

ERNEST: Ah.

DELIA: He was always a difficult boy. I sometimes think if you hadn't ignored him quite as much—

ERNEST: I did?

DELIA: Of course you did. You hardly said a word to him all the time he was growing up.

ERNEST: I seem to remember chatting away to him for hours.

DELIA: Well. Chatting. I meant conversation. Conversation about important things. A father should converse with his son. About things that matter deeply.

ERNEST: Doesn't really leave them much to talk about then, does it?

DELIA: And that if I may say so is typical. No. Let's admit it. We weren't good parents. You did nothing and I tried to make up for it, and that's why he's like he is today. I mean if he'd had a stable childhood, he'd never have completely lost his sense of proportion and married Susannah. I mean, I sometimes feel on the rare occasions one does see them together that she's not really—awful thing to say but—not really resilient enough for Trevor. He wants somebody more phlegmatic. That Jan girl for instance would have been ideal. Do you remember her?

ERNEST: Jan? Jan? Jan?

DELIA: Nice little thing. Beautifully normal. She came to tea, do you remember? You got on very well with her.

ERNEST: Oh yes. She was jolly, wasn't she? She was very interested in my stamps. What happened to her?

DELIA: Oh, she married—someone else, I think. She still writes occasionally.

ERNEST: I must say I preferred her to Susannah. Never really hit it off with her, I'm afraid.

DELIA: Well, she's a very complex sort of girl, isn't she? Hasn't really made up her mind. About herself. I mean, I think a woman sooner or later has simply got to make up her mind about herself. I mean, even if she's someone like Carolyn—you know, Mrs. Brightman's Carolyn—who looks at herself and says, right, I'm a lump. I'm going to be a lump but then at least everyone can accept her as a lump. So much simpler.

ERNEST: I think he should have married this other one.

DELIA: Jan? I don't think she was that keen.

ERNEST: She was altogether much jollier.

DELIA: Well, we're saddled with Susannah as a daughter-in-law—at least temporarily. We'd better make the best of it—I think I've put these eyes on crooked—we'd better make the best of it.

ERNEST: It's their bed. They can lie on it.

DELIA: Yes. I think that's one of the problems.

ERNEST: Eh?

DELIA: B—E—D.

ERNEST: B—E—D? Bed?

DELIA: Enough said.

ERNEST: Good lord. How do you know?

DELIA: One reads between the lines, darling. I've had a little look around their house. You can tell a great deal from people's bedrooms.

ERNEST: Can you? Good heavens. (*He looks about.*)

DELIA: If you know what to look for.

There is nothing obscure or difficult in *Bedroom Farce,* which stands out in the contemporary theatre mainly for its capacity to entertain, to titillate, and to dazzle with cleverness. Indeed, Ayckbourn makes clear his purely comedic intentions in the selection of his title, which suggests an even more frivolous diversion than Ayckbourn actually provides. For what the author has created in *Bedroom Farce* is, ultimately, something more than just another series of hijinks, physical incongruities, and dramatic clichés: it is a wry combination of social satire, middle-class insights, and boisterous good fun. The modern stylization can be seen in the intricacy of the plot design, which is echoed if not exceeded in Ayckbourn's other plays (*Absurd Person Singular* takes place, successively, in the kitchens of three married couples; *The Norman Conquests* consists of three interlocking plays, occurring simultaneously, involving the same cast of characters in three parts of the same house) and reflects a skill at construction that borders on pure genius. This kind of craftsmanship alone would suffice to elevate any comedy far beyond the usual level of television skit or sitcom; in Ayckbourn's case, it enables his stage works to reach the heights of inspired farce.

POLITICAL SATIRE: *SERIOUS MONEY*   Since at least the time of Aristophanes, playwrights have used the theatre as a broad public platform to criticize the social world of their times—most often in a way that is both caustic and entertaining. Causticity gives such criticism its necessary bite, but a playful or whimsical tone renders even the harshest criticism palatable—and, in exceptionally dangerous times, may also protect a playwright from political retribution. We use the term *satire* to distinguish such works, which have been popular in the theatre of most cultures.

British playwright Caryl Churchill (born 1938) has been a unique exemplar of socially conscious dramatic satire since the 1970s, with trenchant and brilliantly innovative works on a wide variety of issues: sexual orientations and their attendant prejudices and hypocrisies (*Cloud 9*), gender discrimination throughout history (*Top Girls*), British-American attractions and antipathies (*Ice Cream*), and the post-cold-war chaos in eastern Europe (*Mad Forest*). In each of these works, Churchill has reinvestigated—and in some cases reinvented—the dramaturgical format itself: in *Cloud 9,* for example, she double-casts actors in both male and female—and youthful and elderly—roles, putting a wholly new slant on the complex perspectives that gender and age cast on our notions of personal identity. And in all of her plays, Churchill reexamines the syntaxes of stage dialogue, often creating new conversational punctuation systems to identify just how characters—like people in real life—frequently overlap, interrupt, and self-abort their own and each other's speeches.

In *Serious Money* (1987), Churchill employs a racy rhyming verse—in an exceptional glib patter that lies somewhere between e. e. cummings and gangsta rap—to explore the vagaries of arbitrage stock trading on the London market and of international finance:

ZACKERMAN [an international banker in London]:
There's some enterprising guys around and here's an example.
You know how if you want to get a job in the states you have to give a urine sample?
        (This is to show you're not on drugs.)
There's a company now for a fifty dollar fee
They'll provide you with a guaranteed pure, donated by a churchgoer, bottle of pee.
        (They also plan to market it dehydrated in a packet and you just add water.)
And AIDS is making advertisers perplexed
Because it's no longer too good to have your product associated with sex.
But it's a great marketing opportunity.

Telephone calls come fast and furious in Caryl Churchill's *Serious Money*, a savage and satirical comedy about stock trading. This 2004 production at the Yale Repertory Theatre was directed by Jean Randich, with costumes by Daniel Urlie and lighting by Paul Whitaker.

Like the guys opening up blood banks
    where you pay to store your own blood
    in case of an accident and so be guaran-
    teed immunity.
        (It's also a great time to buy into
        rubber.)
Anyone who can buy oranges for ten and
    sell at eleven in a souk or bazaar
Has the same human nature and can go
    equally far.
The so-called third world doesn't want our
    charity or aid.
All they need is the chance to sit down in
    front of some green screens and trade.

The witty rhymes, punctuated by paren-thetical "ad libs," and the complicated frenzy of *Serious Money*'s plot and staging (much of the play takes place on a stock brokerage's trading floor, bursting with stock monitors, telephone banks, and continuous, shouted deal-making) create a mesmerizing enchant-ment. Yet Churchill's views of economic ex-ploitation on an international level beam through loud and clear. Satire is a topical dra-matic form that often does not outlive its top-ics, but when the content is compelling and the form brilliant—as it was with Aristophanes and is with Churchill—the play usually sur-vives its merely political utility and makes its way into the lasting theatrical repertoire.

9

The Musical Theatre

MUSICAL THEATRE — A THEATRE THAT EMPLOYS A FULL SINGING SCORE, usually accompanied by an orchestra and often dance as well—would generally have to be considered "antirealistic" in the most obvious sense. Nonetheless, its particularity derives not from a rebellion against verisimilitude (thus it does not fit into the category "antirealistic theatre," as described in the preceding chapter) but rather from its basis in an aesthetics unique to its performance. Hence we will treat musical theatre in a chapter of its own.

It could actually be argued that most drama throughout theatre's history has been in fact musical, that musical theatre is, indeed, the dominant—not merely an alternative—mode of dramatic art. Classic Greek tragedy was sung and danced; it was accompanied by the *aulos* (flute) and other instruments, and Aeschylus, who directed his own plays, was particularly noted for his choreography in the choral entrance of *The Eumenides*. Most Renaissance and commedia dell'arte plays included songs and instrumental music, and twenty-five of Shakespeare's thirty-eight plays contain at least some singing (*The Tempest* alone has nine scripted songs). Moreover, Shakespeare's comedies, as well as those of his contemporaries, seem to have each ended with a full-stage company dance. In the seventeenth century, English dramatist Ben Jonson wrote musical masques (dance-dramas) for the court of King James I, and in France, Molière wrote *comédie ballets* for King Louis XIV, such as *The Bourgeois Gentleman,* whose five acts each end with a fully orchestrated and choreographed mini-opera.

And, of course, all major Asian dramatic forms involve singing, dancing, and instrumental music—sometimes continuously throughout the performance.

And while a spoken text predominates in modern Western drama, singing and dancing make frequent appearances, certainly in the antirealistic theatre. Most of Bertolt Brecht's theatre of alienation plays involve songs (his *The Threepenny Opera, Happy End,* and *The Rise and Fall of the City of Mahagonny* are indeed fully orchestrated musical works), and brief songs also are included in the texts of Samuel Beckett's theatre of the absurd plays *Waiting for Godot* and *Happy Days* and Peter Weiss's *Marat/Sade.*

Still, musical theatre has become a specific genre of its own over the past 150 years of Western drama, not so much as a reaction to (or against) prevailing theatre traditions but as a medium calculated, at first anyway, to provoke audience merriment. Absorbing elements of light opera and ballet and, even more significantly, of popular nineteenth-century entertainments such as the English music hall and American minstrel and variety shows, the modern musical theatre brings to the contemporary dramatic repertory a proven and widely enjoyed form of entertainment with a global commercial appeal.

Nowhere is that commercial and entertainment success better known than in New York, which remains the international capital of the world's musical theatre—although London, Toronto, and even Sydney are currently hot competitors. In New York, during the past decade, as much as 80 percent of Broadway's box-office income has derived from musicals alone, several of which (*Phantom of the Opera, Les Misérables,* and *The Producers*) seem all but permanently installed in the theatres where they play eight times a week. At the time of this writing, twenty full-scale musicals are performing on Broadway, and more are waiting in the wings. And the income from "road" (touring) versions of these shows attests to an even greater dominance of musicals in larger performing halls around the country. Furthermore, New York's less-capitalized off-Broadway theatres are also home to musicals, many of them smaller musical theatre pieces with simpler stagings, reduced casts, and less-than-complete orchestras. *The Fantasticks,* with an eight-member cast and an "orchestra" of piano and harp, opened in 1960 and ran for forty-two years, closing (in 2002) after 17,162 performances.

Not-for-profit regional theatres are increasingly drawn to musicals, too, as are university, community, and dinner theatres and even Shakespeare festivals. And musical theatre is also now a staple of major theatres abroad, including government-subsidized houses such as the Royal National Theatre of England, which in the past two decades has become a major producer of American musicals (*Guys and Dolls, Carousel, Oklahoma!, My Fair Lady, South Pacific, Anything Goes, A Funny Thing Happened on the Way to the Forum*). Indeed, up to a third of the main theatres in Berlin, Budapest, London, Tokyo, Sydney, and Stockholm (many of them government subsidized) are at any given time hosting engagements of such world-popular musicals as *Phantom of the Opera, Rent, Chicago, Jekyll and Hyde, The Lion King, Les Misérables,* and *The Sound of Music.* Such musical theatre engagements, often (but not always) spectacularly produced, can form the commercial backbone of an entire theatre community's offerings.

But commercial appeal is hardly the sum of musical theatre's international importance. Musical theatre is a dramatic form of great variety, vitality, and—on many occasions—artistic significance. The Pulitzer Prize has been awarded to numerous musical dramas (*Of Thee I Sing, South Pacific, Fiorello!, How to Succeed in Business without Really Trying, A Chorus Line, Sunday in the Park with George, Rent*); using techniques as old as Greek tragedy and as inspired as those of Mozart and Wagner, musical theatre authors and artists have created both aesthetic innovations and social impact through

Oklahoma! revolutionized the American musical in 1943. A freshly reconceived production by director Trevor Nunn and choreographer Susan Stroman for England's National Theatre was a popular hit on Broadway when it arrived there in 2003. Here Josefina Gabrielle (*kneeling, in white*) plays Laurey, as the chorus sings their advice to her in "Make Up Your Mind!"

brilliantly integrated disciplines of melody, cadence, choreography, and rhyme.

The Development of the Broadway Musical: America's Contribution

America didn't invent musical theatre, and it no longer dominates the genre the way it did in the middle decades of the twentieth century, but there is no doubt that the Broadway musical—even in its current international form—is America's best-known contribution to world theatre. Moreover, the Broadway musical in the beginning of the twenty-first century seems to be in a renewed period of ascendancy. But the "Broadway musical" is not a purely American product; as we shall see, it is created today by artists from all over the world.

The Broadway musical dates back to the staging of *The Black Crook* at Niblo's Garden in New York City in 1866. This play was in fact a rather ordinary melodrama, but when a French dance company, stranded in the city, was added to the show to give it some extra spice, *Crook* became a rather sexy spectacle, with dances, songs, and a bevy of scantily clad young women. The popularity of staged musical entertainments featuring a wide diversity of performers grew by leaps during the nineteenth and early twentieth centuries. Challenging the old custom of white actors' "blacking up" (with burnt-cork makeup) for minstrel shows, a new black musical comedy arose, employing the emerging ragtime musical syncopations of earlier black vaudeville reviews. Bob Cole's 1898 *A Trip to Coontown* (*coon* was, at the time, a common and generally offensive term for blacks) was one of the most successful: a full-length black musical comedy written and performed by African Americans (some in whiteface!), it played to large mixed-race audiences in New York. Though an unapologetic farce—with ethnic humor, girlie numbers, and neo-operatic inserts—Cole's play included at least one song of direct social protest: "No Coons Allowed!" tells of a young man unable to bring his date to the "swellest place in town" on account of the club's racist policy.

New York also proved a hospitable site for sophisticated musical theatre works from abroad at the end of the nineteenth century. The sensational and still-popular satirical light operas of the English duo W. S. Gilbert and Arthur Sullivan (*HMS Pinafore, The Pirates of Penzance,* and *The Mikado*), the *opéra bouffe* (satirical comic opera) of French composer Jacques Offenbach (*La Perichole, La Belle Hélène, Orpheus in the Underworld*—which introduced the cancan), and the Viennese operetta of Franz Lehar (*The Merry Widow*) all demonstrated that musical theatre could tell a story in a delightfully appealing way. Audiences flocked to these musicals, and American writers and composers emerged to create homegrown products that could compete with these imports. Irish-born Victor Herbert, an émigré to the United States at twenty-seven, became America's first great composer for the stage; Herbert's major hits, *Babes in Toyland* (1903) and *Naughty Marietta* (1910), proved immensely successful, introducing songs such as "Ah, Sweet Mystery of Life" to America's popular music repertoire. More prominent still was Rhode Island–born vaudevillian George M. Cohan, whose *Little Johnny Jones* (1904), in which Cohan also starred, provided what became his—and some of his country's—signature songs: "I'm a Yankee Doodle Dandy" and "Give My Regards to Broadway." By the first decade of the new century, American musical

---

AUTHORSHIP IN MUSICAL THEATRE

A musical generally has three creators: an author for the *book* (the spoken text), another for the lyrics (the words in the songs), and a composer for the music. It is not unusual, however, for a single person to perform two or even three of these tasks: Cole Porter and Stephen Sondheim have written lyrics and music to most of their musicals, and with his 1997 *Rent,* Jonathan Larson added his name to the several triple-threats who have written the book, lyrics, and music for a single show. When working in collaboration, lyricists and composers tend to work in teams, such as the famous pairings of Gilbert and Sullivan, Rodgers and Hammerstein, and Lerner and Loewe.

---

theatre was becoming the world leader in a newly defined theatrical form: musical comedy.

Musical Comedy: Gershwin, Kern, Darktown Follies, *and Rodgers and Hart*

The first third of the twentieth century was the great age of *musical comedy*—a genre that, of course, emphasized comedy as well as singing but also youthful romance; it featured sexy (and lightly clad) girl choruses, liberal doses of patriotic jingoism, and, in response to the "dance craze" of the early 1900s, spectacular dancing—including the show-offy "tap"—to a jazzy or ragtime beat.

By the 1920s and 1930s, American musical comedy had dozens of starring composers, lyricists, and performers. Tourists from all over the country flocked to midtown Manhattan to see such musical works as the brothers George (music) and Ira (lyrics) Gershwin's cool and still-memorable *Lady Be Good, Oh, Kay!, Funny Face,* and *Girl Crazy;* Vincent Youmans's sweetly romantic *Hit the Deck* and *No, No, Nanette* (with "Tea for Two"); Jerome Kern's bouncy *Very Good Eddie* and *Sunny;* Cole Porter's wittily engaging *Anything Goes* and *DuBarry Was a Lady;* and a series of especially droll and delightful musical comedies by Richard Rodgers (music) and Lorenz

Hart (lyrics), including *A Connecticut Yankee, On Your Toes,* and *Babes in Arms.* What all these works had in common were a laughably simple plot, a cast composed strictly of romantic and comedic characters, a wholly unchallenging theme, lots of pretty girls in revealing costumes, and abundantly cheerful singing and dancing that had little or no connection to the plot. And although these works were often silly as dramas, there can be no mistaking the musical glories of the best of them, with music that remains enchanting to the present day. The Gershwin songs ("Embraceable You," " 'S Wonderful," and "The Man I Love") and those of Rodgers and Hart ("The Lady Is a Tramp," "Small Hotel," and "Bewitched, Bothered and Bewildered") and the shows they came from have been regularly revived; the songs themselves have become a staple of the repertories of literally hundreds of modern jazz singers.

Up in Harlem, meanwhile, Bert Williams and J. Leubrie Hill drew large mixed-race audiences for their *Darktown Follies of 1914* (introducing the hit number "After the Ball"). And in 1921 a black musical dominated a full Broadway season for the first time: composer Eubie Blake and lyricist Noble Sissle's wildly successful *Shuffle Along* ran more than 500 performances and introduced such songs as "In Honeysuckle Time" and "I'm Just Wild about Harry." Popular high-stepping, side-slapping "black-bottom" dancing was a feature of many black musicals of the 1920s, as was the epoch-defining dance known as "the Charleston," which, introduced in the 1923 black musical *How Come?* (composed by Maceo Pinkard), started a national craze in the hit show *Runnin' Wild* (by James P. Johnson and Cecil Mack) later that year.

A Golden Age

By 1925 the American musical was beginning to dominate New York's cultural life—and the country's. That September, four great musicals

opened on Broadway in four days: Vincent Youmans and Irving Caesar's *No, No Nanette,* Rudolf Friml's *The Vagabond King,* Jerome Kern and Oscar Hammerstein II's *Sunny,* and Rodgers and Hart's *Dearest Enemy.* Each of these shows was wildly popular and went on to run well into the following year—from almost three hundred performances (*Dearest Enemy*) to more than five hundred (*Vagabond King* and *Sunny*). What is widely considered a "golden age of musicals" had begun.

The golden age ushered in a new genre—musical drama—characterized by increasingly serious plots and sophisticated musical treatments. *Show Boat,* written by Jerome Kern (book) and Oscar Hammerstein II (lyrics) in 1927, was an early masterpiece of musical drama (though its authors insisted on calling it a musical comedy). It represents one of the great pieces of fully acted—and not just sung—vocal literature in the American theatre. Adapted from a gritty novel by Edna Ferber, *Show Boat* has a complex plot that is carried by the music and dancing as well as by the work's spoken dialogue; the musical touches significantly on race relations in America. Indeed, the famous "Ol' Man River" aria (though viewed by some as patronizing at the time of its successful 1993 revival) referred pointedly to the then-current racial divisions as sung by a black actor in front of the show's (largely white) 1927 audience:

> Colored folks work on de Mississippi,
> Colored folks work while de white folks play,
> Pullin' dem boats from de dawn to sunset,
> Gittin' no rest till de Judgment Day—
> Don' look up
> An' don' look down—
> You don' dast make
> De white boss frown.
> Bend your knees
> An' bow your head,
> An' pull dat rope
> Until yo' dead.

Meanwhile, the Gershwin brothers' *Strike Up the Band* and *Of Thee I Sing* moved this fraternal team into the arena of political satire and proved so successful that the latter production received the 1932 Pulitzer Prize in drama—the first musical to do so. The Gershwins followed with the full-out folk opera *Porgy and Bess* (1935), which remains a staple of international opera companies today.

The second serious phase of the musical's golden age came into full flower with Rodgers and Hart's startling *Pal Joey* (1940), adapted from grimly ironic and sophisticated *New Yorker* stories by John O'Hara and featuring an amoral gigolo and his often unsavory companions in a musical pastiche of the contemporary urban nightclub scene. Tame by today's standards, *Joey* shocked prewar audiences with its blithely suggestive lyrics about sexual infidelity and shady business ethics and with a show-stopping song ("Zip!") belted out by an intellectual stripteaser—who sang out her thoughts while doing her act.

Many serious musicals followed, straining the word *comedy* wholly out of the musical's nomenclature. Marc Blitzstein's *The Cradle Will Rock* (1938), concerning the struggle to organize a union of steelworkers in "Steeltown" against the opposition of one Mr. Mister, the town's leading capitalist, was canceled an hour before its New York opening by government officials who objected to the play's "left-wing propaganda" (the government provided funding for the sponsoring theatre). The play was performed later that night across the street, oratorio-style and without scenery or costumes, to tremendous enthusiasm—as memorialized in Tim Robbins's film *Cradle Will Rock* in 1999. *Lady in the Dark* (1941)—with a book by dramatist Moss Hart, lyrics by Ira Gershwin, and music by Kurt Weill (Brecht's colleague, who, like Brecht, had fled to America from Nazi rule in Germany)—concerned itself with psychoanalysis and dream analysis and the perilous situation of a career woman (Liza Elliott) in a world dominated by old-fashioned ideas of marriage and women's roles; the musical numbers were all contained in Liza's three long dream sequences. *Oklahoma!* (1943), with

music by Richard Rodgers and lyrics by Oscar Hammerstein II, dealt with social and sexual tensions in the opening of the western states. Dispensing with the accepted convention of decorative dancing girls, *Oklahoma!* featured content-laden balletic choreography by Agnes de Mille to advance the plot and treated its historical subject—which included an onstage killing and the quick dispensing of frontier justice—with romantic passion and a new level of social intensity.

By the end of the Second World War, seriously themed Broadway musicals dominated the commercial American theatre. Rodgers and Hammerstein followed *Oklahoma!* with one success after another: *Carousel* (dealing with spousal abuse), *South Pacific* (racial prejudice), *The King and I* (gender prejudice and ethnocentricity), *Flower Drum Song* (East-West assimilation), and *The Sound of Music* (Nazism), all marked with social and intercultural conflict, richly romantic settings and songs, beautiful solo numbers and love duets, and thrilling choral, choreographic, and orchestral ensembles. Leonard Bernstein, one of America's leading orchestral conductors and composers, left a considerable mark on the musical's golden age with his *On the Town,* about World War II sailors on leave in Manhattan, and *West Side Story* (with lyrics by Stephen Sondheim), a powerfully emotional retelling of the *Romeo and Juliet* story, with a contemporary Polish American (Tony) as his Romeo and a Puerto Rican American (Maria) as Juliet. And Jerry Bock and Sheldon Harnick conveyed a profoundly moving version of Jewish shtetl life in czarist Russia with *Fiddler on the Roof.*

Not all musicals were deeply sober and serious, of course. More-lighthearted and satirical musicals of the 1940s and 1950s—first-rate works that still featured well-integrated plots, characters, themes, and musical styles—included Frank Loesser's *Guys and Dolls,* based on the idiosyncratic urban stories of Damon Runyon; Cole Porter's *Kiss Me Kate,* based on a backstage romance during a tour of Shake-

The stunning 1994 Broadway revival of Rodgers and Hammerstein's 1945 *Carousel* showed what a powerful impact the golden-age Broadway musicals can still deliver. Although elements of the script — adapted from Ferenc Molnar's Hungarian classic, *Liliom* (1909) — are clearly dated, brilliant design and a contemporary staging and sensitivity bring out the play's still-valid insights and premises, along with Rodgers's glorious musical score. This production, directed by Nicholas Hytner, featured scenery and costumes by Bob Crowley.

speare's *Taming of the Shrew;* and Irving Berlin's *Annie Get Your Gun,* based on the life of American folk heroine Annie Oakley. Richard Adler and Jerry Ross's *Pajama Game* (about union organizing in a pajama factory) and *Damn Yankees* (a Faustian tale about baseball) featured superlative jazz dancing choreographed by Bob Fosse. Alan Jay Lerner (book and lyrics) and Frederick Loewe (music) first successfully collaborated on the fantasy *Brigadoon,* about a mythical Scottish village, and then followed up with their brilliant musical revision of George Bernard Shaw's *Pygmalion,* renamed *My Fair Lady,* which wittily explores and exploits heroine Liza Doolittle's proper and improper pronunciation of spoken English.

The best of these musicals during Broadway's golden age were commercially successful beyond anything in the theatre's previous history. Hit plays ran, not for weeks or months, as before, but for years. They were, indeed, more than just "plays"; they were world-renowned cultural phenomena. For the first time, theatre tickets were sold as far as six months in advance, and business travelers returning from Manhattan were expected to provide a full report on "the new musicals in town." Touring companies brought the best of these shows to

the rest of the country: first-class national tours, with the Broadway stars intact, and, subsequently, "bus and truck" tours, with less-familiar performers — nonetheless advertising "straight from Broadway!" — traveled around the nation. It is likely that most Americans during these years first experienced live theatre in the form of a road version of a Broadway musical, as did the author of this book. Songs from the best musicals — and even some mediocre ones — routinely made the radio "hit parade" (forerunner of the "top ten" or "top forty" listings of today) and gained an instant national audience. Film versions of many musicals — *Oklahoma!, Carousel, My Fair Lady, Guys and Dolls, The Sound of Music* — were also widely popular. For a couple of decades, at least, it seemed as if everyone in America was whistling the latest creation from the tunesmiths of Broadway. And the stars of Broadway musicals past and present — Jimmy Durante, Eddie Cantor, Mary Martin, Ethel Merman, Julie Andrews, Carol Channing, Pearl Bailey, Bob Hope, and John Raitt — achieved national celebrity status; many became the pioneer performers on America's new entertainment medium, television. It is certain that the theatre had never played such a central role in American

Many of the musicals on Broadway at present are revivals of shows from Broadway's
golden age. For the 1998 New York revival of John Kander and Fred Ebb's 1966 musical
Cabaret, the Roundabout Theatre was turned into a cabaret of its own, with the audience
seated at cafe tables instead of orchestra seats, thus emphasizing the participatory
decadence and salaciousness of Nazi-era entertainment. Alan Cumming won the Tony
Award for his performance as the MC; here we see him surrounded by his cabaret's
"Kit Kat" girls.

popular culture before; it is questionable if it ever will again.

The Contemporary Musical

No golden age lasts forever, and in retrospect no such age is unquestionably remembered as golden; the glittery epithet may in fact become little more than a quaint historical milepost. It is unquestionable, however, that the bulk of musicals produced in America today, not just by amateur groups but on Broadway as well, are revivals of the great musicals of the American mid-century. Today, however, a new and

more contemporary musical theatre—at once less sentimental and more ironic, less rhapsodic and more choreographic—has come onto the scene.

The Emergence of Choreographer-Directors: Jerome Robbins, Gower Champion, Bob Fosse, Tommy Tune, Michael Bennett

The past half century has seen a tremendous escalation in the importance of choreography in American musicals. Agnes de Mille was instrumental in initiating this movement, with her plot-advancing dance numbers, already mentioned, in Rodgers and Hammerstein's *Okla-*

homa! But the coming years saw the emergence of several choreographers who became more widely known than the directors they worked with—indeed, who *became* their productions' directors.

Jerome Robbins (1918–1998) was the first of these. Trained in both ballet and acting, his "Small House of Uncle Thomas" ballet—a deliberately quaint, Siamese-themed version of *Uncle Tom's Cabin*—in *The King and I* and his vigorous teenage "street rumble" dances in *West Side Story* earned him national critical fame, leading to his combining directorial and choreographic chores in the seriocomic Broadway musicals *Gypsy,* about the life of striptease artist Gypsy Rose Lee and her mother, and *Fiddler on the Roof,* about Jewish life in prerevolutionary Russia. In 1989 Robbins put together a retrospective collection of his dances in *Jerome Robbins' Broadway,* winning him the Tony Award for best musical.

Gower Champion (1921–1980) and Bob Fosse (1927–1987) were of Robbins's generation but utterly unalike. Champion, a veteran dancer (with his wife, Marge) in many Broadway shows and Hollywood films, returned to the stage in 1960 to both stage and choreograph the energetic, crowd-pleasing *Bye Bye Birdie* and followed this up with the romantic *Carnival* (1961) and the brashly presentational *Hello, Dolly!* (1964), in each case placing dance at the center of his dramatic entertainment. Champion's final show—he died tragically on its opening night—was *42nd Street* (1980), a virtual valentine to the Broadway theatre, and particularly to tap dancing; the show enjoyed a long run and was brought back in a Tony Award–winning revival in 2000–2001. Fosse, also a golden-age choreographer (*Pajama Game* and *Damn Yankees,* 1954 and 1955), went on to develop, in the coming years, a highly idiosyncratic style—quick, jerky moves that suddenly segue to slow, sinuous come-ons; bumps and grinds from the striptease; white gloves and black bowler hats from minstrel and vaudeville; dance-as-sex and sex-as-dance—in, particularly, *Chicago* (1975) and

Dancin' (1978), as well as in the film of *Cabaret* and his own filmed autobiography, *All That Jazz.* A posthumous retrospective of Fosse's dances, simply titled *Fosse,* opened on Broadway in 1999, running two years and winning the Tony Award for best musical.

Tommy Tune (born 1939) and Michael Bennett (1943–1987) are of a later generation. The lanky Tune, a brilliant tap dancer, even performs in some of the productions he also choreographs and/or directs; indeed, he is the only person to have won Tony Awards in four categories—director, choreographer, leading and featured actor. Tune's *My One and Only* (1988), in which he also starred, *Grand Hotel* (1989), and *Will Rogers Follies* (1991) were virtually celebrations of dance entertainment. Bennett's artistic goals were somewhat more conceptual: his masterwork (after choreographing and codirecting Stephen Sondheim's *Company* and *Follies*) was *A Chorus Line* (1975), a musical that, conceived, staged, and choreographed by Bennett, takes place in a dance audition and consists largely of dances interspersed with "interviews" with the auditioning dancers; it was initially developed off-Broadway using improvisations with performers, many of whom landed in the show itself. *A Chorus Line* was for many years Broadway's longest-running show.

This list could not possibly be complete without mentioning Susan Stroman, director-choreographer of *Contact* and *The Producers,* but her work is covered more fully later in the next chapter, "Theatre Today."

Stephen Sondheim

No one has been more influential in the modern musical than the composer and lyricist Stephen Sondheim (born 1930), whose first important work, mentioned earlier, was the composition of lyrics for Leonard Bernstein's 1957 *West Side Story.* After one more assignment as a golden-age lyricist (for Jule Styne's *Gypsy*), Sondheim turned composer as well, winning high praise and success for both the lyrics and

MUSICAL LYRICS THROUGH THE ERAS

A brief sampling of the lyrics from different eras clearly indicates the changing styles of musical theatre popular in America. W. S. Gilbert's lyrics tend toward lighthearted satire and revel in their own cleverness and literary showmanship. With multisyllable rhymes and a mocking attitude toward all pomposity, Gilbert amusingly skewers official British pretension, as in the Major General's self-explanatory "patter song" (so called because its singing requires rapid enunciation) from *The Pirates of Penzance* (1879):

STANLEY: I am the very model of a modern major
           general,
     I've information animal and vegetable and
           mineral,
     I know the kings of England and I quote the fights
           historical,
     From Marathon to Waterloo in order categorical.
     I'm very well acquainted too with matters
           mathematical,
     I understand equations both the simple and
           quadratical,
     About binomial theorems I am teaming with a lot
           of news,
     With many cheerful facts about the square of the
           hypotenuse! . . .

Ira Gershwin's lyrics are openly romantic and tender; rather than call attention to the lyricist's own wit, the clever wordplay is more hidden within the feelings of the characters. The following excerpt from " 'S Wonderful" was coauthored by Ira and his brother George (music) for the musical *Funny Face* (1927). Like most songs, it is divided into a verse, which sets up the situation, and a refrain, which is the musical (and emotional) heart of the song:

PETER: Life has just begun:
     Jack has found his Jill.
     Don't know what you've done,
     But I'm all a-thrill.
     How can words express
     Your divine appeal?
     You could never guess
     All the love I feel.
     From now on, lady, I insist,
     For me no other girls exist.

(*Refrain*)

'S wonderful! 'S marvelous
You should care for me!
'S awful nice! 'S Paradise –
'S what I love to see!
You've made my life so glamorous
You can't blame me for feeling amorous.
Oh, 'S wonderful! 'S marvelous –
That you should care for me! . . .

Perhaps no lyricist in the field has conveyed thwarted love and ironic longing as well as Lorenz Hart, the first partner of Richard Rodgers. In "Bewitched, Bothered and Bewildered" (*Pal Joey*, 1940), Vera, a society lady, drunkenly sings of her going-nowhere affair with a sexy but good-for-nothing nightclub owner:

VERA: After one whole quart of brandy,
     Like a daisy I awake.
     With no Bromo Seltzer handy.
     I don't even shake.
     Men are not a new sensation;
     I've done pretty well, I think.
     But this half-pint imitation's
     Put me on the blink.

(*Refrain*)

     I'm wild again,
     Beguiled again,
     A simpering, whimpering child again –
     Bewitched, bothered and bewildered am I.
     Couldn't sleep
     And wouldn't sleep
     Until I could sleep where I shouldn't sleep –
     Bewitched, bothered and bewildered am I.
     Lost my heart, but what of it?
     My mistake, I agree.
     He's a laugh, but I love it
     Because the laugh's on me . . .

By the time of Hart's death in 1943, Rodgers had begun a new partnership, with Oscar Hammerstein II, already the lyricist for Jerome Kern's *Show Boat* and many other musicals. Hammerstein wrote that he barely dared "place a timid encroaching foot on the territory" of the "masters" Gilbert and Hart and sought to write instead what he himself termed "a more primitive type of lyric . . . expressing my own true convictions and feelings." His lyrics for the opening song in *Oklahoma!* (1943) clearly convey this:

CURLEY:　There's a bright, golden haze on the meadow,
　　There's a bright, golden haze on the meadow.
　　The corn is as high as an elephant's eye,
　　An' it looks like it's climbin' clear up to the sky.

(*Refrain*)

　　Oh, what a beautiful mornin'!
　　Oh, what a beautiful day!
　　I got a beautiful feelin'
　　Ev'rythin's goin' my way . . .

Hammerstein derived the verse of this song from a written stage description in Lynn Riggs's *Green Grow the Lilacs*, the source play for *Oklahoma!* Riggs had described the scene as "a radiant summer morning . . . cattle in the meadow, blades of the young corn . . . their images giving off a visible golden emanation that is partly true and partly a trick of imagination. . . ." Deciding it was a shame to waste Riggs's images on the reading audience only, Hammerstein made them the source of his famous opening lyric.

Stephen Sondheim, who enlarged the musical's palette more profoundly, perhaps, than any artist in the field, is most noted for a deeply ironic and anti-romantic tone that, nonetheless, remains amusing and surprisingly good-spirited; somehow he has managed to leaven his gloomy message with buoyant music, penetrating observation, and fiendishly clever rhymes and rhythm breaks. In "The Little Things You Do Together" (*Company*, 1970), Sondheim mocks the too-easy sentimentality of marital "relationships":

JOANNE　It's the little things you share together,
　　Swear together,
　　Wear together,
　　That make perfect relationships.
　　The concerts you enjoy together,
　　Neighbors you annoy together,
　　Children you destroy together,
　　That keep marriage intact.

(*Refrain*)

　　It's not so hard to be married
　　When two maneuver as one
　　It's not so hard to be married,
　　And, Jesus Christ, is it fun.

Finally, Jonathan Larson in *Rent* has brought a new style to lyric writing altogether and, with it, a new audience for the Broadway musical. With a rock and rap beat (Larson wrote his own music) and with a script and staging that derived in part from cast improvisations, the musical scored an enormous success. "Contact" is one of the show's closing songs. Because it does not easily divide into verse and refrain stanzas, none are noted here:

ROGER, MARK, JOANNE, & BENNY:　Hot-hot-hot-sweat-sweet
　　Wet-wet-wet-red-heat
　　Hot-hot-hot-sweat-sweet
　　Wet-wet-wet-red-heat
　　Please don't stop please
　　Please don't stop stop
　　Stop stop stop don't
　　Please please please please
　　Hot-hot-hot-sweat-sweet
　　Wet-wet-wet-red-heat
　　Sticky-licky-trickle-tickle
　　Steamy-creamy-stroking-soaking

COLLINS:　Touch!
MAUREEN:　Taste!
MIMI:　Deep!
COLLINS:　Dark!
MAUREEN:　Kiss!
COLLINS:　Beg!
MIMI:　Slap!
MIMI, MAUREEN, & COLLINS:　Fear!
COLLINS:　Thick!

COLLINS, MIMI, & MAUREEN:　Red, red
　　Red, red
　　Red, red – please

MAUREEN:　Harder!
ANGEL:　Faster!
MAUREEN:　Wetter!
MIMI:　Bastard!
COLLINS:　You whore
MAUREEN:　You animal
MIMI & ANGEL:　More

MAUREEN, COLLINS, & MIMI:　Fluid no fluid no contact
　　yes no contact

ALL:　Fire fire burn – burn yes!
　　No latex rubber rubber
　　Fire latex rubber latex bummer lover bummer

music to the songs in the highly novel *A Funny Thing Happened on the Way to the Forum,* drawn from the Roman comedies of Plautus.

But in his work from 1970 onward, Sondheim departed from the standard formats of those early shows to develop a new style, marked by a disturbing plot, an ironic and sometimes even cynical tone, a brutal skepticism about conventional morality, and highly sophisticated, adult, intricately rhymed lyrics that are integrated with a score that brings surprising new rhythms to popular music. Sondheim's first works in this style include *Company* (1970), a devilishly clever and incisive look at sexual pairings and partings in the Manhattan of the time; *Follies* (1971; Broadway revival 2001), set at an onstage reunion of able but aging musical theatre performers, also set in Manhattan ("I'm Still Here!" is the famous number from this show); and *A Little Night Music* (1973), adapted from an Ingmar Bergman film about summer sexual dalliances on a country estate in Sweden. These works were widely heralded for their brilliantly acerbic but always entertaining portrayal of the inevitable and eternal conflicts between social mores and romantic idealism (or, more bluntly, between laws and lust). Furthermore, they established Sondheim's supremacy in the American musical form for the entire generation that followed.

Sondheim continued to break new boundaries in three amazing creations. His *Pacific Overtures* (1976) employs kabuki-inspired music and stage techniques to trace the history of relations between Japan and the United States since Commodore Perry's "opening" of Japan in 1853. Sondheim's *Sweeney Todd* (1979) integrates Brechtian alienation techniques and blends elements from Italian grand opera, the English music hall, and Victorian melodrama in a wildly morbid story of a barber's revenge. *Sweeney*'s score is so powerful and its actions and images so compelling that the work has been staged by several European opera companies. Conversely, Sondheim's *Sunday in the Park with George* (1984) is an elegant musical play

about the pointillist painter Georges Seurat; for this production, Sondheim invented a "pointillist" style of music to echo Seurat's painting style.

Sondheim's most controversial works are *Assassins* (1991) and *Passion* (1993). *Assassins* is a musical review of presidential assassinations (and assassination attempts), which cascades through two centuries, portraying the quirks and oddities of John Wilkes Booth, Lee Harvey Oswald, Squeaky Fromm, and John Hinckley, Jr., among other unlikely musical theatre protagonists (if not heroes). *Assassins* was so unconventional and, to some, so alarming that it did not open on Broadway after its limited (and sold-out) off-Broadway premiere, and when a Broadway production was finally put into rehearsal in the early fall of 2001, it was quickly aborted because of the World Trade Center attacks. Happily, however, when *Assassins* was finally staged at Broadway's Studio 54 in the spring of 2004, it won five Tony Awards, including Best Revival of a Musical.

In contrast, *Passion* opened on Broadway and, despite mixed reviews, won four Tony Awards in 1994, including Best Musical. An intermissionless nineteenth-century gothic tragedy—"one long love song," according to Sondheim—*Passion* tells the strange story of Giorgio, a handsome Italian army officer who is deeply in love with the beautiful Clara but is relentlessly pursued by his commanding officer's cousin, Fosca, a homely, ailing, and pathetically obsessional woman. The initial attractiveness of Giorgio and Clara's love (they begin the play in bed together, totally naked, singing in duet, "I'm so happy, / I'm afraid I'll die / Here in your arms") gradually gives way against its own limitations (Giorgio's assignment to the provinces, Clara's nondivorceable marriage) and to the intensity of Fosca's amorous fixations, to which Giorgio ultimately yields—to Clara's despair and to that of most of the audience as well. As there is little to admire or "root for" in this romantic tangle, *Passion*'s success was somewhat limited, but its

With Stephen Sondheim's music, the long-ignored musical version of Aristophanes'
The Frogs, originally produced as a novelty in the Yale University swimming pool, was
too attractive not to revive. This latest version, with six new songs, a revised book
(spoken text) by Nathan Lane, who also starred, direction by Susan Stroman, and
a leaping, multicolored frog chorus, opened on Broadway in 2004.

achievements and innovations are exhilarating nonetheless; it is a profound, intense musical examination of irrational sexual attraction and was again before audiences, along with five other Sondheim shows, in a Sondheim Celebration at Washington's Kennedy Center in 2002.

Sondheim's activity has extended further into the new century. His 1974 musical *The Frogs,* adapted from Aristophanes and previously produced only in Yale University's swimming pool, has now been readapted by actor Nathan Lane and was directed by Susan Stroman (with Lane starring as Dionysus) for its long-delayed Broadway opening in 2004.

European Musicals

But several of the most successful new musicals running on Broadway and around the world at the turn of the century are not American at all:

the megahits of Englishman Andrew Lloyd Webber (particularly *Cats* and *Phantom of the Opera* but also *Jesus Christ Superstar, Evita, Starlight Express, Aspects of Love,* and *Sunset Boulevard*) and of Frenchmen Alain Boublil and Claude-Michel Schönberg (*Les Misérables* and *Miss Saigon*). These works, usually sung-through (that is, entirely sung, without any spoken words at all), are known for their lush musical scores more than either their book (if there is any) or lyrics, which in part explains their international popularity (because they have less of a language barrier to surmount). They are also generally presented in an exceptionally spectacular manner: *Starlight Express* features a cast on roller skates and a roller race-track encircling the audience; in *Phantom of the Opera* a chandelier all but falls in the midst of the audience, and the extraordinarily magical second act is set on a fiery lake beneath the Paris Opera; and in *Miss Saigon* a "helicopter" descends to rescue American and Vietnamese citizens fleeing the U.S. embassy in the last days of the Saigon regime. Lloyd Webber's music-dominant works, combined with the rapid technological advances in audio enhancement, have also inspired gifted sound designers to work their special magic into the acoustics of musical theatre; wireless microphones on the performers and superpotent electronic amplification between performers and house speakers (computer delayed to reach every seat in the house simultaneously) are now commonplace—to the chagrin of many purists and critics—in musical theatre.

Some of the Lloyd Webber and Boublil-Schönberg works will likely run well into the twenty-first century, but the era of lushly sung-through musicals might soon be reaching its end. Despite a series of tryout runs, Boublil and Schönberg's *Martin Guerre* has not yet proven successful, leaving them without a hit since 1991. And Lloyd Webber's *Cats,* though displacing *A Chorus Line* as Broadway's longest-running show, failed to live up to its "Now and Forever" slogan, closing in 2000, while his *Whistle Down the Wind* met with only tepid response in a London reworking (1998).

Mel Brooks: The Producers

Mel Brooks has had a long career in show business, beginning in the 1950s and 1960s as a writer of review sketches and musical librettos for the Broadway stage, as well as award-winning records, television shows, and feature films. But Brooks has almost certainly climaxed his amazing career with his stage version of *The Producers,* which won a record-shattering twelve Tony Awards in 2002. *The Producers* is neither novel nor innovative; indeed, much of the script was taken directly from Brooks's own 1968 screenplay of the same name. Rather, it is an unapologetic return to classic musical comedy of the 1930s, with corny jokes, a "dumb blonde" secretary, scantily clad chorus girls, and a vaudeville style remi-

Nathan Lane plays the fictional Broadway producer Max Bialystock in Mel Brooks's 2001 *The Producers,* an outrageously satirical musical farce that, though neither subtle nor particularly innovative, is certainly the biggest American musical hit of the past two decades.

niscent of the Marx Brothers. What make the show work so brilliantly are its outrageously offensive story (two Broadway producers, trying to create an enormous flop so as to bilk unwary investors, present a musical about Adolf Hitler that turns out to be a giant success, landing them in bankruptcy and jail), the absolutely over-the-top performances by Nathan Lane and Matthew Broderick as the corrupt producers, Susan Stroman's exuberant direction and choreography, and the very funny scenery and costumes by, respectively, Robin Wagner and William Ivey Long. *The Producers* is a production that, by virtually universal agreement, shows conventional theatrical craft at the absolute top of its form, and the immense entertainment potential that musical theatre can offer.

Directions in the Modern Musical

Modern musicals—*The Producers, Hairspray!,* and *Mamma Mia* notably excepted—have increasingly tackled serious subjects. Gang violence (*The Beautiful Game*), unemployment (*The Full Monty*), Nazism (*Cabaret* and *Grand Hotel*), homosexuality (*A Chorus Line, Falsettos, Kiss of the Spider Woman, La Cage aux Folles, The Wild Party,* and *The Boy from Oz*), environmental degradation (*Urinetown*), and race-ethnic relations (*Big River, Jelly's Last Jam, Zoot Suit, Ragtime,* and *Caroline, or Change*) have been explored in many musical dramas with sharp, even brutal, insight and penetration. A nightmarish seagoing disaster and the ensuing physical and class struggle for survival were the focus of *Titanic,* which preceded by more than a year—and exceeded in social insight—the notable film of the same name.

More than a dozen major "black musicals" (musicals largely by, about, and performed by African Americans), including *Bubbling Brown Sugar* and *Eubie* (both based on the music of Eubie Blake), *Ain't Misbehavin'* and *Sophisticated Ladies* (featuring, respectively, the music of Fats Waller and Duke Ellington), *Dreamgirls* (celebrating a Supremes-like singing group), and *Bring in 'Da Noise, Bring in 'Da Funk* (a capsule history of racial injustice in America, conceived and directed by George C. Wolfe and choreographed by Savion Glover, who also performs), have explored African American culture and cultural issues, often passionately, through the medium (among others) of black performance culture.

Rock and other forms of music particularly popular with American youth were introduced into the mainstream first in the 1968 Broadway musical *Hair* (which also introduced full frontal nudity to the genre) and then in more recent musicals such as *The Who's Tommy* and the 1997 sensation (and winner of that year's Tony Award for best musical) *Rent.* And family musicals were pioneered in the late 1990s by none other than the Disney Corporation, which constructed and renovated Broadway theatres to present stage adaptations of their animated films *Beauty and the Beast* and *The Lion King.* The latter, fabulously successful and winner of the 1998 Tony Award for best musical, was directed by avant-garde director-designer Julie Taymor (see the following chapter) and brilliantly recaptures both African jungle and universal myth, creating a magnificent and unique blend of African, Asian, and American performance styles.

Musicals of the New Century

The trend for Broadway musicals opening in New York during the twenty-first century, however, has not only been serious but, in many cases, downright grim. John Lachiusa and George C. Wolfe's 2000 *The Wild Party* (the second Broadway musical that season with that title, based on the same 1928 poem) cynically depicts the raucous goings-on at a late-night drinking party, providing a virtual menu of sexual infidelities and emotional betrayals. "People like us, we take lovers like pills / Just hoping to cure what we know we can't fix," says one character at the party; "You're out in the clubs / Paradin' your meat / Spending all your advance / On snatch off the street / You seen more ass / Than a toilet seat," says another. And the party ends with the conclusion:

> You can make a fortune doing next to nothing:
> You can sit there on your ass and screw your friends:
> But you better know how to kick—kick— kick your way
> Outta the burning room
> When it ends.

And Ben Elton's lyrics for the ironically named *Beautiful Game* (with music by Andrew Lloyd Webber), also premiering in 2000, address English-Irish terrorism with this prisoner's lament:

> You're in the death zone. Satan sits on his throne.

Even the strongest are frightened.
This is the dark zone. We see in
    monochrome.
Nothing is good or enlightened.
Happiness is ended. All hope is suspended.
We are the damned, we are all despised.

More recent musicals extend cultural malaise to personal and individual anguish. Richard Thomas's *Jerry Springer* presents—with almost unlimited sleaze—a chamber of horrors at America's outermost sexual fringes, with rambunctious (and regularly scatological) song titles and lyrics such as "Chicks with Dicks," "Sex with My Sister," and "I got shit pouring outta my ass" in the first act alone. And the second act takes place in Hell. It's "the most explosive theatrical event in years" says the *London Observer*. Tony Kushner's *Caroline, or Change* is awash in bleak depression from beginning to end, with its characters' hopes continually dashed and the title character never smiling during the entire play (nor, in the performance this writer attended, even during the curtain call ovation). Caroline's defining solo, at her ironing board, is virtually a funeral dirge:

I'm gonna slam that iron
down on my heart
gonna slam that iron
down on my throat
gonna slam that iron
down on my sex

Below left: Tonya Pinkins plays Caroline, and Harrison Chad is the ever-optimistic Jewish boy from Louisiana, in Tony Kushner's *Caroline, or Change* at the New York Public Theater in 2003.

Below right: Avenue Q, an ironic and risqué musical of current life – animated by both humans and puppets – walked away with five Tony Awards in 2004.

Hairspray, an immensely lively musical celebration of Baltimore in the 1960s, took the 2003 Tony Award for Best Musical. Jaret Winokur (*left*), plays Tracy Turnblad, and Harvey Fierstein plays her sister Edna Turnblad.

gonna slam it
slam it
slam it down
'til I drown
the fire out
'til there ain't no air left anywhere!

Dare we applaud? Of course, we do—but we sure don't feel like it.

Even the bright, often bouncy *Avenue Q*, which won the 2004 Tony Award for best musical, takes an unswervingly skeptical look at contemporary urban racism, sexual identity crises, and an addiction to pornography, with out-front lyrics like:

TREKKIE AND GUYS: The internet is for porn!
KATE: Gross!
TREKKIE AND GUYS: The internet is for porn!
KATE: I hate porn
TREKKIE AND GUYS: Grab your dick and double click
KATE: I hate you men!
TREKKIE AND GUYS: For porn, porn, porn!
    (*harmonizing*) porn, porn, porn, porn

Seriousness has, of course, been a staple of musical theatre since at least *Show Boat*, as discussed earlier in this chapter, but almost always as leavened by comic (or at least satirical) musical numbers, dances, and scenes. The sustained grimness of *Caroline,* the sleaziness of *Jerry Springer,* and the bleak cynicism of *The Wild Party* and other recent works have divided traditional audiences and critics but also brought new audiences into theatre houses—and even expanded the theatre's reach into surprising new venues. The producers of *Rent* built a strikingly younger-than-usual theatre audience in many cities around the world by selling front-row seats for a fraction of their usual price on the day of performance, thus also virtually guaranteeing their show a nightly standing ovation, as the grateful first-row audience—almost entirely composed of young people willing to wait in line earlier in the day—rises en masse to their feet at the curtain call. And Broadway veterans were astounded when the producers of *Avenue Q* decided not to take their Tony-winning show on the road to play in America's traditional touring cities (such as Chicago, Los Angeles, and San Francisco) but rather to reopen it in a theatre especially designed and built for it in Las Vegas. The musical theatre may be increasingly scabrous, cynical, and sardonic, but it has found an audience willing to go with it in these directions—at least some of the time.

All in all, the musical theatre is alive and well in the cities that can afford to mount and present such works, and the stage musical continues to reinvent itself in both subject matter and style of presentation. *Rent, The Producers,* and *The Lion King* are unique not merely because of their forms but also because of their audience appeal; the first draws huge numbers of young people in their teens, twenties, and thirties, and the latter two attract audience members ages five to ninety-five. The musical's only drawback, in the minds of many, is its very success; musicals so dominate the Broadway theatre that straight plays tend to play a secondary role. But of course straight theatre has its solid base in America's not-for-profit theatres, including those in New York, and need not compete at every level of the mass-market economy. Moreover, playwrights of the nonmusical stage, such as Tony Kushner (*Caroline, or Change*), Terrence McNally (author of *Ragtime, Kiss of the Spider Woman,* and *The Full Monty*), Marsha Norman (*The Secret Garden*), and David Henry Hwang (*Aida* and *Flower Drum Song*), are increasingly tapped for new musical-theatre assignments, as are literally hundreds of actors, directors, and designers who work in both spoken and sung dramas. It appears that at the dawning of the twenty-first century, the Broadway musical is the commercial leader of a vibrant all-genre American theatrical establishment.

10

Theatre Today: What, Who, and Where?

T HE THEATRE OF TODAY EXISTS ONSTAGE, not in the pages of this or any other book. The theatre of today is being performed right now, in the multimillion-dollar theatres of the world's great cities as well as on the simpler stages at schools, community theatres, nightclubs, roadhouses, and experimental theatre clubs everywhere.

The theatre of today is all around us, simply waiting to be discovered, seen, heard, felt, and experienced. The easiest and best way to apprehend its fundamental impulse is to go out and see it firsthand.

What's Happening?

What's happening in the theatre today? It's not easy to say. We cannot evaluate the current theatre with the same objectivity that we can the theatre of the past—even the recent past. Theatre is a business as well as an art, and the flurry of promotion, publicity, and puffery that surrounds each current theatrical success makes a cool perspective difficult. Whereas poets and painters are often ignored until years following their deaths, the opposite is more often true of theatre artists: they are frequently lionized in their own time, only to be forgotten a few years later. A permanent place in the repertory of world theatre is the achievement of very few indeed; among the playwrights once deemed equal to Shakespeare are such now-dimly remembered figures as John Fletcher, Joseph Addison, Edward George Bulwer-Lytton, August Friedrich, August von Kotzebue, Eugène Brieux, and Maxwell Anderson. Which of our present-day writers and actors and other theatre artists will achieve more than ephemeral glory? Which, if any, will leave a mark on future generations? No one can answer either question with any certainty. But there are some directions in today's theatre that show signs of becoming established, and these are worthy of examination.

The Modern and the Postmodern

From a practical point of view—looking at stage practice rather than theory—theatre is a fairly conservative institution. Certainly, theatre companies the world over will continue to present plays from the past as well as from our own time—and will also conserve (the root of *conservative*) many of the theatre's traditional ways of working. In fact, virtually all the plays mentioned in the previous chapters are being performed somewhere in the world today, and the vigorous debates among today's actors and directors often repeat, almost verbatim, dialogues from the days of Aristophanes, Shakespeare, and Stanislavsky.

Nevertheless, in the first decade of the twenty-first century, a new era seems to be emerging. The twentieth century was a particularly violent one: two world wars and one cold one, assassinations of great political and cultural leaders (Martin Luther King, Jr., John and Robert Kennedy, Mohandas Gandhi, Anwar Sadat, Yitzhak Rabin, John Lennon), both Nazi and nuclear holocausts, the proliferation of alluring but dangerous drugs and sex-linked diseases, and the threatened destruction of our planet's vital resources. The arts responded to these social changes with an artistic freedom that was frightening in its extremity—nowhere more so than in the theatre, where, by the 1970s, Dionysian ecstasy had returned to the stage with a force almost equal to that of the dithyramb. As play-

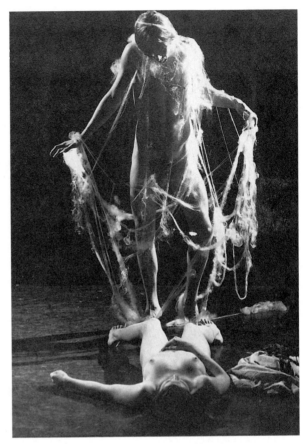

The Company Theatre of Los Angeles was only one of many theatre companies in the 1960s and 1970s to experiment with total nudity and participatory improvisation onstage. This original production, titled *The Emergence*, was one of the finest and most visually eloquent productions of the turbulent times.

licensing laws fell in England and legal censorship became locally unenforceable in America, profanity, nudity, copulation, violence, and libelous accusation—all unknown on the legitimate stage since ancient times—became almost commonplace. Plays popular in America in the last third of the century included one accusing the sitting president of murder (*MacBird*), another accusing a recent pope of genocide (*The Deputy*), another featuring a farm boy copulating with his pig (*Futz*), another of teenage boys stoning a baby to death in its crib (*Saved*), and another that concluded with the actors and some of the audience undressing and marching naked out into the street (*Paradise Now*). Most of this reached right into the theatre's mainstream when the rock Broadway musical *Hair* (1968) concluded with the actors—who had already sung rapturously about sodomy, fellatio, and cunnilingus—brazenly stripped off their clothes and grinningly faced the audience. Nor were theatre audiences themselves immune from such changes in theatrical convention; often in the 1970s and 1980s, spectators found themselves physically sat upon, fondled, assaulted, hurled about, handed lit joints (of marijuana), and, in at least one case (in Finland), urinated upon. These and other extreme behaviors had become part of the license claimed by a theatre purportedly trying to make itself heard above the societal din of war, riots, and corruption. Or, many asked, were its adherents only clamoring for personal attention? In any event, it was an era of dramaturgical violence and abandon that brought the age of "modernism" to a crisis, if not to a conclusion.

The Directions of Today's Theatre

Well before the century's end, however, this mood of violent protest was largely spent. The novelty of stage sex and profanity had mostly passed, much of it being filtered into more mainstream artistic forms, and the latent voyeurism of the audience had been more than satisfied; an increasingly serious and sober public soon began demanding a more focused response to major issues than the theatre had been providing. And many artists (and critics) were beginning to freshly examine and reveal the hidden prejudices and privileges—in terms of gender, race, class, and sexual orientation—that continued to undermine even modernism's seeming freedom and fairness.

At the same time, the end of the twentieth century had brought with it an explosion of new social and political alignments, and a sometimes overwhelming spectrum of new technologies. With the cold war ended, and its empires and military alliances dissolved or reconfigured, a newly globalized economy challenged local cultures with enhanced but often troubling prospects, while astonishing advances in telecommunications—e-mail, mobile phones, satellite television broadcasting, broadband webcasting—revolutionized the way global citizens connect with each other. And the succeeding century's political landscape was staggered, a bare year into its life, when a hideous terrorist attack on New York and Washington was soon followed by militarily imposed and passionately resisted regime changes in the Middle East and Central Asia, threatening at times to catapult civilization into the chaos of a global war on terror fueled by contrary military, economic, and religious imperatives. The theatre—as a tool of live communication—has responded quickly to a vast store of new subjects and fresh opportunities. Once again, as in the days of the ancient Greeks and Shakespearean England, the stage has surfaced as an arena where new thoughts, fashions, feelings, morals, theologies, and aesthetics can be enacted, and new technologies explored, in order to bring lucidity and structure to the confusions that beset us all.

Although generalizations about an era still upon us must be tentative, there are clearly three major movements, or themes, in the current theatre, the theatre of the age we increasingly call "postmodern." These movements might be categorized as a theatre of postmodern experiment, an open theatre, and a theatre of revival. While we will go back a few years in looking at the sources of these movements, there is no question but that they are truly flowering in the theatre of the immediate present: the middle of the first decade of the 2000s.

A Theatre of Postmodern Experiment

The notion of a postmodern era is not as historically defined as the name suggests. As the term has developed since the 1970s, *postmodernism* indicates a way of thinking, or even of nonthinking, more than it defines a particular period in time.

The postmodern defies complete analysis, because postmodernism literally defies (repudiates) the act of analyzing. A postmodern approach essentially dismisses logic and cause-and-effect determinism, replacing both with more parallel, almost random, reflections. These reflections are of two sorts: self-reflections, whereby a work of art pays homage to itself, and reflections of the past, whereby the art pays homage to past texts and models.

One can see postmodernism, therefore, in Andy Warhol's repeated and repainted images (of Campbell soup cans, head shots of Marilyn Monroe, electric chairs), each of which emphasizes the artist's redefining an existing artifact as an independent work of "art." One may see it also in Philip Johnson's AT&T building in New York (1984), with its neo-Renaissance facade and "Chippendale highboy" roofline. Whereas modernism repudiated the past, postmodernism gaily embraces it, quotes it, and even recycles it.

A postmodernist work of art, therefore, is not about "something" so much as it is about itself—about "art." Moreover, a postmodern work might also be said to "deconstruct" itself, so as to make us think about ourselves as much as what we're seeing. Indeed, postmodern art is about us as well as it is about art. How do we view art? And, we might say, how does art view us? Are there any hidden assumptions about "what art is" that exclude us from enjoying it —or that "privilege" other audiences? Inasmuch as a postmodern work is self-referential (refers to itself), it also contains its own critique; it parodies itself; it throws us back, sometimes in amusement and sometimes in irritation, upon our own thoughts.

Postmodern artists—and postmodern critics—are as deeply concerned with the social orders from which art springs, with the processes of creating art, and with the open or hidden assumptions that inform art as with the art products themselves. Such definitions of the postmodern are admittedly complex, probably humorous (if not bewildering) to a first-time reader, and are themselves subject to parody—which is itself a postmodern approach!

In theatre, which is a practical art, the notion of postmodernism can be understood concretely. Postmodern drama springs directly from the antirealistic theatre, but unlike most antirealistic theatres, it has little, if any, of the modernist's aesthetic or social optimism. Whereas the symbolists and surrealists were working to reveal inner truths, a "higher order" of reality, and whereas the Brechtian epic theatre was struggling to change (or save) the world and to create a higher level of society, none of these goals are deemed within the reach of the postmodernist, who presupposes no higher levels of reality or social order. Because there is no higher reality to symbolize, the postmodernist abjures symbols (the postmodern is the art, one critic suggests, of the *métaphore manquée,* or "missing metaphor"). Because social progress is impossible (and social decline possibly inevitable), the postmodernist can contemplate the future only warily, if at all.

The postmodern writer or director, therefore, is more likely to explore the discontinuity of observable reality rather than attempt to find any integrated synthesis or meaning. Postmodern art celebrates the apparent randomness of arbitrary juxtaposition, and it prides itself not on logic and conviction but, rather, on delightful surprise, even shock, and tantalizing (if bewildering) irrelevancies. Students of the postmodern find its salient features, for example, in the action painting of Jackson Pollock, who randomly dripped paint from buckets with holes in their bottoms; in break dancing, which is improvised, haphazard, and disjunctive; and in the music (or, as some say, cacophony) of John Cage, which consists of apparently indiscriminate sounds, few of which come from conventional "musical" instruments. Television, with its night-and-day agglomeration of dramatic fragments inter-mixed with commercials, promos, newsbreaks, announcements, station identifications, and old film clips, is a perfectly postmodern creation, made all the more discontinuous by a technology that permits the viewing of two or more agglomerations (split-screen, or picture-in-picture) simultaneously and remote-control shuttling between a hundred-odd channels at lightning speed.

The first great postmodern theatre (although its creators refused to call it "theatre," and the term *postmodern* had yet to be invented) was the short-lived arts phenomenon called *dada,* which flourished—beginning at the Cabaret Voltaire, in Zurich, Switzerland, in 1916—in the years immediately following World War I. As critic Mel Gordon describes it, dada was a "chaotic mix of balalaika music, Wedekind poems, dance numbers, cabaret singing, recitations from Voltaire, and shouting in a kaleido-scopic environment of paintings." So-called chance poetry, created by dada poet Tristan Tzara by pulling words out of a hat, led to cabaret performances of chance drama. The dadaists—as they came to be called (the name was chosen at random from an unabridged dictionary)—found themselves the artistic darlings of Berlin and Paris in the early 1920s. And while dada was short-lived, it clearly stimulated the experimentalism of the theatre of the absurd, which was its longer-lasting successor.

Today's theatrical postmodernism follows in the wake of the absurd. The late plays of Samuel Beckett best exemplify the pessimism and flight from meaning characteristic of the postmodern. Although Beckett explored mean-inglessness from his earliest writings, by the 1980s his vision had become grim, if not completely nihilistic. In his very short play *Rock-abye* (1981), Beckett's sole visible character is an old lady with "huge eyes in white expressionless face." On a dark stage she rocks alone, dimly lit in a rocking chair; during the play she says but one word ("More") in what is apparently a beyond-the-grave dialogue with her prerecorded voice. The play ends with the recorded voice saying:

> rock her off
> stop her eyes
> fuck life
> stop her eyes
> rock her off
> rock her off

And the rocking stops as the lights fade out.

But contemporary postmodernism also owes a debt to the other mainstream of antirealistic theatre, the theatre of alienation as created and promoted by Bertolt Brecht. If Beckett's theatre stimulates the postmodern's intellectual pessimism, Brecht's theatre stimulates its parodic delight, as his plays deconstruct themselves into storytelling lectures and seek to disconnect the actor from his or her character in order to toss the play's issues directly into the audience. Postmodern directors and dramatists who are influenced by Brecht therefore openly—and even gaily—employ the theatre as an ironic metaphor, jumping back and forth between simulations of reality (realism) and comments on that very simulation. Many post-Brechtian and postmodern theatrical techniques stem from this: deliberate cross-gender casting—as for, example, actors switching roles as well as genders between the first and second acts of Caryl Churchill's *Cloud Nine* (1983), or a young actress with an obviously fake beard playing the old Jewish rabbi at the opening of Tony Kushner's *Angels in America* (1993)—forces us to confront a profound separation between the actor and his or her role. This was taken a step further in Matthew von Waaden's off-Broadway production of *Eat the Runt* in 2001, where the theatre spectators actually cast the eight roles—regardless of gender—from among the actors who presented themselves onstage right before the play began.

Increasingly, the raw mechanics of theatrical practice have come into play in even mainstream plays and productions; clearly visible microphones, worn on the actor's body, are increasingly employed in musicals and even some straight plays, for example, making us continually aware that the characters are played by technologically augmented actors, while the sound mixer who adjusts their volume levels is no longer hidden away backstage but plunked right in the midst of the audience. (In the Broadway musical *The Full Monty,* the conductor—who dances to the music she conducts—is fully visible from every seat in the house and is illuminated by a spotlight during much of the show.)

Plays increasingly comment on their own dramatization. A character asks another, "Why did you just walk downstage right?" during *The Producers* (2001), and in *Urinetown* (2001) a character asks another, "Is this where you tell the audience about the water shortage?" and the other replies, "Everything in its time . . . nothing can kill a show like too much exposition."

And today's plays have more and more frequently adopted the theatre as their primary setting and subject: in one of the classic postmodern deconstructions of theatrical "reality," the opening scene of Tom Stoppard's *The Real Thing* (1982) is revealed to have been a staged play when, at the beginning of scene 2, we see the "characters" of scene 1 appear as the actors

The 2005 campy-medieval pastiche, *Monty Python's Spamalot* (adapted from the legendary 1975 film *Monty Python and the Holy Grail*), is an outrageous parody of – and an implicit homage to – the modern Broadway musical. Like *The Producers, Spamalot* is a Broadway musical about Broadway musicals and, as directed by Mike Nichols, became, as did its predecessor, the sell-out hit of its season. With, from left, Hank Azaria, David Hyde Pierce, Tim Curry, Christopher Sieber and Steve Rosen.

who played them. Shakespeare is fodder for many deconstructed variations: Amy Freed's *The Beard of Avon* (2001) shows Shakespeare writing — or perhaps not writing — the plays attributed to him; Paul Rudnick's *I Hate Hamlet* (1992) shows actors rehearsing and presenting a production of *Hamlet;* Lee Blessing's 1992 *Fortinbras* (as well as Tom Stoppard's seminal 1967 *Rosencrantz and Guildenstern Are Dead*) expands on previously untold stories of the same play; Steven Berkoff's *Sit and Shiver* (2004) concludes with a speech from *King Lear;* and Athol Fugard's *Exits and Entrances* (2004) centers on a delivery of the "To be or not to be?" soliloquy from *Hamlet.* Even Neil Simon's *Laughter on the 23rd Floor* and musical stage version of *The Goodbye Girl* include scenes parodying performances of Shakespeare — *Julius Caesar* and *Richard III,* respectively. And musicals, particularly in the postmodern era, are almost all about show business: *The Producers, Tick, Tick . . . Boom!, George Gershwin Alone,* and *A Class Act* (all 2001) are Broadway musicals about Broadway musicals, while *Urinetown* (2001) and *The Musical of Musicals — The Musical!* (2004) are off-Broadway parodies of Broadway musicals. *The Boy from Oz* (2003), meanwhile, is a Broadway musical about the late star (Peter Allen, as played by Hugh Jackman) of an earlier Broadway musical. It is certainly clear that twenty-first-century postmodernist drama is delightedly cannibalizing — ingesting, chewing, and eventually regurgitating, in various ironic transformations — its past glories.

Two of postmodernism's most noted dramatic themes are its rejection of linear storytelling and its enhanced appeal to the senses — particularly visual and aural (but also, in some cases, tactile and olfactory). These, together with some of their applications, are worth specific discussion.

A NONLINEAR THEATRE Aristotle proposed that plays should contain a "beginning, middle, and end," and they generally still do — but no longer always in that order, for the conventional development of plot — from an inciting incident through intensifying action, climax, and denouement — is no longer uniformly presented in linear fashion. Temporary "flashbacks," of course, have been used in drama, as well as film, for several decades (they appear prominently in Arthur Miller's *Death of a Salesman,* for example, and the action of Tennessee Williams's *The Glass Menagerie* is, in effect, almost entirely a flashback), but flashbacks are generally framed as such, as by a narrative or musical transition, or, in film, a blurry crossdissolve, which makes clear that the story is now shifting to an earlier time period.

In postmodern drama, however, shuttling from one time zone to another is usually instant and unnarrated: the audience is simply expected to figure it out. Moreover, we are not necessarily "returned" to the present when a postmodern flashback concludes; a play can proceed, in the current theatre, in almost any order the playwright wishes to construct. Such time-warping is no longer surprising. When Harold Pinter, in *Betrayal* (1978), organized his play's nine scenes in mostly reverse chronological order, it was considered revolutionary and reviewers talked of little else, yet when David Auburn, in his 2001 Pulitzer Prize–winning *Proof,* began his second act with a scene chronologically four years earlier than the first (requiring that a ghost in act 1 be instantly seen — with no change of costume or makeup and without explanation — as a living man in act 2), virtually no reviewer thought this reordering of events even worth mentioning; indeed, the *New York Times* theatre critic called the play "as accessible and compelling as a detective story." Postmodern plays are therefore freed from the necessity to align themselves with a forward-moving arrow of time, and even from the need to explain when the arrow reverses direction.

A few other examples of postmodern nonlinear theatre: In Tony Kushner's Pulitzer Prize–winning 1993 *Angels in America,* the action

In David Auburn's *Proof,* which won the 2001 Pulitzer Prize, a daughter (played here by Mary Louise Parker in the Broadway original) converses with her dead father (played by Larry Bryggman) before the audience knows he's dead. The shifting of time during the play makes it a riveting intellectual – as well as emotional – experience.

makes quantum moves in time—between previous centuries, the present, and the afterlife—with never so much as a program note, while actors jump back and forth between different roles and occasionally between different genders as well. In Tom Stoppard's 1998 *The Invention of Love,* the principal character, poet and scholar A. E. Housman, is divided into a younger and an older self, each played by a different actor; the play's scenes alternate back and forth between Housman's student days, professorial years, and boat-borne journey to purgatory after death, with the younger and elder Housmans even crossing paths for conversation as the eras of their lives intertwine. And in Doug Wright's *I Am My Own Wife* (2003), we continually swing forward and back through the life of the play's main character, German transvestite Charlotte von Mahlsdorf, with the play's sole actor (Jefferson Mays in the premiere) performing Charlotte not only in two genders but in two languages and at multiple ages—as well as playing playwright Wright (and thirty-three other characters) besides. None of these non-linear—or gender or language or character—shifts represent sheer dramaturgical novelty; rather, each indicates a theatre—and an audience—prepared for instant cross-association, able to keep several ideas and chronologies in mind at the same time, and meld them into a satisfying dramatic experience.

A Theatre of the Senses   Theatre has always appealed to the senses as well as the intellect, certainly since Sophocles introduced painted scenery in ancient Greece and Aeschylus choreographed his Furies with such whirling passion that audiences fainted and had miscarriages, but the visual, aural, and generally sensory role of theatrical performance has been profoundly enhanced in the current era. Certainly the theatre's scenic design has expanded in the past decades from a primary focus on identifying locales and underlining dramatic themes to making bold, flamboyant, semi-autonomous statements, often in an analogous juxtaposition, or even at a (presumably clarifying) dissonance, from the play's actions. And stage lighting, never wholly realistic to begin with, has become even more directly expressive in making its presence crucial to the intellectual, as well as the mere physical, illumination that a play provides—perhaps in part a technological response to Antonin Artaud's hyperbolic call for "light in waves, in sheets, in fusillades of

Tom Stoppard's *The Invention of Love* portrays various events in the life of the English classical scholar and poet A. E. Housman from age eighteen to seventy-seven, not only by jumping backward and forward in time but also through intriguing same-time conversations between the young Housman (played by Robert Sean Leonard, *right*) and Housman as a just-deceased old man (played by Richard Easton), here shown – along with their reflections – sitting on a fallen antique monument (another postmodern touch) on the River Styx in Hades (the land of the dead). Both Leonard and Easton won Tony Awards for their Housman portrayals in the 2001 Broadway season. Sets and costumes are by Bob Crowley and lighting by Brian MacDevitt.

fiery arrows." The use of scenery and lighting simply as scenery and lighting—as contrasted to its use to depict "a living room in Manhattan during late afternoon"—has now become fundamental to the theatre, leading to design innovations that create bold surprises, provoca-tive, meaningful imagery, and a deeply sensual impact. Thus design has become self-con-sciously "sensational" in the best sense of that term, creating sensory impact—rather than mere realistic or historical detail—at every mo-ment of the production.

Jefferson Mays, as German transvestite Charlotte von Mahlsdorf, holds a treasured antique record player in Doug Wright's multiple-award-winning *I Am My Own Wife*. Charlotte is one of thirty-three roles Mays plays in the show, which crosses gender, linguistic, and time barriers.

Such postmodern designs may make references to elements wholly outside the play and outside the play's historical period; they may employ vivid colors, written texts, mythic or religious or erotic images; they may take the form of wall-sized photographs, surrounding projections and illuminations, kinetic sculptures, or video images (sometimes of the play's actions and sometimes extraneous to them). Any or all of these design elements create a structure of meaning meant to be viewed as integral to—not merely background to—the performance of the actors.

Sound design has been particularly enhanced in the postmodern era. Virtually unknown by anything resembling that name a generation ago, sound design has become a fundamental partner of the theatrical design team in the past decade, expanding from sound effects to sound surround, employing at various points continuous underscoring, live stage orchestras, rock-concert-level amplification, and body microphones for the actors. And increasing use of theatrical smoke, fog, wind, and even rain (in, for example, De La Guarda's 1998 *Villa Villa*, described later in the chapter), often sent directly into or onto the audience, has profoundly increased the all-sensory impact of contemporary theatre stagings.

Much of today's drama has become sexually sensual as well. Total nudity, introduced to drama mainly as a risqué novelty in the 1960s, swiftly entered the theatre's mainstream of serious works in the succeeding decades. Coming of age with Peter Shaffer's Tony Award–winning 1973 *Equus* (in which a young boy and girl strip to make love in a stable), wholly unclothed actors subsequently appeared in such mainstream plays as David Storey's 1973 *The Changing Room* (quarrels in the locker room of an English rugby team), David Henry Hwang's 1988 *M. Butterfly* (a transvestite proves his real gender by disrobing), Terrence McNally's 1994 *Love! Valour! Compassion!* (gay men sunbathe in a country retreat), and Stephen Sondheim's 1994 musical, *Passion* (which begins with a postcoital man and woman in bed, totally nude but for their body microphones, singing about their relationship). Theatrical nudity has now in fact become all but commonplace, appearing in America in the 2000s in widely acclaimed productions of David Hare's *The Blue Room*, Rebecca Gilman's *Blue Surge*, Margaret Edson's *Wit*, Edward Albee's *The Play about the Baby*, John Barton's *Tantalus*, and, with uninhibited blatancy, Richard

Greenberg's 2003 *Take Me Out,* in which a team of major-league baseball players joke, chat, and argue—all while taking long showers after a game.

Nudity is not specific only to postmodernism, of course. But it creates a postmodern shock wave: though not necessarily (and in some cases not remotely) used for erotic reasons, onstage nudity creates a sudden jolt in which, for a moment at least, time seems to stop, logic and analysis are temporarily suspended, and the fiction of drama is forced to contend with the blatancy of sheer naked humanity—the "bare forked animal" that Shakespeare wrote of in *King Lear* but was unable to show. Nudity forces us to confront the reality within the theatrical fiction: that within the construct of a dramatic character lies the exposed and defenseless reality of a live and very naked actor.

An Open Theatre

It is safe to say that the theatre of the present century will be open to an infinitely wider range of interests, cultures, and individuals than has been any other period in the theatre's history. The deconstruction of the theatre, promoted by its most stellar luminaries—Beckett and Brecht among them—made us painfully conscious of the theatre's challenge to fully reflect the humanity inside us and the society around us. For although Shakespeare (for example) was certainly able to create magnificent female and ethnic characters (Beatrice and Cleopatra, Othello and Shylock) and his acting company was clearly able to bring them vividly to life, the notion of an all-white (not to mention all-male) theatre company claiming to hold "a mirror up to nature" has proven

---

*Shakespeare himself seems to have been frustrated at the convention of his day that disallowed women on the stage, judging by Cleopatra's complaint that, upon capture, the Romans' "quick comedians . . . will stage us . . . , and I shall see some squeaking Cleopatra boy my greatness . . ." (*Antony and Cleopatra,* 5, ii, 222–23).

generally unsustainable.* For how could an exclusively male or exclusively white or even a single-ethnic company wholly mirror the hopes and concerns of women as well as men, Asians and blacks as well as whites? Postmodern authors and directors, therefore, have increasingly sought to open the theatre to all comers. Using the deconstructed disconnect between actor and character, the postmodern theatre shows roles as "roles" rather than characters indissolubly linked to the physical characteristics of the actors who play them. Thus, casting considerations have broadened to bend gender distinctions, cross racial lines, and span age ranges, as will be detailed below.

A brilliantly innovative American company named The Open Theatre, created by Joseph Chaikin in 1963, happily gives a name to this theatrical movement. For a decade, Chaikin's Open Theatre combined social improvisation with Brechtian techniques, developing plays in which performers glided into and out of the characters they played (they also played scenery and props; often they played themselves) and using story and character merely as vehicles for direct interactions with audiences. These plays, including Megan Terry's *Viet Rock,* Susan Yankowitz's *Terminal,* and the company-authored *Mutation Show,* were continually evolving workshop performances that addressed immediate audience concerns. The company toured Europe—as well as American cities, campuses, and prisons. They made fraternal and sororal alliances with the New Lafayette Theatre in Harlem, El Teatro Campesino in California, and the Women's Collective Theatre. The Open Theatre ended its existence in 1973, but its influence has been extraordinary, and its name may well stand to represent the larger "opening" of our contemporary stage.

For today's newest and most provocative theatre is truly open, or is at least opening, to voices heretofore shut out or severely limited in the largely Western, white, and male-dominated theatre of yesterday and even of "modern" yesterday. And that opening is occurring on all levels.

A THEATRE BY AND ABOUT WOMEN Save for rare exceptions such as in the commedia dell'arte, women were virtually unrepresented in the theatre until the seventeenth century, and from then until the 1950s they were largely relegated to acting, copying scripts, and building costumes. Today, however, women are a major force in every one of the theatrical arts. Six American women—Paula Vogel, Beth Henley, Marsha Norman, Wendy Wasserstein, Margaret Edson, and Suzan-Lori Parks have received the esteemed Pulitzer Prize for playwriting since 1981 (more than during the previous 65-year history of this honor). And women directors dramatically moved to the forefront in 1998, when Julie Taymor and Garry Hynes became the first and second women in history to win Broadway's Tony Award in directing; this list quickly doubled when Susan Stroman took the 2001 award for *The Producers* (which she also choreographed) and Mary Zimmerman the 2002 award for *Metamorphoses* (which she also wrote). At the same time, women are increasingly assuming the artistic directorships at major American repertory companies: fully one-third of America's 200-plus professional regional theatres are currently headed by women, an astounding record of achievement in a field in which women were all but invisible three or four decades ago.

Meanwhile, over one hundred separate feminist theatre ensembles—groups of women presenting plays by, about, and for women—have been founded in the United States since 1970. The goal of each is to present plays about sex-role stereotyping, abortion, pregnancy, motherhood, rape, the mother-daughter relationship, lesbianism, domestic violence, historically important women, battered women, and women in prison. "The content of almost all feminist drama," says Elizabeth J. Natalle, "comes out of the personal lives of the theatre group members. Feminist theatre groups write

their own drama, and the reality they depict comes from their own experience"—and from the experience of the audience as well. Natalle explains: "In feminist theatre the audience is more than just a passive body viewing the action on stage. . . . Audience members [play] an active role in the creation of a total theatre experience." Natalle goes on to show how, in a play about rape, for example, the audience is invited "to stop the play at any moment and give witness to their own rapes, both literal and metaphoric."

A THEATRE OF ETHNIC DIVERSITY It is a typically postmodern phenomenon that the leading American playwright of the current era is certainly August Wilson, of mixed racial heritage and generally identified as African American. Wilson's *Ma Rainey's Black Bottom, Fences, The Piano Lesson, Joe Turner's Come and Gone, Two Trains Running, Seven Guitars, Jitney, King Hedley II,* and *Gem of the Ocean* are among the most powerful and evocative dramas of our times, concerning, as they do, an entire twentieth-century history of black America. Significantly, Wilson's plays have been commercial as well as artistic hits, playing to huge audiences of all races both on Broadway and in a great many American regional theatres. Wilson is certainly the most honored playwright of recent years (see the chapter titled "The Playwright"), yet he is but one of a number of minority voices that surfaced in the theatre of the 1990s and beyond.

An African American Theatre African American theatre has existed since the earliest American times, and black-themed, black-authored drama made particularly strong creative inroads in the earlier years of the twentieth century (Langston Hughes's *Mulatto* in the 1930s and Lorraine Hansberry's *A Raisin in the Sun* in the late 1950s), becoming a truly revolutionary force with the plays of Amiri Baraka (then LeRoi Jones) in the early 1960s. With his boldly defiant *Dutchman* and *The Toilet,* Baraka confronted American

This Broadway revival of Lorraine Hansberry's classic *A Raisin in the Sun* – directed by Kenny Leon and starring Sean Combs (*left*) as Walter Lee Younger, Audra McDonald as his wife, and Sanaa Lathan as his sister, Beneatha – attracted large crossover audiences on Broadway in 2004.

racism head-on, not shrinking from its potentially violent ramifications. In light of the 1965 Watts riots, Baraka's voice proved prophetic; in light of the 1992 Los Angeles uprisings, we can understand that the problems he revealed have still not been solved.

The Negro Ensemble Company, created by Douglas Turner Ward, and the New Lafayette Theatre in Harlem, with Ed Bullins as chief playwright-in-residence, soon followed Baraka's successes, inching the African American experience into the global arts marketplace. In 1970 Charles Gordone's *No Place to Be Somebody,* produced by Joseph Papp at the New York Public Theatre,

won the Pulitzer Prize in drama, at once putting black and minority playwrights into the American forefront. Black authors achieving national success in subsequent years included Lonne Elder III (*Ceremonies in Dark Old Men*), Adrienne Kennedy (*Funnyhouse of a Negro*), and Ntozake Shange (*for colored girls who have considered suicide/when the rainbow is enuf*). Meanwhile, in Africa, Nigerian dramatist Wole Soyinka received the Nobel Prize for Literature in 1986.

Beginning in the 1970s, Broadway inaugurated an era of lavishly produced black (or largely black) musicals, including *Purlie, Bubbling Brown Sugar, The Wiz, Ain't Misbehavin',*

One of the most influential black-themed American plays is Ntozake Shange's "choreo-poem" titled *for colored girls who have considered suicide/when the rainbow is enuf*, which received Tony, Drama Desk, and Obie awards for its 1976 premiere and spurred a new growth in black theatre – especially black female theatre; it has also been accounted as the beginning of hip-hop. The twenty-fifth anniversary production in 2001 at the (New York) American Place Theatre, featured Eleanor McCoy (*in red*), Katherine J. Smith (*in orange*), and J. Ieasha Prome (*in yellow*), as directed and choreographed by George Faison.

Sophisticated Ladies, Dreamgirls, Raisin, Timbuktu, Five Guys Named Moe, Bring in 'Da Noise, Bring in 'Da Funk, and *Harlem Song.* In more recent years, dramatic plays written by, concerning, and largely performed by African Americans have come to the fore, particularly August Wilson's astonishing ten-play cycle of black American life (culminating in the 2004 *Gem of the Ocean* and 2005 *Radio Golf*), but also Suzan-Lori Parks's *Venus* and *Topdog/Underdog,* Charles Randolf-Wright's *Blue,* Regina Taylor's *Urban Zulu Mambo,* and Lynn Not-

tage's *Intimate Apparel* (which won the 2004 New York Drama Critics' Circle prize for Best Play) and *Fabulation, or the Re-Education of Undine.* Most of these plays—and all of the musicals—have attracted large crossover (multiethnic) audiences, as did the 2004 revival of Hansberry's *A Raisin in the Sun,* with Phylicia Rashad, Audra McDonald, and rap mogul Sean Combs in the major roles.

No one should suppose, however, that an African American theatre exists to universal satisfaction. In the 1990s August Wilson publicly lamented the decline of black-specific theatres that flourished in the 1960s, demanding that African American theatre artists come "face to face" with each other to create a truly postcolonial black theatre. To that end, Wilson premiered *Jitney* at the black-run Crossroads Theatre of New Jersey instead of the Yale Repertory Theatre, his former premiere site. Wilson's ideas, still debated furiously, provide a brilliant departure point for any discussion as to how theatre best represents the concerns of the community for which it is intended.

A Latino Theatre   A Spanish-speaking theatre has existed in North America since the late sixteenth century; indeed, the first play ever staged in what is now the United States was *Los Moros y Los Cristianos* (*The Moors and the Christians*) at the San Juan Pueblo outside of Santa Fe, then part of Mexico. By the mid-nineteenth century, serious and talented professional Mexican touring companies had established residence in Los Angeles and San Francisco and were touring to Texas, Arizona, and New Mexico. On the East Coast, Spanish-speaking theatre—largely imported from Spain and Cuba—had become established in New York and Tampa well before 1900, with stable Spanish-language companies presenting the classical plays of Pedro Calderón de la Barca

Many regional American theatres, including South Coast Repertory, present *A Christmas Carol* for Christmas audiences, but SCR also presents Octavio Solis's *La Posada Magica* at the same time on their smaller stage. The play depicts a young Mexican girl joining her neighborhood *posada*, a reenactment of Joseph and Mary's travel to Bethlehem. Tiffany Ellen Solano (*left*) plays the girl in this 2003 SCR production, directed by the author, with Elsa Martinez and Mauricio Mendoza as Mary and Joseph.

and Lope de Vega, mixed with melodramas and *zarzuelas* (light operettas). Spanish-speaking theatre of this time largely served a community function, preserving traditional Latino culture in Anglo-dominated environments.

With the founding of El Teatro Campesino by Luis Valdez in 1965, however, a contemporary Chicano theatre with a powerful creative and political thrust burst into prominence in California and ultimately won national acclaim. Valdez, a Mexican American, created his Teatro with and for migrant farmworkers in rural California. "In a Mexican way," wrote Valdez in 1966, "we have discovered what Brecht is all about. If you want unbourgeois theatre, find unbourgeois people to do it." Valdez's short, didactic *actos* of the farmworkers' situation have been performed—in English and in Spanish—on farms, in city squares, and, eventually, in theatres all over California and on national and European tours as well; his full-length plays *Zoot Suit* and *I Don't Have to Show You No Stinkin' Badges* have been performed for major metropolitan audiences; and his film *La Bamba* has brought his Teatro to international acclaim (and some financial stability). "Our theatre work is simple, direct, complex and profound, but it works," Valdez explains. Other noted Latina and Latino dramatists include Cuban-born Maria Irene Fornés (whose *Fefu and Her Friends,* 1977, is an often-produced appraisal of friendship and women's roles), Puerto Rican–born José Rivera (*Marisol,* 1992), and Chicano authors Josefina López (*Real Women Have Curves,* 1990) and Carlos Morton (*The Miser of Mexico,* 1989). And recently rising to exceptional prominence, Cuban-born Nilo Cruz received the 2003 Pulitzer Prize for Drama with his enchanting Cuban-American-themed *Anna in the Tropics,* which portrays Cuban émigré workers in a Florida (Ybor City) cigar factory and the handsome *lector* who reads novels aloud to them—enchanting the female employees as he does so—during their daily labors. Cruz, who emigrated to the United States when he was nine, began writing for the Prometeo theatre group on his Miami-

David Zayas plays Cheche, a hot-headed Cuban-American cigar manufacturer who urges his company to discard tradition and adapt to modern American factory techniques, in the 2003 Broadway production of Nilo Cruz's Pulitzer Prize–winning *Anna in the Tropics.*

Dade Community College campus; subsequently he studied advanced playwriting with Fornés in New York. His was the first Pulitzer drama prize to be awarded to a yet-unproduced play, but *Anna in the Tropics* has since been performed with distinction on Broadway (with Jimmy Smits as the lector) and by many American regional companies, including the New Theatre of Coral Gables, Florida, which initially premiered it.

An East-West Theatre The Eastern voice stunned American drama in the late 1980s with

"Fusion theatre," which combines different performance traditions (usually Eastern and Western), is now widespread. Admired for its global, nonparochial perspective, it is sometimes criticized for appropriating the cultures from which it borrows. Shown here is a 2003 fusion production at New York's Lincoln Center of *Orphan of Zhao*. Chen Shi-Zheng, a Chinese-born American directed this twelfth-century Chinese tragic masterpiece in a free adaptation by noted American playwright David Greenspan. The music, composed by Stephin Merritt, featured both Chinese and Western instruments.

David Henry Hwang's *M. Butterfly*, which boldly reinterpreted the Madame Butterfly myth, effectively exploding narrow and deprecatory "Orientalist" stereotypes and misperceptions of Asian culture. Hwang's incorporation of Beijing Opera technique into Western drama draws on a tradition that predates postmodernism—Ezra Pound, Bertolt Brecht, W. S. Gilbert, and Antonin Artaud all drew heavily on Asian dramatic styles in their antirealistic works of the modernist period. But Hwang, who is of Asian (Chinese) background himself (see the chapter titled "The Playwright"), employs Asian and Western performers in this deliberately confrontational play, which poses East against West (and maleness against femaleness) in a continually informing, continually surprising way. Hwang's play brought postmodernism into Broadway commercialism—as a certified Broadway hit spectacle. Hwang returned to Broadway in 1998 with the Chinese family drama *Golden Child*, which was nominated for a best-play Tony Award, and authored the book for the Disney musical *Aida*, treating African legends. Other Asian American authors include Philip Kan Gotanda, whose 1998 *Ballad of Yachiyo*, about Japanese emigrants in Hawaii and an embittered potter and his idealistic apprentice, played widely in the present decade in the United States and London; his 2004

After the War, commissioned by San Francisco's American Conservatory Theatre, will treat the interactions between San Francisco's Japanese Americans and the African American jazz scene after World War II. Lonnie Carter's 2003 *The Romance of Magno Rubio,* about Filipino farmworkers in California in the 1930s and their struggles to ascend social and economic ladders while retaining their sense of community, won eight Obie (off-Broadway) Awards with its largely Filipino cast (a considerable portion of the play is in the Tagalog language) in New York. And Elizabeth Wong's *China Doll, Letters to a Student Revolutionary, Kimchee and Chitlins,* and *Dating and Mating in Modern Times* have explored all aspects of Chinese American relations in the context of the multiplicity of world cultures represented in the American environment. All of these dramatists—and several dozen others with like interests—have risen to prominence over the past decade, with the help of such nurturing companies as the East-West Players in Los Angeles and the Pan Asian Repertory Theatre in New York.

Asian performance techniques have also broadly influenced Western theatre, even for Western plays. French director Ariane Mnouchkine (also see later discussion) introduced Japanese kabuki music and movement to her production of Shakespeare's *Richard II,* Indian kathakali technique to her *Twelfth Night,* and Middle Eastern music and dancing to her production of Molière's *Tartuffe,* thereby setting each play's Western orientation in bold relief and universalizing many of the play's themes. English director Peter Brook (also see later discussion) directed a 2001 production of *Hamlet* that included a continuous score played live by Japanese composer Toshi Tsuchitori, who had also contributed the Indian-inspired orchestration for Brook's celebrated production—with an international cast—of the Indian Sanskrit epic *The Mahabharata.* Japanese director Tadashi Suzuki's acting theories and teachings, as well as his bilingual productions, have broadly influenced acting and actor training in both

Europe and America. And the late Jerzy Grotowski completed his life's work by training an international group of performers in prehistoric performance techniques drawn largely from Asia and Africa, attempting to create an "objective drama" that sought to dissolve the unconsciously applied linguistic and cultural codes separating human beings from their true biological (and, some might say, spiritual) selves. These East-West movements have occasioned lively debate in recent years: proponents of such "fusion art" applaud the integration of disparate cultural and aesthetic values; dissenters, however, criticize this as a neocolonialist appropriation of one culture by another. The debate—as well as that led by August Wilson, mentioned earlier—bespeaks the vital social and ethical complexity of today's theatre.

A GLOBAL THEATRE—AND A MACARONIC DRAMA Theatre is—and during most of its history has been—an international medium. In the time of the ancient Greeks, virtually all of the Hellenic city-states were represented in the annual Great Dionysia, Athens's springtime theatre festival, which also attracted traders and visitors from throughout the Mediterranean world. In Shakespeare's time, plays—including many of his own—were set in, among other locales, what is now Italy, France, Egypt, Bohemia, Greece, Austria, Denmark, Scotland, and an island that is quite possibly intended to be Bermuda; audiences to these plays included many foreigners, who in some cases provided much of what we know about theatergoing in Shakespeare's day.

While theatre retreated to a more parochial insularity in subsequent centuries, the twenty-first century has seen the theatre reemerge into an art form with an international audience. Part of this results from the globalization of today's world economy and part from the likewise global proliferation of art and culture through film, television, and increasingly intercontinental theatrical touring, but most has been occasioned by the expansion of world tourism and

Maggie Gyllenhaal plays the daughter of an Englishwoman who has disappeared in Afghanistan, while Dariush Kashani is an Afghan merchant and Firdous Bamji a Tajik poet in Tony Kushner's multilingual and multicultural *Homebody/Kabul*, presented at the Mark Taper Forum in Los Angeles in 2003 prior to its Broadway premiere.

cross-migration that began with radically expanded airplane travel after World War II, coupled with the worldwide social and economic upheavals in and after the cold war. For all of these reasons, it is virtually impossible to spend an hour on the sidewalks of any major world city—New York, Los Angeles, Chicago, London, Tokyo, Toronto, Berlin, Sydney—without hearing a broad mix of languages from at least the three major continents. And the theatre of today often reflects both the internationalism and the interlinguistics of today's supremely globalized world.

Critic Marvin Carlson has imaginatively used the term *macaronic*—originally equating the mixture of Latin and early Italian spoken in medieval Italy to a *maccarone* (macaroni) of

thrown-together pasta—to indicate plays including speeches in different languages.* The European theatre has long been macaronic: even Shakespeare's plays include many lines (and in two cases entire scenes) in French, Italian, Latin, or Welsh. More recent plays take this much further. Canadian playwright David Fennario's 1979 *Balconville*, about the relationship of French-speaking and English-speaking Canadians, is presented in both languages of that officially bilingual country. The 1993 French comic play *Les Aviateurs* is performed entirely in English—the language of

*"The Macaronic Stage," in *East of West*, ed. Claire Sponsler and Xiamei Chen (New York: Palgrave, 2000), 15–31.

aviation—though it is a thoroughly French play, initially produced at a local Paris theatre. *Endstation Amerika*, Frank Castorf's 2002 adaptation of Tennessee Williams's *A Streetcar Named Desire* at the Berlin Volksbühne (discussed later in this chapter), was performed in German, French, and English. In the United States, Luis Valdez's *Zoot Suit* (1978) and *I Don't Have to Show You No Stinkin' Badges* (1986), about Chicano assimilation in California, were written almost equally in Spanish and English, pioneering a bilingual "Spanglish" text that conveyed the ethnic authenticity of the cast, as well as the reality of their assimilation of a second language. And nearly a third of *The Romance of Magno Rubio* (see above) is written in Tagalog. It is both realistic and exceptionally poignant for the characters in these plays to speak in both their old and new languages at various times, truthfully reflecting different states of emotion and cultural identity.

More flagrantly macaronic, however, are two recent plays, *Homebody/Kabul* (2004), by American playwright Tony Kushner, which is presented—usually with great vehemence—in French, Arabic, Pashto, Dari, English, and Esperanto, and *Pentecost* (1995), by British playwright David Edgar, set in an unnamed eastern European country in which Bulgarian, Hungarian, Kurdish, Romany, Azeri, Mozambican, Hindi, Afghan, Bosnian, Palestinian, and Kuwaiti refugees speak, among them, at least eleven languages. The biblical word *pentecost* refers to ecstatic multilingual utterances proclaiming the gift of tongues; in this play, and in *Homebody/Kabul*, English appears both as the native language of a small group of characters and as the second language of the rest.

As macaronic theatre has begun to receive broad exposure, the theatre is now learning to cope with the demands of macaronic multicultural dramatic speech. Casting directors are seeking bilingual performers with native languages different from their own; playwrights and directors are learning to shape their plays to make the key lines and actions of multilin-

gual texts comprehensible to single-language audiences; and actors are discovering how to heighten the transmission of meaning by gesture, tone of voice, and implication. But since many of us are facing the same challenges in our increasingly multicultural daily lives, the macaronic theatre is simply holding its mirror up to our evolving nature. It is hard to overestimate the importance of this movement, which can brilliantly depict the conflicts between cultural survival and assimilation and give voices to the multiple perspectives of societies ravaged by the factionalism and terrorism spreading through the post–cold war and post–September 11 world.

A THEATRE OF DIFFERENCE   Gender and ethnicity are not the only bases for the new voices that have entered the mainstream of postmodern theatre. The issue of sexual preference had been buried deeply in the closet during most of the theatre's history, and as late as 1958 the representation of homosexuality was actually illegal in England and widely (if not legally) suppressed in America. The love that "dared not speak its name" came to the stage in those eras only through authors' implications and audiences' inferences, and gay playwrights, such as Oscar Wilde, Tennessee Williams, Gertrude Stein, Edward Albee, William Inge, and Gore Vidal, were forced to speak—at certain critical moments in their work—only by innuendo and through oblique code words.

All of this changed dramatically in the late 1960s, when gay and lesbian life—and gay and lesbian issues—began to be treated as serious dramatic subjects, most notably by Mart Crowley in his groundbreaking American comedy *The Boys in the Band* (1968). Since that time, sexual-preference issues have become principal or secondary topics in hundreds of plays, including mainstream Broadway musicals (*La Cage aux Folles, Falsettos, Kiss of the Spider Woman, The Wild Party, Jerry Springer*), popular comedies (*Love! Valour! Compassion!, Jeffrey, The Lisbon Traviata*), and serious dramas (*Bent, M. Butterfly, Gross Indecency, Breaking the Code, The Laramie*

Project, Take Me Out, I Am My Own Wife). Gay actors came out of the closet (most of them theatrically) to advocate gay rights worldwide, as did the British classical star Sir Ian McKellen in his one-man performance "A Knight Out" at the Gay Games in New York in 1994. In the wake of a new and terrible illness, a growing genre of AIDS plays (*The Normal Heart, As Is*) addressed the tragic human consequences of this disease, whose initial victims in the United States and Europe were predominantly gay. And in 1992, Tony Kushner's extraordinary "gay fantasia on national themes," titled *Angels in America*, proved one of the most celebrated stage productions of the decade in both England and the United States. Sexual preference has emerged over the past decade as a defining

issue for many theatre groups, theatre festivals, and theatre publications, each seeking to examine the political, cultural, and aesthetic implications of gay- and lesbian-themed drama.

Persons differently abled are also represented in new theatre companies created specifically for these voices and for expanding audiences. Theatre by the Blind, in New York, employs sightless actors for all of its productions, and the National Theatre of the Deaf is only one of four American companies (Deaf West, Sign Rise Theatre, and the Fairmount Theatre of the Deaf are the others) that create theatre of and for the hearing-impaired, employing American Sign Language (ASL) as the primary verbal dramatic medium. With Mark Medoff's play *Children of a Lesser God*, the hearing-impaired found a

Diana Son's *Stop Kiss* is a contemporary drama about two women who discover their repressed sexuality – and homophobia – at the same moment. Julie Oda (*left*) and Tyler Layton play the pair in Loretta Greco's 2000 production at the Oregon Shakespeare Festival. The geometric scenic design, which serves the play's multiple settings, is by Robert Brill.

Deaf West is a Los Angeles theatre for the hearing-impaired, and its production of the musical *Big River*, in which characters alternately speak, sing, and sign their roles, began on the company's tiny home stage. From there it moved to the much larger Mark Taper Forum and then to Broadway, winning critical acclaim, not merely for overcoming its "handicapped" label but for creating an altogether new theatre aesthetic of hearing and "seeing" musical drama at the same time. Tyrone Giordano (*left*) plays Huckleberry Finn, with Michael McElroy as Jim, at the American Airlines Theater in 2003.

broad popular audience, and a number of hearing-impaired actors and actresses found national recognition. In 2001 the opening at the Mark Taper Forum of John Belluso's *The Body of [Randolph] Bourne,* which treats the esteemed cultural critic's physical disfiguration, was wisely accompanied by a quadrupling of the Taper's wheelchair-accessible seating and a renovation of the theatre's backstage area to better accommodate performers with disabilities. The Coalition for Inclusive Performing Arts (CIPA), based in the National Arts and Disability Center at UCLA (http://nadc.ucla.edu), is currently devoted to full inclusion of children and adults with disabilities into the theatre community.

A THEATRE OF NONTRADITIONAL CASTING
Across the country, color-blind casting—once thought of as daring—has become almost routine, particularly in the classics. African Americans are playing roles once thought to be reserved for whites—while, conversely, the white Patrick Stewart has played the black Othello (without makeup!) opposite a black Desdemona. The New York Shakespeare Festival has been a leader in such alternative casting, choosing Angela

In Shakespeare's *Othello*, the title character is black and the society in which he lives is white. In this noteworthy Shakespeare Theatre (Washington, D.C.) production in 1998, Patrick Stewart played Othello; everyone else in the cast was black. The goal, mainly achieved, was to put racial discrimination into bold, even shocking, relief.

Fran Bennett plays the title role in Travis Preston's 2002 avant-garde production of *King Lear*, staged by the Center for New Theatre at CalArts in the long-abandoned Edison Electric Building in Los Angeles. This was not Bennett's first male role in *Lear*: she had performed the Duke of Gloucester for the Company of Women in 1996.

Bassett as their 1998 Lady Macbeth, Morgan Freeman as their Petruchio, and Denzel Washington as their Richard III. And in 2003, Fran Bennett, a black woman, played the title role in Travis Preston's provocative *King Lear* in an abandoned Los Angeles factory.

But such nontraditional casting is not limited to large metropolitan venues: the Oregon Shakespeare Festival, in a state with less than 4 percent African Americans and Asian Americans *combined,* has, under the leadership of Libby Appel, routinely assembled acting companies of whom fully a third are non-Caucasian and prominently features nonwhite actors as English royalty and Renaissance Italian lovers and, indeed, in whatever roles the company has to offer. The Non-Traditional Casting Project (http://www.ntcp.org), with headquarters in New York, coordinates a national oversight of this color-blind casting process.

Cross-gendered casting is also commonplace in the postmodern age, as in the case of Bennett's King Lear. The New York Shakespeare Festival was also a pioneer in this area, featuring New York's first female Hamlet in modern times, and by now female Hamlets, Prosperos, Richard IIs, and Richard IIIs are everywhere apparent—as are male Cleopatras, Olivias, and Rosalinds. Indeed, on mainstream Broadway in 2001, the males Sean Campion and Conleth Hill played, between them, all sixteen male and female roles in Marie Jones's *Stones in His Pockets,* and female Lily Tomlin played all seventeen male and female roles in her revival of Jane Wagner's *The Search for Intelligent Signs in the Universe.*

Multiculturalism extends, of course, to play selection. The canon of past dramatic works is now being exhumed and expanded to "discover" women and minority voices that were suppressed or ignored in the past; revivals today are likely to focus on previously unheralded female authors, such as Aphra Behn (one of the most prolific Restoration dramatists), Alice Brown, Rachel Crothers, Sophie Treadwell, Susan Glaspell, and Zoe Atkins, demonstrating how women and minorities have often been neglected and marginalized in past cultural undertakings. Theatres devoted to the exploration of minority voices are likewise expanding the standard canon with new works. The Ma-Yi Theatre Company, Pan Asian Repertory Theatre, INTAR Hispanic American Arts Center, Repertorio Español, Thalia Spanish Theatre, Pregones Theatre, and Ping Chong and Company of New York; the Pangea World Theatre, Mixed Blood Theatre, and Theater Mu of Minneapolis; the GALA Hispanic Theatre and African Continuum Theatre Company of Washington, D.C.; the Arizona Jewish Theatre Company of Phoenix; the Borderlands Theatre of Tucson; the Traveling Jewish Theatre of San Francisco; the Teatro Visión of San Jose; the St. Louis Black Repertory Company; the San Diego Asian American Repertory Theatre; and the Deaf West Theatre, East West Players, and Cornerstone Theatre of Los Angeles are only some of a long list of professional theatre companies seeking to make minority voices competitive in the American theatre world.

And for each professional company, there are a dozen amateur and university companies now forming. It is abundantly clear, as the new millennium begins, that the theatre will never again revert to the protected confines of a privileged elite. Nor can it live successfully in social isolation in some "underprivileged" ghetto. Isolation, at the top or bottom, has no place in the postmodern—or post-postmodern—culture. One of the great achievements of the current era has been the relentless (if still incomplete) democratization of art and the multiplicity (if not the integration) of struggling, and often competing, voices.

A THEATRE OF POLITICAL IMMEDIACY   Theatre has always dealt with current politics—indeed, the potentially short lead time between initial conception and finished product is one of the advantages live theatre has over film. But the new century, particularly after the events of September 11, 2001, has seen a virtual explosion of up-to-the-minute dramas performed on major stages around the world. Many of these may be called "verbatim theatre," as they have been developed from transcripts of real-life speeches and interviews. A few examples:

- *The Guys,* by Anne Nelson, opened at the Flea Theater in New York's Tribeca district less than three months after—and a dozen blocks from—the horrific attacks on the World Trade Center. Nelson wrote the play based on conversations she had had with a surviving fire captain and the stories he had told her of eight of his men killed in the buildings' collapse. Edited by actress Sigourney Weaver, and with Bill Murray as the captain, the play was a powerful emotional experience for the New York audience in the theatre season that began so shatteringly.

- *Guantanamo,* staged in a fringe neighborhood playhouse in London in 2004, moved just three weeks later to London's fashionable West End and two months after that to New York's off-Broadway. Conceived and directed by Nicolas Kent at his Tricycle Theatre in England, *Guantanamo* is assembled from transcripts of interviews Kent and his writing team conducted with families of detainees held at the U.S. prison in Cuba, interspersed with speeches by U.S. defense

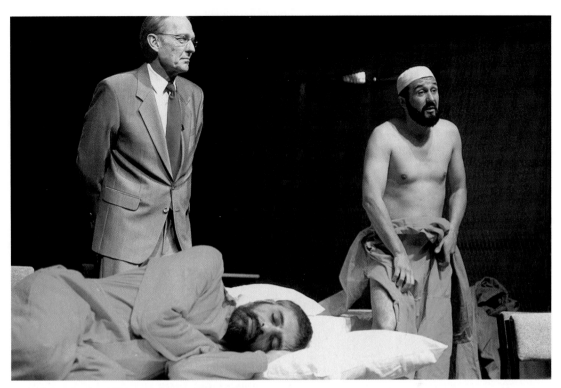

In Nicolas Kent's *Guantanamo*, staged in 2004 at the Tricycle Theatre in London, William Hoyland plays U.S. defense secretary Donald Rumsfeld, and Paul Bhattacharjee (*lying down*) and Daniel Cerqueir play detainees at the news-prominent U.S. naval-base prison in Cuba.

secretary Donald Rumsfeld and British foreign secretary Jack Straw, among others. "Anyone who is seriously interested in the values that sustain civilization [should] see this production," said the London *Financial Times* review.

- *The Private Room,* by American playwright Mark Lee, is set in Guantanamo as well, in a Camp Delta interrogation room, as well as in an exclusive dining room in New York's financial district. Lee connects these two "private rooms" by creating a Wall Street clerk who finds herself, as an army reservist, assigned to Guantanamo and thus torn between conflicting values of superpower politics, militarism, and economics. The play opened in London in

2004 and will doubtless be in the United States by the time this book is published.

- *Embedded* was created by actor Tim Robbins for the Actors' Gang in Los Angeles in 2003. Portraying a U.S. attack on the fictional country of "Gomorrah," where the military embeds reporters with the advancing forces and pressures them to cover U.S. actions favorably while suppressing reports of casualties, the half-masked characters clearly are meant to be seen as Rumsfeld (called "Rum-Rum") and Cheney ("Dick"). Despite mixed reviews, *Embedded* had extended runs in both Los Angeles and New York, where it transferred in 2004, stirring intense public debate in both cities.

In Tim Robbins's *Embedded*, which Robbins terms "a ripped-from-the-headlines satire," V. J. Foster is U.S. colonel Hardchannel and Kate Mulligan the reporter given basic training before heading off to the front. This 2004 production was staged at the Joseph Papp Public Theatre in New York.

- *The Arab-Israeli Cookbook,* a 2004 piece of verbatim theatre by Robin Soans, is shaped out of kitchen interviews with forty-two Israelis and Palestinians—Jews, Muslims, and Christians—each sharing, along with their recipes, their individual hopes, horrors, and humiliations while living with checkpoints, suicide bombers, and an apparently unending intifada. Without taking sides in the conflict, Soans's *Cookbook,* performed with eight actors at London's Gate Theatre, proved, in the words of one critic, "a testament of survival . . . under the constant threat of sudden death."

- *Sin, a Cardinal Deposed* is the creation of playwright Michael Murphy, who compressed and rearranged 1,000 pages of Boston Archdiocese Cardinal Law's court deposition, plus letters and public documents from priests, doctors, and sexual-abuse victims. The verbatim script was performed by six actors of the Bailiwick Theatre in Chicago in 2004 to great—and often tearful—acclaim. Said one attendee to a producer who was bringing the production to Boston, "You're going to need bodyguards at the stage door."

- *Stuff Happens,* written by celebrated British playwright Sir David Hare for the English National Theatre, deals with the creation of the British-American coalition during the buildup to the Iraq War; the play's title comes from Donald Rumsfeld's 2003 response, during a press conference, to the looting of Baghdad. Hare's play—created by Hare and National Theatre artistic director Nicholas Hytner out of company workshops—asks "How does the world settle its differences, now there is only one superpower? What happens to leaders risking their credibility with skeptical publics?"

In addition to these new plays of great immediate political pertinence, the 2003–4 season was replete with directors' stagings of classic dramas, particularly Greek tragedies, that were openly reflective of the war in Iraq and the larger one on terrorism that were being fiercely fought and debated during the periods of production. Such productions included Kate Whoriskey's *Antigone* at South Coast Repertory in California, Katie Mitchell's *Iphigenia at Aulis* at the National Theatre of England, and Luc Bondy's production of Martin Crimp's *Cruel and Tender,* adapted from Sophocles' *Women of Trachis.* All of these productions have clearly drawn the linkages between the wars and warriors of ancient Greece and those of the current day.

A DANGEROUS THEATRE   In addition to being politically immediate, late modern and postmodern theatre has increasingly been seen as dangerous. The nudity and sensory assault of much contemporary drama have caused consternation in many quarters; subjects such as political torture (*Death and the Maiden*), the Nazi Holocaust (*Ghetto, The Deputy*), prison atrocities (*Bent, The Island*), and urban mayhem (*Aven "U" Boys*) have also proliferated in today's theatre. Simulated homosexual intercourse in *Angels in America* has caused the play to be banned in many communities; vulgar language in, for example, David Mamet's 1983 *Glengarry Glen Ross* ("*Fuck* marshalling the leads. What the fuck talk is that? What the fuck talk is that?") and the very title of Mark Ravenhill's *Shopping and Fucking* have occasioned barrages of angry letters to theatre producers and the editorial pages of many newspapers. Accusations of religious defamation led to bomb

One of the most gripping contemporary plays about urban British violence is Mark Ravenhill's shockingly titled *Shopping and Fucking.* Andrew Clover is the besieged actor in the original London production, at the Royal Court Theatre, in 1996.

threats at the 1998 New York opening of Terrence McNally's *Corpus Christi,* which concerns a Jesus-like character who has sexual relations with his disciples, and more recently, legal threats put forth by twenty-one members of the Indiana legislature in the summer of 2001 prevented Purdue University from producing the same play. And Neil LaBute's violent, baby-murdering *The Distance from Here* was met with outrage by some subscribers and loud screams from at least one audience (as well as plaudits from many critics) at its American premiere at the Manhattan Theatre Club in 2004. The theatre continually treads on toes—but sometimes the toes kick back.

Political censorship and even judicial intervention have, of course, been with the theatre since its inception. The ancient Greek playwright Phrynicus was heavily fined for producing his *Capture of Miletus,* which offended sixth-century (B.C.) Athenian officers by vividly portraying a Greek military defeat. Shakespeare seems to have deleted several oaths from his manuscript of *Othello* because they were deemed sacrilegious by authorities; and his contemporaries Ben Jonson, John Marston, and John Chapman were all jailed for writing satirical plays. Molière rewrote *Tartuffe* at least three times to get it past the king's aunt's religious scruples. Almost every country has regulated what can and cannot be seen on the stage, right up to modern times: in twentieth-century England, for example, authorities temporarily suppressed such nonclassic plays as August Strindberg's *Miss Julie,* Eugene O'Neill's *Desire under the Elms,* Luigi Pirandello's *Six Characters in Search of an Author,* and Arthur Miller's *A View from the Bridge.* Samuel Beckett's *Endgame* was officially censored (for disputing the existence of God) as late as 1958. Even W. S. Gilbert and Arthur Sullivan's *The Mikado* was suppressed by the British so that it would not offend the visiting crown prince of Japan in 1907. Nor is such outright censorship, even now, wholly in the past. Many Asian countries maintain censorship boards; in fact, the Chinese government initiated a huge international uproar in 1998 by canceling a planned American tour of the Shanghai-based production of *The Peony Pavilion*—a 22-hour kunqu (Chinese Opera) directed by an American of Chinese descent. According to Chinese officials, the production did not give a truthful representation of the kunqu form and was too "erotic" by Chinese standards.

There is no outright artistic censorship in the United States, owing to the First Amend-

What is and is not permissible in the theatre varies widely from culture to culture. Chen Shi-zheng's Shanghai production of the sixteenth-century Chinese masterpiece *The Peony Pavilion* had to cancel its 1998 tour to New York when Chinese authorities complained that certain scenes were so nontraditional that they would give a false impression of the kunqu form to foreign audiences.

ment of the U.S. Constitution. But of course government funding is subject to approval by local and national legislators, who often balk at the works of artists of whom they disapprove. Thus performance artist Karen Finley (who in her most famous one-woman show smears her naked body with chocolate—see later discussion) was engaged in a decade-long battle to reinstate her NEA grant, which had been cancelled following vigorous complaints from local and national government officials who disapproved of her performance—or of what they had heard about that performance, since few, if any, had seen it. The argument against *Corpus Christi* at Purdue was not about censorship but about money: raising the issue of a state university using public funds to present a play that outraged members of the community—and not a few state legislators. No one can fully respond to the facts of any of these cases without a more complete understanding of them than one gets from the newspapers (or this book). Certainly a government, especially one democratically elected and proceeding according to recognized law, has the right as well as the responsibility to make well-considered funding decisions—for the arts as well as for everything else. But one certainly hopes that such legislators will not assume the roles of sole arbiters of artistic merit and propriety. And surely no one believes that bomb threats should determine what sort of dramatic material adults should be permitted to produce—and to see—on any American or world theatre stage.

The good news from these contemporary episodes, one might say, is that even in a world that continually blasts us with high-tech media and mega-information—through our ubiquitous TVs, films, magazines, computers, video games, talk radio, and CDs—the theatre remains a forum that is both provocative and perilous, still daring enough to provoke outrage and outrageous enough to be thought a danger. This—the theatre's leading edge—is worth protecting fiercely, though it may give many theatre artists, and legislators, a few sleepless nights.

A Theatre of Revival

It would be a mistake, however, to think that all current theatre is at the edge of postmodernity. It definitely is not. Indeed, much of the work seen on today's stages consists of revivals of earlier works, including musicals, classics, and popular plays of previous decades that remain in theatrical repertories—and the theatergoing public's awareness.

This does not mean, however, that such works are simply remounted in their earlier fashion, for the distinguishing characteristic of theatre everywhere is that it is a *live* performance, and for that reason virtually every play, when remounted upon the stage, is—consciously or unconsciously, subtly or outrageously—partly or wholly reconceived for its current audience. That is why such remountings are called "revivals," because they give new life (from the French *vivre,* "to live") to older masterworks. No theatre revival can succeed simply as a museum piece; theatrical revivals, like original works, only triumph in the theatre by freshly intriguing the imaginations and engaging the emotions of its present-day audience.

Shakespearean festivals are only one visible national indication of a theatre of revival: at last count, there were over a hundred theatre companies, in virtually every state in America, devoted at least in part to producing the 400-year-old works of England's most celebrated dramatist. Meanwhile, on Broadway, new stagings of old American musicals have threatened to dominate the street, with new productions of *Follies, Forty-Second Street, The Music Man, Kiss Me Kate, Cabaret, Chicago, Annie Get Your Gun, Oklahoma!, The Rocky Horror Picture Show, Wonderful Town, Gypsy,* and *Fiddler on the Roof* running on New York's Great White Way in the century after their premieres. Nor are America's classic dramas ignored, with Arthur Miller's *After the Fall,* Eugene O'Neill's *Long Day's Journey into Night,* Sam Shepard's *Fool for Love,* and Tennessee Williams's *Cat on a Hot Tin Roof* and *A Streetcar Named Desire* also playing in America's most prestigious venues during the 2003–4 and 2004–5 seasons. Restagings of modern world classics, indeed, constitute roughly half to two-thirds of the offerings among America's regional, community, and academic theatres at any given time. And new plays mimicking these modernist classics—serious dramas as well as comedies—might in any year make up another quarter of the bill.

One might even call the most successful of our new century's productions thus far, Mel Brooks's musical *The Producers,* a revival, as it not only is based on Brooks's 1968 movie but also revives (and quotes) well over a hundred gags, techniques, and themes of American musical comedies since the 1938 Olson and Johnson *Hellzapoppin!*

The theatre of revival—including new plays mimicking earlier forms—has broad and legitimate appeal. For most audiences, it is familiar, entertaining, and aesthetically satisfying; on the best occasions, it profoundly addresses serious and tangible problems that face humanity around the world. The theatre of revival is not merely a theatre of nostalgia; at its best it can be a forum for insight, information, ideas, empathy, catharsis, wit, rapture, virtuosity, and laugh-'til-you-cry comedy. The tears of audiences emerging from the recent *Fiddler on the Roof* are real tears, and the laughs from the *Wonderful Town* revival virtually shake theatre seats. Finely crafted revivals also provide a box-office and public-relations lift to the whole theatre world, providing both employment for veteran artists and training for beginners while raising the visibility and importance of dramatic art throughout national and world cultures. Though not at the cutting edge of innovation, and therefore easily derided by many avant-gardists, the traditional (or derrière-garde) theatre of revival needs no apologists; it is a vital, vibrant, thriving glory of the current stage.

Who's Doing Today's Theatre?

No book can tell you what's happening, or who's doing it, in the theatre right now—for by the time you read about it, it's already happened. The artist who sprang to prominence last year may sink to total obscurity next month. No one can safely predict the theatre of tomorrow.

What we can do, however, is list a few promising artists and artistic trends that may be at the forefront of theatrical life during the first years of the new century. Even if the list is less than prophetic, it should give a general picture of the diversity of the theatre of our times and of the sorts of dramatic possibilities that theatre artists and enthusiasts are currently anticipating.

Robert Wilson and Performance Art

The term *performance art* came into common parlance in the 1960s, describing presentations, usually in art galleries or museums, that combined elements of the visual arts, dance, theatre, mime, poetry, and video. In general, these works lack—indeed, deliberately avoid—the traditional dramatic elements of plot, character, and dramaturgical structure (exposition, climax, denouement). Taking a page, instead, from Antonin Artaud and his notion of "no more masterpieces" (see the chapter titled "The Modern Theatre"), performance art focuses on the vibratory rather than the semantic aspect of words in a text (that is, on their sound rather than their meaning) and on the impressions of imagery rather than the development of character relationships or logical argument. "Performance art, properly speaking, means nothing," said one important practitioner.* Rather, autobiographical narratives, body art, ceremonial ritual, current political commentary, and full sensory involvement (taste, feel, and smell, along with sound and sight) are common in performance art, and on-the-spot improvisation is often featured as well. Since the form is self-identified as nontheatrical, even antitheatrical, trained theatre performers are generally abjured.

Despite its stated nontheatricality, however, performance art has had an enormous influence on the theatre of today. Virtually all the photos of recent theatre productions through-

---

*Jeff Nuttal, in Patrice Pavis, *Dictionary of the Theatre* (Toronto: University of Toronto Press, 1998), 261.

out this book—even in mainline Broadway or regional theatres—indicate a heightened visual and sensual creativity in contemporary stage production as compared to what could be seen twenty years ago (and certainly to what was seen in the first edition of this book in 1981). Explosive, arresting, shocking, provocative, and hilarious imagery is in; solely formal, logical, narrative, "storytelling" imagery is out. Performance art has infiltrated theatre art in ways that make the two, at times, almost indistinguishable.

Pure performance art, however, by its nature tends to be transitory. The works are often brief (fifteen minutes is a common maximum), attended by small audiences, and engaged for short runs. Most performance artists prefer it this way. But several have moved into the more rigorous demands of full theatrical presentation, with varying degrees of success. Karen Finley (discussed shortly) was one of the first, and she continues to perform successfully around the United States, occasionally in theatres. Laurie Anderson, who experiments with voice amplification, plotlines, and whole casts of characters, has made a more complete move into theatrical venues; her *Moby Dick,* scripted after Melville's novel, has performed around the world. Visual artist Michael Counts, taking over a 40,000-square-foot warehouse in Brooklyn in 1995, created astounding, walk-through installation performances in the first years of the 2000s—until he ran out of money with a breathtaking but budget-breaking extravaganza, *So Long Ago I Can't Remember,* and had to close shop (temporarily, one hopes).

But the one artist who has most successfully blended performance art with theatre is the Texas native Robert Wilson. Born in 1941 and emerging in the European avant-garde in the early 1970s, Wilson remains at the very top of his field—as writer, director, designer, and sometimes even actor—with half a dozen new productions in preparation at this writing.

Wilson first came to prominence in Germany, where his highly original collages of po-

Laurie Anderson is a long-recognized performance artist, specializing in the integration of visual excitement and electronic sound perturbations. In her "techno-opera" of *Moby Dick,* as presented at the Brooklyn Academy of Music in 1999, Anderson serves as singer, speaker (in many voices), composer, violinist, keyboardist, guitarist, and operator of an electronic, sound-generating Talking Stick, mostly while perched on a supersized chair of her own invention.

etic texts recited against brilliantly evocative *tableaux vivants* ("living pictures") gained serious attention from enthusiasts of the avant-garde. The extraordinary length of these pieces, which Wilson both wrote and directed, earned him early notoriety: *The Life and Times of Joseph Stalin* (1973) lasted twelve hours; *Ka Mountain* (1972) lasted twenty-three. Wilson became a

Artist Michael Counts's astonishing, if short-lived, Brooklyn (New York) performance art/theatre troupe, GAle GAtes et al., received national acclaim for *1839,* a seemingly free association of the complex relationships between narrative, images, and human memory, employing both Greek tragedy and high-tech sound and videography and creating intriguingly beautiful stage pictures such as this one. The play's title refers to the date Louis Daguerre invented the world's first camera.

world figure when he was invited to create the central performance work of the 1984 Los Angeles Olympic Arts Festival, for which he composed *The CIVIL warS,* a massive piece to be rehearsed in several countries around the world; funds could not be raised for the performance, however, and only fragments of the work were ever performed. Since then, however, Wilson's work has stayed within more practical time and space limits, as he has begun to direct—however unconventionally—more conventional works, including operas, and original pieces of mixed genre.

Wilson's work is not performance art in the strictest sense: his pieces have a theme, they are not improvised, and the performers usually (but not always) play characters other than themselves. But he shares with performance art a disdain for logical language and plot construction and a corresponding preference for combining music, movement, sculpture, video, painting, lighting, poetry, and human expressiveness. "I hate ideas," Wilson has said, and in their place he presents visions, dreams, and impressions. Frequent collaborators such as nō and kabuki specialist Suzushi Hanayagi and the autistic poet Christopher Knowles—a longtime Wilson friend—make non-Western and nontraditional contributions to most of Wilson's work, as do overscale props, ideographic and kinetic scenery, free intermixing of humans and puppets, utterly nontraditional casting, and, most characteristically, stage movements in extremely slow motion, as if the characters are wholly under water. Every aspect—even the sheer duration—of Wilson's work forces a re-examination of the nature of performance and the relationship of audience and art, meaning and aesthetics, making us question the very foundations of dramaturgy: Why do we watch theatre? What are we looking for? What do we care about?

Wilson now directs plays. Starting with Euripides' *Alcestis,* a visually stunning and magical production (featuring a mountain falling down in slow motion) at the American Repertory Theatre in Cambridge, Massachusetts, Wilson now works with professional actors, often in normal proscenium theatres. His 1995 adaptation of *Hamlet,* with Wilson himself playing

the title and various other roles, was set in a minimalist construction of black slabs against a horizon shifting from white to blue to red according to the prince's mood, presenting Shakespeare's text as a deathbed meditation on the play's confounding events and discoveries. His 1999 *The Days Before: Death, Destruction and Detroit III,* based on the Apocalypse and accompanied by seemingly unrelated texts by Italian philosopher Umberto Eco, seeks to create a "celebration of humanity" out of the grim Eco texts (read by actors Tony Randall and Fiona Shaw), nō dance, baboonlike "soldiers," Tibetan chanting, costumes parading across the stage (with no actors in them), a wing-flapping owl, and a rapacious red rooster. Wilson returned to animals for his recent production *Les Fables de La Fontaine,* at the Paris Comédie Française in 2004, for which Wilson selected and adapted nineteen of the beloved children's stories by

Robert Wilson's production of *Time Rocker,* an experimental musical work by Lou Reed and Darryl Pinckney, was originally created in Hamburg before its 1997 opening at the Paris Odeon – the Theatre of Europe. Wilson served, as he customarily does, as director and designer; his startlingly original theatrical visualizations, exemplified by this production photograph, have become celebrated worldwide.

the seventeenth-century French fabulist Jean de La Fontaine. Using fifteen actors from France's oldest and most celebrated theatre company (founded in 1680 by veterans of Molière's own troupe), Wilson clothed his cast in brilliantly imaginative animal masks and costumes, backed them with vivid lighting and stunning geometric designs, and, rare for him, directed them toward bold and sprightly movements, so that they virtually leaped and whirled their way through ancient fables such as "The Crow and the Fox," "The Grasshopper and the Ant," and "The Frog Who Wanted to Be as Big as the Ox." *The Fables* proved an enormous success in its premiere season and has now become a staple of the company's permanent repertory.

Wilson's newest work is *The Black Rider: The Casting of the Magic Bullets,* a musical theatre collaboration with composer Tom Waits and an international cast, which had its North American premiere at the American Conservatory Theatre in San Francisco. "If I had studied theatre," Wilson has said, "I would never make the

Nicolas Lormeau plays the Monkey Judge in Robert Wilson's 2004 creation of *Les Fables de La Fontaine* at the Comédie Française in Paris.

work I do." Though it may not be theatre, virtually everyone working in the contemporary theatre world knows of Wilson's work, and a great many are deeply influenced by it.

Bill Rauch and a Theatre of Community

While most of the theatre discussed and pictured in this book was created by trained professional artists, we must never forget that theatre's origins are located in performances created not by such professionals but by social communities—religious and ethnic—whose works were intended not for the entertainment of spectators but for the benefit, and often the rapture, of their own participants. The African dance-drama, the Egyptian resurrection plays, the Greek dithyrambs, and the medieval *Quem Queritis* trope were basically celebrations of their societies' cultures, and their performers were the primary celebrants.

Such theatres—whose works are created not only *for* a community but *by* that same community—continue today. Though they may eventually attract audiences, attain box-office income, and pay professional salaries, they are primarily expressions and celebrations—and sometimes critiques—of the cultures of their creators. In America, such groups have existed in tribal Native American cultures since before the landing of Columbus. In twentieth-century America, a number of "workers' theatres" in the 1930s created theatre pieces by and for the American worker, the most famous being Clifford Odets's *Waiting for Lefty* in 1935, produced by the Group Theatre, one of the country's first prominent theatre ensembles dedicated to social causes. Other focused theatre ensembles followed, many devoted not merely to creating theatre works by and for members of their community but also to touring their productions to localities previously unserved by the theatre at all. El Teatro Campesino (the "farmworkers' theatre"), founded by Luis Valdez in 1965, was one of these ensembles, bringing Chicano labor concerns to farming communities throughout

California's agricultural valleys. The Free Southern Theatre was another; founded in New Orleans by African American playwright John O'Neal in 1965, this racially integrated company toured black rural areas in the southeast United States as part of what became known as the Black Arts Movement of those turbulent times.

Unique in this movement, however, is the Cornerstone Theater, founded in 1986 by Harvard graduates Bill Rauch and Alison Carey. While the Cornerstone is an ensemble organization, with leadership generally shared among its members, its key figure since its founding has been Rauch, the company's artistic director as well as its principal stage director. Rauch's primary goal is to bring Cornerstone's core of professionally trained actors and designers into various communities around the country—often those without theatres of their own—and to ally with specific cultural groups in order to create new theatrical works (often based on classic dramas) specifically adapted to reflect each group's interests, fears, and aspirations. These works are then performed—by the merged Cornerstone and community groups—within the community, usually on a free or pay-what-you-can basis. The response is usually electric: not only are these works heralded as absorbing and entertaining; they initiate new cultural discourse and even social change in virtually every community where they have been engaged. Ben Cameron, director of the Theater Communications Group (the national organization of nonprofit professional theaters), reports that "Cornerstone is re-envisioning community activism. No one has ever done this work in this way. It's galvanizing, thrilling work."

Examples of Cornerstone's work are as varied as American culture itself. Here are a few examples:

- *Tartoof (Or, an Imposter in Norcatur):* Moliere's *Tartuffe,* adapted to examine a disintegrating farm family with a cast and crew of fifty-five Kansans and performed in Norcatur, Kansas (population 215).

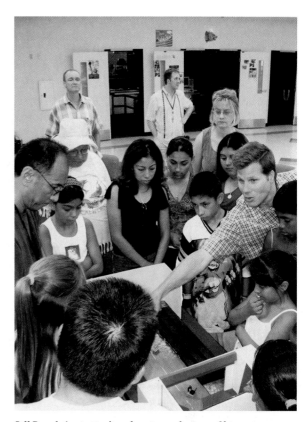

Bill Rauch (*pointing*) and costume designer Shigeru Yagi (*left, with glasses*) show the community actors a model of the scenery at the first rehearsal of *Waking Up in Lost Hills: A Central California Rip Van Winkle,* Cornerstone's 2004 theatre project in the Lost Hills farming village in California's Central Valley.

- *Three Sisters from West Virginia:* Chekhov's play, set in a contemporary Rust Belt city and performed in the basement of city hall in Montgomery, West Virginia (population 3,104), focusing on Appalachian out-migration.

- *Romeo & Juliet:* performed by a racially integrated cast in Port Gibson, Mississippi (population 2,371).

- *The House on Walker River:* an adaptation of Aeschylus's trilogy *The Oresteia,* in Schurz, Nevada (population 325), on the Walker River Paiute Indian Reservation.

At the Guthrie Theatre in 2003, Rauch directed Joan Holden's *Nickel and Dimed*, adapted from the nonfiction book by Barbara Ehrenreich. Both book and play describe the lives of America's working poor, and in the spirit of "theatre of community" the Guthrie lowered its ticket price to $2 for the region's working poor. Here Robynn Rodriguez plays Barb, a hotel room cleaner who makes $5.15 an hour and refuses to remain quiet about it.

- *A Community Carol* (created at Arena Stage): an adaptation of Dickens's classic *A Christmas Carol* involving residents of primarily African American communities east of the Anacostia River.

- *Steelbound:* adapted from Aeschylus's *Prometheus Bound,* featuring steelworkers at the defunct Bethlehem Steel plant in Pennsylvania and coproduced with the local Touchstone Theatre in a vacant factory building.

- *Candude, Or the Optimistic Civil Servant:* a musical adaptation of Voltaire's *Candide,* presented with and for employees of the Los Angeles Police Department, Metropolitan Transportation Authority, Los Angeles Public Library, and U.S. Postal Service as a roving, site-specific journey through Los Angeles's Central Library.

- *The Toy Truck:* adapted from a Sanskrit epic and performed in English, Spanish, Mandarin, and Korean with residents of the nation's largest low-income housing complex for seniors.

- *Ghurba:* a play based on stories of the Arab experience in Los Angeles, told through interviews with local residents citywide.

- *Los Vecinos:* an adaptation of the Mexican shepherds' play *La Pastorela,* performed by residents of East Los Angeles at the Boyle Heights Community Service Organization.

- *Mall Plays:* a festival of nine original works by previous community collaborators, performed in different Southern California shopping malls.
- *Waking Up in Lost Hills: A Central California Rip Van Winkle:* a Spanish/English *Rip Van Winkle,* created in collaboration with an almond-producing town in California's Central Valley.

Obviously these works are more than just "theatre"; they are social, cultural, and, in the broadest sense of the word, political events that have the potential—fulfilled much more often than not—of radically expanding interaction within and among previously disparate social groups. Theatre, Rauch declares, is "a rehearsal for changing the world." In asserting this, he reaches back to the most ancient role of theatre as the broadest possible community forum—not merely an entertainment for an elite "theatergoing" class, but a participatory ceremony involving truth, fiction, struggle, and art, welded together into performance and witnessing.

Moreover, Cornerstone's plays are also fresh *textual* creations, either adaptations of classics or wholly original texts, as developed in collaborations between Rauch, his professional company, and the nontheatrical members of the communities where he creates these works. Since the communities cocreate the plays, they also "co-own" them. Many of these works also win critical acclaim, prizes, and a life beyond their initial presentations. Rauch's production of *Chalk Circle,* an adaptation of Brecht's play performed by members of south Los Angeles's African American and Latino communities at the Watts Labor Community Action Committee Center, won the city's 1996 Ovation Award for Best Production of the Year, and his *Good Person of New Haven,* adapted from another Brecht play and produced in conjunction with the Long Wharf Theatre of New Haven and local amateur performers, was reviewed nationally and discussed at both academic and public conferences.

Cornerstone, which was an itinerant company during its first five years, moved to Los Angeles in 1992. Although it does not permanently occupy any single theatre and continues to tour nationally, it is now more connected with mainstream theatres, with which (like the Long Wharf) it occasionally presents collaborative "bridge" productions. Rauch himself has expanded his directing career to many of these companies, including the Oregon Shakespeare Festival (where he has directed Shakespeare, Ibsen, and two new plays by the Pulitzer Prize–winning playwright Robert Shenkkan), the California Mark Taper Forum and South Coast Repertory, and the Guthrie Theatre in Minneapolis. Rauch's conception and codirection (with Tracy Young) of his own play *Medea/Macbeth/ Cinderella* (combining elements of all three of these classic works) for the Yale Repertory Theatre won him the Connecticut Critics Circle Awards for both Best Play and Best Director of the Year. He has also begun to direct for television. Yet Rauch's primary commitment, even with these new venues, is to engage new communities with theatre at every level—the script, the performance, and the audience. As he says, "I am moved to make plays with the majority of our population who claim they have no stories to tell because I have learned that they always do. I am moved to make plays with people who have often never even seen a play because everyone is an artist, even if most of us have not had the opportunities and the privilege to find our artistic voice."

Susan Stroman, Matthew Bourne, Pina Bausch, Martha Clarke: Dance Theatre and Dance Play

Choreographers—and choreographer-directors—have become increasingly important in the musical theatre (see the previous chapter), but two of today's younger choreographer-directors have reconfigured the nature of theatre itself. They have also helped a new field, dance theatre, emerge into American consciousness.

Susan Stroman, by the first year of the new millennium, had virtually seized at least temporary control of the Broadway musical stage, winning every award in sight for her extraordinary choreography and direction of the hit Broadway productions of *The Producers, Contact,* and *The Music Man,* plus her choreography for the London (and then Broadway) revivals of Rodgers and Hammerstein's great 1943 classic, *Oklahoma!*—all within a three-year period! And in 2004, she directed and choreographed Nathan Lane and Stephen Sondheim's musical adaptation of Aristophanes' *The Frogs* at New York's Lincoln Center, for Broadway's first-ever production of an ancient Greek Old Comedy.

No overnight sensation, the Delaware native had arrived in New York back in the mid-1970s, dancing in road companies of *Chicago* and *Sugar Babies* until receiving her first choreographic assignment in the 1987 off-Broadway production of *Flora, the Red Menace.* She gained worldwide attention, and her first Tony Award, with her 1995 *Crazy for You*—a Broadway adaptation of George Gershwin's earlier *Girl Crazy* —which she followed with Broadway productions of *Show Boat, Big,* and *Steel Pier,* plus dance works for the New York City Ballet and the Martha Graham Company, before her meteoric four-show ascendancy of 1999–2001. What is remarkable about Stroman's choreography is its great humor, exuberance, inventiveness, and down-to-earth accessibility— across an enormously wide-ranging stylistic palette. A brilliantly clever deployment of props is as close as Stroman comes to having a trademark: dozens of farm implements in the country dance of *Crazy for You,* trays filled with dishes in the restaurant scene of *Contact,* eye-popping rope tricks in *Oklahoma!,* and old ladies "tap dancing" with metal walkers in *The Producers,* where pigeons also flap in comic unison and chorus girls pop out of file cabinets. But trademarks are not really what Stroman offers; rather, her work seems less about herself and more about a clever integration of choreography with storytelling. In her revival of *Music Man,* for example, she had Harold Hill, the

Susan Stroman directed and choreographed *Contact,* one of the biggest Broadway musical hits of the current century. Debra Yates is the dazzling dancer in the yellow dress who attracts the life-changing attention of Boyd Gaines (*spotlighted behind her*), who plays a burnt-out advertising exec.

title character, "teach" other characters the dance steps that eventually figured into the "Shipoopi" number, thus making what was previously strictly a dance interlude an integral part of the plotline. Now the *Music Man* characters "really have a musical journey," Stroman notes.

Contact has perhaps been Stroman's most important production to date. Billed as a "dance play" (with no singing, no original music, and

Matthew Bourne's *Car Man*, a sexy, powerful dance adaptation of Bizet's opera *Carmen*, is set in a diner that doubles as an auto repair shop (hence "car" man) in a mythic Harmony, USA of the 1960s. The original role of Carmen is split in two: Michaela Meazza plays Lena and Wean Wardrop is Luca in the 2000 London premiere.

Matthew Bourne's latest work to date, *Play without Words*, is a wordless movement theatre piece about class and sex in London's "swinging sixties," staged in 2002 by the esteemed director-choreographer at England's National Theatre.

only minimal speaking), it was nonetheless classified, by the Tony Awards committee among others, as musical theatre on the sheer strength of its vivid storytelling and the implicit passion of its characters. *Contact* consists of three separate pieces connected only by the theme of romantic linkups: *Swinging,* in which Fragonard's famous eighteenth-century French painting of a girl on a swing comes to life as a three-way sex romp; *Did You Move?,* a housewife's seriocomic fantasy in a chaotic, outer-borough, 1950s New York restaurant; and the title piece, *Contact,* in which an alcoholic and burnt-out advertising executive tries to commit suicide—after failing

to make contact, in a high-voltage dance club, with a supersexy lady dazzlingly dressed in brilliant yellow. Opening in the small downstairs theatre in New York's Lincoln Center, *Contact* quickly moved to the larger upstairs space and subsequently to a national tour, thrilling its audiences with the complexity, conviction, and intensity of its acting—rare for musical theatre of any sort and exceptionally rare for a theatre piece based principally on movement.

English-born Matthew Bourne has been choreographing for the stage since the late 1980s, with assignments at the London Palladium (*Oliver!*), Royal Shakespeare Company (*As You Like It*), Malmo (Sweden) City Theatre (*Show Boat*), and Los Angeles Ahmahnson (*Cinderella*), but his move into innovative dance theatre began with a series of radical adaptations of classical nineteenth-century ballets, including *Cinderella, La Sylphide,* the *Nutcracker,* and, most notably, *Swan Lake,* for which Bourne replaces the airy and delicate swan-ballerinas with bare-chested, buzz-cut men, muscular but amply feathered around the loins. "See it, or live to regret it!" said the *London Independent* after the British opening. Bourne's beautifully danced and beautifully acted version of this classic—possibly the world's best-known ballet, with music by Tchaikovsky—presents a young prince alternately coddled by his parents and servants (parodying current English royalty), seduced in a dream-fantasy by a flock of male swans, both brutal and tender; the famous pas de deux then becomes a homoerotic opus, turning romanticism on its head—and then back on its feet. *Swan Lake* won Bourne Tony Awards for both choreography and direction in 1999, an extraordinary achievement for a work that consists of nothing but dance.

Bourne followed *Swan Lake* with *Car Man: An Auto-Erotic Thriller* in 2000, restaging Bizet's opera *Carmen* and moving it from Spain to a diner/auto repair shop in a mythic 1960s Harmony, USA. *Car Man* is flagrantly sexual, violent, and raw; characters copulate on kitchen tables and bloody fights redden the stage.

Pina Bausch's latest work is *Nefes* (Turkish for "breath"), created by Bausch's Tanztheater Wuppertal, with music by Tom Waits. *Nefes*, shown here on its Paris tour, is a response to violence between both East and West and males and females. Peter Pabst's spare setting is a wooden slat floor over which water flows into a puddle; from it performers bathe, drink, and anoint themselves.

Bizet's music is reorchestrated for a percussion-heavy score, which blares forth (presumably) from an onstage jukebox, while the title role is now divided in two: one male and one female. And after *Car Man* came *Play without Words,* a dance-drama concerning social and sexual relationships during Britain's swinging sixties that premiered at England's National Theatre in 2003. Combining jazzy eroticism with a penetrating cultural critique, *Play* won Bourne Olivier Awards—the English theatre's most prestigious honor—for both Best Entertainment and Best Choreography and toured the United Kingdom after its limited London run, quite probably on its way to the United States and elsewhere abroad.

Bourne and Stroman have brought dance theatre squarely into the American dramatic mainstream. They did not, however, invent it: Pina Bausch defined such a form with her Tanztheater Wuppertal in Germany during the 1970s with works that were both playful and experimental but always underlaid with strains of contemporary human anguish. Recent glorious revivals of her *Sacre du Printemps* (about youthful sexual desire) and *Café Müller* (about troubled sexual relationships) added further luster to her legend, maintaining her at the forefront of the avant-garde, and her *Only You* (1997) and *The Window Washer* (1998) continue to dazzle audiences and influence stage directors around the world. Martha Clarke, a

Martha Clarke's production of Shakespeare's *A Midsummer Night's Dream* at the American Repertory Theatre in 2004 employs the dazzling aerial choreography – with technology operated by the cast in full view of the audience – that distinguishes much of her work.

veteran of the Pilobolus dance troupe, created two stunning dance-theatre pieces in the late 1980s: *The Garden of Earthly Delights,* based on a painting by Hieronymus Bosch, and *Vienna: Lusthaus,* evoking the artistic and sexual ferment of Vienna at the time of painter-designer Gustav Klimt. Clarke's latest work, *Belle Epoque,* portrays the jaded and erotic *demimonde* of the Moulin Rouge nightclub, as painted by nineteenth-century Parisian poster artist Henri de Toulouse-Lautrec; the dance-drama (a collaboration, as with *Vienna: Lusthaus,* with playwright Charles L. Mee) premiered at New York's

Lincoln Center in 2004. Dance theatre now has both history and Tony-certified prominence in the United States, and we can expect its achievement and influence to grow in the coming years.

STOMP, Blue Man Group, De La Guarda: Movement Art

Somewhere between performance art and dance theatre is a group performance based primarily on surprising movement techniques, where rhythm, sound, color, and pure athleticism reign over plot, character, and language. Many of these groups enjoy enormous popularity.

Collaborators since the early 1980s, Luke Cresswell, a percussionist and composer, and Steve McNichols, an actor and writer, created STOMP, a purely percussive performance piece in 1991; it proved a great success in both London and New York and has run ever since in those cities and many others around the world. STOMP employs, instead of drums, an assortment of garbage-can lids, pipes, brooms, and other everyday objects; its rhythms are furious, its choreography explosive, and its intensity relentless—and often comic. There is no story, no characters, and no dramatic impact, but the performers are young, diverse, and exciting and the sheer theatricality is captivating.

Blue Man Group is a similar storyless, percussion enterprise that also employs riotous clowning, interaction with the audience, and amazing food fights; it is performed by three head-shaved actors covered from the neck up in superglossy blue makeup. The group was created in New York City by former school pals Chris Wink, Matt Goldman, and Phil Stanton, first as improvised street theatre and then as staged performance art. The opening of their first full show, *Tubes,* at the small off-Broadway Astor Place Theatre in 1991 made the group a near-permanent fixture in the New York theatre scene—and a few years later the Boston and Chicago scenes as well. Now with television appearances (on *The Tonight Show,* at the Grammy Awards, and in frequent Intel commercials) and an expanded show, *Live at Luxor,* at a 1,200-seat Las Vegas showroom, the avant-garde troupe has become a very big business, with an annual budget of $28 million and a reported staff of 473. Blue Man Group revels in low technology: actors bang on homemade instruments, hurl marshmallows at each other (catching them in their mouths), and hold printed cards up to the audience to convey verbal thoughts or admonitions; they also invite audience members onstage—on some occasions to be hung upside down and pelted with various substances. Both of their shows, however, are continuously evolving, according to BMG's founders, and therefore anything you read about the shows may have changed before you see them.

De La Guarda, the most recent of these three movement art groups, opened their *Villa Villa* in New York's Daryl Roth Theatre in 1998; it is, at the moment of writing, still running and the group, like BMG, has opened another version in Las Vegas. *Villa Villa* combines dazzling elements of disco rock, rave parties, soaring aerial acrobatics, and all-weather immersion for cast and audience alike. This textless, intermission-less, ninety-minute wonder, which takes place largely above and sometimes amidst the audience—who are penned into a standing-room-only boxlike space—is most notable for its actors first whizzing around overhead, atop a translucent "cloud" of theatrical scrim, where only their angel-like silhouettes are glimpsed, and then plunging down through the "clouds" to grab audience members (presumably by pre-arrangement) and carry them up into the sky. Such soaring performers combine and recombine like swarming bees, hurling themselves into each other and the walls, often with orgasmic intensity (and accompanying gasps), all to pounding rock music played from above, fierce winds, and very wet rain that fills the room. The total effect is a vividly sensual kinetic surround; while there is no plot, there are implicit real-life inter-actions—flirtations, couplings, and dissolutions—among the cast, all costumed in ordinary street clothes. Created by unemployed recent theatre graduates from Buenos Aires, Argentina, De La Guarda's *Villa Villa* is destined, like the other shows in this section, for a long run and major influence in world theatrical movements.

Sherry Glaser, John Leguizamo, Karen Finley, Eric Bogosian, Anna Deveare Smith: Solo Performance

Although Anton Chekhov wrote a short play for a single actor (*On the Harmfulness of Tobacco,* in which the character is a lecturer addressing his audience), it has only been in recent times that authors have seriously entertained the possibilities of full-length plays employing a single actor. Sometimes these are little more than star vehicles or extended monologues, often based on historical characters, as, for example, Hal Holbrook's long-running portrayal of America's great writer in *Mark Twain Tonight,* James Whitmore's rendition of America's feisty thirty-third president in *Give 'Em Hell, Harry!,* and Julie Harris's recurrent tours as Emily Dickinson in *The Belle of Amherst.* More fully dramatized works followed in the 1990s, when Jay Presson Allen wrote two intriguing and generally successful Broadway plays for solo actors: *Tru,* about novelist and society darling Truman Capote in his despairing last days, performed by Robert Morse; and *The Big Love,* about the mother of Errol Flynn's mistress, played by Tracey Ullman. Also noteworthy in the 1990s were Willy Russell's *Shirley Valentine* (in which a frustrated middle-aged housewife tells us of leaving her English husband for a boatman on a Greek island), Lily Tomlin's portrayal of all seventeen characters in Jane Wagner's previously mentioned *Search for Signs* (reprised on Broadway in 2001), and Patrick Stewart's one-man presentation of Charles Dickens's *A Christmas Carol,* in which the celebrated Shakespearean actor (and *Star Trek* star) played all the roles.

The most recent strain of one-person shows, however, makes serious attempts at complex (and often comic) dramaturgy, often with an autobiographical basis. Sherry Glaser's seemingly plain but dramatically astonishing *Family Secrets,* for example, recounts the author's family story through the lively and racy monologues of five characters: Glaser, her mother, her sister, her father, and her grandmother—all played by Glaser, who transforms herself onstage, often in midsentence, with simple costume and makeup changes. Glaser's family secrets—some hilarious, some painful, and all poignant and provocative—revolve around sexual identity and ambiguity, religious absorption and assimilation, mental illness, menstruation, and childbirth.

Colombian-born and NYU-educated (as a theatre major) John Leguizamo has become one of America's leading solo writer-performers; his *Freak,* set in Leguizamo's childhood borough of Queens (New York), is a hugely comic and often deeply poignant autobiographical journey in which Leguizamo plays at least a dozen entirely distinct—and indelibly memorable—roles. The play was nominated for a 1998 Broadway Tony Award, and his solo follow-up, *Sexaholix . . . A Love Story,* received wide praise at its 2001 Broadway premiere. Both of Leguizamo's solo performances have been subsequently

The late Spalding Gray reinvented solo performance in the 1980s and 1990s by simply (though with immense artistry) telling stories of his life. He is shown here – alone with desk, microphone, and water glass – in his *Morning, Noon and Night* at New York's Lincoln Center in 1999.

filmed for television. Leguizamo now performs mainly in films and as a stand-up entertainer, but his stand-up routines often evolve into titled solo plays, as was the case with *Sexaholix.*

Karen Finley's 1990 solo performance, *We Keep Our Victims Ready,* in which the artist smeared her naked body with chocolate to represent the exploitation and sexual abasement of women, earned unwanted notoriety when national columnists portrayed her performance as indecent. The ensuing furor cost Finley future grants and even occasioned congressional threats, fortunately short-lived, to terminate the National Endowment for the Arts funding that had supported her work. But Finley has prevailed over many of her detractors with subsequent performances that expand upon the themes of self-exposure and self-degradation, presenting human eroticism together with its inherent ironies. In a 1999 performance of *Shut Up and Love Me* (and Finley's performances are never the same from night to night or year to year), the artist again smeared herself with chocolate, this time inviting audience members to lick it off her (at $20 a lick, to compensate for the loss of her funding); in a 2001 performance of the same work, she covered herself entirely in honey, turning herself into what one reviewer called "the ultimate objectified woman." By confronting viewers with their own lust—and consequent disgust—Finley creates a vividly memorable unease. In her latest work, *Make Love, the Distribution of Empathy* (in development and touring at this writing), Finley—now known as the "godmother of performance art"—combines post–September 11 reflections with representations of Liza Minnelli, as performed by Finley and several collaborators, male and female, including Finley's ten-year-old daughter. "What I'm dealing with now is unresolved childhood traumas disguised as national mourning," Finley reports about this show, in which Minnelli represents the irrepressible spirit of survival through performance.

Eric Bogosian's series of intense and penetrating performances, savage and comic by turns, has created an indelible cast of American low-life characters—pimps and whores, addicts and agents, executives and rock stars, panhandlers and jocks—in his increasingly brilliant collection of solo evenings, variously titled *Drinking in America; Sex, Drugs, and Rock & Roll; Pounding Nails in the Floor with My Forehead;* and *Wake Up and Smell the Coffee.*

Anna Deveare Smith, in two works, *Fires in the Mirror* and *Twilight: Los Angeles 1992,* has taken the personal one-woman play to new levels altogether, with performances of the latter play moving from the Mark Taper Forum in Los Angeles (which commissioned it) to the New York Public Theatre and then to Broadway, where it was nominated for two Tony Awards and the Pulitzer Prize. Smith writes of and performs specific urban events that focus on fundamental problems of contemporary American society, particularly racism. *Fires* centers on the many days of rage in Crown Heights, Brooklyn, that followed the violent deaths of Gavin Cato (an African American) and Yankel Rosenbaum (a Hassidic Jew). *Twilight* concerns the Los Angeles riots that followed the acquittal of white police officers charged with the beating of a black motorist, Rodney King. In both pieces, Smith excerpted personal interviews with hundreds of individuals who lived through these city-defining events. Using minimal props and costume elements, Smith transforms herself into an entire cast of characters for each social upheaval, creating, in one critic's words, "pure, unbiased, tumultuous symphonies." Smith's most recent performance reaches further back into history. Premiered as a solo work at New York's Public Theatre in 2000 (although earlier staged by Smith elsewhere with a cast of actors), *House Arrest* concerns American presidents (notably Jefferson, Lincoln, F. D. Roosevelt, Kennedy, and Clinton) amidst a host of cultural and media celebrities (Walt Whitman, Studs Terkel, Arianna Huffington) who expose the presidents' contradictions. Smith limits herself to dramatizing actual historical documents and verbatim transcriptions in this solo work, which powerfully illumines darker corners of American thoughts and practices concerning the interfaces of race, sex, politics, idealism, and democracy over the past 150 years. Smith's newest play, *Piano,* published in 2004 by Random House, concerns "race, sex and exploitation" in Cuba prior to the Spanish-American War and has been presented at the Institute on the Arts and Civic Dialogue. She spends a good deal of her time now, however, as an actor (on television's *West Wing* and *The Practice* and in the feature film *The Human Stain*) and as a professor at New York University.

Two American Directors: Julie Taymor and Mary Zimmerman

Nothing really prepared the theatre world for the colossal triumph of Julie Taymor's Disney-produced *The Lion King* in 1998. Taymor, born in Newton, Massachusetts, in 1953, was known at the time strictly as an avant-garde director, designer, and choreographer who, having studied in Paris and Indonesia, had developed a professional reputation for cutting-edge productions of classical plays (*Titus Andronicus, The Tempest, The Taming of the Shrew, King Stag*), primarily at off-Broadway's Theatre for a New Audience and the American Repertory Theatre in Cambridge, Massachusetts. *The Lion King,* with its giant corporate producer, far exceeded any scale on which Taymor had previously operated; its production budget ($20 million—an all-time Broadway record) was doubtless more than the budgets for all her previous productions combined. But *Lion King* turned the commercial and avant-garde American theatre upside down.

With *The Lion King,* Taymor animated the vast African plain, employing more than fifty performers and a hundred puppets to represent twenty-five species of animals, birds, fish, and insects. In the spectacular opening scene, 26-foot giraffes lope soulfully across the stage,

gazelles leap in staggered unison, and a 13-foot-long elephant, more than 11 feet high, makes an astonishing entrance down the auditorium aisle—while birds fly and court in midair, warthogs wobble close to the ground, wildebeests stampede, grasses spring from the soil, flowered vines descend from the trees, and an enormous, latticed sun rises to reveal the radiant African dawn.

In this glorious work, Taymor ingeniously mixes Javanese rod puppetry, Balinese headdresses, African masks, American and British music (much of it written by Elton John), and the Disney style of family entertainment; she also incorporates South African music and lyrics in various African languages—particularly the click language of Xhosa (performed by Tsidii Le Loka from South Africa, as Rafiki the baboon sorceress)—with the confidence that a literal understanding of a musical's libretto (text) is not at all times strictly necessary. But the individual signature of Taymor in *The Lion King* is how she openly reveals the theatricality of the puppetry and the musicality of the production rather than hiding them to maintain a realistic illusion. Her puppets' heads are located well above the faces of the actors who wear them so that the audience is continually aware of the actors manipulating (and often speaking for) each animal; all of the strings, wheels, and sticks of the puppetry mechanics are in full sight. And the orchestra is not wholly buried in a pit below the stage but, rather, extends to costumed African drummers and chanters in the audience boxes that frame the action.

The Lion King opened to rapturous reviews from even the most hardened New York critics—winning for Taymor Tony Awards for both directing and costume design. At the time of this writing, it is playing in eight cities in the United States and abroad in London, Hamburg, Sydney, Scheveningen (Netherlands), Tokyo, and Nagoya (Japan). "I think *The Lion King* bridges the divide between Broadway and avant-garde theatre," Taymor has said, "and

I am delighted that my work, which has been characterized as 'too downtown' or 'too sophisticated,' is now going to be seen by the widest possible audience." Most in the theatre world are equally delighted at (if not a little nervous because of) this merger of experimental and intercultural innovation with broad public appeal and international corporate financing, which Taymor shows no sign of abandoning; indeed, she is next scheduled to direct the Broadway musical of *Spiderman* and has recently extended her directing career into major feature films—*Titus* in 1999 and *Frida,* about the life of Mexican artist Frida Kalho, in 2002.

Mary Zimmerman's most unique theatre works are theatrical adaptations of nondramatic texts, including, so far, *The Notebooks of Leonardo da Vinci, The Odyssey,* and Ovid's *Metamorphoses.* A professor of performance studies (not drama) at Northwestern University, Zimmerman follows that program's emphasis (made famous by Frank Galati) of adapting narrative texts for theatrical performance, while lending them an exceptionally striking visual and choreographic presence. *Metamorphoses* is perhaps her most impressive work to date, in which Ovid's famous (and some not-so-famous) stories are staged on, in, and around a square-bordered pool of water that—backed by a stately door, horizontal screen of painted clouds, and towering waterfall—occupies virtually the entire stage. In Zimmerman's pool, Ovid's legendary

Julie Taymor's *The Lion King* forges a profound alliance between experimental theatre, African ritual, Asian dance and puppetry, and American mass-market entertainment (namely, the Disney Corporation and Broadway). Here, South African vocalist Tsidii Le Loka plays the role of Rafiki, the singer-narrator, amidst leaping gazelles and a menagerie of other animals.

and often fantastical characters do everything: swim, float, splash, thrash, drown, paddle, bathe, fight, make love, wash their clothes, study their reflections, and, in general, get sopping wet. Yet Zimmerman does not simply rely on theatrical novelty or physical sensationalism; in *Metamorphoses* the despair of Alcyon for her drowned lover, Ceyx, is heartbreaking, while their resurrection as a pair of seabirds is ethereally lovely. And the passionate carnality of Eros and Psyche, and of Myrrha and her father, Cinyras, contains lusty fires that mere water cannot douse. *Metamorphoses* came to New York in 2001 and *Notebooks* in 2003. Zimmerman's *The Secret in the Wings,* based on fairy tales, will be appearing at the Seattle Repertory when this book is published. Zimmerman's

narrative adaptations have visual poetry galore, creating stories of genuinely mythic poignancy.

Three European Directors: Peter Brook, Ariane Mnouchkine, Frank Castorf

Today's European theatre is generally more highly subsidized by government support than is American theatre, and it is likewise more responsive to cultural (as opposed to commercial) expectations from its audience. For these and other reasons, most European stage directors have greater opportunity (and perhaps desire) than their American counterparts to create radical staging innovations in working with—and often deconstructing—classical dramatic texts.

Mary Zimmerman's *The Notebooks of Leonardo da Vinci,* mixing Renaissance science with postmodern observation, was warmly received at its 2003 New York premiere, directed by the author.

Three such directors, each at the helm of a permanent company of actors and designers and thus able to expend greater sums over a much larger rehearsal/preparation period than exists in the United States, have among them created an immensely original body of startling theatre works that tour internationally. Peter Brook and Ariane Mnouchkine, born in 1925 and 1939 respectively, are the elders of this group, each making their longtime headquarters in Paris, where they work with international casts in unconventional performing spaces. The younger Frank Castorf, born in 1951, makes his base in Berlin and represents a new type of German-language director, noted for radically reconfiguring classic dramatic texts and/or crisscrossing the boundaries of artistic and literary disciplines in the creation of both wholly new works and adaptations.

PETER BROOK: THE INTERNATIONAL CENTER OF THEATRE RESEARCH

No director was more influential in the latter half of the twentieth century or is more provocative in the current theatre than the English-born Peter Brook. Brook began his directorial career with freshly conceived experimental productions of Shakespeare, Marlowe, Sartre, and Jean Cocteau, receiving sufficient attention to be appointed, at the age of twenty, to direct at the Shakespeare Memorial Theatre at Stratford-upon-Avon, where his 1955 *Hamlet* was the first English play to tour the Soviet Union. Within a short time, Brook was staging plays (including classics), a Broadway musical (*House of Flowers*), and operas at the major performing venues—Covent Garden, Broadway, the Metropolitan Opera—of London and New York.

Brook's heart remained in experimental theatre, however, and in three landmark productions with the newly founded Royal Shakespeare Company at Stratford in the 1960s, he received immense international acclaim. These productions—Shakespeare's *King Lear* (1962), deeply influenced by Beckett and the theatre of the absurd; Peter Weiss's *Marat/Sade* (1964), a produc-

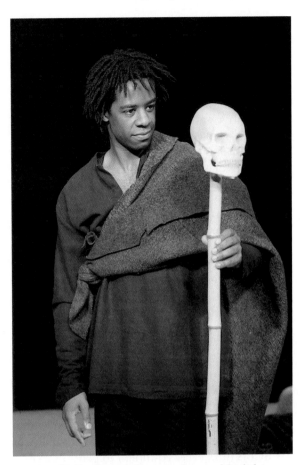

Peter Brook's *Hamlet*, with Jamaican-born and English-trained Adrian Lester in the title role, was coproduced by Brook's International Center of Theatre Research and the Vienna *Festwochen* with an international cast and toured widely in 2001, including stops in Seattle and New York. Design is by Chloe Obolensky.

tion blending Artaud's notion of a theatre of cruelty with Brecht's theatre of alienation; and *US* (1966), a company-improvised documentary commenting on American (i.e., "U.S." as "us") involvement in Vietnam—toured widely, and both *Lear* and *Marat/Sade* were subsequently filmed, thereby receiving even wider exposure.

Brook's subsequent publication of *The Empty Space*, in 1968, extended his reputation to theory, presenting a brilliant analysis of modern drama. Brook divides the current theatre into three categories: "deadly, holy, and rough" (corresponding, more or less, to conventional, Artaudian, and Brechtian). Rejecting all three, he culminates his study with a manifesto on behalf of an "immediate" theatre, one not preplanned by the director but developed through a creative and improvisational process, "a harrowing collective experience" rather than a dispassionate assemblage of the separate contributions of cast and designers. Brook then proved his point with an amazingly comic, penetrating, original, and "immediate" version of Shakespeare's *A Midsummer Night's Dream* in 1970, a production that—staged without sentimentality on a bare white set—combined circus techniques with uninhibited sexual farce, creating fresh interactions between the play's very familiar (though often shallowly realized) characters. Brook's *Dream* captivated critics and audiences throughout Europe and America during the early 1970s, further establishing him as one of the most creative and talented theorist–theatrical practitioners of all time.

Brook walked away from all of this, however, in 1971, moving to Paris and creating the International Center of Theatre Research, which he continues to head. Engaging a company of actors from every continent to perform mostly in French, in a long-abandoned, dirt-floored theatre (the Bouffes du Nord, located in the African quarter of Paris), Brook has produced a series of intercultural works of extraordinary interest, including *The Iks* (about a northern Ugandan tribe), *The Conference of the Birds* (based on a twelfth-century Persian poem), Alfred Jarry's *Ubu Roi,* Georges Bizet's opera *Carmen,* a production of Shakespeare's *The Tempest,* and, most remarkably, *The Mahabharata,* which opened in Paris in 1986 and which Brook filmed for worldwide audiences in 1991. *The Mahabharata* is the national novel of India, ancient, archetypal, and immense (it is the longest single work of world literature); Brook had it adapted into a nine-hour play, which he initially staged with an international cast in a rock quarry in the south of France, and subsequently at his

Bouffes du Nord. Brook blends the text with a myriad of natural (but not naturalistic) elements: actors wade in pools and rivers of real water trapped by circles of real fire; chariot wheels are mired in the real mud of the Bouffes du Nord stage; armies clash by torchlight; and candles float in the pond. The multifaceted reality of this Indian epic—directed by an Englishman, in French, with an intercontinental cast—lends a universality to the production that leaves the audience fulfilled in ways previously unrealized in the theatre's history.

Brook's most recent work studies the individual human mind and includes notable productions of such works as *The Man Who,* a 1994 adaptation of Dr. Oliver Sacks's study of neurological illness; a 1998 Parisian staging of a new play, *I Am a Phenomenon,* concerning a Russian man with a wizardlike memory; and *Le Costume,* a South African play by Can Themba about a ménage à trois that consists of a man, his wife, and her lover's suit of clothes. His substantially abridged *Hamlet,* which toured to the United States in 2001, became his first production in English in decades and featured an intercultural cast: Jamaican-born Adrian Lester in the title role, the Indian Shantala Shivalingappa as Ophelia, and the English Natasha Parry (Brook's wife) as Gertrude, all of whom are accompanied by a string and percussion score composed and performed onstage by Japanese musician Toshi Tsuchitori. And Brook's most recent production, *Tierno Bokar* (2004), continues his interculturalism. Based on the writing of the late African writer Amadou Hampaté Bâ and coauthored by the British Brook and the French Marie-Hélène Estienne, the play takes place in an Islamic and animist African village, torn asunder in the global tumult of World War II. Furthering its internationalism, *Tierno Bokar* opened in Germany, toured to Spain, and then opened in Paris at Brook's Bouffes du Nord. At 79, Brook remains one of the most adventurous and fascinating creators of the theatrical avant-garde.

ARIANE MNOUCHKINE: THÉÂTRE DE SOLEIL

Like Brook, director Ariane Mnouchkine disdains conventional theatres, and her troupe, the Théâtre de Soleil, performs in the Cartoucherie—an abandoned munitions factory just outside of Paris. Even more than Brook, Mnouchkine is celebrated for mixing Eastern themes and performing traditions with Western works. And she has gone much further than Brook in dispensing with traditional theatrical hierarchy in favor of creative collaboration: in the Soleil, all productions emerge from an extended process of improvisation, discussion, and group study, with all twenty-five members of her company—who live and work together as a community—sharing the various responsibilities of research, scriptwriting, staging, interpretation, design, construction, and even house management. Indeed, all company members are allocated the same salary—including Mnouchkine, who, perhaps alone among the world's artistic directors, has steadily worked to diminish the formal status of the director in the theatre. (Even today, at the height of her fame, Mnouchkine might be tearing the tickets at the door or clearing away paper plates at the theatre's buffet bar.) The audience, too, is treated as a participant at Soleil performances; before each show, the actors put on their costumes and makeup in open dressing areas located beneath the audience gallery, where they chat quietly with each other and with entering spectators.

Under Mnouchkine, the Soleil earned national esteem in the early 1970s for a trilogy of plays, titled *1789, 1793,* and *The Golden Age,* that traced major events of the French Revolution. And the Soleil's reputation broadened immeasurably in the early 1980s with a trilogy of Asian-inspired Shakespearean productions—particularly a kabuki-inspired *Richard II* and a kathakali-inspired *Twelfth Night* that were also performed to great acclaim at the 1984 Los Angeles Olympics. In the 1990s, Mnouchkine extended her play groupings to a tetralogy of ancient Greek plays—Euripides' *Iphigeneia at Aulis* followed by the three plays of Aeschylus's *Oresteia,* collectively titled *The House of Atreus* (*Les Atrides*). "You will be fortunate if you ever see a more exhilarating production of the first great tragedies in European drama," said the *New York Times* of this production.

Mnouchkine's work seeks a new language of theatre, based in equal parts on Artaudian freedom, Brechtian political commitment, collective improvisation, a commitment to multiplay series, and a passionate commitment to interculturalism, whereby Eastern performance traditions are blended with Western texts. A 1995 production of Molière's *Tartuffe,* employing an international and interracial cast, is a thrilling revisitation of religious hypocrisy as seen in the light of North African Islamic fundamentalism.

Four subsequent Asian-themed plays by Hélène Cixous—*Norodom Sihanouk,* about Cambodia; *L'Indiade,* about India; *Suddenly, Nights of Awakening,* about Tibet; and *Drums on the Dyke,* about China—each dealing with political, gender, and ethnic issues, combine ancient themes with contemporary struggles on Mnouchkine's stylized stage. *Drums on the Dyke,* for example, a play for masked actors who are "operated" like marionettes, with continuous music and sound played on Asian instruments, is based on a 4,000-year-old work by legendary Chinese poet Hsi-Xhou, exploring the relations between humans and nature as the ancient Chinese try to contain the rampaging Yellow and Blue rivers. In fact, however, the play was inspired by the current Beijing government's deliberate flooding of large areas of farmland without warning its local citizens. Like its name, the Soleil (meaning "the sun") brings both light and heat to the pressing issues of our time.

FRANK CASTORF: BERLIN VOLKSBÜHNE

After studying dramaturgy at Humboldt University in East Berlin, Frank Castorf earned a strong public following with startling productions of classical dramas (Sophocles' *Ajax,* Ibsen's *A Doll's House* and *Enemy of the People,*

Ariane Mnouchkine, one of the truly revolutionary directors of modern France, has mounted dozens of astonishing productions at her company's home in the Paris suburb of Vincennes, as well as throughout Europe, Asia, the United States, and Canada. Mnouchkine's fame is largely based on her many East-West "fusion" productions. Mnouchkine's *Les Atrides*, shown here, was a pan-Asian version of the Greek Atreus plays (mainly Aeschylus's *Oresteia* and Euripides' *Iphigenia at Aulis*), with Armenian, Brazilian, Indian, and even French actors; it toured Europe and America in the late 1980s.

Shakespeare's *Othello* and *Hamlet,* Goethe's *Tasso*) and adaptations of novels (Anthony Burgess's *A Clockwork Orange*) at major theatres throughout Germany in the 1980s, leading to his current appointment, as artistic director of the Berlin Volksbühne ("people's theatre") in 1992. There, and increasingly in guest productions throughout Europe, Castorf's reputation has soared, as has the controversy his works induce. "A master of ruination" is one of the critical brickbats he has faced.

Castorf's first directorial act is to dismember the script. Improvising with the actors, he fragments and reconstructs the text as virtually a new work, often unrecognizable from its for-

mer self. Characters are deleted, combined, and added; speeches are rewritten, translated into different languages, or turned into songs; words are changed, chanted, and often repeated (all but endlessly); gestures and stage business are freely invented; music and songs are freely interpolated; and whole story lines are eliminated while wholly new ones emerge. Castorf's production of *Endstation Amerika* (2001) is a classic example of this process: An adaptation of Tennessee Williams's *A Streetcar Named Desire* (the Williams estate required that the title be changed for this presentation), the cast has been drastically pared to six characters—Stanley and Stella, Blanche and Mitch, Steve and

Eunice—of whom are given approximately the same weight in the play's action, which now centers on three dysfunctional couples. Themes of sexual longings and abuse remain but are largely switched around: Stanley (played by the young and sultry Marlon Brando in the famous 1948 New York premiere) is here presented as a violent, middle-aged, beer-bellied thug, a Polish veteran of the anticommunist Solidarity movement, while a hyperanimated Stella, not a predatory Blanche, is now his principal victim. Music adds a constant (and wholly new) theme: Steve lugs his base viol around the house, joining with Stanley on his guitar, in a rendition (in

English) of Lou Reed's "Just a Perfect Day." Eunice spouts cultural commentary in French, while Mitch, as if imagining himself a character in Alfred Hitchcock's *Psycho,* carts what he believes is his mother's corpse around the stage in a wheelchair. Responding to Blanche's accusation that he's an animal, Stanley saunters into their home in a head-to-toe gorilla suit. *Endstation*'s design is deconstructed as well. The garish and trashy set consists of a narrow one-room flat, divided from right to left into kitchen, bathroom door, and double bed, but we're invited to see right into the bathroom—where Stella changes her clothes and Mitch takes a (real)

Frank Castorf's radical reconstruction of Tennessee Williams's *A Streetcar Named Desire,* retitled *Endstation Amerika* at the Berlin Volksbühne in 2001, alters dialogue, characters, situation, and language but retains, and in some cases expands and intensifies, fundamental aspects of the characters' relationships. *From left:* Stanley (Henry Hübchen) is now a rock guitarist, Stella (Kathryn Angerer) is his abused and deeply disturbed wife, and Mitch (Bernhard Schütz) and Steve (Fabian Himrichs) complete Stanley's musical combo. The video monitor shows what is happening in the bathroom behind the door.

shower—on a large-screen video monitor facing the audience. When, in the final scene, the reality of the characters' lives turns topsy-turvy, the entire set suddenly tilts a full 45 degrees backward, with the actors sliding awkwardly against its back wall. At the play's end, the actors are scrambling up the "floor"—which is now a virtual fourth wall of their apartment—to show their heads while they speak to one another and to nod at the audience during the riotous curtain call. And amazingly, all of this works, in its fashion, showing a world in which there is tenderness and carnality, romance and commercialism, interethnic violence and attraction that Williams himself probably would have admired (even if his estate attorneys did not).

Since taking over the Volksbühne, Castorf has vastly expanded the theatre's namesake mission. Intermixed with the company's stage productions, an ambitious series of public discussions, symposia, lectures, films, and rock and electronic music concerts are also presented there on a regular basis, and new films are beginning to emerge from an on-premises film studio initiated in 2000. The Volksbühne, located in the heart of old—and newly fashionable—Mitte ("central") Berlin, is clearly a place not merely for deconstructing classic dramas but also for reconstructing—or at least reinvigorating—urban German culture at large.

Theatre of Today: Where Can You Find It?

The current theatre happens all over the world: in villages, campuses, prisons, resorts, and parks; at local and international festivals; on ocean liners and at suburban dinner theatres; on temporary stages in rural churchyards or within historic ruins; and, increasingly, at so-called site-specific venues, such as a Manhattan apartment, a worker's meeting hall, or, in the case of one recent Russian production, an interurban railway car.

But mostly current theatre is found in cities—particularly in the traditionally great theatrical capitals such as New York City, Moscow, London, Paris, Vienna, Toronto, Tokyo, Budapest, and Berlin, as well as in cities of more modest theatrical repute, such as Kyoto, Zurich, Munich, Edinburgh, Milan, Buenos Aires, Johannesburg, Helsinki, Mexico City, Chicago, San Francisco, Seattle, Minneapolis, New Haven, Louisville, Los Angeles, Hartford, Boston, and Washington, D.C.

In the United States, New York City is without question the primary locus of the nation's theatrical activity. Every year Manhattan is the site of more performances, more openings, more revivals, more tours, and more dramatic criticism than any half-dozen other American cities put together; theatrically, it is the showcase of the nation. In the minds of many Americans, the Big Apple is simply *the* place to experience theatre; thus the town's hundred-plus playhouses are a prime tourist attraction and a major factor in the local economy. And in the minds of most theatre artists—actors, directors, playwrights, and designers—New York is the town where the standards are the highest, the challenge the greatest, and the rewards the most magnificent. "Will it play in Peoria?" may be the big question in the minds of film and television producers, but "Will it make it in New York?" remains a cardinal concern in the rarefied world of American professional theatre. Therefore the reality of New York is surrounded by a fantasy of New York, and in a "business" as laced with fantasy as is the theatre, New York commands a strategic importance of incomprehensible value.

Broadway

Mapmakers know Broadway as the longest street in Manhattan, slicing diagonally down the entire length of the New York City island borough. Virtually everybody else, however, knows it as the historic apex of the American theatre, the "Great White Way" (referring to its bright lights), and few tourists anywhere in the world head to New York City without hoping to catch a Broadway play. What a "Broadway play" is today, however, is not always what it was in the past.

New York theatre has always been near Broadway, but at first it was much farther downtown, beginning with the 1798 Park, which was built at the junction of Broadway and the Bowery. Early-nineteenth-century theatres congregated twenty-some blocks north around Union Square at 14th Street, and Edwin Booth's magnificent Booth's Theatre was built in 1869 just off Broadway on 23rd Street. It wasn't until 1893 that the American theatre began to develop around Longacre (now Times) Square, at Broadway and 42nd Street, but the great number of theatres built in that district, almost all within a couple of decades, made for a concentration of theatrical excitement still unique in the world. Between the 1920s and 1960s, it was the place where Eugene O'Neill, Arthur Miller, Tennessee Williams, William Inge, and Edward Albee all saw their masterpieces first produced; where memories of George M. Cohan, Ethel Merman, Mary Martin, and Barbra Streisand—Broadway Babies all —sang and danced through the twentieth century; and where John Barrymore, Marlon Brando, Helen Hayes, Henry Fonda, Alfred Lunt, Lynn Fontanne, and thousands of others acted their way into America's hearts and, subsequently, into Hollywood's films.

Much of the Broadway theatre district fell into urban decay after World War II, however, becoming a haven for sex shops, crack houses, porno movie theatres, and videogame parlors for the best part of a generation. Theatres closed down or were converted to movie houses, churches, or television studios, and tourists were frightened away by what had seemingly become a sleazy, crime-ridden part of town. Massive redevelopment, however, at the end of the century, including the reclaiming of 42nd Street from drugs and prostitution by the restoration and construction of the New Amsterdam, New Victory, and American Airlines

Theatres, restored the district to much of its former glory—only to be halted, if temporarily, by the crushing impact of the September 11 attacks on New York in 2001, which closed the theatres for four days and threatened to challenge the city's effort to reclaim its artistic centrality for an indefinite period.

Happily, the Broadway district has recovered intact, and at the time of writing is enjoying its most commercially successful years in history, with attendance averaging over 206,000 per week—up 33 percent since the mid-1990s— and ticket income more than doubled; there is little question but that the district is once again a glamorous, vibrant center for mainstream legitimate theatre and, arguably, the single most important focal point of America's cultural life.

Broadway's lure is its dazzling visual and social excitement, its heady mix of bright lights and famed celebrities, and its trend-setting fashions, big-buck entertainments, and high-toned Tony Awards. The stakes are higher on Broadway than anywhere else in theatre; if you can make it there, as the song says, you'll make it anywhere, and the energy that this lyric connotes—and attracts—makes the Broadway district unforgettably fascinating.

It is no longer, however, the place where new plays ordinarily originate, as it was in 1947, when Tennessee Williams's *A Streetcar Named Desire* and Arthur Miller's *All My Sons* debuted there. Rather, Broadway has primarily become the staging ground for extravagantly produced musicals, both new ones (such as *Mamma Mia, Hairspray,* and *Avenue Q*) and revivals (*Fiddler on the Roof*). Secondarily, it is the showcase for the best (or at least most commercially promising) new plays from America's off-Broadway and regional theatres (such as David Auburn's *Proof* from the Manhattan Theatre Club, Tony Kushner's *Caroline, or Change* from the New York Public Theatre, and Bryony Lavery's *Frozen* from MCC Theatre), as well as new plays from abroad (such as Tom Stoppard's *The Invention of Love,* Michael Frayn's *Copenhagen,* Martin McDonagh's *The Beauty*

Rain does little to dissuade eager theatergoers from lining up at the New York TKTS booth, where half-price, same-day tickets go on sale for dozens of Broadway and off-Broadway shows playing that day. The booth is located at Broadway and 47th Street, within a five-minute walk of about twenty theatres and flanked by ads for currently running shows.

Queen of Leenane, Marie Jones's *Stones in His Pockets,* and Yasmina Reza's *Art*). Finally, it is the site of major revivals of classic dramas from the American and international repertory (Arthur Miller's *After the Fall,* Eugene O'Neill's *Long Day's Journey into Night,* and Tom Stoppard's *Jumpers*). Occasionally, too, you will find a star-heavy revival of a world classic on Broadway, as in 2004, with Olympia Dukakis in Aeschylus's *Agamemnon* and Christopher Plummer in Shakespeare's *King Lear.*

As mentioned, rarely does a new play by a young playwright premiere on Broadway; the costs are ordinarily far too high to risk on an unknown author. And despite high ticket prices,

which in 2004 ascended to as much as $90 for straight plays and $100 for musicals (and a near-astronomical $480 for selected seats at *The Producers*), most new productions on Broadway are, in fact, financial failures. Increasingly, therefore, Broadway producers await the new plays whose worth has first been "proven" in the subsidized European (chiefly English) theatre or on the not-for-profit American regional stage. Only the star-studded revival or Tony Award–winning new musical is otherwise likely to be "bankable" and offer sufficient opportunity for commercial success. And Broadway, once at the cutting edge of the American theatre, is its glamorous but somewhat expectable museum.

Anika Noni Rose exults with her 2004 Tony Award for Best Featured Actress in a Musical, which she won for playing Caroline's daughter in Tony Kushner's *Caroline, or Change.*

Off-Broadway and Off-Off-Broadway

Not all of New York theatre is performed within the geographic and commercial confines of the Broadway district, however. There are literally hundreds of theatres far from the Great White Way. The symbolic centrality of Broadway, however, is so strong that these theatres are named not for what they are but for what they are not: they are "off-Broadway" theatres. *Off-Broadway,* a term that came into theatrical parlance during the 1950s, refers to professional theatres operating on significantly reduced budgets. They are found primarily in Greenwich Village, with some in the area south of Houston Street (SoHo) and others on the upper East and West

sides of Manhattan. A few houses in the Broadway geographic area itself actually fall into this category (American Place, Manhattan Theatre Club, New 42nd Street), but only because they operate under off-Broadway financing structures. Yet another category of theatre is known as *off-off-Broadway,* a term dating from the 1960s that denotes semiprofessional or even amateur theatres located in the metropolitan area, often in church basements, YMCAs, coffeehouses, and converted studios or garages.

Off- and off-off-Broadway theatres generate a great deal of fertile and vigorous activity. Leaner and less costly than the Broadway stage, they attract specialized cadres of devotees, some of whom would never allow themselves to be seen in a Broadway house. Much of the original creative work in the American theatre since World War II has been done in these theatres, and their lower ticket prices, and in many cases subscription seasons, have lured successive generations of theatre audiences their way to see original works before they are showcased to the Broadway masses, works still raw with creative energy and radiating the excitement of their ongoing development. Indeed, the American Theatre Wing has come under increasing criticism for limiting its annual Tony Awards solely to plays presented on Broadway, since in any given year the majority of critically well-received dramas—if not musicals—are more likely to be seen off Broadway than on.

In composite, the New York theatre provides almost every conceivable opportunity for theatrical exploration and achievement, offering close to a thousand new productions each year. And thanks to coverage in the national media—weekly news magazines, monthly journals, television talk shows and specials, and the annual televising of the Tony Awards ceremonies—the New York theatrical season does not long remain a strictly local phenomenon; it becomes a focal point of American cultural activity, and, before long, the world is privy to its innovations, its successes, its radical ideas, its catastrophes, and its gossip.

The Nonprofit Professional Theatre

But the nonprofit (or, technically, "not-for-profit") professional theatre is where, for the past forty years or so, America's theatre has been truly happening. The nonprofit theatre, often called the "regional" or "resident" theatre (because the theatres generally are in regions outside of New York, with resident staffs and at least some resident company members), is a phenomenon of the last third of the twentieth century, an outpouring of theatrical activity that at first diversified the American theatre and has since remade it.

Nonprofit means "noncommercial," not "nonprofessional." Nonprofit theatres are fully professional but have funding sources other than the box office, including some mix of state or local grants, national foundation or corporate support, and private donations. But in return for having no owners and making no profits, the nonprofit theatre is exempt from most taxes, and its donors receive tax deductions for their support. In all other aspects, the theatres are professional in every sense, employing professional artists, sometimes year-round, at every level. There were no such theatres at the end of World War II, and only four—one each in Washington, Houston, San Francisco, and Minneapolis—by the mid-1960s. But there are well over *four hundred* today—many with multiple stages—and they exist in every major city in America, including New York. They produce over two thousand productions each year (which translates into tens of thousands of performances), providing Americans in every part of the country an opportunity to see professional theatre, often at its best.

Nonprofit theatres vary enormously in character: some concentrate on classics, some on the contemporary international repertoire, some on American classics, others on new plays. Some operate on tiny stages with tiny bud-

gets, and although they engage professional artists, they can reduce their costs by negotiating salary waivers with the professional unions. Other theatres operate several stages simultaneously and are enormous operations: the New York Shakespeare Festival has an annual budget of more than $10 million and often has its productions running in many parts of the city. Among America's best-known regional theatres are these in the following eight cities.

BOSTON   The American Repertory Theatre, actually in Cambridge, was founded by Robert Brustein in 1980. The ART has been one of America's most experimental companies since its founding and has been known particularly for giving free rein to many of the most creative directors working in the United States, including Andrei Serban, Peter Sellers, Adrian Hall, Jonathan Miller, Anne Bogart, Susan Sontag, Des McAnuff, JoAnne Akalaitis, and Robert Wilson.

CHICAGO   With as many as two hundred theatre companies, a thriving "loop" theatre district (six major theatres within five blocks in the heart of downtown), seven half-price ticket booths, 1,400 professional actors, and at least a score of nationally distinguished directors and playwrights, Chicago rightfully stands as America's "second city" for theatrical culture. Indeed, in 2004, the distinguished British drama critic of the *Guardian*, Michael Billington, described the city as "the current theater capital of America." Chicago has certainly been the breeding ground for literally hundreds of bright and creative American actors and directors, including Alan Arkin, Gilda Radner, Dan Aykroyd, Alan Alda, Mike Nichols, and Elaine May (all former members of the famed Second City improvisational troupe) and the more recent Dennis Franz, Joe Mantegna, David Schwimmer, John Mahoney, John Malkovich, Gary Sinese, and Joan Allen. Chicago is also the home (and setting) for plays by David Mamet and dramatizations by Mary Zimmerman (see earlier discussion) and Frank Galati. The Goodman Theatre, now in sparkling new quarters, is Chicago's oldest and largest nonprofit company and is known for its production of new plays, particularly Mamet's, while the Steppenwolf is known for intense naturalistic acting and for pioneering what is frequently called a "Chicago style" of fervently emotional performances. With many smaller distinguished theatres as well (one of which, Victory Gardens, won the 2001 Tony Award for Outstanding Regional Theatre), Chicago has now become a "destination town" for theatergoers from all over the Midwest and beyond.

LOS ANGELES The Mark Taper Forum was founded in 1967 by Gordon Davidson, who served as its artistic director until his retirement in 2005. The Taper has been distinguished during his tenure for its production of new American plays, many of which have subsequently received national recognition: George C. Wolfe's *Jelly's Last Jam*, Tony Kushner's *Angels in America*, Robert Schenkkan's *The Kentucky Cycle*, Mark Medoff's *Children of a Lesser God*, Luis Valdez's *Zoot Suit*, Marsha Norman's *Getting Out*, Michael Christopher's *The Shadow Box*, and Daniel Berrigan's *The Trial of the Catonsville Nine* had either their premieres or major developmental productions at the Taper. These works constitute a remarkable diversity of authorial interests and backgrounds. Forty-five miles south of Los Angeles, South Coast

The catastrophe of wasted and misused power is a constant theme of Shakespeare's *King Lear*, as director Adrian Hall underlines in his stark American Repertory Theatre production of 1990, with bleak scenery and costumes by, respectively, Eugene Lee and Catherine Zuber.

Repertory vies for attention with its only slightly older rival. Founded by David Emmes and Martin Benson, who remain as the company's artistic codirectors, SCR's success has been built on excellent productions and a superb knack at finding (and commissioning) outstanding new plays, including David Henry Hwang's *Golden Child,* Richard Greenberg's *Three Days of Rain,* Margaret Edson's *Wit,* Amy Freed's *Freedomland* and *The Beard of Avon,* and Lynn Nottage's *Intimate Apparel,* all of which have had "legs"—

a theatre term for an extended life elsewhere, particularly in New York.

Los Angeles is known beyond its mainstream theatres, however, for its nearly one hundred small theatres that operate under the Actors' Equity Association's "99-Seat Theatre Plan" (popularly known as "equity waiver"), where plays, performed by professional—but basically unpaid—actors, can be given limited runs without running afoul of union salary regulations. The equity-waiver circuit often produces important

Jean Verdun's *Tibi's Law* is a new French play set in rural Africa; it premiered not in France but in the 44-seat "equity-waiver" Stages Theatre Center in Hollywood, California, in 2003, echoing the play's theme of globalization and the third world by such a transnational opening. American slam poet Saul Williams plays the title role of an African "sayer" who officiates at the funerals of Africans killed by disease, poverty, and thoughtless police raids, while Erinn Anova plays his long-lost girlfriend, Mara. The audience is cast in the role of global tourists, sent to these funerals by travel agents so they may see, between safaris to the wild-game parks, the "real Africa." Setting is by Grant Van Szevern and lighting by Leigh Allen.

plays that transfer to New York (as with *The Guys, Embedded,* and *The Mystery Plays* at Tim Robbins's Actors' Gang) and not infrequently presents important world premieres of plays that enter the international theatre repertoire (Jean Verdun's *Tibi's Law* at Stages Theatre Center in 2003 and Athol Fugard's *Exits and Entrances* at the Fountain Theatre in 2004).

LOUISVILLE   The Actors Theatre of Louisville, under the guidance of longtime artistic director Jon Jory (who, however, retired from ATL in 2000), has achieved a fine reputation both for a "Classics in Context" series and, even more significantly, for its annual Humana New Play Festival, in which five to ten new plays are produced simultaneously, attracting a large audience of theatre critics from around the country. Many of these plays, including *The Gin Game, Getting Out, Crimes of the Heart, Agnes of God, Extremities, Talking With, Marisol,* and *Execution of Justice,* have enjoyed long subsequent lifetimes in the national American repertory.

MINNEAPOLIS   The Guthrie Theatre was founded by the celebrated English director Tyrone Guthrie in 1963 and, with a continuing series of distinguished artistic directors, has maintained the highest artistic and creative standards in staging world theatre classics from all periods in the heart of America's Midwest. And the Theatre de la Jeune Lune, created in France by both Parisians and Minnesotans in 1978 and relocated to Minneapolis in 1985, has produced innovative works seeking to blend classical farce, circus, vaudeville, and commedia dell'arte, several of which have toured widely throughout the country.

NEW YORK CITY   The New York Shakespeare Festival was founded by Joseph Papp in 1954 with the goal of presenting free Shakespeare productions on trestles in Central Park. By the time Papp died in 1991, the company had a permanent theatre (the Delacorte) in the park plus six performance spaces in its downtown New York Public Theatre. The Public Theatre has also mounted full-scale Broadway productions, including *A Chorus Line, The Pirates of Penzance, Macbeth, Bring in 'Da Noise, Bring in 'Da Funk, The Tempest, On the Town, The Wild Party,* and, most recently, *Caroline, or Change.* In 2005, Oscar Eustis was appointed as the Public Theatre's new artistic director—"the most important job in American theatre," Eustis declared.

There are more than fifty other nonprofit theatres in New York City. Playwrights Horizons has spawned productions of astonishing merit, including Christopher Durang's *Sister Mary Ignatius Explains It All for You,* Scott McPherson's *Marvin's Room,* Wendy Wasserstein's *The Heidi Chronicles,* Alfred Uhry's *Driving*

A Christmas Carol is the title of many adaptations of Charles Dickens's novel of that name, as well as a mainstay for many regional theatres during the otherwise slow Christmas season, including this production at the Guthrie.

This production of Molière's *The Miser,* directed by French-born Dominique Serrand for Minneapolis's Theatre de la Jeune Lune, blends Renaissance scenic and costume formats with contemporary images and shapings. The staging is both visually spectacular and absurdly comic. The scenery is by Riccardo Hernandez, costumes by Sonya Berlovitz, and lighting by Marcus Dillard, all as seen here in its 2004 coproduction at the American Repertory Theatre in Cambridge, Massachusetts. Stephen Epp, in yellow, (who along with Serrand is one of the company's artistic directors) plays Harpagon, the title character.

Miss Daisy, William Finn's *Falsettos,* Stephen Sondheim and James Lapine's *Sunday in the Park with George,* Richard Nelson's adaptation of *James Joyce's The Dead,* and Doug Wright's 2004 Pulitzer Prize– and Tony Award–winning *I Am My Own Wife.* The Manhattan Theatre Club, which has been under the artistic directorship of Lynne Meadow since 1972, has regularly presented major new works by Terrence McNally (*Love! Valour! Compassion!, A Perfect Ganesh*), Beth Henley (*Crimes of the Heart, Miss Firecracker Contest*), Athol Fugard (*The Blood Knot*), Donald Margulies (*Sight Unseen, Collected Stories*), Arthur Miller (*The Last Yankee*), and Richard Greenberg (*Eastern Standard*), while more recently David Auburn's *Proof* won the 2001 Pulitzer Prize; indeed, MTC productions have among them won, as of 2004, eleven Tony Awards and three Pulitzer Prizes. The Lincoln

Center Theatre Company is also a nonprofit operation; it has premiered major plays by John Guare, Wendy Wasserstein, John Robin Baitz, and Richard Nelson, as well as lavish musical theatre revivals and an annual international summer theatre festival. The Wooster Group and La Mama Theatre, on the other hand, are among many veteran New York theatres that specialize in highly experimental new plays, both American and foreign, and reinvestigations of older classics.

SEATTLE   With seven professional companies, Seattle is arguably the most exciting theatre city on the West Coast. Its major stages include the Seattle Repertory Theatre, which premiered the Broadway-bound productions of Wendy Wasserstein's *The Heidi Chronicles* and *The Sisters Rosensweig,* as well as Herb

The Delacorte Theatre in Manhattan's Central Park was created in 1962 by Joseph Papp to provide free Shakespearean performances – often with stars – to New Yorkers and tourists each summer. Here it is shown in the 2004 production of *Much Ado about Nothing*, with Jimmy Smits (*front right, with back to audience*) as Benedick.

Gardner's *Conversations with My Father;* the Intiman, which initially premiered Schenkkan's *The Kentucky Cycle;* and the more avant-garde Empty Space and ACT Theatre (formerly A Contemporary Theatre).

WASHINGTON, D.C.   The Arena Stage, founded in 1950 and one of America's oldest and most distinguished theatres owes its name to the shape of the original stage, in which the audience surrounds the actors. Now several times removed from its original location, and augmented by more conventional staging configurations, Washington's Arena is increasingly dedicated to echoing the racial and ethnic mix of its city, emphasizing its "longstanding commitment to encourage participa-

tion by people of color in every aspect of the theatre's life."

But there are hundreds of theatre towns in the United States. The American nonprofit professional theatre, which was a "movement" during the 1960s and 1970s, has become, quite simply, America's national theatre: it is the theatre where the vast majority of America's plays are first shaped and first exposed. More and more, the American national press is attuned to major theatre happenings in the nonprofit sector; more and more the Broadway audience, while admiring the latest "hit," is aware that they are seeing that hit's second, third, or fourth production. National theatre prizes such as the Pulitzer, once awarded only for New York productions, are now seized by theatres around the country; world-renowned actors, once seen live only on the Broadway stages and on tour, are appearing in the country's more than four hundred nonprofit theatres in the fifty states. Most important: for the first time in America's history, the vast majority of Americans can see first-class professional theatre created in or near their hometowns, and professional theatre artists can live in any major city in the country—not only in New York.

Shakespeare Festivals

In Broadway's mid-century heyday there was also *summer stock,* a network of theatres, mainly located in resort areas throughout the mountains of the Northeast, that provided summer entertainment for tourists and assorted local folks. This "straw-hat circuit," as it was called, produced recent and not-so-recent Broadway shows, mainly comedies, with a mix of professional theatre artists from New York and young theatrical hopefuls from around the country; it was both America's vacation theatre and professional training ground.

Summer stock is mostly gone today, but in its place has arisen another phenomenon that, like summer stock, is unique to the United States. This is the vast array of Shakespeare festivals, begun during the Great Depression and now flourishing in almost every state in the nation. The Oregon Shakespeare Festival, in rural Ashland, is the much-heralded (and Tony Award–winning) grandparent of this movement. Founded by local drama teacher Angus Bowmer, whose three-night amateur production of *The Merchant of Venice* in 1935 was preceded by an afternoon boxing match "to draw the crowds," the OSF, which immediately discovered that Shakespeare outdrew the pugilists, now produces (under Libby Appel, who became artistic director in 1996) 750 fully professional performances of eleven plays (and a free, outdoor "Greenshow") each year, attracting

350,000 spectators during a ten-month season —all in a town of less than 20,000 people! There are over a hundred other North American Shakespeare festivals, many of which are largely or partially professional; particularly notable are the Stratford Festival in Canada, the Utah Shakespearean Festival (also Tony Award–winning), and the Alabama, New Jersey, California, Colorado, Illinois, Santa Cruz (California), and New York Shakespeare festivals. Characteristic of all of these operations is a core of two to four Shakespearean productions, normally performed outdoors, together with more contemporary plays, often performed on adjacent indoor stages: a setup resembling that of Shakespeare's original company, the King's Men, which, by the end of Shakespeare's career, was performing plays of many authors at both the outdoor Globe and the indoor Blackfriars.

In addition to providing exciting classical (and sometimes contemporary) theatre to audiences around the nation, often in rural areas and always at reasonable prices, Shakespeare festivals provide a wonderful bridge, for aspiring performers and designers, from college or community training to actual professional employment. And more than the old summer stock, the festivals offer opportunities to work in an ambitious theatre repertory as well.

Summer and Dinner Theatres

There remain some notable professional summer theatres without the word *Shakespeare* in their names. The Williamstown Theatre Festival in Massachusetts is probably the best of these, employing many of New York's better-known actors, designers, and directors, eager to leave the stifling city in July and August to spend a month or two in this beautiful Berkshire village, where they may play Chekhov (for which the theatre is justly famous), Brecht, O'Neill, and Williams in elegantly mounted productions. The Berkshire Theatre Festival in Stockbridge, Massachusetts, is also a highly accomplished professional summer theatre, located in a culturally rich area just two hours north of New York, where, in the afternoons, visitors can also drop in at Tanglewood to see the Boston Symphony Orchestra rehearsing in their shirtsleeves.

Dinner theatres were introduced to suburban America in the 1970s, offering a "night-on-the-town" package of dinner and a play in the same facility. Their novelty has worn thin, however, and only a few remain, generally offering light comedies, mystery melodramas, and pared-down productions of golden-age Broadway musicals. Never high in its artistic aspirations (the format virtually excludes adventurous dramaturgy, challenging themes, or even elaborate staging), dinner theatre nevertheless has played a role in bringing theatre to those otherwise unacquainted with it and in providing employment (and certainly performance experience) to hundreds of theatre artists each year.

The Utah Shakespearean Festival presents a free outdoor "Greenshow" of Renaissance music, skits, and dance each evening to get the audience in the mood for their summer productions in the festival's largely accurate reproduction of an outdoor Elizabethan theatre.

Amateur Theatre: Academic and Community

There is an active amateur theatre in America, some of which operates in conjunction with educational programs. More than one thousand U.S. colleges and universities have drama (or theatre) departments offering degrees in theatre arts, and another thousand collegiate institutions put on plays, or give classes in drama, without having a full curriculum of studies. And several thousand high schools, summer camps, and private schools teach drama and mount plays as well. Much of this dramatic activity is directed toward general education, as the staging of plays has been pursued at least since the Renaissance as an excellent way to explore dramatic literature, human behavior, and cultural history, as well as to teach skills such as public speaking, self-presentation, and foreign languages. Practical instruction in drama has the virtue of making the world's greatest literature physical and emotional; it gets drama not only into the mind, but into the muscles—and into the heart and loins as well. Some of the world's great theatre has, in fact, emerged from just such academic activity. Four or five "University Wits" dominated Elizabethan playwriting before Shakespeare arrived on the scene, and Shakespeare's company competed with publicly presented school plays that had become popular in London (such plays "are now the fashion," says a character in *Hamlet*) during his career. Several plays that changed theatre history—such as Alfred Jarry's *Ubu Roi*, Tom Stoppard's *Rosencrantz and Guildenstern Are Dead*, and Arthur Kopit's *Oh Dad, Poor Dad . . .*—were first conceived as extracurricular college projects.

The founding of the Yale Drama Department (now the Yale School of Drama) in 1923 signaled an expanded commitment on the part of American higher education: to assume not merely the role of theatre educator and producer but also that of theatre trainer. Today, the vast majority of American professional theatre artists receive their training in American college and university departments devoted, in whole or in part, to that purpose. As a result, academic and professional theatres have grown closer together, with many artists working interchangeably in both kinds of institutions. For this reason, the performances at many university theatres may reach sophisticated levels of excellence and, on occasion, equal or surpass professional productions of the same dramatic material.

Community theatres are amateur groups that put on plays for their own enjoyment and for the entertainment or edification of their community. There are occasions when these theatres, too, reach levels of excellence. Some community theatres are gifted with substantial funding, handsome facilities, and large subscription audiences, and some (such as the Laguna Playhouse in California) become professional. One should always remember that many of the greatest companies in the theatre's history, including Konstantin Stanislavsky's Moscow Art Theatre and André Antoine's Parisian Théâtre Libre, began, essentially, as amateur community theatres. One should also remember that the word *amateur* means "lover" and that the artist who creates theatre out of love rather than commercial expedience may in fact be headed for the highest, not lowest, levels of art. Community theatre has, then, a noble calling: it is the theatre a community makes out of itself and for itself, and it can therefore tell us a lot about who we are and what we want.

International Theatre

One of the greatest movements in current theatre is its growing internationalism; few spectator experiences are as challenging and fascinating as seeing plays from a culture—and a country—other than your own.

International theatre festivals are common abroad: there are now major festivals in Avignon, France; Edinburgh, Scotland; Spoleto, Italy;

This University of California-Irvine production of Shakespeare's *As You Like It* featured giant (and bleating!) yellow balls that represent sheep in the pastures of Arden. The set designer was Douglas-Scott Goheen.

Tampere, Finland; Amsterdam, Holland; Ibiza, Spain; Berlin, Germany; Toga, Japan; Adelaide, Australia; Pècs, Hungary; Sibiu, Romania; Curitiba, Brazil; and the city-state of Singapore. North America has been relatively slow to respond, but there is now a major international festival at Lincoln Center in New York every summer, and there have been successful international festivals in Baltimore, Denver, Chicago, Montreal, and Los Angeles over the years as well, often with audio translations (by earphones) or supertitles above the stage. A distinguished organization—the International Theatre Institute (www.iti-worldwide.org)—has been the coordinating overseer of much of this activity and can provide current information. It is possible that nothing could prove more valuable for the world today than global theatre exchanges, for drama's capacity to serve as a vehicle for international communication—a communication that goes beyond mere rhetoric—is one of its greatest potential gifts to humanity. Drama, in performance, can transcend ideologies, making antagonists into partners and strangers into friends. As theatre once served to unite the thirteen tribes of ancient Greece, so it may serve in the coming decades to unite a world too often fractured by prejudice and divided by ignorance. The theatre's greatest virtue is to explore the fullest potential of humankind and to lay before us all the universality of the worldwide human experience: human hopes, fears, feelings, and compassion for the living. Nothing could be more vital in the establishment of true world peace than a shared, cross-cultural awareness of what it means to be human on this planet.

A trip to an international drama festival, either in the United States or abroad, is the best way to sample the theatres of several other countries, but in truth nothing can match a theatre tour abroad, whereby the adventurous theatergoer can see not only the dramatic productivity of a given culture but also the "theatre scene" in its own local setting. Each year millions of Americans find a way to go to London for this purpose; indeed, Americans often account for up to a third of the theatre audiences at mainstream London productions, which, in addition to classics and musicals, may in any given year feature new works by such celebrated current English dramatists as Tom Stoppard, Harold Pinter, Mark Ravenhill, Alan Ayckbourn, David Hare, and Caryl Churchill. Highlighting England's theatre scene is the Royal National Theatre, operating three stages in a large complex on the south side of the Thames; the nearby Globe—a replica of Shakespeare's original playhouse—which offers Shakespearean-era drama during the summers; and the more commercial West End theatre district, on and around Shaftesbury Avenue, comparable to New York's Broadway in its mix of musicals, dramas, and the occasional classical revival. There is also a London "fringe" of smaller theatres, roughly comparable to off-Broadway, which is often where the most exciting action is, particularly at the always-adventurous Almeida Theatre, Donmar Warehouse, and Royal Court. Also often in London, though no longer on a regular basis, is the legendary and ambitious Royal Shakespeare Company, which you are more likely to catch at its home base in

Both scenic and historic sites host summer theatre festivals all over Europe. The Minack Theatre on England's rocky coast of Cornwall here presents a well-attended outdoor production of Gilbert and Sullivan's *Iolanthe*.

Shakespeare's birthplace, Stratford-upon-Avon, only a little more than an hour's train ride away. Tickets in London are somewhat cheaper than in New York, and an official half-price, day-of-performance ticket office, comparable to New York's TKTS booth, can be found in the small park centering Leicester (pronounced "Lester") Square, with several commercial discount booths (though with higher prices) nearby.

The international theatergoer can also travel to other English-speaking dramatic centers. Ireland has provided a vast repertoire to the stage since the seventeenth century; indeed, most of the great "English" dramatists of the eighteenth and nineteenth centuries—George Farquhar, Oliver Goldsmith, Richard Sheridan, Oscar Wilde, and George Bernard Shaw—were in fact Irish. In the twentieth century, a truly Irish drama became immensely popular under the hands of William Butler Yeats, Sean O'Casey, and Brendan Behan. But possibly no period of Irish drama is as rich as the current one, which includes major established playwrights such as Brian Friel (*Philadelphia, Here I Come; Translations; Dancing at Lughnasa*) and newer ones such as Sebastian Barry (*The Steward of Christendom, Whistling Psyche*) and English-Irish Martin McDonagh (*The Beauty Queen of Leenane, The*

Theatre is immensely popular in London today, where avid theatergoers mob a dozen or more discount ticket brokers in the theatre district, mainly around Leicester Square, where three such commercial outlets are virtually side by side.

Cripple of Inishmaan, The Pillowman). The production of these works, issuing from theatres as abundantly active as the Gate Theatre of Dublin and the Druid Theatre of Galway, foretells a brilliant future for Irish theatre.

Plays have been staged in Canada since the beginning of the seventeenth century. Today, theatre flourishes in every Canadian province. Toronto alone claims two hundred professional theatre companies and is now, after Lon-don and New York, the largest theatre metropolis in the English-speaking world. With its celebrated dramatists David French (writing in English) and Michael Trombley (in French), an internationally prominent director in Robert Lepage, two major summer festivals in Ontario—one for Shakespeare in Stratford, the other for George Bernard Shaw in Niagara-on-the-Lake—and a strong network of repertory companies and avant-garde groups

Tourist literature portrays the island of Ireland as a peaceful and beautiful land, but unfortunately it has suffered fiercely contentious rule for most of its political history. Martin McDonagh, English-born but of Irish parents, writes about the island's notorious "troubles," as they are famously called there, and his 2002 *The Lieutenant of Inishmore*, a dark (and many say tasteless) comedy of violence, torture, and killings (of both humans and animals), both shocked and fascinated London audiences. Paul Lloyd (*hanging upside down*) and Peter McDonald are shown here in one of the play's grimmer scenes.

The most important playwright in France today is probably Michel Vinaver, whose *L'émission de télévision* ("television broadcast"), a comedy about unemployment, mass communications, and political/sexual rivalry, captivated Paris in 2004. The elegantly modernist production was directed by Christophe Lesage at the Théâtre de l'Est Parisien .

throughout the provinces, Canada today enjoys a virtual flood of new Canadian playwrights, directors, and theatre critics who are developing global reputations.

Half a world away, another former British colony, Australia, has a fine theatrical tradition and a lively contemporary scene. Established playwrights David Williamson and Louis Nowra, now supplemented by a host of younger writers, flourish in both standard repertory and offbeat, alternative theatres in Melbourne, Sydney, and Brisbane, as well as Australia's great biennial Adelaide Arts Festival.

Nor is English playwriting limited to Europe and North America. The Market Theatre of Johannesburg, South Africa, has won its reputation not only for the outstanding quality of its productions but also for its courageous and effective confrontation of that country's now-concluded policy of apartheid; its most notable productions include Athol Fugard's *Sizwe Banzi Is Dead, The Island, Master Harold . . . and the Boys, A Lesson from Aloes, Valley Song, My Children! My Africa!,* and *Playland.* Since the demise of apartheid, Fugard has written new plays, often autobiographical, dealing with his continuing struggles to reconcile contemporary Africa with both its roots and its future; these include the notable *Valley Song* (1996) and *Exits and Entrances* (2004).

Meanwhile, one of Fugard's longtime South African colleagues, the distinguished actor John Kani (and the initial creator of Fugard's Sizwe Banzi role), has written a new play, *Nothing but the Truth,* concerning black South Africans who went abroad to protest apartheid and returned

Above left: New Latin American theatre is usually experimental and often intensely political. Here, in the 1998 Teatro Ubu (San José, Costa Rica) premiere of Argentinian-Quebecois Luis Thenon's *Los Conquistadores,* Maria Bonilla (director-actor at Costa Rica's National Theatre) kneels in anguish at the plight of her son, whom she discovers listed among citizens who mysteriously "disappeared" but were generally known to have been tortured and killed by official goon squads.

Above right: While traditional theatre is found in most Asian countries, modern plays abound there as well. Suk-Man Kim's historical drama *Mr. Han* treats a Korean doctor and his family before, during, and after the brutal Korean War, which divided the country. In this scene from the Korean National Theatre production, Korean and American military officers trace an imposed line of demarcation on the map they irreverently stand upon.

to confront those that stayed home and suffered under it. Kani's play premiered at the Market Theatre in Johannesburg in 2003 and came to New York and Los Angeles in 2004. Black African writers of English drama also include the South African Mbongeni Ngema, the Kenyan Ngugi wa Thiong'o, and the Ghanaian Christina Ama Ata Aidoo and Mohammed ben Ab-

dallah, all of whom address African issues in the context of postcolonial globalization.

And for those able to manage a foreign language, France and Germany—the countries that spawned the theatre of the absurd and the theatre of alienation, respectively—are immensely rewarding theatre destinations, each country providing an outstanding mix of traditional

Israel's Gesher Theater tours regularly and is particularly well known in New York, where in 2004 it performed (in Hebrew and Russian) *The Slave*, adapted from the novel by Isaac Bashevis Singer. The play, staged by the company's founding and artistic director Yevgeny Arye, portrays a mixed marriage (a Jewish slave marries his master's daughter in seventeenth-century Poland) and its tragic aftermath. *Gesher* is Hebrew for "bridge," and the company's stated goal is to provide cultural connections – initially between Israel and its own Russian émigrés, and secondarily between Jewish and non-Jewish populations in the Middle East and around the world. In a larger context, however, "bridge" theatres everywhere have the potential to improve communication between people of all races, religions, and ethnicities.

and original theatre, though rarely in English. French and German theatre, along with that of most European countries, also enjoys strong government support, which keeps ticket prices at a fraction of what they are in the United States and England. France has five fully supported national theatres, four of them in Paris —including the historic Comédie Française, founded in 1680 out of the remains of Molière's company shortly after his death, and the Odeon, which is now a "theatre of nations," presenting plays from all over the world—plus more than a dozen regional ones. Germany, where major dramatic activity is spread more broadly throughout the country (there is no recognized German cultural "capital" compara-

ble to London or Paris), supports more than 150 theatres, and about 60 theatre festivals, in just about every large city on the map.

We end this mini-travelogue with the reminder that only cultural insularity causes us to imagine ourselves as the center of the universe, as the true and legitimate heirs of those who invented theatre. The truth, however, is that theatre is happening throughout the world and in forms so diverse as to defy accounting or assimilation. Every component of theatre—from architecture to acting, from dramaturgy to directing—is in the process of change: theatre is always learning, rebelling from convention, building anew. The theatre's diversity is its very life, and change is the foremost of its vital signs. We must think not to pin it down but rather to seek it out, to produce it ourselves, and to participate in its growth.

Conclusions on the Current Theatre?

Can there be any conclusions concerning the current theatre? No, there cannot—simply because what is current is never concluded. The current theatre is in process; it is like a book we are just beginning to read. The plays and playwrights discussed in this chapter may not, in the end, be accorded significant positions in our era of theatre; even the movements they now seem to represent may prove minor and transitory. We are not in a position even to hazard guesses at this point. We can only take note of certain directions and look for clues as to where the future will lead us.

Meanwhile, the evidence plays nightly on the stages of the theatre worldwide. It is there to apprehend, to enjoy, to appreciate, and, finally, to be refined by opinion and encapsulated into critical theory and aesthetic categorization—if that is our wish. More than being a play, or a series of plays, or a spectrum of performances, the current theatre is a worldwide event, a communication between people and peoples that raises the level of human discourse and artistic appreciation wherever it takes place. The current theatre responds to the impulses of creativity and expression and to the demands of human contact and understanding. It synthesizes the impulses of authors and artists, actors and audiences, to foster a medium of focused interaction that incorporates the human experience and embodies each culture's aspirations and values. No final chapter can be written on this medium, no last analysis or concluding categorization. All that is certain is that the art, and the feeling, of theatrical life will endure.

11

The Critic

I T IS ELEVEN O'CLOCK; THE LIGHTS FADE a final time, the curtain falls, the audience
applauds, and the play is over. The actors go back to their dressing rooms, take off their
makeup, and depart. The audience disperses into the night.

But the theatrical experience is not over; in important ways, it is just beginning. A play
does not begin and end its life on a stage. A play begins in the mind of its creator, and its
final repository is in the minds and memories of its audiences. The stage is simply a focal
point where the transmission takes place—in the form of communication we know as theatrical performance.

After the performance is over, the play's impact remains. It is something to think about,
talk about, fantasize about, and live with for hours, days, and years to come. Some plays we
remember all our lives: plays whose characters are as indelible in our memories as the people
in our personal lives, plays whose settings are more deeply experienced than were many of
our childhood locales, and plays whose themes abide as major object lessons behind our decision making. Should we take up arms against a sea of troubles? Can we depend on the kindness of strangers? What's in a name? Shall we be as defiant as Prometheus? as determined as
Oedipus? as passionate as Romeo? as accepting as Winnie? as noble as Hecuba? What is
Hecuba to us, or we to Hecuba? We talk about these matters with our friends.

And we also talk about the production—about the acting, the costumes, the scenery, the sound effects. Were we convinced? impressed? moved? transported? changed? Did the production hold our attention throughout? Did our involvement with the action increase during the play, or did we feel a letdown after the intermission? Did we accept the actors as the characters they were playing, or were we uncomfortably aware that they were simply "acting" their parts rather than embodying their roles?

The formalization of postplay thinking and conversation is known as *dramatic criticism.* When it is formalized into writing it can take many forms: production reviews in newspapers or periodicals, essays about plays or play productions written as academic assignments, commentaries in theatre programs or theatre journals, magazine feature articles on theatre artists, and scholarly articles or books on dramatic literature, history, or theory. All of these and more fall under the category of dramatic criticism, which is nothing other than an informed, articulate, and communicative response to what the critic has seen in the theatre or read in the theatre's vast literature.

Critical Perspectives

What makes a play particularly successful? What gives a theatrical production significance and impact, and what makes it unforgettable? What should we be looking for when we read a play or see a dramatic production? We have, of course, complete freedom in making up our minds, for response, by definition, can never be dictated; the price of theatrical admission carries with it the privilege of thinking what we wish and responding as we will. But five perspectives can be particularly useful in helping us focus our response to any individual theatrical event. These perspectives relate to a play's social significance, its human or personal significance,

its artistic quality, its theatrical expression, and its capacity to entertain.

A Play's Relation to Society

Theatre, as we have seen throughout this book, is always tied to its culture. Many theatres have been directly created or sustained by governments and ruling elites: the Greek theatre of the fifth century B.C. was a creation of the state; the medieval theatre was generated by the church, the township, and the municipal craft guilds; and the Royal theatre was a direct extension of a monarchical reign. Even in modern times, government often serves as sponsor or cosponsor or silent benefactor of the theatre. But the intellectual ties between a theatre and its culture extend well beyond merely political concerns: thematically, the theatre has at one time or another served as an arena for the discussion of every social issue imaginable. In modern times, the theatre has approached from different perspectives such issues as alcoholism, homosexuality, venereal disease, prostitution, public education, racial prejudice, capital punishment, thought control, prison reform, character assassination, civil equality, political corruption, and military excess. The best of these productions have presented the issues in all of their complexity and have proffered solutions not as dogma but as food for thought—for great theatre has never sought to purvey pure propaganda.

The playwright is not necessarily brighter than the audience nor even better informed: he and his collaborators, however, may be able to focus public debate, stimulate dialogue, and turn public attention and compassion toward social injustices, inconsistencies, and irregularities. The theatre artist traditionally is something of a nonconformist; her point of view is generally to the left or right of the social mainstream, and her perspective is of necessity somewhat unusual. Therefore, the theatre is in a strong position to force and focus public confrontation with social issues,

Political street theatre is an open interaction between actor-activists and audiences; the elements of theatre – acting, costumes, playwriting, and directing – are all subservient to the goals of reforming society, and the theatre artists are fully engaged in this goal rather than financial gain or career advancement in the commercial theatre. Here a Filipino troupe – with one masked as President Gloria Arroyo – protests what they consider government abuses of human rights in this political street drama in Manila.

and at its best it succeeds in bringing the audience into touch with its own thoughts and feelings about those issues.

A Play's Relation to the Individual

The theatre is a highly personal art, in part because it stems from the unique (and often oblique) perspectives of the playwrights who initiate it and the theatre artists who execute it and in part because its audiences all through history have decreed that it be so.

The greatest plays transcend the social and political to confront the hopes, concerns, and conflicts faced by all humankind: personal identity, courage, compassion, fantasy versus practicality, kindness versus self-serving, love versus exploitation, and the inescapable problems of growing up and growing old, of wasting and dying. These are some of the basic themes of the finest of plays and of our own stray thoughts as well; the best plays simply link up with our deepest musings and help us put our random ideas into some sort of order or philosophy. The theatre is a medium in which we invariably see reflections of ourselves, and in the theatre's best achievements those reflections lead to certain discoveries and evaluations concerning our own individual personalities and perplexities.

THE INDOMITABLE THEATRE

There are places in the world where theatre has, at times, been made illegal, for either political or religious reasons. But the theatre's spirit has never been totally extinguished. Although all English theatres were closed by a parliamentary ordinance in 1642, as the Puritans seized national power and the London theatres — including Shakespeare's Globe — were burned to the ground, theatre was restored upon the restoration of the monarchy in 1660, reaching new glories within its first decade. China abolished its ancient xiqu — apart from eight new plays strictly spouting the party line — during the Cultural Revo-

lution in the 1960s and 1970s, only to see this glorious traditional drama quickly return with the emergence of new leaders. And the Taliban government of Afghanistan outlawed theater when it assumed rule over that long-tortured country in 1995, punishing actors with beatings and imprisonment. By the time the Taliban was routed in 2001, Kabul's National Theatre was in ruins — its roof bombed into oblivion, its walls bullet-scarred or fallen, and its stage literally blasted away — yet the Afghan theatre quickly reemerged with the advent of a new government in 2002.

The Afghanistan National Theatre reopened in 2002 in the ruins of its old building after the overthrow of the Taliban government (which forbade drama). Here, actress Roya Naqibullah (in white) cries, "We're still alive and peace will definitely come. God, please have mercy on us," in the company's first post-Taliban production.

By 2003, Afghanistan had its first avant-garde theatre troupe, the Takamol Theatre in Kabul, seen here in a publicity photo of the animated and ambitious company led by Aziz Baraki (center).

A Play's Relation to Art

The theatre is an art of such distinctive form that even with the briefest exposure we can begin to develop certain aesthetic notions as to what that form should be. We quickly come to know—or think we know—honesty

onstage, for without being experts we feel we can recognize false notes in acting, in playwriting, and even in design.

Beyond that, we can ask a number of questions of ourselves. Does the play excite our emotions? Does it stimulate the intellect? Does it surprise us? Does it thrill us? Does it seem complete and all of a piece? Are the characters credible? Are the actors convincing? enchanting? electrifying? Does the play seem alive or dead? Does it seem in any way original? Is it logically sound? Is the action purposeful, or is it gratuitous? Are we transported, or are we simply waiting for the final curtain? In the last analysis, does the play fit our idea of what a play should be—or, even better, does it force us, by its sheer luster and power, to rewrite our standards of theatre?

Aesthetic judgments of this sort are necessarily comparative, and they are subjective as well. What seems original to one member of the audience may be old hat to another; what

seems an obvious gimmick to a veteran theatergoer can seem brilliantly innovative to a less jaded patron. None of this should intimidate us. An audience does not bring absolute standards into the theatre—and certainly such standards as it brings are not shared absolutely. The theatrical response is a composite of many individual reactions. But each of us has an aesthetic sensibility and an aesthetic response. We appreciate colors, sights, sounds, words, actions, behaviors, and people that please us. We appreciate constructions that seem to us balanced, harmonic, expressive, and assured. We appreciate designs, ideas, and performances that exceed our expectations, that reveal patterns and viewpoints we didn't know existed. We take great pleasure in sensing underlying structure: a symphony of ideas, a sturdy architecture of integrated style and action.

A Play's Relation to Theatre

As we've already discussed, plays are not simply things that happen *in* the theatre; they *are* theatre—which is to say that each play or play production redefines the theatre itself and makes us reconsider, at least to a certain extent, the value and possibilities of the theatre itself. In some cases the playwright makes this reconsideration mandatory, by dealing with theatrical matters in the play itself. Some plays are set in theatres where plays are going on (Luigi Pirandello's *Six Characters in Search of an Author,* Michael Frayn's *Noises Off,* Mel Brooks's *The Producers*); other plays are about actors (Jean-Paul Sartre's *Kean*) or about dramatic characters (Tom Stoppard's *Rosencrantz and Guildenstern Are Dead*); still other plays contain plays within themselves (Anton Chekhov's *The Seagull,* William Shakespeare's *Hamlet*) or the rehearsals of such plays (Shakespeare's *A Midsummer Night's Dream,* Molière's *The Versailles Rehearsal,* Jean Anouilh's *The Rehearsal*).

We use the term *metatheatre,* or *metadrama,* to describe those plays that specifically refer back to themselves in this manner, but in fact

Michael Frayn's *Democracy* addresses crucial political issues of postwar Germany, as well as the global politics that affect all of us. Roger Allam plays onetime German chancellor Willy Brandt in this multiple-award-winning London premiere, directed by Michael Blakemore in 2003 and restaged in the United States in 2004–5.

all plays and play productions can be analyzed and evaluated on the way they use the theatrical format to best advantage and the way they make us rethink the nature of theatrical production, for all plays stand within the spectrum of a history of theatre and a history of theatrical convention (see Chapter 2). All plays and productions can be studied, often with illuminating results, from the perspective of how they adopt or reject prevailing theatrical conventions, how they fit into or deviate from prevailing dramatic genres, and how they echo various elements of past plays or productions—and what theatrical effects, good and bad, such historical resonances may have.

A Play as Entertainment

Finally, we look upon all theatre as entertainment. Great theatre is never less than pleasing. Even tragedy delights. People go to see *Hamlet* not for the purpose of self-flagellation or to wallow in despair but, rather, to revel in the tragic form and to experience the liberating catharsis of the play's murderous finale. Hamlet himself knows the thrill of staged tragedy:

HAMLET: What players are they?

ROSENCRANTZ: Even those you were wont to take such delight in, the tragedians . . .

What is this entertainment value that all plays possess? Most obviously the word *enter-*

Tom Stoppard's *Rosencrantz and Guildenstern Are Dead*, originally written as a college project, was the first of the playwright's brilliant metatheatrical plays that turn the theatre inside out, in this case by making minor characters in Shakespeare's *Hamlet* into title roles. The leads are played here by Adrian Scarborough (*left*) and Simon Russell Beale in a 1995 London production.

tainment suggests "amusement," and so we think immediately of the hilarity of comedy and farce; indeed, most of the literature regarding theatrical entertainment concentrates on the pratfalls and gags that have been part of the comic theatre throughout its history. But entertainment goes far beyond humor. Another definition for *entertainment* is "that which holds the attention" (from the French *entre* [between] and *tenir* [to hold], thus "to hold together" or "to bring together"). This definition casts more light on our question. It means that entertainment includes the enchantment of romance; the dazzle of brilliant debate, witty epigram, and biting repartee; the exotic appeal of the foreign and the grotesque;

the beauty and grandeur of spectacle; the nuance and crescendo of a musical or rhythmic line. It accommodates suspense and adventure, the magic of sex appeal, and the splendor of sheer talent. Finally, of course, it includes any form of drama that profoundly stirs our feelings and heightens our awareness of the human condition. It is no wonder that Hamlet delights in the performance of tragedians—and that we delight in *Hamlet*—for the mixture of ideas, language, poetry, feelings, and actions that constitute great tragedy confers one of life's sublime entertainment experiences.

Indeed, the theatre is a storehouse of pleasures, not only for the emotional, intellectual, spiritual, and aesthetic stimulation it provides

Of course a great deal of theatre is created mainly, if not solely, to provide sheer audience entertainment. Although it deals with appalling subject matter, Mel Brooks's farcically satirical *The Producers* was designed purely for pleasure — as if to allow its audience to shake off, once and for all, the horrors of Adolf Hitler's regime. Matthew Broderick is here shown surrounded by a bevy of beautiful chorus girls.

but also for its intrinsic social excitement. Theatre is a favored public meeting place for people who care about each other. "Two on the aisle" implies more than a choice seating location; it implies companionship in the best theatrical experience, for the theatre is a place to commune in an especially satisfying way with strangers. When in the course of a dramatic performance we are gripped by a staging of romantic passion or stunned by a brilliantly articulated argument or moved by a touching denouement, the thrill is enhanced a hundredfold by the certainty that we are not alone in these feelings, that possibly every member of the audience has been stirred to the same response. Theatre, in its essence, serves to rescue humankind from an intellectual and emotional aloneness; and therein lies its most profound "entertainment" value.

Critical Focus

These five perspectives on the theatre experience—on its social, personal, artistic, theatrical, and entertainment values—are all implicit in the responses of any audience, regardless of its training or theatrical sophistication. These are the five angles from which we view and judge plays—and judge them we do, for our involvement with a play naturally generates a series of comparisons: the play vis-à-vis other plays, the play vis-à-vis our personal experiences, the play vis-à-vis other things we might have done that evening. Judging plays and performances, which has been done formally since ancient Greek times and continues today through the well-publicized Tony and Obie awards, Pulitzer Prizes, and Critics Circle citations, is one of the fundamental aspects of theatrical participation—and yet it is a participation open to amateur and professional alike.

Professional Criticism

Professional criticism takes the basic form of production reviews and scholarly books and articles written, for the most part, by persons who specialize in this activity, often for an entire career.

Newspaper reviews of play productions are common throughout the theatre world; indeed, the box-office success of most theatres depends on receiving favorable press coverage. In the commercial Broadway theatre, favorable reviews—particularly from the influential *New York Times*—are all but absolutely necessary in order to guarantee a successful run. Where theatre audiences are generated by subscriptions and where institutional financing secures the production funds, newspaper reviews play a less-crucial, short-term role, but they still bear weightily in a theatre's ultimate success or failure.

In New York, newspaper reviews have traditionally been written immediately following the opening-night performance and are published the following morning; actors and producers gather after opening night at Sardi's restaurant, in the Broadway theatre district, awaiting the first edition of the next morning's *Times* to see how their show fared with the current critic. This is "instant criticism," and the

> ## A Critic's Tastes
>
> Somebody recently wrote one of my editors to the effect that I had no sense whatever of the tastes of my readers or the public at large. He was, unintentionally, paying me a great tribute which I can only hope I deserve. For it is extremely hard not to be influenced by the tastes of one's milieu; yet resisting them is precisely the critic's duty. It is only in being uncompromisingly himself that a critic performs a true service, and as a man of taste (not infallible taste, for there can be no such thing), goes down in history, or as a man of no taste, goes down the drain.
>
> – John Simon

journalist who tackles these assignments has to be very fluid at articulating his or her immediate impressions. Outside of New York, newspaper critics frequently take two or three days to review a production, allowing themselves the luxury of considered opinions and more polished essays. Some New York newspaper critics have recently begun to emulate this practice; although their reviews are still published the day after opening night, they have actually attended a preview performance two or three days earlier and have had the opportunity to write their review at some leisure.

Still, the journalist's review must be limited to a brief, immediate reaction rather than being a detailed or exhaustive study. It provides a first-hand, audience-oriented response to the production, often vigorously and wittily expressed, and may serve as a useful consumer guide for the local theatergoing public. Writing skill rather than dramatic expertise is often the newspaper critic's principal job qualification, and at many smaller papers, staff reporters with little dramatic background are assigned to the theatre desk. But many fine newspaper critics throughout the years—New York's Ben Brantley and Chicago's Michael Phillips, for example—have proven extremely subtle and skillful at transcending the limitations of their particular profession and have written highly intelligent dramatic criticism that remains pertinent long

CONTRASTING REVIEWS

Sixteen Wounded was a new play by a new playwright that opened – and quickly closed – on Broadway in the spring of 2004. Reviews were "mixed," which is not a good sign for a straight (that is, nonmusical) play, particularly when one of the more negative reviews is from the very influential *New York Times,* as was true in this case.

These two reviews – the first from *USA Today,* the second from the *New York Times* – give contrasting literate and intelligent, but divergent, opinions by experienced critics.

"Wounded" Finds Way to Mend the Heart

BY ELYSA GARDNER
NEW YORK – You could hardly define 30-year-old playwright Eliam Kraiem as a radical in terms of his political philosophy or dramatic approach.

Yet the premise of *Sixteen Wounded* (★★★¹/₂ out of four), Kraiem's eloquent, acutely moving new work, is one that may seem subversive to some in our current political climate: Not all people or impulses can be written off as either good or evil.

That lesson is learned by Mahmoud, a young Palestinian living in Amsterdam, when he befriends Hans, a Jewish baker, in the play that opened Thursday at Broadway's Walter Kerr Theatre. The two meet in the early 1990s, an innocent time in retrospect before "suicide bomber" had entered the common vernacular and when a peace accord between Israel and the Palestinians seemed more feasible than a sci-fi movie.

But the camaraderie between Kraiem's protagonists is, predictably, a troubled one. Each man has witnessed and endured debilitating oppression because of his heritage. "I can be whatever I want," Mahmoud tells Hans, but it's the wishful boast of a man trying in vain to escape the legacy of a haunted past.

What that past entails won't surprise many theatergoers. But Kraiem articulates the challenges, desires and obligations that both bind and divide Hans and Mahmoud with such unaffected poignancy and insight that the effect is never tedious or pedantic.

Under Garry Hynes' sensitive, adroit direction, *Wounded* also is beautifully played. Judd Hirsch's deceptively weary Hans is a study in marvelously nuanced character acting, while Omar Metwally plays Mahmoud with riveting vulnerability and charisma.

The leading men are ably assisted by Jan Maxwell as a weathered beauty with her own tortured history and Martha Plimpton as young dancer Sonya [Nora] who, for a while, offers Mahmoud a fresh lease on life.

It's fair to say that Mahmoud and Sonya [Nora] don't ride off into the sunset at the end. But however distressing the developments in *Wounded* might be, Kraiem's tender humanism leaves room for hope, even in a world more complicated than some would like to acknowledge.

– *USA Today,* April 16, 2004

Personal Friends, Political Pawns

BY BEN BRANTLEY
From the moment in the first scene when the fiery young Palestinian crashes through the shop window of the curmudgeonly old Jewish baker, life moves at a disorientingly fast clip in Eliam Kraiem's "Sixteen Wounded," the political melodrama with the pace of a sitcom that opened last night at the Walter Kerr Theater.

After meeting cute, if bloody, amid shattered glass in Amsterdam in 1992, Hans (Judd Hirsch), the baker, and Mahmoud (Omar Metwally), his unexpected visitor, sit down to a cozy game of backgammon and almost instantly develop a friendship that bridges a vast ethnic divide. Oh, sure, there are some rocky moments early on, as when Mahmoud realizes that Hans is a Jew and spits on the mezuza nailed to the old guy's door.

But they both get over that uncomfortable episode quickly as Mahmoud, a medical student, agrees to keep working for Hans in the bakery shop where the grumpy but warm-hearted old fellow has cloistered himself. Even when weightier things come between them, like a time bomb, they're able to reach inside themselves and discover their abiding mutual affection. That's just the way these lovable if tragic lunkheads are. And when Nora (Martha Plimpton), Hans's spunky and sexy employee, shows up, you know it's just a matter of very limited time before she and the hunky Mahmoud fall for each other.

Basically, there's not a major emotional reversal – and they happen with head-spinning frequency in this play, directed by Garry Hynes – that couldn't be clocked with an egg timer, with a minute or two to spare. Yet as the characters race through their frenzied, predestined dance of friendship, love, loss and destruction, the overall effect is of a turtle race in slow motion. And while the theme of Arab-Jewish relations is normally guaranteed to whip up passionate feelings, "Sixteen Wounded" generates less urgency than your average episode of "Friends."

These are sad tidings to report in a season when Broadway is suffering from a drought of new plays, and especially of works with the courage and honorable intentions of this one. After 9/11 and the invasion of Iraq, it has been heartening to see how many American dramatists, from John Patrick Shanley and Craig Lucas to A. R. Gurney and Tim Robbins, have felt compelled to address the terrifying state of international politics today.

But these works have all been staged in theaters other than the palaces of Broadway, where only the presence of a movie star — preferably naked and of tabloid notoriety — can promise success for a nonmusical. Though "Sixteen Wounded" does star Mr. Hirsch, popular to television audiences from "Taxi," its cachet is, first and foremost, its topicality. Which means that to draw crowds it needs to be garlanded, through word of mouth as well as critical reviews, with adjectives like searing, unflinching, shattering and revelatory, all followed by exclamation points.

None of these words apply to "Sixteen Wounded," previously staged (in a somewhat different version) at the Long Wharf Theater in New Haven. For his Broadway debut, the 30-year-old Mr. Kraiem has boldly taken on a subject that has baffled masterminds of world diplomacy. And it's fair to say that he does not undervalue the Gordian complexity of that subject. "Sixteen Wounded" fully acknowledges that any debate about the Middle East among ardent partisans is going to produce no winners.

But for politically themed, slice-of-life theater like this to work, you have to feel emotionally invested in the individuals who are shaped and manipulated by historical forces. And aside from the always excellent Jan Maxwell, who plays a prostitute with whom Hans shares a Sunday kind of love, the performers here are hard pressed to make you care about the people they embody.

The production has gone to some trouble to create an authentic environment, from the designer Francis O'Connor's hunger-inspiring, fully stocked baker's kitchen to the convincing showers of rain and snow created to evoke the changing seasons. But even doing in-the-moment activities like kneading dough or playing backgammon, the cast members register mostly as mechanical cogs in a clockwork plot. (The five-member ensemble also features Waleed F. Zuaiter, who appears in the second act to hurry along the play's inevitably unhappy denouement.)

This sense of affectlessness has much to do with the shortcuts that Mr. Kraiem takes in pushing his characters into relationships. Though Hans advises the restless young Mahmoud that patience is necessary in all things, from the game of dominoes to the art of baking, "Sixteen Wounded" does not itself practice this virtue. Structured as an elliptical series of black-out vignettes that take place over two years, the play works on the assumption that the audience will fill in a lot of blanks on what's occurred among these characters in the time between scenes.

Yet even within a single episode, characters are asked to exchange deep secrets, to process that information and then come to terms with it, switching psychological gears in ways more suited to Jim Carrey at his most manic. Perhaps this accounts for the odd disjointedness of Mr. Hirsch's performance, in which lines seem to erupt from him at different pitches like a scale of stylized belches. Mr. Hirsch is an actor of probing intelligence, and presumably he is trying to convey the detachment of a man who has buried his real identity, as he reveals in the second act.

But the ultimate impact of "Sixteen Wounded" rests entirely on your belief in the familial love that develops between Hans and Mahmoud and, to a lesser extent, between Mahmoud and Nora. While Mr. Metwally is a handsome and engaging young actor, he never conveys the hair-trigger intensity and feverish warmth Mahmoud is said to possess.

The usually first-rate Ms. Plimpton here lets her mask of a European accent do most of the work in creating her character. (It is supposedly a Dutch accent, but to me she sounded like Ingrid Bergman with a megaphone.) And Ms. Hynes, who brought such gooseflesh-making verisimilitude to "The Beauty Queen of Leenane," appears at some point to have simply given up on forging credible connections among the characters.

It is to the play's advantage, by the way, that it begins with Ms. Maxwell alone on the stage as Sonya, the Russian prostitute who has just finished her weekly assignation with Hans. As she zips up her boots with grim, bored efficiency, Sonya radiates the compelling weariness of someone who has come to see life as a matter of just going through the motions, of surviving from day to day.

Whenever Ms. Maxwell and Mr. Hirsch are alone on-stage together, you began to feel inklings of complexity in their characters, a sense of lonely people forced by circumstance to detach themselves from their core identities and deepest feelings. Mr. Kraiem's point seems to be that even in the homey isolation that Hans has created for himself in his baker's shop, there's no escape from a vicious world of conflict, where to feel too much of anything is to court infinite pain.

This premise could be the basis for a seriously moving play. But it's an idea that registers fully only when Ms. Maxwell is around. That her character has the least to do with the play's central plot tells you a lot about how far "Sixteen Wounded" remains from achieving its admirable ambitions.

— *New York Times*, April 16, 2004

after its consumer-oriented function has run its course.

More scholarly critics, writing without the deadlines or strict space restrictions of journalists, are able to analyze plays and productions within detailed, comprehensive, and rigorously researched critical contexts. They are therefore able to understand and evaluate, in a more complex way, the achievements of playwrights and theatre artists within any or all of the five perspectives we have discussed. Scholarly critics (and by *scholarly* we mean only "one who studies") seek to uncover hidden aspects of a play's structure, to analyze its deep relationships to social or philosophical issues, to probe its various meanings and dramatic possibilities, to define its place in cultural history, to amplify its resonance of earlier works of art, to shape its future theatrical presentations, and to theorize about larger issues of dramaturgy, art, and human understanding. Such criticism is itself a literary art, and the great examples of dramatic criticism have included brilliantly styled essays that have outlasted the theatrical works that were their presumed subjects: Aristotle, Goethe, Shaw, and Nietzsche are among the drama critics who, simply through their analyses of drama, have helped shape our vision of life itself.

The scholarly critic, ordinarily distinguished by her or his broad intellectual background and exhaustive research, writes with a comprehensive knowledge of the specific subject—a knowledge that includes the work of all important previous scholars who have studied the same materials. The professional scholar is not content to repeat the opinions or discoveries of others but seeks to make fresh insights from the body of literature (playtexts and productions, production records, previous scholarship) that constitutes the field of study.

Scholarly critics tend to work within accepted methodologies, which develop and change rapidly in contemporary academic life. Traditional methodologies include historical and biographical approaches ("the man and his work"), thematic and rhetorical analyses, studies of character and plot, examinations of staging and theatrical styles, and detailed exegeses of meaning, or *explication de texte*. More contemporary methodologies include systems and theories developed since the 1970s, particularly structuralist, semiotic, and deconstructive approaches; these bypass traditional questions of history, biography, character, theme, and meaning and focus instead on the internal relationships of various dramatic ingredients and their particular combination in a self-referential dramaturgic system. Contemporary methodologies, which draw heavily from the fields of philosophy, linguistics, anthropology, and critical theory, are intellectually demanding and difficult to master; they provide, however, stunning insights to those properly initiated.

Student Criticism

One does not expect of beginning theatre students a thoroughly comprehensive background in the subject; indeed, students writing class papers are likely to be looking seriously at the subject for the very first time. Naturally, different standards apply.

Such beginning students will characteristically analyze plays from any of the five perspectives cited earlier but without the need for a very sophisticated or advanced methodology. Some simple but effective methodologies, for writing both class essays and production reviews for local or school newspapers, are provided in the Online Learning Center for *Theatre* at www.mhhe.com/cohen and *Enjoy the Play,* accompanying this text.

We Are the Critics

Whether we are professional writers, students, or just plain theatergoers, we are all the critics of the theatre. We the audience are a party to the theatrical experience, not a mere passive receptacle for its contrived effects. The

IS IT ART ... OR TRASH?

The theatre critic spends most of his time with trash. But the trash is as much a part of his subject as the non-trash.... Part of his function is to make sure that false messiahs and peddlers and charlatans are shown as such. Hope — non-delusionary, non-inflationary, non-self-aggrandizing hope — is the core of the critic's being: hope that good work will recurrently arrive, hope that (partly by identifying trash) he may help it to arrive, hope that he may have the excitement and privilege of helping to connect that good work with its audience.

— Stanley Kauffman

theatre is a forum of communication, and communication demands mutual and active participation.

To be an *observant* critic, one need only go to the theatre with an open mind and sharply tuned senses. Unfettered thinking should be a part of every theatrical experience, and provocative discussion should be its aftermath.

To be an *informed* critic, one needs sufficient background to provide a context for opinion and evaluation. A play may be moving, but is it as moving as *The Three Sisters*? as passionate as *The Trojan Women*? as romantic as *Romeo and Juliet*? as funny as *The Bourgeois Gentleman*? as intriguing as *Happy Days*? An actor's voice may be thrillingly resonant, but how does it compare with the voice of Ian McKellen? If our opinions are to have weight and distinction, they may do so only against a background of knowledge and experience. If we are going to place a performance on a scale of one to ten, our friends (or readers) must know just what is our "one" and what is our "ten."

To be a *sensitive* critic, one must be receptive to life and to artistic experience. The most sensitive criticism comes from a compassionate approach to life, to humankind, and to artistic expression; this approach elicits and provokes a personalized response to dramatic works. Sensitive criticism admits the critic's needs: it begins from the view that life is difficult and problematical and that relationships are demanding. Sensitive critics are questing, not smug; humane, not self-absorbed; eternally eager for personal discovery and the opportunity to share it. They recognize that we are all groping in the dark, hoping to encounter helping hands along the way in the adventure of life — that this indeed is the hope of theatre artists too.

To be a *demanding* critic is to hold the theatre to the highest standards of which it is capable, for, paradoxically, in the theatre's capacity to entertain, to supply immediate gratification, lies the seed of its own destruction. As we have seen so often in the preceding pages, the theatre wants to be liked. It has tried from its very beginning to assimilate what is likable in the other arts. Almost scavenger-like, it has appropriated for itself in every era the most popular music and dance forms, the most trendy arguments, vocabularies, philosophies, and fashions in dress. In the process, alas, it often panders to tastelessness and propagates the meanest and most shallow values of its time. And here the drama critic in each of us can play a crucial role. The very need of the theatre to please its patrons tends to beget a crass insecurity: a tendency to resort to simple sensationalism in exchange for immediate approval. Cogent, fair-minded, penetrating criticism keeps the theatre mindful of its own artistic ideals and its essential responsibility to communicate. It prevents the theatre from either selling out completely to the current whim or bolting the other way into a hopelessly abstract and arcane self-absorption.

To be an *articulate* critic is to express one's thoughts with precision, clarity, and grace. "I loved it" or "I hated it" is not criticism but rather a crude expression of opinion and a wholly general opinion at that. Articulation means the careful building of ideas through a presentation of evidence, logical argument, the use of helpful analogy and example, and a style of expression neither pedantically turgid nor idiosyncratically anarchic. Good criticism should be a pleasure to write, a pleasure to read; it should make us want to go deeper into the mysteries of the theatre and not suffocate us with the prejudices or egotistical displays of the critic.

In sum, the presence of a critical focus in the audience — observant, informed, sensitive, demanding, and articulate — keeps the theatre honest. It inspires the theatre to reach its highest goals. It ascribes importance to the theatrical act. It telegraphs the expectations of the audience to producer, playwright, director, and actor alike, saying, "We are out here, we are watching, we are listening, we are hoping, we care: we want your best — and then we want you to be better yet." The theatre needs such demands from its audience. The theatre and its audience need to be worthy coparticipants in a collective experience that enlarges life as well as art.

If we are to be critics of the theatre, then, we must be knowledgeable, fair, and open-minded; receptive to stimulation and excitement; open to wisdom and love. We must also admit that we have human needs.

In exchange, the theatre must enable us to see ourselves in the characters of the drama and in the performers of the theatre. We must see our situations in the situations of plays and our hopes and possibilities in the behavior staged before us. We must be drawn to understand the theatre from the *inside* and to participate in thought and emotion in a play's performance.

Thus do we become critics, audience, and participants in one. The theatre is then no longer simply a remote subject encountered in a book, in a class, or in the entertainment columns of the world press; the theatre is part of us.

It is *our* theatre.

Glossary

Terms within the definitions that are themselves defined in this glossary are in *italic*.

absurd The notion that the world is meaningless, derived from an essay, "The Myth of Sisyphus," by Albert Camus, which suggests that man has an unquenchable desire to understand but that the world is eternally unknowable. The resulting conflict puts man in an "absurd" position, like Sisyphus, who, according to Greek myth, was condemned for eternity to push a rock up a mountain, only to have it always fall back down before it reached the top. The philosophical term gave the name to a principal postwar dramatic genre: theatre of the absurd.

act (verb) To perform in a play. (noun) A division of a play. Acts in modern plays are bounded by an *intermission* or by the beginning or end of the play on each side. Full-length modern plays are customarily divided into two acts, sometimes three. Roman, Elizabethan, and neoclassic plays were usually printed in five acts, but the actual productions were not necessarily divided by intermissions, only stage clearings.

ad-lib A line improvised by an actor during a performance, usually because the actor has forgotten his or her line or because something unscripted has occurred onstage. Sometimes an author directs the actors to ad-lib, as in crowd scenes during which individual words cannot be distinguished by the audience.

aesthetic distance The theoretical separation between the created artifice of a play and the "real life" the play appears to represent.

agon "Action," in Greek; the root word for "agony." Agon refers to the major struggles and interactions of Greek *tragedies*.

alienation effect A technique, developed by German playwright Bertolt Brecht (1898–1956), by which the actor deliberately presents rather than represents his or her character and "illustrates" the character without trying to embody the role fully, as *naturalistic* acting technique demands. This technique may be accomplished by "stepping out of character"—as to sing a song or to address the audience directly—and by developing a highly objective and *didactic* mode of expression. The actor is alienated from the role (*estranged* and *distanced* are perhaps better terms—all translations of the German word *Verfremdung*) in order to make the audience more directly aware of current political issues. This technique is highly influential today, particularly in Europe.

amphitheatre In Rome, a large elliptical outdoor theatre, originally used for gladiatorial contests. Today the term is often used to designate a large outdoor theatre of any type.

anagnorisis "Recognition," in Greek. Aristotle claimed that every fine *tragedy* has a recognition scene, in which the *protagonist* discovers either some fact unknown to her or him or some moral flaw in her or his character. Scholars disagree as to which of these precise meanings Aristotle had in mind. See also *hamartia*.

antagonist In certain Greek tragedies, the opponent of the *protagonist*.

Apollonian That which is beautiful, wise, and serene, in the theories of Friedrich Nietzsche, who believed *drama* sprang from the junction of Apollonian and *Dionysian* forces in Greek culture.

apron The part of the stage located in front of the *proscenium;* the forwardmost portion of the stage. The apron was used extensively in the English

Restoration period, from whence the term comes. Today, it is usually called the *forestage.*

aragoto The flamboyant and exaggerated masculine style of acting employed in certain *kabuki* roles.

arena stage A stage surrounded by the audience; also known as "theatre-in-the-round." *Arena* is a Latin term meaning "sand," and it originally referred to the dirt circle in the midst of an *amphitheatre.*

aside A short line in a play delivered directly to the audience; by dramatic convention, the other characters onstage are presumed not to hear it. Popular in the works of William Shakespeare (1564–1616) and of the *Restoration* period, the aside has made a comeback in recent years and is used to good effect, in conjunction with the longer *direct address,* by contemporary American playwrights such as Lanford Wilson (born 1937) and Neil Simon (born 1927).

audition The process whereby an actor seeks a role by presenting to a director or casting director a prepared reading or by "reading cold" from the text of the play being presented.

avant-garde In military terms, the "advance-battalion" of an army that goes beyond the front lines to break new ground; in theatre terms, those theatre artists who abandon conventional models and create works that are in the forefront of new theatrical movements and styles.

backstage The offstage area hidden from the audience that is used for *scenery* storage, for actors preparing to make entrances, and for stage technicians running the show. "Backstage plays," such as *The Torchbearers* and *Noises Off,* "turn the set around" and exploit the furious backstage activity that takes place during a play production.

biomechanics An experimental acting system, characterized by expressive physicalization and bold gesticulation, developed by the Russian director Vsevolod Meyerhold (1874–1940) in the 1920s.

black musical See *black theatre.*

black theatre In America, theatre that is generally by, with, and about African Americans.

black-box theatre A rectangular room with no fixed seating or stage area; this theatre design allows for a variety of configurations in staging plays.

blocking The specific staging of a play's movements, ordinarily by the director. "Blocking" refers to the precise indications of where actors are to move, moment by moment, during the performance. Often this is worked out ("blocked out") on paper by the director beforehand.

book In a *musical,* the *dialogue* text, apart from the music and song lyrics.

border A piece of flat *scenery,* often black velour but sometimes a *flat,* which is placed horizontally above the set, usually to *mask* the lighting instruments. Borders are often used with side *wings,* in a scenery system known as "wing and border."

box set A stage set consisting of hard scenic pieces representing the walls and ceiling of a room, with one wall left out for the audience to peer into. This set design was developed in the nineteenth century and remains in use today in realistic plays.

Broadway The major commercial theatre district in New York, bordered by Broadway, 8th Avenue, 42nd Street, and 52nd Street.

bunraku A Japanese puppet theatre, founded in the seventeenth century and still performed today.

burlesque Literally, a *parody* or mockery, from an Italian amusement form. Today the term implies broad, coarse humor in *farce,* particularly in parodies and *vaudeville*-type presentations.

business The minute physical behavior of the actor, such as fiddling with a tie, sipping a drink, drumming the fingers, lighting a cigarette, and so forth. Sometimes this is controlled to a high degree by the actor and/or the director for precise dramatic effect; at other times the business is *improvised* to convey a *naturalistic verisimilitude.*

callback After the initial *audition,* the director or casting director will "call back" for additional— sometimes many—readings those actors who seem most promising. Rules of the actors' unions require that actors be paid for callbacks exceeding a certain minimum number.

caricature A character portrayed very broadly and in a stereotypical fashion, ordinarily objectionable in *realistic* dramas. See also *character.*

catharsis In Aristotle's *Poetics,* the "purging" or "cleansing" of terror and pity, which the audience develops during the *climax* of a *tragedy.*

character A "person" in a play, as performed by an actor. Hamlet, Oedipus, Juliet, and Willy Loman are characters. Characters may or may not be based on real people.

chiton The full-length gown worn by Greek tragic actors.

chorus (1) In classic Greek plays, an ensemble of characters representing the general public of the play, such as the women of Argos or the elders of Thebes. Originally, the chorus numbered fifty; Aeschylus is said to have reduced it to twelve and Sophocles to have increased it to fifteen. More recent playwrights, including Shakespeare and Jean Anouilh (1910–1987), have occasionally employed a single actor (or small group of actors) as "Chorus," to provide narration between the scenes. (2) In *musicals,* an ensemble of characters who sing and/or dance together (in contrast to soloists, who sing and/or dance independently).

chou In *xiqu,* clown characters and the actors who play them.

classical drama Technically, plays from classical Greece or Rome. Now used frequently (if incorrectly) to refer to masterpieces of the early and late Renaissance (Elizabethan, Jacobean, French *neoclassical,* and so on).

climax The point of highest tension in a play, when the conflicts of the play are at their fullest expression.

comedy Popularly, a funny play; classically, a play that ends happily; metaphorically, a play with some humor that celebrates the eternal ironies of human existence ("divine comedy").

comic relief In a *tragedy,* a short comic scene that releases some of the built-up tension of the play—giving the audience a momentary "relief" before the tension mounts higher. The "porter scene" in Shakespeare's *Macbeth* is an often-cited example; following the murder of Duncan, a porter jocularly addresses the audience as to the effect of drinking on sexual behavior. In the best tragedies, comic relief also provides an ironic counterpoint to the tragic action.

commedia dell'arte A form of largely improvised, masked street theatre that began in northern Italy in the late sixteenth century and still can be seen today. The principal characters—Arlecchino, Pantalone, Columbine, Dottore, and Scapino among them—appear over and over in thousands of commedia stories.

company A group of theatre artists gathered together to create a play production or a series of such productions. See also *troupe.*

convention A theatrical custom that the audience accepts without thinking, such as "when the curtain comes down, the play is over." Each period and culture develops its own dramatic conventions, which playwrights may either accept or violate.

cue The last word of one speech that then becomes the "cue" for the following speech. Actors are frequently admonished to speak "on cue" or to "pick up their cues," both of which mean to begin speaking precisely at the moment the other actor finishes.

cycle plays In medieval England, a series of *mystery plays* that, performed in sequence, relate the story of the Judeo-Christian Bible, from the Creation of the universe to Adam and Eve to the Crucifixion to Doomsday. The York Cycle includes forty-eight such plays.

cyclorama In a *proscenium theatre,* a large piece of curved *scenery* that wraps around the rear of the stage and is illuminated to resemble the sky or to serve as an abstract neutral background. It is usually made of fabric stretched between curved pipes but is sometimes a permanent structure made of concrete and plaster.

dada A provocative and playful European art movement following World War I—characterized by seemingly random, unstructured, and "antiaesthetic" creativity—that was briefly but deeply influential in poetry, painting, and theatre.

dan In *xiqu,* the female roles and the actors who play them.

denouement The final *scene* or scenes in a play devoted to tying up the loose ends after the *climax* (although the word originally meant "the untying").

deus ex machina In Greek *tragedies,* the resolution of the *plot* by the device of a god ("deus") arriving onstage by means of a crane ("machina") and solving all the characters' problems. Today, this term encompasses any such contrived play ending, such as the discovery of a will. This theatrical element was considered clumsy by Aristotle and virtually all succeeding critics; it is occasionally used ironically in the modern theatre, as by Bertolt Brecht in *The Threepenny Opera.*

dialogue The speeches—delivered to each other—of the *characters* in a play. Contrast with *monologue.*

diction One of the six important features of a *drama,* according to Aristotle, who meant by the term the intelligence and appropriateness of the play's speeches. Today, the term refers primarily to the actor's need for articulate speech and clear pronunciation.

didactic drama Drama dedicated to teaching lessons or provoking intellectual debate beyond the confines of the play; the dramatic form espoused by Bertolt Brecht. See also *alienation effect.*

dim out To fade the lights gradually to blackness.

dimmer In lighting, the electrical device (technically known as a "potentiometer") that regulates the current passing through the bulb filaments and, thereby, the amount of light emitted from the lighting instruments.

Dionysia Or "Great Dionysia" or "City Dionysia"; the weeklong Athenian springtime festival in honor of *Dionysus,* which was, after 534 B.C., the major play-producing festival of the Greek year.

Dionysian Passionate revelry, uninhibited pleasure-seeking; the opposite of *Apollonian,* according to Friedrich Nietzsche, who considered *drama* a merger of these two primary impulses in the Greek character.

Dionysus The Greek god of *drama* as well as the god of drinking and fertility. Dionysus was known as Bacchus in Rome.

direct address A character's speech delivered directly to the audience, common in Greek Old Comedy (see *parabasis*), in Shakespeare's work (see *soliloquy*), in *epic theatre,* and in some otherwise *realistic* modern plays (such as Neil Simon's *Broadway Bound*).

discovery A *character* who appears onstage without making an entrance, as when a curtain opens. Ferdinand and Miranda are "discovered" playing chess in Shakespeare's *The Tempest* when Prospero pulls away a curtain that had been hiding them from view.

dithyramb A Greek religious rite in which a *chorus* of fifty men, dressed in goatskins, chanted and danced; the precursor, according to Aristotle, of Greek *tragedy.*

documentary drama Drama that presents historical facts in a nonfictionalized, or only slightly fictionalized, manner.

domestic tragedy A *tragedy* about ordinary people at home.

double (1) An actor who plays more than one role is said to "double" in the second and following roles. Ordinarily the actor will seek, through a costume change, to disguise the fact of the doubling; occasionally, however, a production with a *theatricalist* staging may make it clear that the actor doubles in many roles. (2) To Antonin Artaud, the life that drama reflects, as discussed in his book *The Theatre and Its Double.* See also *theatre of cruelty.*

downstage That part of the stage closest to the audience. The term dates back to the eighteenth century, when the stage was *raked* so that the front part was literally below the back (or *upstage*) portion.

drama The art of the theatre; plays, playmaking, and the whole body of literature of and for the stage.

dramatic Plays, scenes, and events that are high in conflict and believability and that would command attention if staged in the theatre.

dramatic irony The situation when the audience knows something the characters don't, as in Shakespeare's *Macbeth,* when King Duncan remarks on his inability to judge character—while warmly greeting the man (Macbeth) we already know plans to assassinate him.

dramaturg A specialist in *dramatic* construction and the body of dramatic literature; a scientist of the art of *drama.* Dramaturgs are frequently engaged by professional and academic theatres to assist in choosing and analyzing plays, develop production concepts, research topics pertinent to historic period or play production *style,* and write program essays. The dramaturg has been a mainstay of the German theatre since the eighteenth century and is becoming increasingly popular in the English-speaking world. Sometimes identified by the anglicized spelling "Dramaturge."

dramaturgy The science of *drama;* the art of play construction; sometimes used to refer to play structure itself.

dress rehearsal A *rehearsal,* perhaps one of several, in full costume; usually also with full *scenery, properties,* lighting, sound, and technical effects. This is ordinarily the last rehearsal(s) prior to the first actual performance before an audience.

drop A flat piece of *scenery* hung from the *fly gallery,* which can "drop" into place by a flying system.

empathy Audience members' identification with dramatic characters and their consequent shared feelings with the plights and fortunes of those characters. Empathy is one of the principal effects of good drama.

ensemble Literally, the group of actors (and sometimes directors and designers) who put a play together; metaphorically, the rapport and shared sense of purpose that bind such a group into a unified artistic entity.

environmental theatre Plays produced not on a conventional stage but in an area where the actors and the audience are intermixed in the same "environment" and where there is no precise line distinguishing stage space from audience space.

epic theatre As popularized by Bertolt Brecht, a *style* of theatre in which the play presents a series of semi-isolated episodes, intermixed with songs and other forms of *direct address,* all leading to a general moral conclusion or set of integrated moral questions. Brecht's *Mother Courage* is a celebrated example. See also *alienation effect.*

epilogue In Greek *tragedy,* a short concluding *scene* of certain plays, generally involving a substantial shift of tone or a *deus ex machina.* Today, the epilogue is a concluding scene set substantially beyond the time frame of the rest of the play, in which characters, now somewhat older, reflect on the preceding events.

existential drama A play based on the philosophical notions of existentialism, particularly as developed by Jean-Paul Sartre (1905–1980). Existentialism, basically, preaches that "you are your acts, and nothing else" and that people must be held fully accountable for their own behavior. *No Exit* contains Sartre's most concise expression of this idea.

exodos In Greek *tragedy,* the departure ode of the *chorus* at the end of the play.

exposition In play construction, the conveyance, through *dialogue,* of story events that have occurred before the play begins.

expressionism An artistic *style* that greatly exaggerates perceived reality in order to express inner truths directly. Popular mainly in Germany between the world wars, expressionism in the theatre is notable for its gutsy dialogue, piercing sounds, bright lighting and coloring, bold scenery, and shocking, vivid imagery.

farce Highly comic, lighthearted, gleefully contrived drama, usually involving *stock situations* (such as mistaken identity or discovered lovers' trysts), punctuated with broad physical stunts and pratfalls.

flat A wooden frame covered in fabric or a hard surface and then painted, often to resemble a wall or portion of a wall. The flat is a traditional staple of stage *scenery,* particularly in the realistic theatre, since it is exceptionally lightweight, can be combined with other flats in various ways, and can be repainted and reused many times over several years.

fly (verb) To raise a piece of *scenery* (or an actor) out of sight by a system of ropes and/or wires. This theatre practice dates back at least to ancient Greek times (see also *deus ex machina*).

fly gallery The operating area for flying scenery, where fly ropes are tied off (on a pinrail) or where ropes in a counterweight system are clamped in a fixed position.

follow-spot A swivel-mounted lighting instrument that can be pointed in any direction by an operator.

footlights In a *proscenium theatre,* a row of lights across the front of the stage, used to light the actors' faces from below and to add light and color to the setting. Footlights were used universally in previous centuries but are employed only on special occasions today.

forestage A modern term for *apron,* the small portion of the stage located in front of the *proscenium.*

found object In scene or costume design (and art in general), an item that is found rather than created and subsequently incorporated into the finished design.

full house Audience seating filled to capacity. See also *house*.

genre French for "kind"; a term used in dramatic theory to signify a distinctive class or category of play, such as *tragedy, comedy, farce,* and so on.

geza The *stage right,* semi-enclosed musicians' box in *kabuki* theatre. This term also refers to the music that is played in this box.

gidayu The traditional style of chanting in *kabuki* and *bunraku* theatre. This term also refers to the singer-chanter himself.

greenroom A room near the stage where actors may sit comfortably before and after the show or during scenes in which they do not appear. This room is traditionally painted green; the custom arose in England, where the color was thought to be soothing.

ground plan A schematic drawing of the stage setting, as seen from above, indicating the location of stage-scenery pieces and furniture on (and sometimes above) the floor. A vital working document for directors in *rehearsal,* as well as for technicians in the installation of *scenery.*

hamartia In Aristotle's *Poetics,* the "tragic flaw" of the *protagonist.* Scholars differ as to whether Aristotle was referring primarily to a character's ignorance of certain facts or to a character's moral defect.

hanamichi In the *kabuki* theatre, a long narrow runway leading from the stage to a door at the back of the auditorium that is used for highly theatrical entrances and exits right through the audience.

Hellenistic theatre Ancient Greek theatre during the fourth and third centuries B.C. The surviving stone theatres of Athens and Epidaurus date from the Hellenistic period, which began well after the great fifth-century tragedies and comedies were written. The Hellenistic period did produce an important form of comedy (*New Comedy*), however, and Alexandrian scholars during this period collected, edited, and preserved the masterpieces of the golden age.

high comedy A comedy of verbal wit and visual elegance, usually peopled with upper-class characters. The *Restoration* comedies of William Congreve (1670–1729) and the Victorian comedies of Oscar Wilde (1854–1900) are often cited as examples.

hikimaku The traditional striped curtain of the *kabuki* theatre.

himation The gownlike basic costume of the Greek tragic actor.

house The audience portion of the theatre building.

hubris In Greek, an excess of pride; the most common *character* defect (one interpretation of the Greek *hamartia*) of the *protagonist* in Greek *tragedy.* "Pride goeth before a fall" is an Elizabethan expression of this foundation of tragedy.

improvisation *Dialogue* and/or stage *business* invented by the actor, often during the performance itself. Some plays are wholly improvised, even to the extent that the audience may suggest situations that the actors must then create. More often, improvisation is used to "fill in the gaps" between more traditionally memorized and rehearsed scenes.

inciting action In play construction, the single action that initiates the major conflict of the play.

ingenue The young, pretty, and innocent girl role in certain plays; also used to denote an actress capable of playing such roles.

interlude A *scene* or staged event in a play not specifically tied to the *plot;* in medieval England, a short moral play, usually comic, that could be presented at a court banquet amid other activities.

intermission In England, "interval"; a pause in the action, marked by a fall of the curtain or a fade-out of the stage lights, during which the audience may leave their seats for a short time, usually ten or fifteen minutes. Intermissions divide the play into separate *acts.*

jing In *xiqu,* the "painted-face" roles, often of gods, nobles, or villains.

jingju "Capital theatre" in Chinese; the Beijing (or Peking) Opera, the most famous form of *xiqu.*

kabuki One of the national theatres of Japan. Dating from the seventeenth century, the kabuki features magnificent flowing costumes; highly stylized scenery, acting, and makeup; and elaborately styled choreography.

kakegoe Traditional shouts that *kabuki* enthusiasts in the audience cry out to their favorite actors during the play.

kathakali A traditional dance-drama of India.

kōken Black-garbed and veiled actors' assistants who perform various functions onstage in *kabuki* theatre.

kunju (sometimes *kunqu*) The most ancient and classical form of Chinese *xiqu* still performed, dating from the sixteenth century.

lazzo A physical joke, refined into traditional *business* and inserted into a play, in the *commedia dell'arte.* "Eating the fly" is a famous lazzo.

Lenaea The winter dramatic festival in ancient Athens. Because there were fewer foreigners in town in the winter, comedies that might embarrass the Athenians were often performed at this festival rather than at the springtime *Dionysia.*

liturgical drama *Dramatic* material that was written into the official Catholic Church liturgy and staged as part of regular church services in the medieval period, mainly in the tenth through twelfth centuries.

low comedy Comic actions based on broad physical humor, scatology, crude punning, and the argumentative behavior of ignorant and lower-class *characters.* Despite the pejorative connotation of its name, low comedy can be inspired, as in the "mechanicals" scenes of Shakespeare's *A Midsummer Night's Dream.* Good plays, such as this one, can mix low comedy with *high comedy* in a highly sophisticated pattern.

mask (noun) A covering of the face, used conventionally by actors in many periods, including Greek, Roman, and *commedia dell'arte.* The mask was also used in other sorts of plays for certain occasions, such as the masked balls in Shakespeare's *Romeo and Juliet* and *Much Ado about Nothing.* The mask is a symbol of the theatre, particularly the two classic masks of Comedy and Tragedy. (verb) To hide backstage storage or activity by placing in front of it neutrally colored *flats* or drapery (which then become "masking pieces").

masque A minor dramatic form combining dance, music, a short allegorical *text,* and elegant *scenery* and costuming; often presented at court, as in the royal masques written by Ben Jonson (1572–1637), with scenery designed by Inigo Jones (1573–1652), during the Stuart era (early seventeenth century).

melodrama Originally a term for *musical* theatre, by the nineteenth century this became the designation of a suspenseful, plot-oriented *drama* featuring all-good heroes, all-bad villains, simplistic *dialogue,* soaring moral conclusions, and bravura acting.

metaphor A literary term designating a figure of speech that implies a comparison or identity of one thing with something else. It permits concise communication of a complex idea by use of associative imagery, as with Shakespeare's "morn in russet mantle clad."

metatheatre Literally, "beyond theatre"; plays or theatrical acts that are self-consciously theatrical, that refer back to the art of the theatre and call attention to their own theatricality. Developed by many authors, including Shakespeare (in plays-within-plays in *Hamlet* and *A Midsummer Night's Dream*) and particularly the twentieth-century Italian playwright Luigi Pirandello (*Six Characters in Search of an Author, Tonight We Improvise*), thus leading to the term "Pirandellian" (meaning "metatheatrical"). See also *play-within-the-play.*

mie A "moment" in *kabuki* theatre in which the actor (usually an *aragoto* character) suddenly freezes in a tense and symbolic pose.

mime A stylized art of acting without words. Probably derived from the *commedia dell'arte,* mime was revived in France during the mid-twentieth century and is now popular again in the theatre and in street performances in Europe and the United States. Mime performers traditionally employ whiteface makeup to stylize and exaggerate their features and expressions.

modern classic A term used to designate a play of the past hundred years that has nonetheless passed the test of time and seems as if it will last into the century or centuries beyond, such as the major works of Anton Chekhov, George Bernard Shaw, and Samuel Beckett. Contrast with *classical drama.*

monologue A long unbroken speech in a play, often delivered directly to the audience (when it is more technically called a *soliloquy*).

morality play An allegorical medieval play form, in which the characters represent abstractions (Good Deeds, Death, and so on) and the overall impact of the play is moral instruction. The most famous of these plays in English is the anonymous *Everyman* (fifteenth century).

motivation That which can be construed to have determined a person's (or *character's*) behavior. Since Konstantin Stanislavsky (1863–1938), actors have been encouraged to study the possible motivations of their characters' actions. See also *objective*.

musical A generic name for a play with a large number of songs, particularly when there is also dancing and/or a *chorus*.

musical comedy A popular form of twentieth-century theatre, with singing and dancing, designed primarily for entertainment.

mystery play The most common term referring to medieval plays developed from liturgical drama that treated biblical stories and themes. (They were also known as "pageant plays" in England, as "passion plays" when dealing with the Crucifixion of Jesus, and as "Corpus Christi plays" when performed in conjunction with that particular festival.) Unlike *liturgical dramas,* which were in Latin, mystery plays were written in the vernacular (English, French, German, Italian, Spanish, and Russian versions exist) and were staged outside the church.

naturalism An extreme form of *realism,* which advanced the notion that the natural and social environment, more than individual willpower, controlled human behavior. Its proponents, active in the late nineteenth and early twentieth centuries, sought to dispense with all theatrical convention in the search for complete verisimilitude: a *slice of life,* as the naturalists would say.

neoclassicism Literally, "new classicism," or a renewed interest in the literary and artistic theories of ancient Greece and Rome and an attempt to reformulate them for the current day. A dominant force in seventeenth-century France, neoclassicism promoted restrained passion, balance, artistic consistency, and formalism in all art forms;

it reached its dramatic pinnacle in the tragedies of Jean Racine (1639–1699).

New Comedy Greek comic dramas—almost all of which are now lost—of the late fourth to the second centuries B.C. Considerably more realistic than the Old Comedy of Aristophanes, New Comedy employed *stock characters* and domestic scenes; it strongly influenced Roman author Plautus and, through him, Renaissance comedy.

nō The classical dance-drama of Japan. Performed on a bare wooden stage of fixed construction and dimension and accompanied by traditional music, nō is the aristocratic forebear of the more popular *kabuki* and remains generally unchanged since its fourteenth-century beginnings.

objective The basic "goal" of a *character.* Also called "intention" or "victory." Since Konstantin Stanislavsky, the actor has been urged to discover his or her character's objectives and, by way of "living the life of the character," to pursue that character's objective during the course of the play.

off-Broadway The New York professional theatre located outside the *Broadway* district; principally in Greenwich Village and around the upper East and West Sides. Developed in the 1950s, when it was considered highly experimental, the off-Broadway theatre is now more of a scaled-down version of the Broadway theatre, featuring *musicals* and commercial *revivals* as much as (or more than) original works.

off-off-Broadway A term designating certain theatre activity in New York City, usually nonprofessional (although with professional artists involved) and usually experimental and *avant-garde* in nature. Off-off-Broadway developed in the 1970s as a supplement to the commercialism of both Broadway and, increasingly, off-Broadway.

Old Comedy Ancient Greek comedy of the fifth century B.C., mainly known to us through the bawdy, satirical, and even slapstick comedies of Aristophanes.

onnagata "Women-type" roles in *kabuki,* which, like all the roles, are played by men.

open the house A direction to admit the audience. See also *house.*

orchestra (1) In the ancient Greek or Roman theatre, the circular (in Rome, semicircular) ground-level acting area in front of the stagehouse, or *skene.* It was used primarily by the *chorus.* (2) In modern theatre buildings, the main ground-level section of the audience, which usually slopes upward at the rear. Distinct from the mezzanine and balconies and ordinarily containing the more expensive seats.

parabasis A "coming-forward" of a *character* in Greek Old Comedy who then gives a *direct address* to the audience in the middle of the play. In Aristophanes' plays, the parabasis is often given in the author's name and may have been spoken by Aristophanes himself. The parabasis was often unrelated to the *plot* and dealt with the author's immediate political or social concerns.

parados The ode sung by the chorus entering the orchestra in a Greek tragedy; the space between the stagehouse (*skene*) and audience seating area (*theatron*) through which the chorus entered the orchestra.

parody Dramatic material that makes fun of a dramatic genre or mode or of specific literary works; a form of theatre that is often highly entertaining but rarely has lasting value.

pathos "Passion," in Greek; also "suffering." The word refers to the depths of feeling evoked by *tragedy;* it is at the root of our words "sympathy" and "empathy," which also describe the effect of drama on audience emotions.

peripeteia In the Anglicized form, "peripety"; the reversal of the *protagonist's* fortunes that, according to Aristotle, is part of the *climax* of a *tragedy.*

pièce bien faite See *well-made play.*

play-within-the-play A play that is "presented" by characters who are already in a play; like "The Murder of Gonzago," which is presented by "players" in *Hamlet.* Many plays are in part about actors and plays and contain such plays-within-plays; these include Anton Chekhov's *The Seagull,* Jean Anouilh's *The Rehearsal,* and Shakespeare's *A Midsummer Night's Dream* and *The Taming of the Shrew.*

plot The events of the play, expressed as a series of linked dramatic actions; more generally, and in common terms, the story of the play. The plot is the most important aspect of play construction, according to Aristotle.

postmodern A wide-ranging term describing certain post–World War II artistic works, characterized by nonlinearity, self-referentiality if not self-parody, and multiple/simultaneous sensory impressions.

practical In stage terminology, a *property* that works onstage the way it does in life. For example, a "practical" stove, in a stage setting, is one on which the characters can actually cook. A "nonpractical" stove, by contrast, is something that only looks like a stove (and may in fact be a stove without insides).

problem play A realistic play that deals, often narrowly, with a specific social problem. George Bernard Shaw's *Mrs. Warren's Profession,* for example, is virtually a dramatic tract on prostitution. The term was most popular around the beginning of the twentieth century; today it is mostly descriptive of certain movies for television.

producer (1) In America, the person responsible for assembling the ingredients of a play production: financing, staff, theatre, publicity, and management. Not ordinarily involved in the day-to-day artistic direction of the production, the American producer nonetheless controls the artistic process through her or his authority over personnel selection and budgeting. (2) Until recently in the English theatre, the theatre artist Americans refer to as the director.

prologue In Greek *tragedy,* a speech or brief *scene* preceding the entrance of the *chorus* and the main action of the play, usually spoken by a god or gods. Subsequently, the term has referred to a speech or brief scene that introduces the play, as by an actor in certain Elizabethan plays (often called the chorus) and in the *Restoration.* The prologue is rarely used in the modern theatre.

properties Or "props"; the furniture and hand-held objects (hand props) used in play productions. These are often real items (chairs, telephones, books, etc.) that can be purchased, rented, borrowed, or brought up from theatre storage; they may also, particularly in period or stylized plays, be designed and built in a property shop.

proscenium arch The arch separating the audience area from the main stage area. The term derives from the Roman playhouse, in which the proscenium (literally, *pro skene,* or "in front of the stage") was the facing wall of the stage. Modern *thrust* and *arena stages* have no proscenium.

proscenium theatre A rectangular-roomed theatre with the audience on one end and the stage on the other, with both areas separated by a *proscenium arch*. The proscenium theatre was first popular in the late seventeenth century and reached its apogee in the late nineteenth and early twentieth centuries. Still the basic theatre architecture of America's Broadway and of major European theatre companies.

protagonist In Greek *tragedy,* and subsequently in any drama, the principal *character,* often opposed by an *antagonist.*

raked stage A sloped stage, angled so that the rear (*upstage*) area is higher than the forward (*downstage*) area. A raked stage was standard theatre architecture in the seventeenth century and is often used today in scene design but rarely in a theatre's permanent architecture.

realism The general principle that the stage should portray, in a reasonable facsimile, ordinary people in ordinary circumstances and that actors should behave, as much as possible, as real people do in life. Although realism's roots go back to Euripides, it developed as a deliberate contrast to the florid *romanticism* that swept the European theatre in the mid-nineteenth century. See also *naturalism,* which is an extreme version of realism.

recognition See *anagnorisis.*

rehearsal The gathering of actors and director to put a play into production; the period in which the director stages the play and the actors develop and repeat their *dialogue* and actions; etymologically, a "reharrowing," or repeated digging into. In French, the comparable term is *répétition.*

repertory The plays a theatre company produces. A company's current repertory consists of those plays available for production at any time.

Restoration In England, the period following the restoration of the monarchy in 1660. In the theatre, the period is particularly noted for witty and salacious comedies, through to William Congreve's brilliant *The Way of the World* in 1700.

revival The remounting of a play production after its initial closing, usually by the same theatre *company* and/or employing many or most of the same artists. The term is not normally used to describe fresh restagings, by other artists, of older plays.

rising action In *dramatic* structure, the escalating conflict; events and actions that follow the *inciting action.*

ritual A traditional cultural practice, usually religious, involving precise movements, music, spoken text, and/or gestures, that serves to communicate with deities. Ritual is often incorporated into plays, either as *conventions* of the theatre or as specific dramatized actions.

romanticism A nineteenth-century European movement away from *neoclassic* formalism and toward outsized passions, exotic and grotesque stories, florid writing, and all-encompassing worldviews. Supplanted in the late century by *realism,* romanticism survives today primarily in grand opera and nineteenth-century-based *musicals.*

rotating repertory The scheduling of a series of plays in nightly rotation. This is customary in most European theatres and in many American Shakespeare festivals; it is otherwise rare in America. See also *repertory.*

samisen The three-stringed banjolike instrument used in *kabuki* and *bunraku.*

satire A play or other literary work that ridicules social follies, beliefs, religions, or human vices, almost always in a lighthearted vein. Satire is not usually a lasting theatre form, as summed up by dramatist George S. Kaufman's classic definition: "Satire is what closes on Saturday night."

satyr A mythological Greek creature, half man and half goat, who attended *Dionysus* and represented male sexuality and drunken revelry; goatskin-clad followers of Dionysus who served as the *chorus* of the *satyr play.*

satyr play The fourth play in a Greek *tetralogy.* Satyr plays were short bawdy *farces* that parodied the events of the trilogies that preceded them.

scansion The study of verse for patterns of accented and unaccented syllables; also known as "metrics."

scene (1) The period of stage time representing a single space over a continuous period of time, now usually marked either by the rise or fall of a curtain or by the raising or lowering of lights, but in the past often marked simply by a stage clearing; often the subdivision of an *act.* (2) The locale where the events of the play are presumed to take place, as represented by *scenery* (as in "the scene is the Parson's living room"). (3) Of scenery, as "scene design."

scenery The physical constructions that provide the specific acting environment for a play and that often indicate, by representation, the locale where a scene is set; the physical *setting* for a scene or play.

scenography *Scene* design, particularly as it fits into the moving pattern of a play or series of plays. Scene design is four-dimensional, comprising three physical dimensions plus time.

scrim A theatrical fabric woven so finely that when lit from the front it appears opaque and when lit from behind it becomes transparent. A scrim is often used for surprise effects or to create a mysterious mood.

script A play's *text* as used in and prior to play production, usually in manuscript or typescript rather than in a published version.

semiotics The study of signs, as they may be perceived in literary works, including plays. Semiotics is a contemporary tool of dramaturgical analysis that offers the possibility of identifying all the ingredients of *drama* (staging as well as language) and determining the precise conjunctions between them.

setting Or "set," the fixed (stable) stage *scenery.*

sheng In *xiqu,* the male roles and the actors who play them.

shite The principal *character* (the "doer") in *nō.*

skene The Greek stagehouse (and root word of our *scene*). The skene evolved from a small changing room behind the *orchestra* to a larger structure with a raised stage and a back wall during the Greek period.

slapstick Literally, a prop bat made up of two hinged sticks that slap sharply together when the bat is used to hit someone; a staple gag of the *commedia dell'arte.* More generally, slapstick is any sort of very broad physical stage humor.

slice-of-life Pure *naturalism:* stage action that merely represents an ordinary and arbitrary "slice" of the daily activity of the people portrayed.

soliloquy A *monologue* delivered by a single actor with no one else onstage, sometimes

played as the *character* "thinking aloud" and sometimes as a seeming *dialogue* with the (silent) audience.

stage business See *business.*

stage directions Scene descriptions, *blocking* instructions, and general directorial comments written, usually by the playwright, in the *script.*

stage left Left, from the actor's point of view.

stage right Right, from the actor's point of view.

stock character A *character* recognizable mainly for his or her conformity to a standard ("stock") dramatic stereotype: the wily servant, the braggart soldier, the innocent virgin, and so on. Most date from at least Roman times.

stock situation One of a number of basic *plot* situations, such as the lover hiding in the closet, twins mistaken for each other, and so on, which, like *stock characters,* have been used in the theatre since Plautus and before.

style The specific manner in which a play is shaped, as determined by its *genre,* its historical period, the sort of impact the director wishes to convey to the audience, and the skill of the artists involved. The term generally refers to these aspects inasmuch as they differ from *naturalism,* although it could be said that naturalism is a style.

stylize To deliberately shape a play (or a setting, a costume, or so on) in a specifically nonnaturalistic manner.

subplot A secondary *plot* in a play, usually related to the main plot by play's end. The Gloucester plot in *King Lear* and the Laertes plot in *Hamlet* are examples.

subtext According to Konstantin Stanislavsky, the deeper and usually unexpressed "real" meanings of a *character's* spoken lines. Of particular importance in the acting of realistic plays, such as those of Anton Chekhov, where the action is often as much between the lines as in them.

surrealism An art movement of the early twentieth century, in which the artist sought to go beyond *realism* into superrealism (of which surrealism is a contraction).

symbolism The first major antirealistic movement in the arts and in the theatre. Symbolism, which emphasizes the symbolic nature of theatrical presentation and the abstract possibilities of drama, flourished as a significant movement from the late nineteenth century to the early twentieth century, when it broke into various submovements: *expressionism, surrealism, theatricalism,* and so on.

tableau   A "frozen moment" onstage, with the actors immobile, usually employed at the end of a *scene,* as the curtain falls or the lights dim.

tetralogy   Four plays performed together in sequence. In ancient Greek theatre, this was the basic pattern for the tragic playwrights, who presented a *trilogy* of tragedies, followed by a *satyr play.*

text   A playscript; sometimes used to indicate the spoken words of the play only, as apart from the stage directions and other material in the script.

theatre of alienation   See *alienation effect, epic theatre.*

theatre of cruelty   A notion of theatre developed by the French theorist Antonin Artaud (1896–1948). Artaud's goal was to employ language more for its sound than for its meaning and to create a shocking stream of sensations rather than a coherent *plot* and cast of *characters.* Although Artaud's practical achievement was slight, his theories have proven extraordinarily influential.

theatre of the absurd   See *absurd.*

theatre-in-the-round   See *arena stage.*

theatricalist   A style of contemporary theatre that boldly exploits the theatre itself and calls attention to the theatrical contexts of the play being performed. This term is often used to describe plays about the theatre that employ a *play-within-the-play.*

theatron   From the Greek for "seeing place"; the original Greek theatre.

thespian   Actor; after Thespis, the first Greek actor.

thrust stage   A stage that projects into the seating area and is surrounded by the audience on three sides.

tragedy   From the Greek for "goat song"; originally meant a serious play. The tragedy was refined by Greek playwrights (Thespis, sixth century B.C., being the first) and subsequently the philosopher

Aristotle (384–322 B.C.) into the most celebrated of dramatic genres: a play that treats, at the most uncompromising level, human suffering. The reason for the name is unclear; a goat may have been the prize, and/or the *chorus* may have worn goatskins.

tragic flaw   See *hamartia.*

tragicomedy   A play that begins as a *tragedy* but includes comic elements and ends happily. Tragicomedy was a popular *genre* in the eighteenth century but is rarely employed, at least under that name, in the modern theatre.

traveler   A curtain that, instead of flying out (see *fly*), moves horizontally and is usually opened by dividing from the center outward.

trilogy   Three plays performed in sequence; the basic pattern of ancient Greek tragedies, of which one—Aeschylus's *The Oresteia (Agamemnon, The Libation Bearers,* and *The Eumenides)*—is still extant.

trope   A written text, usually in dialogue form, incorporated into the Christian church service. In the tenth century A.D. these became the first *liturgical dramas.*

troupe   A group of actors who perform together, often on tour. See also *company.*

unit set   A set that, by the moving on or off of a few simple pieces and perhaps with a change of lights, can represent all the scenes from a play. The unit set is a fluid and economical staging device, particularly useful for Shakespeare productions.

unities   The unity of place, unity of time, unity of action, and unity of tone were the four "unities" that *neoclassic* critics of the seventeenth century claimed to derive from Aristotle; plays said to "observe the unities" were required to take place in one locale, to have a duration of no more than one day (in an extreme interpretation, in no more time than the duration of the play itself), and to concern themselves with no more than one single action. Aristotle made no such demands on playwrights, however, and very few authors have ever succeeded in satisfying these restrictive conventions.

upstage   (noun) In a *proscenium theatre,* that part of the stage farthest from the audience; the rear of the stage, so called because it was in fact raised ("up") in the days of the *raked stage.* (verb) To stand upstage of another actor. Upstaging is often considered rude, inasmuch as it forces the *downstage* actor to face upstage (and away from the audience) in order to look at the actor to whom she or he is supposed to be speaking. Figuratively, the term may be used to describe any sort of acting behavior that calls unwarranted attention to the "upstaging" actor and away from the "upstaged" one.

vaudeville A stage variety show, with singing, dancing, comedy skits, and animal acts; highly popular in America from the late 1880s to the 1930s, when it lost out to movies, radio, and subsequently television.

verisimilitude The appearance of actual reality (as in a stage setting).

wagoto In *kabuki,* "gentle-style" acting performed by certain male romantic characters.

waki The secondary *character* in *nō.*

well-made play *Pièce bien faite* in French; in the nineteenth century, a superbly plotted play, particularly by such gifted French playwrights as Eugène Scribe (1791–1861) and Victorien Sardou (1831–1908); today, generally used pejoratively, as to describe a play that has a workable *plot* but shallow characterization and trivial ideas.

West End The commercial theatre district of London, England.

wings In a *proscenium theatre,* the vertical pieces of *scenery* to the left and right of the stage, usually parallel with the footlights.

xiqu Chinese for "tuneful theatre"; the general term for all varieties of traditional Chinese theatre, often called "Chinese Opera."

zadacha Russian for "task"; (though commonly translated as "objective"); according to Konstantin Stanislavsky, the character's (fictional) tasks (or goals) that the actor must pursue during the play.

Brief Bibliography

The following brief bibliography lists selected sources for further research, with an emphasis on recent works. For a fuller bibliography, go to the Online Learning Center at www.mhhe.com/cohen.

Broad Surveys of Drama and Theatre

Auslander, Philip. *From Acting to Performance*. New York: Routledge, 1997.

Banham, Martin, ed. *The Cambridge Guide to Theatre*. Cambridge: Cambridge University Press, 1995.

Beckerman, Bernard. *Dynamics of Drama: Theory and Method of Analysis*. New York: Knopf, 1970.

Bentley, Eric. *The Life of the Drama*. New York. Atheneum, 1964.

Boardman, Gerald and Thomas S. Hischak. *The Oxford Companion to American Theatre*. Oxford University Press, 2004.

Brockett, Oscar G. *History of the Theatre*. 9th edition. Boston: Allyn & Bacon, 2003.

Esslin, Martin. *An Anatomy of Drama*. New York: Hill & Wang, 1976.

Kennedy, Dennis. *The Oxford Encyclopedia of Theatre and Performance*. Oxford: Oxford University Press, 2003.

Pavis, Patrice. *Dictionary of the Theatre: Terms, Concepts, and Analysis*. Toronto: University of Toronto Press, 1998.

Pottlitzer, Joanne. *Hispanic Theater in the United States and Puerto Rico*. New York: Ford Foundation, 1988.

Sanders, Leslie C. *The Development of Black Theatre in America*. Baton Rouge: Louisiana State University Press, 1998.

Styan, J. L.. *Drama, Stage and Audience*. Cambridge: Cambridge University Press, 1960.

Specialized Studies

THE ANCIENTS

Ashby, Clifford. *Classical Greek Theatre: New Views of an Old Subject*. Iowa City: University of Iowa Press, 1999.

Beacham, Richard C. *The Roman Theatre and Its Audience*. Cambridge, MA: Harvard University Press, 1992.

Rehm, Rush. *The Play of Space: Spatial Transformation in Greek Tragedy*. Princeton: Princeton University Press, 2002.

——. *Radical Theatre: Greek Tragedy and the Modern World*. London: Duckworth, 2003.

Taplin, Oliver. *Greek Tragedy in Action*. London: Routledge, 1985.

——. *The Stagecraft of Aeschylus*. Oxford: Clarendon Press, 1977.

Wiles, David. *Greek Theatre Performance*. Cambridge: Cambridge University Press, 2000.

Zimmerman, Bernhard. *Greek Tragedy: An Introduction*. Translated by Thomas Marier. Baltimore: Johns Hopkins University Press, 1991.

THE MIDDLE AGES

Chambers, E. K. *The Medieval Stage*. 2 vols. Oxford: Clarendon Press, 1903.

Clopper, Lawrence M. *Drama, Play and Game: English Festive Culture in the Medieval and Early Modern Period*. Chicago: University of Chicago Press, 2001.

Gusick, Barbara I., and Edelgard E. DuBruck. *New Approaches to European Theatre of the Middle Ages*. New York: Peter Lang, 2004.

Ogden, Dunbar H. *The Staging of Drama in the Medieval Church*. Newark: University of Delaware Press. 2002.

THE SHAKESPEAREAN ERA

Bloom, Harold. *Shakespeare: The Invention of the Human*. New York: Riverhead Books, 1998.

Chambers, E. K. *The Elizabethan Stage*. 4 vols. London: Oxford University Press, 1923.

Dessen, Alan C. *Rescripting Shakespeare: The Text, the Director, and Modern Productions*. Cambridge: Cambridge University Press, 2002.

Greenblatt, Stephen. *Will in the World: How Shakespeare Became Shakespeare*. New York: W. W. Norton, 2004.

Gurr, Andrew. *Playgoing in Shakespeare's London*. 2nd ed. Cambridge: Cambridge University Press, 1996.

Kiernan, Pauline. *Staging Shakespeare in the New Globe*. New York: St. Martin's Press, 1958.

Mann, David. *The Elizabethan Player*. New York: Routledge, 1991.

Worthen, W. B. *Shakespeare and the Force of Modern Performance*. Cambridge: Cambridge University Press, 2003.

ASIAN THEATRE

Brandon, James R., ed. *Nō and Kyōgen in the Contemporary World*. Honolulu: University of Hawai'i Press, 1997.

Gunji, Masakatsu. *Kabuki*. Tokyo: Kodansha International, 1988.

Leiter, Samuel L. *Frozen Moments: Writings on Kabuki 1966–2001*. Ithaca, NY: Cornell University Press, 2002.

——. *New Kabuki Encyclopedia*. Westport, CT: Greenwood Press, 1997.

Richmond, Farley P., Darius L. Swann, and Phillip B. Zarilli, eds. *Indian Theatre: Traditions of Performance*. Honolulu: University of Hawai'i Press, 1990.

Van Erven, Eugène. *The Playful Revolution: Theatre and Liberation in Asia*. Bloomington: Indiana University Press, 1992.

Wang-ngai, Siu, with Peter Lovrick. *Chinese Opera*. Vancouver: University of British Columbia Press, 1997.

ROYAL THEATRE

Holland, Peter. *The Ornament of Action: Text and Performance in Restoration Comedy*. New York: Cambridge University Press, 1979.

Lawrenson, T. E. *The French Stage in the XVIIth Century*. Manchester, England: Manchester University Press, 1957.

McBride, Robert. *Aspects of 17th Century French Drama and Thought*. Totowa, NJ: Rowman & Littlefield, 1980.

MODERN AND POSTMODERN THEATRE

Artaud, Antonin. *The Theatre and Its Double*. Translated by Mary C. Richards. New York: Grove Press, 1958.

Bigsby, C. W. E. *A Critical Introduction to Twentieth-Century American Drama*. 3 vols. Cambridge: Cambridge University Press, 1985.

Birringer, Johannes H. *Theatre, Theory, Postmodernism*. Bloomington: Indiana University Press, 1991.

Brecht, Bertolt. *Brecht on Theatre*. Translated by John Willett. New York: Hill & Wang, 1965.

Brook, Peter. *The Empty Space*. New York: Atheneum, 1968.

Esslin, Martin. *The Theatre of the Absurd*. Rev. ed. New York: Doubleday, 1969.

Marranca, Bonnie, and Gautam Dasgupta, eds. *Interculturalism and Performance*. New York: PAJ Publications, 1991.

Natalle, Elizabeth J. *Feminist Theatre: A Study in Persuasion*. Metuchen, NJ: Scarecrow Press, 1985.

Shaw, George Bernard. *The Quintessence of Ibsenism*. London: Constable, 1913.

MUSIC THEATRE

Everett, William A., and Paul R. Laird. *The Cambridge Companion to the Musical*. Cambridge: Cambridge University Press, 2002.

Hischack, Thomas S. *Boy Loses Girl: Broadway's Librettists*. Lanham, MD: Scarecrow Press, 2002.

Most, Andrea. *Making Americans: Jews and the Broadway Musical*. Cambridge, MA: Harvard University Press, 2004.

PRACTICAL THEATRE ARTS

Aronson, Arnold. *American Set Design*. New York: Theatre Communications Group, 1985.

Benedetti, Jean. *Stanislavsky*. London: Methuen, 1988.

Carnicke, Sharon Marie. *Stanislavsky in Focus*. Amsterdam: Harwood Press, 1998.

Chaikin, Joseph. *The Presence of the Actor*. New York: Atheneum, 1972.

Cohen, Robert. *Acting Power*. Palo Alto, CA: Mayfield, 1978.

Izenour, George. *Theatre Design*. 2d ed. New Haven, CT: Yale University Press, 1996.

Pecktal, Lynn. *Costume Design*. New York: Back Stage Books, 1993.

Reid, Francis. *Designing for the Theatre*. New York: Routledge, 1996.

——. *The Stage Lighting Handbook*. 5th ed. New York: Routledge, 1996.

Roach, Joseph R. *The Player's Passion: Studies in the Science of Acting*. Newark: University of Delaware Press, 1985.

Sofer, Andrew. *The Stage Life of Props*. Ann Arbor: University of Michigan Press, 2003.

Svoboda, Joseph. *The Secret of Theatrical Space*. New York: Applause Theatre Books, 1993.

Walne, Graham, ed. *Effects for the Theatre*. New York: Drama Book Publishers, 1995.

Text Credits

Photo Credits

Brief Index